W9-BYH-470

Jamsa's 1001 C/C++ Tips

Kris Jamsa

JAMSA P·R·E·S·S

. . . a computer user's best friend

a division of Kris Jamsa Software, Inc.

Published by
Jamsa Press
2821 High Sail Ct.
Las Vegas, NV 89117
U.S.A.

For information about the translation or distribution of any Jamsa Press book, please write to Jamsa Press at the address listed above.

Jamsa's 1001 C/C++ Tips

Copyright © 1993 by Jamsa Press. All right reserved. Except as permitted under the Copyright Act of 1976, no part of this publication may be reproduced or distributed in any format or by any means, or stored in a database or retrieval system, without the prior written permission of Jamsa Press.

Printed in the United States of America.
98765432

ISBN 0-9635851-2-6

Publisher
  Debbie Jamsa

Technical Editor
  Ken Cope

Copy Editor
  Paul Medoff

Layout Design and Illustrator
  Phil Schmauder

Composition
  Kevin Hutchinson

Indexer
  Janis Paris

Cover Design
  Jeff Wolfley & Associates

Cover Photograph
  O'Gara/Bissell

This book identifies product names and services known to be trademarks or registered trademarks of their respective companies. They are used throughout this book in an editorial fashion only. In addition, terms suspected of being trademarks or service marks have been appropriately capitalized. Jamsa Press cannot attest to the accuracy of this information. Use of a term in this book should not be regarded as affecting the validity of any trademark or service mark.

Except for the limited warranty covering the physical disks(s) packaged with this book as provided in the end user license agreement at the back of this book, the information and material contained in this book are provided "as is," without warranty of any kind, express or implied, including without limitation any warranty concerning the accuracy, adequacy, or completeness of such information or material or the results to be obtained from using such information or material. Neither Jamsa Press nor the author shall be responsible for any claims attributable to errors, omissions, or other inaccuracies in the information or material contained in this book, and in no event shall Jamsa Press or the author be liable for direct, indirect, special, incidental, or consequential damages arising out of the use of such information or material.

This publication is designed to provide accurate and authoritative information in regard to the subject matter covered. It is sold with the understanding that the publisher is not engaged in rendering professional service or endorsing particular products or services. If legal advice or other expert assistance is required, the services of a competent professional should be sought.

Planting 1001 Trees

Some time ago, I encountered a note from another publisher about the number of trees required to produce a book such as this. I was astounded to learn it requires about 500 trees for every 10,000 books printed. That publisher had instituted a policy of planting 2 trees for every tree felled in the production of their book.

I was greatly impressed by this policy and have decided to follow suit. I hope that some day all publishers will do the same. For each 10,000 copies of *Jamsa's 1001 C/C++ Tips* that are printed, Jamsa Press will donate 1,001 trees for planting. If you would like to become involved in this effort, please write to:

> The Basic Foundation
> P.O. Box 47012
> St. Petersburg, FL 33743

You can plant a single tree for only $5.00, or 1,001 trees for $255.00.

Acknowledgments

I am thrilled to present to you the third Jamsa Press book. As the number of books in our line begins to grow, I have had the tremendous fortune of adding several excellent new members to the Jamsa Press team. To begin, Kevin Hutchinson did an outstanding job working on this book's design and managing the flow of tips to and from various editors. This was Kevin's first project, and he mastered it with ease and the expertise of a seasoned veteran. Second, Ken Cope, this book's technical editor did an outstanding job of tracking the ins and outs of numerous compilers and programming environments. Ken, too, was working on his first book. His programming knowledge and technical expertise make him a natural for the computer book business. Once again, Paul Medoff, this book's copy editor did a tremendous job, not only of correcting this book's grammatical errors, but also in providing insights into the programs, algorithms, and various technical concepts. Very few individuals possess Paul's capabilities. Janis Paris did a great job meeting frantic deadlines while still providing a high-quality index. Finally, Phil Schmauder, this book's project manager, illustrator, and desktop publisher has again exceeded my greatest expectations. I am constantly amazed by Phil's ability to master any aspect of book publishing quickly. Thank you all once again for another great job.

Table of Contents

Getting Started with C

All references are to tip numbers

All references are to tip numbers

Macros & Constants

All references are to tip numbers

Strings

Functions

All references are to tip numbers

All references are to tip numbers

Keyboard Operations

Math

Files, Directories, & Disks

All references are to tip numbers

Arrays, Pointers, & Structures

All references are to tip numbers

DOS & BIOS Services

Memory Management

Date & Time

I/O Redirection & Command Line Processing

Programming Tools

All references are to tip numbers

Advanced C

Getting Started with C++

All references are to tip numbers

All references are to tip numbers

Object-Oriented C++

C 1

An Introduction to Programming

Computer programs, also known as *software,* are made up of a series of instructions that the computer executes. When you create a program, you must specify the instructions that the computer must execute to perform the desired operations. This process of defining the instructions the computer is to execute is called *programming.* You store the instructions in an ASCII file whose name normally contains the extension C for a C program and CPP for a C++ program. For example, if you create a C program that performs payroll operations, you might name the file containing the program instructions PAYROLL.C. When you create programs, you specify the desired instructions using a *programming language.* C and C++ are only two of many programming languages. Many programmers use programming languages such as BASIC, Pascal, and FORTRAN. Different programming languages provide unique features and have their own strengths (and weaknesses). In any case, programming languages exist to let us define the instructions we want the computer to execute.

The instructions a computer executes are actually a set of 1's and 0's (binary digits) that represent electronic signals that occur inside the computer. To program the earliest computers (in the 1940s and 50s), programmers had to understand how the computer interpreted different combinations of 1's and 0's. In fact, these early programmers wrote all of their programs using these binary digits. As programs became larger, it became very impractical to make programmers work in terms of the computer's 1's and 0's. Instead, programming languages were created that let programmers express the computer instructions in a form more meaningful to the programmer. After the programmer placed their instructions in a file (called a *source file*), a second program, called a *compiler,* converted the programming language instructions into the 1's and 0's (called *machine code*) understood by the computer. The files on your disk with the EXE and COM extensions contain the machine code (1's and 0's) the computer will execute. Figure 1 illustrates the process of compiling a source code file into an executable program.

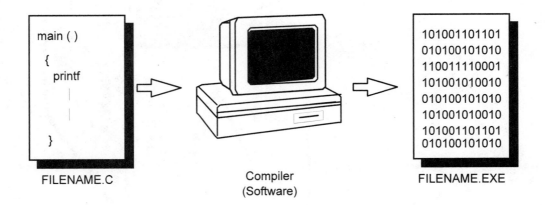

```
main ( )

{
    printf



}
```

FILENAME.C

Compiler
(Software)

FILENAME.EXE

Figure 1 *A compiler converts source code instructions into machine code.*

After you create a source code file, you run a compiler to convert the instructions into a format the computer can execute. If you are using Borland's C++, for example, you invoke the compiler using the BCC command, as shown here:

```
C:\> BCC SourceFile.C  <ENTER>
```

To compile the program PAYROLL.C, for example, you would invoke the compiler as shown here:

```
C:\> BCC PAYROLL.C  <ENTER>
```

The following tips walk you through the steps required to create and compile a C program.

Creating an ASCII Source File

C 2

When you create a program, you must place the instructions that you want the computer to execute in a file called a *source file*. To create the file, you should use an ASCII editor, such as the EDIT command provided with DOS. You should not create programs using a word processor such as Word or WordPerfect. As you know, word processors let you format documents by aligning margins, italicizing and underlining text, and so on. To perform these operations, word processors embed special characters within your documents. Although these characters are meaningful to your word processor, they will confuse the compiler that converts your source file to machine code, causing errors. When you create your source file, make sure you assign a meaningful name that accurately describes the program's function to the file. For example, you might name the source code for a billing program BILLING.C, and the source file for a game program FOOTBALL.C.

Using EDIT or another ASCII-based editor, create the source file FIRST.C, which contains the instructions for your first C program:

```
#include <stdio.h>

void main ()
 {
   printf ("1001 C & C++ Tips!");
 }
```

Although this program contains six lines, only the *printf* statement actually performs any work. When you execute this program, *printf* will display the message *1001 C & C++ Tips!* on your screen. Every programming language (in fact every language, such as English, French, and German), has a set of rules, called *syntax rules* that you must follow when using the language. When you create C programs, you must obey the syntax rules of the C programming language. Examples of syntax rules include the parentheses that follow the name "main" and the semicolon at the end of the *printf* instruction. When you type in your program, you must be very careful that you do not omit any of these elements. Double-check your typing to ensure that you have successfully typed in the C program instructions exactly as they appear above. If the instructions are correct, save the contents of the file to your disk. In Tip 3 you will learn how to compile your source file, converting your C programming instructions to the machine language your computer can understand and execute.

Compiling Your C Program

In Tip 2 you created the C source file, FIRST.C, which contains the *printf* instruction that will display the message *1001 C & C++ Tips!* on your screen when you execute the program. As you read, a source file contains instructions in a format we can understand (or at least we'll be able to understand after learning C). An executable program, on the other hand, contains instructions expressed as 1's and 0's the computer understands. The process of converting your C source file to machine code is *compiling*. Depending on the C compiler you are using, the command you must perform to compile your source file will differ. Assuming you are using Borland's C++, you can compile the program, FIRST.C, that you created in Tip 2 using the BCC command as shown here:

```
C:\> BCC FIRST.C  <ENTER>
```

If you successfully typed in the C statements as shown in Tip 2, the C compiler will create an executable file named FIRST.EXE. You can then execute the program by typing the FIRST command:

```
C:\> FIRST  <ENTER>
1001 C & C++ Tips!
```

If the C compiler does not create the file FIRST.EXE, but instead, displays error messages on your screen, you have probably violated a C syntax rule, as discussed in Tip 4.

Understanding Syntax Errors

As you read in Tip 2, every programming language has a set of rules, called *syntax rules,* that you must obey as you specify your program statements. If you violate a syntax rule, your program will not successfully compile. Instead, the compiler will display error messages on your screen that specify the line of your program that contains the error and a brief description of the error. Using your editor, create the file SYNTAX.C, which contains a syntax error. The program fails to include an ending quote at the end of the message *1001 C & C++ Tips!*:

```
#include <stdio.h>

void main ()
  {
    printf ("1001 C & C++ Tips!);
  }
```

When you compile this program, your compiler will display a syntax error message when it encounters line 3. Depending on your compiler, the actual error message will differ. In the case of Borland's C++ compiler, your screen will display the following error message:

```
C:\> BCC SYNTAX.C  <ENTER>
Error syntax.c 5: Unterminated string or character constant
Error syntax.c 6: Function call missing ) in function main
Error syntax.c 6: Compound statement missing } in function main
*** 3 errors in Compile ***
```

Although the source code SYNTAX.C only contains one error, the C compiler displays three error messages. In this case, the missing quote caused a series of cascading (one error leads to another) errors within the compiler.

When your program contains syntax errors, you should write down the line number of each error and a brief description. Next, edit your source file, moving your cursor to the first line number the compiler displays. Correct the error and move the cursor to the to the next line number. Most editors will display the current line number to help you locate specific lines within the file. In the case of the file SYNTAX.C, edit the file and add the missing quote. Save the file to disk and use your compiler to compile it. With the syntax error corrected, the compiler will create the file SYNTAX.EXE, which you can execute as shown here:

```
C:\> SYNTAX  <ENTER>
1001 C & C++ Tips!
```

The Structure of a Typical C Program

In Tip 2 you created the source file FIRST.C, which contained the following statements:

```
#include <stdio.h>

void main ()
  {
    printf ("1001 C & C++ Tips!");
  }
```

These statements are similar to those found in most C programs. In many cases, a C source file may begin with one or more #*include statements*. The #include statement directs the C compiler to use the contents of a specific file. In the case of the file FIRST.C, the #include statement directs the C compiler to use a file named stdio.h. The files specified in an #include statement are ASCII files that contain C source code. You can print or display the contents of these files by following the steps discussed in Tip 13. Such files, which normally use the h extension are called *include files* or *header files*. They contain statements that are commonly used in your programs. By directing the C compiler to include the file's contents, you don't have to type the statements into your programs yourself. Following the #include statements, you will normally find a statement similar to the following:

```
void main ()
```

Each C program you create will include a line similar to this. As you read in Tip 1, a C program contains a list of instructions you want the computer to execute. As the complexity of your programs increase, you will break them into small pieces that are easier for you (and others who read your programs) to understand. The instructions you want the computer to execute first are called your *main program*. The statement **void main ()** identifies these statements to the C compiler. Next, you need a way to tell the C compiler which instructions correspond to each part of your program. To assign program statements to a specific part, you place the statements within an open ({) and closing brace (}). The braces are a part of C syntax. For every open brace, you must have one closing the group of statements.

C 6 Adding Statements to Your Program

As you have read, the program FIRST.C used the *printf* statement to display a message on your screen. The following C program, 3_MSGS.C, uses three *printf* statements to display the same message. Each of the statements are contained within the program's opening and closing braces.

```
#include <stdio.h>

void main ()
 {
   printf ("1001 ");
   printf ("C and C++ ");
   printf ("Tips!");
 }
```

Note the use of the space character within the *printf* statements to ensure that the text is correctly displayed on your screen. As the number of statements in your programs increases, so too does the likelihood of syntax errors. Double check your program to insure that you have correctly typed each statement and then save the file to disk. When you compile and execute 3_MSGS, your screen will display the following output:

```
C:\> 3_MSGS  <ENTER>
1001 C & C++ Tips!
```

Displaying Output On a New Line

Several of the previous programs have displayed the message *1001 C & C++ Tips!* on your screen display. As your programs become more complex, you might want the programs to display their output on two or more lines. In Tip 5, you created the program 3_MSGS.C that used three *printf* statements to display a message on your screen:

```
printf("1001 ");
printf("C and C++ ");
printf("Tips!");
```

Unless you tell *printf* to do otherwise, *printf* will continue its output on the current line. The goal of the following program, ONE_LINE.C, for example, is to display output on two successive lines:

```
#include <stdio.h>

void main ()
  {
    printf("This is line one.");
    printf("This is the second line.");
  }
```

When you compile and execute this program, your screen will display the following output:

```
C:\> ONE_LINE  <ENTER>
This is line one.This is the second line.
```

When you want *printf* to begin its output on a new line, you need to include the special *newline character* (\n) within the text you direct *printf* to display. When *printf* encounters the \n character, it will advance the cursor to the start of the next line. The following program, TWO_LINE.C, uses the newline character to display the second line of text on a new line as desired:

```
#include <stdio.h>

void main ()
  {
```

```
    printf("This is line one.\n");
    printf("This is the second line.");
}
```

When you compile and execute the program TWO_LINE.C, your screen will display the following output:

```
C:\> TWO_LINE  <ENTER>
This is line one.
This is the second line.
```

Many of the programs presented in this book make use of the newline character.

C 8 C Considers Upper- and Lowercase Letters as Different

As you type in your programs, you must keep in mind that C considers upper- and lowercase letters as different. As a rule, C programs make extensive use of lowercase letters. Because the following program, UPPERERR.C, uses the uppercase letter M in the name *Main*, the program will not successfully compile:

```
#include <stdio.h>

void Main ()
 {
   printf("This program does not compile.");
 }
```

When you compile this program, your compiler will display a message stating that the function *main* was not found (or possibly that it was an unresolved external). In this case, to correct the error, you simply need to change *Main* to *main*.

C 9 Understanding Logic Errors (Bugs)

In Tip 4 you learned that if you violate one of the C language rules, the compiler will display a syntax error message and your program will not successfully compile. As your programs become more complex, there will be many times when the program successfully compiles, but does not correctly perform the task you wanted. For example, assume that you want the following program, ONE_LINE.C, to display its output on two lines:

```
#include <stdio.h>

void main ()
  {
    printf("This is line one.");
    printf("This is the second line.");
  }
```

Because the program does not violate any of C's syntax rules, the program will successfully compile. When you execute the program, however, it does not display its output on two lines, but instead, displays the output on one line, as shown here:

```
C:\> ONE_LINE   <ENTER>
This is line one.This is the second line.
```

When your program does not work as you desire, the program contains *logic errors* or *bugs*. When your program contains a logic error (and eventually your programs will), you must try to figure out the cause of the error and correct it. The process of removing logic errors from your program is *debugging*. Later in this book, you will learn several different techniques you can use to help locate logic errors within your programs. For now, however, the best way to locate such errors is to print a copy of your program and examine the program line by line until you locate the error. This line-by-line examination of the program is called *desk checking*. In the case of the program ONE_LINE.C, your desk checking should reveal that the first *printf* statement does not contain the newline character (\n).

Understanding the Program Development Process

When you create programs, you will normally follow the same steps. To begin, you will use an editor to create your source file. Next, you will compile the program. If the program contains syntax errors, you must edit the source file and correct the errors. After the program successfully compiles, you can run it. If the program runs successfully, you are done. If the program does not work as you expected, you must desk-check the source code as discussed in Tip 8 to locate the logic error. After you correct the error, you must compile the source code to create a new executable file. You can then test the new program to ensure that it performs the desired task. Figure 10 illustrates the program development process.

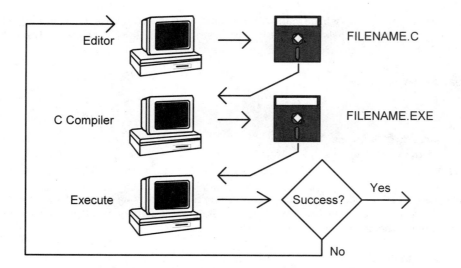

Figure 10 *The program development process.*

C 11   Understanding the File Types

When you create a C program, you place your statements in a source file that uses the C extension. If your program successfully compiles, the compiler will create an executable program file with the EXE extension. As you read in Tip 5, many programs use header files (that use the h extension) that contain commonly used statements. If you examine your directory after compiling a program, its likely that you will find one or more files with the OBJ extension. These files, called *object files*, contain instructions, in the form of 1's and 0's, that the computer understands. You cannot execute object files, however, because their contents are not quite complete.

To reduce the number of statements you must include in your programs, the C compiler provides routines such as *printf* that perform commonly used operations. After the compiler examines your program's syntax, it creates a object file. In the case of the program FIRST.C, the compiler would create an object file named FIRST.OBJ. Next, a program called a *linker* combines the program statements in your object file with the functions such as *printf*, provided by the compiler to build the executable program. In most cases, when you invoke the compiler to examine your source code, the compiler will automatically invoke the linker for you if your program successfully compiles. Figure 11 illustrates the process of compiling and linking a program.

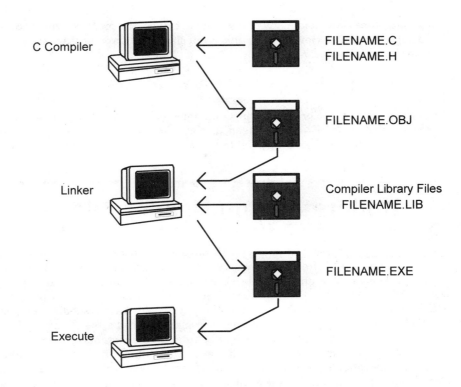

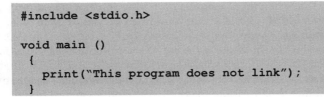

Figure 11 *The process of compiling and linking a program.*

Better Understanding the Linker

In Tip 11 you learned that when you compile your C program, a second program called a linker combines your program statements with predefined routines (provided by the compiler) to convert an object file to an executable program. As was the case with the compilation process, which can detect syntax errors, the linker process can also encounter errors. Consider, for example, the following program, NO_PRINT.C, which erroneously uses *print* instead of *printf*:

```c
#include <stdio.h>

void main ()
  {
    print("This program does not link");
  }
```

Because this program does not violate any of the C syntax rules, the program will successfully compile (producing an OBJ) file. However, the linker will display an error message similar to the following, due to the undefined *print*:

```
Error: Undefined symbol _print in module no_print.c
```

Because the C compiler does not provide a function named *print*, the linker cannot create the executable program NO_PRINT.EXE and instead, displays the undefined symbol error message. To correct the error, edit the file, changing *print* to *printf*, and recompile and link your program.

C13 Understanding Header Files

Each of the programs presented throughout this book use one or more #include statements to direct the C compiler to use the statements contained in a *header file*. A header file is an ASCII file whose contents you can print or display on your screen. If you examine the directory that contains your compiler (the directory BORLANDC in the case of Borland's C++ compiler), you will find a subdirectory named INCLUDE. The INCLUDE subdirectory contains the compiler's header files. Take time now to locate your compiler's header files. You might even want to print the contents of a commonly used header file such as stdio.h. What you will find within the include file are C programming statements. When the compiler encounters a #include statement within your program, the compiler compiles the code contained in the header just as if you had typed the file's contents into your program source code. Header files contain commonly used definitions and provide the compiler with information about compiler-provided functions such as *printf*. For now, you may find the contents of a header file difficult to understand. As you become more conversant in C and C++, however, you should print a copy of and examine each header file you use. The header files contain a wealth of information and provide you with programming techniques that will make you a better C programmer.

C14 Helping the Compiler Locate Header Files

In Tip 12 you learned that when the C compiler encounters an #include statement, the compiler adds the header file's contents within your program, just as if you typed its contents into your source file. Depending on your compiler, your environment entries may contain an INCLUDE= entry that tells the compiler the name of the subdirectory containing the header files. If, when you compile a program, your compiler displays an error message stating it is unable to open a specific header file, first check the subdirectory that contains your compiler's header files to ensure that the file exists. If you find the file, issue the SET command, as shown here:

```
C:\> SET  <ENTER>
COMSPEC=C:\DOS\COMMAND.COM
PATH=C:\DOS;C:\WINDOWS;C:\BORLANDC\BIN
PROMPT=$P$G
TEMP=C:\TEMP
```

If your environment does not contain an INCLUDE= entry, check the documentation that accompanied your compiler to determine if your compiler requires such an entry. Normally, the compiler's installation will place a SET command in your AUTOEXEC.BAT file that assigns the INCLUDE= entry to the subdirectory containing the header files, as shown here:

```
SET  INCLUDE=C:\BORLANDC\INCLUDE
```

If your compiler uses the INCLUDE entry and your AUTOEXEC.BAT file does not define the entry, you can create the entry yourself, placing it in your AUTOEXEC.BAT file.

Speeding Up Compilations

When you compile a source file, the C compiler might create one or more temporary files that exist only while the compiler and linker is working. Depending on your compiler, you may be able to use the TEMP environment entry to specify where the compiler creates these temporary files. If your computer has enough memory for you to create a RAM drive, you might consider assigning the TEMP entry to point to the drive. In this way, the compiler will create its temporary files on the very fast RAM drive, which speeds up the compilation process. Assuming that you have created the RAM drive D, you can assign the TEMP entry to drive by placing a SET command within your AUTOEXEC.BAT file as shown here:

```
SET  TEMP=D:
```

Commenting Your Programs

As a rule, each time you create a program you need to ensure that you include *comments* in the program that explain the processing the program performs. In short, a comment is simply a message that helps you (or someone) read and understand the program. As your programs increase in length, the programs become more difficult to understand. Because you may eventually create hundreds and possibly thousands of programs, it will be impossible for you to remember the purpose of every statement within every program. If you include comments in your program, you won't have to remember each program's details. Instead, the program's comments will explain the processing.

Most newer C and C++ compilers provide two ways for you to place comments within your source file. First, you place two forward slash (//) characters together, as shown here:

```
// This is a comment
```

When the C compiler encounters the double slashes, it ignores the text that follows to the end of the current line. The following program, COMMENT.C, illustrates the use of comments.

```c
// Program: COMMENT.C
// Written by: Kris Jamsa
// Date written: 06-30-93

// Purpose: Illustrates the use of comments in a C program.

#include <stdio.h>

void main ()
  {
    printf("1001 C & C++ Tips!");  // Display a message
  }
```

In this case, you immediately know who wrote the program, when, and why by reading these simple comments. Get in the habit of placing similar comments at the start of your programs. Should other programmers who must read or change the program have questions, they quickly know the program's original author.

When the C compiler encounters the double slashes (//), it ignores the text on the line that follows. Most newer C source files use the double slashes to designate a comment. If you are reading an older C program, you may encounter comments that appear between a set of slashes and asterisks, as shown here:

```
/* This is a comment */
```

When the compiler encounters the opening comment symbol (/*) it ignores all text up to and including the closing comment symbol (*/). Using the */* comment */* format, a single comment can appear on two or more lines. The following program, COMMENT2.C, illustrates the use of the */* comment */* format:

```c
/* Program: COMMENT.C
   Written by: Kris Jamsa
   Date written: 06-30-93

   Purpose: Illustrates the use of comments in a C program. */

#include <stdio.h>

void main ()
```

```
{
    printf("1001 C & C++ Tips!");   /* Display a message */
}
```

As you can see, the program's first comment contains five lines. When you use the */* comment
/, make sure that every starting comment symbol (/*) has a corresponding ending symbol (*/).
If the ending symbol is missing, the C compiler will ignore much of your program, eventually
resulting in syntax errors that can be difficult to detect.

Most C compilers will not let you place one comment within another (called nesting comments),
as shown here:

```
/* This comment has /* a second */ comment inside */
```

Improving Your Program Readability

In Tip 15 you learned how to use comments within your programs to improve
their readability. Each time you create a program, assume that you or another
programmer will eventually have to change the program in some way. As such, it's essential that
you write your programs so they are easy to read. The following C program, HARDREAD.C,
displays a message on your screen:

```
#include <stdio.h>
void main() {printf("1001 C & C++ Tips!");}
```

Although this program will compile and successfully display the desired message, the program
is difficult, at best, to read. A *good* program not only works, but is also easy to read and understand.
The key to creating readable programs is including comments that explain the program's
processing and the use of blank lines to improve the program's format. In later tips you will learn
the important role indentation plays in producing readable program code.

Pay Attention to Compiler Warning Messages

When your program contains one or more syntax errors, the C compiler will
display error messages on your screen and will not create an executable program.
As you create programs, there may be times when your compiler displays one or more *Warning*

messages on your screen, but still creates the executable program file. For example, the following C program, NO_STDIO.C, does not include the header file stdio.h:

```
void main ()
 {
   printf ("1001 C & C++ Tips");
 }
```

When you compile this program, your compiler might display a warning message similar to the following:

```
Warning no_stdio.c 3: Call to function 'printf' with no prototype
```

As a rule, when the compiler displays a warning message, determine the cause of the compiler complaint and correct it. Although the warnings might never cause an error during your program's execution, some warnings leave open the opportunity for errors that are very difficult to debug later. By taking time to locate and correct the cause of compiler warnings, you will learn much more about the inner workings of C and C++.

C19 Controlling Compiler Warnings

In Tip 18 you learned that you should pay attention to the warning messages that your compiler displays on your screen. To help you make better use of compiler warnings, many compilers let you set the desired message level. The higher the level, the more messages the compiler will generate. If you are using Borland C++, for example, the following warning levels apply:

Level	Messages
1	Only severe messages
2	Severe and middle-level warnings
3	All warning messages

Depending on your compiler, the command-line switch you use to control the warning level may differ. Refer to the documentation that accompanied your compiler. In addition, some compilers may let you disable specific warning messages. In the case of Borland C++, the following command line uses the *–w* switch to disable the *Identifier is declared but never used* warning:

```
C:\> BCC -wuse FILENAME.C  <ENTER>
```

Refer to the documentation that accompanied your compiler to determine if you can turn off specific warning messages.

Using Comments to Exclude Program Statements

C 20

In Tip 16 you learned that you should place comments within your programs to improve your program's readability. As your programs become more complex, you may use comments to help you debug (remove errors) from your programs. When the C compiler encounters the double slashes (//), the compiler ignores the current line text that follows. Likewise, when the compiler encounters the starting comment symbol (/*), the compiler ignores all of the text that follows, up to and including the closing comment symbol (*/). As you test your programs, there may be times when you want to eliminate one or more statements from your program. One way to eliminate the program statements is to simply delete the statements from your source file. A second way to eliminate statements is to "comment them out." The following program, NOOUTPUT.C, comments out all of the *printf* statements:

```c
#include <stdio.h>

void main ()
  {
    // printf("This line does not appear");

    /* This is a comment

       printf("This line does not appear either");

    */
  }
```

Because both *printf* statements appear within comments, the compiler ignores both of them. As a result, when you execute the program, no output appears:

```
C:\> NOOUTPUT   <ENTER>

C:\>
```

As your programs become more complex, using comments to disable statements is very convenient.

Most C compilers will not let you place one comment within another (called nesting comments), as shown here:

```c
/* This comment has /* a second */ comment inside */
```

When you use comments to disable statements, be careful that you do not inadvertantly nest comments.

C 21 What's in a Name?

As you examine the tips presented throughout this book, you will encounter variable names and functions whose names begin with an underscore, such as _dos_getdrive_ or _chmod_. Such variables and functions can normally only be used within the DOS environment. If you are writing programs that will execute under DOS, UNIX, and possibly some other operating system, you should avoid using these functions because they will not be available under the other systems. As such, to move your program from DOS to another operating system, you will have to perform additional programming. Some functions may have two implementations, one with an underscore (_chmod_), and one without (_chmod_). As a rule, use the function or variable that does not use the underscore, in this case, _chmod_.

C 22 Understanding the Semicolon

As you examine C programs, you will find that the programs make extensive use of semicolons. The semicolon in C has special meaning. As you know, a program is a list of instructions that you want the computer to perform. When you specify those instructions in C, you use the semicolon to separate one statement from another. As your programs become more complex, you may find that a statement does not fit on one line. When the C compiler examines your program, it uses the semicolon to distinguish one statement from the next. The use of the semicolon is defined by the C language syntax. If you omit the semicolon, a syntax error will occur, and the program will not successfully compile.

C 23 Understanding Variables

To perform useful work, programs must store information, not only within a file, such as document that you edit over multiple computer sessions, but also internally. As you know, each time you run a program, the operating system loads your program's instructions into the computer's memory. As the program runs, its stores values in memory locations. For example, assume that a you have a program that prints a document. Each time you run the program, it displays a message asking you the name of the file, as well as the number of copies you want to print. As you type in this information, the program stores the values you enter in specific memory locations. To help your program track the memory locations in which it has placed data, each memory location has a unique *address*, such as location 0, 1, 2, 3, and so on. Because there can be billions of such addresses, you can guess that keeping track of the individual storage locations can become very difficult. To simplify the storage of information, programs define *variables*, which are simply names that the program associates with specific locations in memory. As the word *variable* implies, the value that the program stores in these locations can change or vary throughout the program's lifetime.

Each variable has a specific *type*, which tells the computer how much memory the data requires and the operations that can be performed on the data. Given the previous example, the program might use a variable named *filename* (that stores the name of the file you want to print) and one named *count* (that stores the number of copies you want to print). Within your program, you reference variables by name. Therefore, you should assign meaningful names to each variable. Within your C programs, you normally declare your variables immediately following *main*, before your program statements, as shown here:

```
void main ()
{
  // Variables go here

  printf("1001 C & C++ Tips!);
}
```

The following program, for example, shows how you would declare three integer variables (variables that store counting numbers such as 1, 2, and 3):

```
void main ()
{
    int age;        // The user's age in years
    int weight;     // The user's weight in pounds
    int height;     // The user's height in inches

    // Other program statements go here
}
```

Each variable has a type that defines the amount of memory the variable requires, as well as the operations the program can perform on the data. To declare an integer variable, your C programs use the type *int*. Once you declare a variable (tell the program the variable's name and type), you can then assign value to the variable (store information).

Assigning a Value to a Variable

C24

A variable is a name that your program associates with a storage location in memory. After you declare a variable within your program, you can assign it a value. In C, you assign a value to a variable using the equal sign (called the *assignment operator*). The following program declares three variables of type *int* and then assigns each variable a value:

```
void main ()
{
    int age;        // The user's age in years
    int weight;     // The user's weight in pounds
    int height;     // The user's height in inches
```

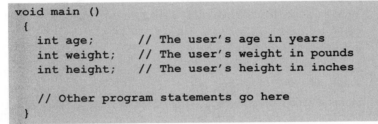

```
    age = 41;        // Assign the user's age
    weight = 165;    // Assign the user's weight
    height = 73;     // Assign the user's height

    // Other program statements
}
```

25 Understanding Variable Types

When you declare variables within your programs, you must tell the C compiler the variable's name and type. A type defines the set of values the variable can store, as well as the set of operations that can be performed on the data. As defined in Table 25, C supports four basic types.

Type Name	Purpose
char	Stores a single character, such as a letter from A through Z
int	Stores counting numbers (called integers) such as 1, 2, and 3, as well as negative numbers
float	Stores a single-precision floating-point numbers (with a decimal point), such as 3.14 or −54.1343
double	Stores a double-precision floating-point numbers (which is more precise for very large or very small numbers)

Table 25 *The four basic types supported by C.*

Several of the tips presented throughout this book examine each of these types in detail.

26 Declaring Multiple Variables of the Same Type

When you declare a variable within your program, you must tell the C compiler the variable's name and type. The following statements declare three variables of type *int*:

```
int age;
int weight;
int height;
```

When you declare variables of the same type, C lets you list the variable names on one or more lines, with each variable name separated by commas, as shown here:

```
int age, weight, height;
float salary, taxes;
```

Commenting Your Variables at Declaration

27

In C programs, comments help someone who is reading your program better understand it. When you choose variable names, you should select names that meaningfully describe the value the variable will store. For example, consider the following declarations:

```
int age, weight, height;
int x, y, z;
```

Both declarations create three variables of type int. In the case of the first declaration, however, you have an idea of the variable's use simply by examining the variable's name. In addition to using meaningful names, it is a good rule to place a comment next to each variable declaration that further explains the variable, as shown here:

```
int age;        // The user's age in years
int weight;     // The user's weight in pounds
int height;     // The user's height in inches
```

Assigning Values to Variables at Declaration

28

After you declare a variable within your program, you can use the C assignment operator (the equal sign =) to assign a value to the variable. As it turns out, C lets you assign a value to a variable within the variable's declaration. Programmers refer to the process of assigning variable's first value as *initializing* the variable. The following statements, for example, declare and initialize three variables of type int:

```
int age = 41;       // The user's age in years
int weight = 165;   // The user's weight in pounds
int height = 73;    // The user's height in inches
```

C 29 Initializing Multiple Variables During Declaration

In Tip 26 you learned that C lets you declare two or variables on the same line, as shown here:

```
int age, weight, height;
```

When you declare multiple variables on the same line, C lets you initialize one or more of the variables:

```
int age = 44, weight, height = 73;
```

In this case, C will initialize the variables *age* and *height*, leaving the variable *weight* undefined.

C 30 Using Meaningful Variable Names

When you declare variables in your programs, you should choose meaningful variable names that describe the variable's use. As discussed in Tip 8, the C compiler distinguishes between upper- and lowercase letters. Your variable names can use a combination of upper- and lowercase letters. If you use upper- and lowercase letters in your variable names, you must always specify the same upper- and lowercase letter combinations. As you get started, you should probably stick to lowercase letters.

Each variable you declare within your programs must have a unique name. In general, you can use an unlimited number of characters in a variable name. Your variable names can contain a combination of letters, numbers, and the underscore character (_) however, the names must start with a letter or underscore. The following statements illustrate valid variable names:

```
int hours_worked;
float tax_rate;
float _6_month_rate;   // Starting _underscore is valid
```

Finally, C predefines several *keywords* that have special meaning to the C compiler. As you create variable names you cannot use these keywords. Tip 31 lists C's keywords.

Understanding C's Keywords

31

The C programming language defines several keywords that have special meaning to the compiler. As you choose variable names (and create your own functions), you cannot use these keywords. Table 31 lists C keywords.

auto	default	float	register	struct	volatile
break	do	for	return	switch	while
case	double	goto	short	typedef	
char	else	if	signed	union	
const	enum	int	sizeof	unsigned	
continue	extern	long	static	void	

Table 31 *The C keyword list.*

Understanding Variables of Type int

32

A *variable* is a name that the C compiler associates with one or more memory locations. When you declare a variable within your program, you must specify the variable's type and name. A variable's *type* specifies the kind of values that variable can store and the set of operations that the program can perform on the data. C uses the type int to store integer values (positive and negative counting numbers). The C compiler normally allocates a sixteen bits (2 bytes) to store values of type int. A variable of type int can store values in the range –32,768 through 32,767. Figure 32 illustrates how C represents an integer value.

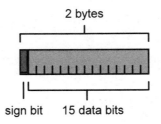

Figure 32 *How C represents an integer value.*

Values of type int are whole numbers, they do not include a fractional portion as do floating-point numbers. If you assign a floating-point value to a variable of type int, most C compilers will simply truncate the fractional portion. If you assign a variable of type int a value outside of the range –32,768 through 32,767, an overflow condition will occur, and the value assigned will be in error.

C 33 Understanding Variables of Type char

A *variable* is a name that the C compiler associates with one or more memory locations. When you declare a variable within your program, you must specify the variable's type and name. A variable's *type* specifies the kind of values that variable can store and the set of operations that the program can perform on the data. C uses the type char to store character (byte) values (positive and negative counting numbers). The C compiler normally allocates a eight bits (1 byte) to store values of type char. A variable of type char can store values in the range –128 through 127. Figure 33 illustrates how C represents a value of type char.

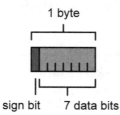

Figure 33 *How C represents a value of type char.*

Programs can assign a value to a variable of type char in one of two ways. First, the program can assign a character's ASCII value. For example, the letter A has the ASCII value 65:

```
char letter = 65;  // Assign letter the character A
```

Second, your program can use a character constant, which appears within single quotes, as shown here:

```
char letter = 'A';
```

Variables of type char only hold one letter at a time. To store a multiple characters, you must declare a character string, as discussed in the Strings section of this book.

Understanding Variables of Type float

A *variable* is a name that the C compiler associates with one or more memory locations. When you declare a variable within your program, you must specify the variable's type and name. A variable's *type* specifies the kind of values that variable can store and the set of operations that the program can perform on the data. C uses the type *float* to store floating-point values (positive and negative numbers that contain fractional portions). The C compiler normally allocates a 32 bits (4 bytes) to store values of type float. A variable of type float can store values with 6 to 7 decisions of precision, in the range 3.4E–38 through 3.4E+38. Figure 34 illustrates how C represents a value of type float.

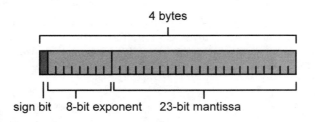

Figure 34 *How C represents a value of type float.*

Understanding Variables of Type double

A *variable* is a name that the C compiler associates with one or more memory locations. When you declare a variable within your program, you must specify the variable's type and name. A variable's *type* specifies the kind of values that variable can store and the set of operations that the program can perform on the data. C uses the type *double* to store floating-point values (positive and negative numbers that contain fractional portions). The C compiler normally allocates a 64 bits (8 bytes) to store values of type float. A variable of type double can store values with 14 to 15 digits of precision, in the range –1.7E-308 through 1.7E+308. Figure 35 illustrates how C represents a value of type double.

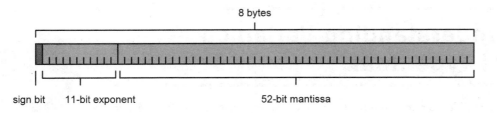

Figure 35 *How C represents a value of type double.*

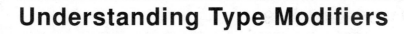

C 36
Assigning Values to Floating-Point Values

A *floating-point* value is a value that contains a fractional part, such as 123.45. When you work with floating-point values within your programs, you can refer to the values using their decimal format, such as 123.45, or you can use the value's exponential format, 1.2345E2. Thus, the following statements assign the variable *radius* the same value:

```
radius = 123.45;
radius = 1.2345E2;
```

In a similar way, the following statements assign the variable *radius* the same value:

```
radius = 0.12345;
raidus = 12.345E-2;
```

C 37
Understanding Type Modifiers

C provides four basic data types, int, char, float, and double. As you learned, each type defines a set of values the variable can store and the set of operations that can be performed on the data. As you have learned, variables of type int can store values in the range –32,768 through 32,767. Likewise, variables of type char can store values in the range –128 through 127. To help you change the range of values that variables of type int and char can store, C provides a set of *type modifiers*: unsigned, long, register, signed, and short. To modify a type, place the type modifier in front of type name in a variable declaration, as shown here:

```
unsigned int inventory_count;
register int counter;
long int very_large_number;
```

Several of the tips that follow discuss these type modifiers in detail.

Understanding the unsigned Type Modifier

38

A type modifier changes (modifies) the range of values a variable can store or the way the compiler stores a variable. As discussed, variables of type int can store positive and negative values in the range –32,768 through 32,767. Within the representation of the a value of type int, the value's most significant bit indicates the value's sign (positive or negative), as previously shown in Tip 32. In some cases, the value your program needs to store may never be negative. The *unsigned* type modifier tells the compiler not to use the most significant bit as a sign bit, but rather, to allow the bit to be used to represent larger positive values. A variable of type unsigned int can store values in the range 0 through 65,535. Figure 38.1 illustrates how the C compiler stores an unsigned int.

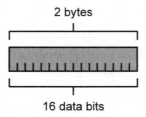

Figure 38.1 *How the C compiler represents values of type unsigned int.*

As discussed in Tip 33, variables of type char can hold values in the range –128 through 127. Using the unsigned type modifier with variables of type char, you can create variables that can store values in the range 0 through 255. Figure 38.2 illustrates how the C compiler represents an unsigned char.

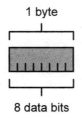

Figure 38.2 *How the C compiler represents variables of type unsigned char.*

The following statements illustrate declarations of variables whose type is unsigned int or unsigned char:

```
void main ()
  {
    unsigned int current_seconds;
    unsigned int status_indicator;
    unsigned char menu_border;     // Extended ASCII character
  }
```

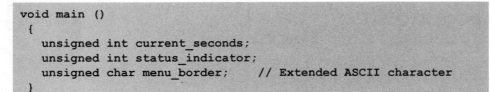

39 Understanding the long Type Modifier

A type modifier changes (modifies) the range of values a variable can store or the way the compiler stores a variable. Variables of type int can store positive and negative values in the range –-32,768 through 32,767. As previously shown in Tip 31, the C compiler represents values of type int using 16 bits, with the most significant bit indicating the value's sign. In many cases, your programs will need to store integer values that are larger or more negative than the range of values a variable of type int can hold. The *long* type modifier tells the compiler to use 32 bits (4 bytes) to represent the integer values. A variable of type long int can store values in the range –2,147,483,648 through 2,147,483,647. Figure 39 illustrates how the C compiler stores a long int.

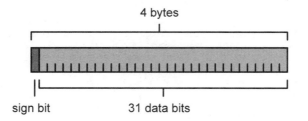

Figure 39 *How the C compiler represents values of type long int.*

The following statements illustrate declarations of type long int:

```
void main ()
  {
    long int seconds_since_january_1;
    long int company_profit;
  }
```

Combining the unsigned and long Type Modifiers

C 40

In Tip 38 you learned that unsigned type modifier directs the C compiler not to interpret a value's most significant bit as a sign indicator, but rather, to use it represent a larger value. Likewise, in Tip 39 you learned that the long type modifier directs the compiler to double the number of bits it uses to represent an integer value. In some cases, your programs may need to store very large positive values. By combining the unsigned and long type modifiers, you can direct the C compiler to allocate a 32-bit variable capable of values in the range 0 through 4,292,967,265. Figure 40 illustrates how the C compiler would represent an unsigned long int.

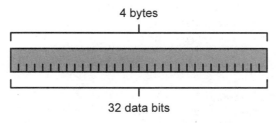

Figure 40 *How the C compiler represents values of type unsigned long int.*

The following statements illustrate a declaration of variables of type unsigned long int:

```
void main ()
 {
    unsigned long int very_large_value;
    unsigned long int national_debt;
 }
```

Working with Large Values

C 41

As you have learned, variables of type int can store values in the range -32,768 through 32,767. Likewise, variables of type long int can store values in the range −2,147,483,648 through 2,147,483,647. When you work with large values in your programs, do not include the commas, as shown here:

```
long int big_number = 1234567;
long int one_million = 1000000;
```

If you include commas within your numbers, the C compiler will generate a syntax error.

C42 Understanding the register Type Modifier

A variable is the name that your program associates with a memory location. When you declare a variable, the C compiler allocates memory to hold the variable's value. When your program needs to access the variable, slight overhead occurs (time is consumed) when the CPU accesses memory. Depending on the variable's use, there may be times when you can increase your program's performance by directing the compiler to store the variable in a register (which resides within the CPU itself) as often as possible. Because the compiler can access the value much faster when it resides in a register, your program will execute faster. The *register* type modifier directs the compiler to keep the variable in a register as often as possible. Because the number of registers in the CPU are limited, the compiler cannot permanently assign the variable to a register. Instead, the compiler will try to keep the variable in a register as often as possible. The following statements illustrate use of the register type modifier:

```
void main ()
  {
    register int counter;
    register unsigned status_flags;
  }
```

The register type modifier should be used with variables that your program repeatedly accesses, such as a counter (loop variable).

C43 Understanding the short Type Modifier

The C compiler normally represents values of type int using 16 bits. As such, the values of type int can store values in the range –32,768 through 32,767. If you are using a 32-bit compiler, however, the compiler may represent an integer value using 32 bits, which means a variable of type int could store values in the range –2,147,483,648 through 2,147,483,647. If you store a value that is outside of the range an integer can store, an *overflow condition* occurs, and the value assigned is in error. Some programs are written with the knowledge that when an overflow occurs, the errant value assigned is done so consistently. In other words, the program is written to use overflow. Should you move a program that uses values of type int in this way from a 16-bit to 32-bit environment, the overflow would no longer occur because the 32-bit integer can store the larger value. If you write a program that is based on overflow, you can use the *short* type modifier to ensure that the compiler represents a variable using 16 bits. The following statements illustrate declarations of variables of type short int:

```
void main ()
  {
    short int key_value;
    short int small_number;
  }
```

Omitting int from Modified Declarations

C 44

Several of the tips in this section have discussed the use of type modifiers such as long, short, and unsigned. The following statements illustrate the use of these modifiers:

```
unsigned int status_flags;
short int small_value;
long int very_big_number;
```

When you use these type modifiers, most compilers will let you omit the *int*, as shown here:

```
unsigned status_flags;
short small_value;
long very_big_number;
```

Understanding the signed Type Modifier

C 45

C compilers normally represent variables of type char using eight bits, with the most significant bit used to represent the values sign. As such, variables of type char can store values in the range −128 through 127. As you have learned, using the unsigned qualifier, you can direct the C compiler not to interpret the sign bit, but rather to use the bit to represent a larger positive value. Using the unsigned type modifier, a variable of type char can store values in the range 0 through 255. If you are using a variable of type char and you assign to the variable a value outside the range of valid values, overflow will occur, and the value assigned will be in error. In some cases, however, programs are written with overflow in mind. If you plan to move such a program to a different compiler, that may represent variables of type char as unsigned, you can use the *signed* type modifier to ensure that compiler represents variables of type char using 8 bits, with 7 bits for the data and 1 bit for sign bit. The following statements illustrates declarations of type signed char:

```
void main ()
 {
   signed char byte_value;
   signed char menu_choice;
 }
```

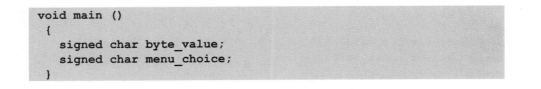

Multiple Assignment Operations

As you have learned, C uses the equal sign (=) as its assignment operator. Normally, your C programs will assign values to variables on distinct lines, as shown here:

```
count = 0;
sum = 0;
value = 0;
```

When you are assigning the same value to multiple variables, C lets you perform the assignments at one time, as shown here:

```
count = sum = value = 0;
```

When C encounters a multiple assignment operation, C assigns values from right to left. As a rule, only use multiple assignments to initialize variables. Using such operations for more complex operations will probably decrease your program's readability. For example, the following program assigns two variables the uppercase equivalent to the character typed by the user:

```
ltr_save = letter = toupper(getchar());
```

Assigning the Value of One Variable Type to a Different Variable Type

A type defines the set of values a variable can store and the set of operations that can be performed on the data. C provides four basic data types (int, float, char, and double). In some cases, you may need to assign the value of a variable of type int to a value of type float, or vice versa. As a general rule, you can successfully assign a value of type int to a variable of type float. When you assign the value of a variable of float to a variable of type int, however, you need to take care. Most compilers will truncate the floating-point value, discarding the fractional portion. However, a different compiler might round the value. If you want to ensure that such assignments are performed consistently, you might consider using the *ceil* and *floor* functions, presented in the Math section of this book.

Creating Your Own Types

A type defines the set of values a variable can store and the set of operations that can be performed on the data. C provides four basic data types (int, float, char, and double). As you have learned, by combining type modifiers you change the range of values a variable can store. As the number of variables your program declares increase, you may find it convenient to create your own variable name, which provides a shorthand name for a commonly used type. For example, consider the following declarations of type unsigned long int:

```
unsigned long int seconds_since_january;
unsigned long int world_population_in_2000;
```

Using C's *typedef* statement, you can define the type name ULINT that is identical to the type unsigned long int, as shown here:

```
typedef unsigned long int ULINT;
```

After the type name exists, you can use it define variables, as shown here:

```
ULINT seconds_since_january;
ULINT world_population_in_2000;
```

As your programs use more complex variable declarations, you may find using to create a new type name is very convenient.

Assigning a Hexadecimal or Octal Value

Depending on your application, there may be times when you need to work with octal (base 8) or hexadecimal (base 16) values. In such cases, you need a way of telling the compiler you want to work with values that aren't decimal. If you precede a numeric value with a 0, such as 077, the C compiler treats the value as octal. Likewise, if you precede a value with 0x, such as 0xFF, the compiler treats the value as hexadecimal. The following statements illustrate the use of an octal and hexadecimal constant:

```
int octal_value = 0227;
int hex_value = 0xFF0;
```

C 50 Understanding Overflow

A variable's type defines the range of values a variable can store and the operations that can be performed on the variable. Variables of type int, for example, can store values in the range –32,768 through 32,767. If you assign a value outside of this range to a variable of type int, an *overflow* error will occur. C uses 16 bits to represent variables of type int. The most significant of the 16 bits is used to determine the variable's sign. If the most significant bit is 0, the value is positive. If the most significant bit is 1, the value is negative. C then uses 15 bits to represent the variable's value. To understand why overflow occurs, you need to consider the value's bitwise implementation. Consider the following values:

```
   0      0000 0000 0000 0000
   1      0000 0000 0000 0001
   2      0000 0000 0000 0010
   3      0000 0000 0000 0011
   4      0000 0000 0000 0100

32,765   0111 1111 1111 1101
32,766   0111 1111 1111 1110
32,767   0111 1111 1111 1111
```

If you add 1 to the value 32,767, you would expect the result to be 32,768. However, to C, the value becomes –32,768, as shown here:

```
32,767   0111 1111 1111 1111
+   1    0000 0000 0000 0001
---------------------------------
-32,768  1000 0000 0000 0000
```

The following program, OVERFLOW.C, illustrates how overflow occurs:

```c
#include <stdio.h>

void main (void)
 {
    int positive = 32767;
    int negative = -32768;

    printf("%d + 1 is %d\n", positive, positive+1);
    printf("%d - 1 is %d\n", negative, negative-1);
 }
```

When you compile and execute this program, your screen displays the following output:

```
C:\> OVERFLOW  <ENTER>
32767 + 1 is -32768
-32768 - 1 is 32767
```

As you can see, adding a value to 32,767 yields a negative number, whereas subtracting a value from −32,768 produces a positive number. One of the problems that makes overflow difficult is that within your program, the error goes essentially unnoticed. In other words, the program's execution continues, although the overflow occurs. As a result, errors resulting from overflow can be very difficult to detect.

Understanding Precision

C 51

Within the computer, numbers are represented using combinations of 1's and 0's (binary digits). Because a type has a fixed number of bits, each type can only hold a specific range of values. If you assign a value outside of the range, an overflow error occurs. Floating-point values can experience overflow and can suffer from insufficient precision, which defines a value's degree of accuracy. Values of type float, for example, provide 6 to 7 significant digits. Assume, for example, you assign the value 1.234567890 to a variable of type float. Because float only provides 7 digits of significance, you can only count on values 1.23456 being accurate. Values of type double, on the other hand, provide 14 to 15 significant digits. As a result, a value of type double could accurately store 1.234567890.

When you work with floating-point numbers, you need to be aware of the fact that the values are represented using a fixed number of bits. As such, it is impossible for the computer to always represent values in an exact manner. For example, the computer may represent the value 0.4 as 0.3999999, or the value 0.1 as 0.099999) and so on. The following program, PRECISE.C, illustrates the difference between double and single precision:

```c
#include <stdio.h>

void main ()
  {
    float accurate = 0.123456790987654321;
    double more_accurate = 0.1234567890987654321;

    printf("Value of float\t %21.19f\n", accurate);
    printf("Value of double\t %21.19f\n", more_accurate);
  }
```

When you compile and execute this program, your screen will display the following output:

```
C:\> PRECISE  <ENTER>
Value of float  0.1234567890432815550
Value of double 0.1234567890987654380
```

C 52 Assigning Quotes and Other Characters

As you work with variables of type char or with character strings, there may be times when you need to assign a single or double quote character. In such cases, you must place the character within single quotes preceded by a backslash (\), as shown here:

```
char single_quote = '\'';
char double_quote = '\"';
```

In addition to the quote characters, you may need to assign one of the special characters listed in Table 52. In such, cases, simply place the character's symbol immediately after the backslash character. In all cases, you must use lowercase letters to represent the special character.

Escape Character	Meaning
\a	ASCII bell character
\b	Backspace character
\f	Formfeed character
\n	Newline character
\r	Carriage return (no linefeed)
\t	Horizontal tab
\v	Vertical tab
\\	Backslash character
\'	Single quote
\"	Double quote
\?	Question mark
\nnn	ASCII value in octal
\xnnn	ASCII value in hexadecimal

Table 52 *Escape characters defined by C.*

C 53 Getting Started with *printf*

Several of the tips presented throughout this book have used the *printf* function to display messages on the screen. When your program uses *printf*, the information you direct *printf* to print is called *printf*'s *parameters* or *arguments*. The following statement uses *printf* to display the message *1001 C & C++ Tips!* on your screen display:

```
printf("1001 C & C++ Tips!");
```

In this case, the character string (the letters that appear within the double quotes) is *printf*'s only argument. When your programs begin to work with variables, you will want to use *printf* to display their values. The *printf* function supports more than one parameter. The first parameter must always be a character string. The parameters that follow can be numbers, variables, expressions (such as 3 * 15), or even other character strings. When you want *printf* to display a value or variable, you must provide *printf* with information about the variable's type within the first parameter. In addition to letting you specify characters within the first parameter, you can include *format specifiers*, which tell *printf* how to print the other parameters. Such format specifics take the form of a percent sign (%) followed by a letter. For example, to display an integer value, you use the %d (d for decimal value). Likewise, to print a floating-point value, you can use %f. The following *printf* statements illustrate the use of *printf* format specifiers:

```
printf("The users age is %d\n", age);
printf("The sales tax is f\n", cost * 0.07);
printf("The user's age: %d weight: %d height: %d\n", age,
  weight, height);
```

As you can see, within *printf*'s first parameter, you can specify one or more format specifiers. Note that the third statement does not fit on one line and continues to the next. When your statements cannot fit on one line, try to find a good place to wrap the line, such as immediately after a comma, and then indent the line that follows. The purpose of the indentation is to improve your program's visual appeal and to make obvious to someone who is reading your program that the line contains a continuation of the previous line. Several of the tips that follow discuss different *printf* format specifiers in detail.

Displaying Values of Type int Using *printf*

C 54

The *printf* function supports format specifiers that provide it with information about its parameter types (such as int, float, char, and so on). To display values of type int with *printf*, you should use the %d format specifier. The following program, INTOUT.C, uses the %d format specifier to values and variables of type int:

```
#include <stdio.h>

void main ()
  {
    int age = 41;
    int height = 73;
    int weight = 165;

    printf("The user's age: %d weight: %d height: %d\n",
      age, weight, height);
```

```
    printf("%d plus %d equals %d\n", 1, 2, 1 + 2);
}
```

When you compile and execute this program, your screen will display the following output:

```
C:\> INTOUT  <ENTER>
The user's age: 41 weight: 165 height: 73
1 plus 2 equals 3
```

Note: *Many C compilers treat the %i format specifier as identical to %d. If you are creating a new program, however, use the %d specifier.*

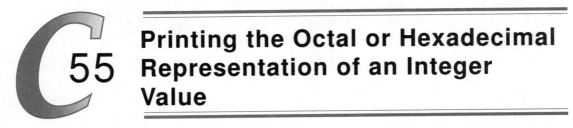

55 Printing the Octal or Hexadecimal Representation of an Integer Value

The *printf* function supports format specifiers that provide it with information about its parameter types (such as int, float, char, and so on). Depending on your program, there may be times when you want to display an integer value in its octal (base 8) or hexadecimal (base 16) format. The %o format specifier directs *printf* to display a value in octal. In a similar way, the %x and %X specifiers direct *printf* to display a value in hexadecimal. The difference between %x and %X is that the latter displays hexadecimal values in uppercase. The following program, OCT_HEX.C, illustrates the use of the %o, %x, and %X format specifiers:

```
#include <stdio.h>

void main ()
  {
    int value = 255;

    printf("The decimal value %d in octal is %o\n",
        value, value);

    printf("The decimal value %d in hexadecimal is %x\n",
        value, value);

    printf("The decimal value %d in hexadecimal is %X\n",
        value, value);
  }
```

When you compile and execute this program, your screen will display the following output:

```
C:\> OCT_HEX  <ENTER>
The decimal value 255 in octal is 377
The decimal value 255 in hexadecimal is ff
The decimal value 255 in hexadecimal is FF
```

Displaying Values of Type unsigned int Using *printf*

56

The *printf* function supports format specifiers that provide it with information about its parameter types (such as int, float, char, and so on). To display values of type unsigned int with *printf,* you should use the %u format specifier. If you use %d instead of %u, *printf* will treat the value specified as type int, quite probably displaying the wrong result. The following program, U_INTOUT.C, uses the %u format specifier, as well as %d, to display the value 42000. The program illustrates the type of error that can occur should you use the wrong format specifier:

```c
#include <stdio.h>

void main ()
  {
    unsigned int value = 42000;

    printf("Displaying 42000 as unsigned %u\n", value);
    printf("Displaying 42000 as int %d\n", value);
  }
```

When you compile and execute this program, your screen will display the following output:

```
C:\> U_INTOUT  <ENTER>
Displaying 42000 as unsigned 42000
Displaying 42000 as int -23536
```

Displaying Values of Type long int Using *printf*

57

The *printf* function supports format specifiers that provide it with information about its parameter types (such as int, float, char, and so on). To display values of type long int with *printf,* you should use the %ld format specifier. If you use %d instead of %ld, *printf* would treat the value specified as type int, quite probably displaying the wrong result. The following program, LONGOUT.C, uses the %ld format specifier, as well as %d to display the value 1000000. The program illustrates the type of error that can occur should you use the wrong format specifier:

```c
#include <stdio.h>

void main ()
  {
    long int one_million = 1000000;

    printf ("One million is %ld\n", one_million);
    printf ("One million is %d\n", one_million);

  }
```

When you compile and execute this program, your screen will display the following output:

```
C:\> LONGOUT  <ENTER>
One million is 1000000
One million is 16960
```

58 Displaying Values of Type float Using *printf*

The *printf* function supports format specifiers that provide it with information about its parameter types (such as int, float, char, and so on). To display values of type float with *printf*, you should use the %f format specifier. The following program, FLOATOUT.C, uses the %f format specifier to display floating-point values:

```c
#include <stdio.h>

void main ()
  {
    float price = 525.75;
    float sales_tax = 0.06;

    printf("The item cost is %f\n", price);
    printf("Sales tax on the item is %f\n", price * sales_tax);
  }
```

When you compile and execute this program, your screen will display the following output:

```
C:\> FLOATOUT  <ENTER>
The item cost is 525.750000
Sales tax on the item is 31.544999
```

As you can see, by default, the %f format specifier provides little output formatting. Several the tips presented in this section, however, present ways to format output using *printf*.

Displaying Values of Type char Using *printf*

59

The *printf* function supports format specifiers that provide it with information about its parameter types (such as int, float, char, and so on). To display values of type char with *printf*, you should use the %c format specifier. The following program, CHAR_OUT.C, uses the %c format specifier to display the letter A on your screen.

```c
#include <stdio.h>

void main ()
  {
    printf("The letter is %c\n", 'A');
    printf("The letter is %c\n", 65);
  }
```

As you can see, the program displays the letter A using the character constant 'A', as well as the ASCII value 65. When you compile and execute this program, your screen will display the following output:

```
C:\> CHAR_OUT  <ENTER>
The letter is A
The letter is A
```

Displaying Floating-Point Values in an Exponential Format

60

The *printf* function supports format specifiers that provide it with information about its parameter types (such as int, float, char, and so on). In Tip 58 you learned that using the %f format specifier, you can display floating-point values. Depending on your program's requirements, there may be times when you will want to display values using an exponential format. To display a floating-point value in an exponential format use the %e or %E format specifier. The difference between %e and %E is that the %E format specifier directs *printf* to use a capital E in the output. The following program, EXP_OUT.C, uses the %e and %E format specifiers to display floating-point values in their exponential format:

```
#include <stdio.h>

void main ()
  {
    float pi = 3.14159;
    float radius = 2.0031;

    printf("The circle's area is %e\n", 2 * pi * radius);
    printf("The circle's area is %E\n", 2 * pi * radius);
  }
```

When you compile and execute this program, your screen will display the following output:

```
C:\> EXP_OUT  <ENTER>
The circle's area is 1.258584e01
The circle's area is 1.258584E01
```

As you can see, by default, the %e and %E format specifiers provide little output formatting. Several the tips in this section, however, present ways to format output using *printf*.

C 61 Displaying Floating-Point Values Using Either Decimal or Exponential Format

In Tip 58 you learned that using the %f format specifier, you can direct *printf* to display floating-point values using their decimal point format. Likewise, in Tip 60 you learned that using the %e and %E format specifiers you direct *printf* to display a floating-point value using an exponential format. In a similar way, *printf* supports the %g and %G format specifiers. When you use these format specifiers, *printf* decides whether it should use the %f or %e format, depending the technique that will display the output in the most meaningful format. The following program, FLT_PT.C, illustrates the use of the %g format specifier:

```
#include <stdio.h>

void main ()
  {
    printf("Displaying 0.1234 yields %g\n", 0.1234);

    printf("Displaying 0.00001234 yields %g\n", 0.00001234);
  }
```

When you compile and execute this program, your screen will display the following output:

```
C:\> FLT_PT  <ENTER>
Displaying 0.1234 yields 0.1234
Displaying 0.00001234 yields 1.234e-5
```

Displaying a Character String Using *printf*

62

A *character string* is a sequence of zero or more characters. The Strings section of this book discusses character strings in detail. One of the most common operations your programs will perform is character string output. The *printf* function supports format specifiers that provide it with information about its parameter types (such as int, float, char, and so on). To display a character string using *printf*, you should use the %s format specifier. The following program, STR_OUT.C, uses the %s format specifier to display a character string:

```c
#include <stdio.h>

void main ()
  {
    char title[255] = "Jamsa's 1001 C/C++ Tips";

    printf("The name of this book is %s\n", title);
  }
```

When you compile and execute this program, your screen will display the following output:

```
C:\> STR_OUT  <ENTER>
The name of this book is Jamsa's 1001 C/C++ Tips
```

Displaying a Pointer Address Using *printf*

63

The *printf* function supports format specifiers that provide it with information about its parameter types (such as int, float, char, and so on). As you have read, a variable is a name that your program corresponds to a memory location. As your program complexity increases, you will eventually work with memory addresses (which are called *pointers*). When you begin to work with pointers, there may be times when you need to display a pointer address. To display a pointer address using *printf,* you should use the %p format specifier. The following program, PTR_OUT.C, uses the %p format specifier to display a memory address:

```c
#include <stdio.h>

void main ()
  {
    int value;

    printf("The address of the variable value is %p\n",
      &value);
  }
```

When you compile and execute this program, your screen will display the following output:

```
C:\> PTR_OUT  <ENTER>
The address of the variable value is FFF4
```

The actual value and the format used to display it when you use the %p format qualifier will differ from one operating system from another. The Pointers section of this book discusses the use of pointers in detail.

C 64 Preceding a Value with a Plus or Minus Sign

As you have learned, *printf* supports various format specifiers that control how output is displayed. By default, when you use *printf* to display a negative value, it will precede the value with a minus sign. Depending on your program, there may be times when you want *printf* to display the sign for positive values as well. To direct *printf* to display a value's sign, simply include a plus sign immediately following the % in the format specifier. The following program, SHOWSIGN.C, illustrates the use of the plus sign within the format specifier:

```c
#include <stdio.h>

void main ()
  {
    int neg_int = -5;
    int pos_int = 5;

    float neg_flt = -100.23;
    float pos_flt = 100.23;
```

```
    printf("The integer values are %+d and %+d\n",
      neg_int, pos_int);

    printf("The floating-point values are %+f %+f\n",
      neg_flt, pos_flt);
  }
```

When you compile and execute this program, your screen will display the following:

```
C:\> SHOWSIGN  <ENTER>
The integer values are -5 and +5
The floating-point values are -100.230003 +100.230003
```

Formatting an Integer Value Using *printf*

C 65

As you read in Tip 54, the %d format specifier directs *printf* to display an integer value. As your programs become more complex, you will want *printf* to format your data better. For example, assume you want to print out a table similar the following:

```
Salesman          Quantity
Jones             332
Smith             1200
Allen             3311
David             43
```

When you use the %d format specifer, you can direct *printf* to display a minimum number characters. The following program, INT_FMT.C, illustrates how you might format integer values using %d:

```c
#include <stdio.h>

void main ()
  {
    int value = 5;

    printf ("%1d\n", value);
    printf ("%2d\n", value);
    printf ("%3d\n", value);
    printf ("%4d\n", value);
  }
```

When you compile and execute this program, your screen will display the following:

```
C:\> INT_FMT  <ENTER>
5
 5
  5
   5
```

As you can see, the digit you place after the % specifies the minimum number of characters *printf* will use to display an integer value. If, for example, you specify %5d and the value you want to display is 10, *printf* will precede the value with three spaces. Note that the value specifies the minimum number of characters the output will consume. If the value you want to display requires more characters than you have specified, *printf* will use the number of characters it will require.

C 66 Zero-Padding Integer Output

In Tip 65 you learned how to format an integer value by placing the desired number of digits immediately after the % in the %d format specifier. Should the integer value *printf* is displaying not require the number of characters specified, *printf* will precede the value with the necessary number of spaces. Depending on your program's purpose, there may be times when you want *printf* to precede the value with zeros (called *zero padding*), as opposed to spaces. To direct *printf* to zero-pad a value, place a 0 immediately after the % in the format specifier, prior to the desired number of digits. The following program, ZERO_PAD.C, illustrates the zero padding:

```
#include <stdio.h>

void main ()
 {
   int value = 5;

   printf ("%01d\n", value);
   printf ("%02d\n", value);
   printf ("%03d\n", value);
   printf ("%04d\n", value);
 }
```

When you compile and execute this program, your screen will display the following:

```
C:\> ZERO_PAD  <ENTER>
5
05
005
0005
```

Displaying a Prefix Before Octal and Hexadecimal Values

In Tip 55 you learned how to use the %o format specifier to display octal values and the %x and %x format specifiers to display hexadecimal values. When your programs output such values, there may be times when you want to precede octal values with a zero, such as 0777, and hexadecimal values with 0x, such as 0xFF. To direct *printf* to precede an octal or hexadecimal value in this way, place a pound sign character (#) immediately after the % in the format specifier. The following program, SHOW_OH.C, illustrates the use of the use the # in the *printf* format specifier:

```c
#include <stdio.h>

void main ()
 {
    int value = 255;

    printf("The decimal value %d in octal is %#o\n",
        value, value);

    printf("The decimal value %d in hexadecimal is %#x\n",
        value, value);

    printf("The decimal value %d in hexadecimal is %#X\n",
        value, value);
 }
```

When you compile and execute this program, your screen will display the following output:

```
C:\> SHOW_OH  <ENTER>
The decimal value 255 in octal is 0377
The decimal value 255 in hexadecimal is 0xff
The decimal value 255 in hexadecimal is 0xFF
```

Formatting a Floating-Point Value Using *printf*

In Tip 65 you learned how to format an integer value by placing the desired number of digits immediately after the % in the %d format specifier. Using a similar technique, *printf* lets you format floating-point output. When you format a floating-point value, you specify two values. The first value tells format the minimum number of characters you want to display. The second value tells format the number of digits you want displayed to the right of the decimal point. The following program, FLT_FMT.C, illustrates to format floating-point values using *printf*:

```
#include <stdio.h>

void main ()
 {
   float value = 1.23456;

   printf ("%8.1f\n", value);
   printf ("%8.3f\n", value);
   printf ("%8.5f\n", value);
 }
```

When you compile and execute this program, your screen will display the following output:

```
C:\> FLT_FMT  <ENTER>
     1.2
   1.235
 1.23456
```

Formatting Exponential Output

69

In Tip 68 you learned how to format floating-point values when you use the %f format specifier. Using similar formatting techniques, you can format floating-point output that is displayed in exponential format. The following program, EXP_FMT.C, illustrates the output of formatted exponential output:

```
#include <stdio.h>

void main ()
 {
   float value = 1.23456;

   printf ("%12.1e\n", value);
   printf ("%12.3e\n", value);
   printf ("%12.5e\n", value);
 }
```

When you compile and execute this program, your screen will display the following output:

```
C:\> EXP_FMT    <ENTER>
      1.2e+00
    1.235e+00
  1.23456e+00
```

Left-Justifying *printf*'s Output

70

By default, when you output text using *printf*'s formatting characters, *printf* displays the text right justified. Depending on your program, there may be times when you want *printf* to left-justify your output. To left-justify text, place a minus sign (–) immediately after the % in the format specifier. The following program, LEFTJUST.C, illustrates the use of the minus sign to left-justify output:

```c
#include <stdio.h>

void main ()
  {
    int int_value = 5;
    float flt_value = 3.33;

    printf("Right justified %5d value\n", int_value);
    printf("Left justified %-5d value\n", int_value);

    printf("Right justified %7.2f value\n", flt_value);
    printf("Left justified %-7.2f value\n", flt_value);
  }
```

When you compile and execute this program, your screen will display the following output:

```
C:\> LEFTJUST   <ENTER>
Right justified     5 value
Left justified 5     value
Right justified    3.33 value
Left justified 3.33     value
```

Combining *printf*
Format Specifiers

71

Several of the tips presented in this section have discussed various *printf* format specifiers. As you use *printf*'s format specifiers, there may be times when you need to take advantage of two or more format specifiers. For example, you may want to display a hexadecimal value, left justified, preceded with the characters 0x. In such cases, simply place each of the specifiers after the %. The following program, FULL_FMT.C, illustrates the use of multiple format specifiers:

```
#include <stdio.h>

void main ()
 {
   int int_value = 5;

   printf("Left justifed with sign %-+3d\n",
     int_value);
 }
```

When you compile and execute this program, your screen will display the following output:

```
C:\> FULL_FMT   <ENTER>
Left justified with sign +5
```

72 Wrapping a Character String to the Next Line

When your programs use *printf*, there may be times when a character string within *printf* will not fit on the current line. In such cases, simply place a backslash (\) at the end of the line, continuing the text at the start of the next line, as shown here:

```
printf("This line is very long and would not \
fit on the same line.");
```

Note: *if you wrap text to the next line, do not include spaces at the start of the new line's text. If spaces are present, the C compiler will include the spaces within the string.*

73 Displaying Near and Far Strings

The Memory section of this book discusses near and far pointers in detail. When your programs work with far string pointers, there are times when you will want to display the string's contents using *printf*. As you will learn, however, if you pass a far pointer to a function that expects a near address, an error will occur. If you want to display the contents of a far string using *printf*, you must tell *printf* that you are using a far pointer. To do so, place an uppercase F (for Far) immediately after the % in the format specifier, as shown here:

```
printf("%Fs\n", some_far_string);
```

Because %Fs tells *printf* you are using a far pointer, the function call is correct. In a similar way, you can tell *printf* that you are passing a near string by placing an uppercase N in the format specifier. However, because near strings are the default, the format specifiers %Ns and %s are the same. The following C program, NEAR_FAR.C, illustrates the use of %Fs and %Ns within *printf*.

```c
#include <stdio.h>

void main ()
  {
    char *near_title = "Jamsa's 1001 C & C++ Tips";
    char far *far_title = "Jamsa's 1001 C & C++ Tips";

    printf("The book's title: %Ns\n", near_title);
    printf("The book's title: %Fs\n", far_title);
  }
```

Working With *printf*'s Escape Characters

74

When you work with character strings, there will be times when you need to use special characters such as the Tab, carriage return, or linefeed characters. To make it easy for you to include these characters within a string (such as characters you want *printf* to output), C defines several *escape characters*. Several of the programs presented in this book have used the newline character to advance output to the start of the next line:

```c
printf("Line 1\nLine 2\Line 3\n");
```

Table 74 lists the escape characters you can use within your character strings (and hence your *printf* output):

Escape Character	Meaning
\a	ASCII bell character
\b	Backspace character
\f	Formfeed character
\n	Newline character
\r	Carriage return (no linefeed)
\t	Horizontal tab
\v	Vertical tab
\\	Backslash character
\'	Single quote
\"	Double quote

***Table 74** Escape characters defined by C.*

\?	Question mark
\nnn	ASCII value in octal
\xnnn	ASCII value in hexadecimal

Table 74 *Escape characters defined by C. (continued)*

C 75 Determining the Number of Characters *printf* Has Displayed

When your programs perform sophisticated screen formatting, there may be times when you need to know the number of characters *printf* has displayed. When you use the %n format specifier, *printf* will assign to the variable (passed by pointer) a count of the number of characters it has displayed. The following program, PRT_CNT.C, illustrates the use of the %n format specifier:

```
#include <stdio.h>

void main()
 {
   int first_count;
   int second_count;

   printf("Jamsa%n's 1001 C & C++ Tips%n\n", &first_count,
     &second_count);

   printf("First count %d Second count %d\n", first_count,
     second_count);
 }
```

When you compile and execute this program, your screen will display the following:

```
C:\> PRT_CNT  <ENTER>
Jamsa's 1001 C & C++ Tips
First count 5 Second count 25
```

C 76 Using *printf*'s Return Value

In Tip 75 you learned how to use *printf*'s %n format specifier to determine the number of characters *printf* has written. Using the %n format specifier is one way to ensure that *printf* has successfully displayed its output. In addition, when *printf* completes, it returns the total number of characters written. If *printf* encounters an error, it will return the constant EOF. The following program, PRINTFOK.C, uses *printf*'s return value to ensure that *printf* was successful:

```
#include <stdio.h>

void main ()
  {
    int result;

    result = printf("Jamsa's 1001 C & C++ Tips!\n");

    if (result == EOF)
      fprintf(stderr, "Error within printf\n");
  }
```

If the user has redirected a program's output to a file or device (such as PRN), and redirected I/O experiences an error (device offline or disk full), your programs can detect the error by testing *printf*'s return value.

Using the ANSI Device Driver

77

Several of the tips presented throughout this book have made extensive use of *printf*'s output formatting capabilities. Although *printf* provides format specifiers that let you control the number of digits displayed, left- or right-justify text, or display output in octal or hexadecimal, *printf* does not provide format specifiers that let you position the cursor to a specific row and column, to clear the screen, or display output in colors. However, depending on the operating system you are using, you can probably perform such operations using the ANSI device driver. The ANSI driver supports different *escape sequences* that direct it to use specific colors, to position the cursor, and even to clear the screen. Escape sequences are so named because they begin with the ASCII escape character (the value 27). If you are using DOS, you can install the ANSI driver by placing an entry such as the following within your CONFIG.SYS file (and then rebooting):

```
DEVICE=C:\DOS\ANSI.SYS
```

After the ANSI driver is installed, your programs can write escape sequences using *printf*.

78 Using the ANSI Driver to Clear Your Screen Display

One of the most common operations your programs will perform when they begin is to clear the screen display. Unfortunately, the C run-time library does not provide a function that does so. However, using the ANSI driver discussed in Tip 79, you can use the following escape sequence to clear your screen display:

```
Esc[2J
```

An easy way to print the Esc character is to use the octal representation of the escape character (\033), as shown here:

```
printf("\033[2J");
```

79 Using the ANSI Driver to Display Screen Colors

Several of the tips presented throughout this book have made extensive use of the *printf* function to display output. Although *printf* provides powerful format specifiers, it does not provide a way for you to display output in color. However, if you are using the ANSI driver, as discussed in Tip 77, you can use the escape sequences listed in Table 79 to display output in color.

Escape Sequence	Color
Esc[30m	Black foreground color
Esc[31m	Red foreground color
Esc[32m	Green foreground color
Esc[33m	Orange foreground color
Esc[34m	Blue foreground color
Esc[35m	Magenta foreground color
Esc[36m	Cyan foreground color
Esc[37m	White foreground color
Esc[40m	Black background color
Esc[41m	Red background color
Esc[42m	Green background color
Esc[43m	Orange background color
Esc[44m	Blue background color

Table 79 *ANSI escape sequences to set screen colors.*

Esc[45m	Magenta background color
Esc[46m	Cyan background color
Esc[47m	White background color

Table 79 *ANSI escape sequences to set screen colors. (continued)*

The following *printf* statement selects the blue background color:

```
printf("\033[44m");
```

In a similar way, the following *printf* statement selects red text on a white background:

```
printf("\033[47m\033[31m");
```

In the previous case, *printf* writes two escape sequences. As it turns out, the ANSI driver lets you specify screen colors separated by semicolons, as shown here:

```
printf("\033[47;31m");
```

Using the ANSI Driver to Position the Cursor

As you have learned, the ANSI driver supports escape sequences that let you clear your screen and display output in color. In addition, the ANSI driver provides escape sequences that let you position the cursor to specific row and column positions. In this way, you display your output at specific screen locations. Table 80 displays the ANSI driver's cursor positioning escape sequences.

Escape Sequence	Function	Example
Esc[#;#H	Set cursor row/column	Esc[10;25H
Esc[#A	Move the cursor up # rows	Esc[1a
Esc[#B	Move the cursor down # rows	Esc[2b
Esc[#C	Move the cursor right # columns	Esc[10c
Esc[#D	Move the cursor left # columns	Esc[10d
Esc[S	Store the current cursor position	Esc[S
Esc[U	Restore the cursor position	Esc[U
Esc[2j	Clear the screen, moving the cursor to the home position	Esc[2j
Esc[K	Clear to end of the current line	Esc[K

Table 80 *ANSI driver cursor-positioning escape sequences.*

Basic Math Operations in C

81

In all but the simplest programs, you will need to perform arithmetic operations such as addition, subtraction, multiplication, or division. To perform these basic math operations, use the operators described in Table 81.

Operator	Purpose
+	Addition
−	Subtraction
*	Multiplication
/	Division

Table 81 *The C basic arithmetic operators.*

The following program, MATH.C, illustrates the use of C's basic arithmetic operators:

```c
#include <stdio.h>

void main ()
 {
   int seconds_in_an_hour;

   float average;

   seconds_in_an_hour = 60 * 60;

   average = (5 + 10 + 15 + 20) / 4;

   printf("The number of seconds in an hour %d\n",
      seconds_in_an_hour);

   printf("The average of 5, 10, 15, and 20 is %f\n",
      average);

   printf("The number of seconds in 48 minutes is %d\n",
      seconds_in_an_hour - 12 * 60);
 }
```

When you compile and execute this program, your screen will display the following output:

```
C:\> MATH <ENTER>
The number of seconds in an hour 3600
The average of 5, 10, 15, and 20 is 12.000
The number of seconds in 48 minutes is 2880
```

Understanding Modulo Arithmetic

82

In Tip 81 you learned that C uses the / operator for division. Depending on your application, there may be times when you need to know the remainder of an integer division. In such cases, you can use C's modulo (remainder) operator. The following program, MODULO.C, illustrates the use of C's modulo operator.

```c
#include <stdio.h>

void main ()
  {
    int remainder;
    int result;

    result = 10 / 3;
    remainder = 10 % 3;

    printf("10 Divided by 3 is %d Remainder %d\n",
      result, remainder);
  }
```

When you compile and execute this program your screen will display the following output:

```
10 Divided by 3 is 3 Remainder 1
```

Understanding Operator Precedence and Associativity

83

In Tip 81 you learned that C uses the operators +, −, *, and / for addition, subtraction, multiplication, and division. When your programs use these operators within arithmetic expressions, you need to understand C's operator precedence, which specifies the order in which C performs its arithmetic operations. For example, consider the following expression:

```c
result = 5 + 2 * 3;
```

Assume that C performs the operations from left to right (the addition before the multiplication), the result of expression is 21:

```
result = 5 + 2 * 3;
       = 7 * 3;
       = 21;
```

However, if C performs the multiplication first, the result is 11:

```
result = 5 + 2 * 3;
       = 5 + 6;
       = 11;
```

To prevent such problems, C defines an operator precedence that defines which operations C executes first. Table 83 illustrates C's operator precedence.

Operator Precedence (High to Low)

```
() [] . ->
++ — + – * & ! ~ (type) sizeof
* / %
+ -
>> <<
== !=
&
^
|
&&
||
? :
= += –= *= /= %= &= ^= |= <<= >>=

,
```

Table 83 *C's operator precedence.*

When you create an expression, C will execute the operations with the highest precedence first. If two operators have the same precedence, C performs the operations from left to right.

C 84 Forcing the Order of Operator Evaluation

As you learned in Tip 83, C performs operations in an expression based on the operator's precedence. In many cases, the order that C will use to evaluate operators is not the order you desire. For example, consider the following expression, whose goal is to calculate the average of three values:

```
average = 5 + 10 + 15 / 3;
```

Mathematically, the average of the values 5, 10, and 15 is 10. However, if you let C evaluate the previous expression, C will assign the variable average the value 20:

```
average = 5 + 10 + 15 / 3;
        = 5 + 10 + 5;
        = 15 + 5;
        = 20;
```

If you examine C's operator precedence table presented in Tip 83, you will find that C's division operator (/) has a higher precedence than the addition operator. Thus, you need a way to change the order in which C performs the operations. When C evaluates an expression, C will always perform operations that appear within parentheses before it performs other operations. By grouping the values you want to sum within parenthesis, C will calculate the correct average, as shown here:

```
average = (5 + 10 + 15) / 3;
        = (15 + 15) / 3;
        = (30) / 3;
        = 10;
```

Within parentheses, C performs operations based on its operator precedence. If multiple expressions are contained within parenthesis, C performs the operations within the innermost parentheses first:

```
result = ((5 + 3) * 2) - 3;
       = ((8) * 2) - 3;
       = (16) - 3;
       = 13;
```

Understanding C's Increment Operator

C 85

One of the most common operations programs perform is incrementing a variable by 1. For example, the following statement increments the variable count by one:

```
variable = variable + 1;
```

Because increment operations are so common, C provides a shorthand notation via its *increment operator*. The following statement uses the increment operator to add 1 to value of variable:

```
variable++;
```

The following program, 0_TO_100.C, uses the increment operator to print the values 0 to 100:

```
#include <stdio.h>

void main ()
  {
    int value = 0;

    while (value <= 100)
      {
        printf("%d\n", value);
        value++;
      }
  }
```

As it turns out, C provides a prefix and postfix increment operator. The following statements both increment the variable count by 1:

```
count++;
++count;
```

The first statement uses C's postfix increment operator, and the second statement uses the prefix operator. It is important to distinguish between the two operators because C treats them differently. When you use the postfix operator, C first uses the variable's value and then performs the increment operation. In the opposite manner, when you use the prefix operator, C first increments the variable's value and then uses the variable. To better understand the difference between the pre- and postfix increment operators, consider the following program, PREPOST.C, which uses both operators:

```
#include <stdio.h>

void main ()
  {
    int value = 1;

    printf("Using postfix %d\n", value++);
    printf("Value after increment %d\n", value);

    value = 1;

    printf("Using prefix %d\n", ++value);
    printf("Value after increment %d\n", value);
  }
```

When you compile and execute this program, your screen displays the following output:

```
C:\> PREPOST <ENTER>
Using postfix 1
Value after increment 2
Using prefix 2
Value after increment 2
```

As you can see, when you use postfix operator, C first uses the variable's value (displaying the value 1) and then increments it (yielding 2). When you use the prefix operator, C first increments the variable (yielding 2) and then uses the value (still 2).

Understanding C's Decrement Operator

C 86

Just as there will be many times when you need to increment a variable's value, there will also be many times when you need to decrement a variable by 1:

```
variable = variable - 1;
```

Because decrement operations are so common, C provides a shorthand notation via its *decrement operator*. The following statement uses the decrement operator to subtract 1 to value of variable:

```
variable--;
```

As was the case with C's increment operator, C provides a prefix and postfix decrement operator. The following statements both decrement the variable count by 1:

```
count--;
--count;
```

The first statement uses C's postfix decrement operator and the second statement uses the prefix operator. It is important to distinguish between the two operators because C treats them differently. When you use the postfix operator, C first uses the variable's value and then performs the decrement operation. In the opposite manner, when you use the prefix operator, C first decrements the variable's value and then uses the variable. To better understand the difference between the pre- and postfix increment operators, consider the following program, POSTPRE.C, which uses both operators:

```
#include <stdio.h>

void main ()
  {
    int value = 1;
```

```
    printf("Using postfix %d\n", value-);
    printf("Value after decrement %d\n", value);

  value = 1;

    printf("Using prefix %d\n", -value);
    printf("Value after decrement %d\n", value);
}
```

When you compile and execute this program, your screen displays the following output:

```
C:\> POSTPRE  <ENTER>
Using postfix 1
Value after decrement 0
Using prefix 0
Value after decrement 0
```

As you can see, when you use the postfix operator, C first uses the variable's value (displaying the value 1) and then decrements it (yielding 0). When you use the prefix operator, C first decrements the variable (yielding 0) and then uses the value (still 0).

87 Understanding a Bitwise OR Operation

As the complexity of your programs increases, you may find that you can increase the program's performance or reduce the program's memory requirement by using *bitwise operations* (operations that manipulate values one or more bit at a time). In such cases, you may take advantage of C's bitwise OR operator (|), which examines the bits in two values and sets to one the bits of the result that are one in either of two values. For example, assume that the two variables contain the values 3 and 4, whose bits are 00000011 and 00000100. The bitwise OR operator returns value 7, as shown here:

```
3       00000011
4       00000100
        ----------------
7       00000111
```

The following program, BIT_OR.C, illustrates the use of C's bitwise OR operator:

```
#include <stdio.h>

void main ()
```

```
   {
     printf("0 | 0 is %d\n", 0 | 0);
     printf("0 | 1 is %d\n", 0 | 1);
     printf("1 | 1 is %d\n", 1 | 1);
     printf("1 | 2 is %d\n", 1 | 2);
     printf("128 | 127 is %d\n", 128 | 127);
   }
```

When you compile and execute this program, your screen will display the following output:

```
C:\> BIT_OR  <ENTER>
0 | 0 is 0
0 | 1 is 1
1 | 1 is 1
1 | 2 is 3
128 | 127 is 255
```

Understanding a Bitwise AND Operation

88

As the complexity of your programs increases, you may find that you can increase the program's performance or reduce the program's memory requirement by using *bitwise operations* (operations that manipulate values one or more bits at a time). In such cases, you may take advantage of C's bitwise AND operator (&), which examines the bits in two values and sets to one the bits of the result that are one in both values. For example, assume that the two variables contain the values 5 and 7, whose bits are 00000101 and 00000111. The bitwise AND operator returns value 5, as shown here:

```
5        00000101
7        00000111
         ----------------
5        00000101
```

The following program, BIT_AND.C, illustrates the use of C's bitwise AND operator:

```
#include <stdio.h>

void main ()
  {
    printf("0 & 0 is %d\n", 0 & 0);
    printf("0 & 1 is %d\n", 0 & 1);
    printf("1 & 1 is %d\n", 1 & 1);
    printf("1 & 2 is %d\n", 1 & 2);
    printf("15 & 127 is %d\n", 15 & 127);
  }
```

When you compile and execute this program, your screen will display the following output:

```
C:\> BIT_AND  <ENTER>
0 & 0 is 0
0 & 1 is 0
1 & 1 is 1
1 & 2 is 0
15 & 127 is 15
```

C 89 Understanding a Bitwise Exclusive OR Operation

As the complexity of your programs increases, you may find that you can increase the program's performance or reduce the program's memory requirement by using *bitwise operations* (operations that manipulate values one or more bits at a time). In such cases, you may take advantage of C's bitwise exclusive OR operator (^), which examines the bits in two values, and sets to one the bits of the result based on the following truth table:

X	Y	Result
0	0	0
0	1	1
1	0	1
1	1	0

For example, assume that the two variables contain the values 5 and 7, whose bits are 00000101 and 00000111. The bitwise exclusive operator returns value 2, as shown here:

```
5      00000101
7      00000111
       ----------------
2      00000010
```

The following program, BIT_XOR.C, illustrates the use of C's bitwise exclusive OR operator:

```c
#include <stdio.h>

void main ()
  {
    printf("0 ^ 0 is %d\n", 0 ^ 0);
    printf("0 ^ 1 is %d\n", 0 ^ 1);
    printf("1 ^ 1 is %d\n", 1 ^ 1);
    printf("1 ^ 2 is %d\n", 1 ^ 2);
    printf("15 ^ 127 is %d\n", 15 ^ 127);
  }
```

When you compile and execute this program, your screen will display the following output:

```
C:\> BIT_XOR   <ENTER>
0 ^ 0 is 0
0 ^ 1 is 1
1 ^ 1 is 0
1 ^ 2 is 3
15 ^ 127 is 112
```

Understanding a Bitwise Inverse Operation

C 90

As the complexity of your programs increase, you may find that you can increase the program's performance or reduce the program's memory requirement by using *bitwise operations* (operations that manipulate values one or more bits at a time). In such cases, you may take advantage of C's bitwise inverse operator (~), which examines the bits in a value, and sets to one the bits of the result that are 0 in the value, and to 0 those bits that are 1. For example, assume an unsigned character variable contains the value 15, the bitwise inverse of the operation would return 240, as shown here:

15   00001111   240   11110000

The following program, BIT_INV.C, illustrates the use of C's bitwise inverse operator:

```c
#include <stdio.h>

void main ()
  {
    int value = 0xFF;

    printf("The inverse of %X is %X\n", value, ~value);
  }
```

When you compile and execute this program, your screen will display the following output:

```
C:\> BIT_INV   <ENTER>
The inverse of FF is FF00
```

C 91 Applying an Operation to a Variable's Value

As you perform arithmetic operations within your programs, you may find that you often assign a variable the result of an expression that includes the variable's current value. For example, consider the following statements:

```
total = total + 100;

count = count - 5;

half = half / 2;
```

For cases when an assignment operation updates a variable with the result of an operation on the variable's current value, C provides a shorthand technique for expressing the operation. In short, you place the operator in front of the assignment operator. Using this technique, the following statements are equivalent to the three statements just shown:

```
total += 100;

count -= 5;

half /= 2;
```

Using this shorthand technique, the following statements are equivalent.

```
variable += 10;        variable = variable + 10;
variable <<= 2;        variable = variable << 2;
variable &= 0xFF;      variable = variable & 0xFF;
variable *= 1.05;      variable = variable * 1.05;
```

C 92 Understanding C's Conditional Operator

As you will learn, C's *if-else* statement, which examines a condition and performs one set of operations if the condition is true and another if the condition is false. In a similar way, C provides a conditional operator that examines a condition and based on whether the condition is true or false, returns one of two values. The format of the condition operator is a follows:

```
(condition) ? TrueResult: FalseResult
```

For example, the following condition tests whether a test score is greater or equal to 60. If the value is greater than or equal to 60, the statement assigns the variable grade a P, for pass. If the value is less than 60, the statement assigns the letter F, for fail:

```
grade = (score >= 60) ? 'P': 'F';
```

The statement is similar to the following *if-else* statement:

```
if (score >= 60)
  grade = 'P';
else
  grade = 'F';
```

The following *printf* statement displays the string "Pass" or "Fail" based on the test score:

```
printf("Score %d Result %s\n", score,
    (score >= 60) ? "Pass", "Fail");
```

Using C's conditional assignment, your programs can reduce *if-else* statements.

Understanding C's sizeof Operator

93

When your programs declare a variable, the C compiler allocates memory to store the variable's value. When you write programs that perform file input/output operations or allocate memory for dynamic lists, it is often convenient to know the amount of memory your program has allocated for a specific variable. C's sizeof operator returns the number of bytes a variable or type requires. The following program, SIZEOF.C, illustrates the use of the sizeof operator:

```
#include <stdio.h>

void main ()
 {
   printf("Variables of type int use %d bytes\n",
     sizeof(int));
   printf("Variables of type float use %d bytes\n",
     sizeof(float));
   printf("Variables of type double use %d bytes\n",
     sizeof(double));
   printf("Variables of type unsigned use %d bytes\n",
     sizeof(unsigned));
   printf("Variables of type long use %d bytes\n", sizeof(long));
 }
```

Depending on your compiler, the output of the SIZEOF program may differ. Using Borland's C++ or Microsoft Visual C++, the program displays the following:

```
C:\> SIZEOF  <ENTER>
Variables of type int use 2 bytes
Variables of type float use 4 bytes
Variables of type double use 8 bytes
Variables of type unsigned use 2 bytes
Variables of type long use 4 bytes
```

C 94 Performing a Bitwise Shift

When you work with values at the bit level, some of the common operations you will perform are bitwise shifts, either to right or left. To help your programs do this, C provides two bitwise shift operators, one that shifts bits to the right (>>) and one to the left (<<). The following expression uses the left-shift operator to shift the values in the variable *flag* two positions to the left:

```
flag = flag << 2;
```

Assuming that the variable *flag* contains the value 2 as shown here:

```
0000 0010
```

When you shift the value two places to the left, the result becomes 8, as shown here:

```
0000 1000
```

When you shift values to left, C zero-fills the lower bit positions. When you shift values to the right, however, the value that C places in the most significant bit position depends on the variable's type. If the variable is an unsigned variable, C zero-fills the most significant bit during a right-shift operation. If the variable is signed, however, C uses the value 1 if the value is currently negative or 0 if the value is positive. The following program, SHIFTEM.C, illustrates the use of C's right-shift and left-shift operators:

```c
#include <stdio.h>

void main(void)
  {
    unsigned u_val = 1;
    signed int value = -1;

    printf("%u (unsigned) shifted left 2 times is %u\n",
      u_val, u_val << 2);
```

```
    printf("%u (unsigned) shifted right 2 times is %u\n",
      u_val, u_val >> 2);

    u_val = 65535;

    printf("%u (unsigned) shifted left 2 times is %u\n",
      u_val, u_val << 2);

    printf("%u (unsigned) shifted right 2 times is %u\n",
      u_val, u_val >> 2);

    printf("%d (signed) shifted left 2 times is %d\n",
      value, value << 2);

    printf("%d (signed) shifted right 2 times is %d\n",
      value, value >> 2);
}
```

Performing a Bitwise Rotation

C95

In Tip 94 you learned how to use C's left-shift and right-shift operators. When you perform a left-shift operation, C zero-fills the least significant bit. When you perform a left-shift operation, on the other hand, the value C places in the most significant bit position depends on the value's type and current value. As you work at the bit level, there may be times when, rather than shifting bits left or right, you may want to simply rotate bits. When you rotate bits to the left, the value's most significant bit becomes the least significant, while the other bits move one position to the right. When you rotate values to the right, the value's least significant bit becomes the most significant. To help you perform this, many C compilers provide the *_rotl* and *_rotr* functions, which rotate an unsigned value left and right:

```
#include <stdlib.h>

unsigned _rotl(unsigned value, int count);
unsigned _rotr(unsigned value, int count);
```

The *count* variable specifies the number of times you want to rotate the value. The following program, ROTATE.C, illustrates the use of the *_rotl* and *_rotr* functions:

```
#include <stdio.h>
#include <stdlib.h>

void main(void)
  {
    unsigned value = 1;
```

```
    printf ("%u rotated right once is %u\n", value,
      _rotr(value, 1));

    value = 5;
    printf ("%u rotated right twice is %u\n", value,
      _rotr(value, 2));

    value = 65534;
    printf ("%u rotated left twice is %u\n", value,
      _rotl(value, 2));
  }
```

When you compile and execute this program, your screen will display the following:

```
C:\> ROTATE  <ENTER>
1 rotated right once is 32768
5 rotated right twice is 16385
65534 rotated left twice is 65531
```

Note: *Many C compilers also provide the _lrotl and _lrotr functions, which rotate unsigned long integer values left or right.*

C 96 Understanding Conditional Operators

All of the programs previously presented in this book have begun their execution with the first instruction in *main* and have executed each instruction that followed in order. As your programs become more complex, there will be times when the program must perform one set of instructions if one condition is true and, possibly, other instructions for another. For example, your program might have different instructions for different days of the week. When a program performs (or does not perform) instructions based on a specific condition, the program is performing *conditional processing*. To perform conditional processing, the program evaluates a condition that results in a true or false. For example, the condition *Today is Monday* is either true or false. To help your programs perform conditional processing, C provides the *if*, *if-else*, and *switch* statements. Several of the tips that follow discuss these statements in detail.

Understanding Iterative Processing

All of the programs previously presented in this book have executed their instructions only one time. In some cases, based on the result of a tested condition, a program may or may not have executed a set of instructions. As your program becomes more complex, there will be times when the program must repeat the same set of instructions a specific number of times or until a specific condition is met. For example, if you are writing a program that calculates student grades, the program must perform the same steps for each student in the class. In a similar way, if a program displays the contents of a file, the program will read and display each line of the file until the end of file is read. When programs repeat one or more statements until a given condition is met, the program is performing *iterative processing*. Each pass the program makes through the statements (it is repeating) is an *iteration*. To help your programs perform iterative processing, C provides the *for*, *while*, and *do while* statements. Several of the tips presented in this book discuss these statements in detail.

Understanding How C Represents True and False

Several of the tips presented in this section have discussed C's conditional and iterative constructs, which perform one set of instructions if a condition is true and, possibly, another if the condition is false. As you work with these constructs, it is important that you understand how C represents a true and false value. To C, any value that is not 0, is true. Likewise, the value 0 represents false. The following condition, therefore, will always evaluate to true:

```
if (1)
```

Many new C programmers write their conditions as follows:

```
if (expression != 0)  // Test if expression is true
```

When you want to test if a condition is true, you can simply include the expression, as shown here:

```
if (expression)
```

If the expression evaluates to a nonzero (true) value, C will execute the statement that follows. If the expression evaluates to zero (false), C will not execute the statement that follows. Operators that work with true and false values are *Boolean* operators. The result of a Boolean expression is always a true or false value.

C 99 Testing a Condition With if

As your programs become more complex, they will perform different statements when one condition is true and another set of statements when the condition is false. When your program must perform such *conditional processing*, you will use the C *if* statement. The format of the *if* statement is as follows:

```
if (condition)
    statement;
```

The condition the if statement evaluates must appear within parenthesis and is either true or false. If the condition is true, C will perform the statement that immediately follows. If the condition is false, your program will not perform the corresponding statement. The following *if* statement, for example, tests whether the variable *age* is greater than or equal to 21. If the condition is true, the program will execute the *printf* statement. If the condition is false, the program will not execute the *printf* statement, continuing its execution at the first statement that follows *printf* (the height assignment statement):

```
if (age >= 21)
    printf("The variable age is 21 or over\n");

height = 73;
```

C 100 Understanding Simple and Compound Statements

When your program performs conditional processing, there will be times when your program performs one statement when a condition is true and, possibly, several other statements if the condition is false. Likewise, when your program performs iterative processing, there will be times when your program repeats one instruction, while at other times, the program might repeat several statements. When you perform conditional and iterative processing, statements are classified as either *simple* or *compound*. A *simple statement* is a single statement, such as a variable assignment, or a call to *printf*. The following *if* statement invokes a simple statement (printf) when the condition is true:

```
if (condition)
    printf("The condition is true\n");
```

A *compound statement* on the other hand, consists of one or more statements contained within right and left braces. The following *if* statement illustrates a compound statement:

```
if (condition)
  {
    age = 21;
    height = 73;
    weight = 165;
  }
```

When your program needs to perform multiple statements based on a condition, or when your program needs to repeat several statements, you will use a compound statement, placing the statements within right and left braces.

Testing for Equality

101

As your programs become more complex, they will compare a variable's value to known conditions and then make decisions as to which statements the program is to execute next. To make such decisions, your programs will use the *if* or *switch* statements. The format of the *if* statement is as follows:

```
if (condition)
    statement;
```

Most if statements will test if a variable's value is equal to a specific value. For example, the following *if* statement tests whether the variable *age* contains the value 21:

```
if (age == 21)
    statement;
```

C uses the double equal signs (==) in tests for equality. When you write tests for equality, make sure you use the double equal sign (==), as opposed to the single equal sign (=) that C uses for an assignment. As you will learn in Tip 113, if you use the assignment operator (=), as opposed to the double equal sign, C considers your condition as correct syntax. Unfortunately, when the statement executes, C does not test to see if the variable equals the value specified, C assigns value to the variable.

> **Note:** *Depending on your compiler warning level, the compiler might display a warning message about the assignment.*

Just as there are times when your programs must test for equality, there will also be times when they must test whether two values are unequal. C uses the symbol != to test inequality. The following statement tests whether the variable age is not equal to 21:

```
if (age != 21)
    statement;
```

The following program, EQL_NEQL.C, uses the C test *if* for equality (==) and inequality (!=):

```c
#include <stdio.h>

void main ()
 {
   int age = 21;
   int height = 73;

   if (age == 21)
     printf("User's age is 21\n");

   if (age != 21)
     printf("User's age is not 21\n");

   if (height == 73)
     printf("User's height is 73\n");

   if (height != 73)
     printf("User's height is not 73\n");
 }
```

When you compile and execute this program, your screen will display the following output:

```
C:\> EQL_NEQL  <ENTER>
User's age is 21
User's height is 73
```

Experiment with this program by changing the value of the *height* and *age* variables.

102 Performing Relational Tests

As your programs become more complex, there will be times when you need to test whether a value is greater than, less than, greater than or equal to, or less than or equal to another. To help you perform such tests, C provides a set of *relational operators*. Table 102 defines C's relational operators.

Operator	Function
>	Greater-than operator
<	Less-than operator
>=	Greater-than-or-equal-to operator
<=	Less-than-or-equal-to operator

Table 102 *C's Relational Operators.*

The following *if* statement uses C's greater-than-or-equal-to operator (>=) to test whether the variable *age* is over 21:

```
if (age >= 21)
    printf("The age is over 21\n");
```

Performing a Logical AND
to Test Two Conditions

103

As you have learned, C's *if* statement lets you test conditions within your programs. As your programs become more complex, you will eventually need to test for multiple conditions. For example, you may want an *if* statement to test whether a user has a dog, if so, whether that dog is a dalmatian. In cases when you want to test if two conditions are true, you can use C's *logical AND* operator. C represents the logical AND with two ampersands (&&). Consider the following *if* statement:

```
if ((user_has_dog) && (dog == dalmatian))
   {
     // Statements
   }
```

When C encounters an *if* statement that uses the logical AND operator &&, C evaluates the conditions from left to right. If you examine the parentheses, you will find that the previous *if* statement is in the following form:

```
if (condition)
```

In this, the condition is actual two conditions connected with the logical AND:

```
(user_has_dog) && (dog == dalmatian)
```

For the resulting condition to evaluate as true when the logical and operator is used, both conditions must evaluate as true. If either condition is false, the resulting condition evaluates as false.

Many of the tips presented throughout this book will use the logical and (&&) operator. In each case, to ensure that each expression evaluates with the correct operator precedence, the programs will place the conditions within parenthesis.

> **Note:** *Do not confuse C's logical AND operator (&&) with C's bitwise AND operator (&). The logical AND operator evaluates two Boolean (true or false) expressions to produce a true or false result. The bitwise AND operator, on the other hand, works bits (1's and 0's).*

C 104 Performing a Logical OR to Test Two Conditions

As you know C's *if* statement lets you test conditions within your programs. As your programs become more complex, you will eventually need to test for multiple conditions. For example, you may want an *if* statement to test whether a user has a dog, or whether the user has a computer. In cases when you want to test whether either of two conditions is true (or if both are true), you can use C's *logical OR* operator. C represents the logical OR with two vertical bars (||). Consider the following *if* statement:

```
if ((user_has_dog) || (user_has_computer))
  {
    // Statements
  }
```

When C encounters an *if* statement that uses the logical OR operator ||, C evaluates the conditions from left to right. If you examine the parentheses, you will find that the previous *if* statement is in the following form:

```
if (condition)
```

In this, the condition is actual two conditions connected with the logical OR:

```
(user_has_dog) || (user_has_computer)
```

For the resulting condition to evaluate as true when the logical OR operator is used, only one of the conditions must evaluate as true. If either condition (or both) is true, the resulting condition evaluates as true. If both conditions evaluate as false, the result is false.

Many of the tips presented throughout this book will use the logical OR (||) operator. In each case, to ensure that each expression evaluates with the correct operator precedence, the programs will place the conditions within parenthesis.

Note: *Do not confuse C's logical OR operator (||) with C's bitwise OR operator (|). The logical OR operator evaluates two Boolean (true or false) expressions to produce a true or false result. The bitwise OR operator, on the other hand, works bits (1's and 0's).*

C 105 Performing a Logical NOT

When your programs use the *if* statement to perform conditional processing, the *if* statement evaluates an expression that yields a true or false result.

Depending on your program's processing, there may be times when you only want the program to perform a set of statements when the condition evaluates as false. For example, assume that you want a program to test whether the user has a dog. If the user does not have a dog, the program should display a message telling them to buy a dalmatian! If the user has a dog, the program should not do anything. When you want your program to perform one or more statements when a condition is false, you should use C's *NOT* operator, which C represents using the exclamation mark (!). Consider the following *if* statement:

```
if (! user_has_dog)
    printf("You need to buy a dalmatian\n");
```

Conditions that use the NOT operator essentially say, "When this condition is not true (in other words, when the condition evaluates to false), perform these statements." Several of the tips presented in this book use the NOT operator within conditions.

Assigning the Result of a Condition

C 106

Several of the tips in this section have presented different conditions that evaluate to a true or false value within an *if, while, for* statement, and so on. In addition to letting you use conditions within C conditional and iterative control structures, C also lets you assign the result of a condition to a variable. Assume, for example, that your program uses the result of the same condition more than once, as shown here:

```
if ((strlen(name) < 100) && (today == MONDAY))
  {
    // Statements
  }
else if ((strlen(name) < 100) && (today == TUESDAY))
  {
    // Statements
  }
else if (strlen(name) >= 100)
  {
    // Statements
  }
```

As you can see, the program makes extensive use of the condition **(strlen(name) < 100)**. Each time the condition appears, the function *strlen* is invoked. In the case of the preceding statements, the function could be invoked three times. The following statements assign the (true or false) result of the condition to the variable *name_ok* and then repeatedly uses the variable, as opposed to the condition, which improves the program's performance.

```
name_ok = (strlen(name) < 100);

if (name_ok && (today == MONDAY))
  {
  }
else if (name_ok && (today == TUESDAY))
  {
  }
else if (! name_ok)
  {
  }
```

C 107 Declaring Variables Within Compound Statements

Tip 100 discusses the difference between simple and compound statements. As you have learned, a compound statement is one or more statements grouped within left and right braces. The following *while* loop (which reads lines from a file and displays them in uppercase) illustrates a compound statement:

```
while (fgets(line, sizeof(line), fp))
  {
    strupr(line);
    fputs(line, stdout);
  }
```

As your programs become more complex, there may be times when the processing performed within a compound statement requires one or more variables whose values are only used within the loop (as might be the case with counter variables). Normally, you would declare such variables at the start of your program, immediately following *main*. If the variable is only used within the compound statement, you can declare the variable at the start of the statement, as shown here:

```
if (condition)
  {
    int counter;
    float total;

    // Other statements
  }
```

In this case, the program declares two variables at the start of the compound statement. Within the compound statement, you can use these two variables just as if they were defined at the start of your program. You cannot, however, refer to these variables outside of the compound statement's opening and closing braces. An advantage of declaring variables within the compound statement is that another programmer who is reading your program code has a better understanding of how and when the variable is used. Several tips presented later in this book focus on a variable's scope, or the locations within your program where a variable is known. As a rule, you try to reduce knowledge of a variable to only those locations that use the variable—in other words, you reduce the variable's *scope*. Declaring variables at the start of a compound statement in this way limits the variable's scope to the compound statement's starting and ending braces.

> **Note:** *If you declare variables within a compound statement that have the same name as variables defined outside of the statement, the C compiler will use the newly declared variables within the compound statement and the original variables outside of the statement.*

Using Indentation to Improve Readability

As you create your programs, one of the best ways you can improve your program readability is to use indentation. As a rule, each time your program uses a brace (such as at the start of a compound statement), you should consider indenting your code two or more spaces. For example, consider the following program:

```
#include <stdio.h>

void main ()
  {
    int age = 10;
    int user_has_dog = 0;    // 0 is false

    if (age == 10)
      {
        printf("Dogs are important pets\n");

        if (! user_has_dog)
          printf("You should get a dalmatian\n");
      }

    printf("Happy is a dalmatian\n");
  }
```

By examining the indentation only, you can quickly get a feel for related program statements. Indentation is meaningless to the compiler. To the compiler, the following program is identical to the one just shown:

```
#include <stdio.h>

void main ()
{
int age = 10;
int user_has_dog = 0;    // 0 is false
if (age == 10)
{
printf("Dogs are important pets\n");
if (! user_has_dog)
printf("You should get a dalmatian\n");
}
printf("Happy is a dalmatian\n");
}
```

As you can see, the indentation makes the first program much easier to understand.

C 109 Use Extended CTRL-BREAK Checking

When you create programs that use the *for*, *while*, and *do* loops for iteration, there may be times when you need to press the **CTRL-BREAK** keyboard combination to end a program stuck in an infinite loop. By default, DOS checks for a **CTRL-BREAK** after each it writes to the screen, disk, the printer, or reads a character from keyboard. If your program does not perform any of these operations, the **CTRL-BREAK** will not end the program's processing. By using the DOS BREAK command, however, you can increase the number of operations that, upon completion, DOS will check for a **CTRL-BREAK**. This additional testing is called extended **CTRL-BREAK** checking. The following BREAK command enables extended **CTRL-BREAK** checking:

```
C:\> BREAK ON   <ENTER>
```

If you want DOS to enable extended **CTRL-BREAK** checking as soon as the system starts, you can place a BREAK=ON entry in your CONFIG.SYS file. Because DOS is performing more extended **CTRL-BREAK** checking, your overall system performance will decrease slightly. However, while you are first getting the feel for iterative processing, you might find that the ability to end a program using **CTRL-BREAK** is more important than the slight loss of performance.

C 110 Testing Floating-Point Values

Several of the tips presented in this section have used the *if* and *while* statements to test a variable's value. For example, the following statements test several integer variables:

```
if (age == 21)
    // Statements

if (height > 73)
    // Statements
```

When you work with floating-point values, however, you need to be careful when you test a variable's value. For example, the following statement tests a floating-point variable named *sales_tax*:

```
if (sales_tax == 0.065)
    // Statements
```

Tip 51 discusses floating-point precision and the fact that the computer must represent floating-point values using a fixed number of bits. It is impossible for the computer to exactly represent all values. In the case of the previous *if* statement, the computer may represent the value 0.065 as 0.0649999. As a result, the *if* statement will never evaluate as true. To prevent such errors within your program, do not test for exact floating-point values. Instead, test for an acceptable range of values, as shown here:

```
if (fabs(sales_tax - 0.065) <= 0.0001)
    // Statements
```

In this case, if the difference between the value in the variable *sales_tax* and 0.065 is less than or equal to 0.0001, the program considers the values as equal.

Looping Forever

C 111

As you have learned, C's *for*, *while*, and *do while* statements let you repeat one or more statements until a given condition is met. Depending on your program, there may be times when you want the program to loop forever. For example, a program that detects radiation leaks at a nuclear reactor should always run. To loop forever, simply place a nonzero constant within the loop, as shown here:

```
while (1)
```

You might want to define constants to improve your program's readability. For example, you might use the constant FOREVER, as shown here:

```
#define FOREVER 1

while (FOREVER)
```

In the case of the nuclear reactor, you might use the following:

```
#define MELT_DOWN 0

while (! MELT_DOWN)
```

C 112 Parts of the *for* Statement Are Optional

In Tip 115 you learned that the *for* statement lets your program repeat one or more statements a specific number of times. As you learned, the *for* loop uses three parts: an initialization, a test, and an increment:

```
for (intialization; test; increment)
```

Depending on your program, there may be times when you don't need to use each of the loop's sections. For example, if the variable *count* has already been assigned the initial value of 0, you can skip the loop's initialization section. Then to display the numbers 0 through 999, your loop would contain the following:

```
for (; count < 1000; count++)
   printf(" %d", count);
```

If you omit one of the *for* loop sections, however, you must include the corresponding semicolon. The following *for* loop skips the initialization and increment sections:

```
for (; count < 1000; )
   printf(" %d", count++);
```

Likewise, the following *for* statement will loop forever:

```
for (;;)
   // Statement
```

Although the *for* statement provides these optional sections, your program will become more difficult to read if you omit them. As a rule, if you don't need all three parts of the *for* loop, use a different looping construct, such as the *while* statement.

Testing an Assignment

C 113

As you have learned, C uses the single equal sign as the assignment operator and the double equal sign to test for equality:

```
score = 100;

if (score == MAX)
   {
     // Statements
   }
```

In this case, the first statement assigns the variable *score* the value 100. Next, the *if* statement tests the variable's value. To help you reduce the number of statements in your program, C lets you test the result of an assignment. For example, the following *if* statement combines the previous assignment and condition test:

```
if ((score = 100) == MAX)
   {
     // Statements
   }
```

In this case, C will first perform the expression contained within the parenthesis, assigning the value 100 to the variable *score*. Then, C will compare the value assigned to the constant *MAX*. If you remove the parentheses, a different assignment and test will occur:

```
if (score = 100 == MAX)
```

In this case, C will test whether the value 100 equals the constant *MAX* and if so, will assign the value 1 (true) to the variable *score*. If the value 100 does not equal *MAX*, the statement assigns the value 0 (false) to the variable *score*.

The most common uses of assignment testing occur when you want to test the value returned by a function, such as *fopen* or *getchar*, as shown here:

```
if ((fp = fopen("CONFIG.SYS", "r")) == NULL)
   {
     // Statements
   }

if ((letter = getchar()) == 'A')
   {
     // Statements
   }
```

C 114 Beware of *if-if-else*

When you use *if-else* statements, a sneaky logic error can cause you much frustration if you don't keep track of which *else* statement corresponds to which *if*. For example, consider the following code fragment:

```
test_score = 100;
current_grade = 'B';

if (test_score >= 90)
  if (current_grade == 'A')
    printf("Another A for an A student\n");
else
  printf("Should have worked harder\n");
```

The first *if* statement tests whether the student's test score was greater than or equal to 90. If so, a second *if* statement tests whether the student already has an A grade, and if so, prints a message. Based upon the indentation, you would expect the *else* statement to display its message when the test score was less than 90. Unfortunately, that's not how this program works. When you place an *else* statement within your program, C associates the *else* with the first *else*less *if*. As such, although the test score was 100, the previous code fragment would print out the message telling the student that they should have worked harder! In other words, the fragment executes statements as follows:

```
if (test_score >= 90)
  if (current_grade == 'A')
    printf("Another A for an A student\n");
  else
    printf("Should have worked harder\n");
```

To prevent C from associating the *else* statement with the wrong *if* in this way, place the second *if* statement within braces, forming a *compound statement*, as shown here:

```
if (test_score >= 90)
  {
    if (current_grade == 'A')
      printf("Another A for an A student\n");
  }
else
  printf("Should have worked harder\n");
```

Performing Statements a Specific Number of Times

C 115

One of the most common operations programs performed is to repeat a set of statements a specific number of times. For example, you might need to calculate the test scores for 30 students, to determine the highs and lows of 100 stock quotes, or even sound your computer's built-in speaker three times. To help your programs repeat one or more statements a specific number of times, C provides the *for* statement, whose format is as follows:

```
for (starting_value; ending_condition; increment_value)
   statement;
```

When your program repeats (loops through) statements a specific number of times, you will normally use a variable, called the *control variable*, that counts the number of times you have performed the statements. The *for* statement contains four parts. The *starting_value* section assigns the control variable its initial value, which is normally 0 or 1. The *ending_condition* value normally tests the control variable's value to determine if the statements have been performed the desired number of times. The *increment_value* section normally adds the value 1 to the control variable each time the statements executes. Finally, the *for* loop's fourth part is the statement or statements you want repeated. Because your program repeatedly performs the statement or statement specified (loops back to the start of the statement), the *for* statement is often called a *for loop*. Consider the following *for* statement, which displays the numbers 1 through 10 on your screen:

```
for (counter = 1; counter <= 10; counter++)
   printf("%d\n", counter);
```

In this case, *counter* is the loop's control variable. The *for* statement first assigns the variable the value 1. Next, the *for* loop immediately tests whether or not *counter's* value is less than or equal to 10 (the loop's ending condition). If *counter* is less than or equal to 10, the *for* loop immediately executes the statement that follows, which in this case is *printf*. After the *printf* statement completes, the *for* loop performs the expression specified in the *increment_value* part of the loop. In this case, the *for* loop increments *counter's* value by 1. The *for* loop then immediately performs the *ending_value* test. If *counter's* value is less than or equal to 10, the loop continues. Thus, the first time through the loop, the *printf* displays the value 1. The second time through the loop, *counter's* value is 2, then 3, and so on. After *printf* displays the value 10, the *increment_value* part of the loop increments *counter's* value, making it 11. When the *for* loop performs the *ending_value* test, it finds that *counter's* value is no longer less than or equal to 10, so the loop ends, and your program resumes its processing at the statement that immediately follows the *for* loop.

To better understanding this processing, consider the following program, FOR_TEST.C:

```
#include <stdio.h>

void main ()
 {
    int counter;

    for (counter = 1; counter <= 5; counter++)
     printf ("%d ", counter);

    printf ("\nStarting second loop\n");

    for (counter = 1; counter <= 10; counter++)
     printf ("%d ", counter);

    printf ("\nStarting third loop\n");

    for (counter = 100; counter <= 5; counter++)
     printf ("%d ", counter);
 }
```

When you compile and execute this program, your screen will display the following:

```
C:\> FOR_TEST   <ENTER>
1 2 3 4 5
Starting second loop
1 2 3 4 5 6 7 8 9 10
Starting third loop
```

As you can see, the first *for* loop displays the numbers 1 through 5. The second *for* loop displays the values 1 through 10. The third *for* loop does not display any values. If you look closely, the loop's control variable is initially assigned the value 100. When the *for* statement tests the value, the ending condition is immediately met, so the loop does not execute.

All of the examples presented in this tip have used single statements within the *for* loop. If you need to repeat more than one statement, simply place the statements within left and right braces, forming a *compound statement*:

```
for (i = 1; i <= 10; i++)
  {
    // Statements
  }
```

Decrementing Values in a *for* Statement

C 116

As you have learned a *for* statement lets you repeat one or more statements a specific number of times. Tip 115 presented several *for* statements. In each case, the *for* loop counted up, from 1 to 5, 1 to 10, and so on. The *for* statement also lets you decrement the control variable. For example, the following *for* loop counts down the numbers 10, 9, 8...2, 1:

```
for (counter = 10; counter >= 1; counter--)
  printf("%d ", counter);
```

As you can see, this *for* statement is almost exactly opposite of those previously shown. The loop initializes the control variable *counter* to a high value and then decrements *counter* by 1 each time the loop repeats.

The following program, FOR_DOWN.C, uses the *for* statement to count down, first from 5 to 1, and then from 10 to 1:

```
#include <stdio.h>

void main ()
 {
   int counter;

   for (counter = 5; counter >= 1; counter--)
    printf("%d ", counter);

   printf("\nStarting second loop\n");

   for (counter = 10; counter >= 1; counter--)
    printf("%d ", counter);

   printf("\nStarting third loop\n");

   for (counter = 0; counter >= 1; counter--)
    printf("%d ", counter);
 }
```

When you compile and execute this program, your screen displays the following output:

```
C:\> FOR_DOWN  <ENTER>
5 4 3 2 1
Starting second loop
10 9 8 7 6 5 4 3 2 1
Starting third loop
```

As you can see, the third loop does not display any values. In this case, the *for* statement initializes *counter* to a variable that is less than the ending value of 1. As such, the loop immediately ends.

117 Controlling the *for* Loop Increment

As you have learned, the *for* loop lets your programs repeat one or more statements a specific number of times. Each of the previous *for* loops have incremented or decremented the loop's control variable by 1. C, however, lets you increment the variable by any amount you desire. For example, the following *for* loop increments the control variable *counter* by 10 with each iteration of loop:

```
for (counter = 0; counter <= 100; counter += 10)
   printf("%d\n", counter);
```

In a similar way, the previous *for* loops have initialized the control variable to 1 or 0. C, again, lets you initialize the variable to any value you desire. The following program, FOR_DIFF.C, uses different increment and initialization values:

```
#include <stdio.h>

void main ()
 {
   int counter;

   for (counter = -100; counter <= 100; counter += 5)
    printf("%d ", counter);

   printf("\nStarting second loop\n");

   for (counter = 100; counter >= -100; counter -= 25)
    printf("%d ", counter);
 }
```

118 *for* Loops Aren't Just for int Variables

As you have learned, the *for* statement lets your programs repeat a set of statements a specific number of times. Each of the *for* statements presented in the previous tips have used only values of type *int*. You can, however, use character and floating-point values within your *for* loops. For example, the following *for* loop displays the letters of the alphabet:

```
for (letter = 'A'; letter <= 'Z'; letter++)
  printf("%c", letter);
```

Likewise, the following loop increments a floating-point value by 0.5:

```
for (percent = 0.0; percent <= 100.0; percent += 0.5)
  printf("%f\n", percent);
```

The following program, FOR_MORE.C, illustrates the use of letters and floating-point values within a *for* loop:

```
#include <stdio.h>

void main ()
 {
   char letter;
   float percent;

   for (letter = 'A'; letter <= 'Z'; letter++)
     putchar(letter);

   for (letter = 'z'; letter >= 'a'; letter--)
     putchar(letter);

   putchar('\n');

   for (percent = 0.0; percent < 1.0; percent += 0.1)
     printf("%3.1f\n", percent);
 }
```

Understanding a NULL Loop

As you have learned, the *for* loop lets you repeat one or more statements until a specific condition is met. In the past, when programmers wanted their program to pause briefly, perhaps to display a message, the programs would place a "do-nothing" or *NULL loop* within their program. For example, the following *for* loop does nothing 100 times:

```
for (counter = 1; counter <= 100; counter++)
  ;   // Do nothing
```

When you place a NULL loop within your program, C will perform the loop's initialization and then repeatedly test and increment the control variable until the ending value is met. This repeated testing consumes processor time, which causes the program to delay. If the program needs a longer delay, you can increase the ending condition:

```
for (counter = 1; counter <= 10000; counter++)
  ;  // Do nothing
```

There are several problems that occur as a result of using such delay techniques. First, if the program is running on a 286, 386, or 486 computer, the length of the delay will differ simply because of the difference in the computer's speed. If you are running the program in a multitasking environment such as Windows, OS/2, or UNIX, do-nothing loops consume processor time that could be much better spent doing meaningful work for another program. If your program needs to use such a delay, see the functions presented in the Date and Time section of this book.

C120 Understanding an Infinite Loop

As you have learned, the *for* loop lets you repeat one or more statements a specific number of times. When the *for* loop's ending condition is met, your program continues its execution at the statement that immediately follows. When you use *for* loops, you need to ensure that the loop's ending condition can be met. Otherwise, the loop will continue to execute forever. Such unending loops are called *infinite* loops because they will continue forever. In most cases, infinite loops occur as the result of a programming error. For example, consider the following loop:

```
for (i = 0; i < 100; i++)
  {
     printf("%d ", i);
     result = value * —i;   // cause of error
  }
```

As you can see, the loop's second statement decrement's the value of the control variable *i*. As such, the loop decrements the value to –1 and then later increments it to 0. As a result, the value never reaches 100, so the loop does not end. When you program enters an infinite loop, you might be able to end the program by pressing **CTRL-C**. The following program, INFINITE.C, illustrates an infinite loop.

```
#include <stdio.h>

void main ()
  {
    int i;
    int result = 0;
    int value = 1;
```

```
  for (i = 0; i < 100; i++)
   {
     printf("%d ", i);
     result = value * —i;
   }

  printf("Result %d\n", result);
}
```

When you compile an execute this program, it will repeatedly display the value 0. To end the program, press **CTRL-C**.

Using C's Comma Operator Within a *for* Loop

121

As you have learned, when you declare variables, C lets you declare multiple variables of the same type by separating the variable names with commas:

```
int age, height, weight;
```

In addition, C lets you initialize variables that are separated by commas:

```
int age = 25, height = 73, weight = 160;
```

In a similar way, C lets you initialize and increment multiple variables within a *for* loop by separating the operations with commas. Consider the following loop, which works with the variables *i* and *j*:

```
for (i = 0, j = 100; i <= 100; i++, j++)
  printf("i = %d j = %d\n", i, j);
```

The most common reason for working with multiple variables within a *for* loop in this way is when you work with arrays, as discussed in the Arrays, Pointers, & Structures section of this book. The following program, FOR_2VAR.C, illustrates the use of the C's comma operator within a *for* loop:

```
#include <stdio.h>

void main()
  {
    int i, j;

    for (i = 0, j = 100; i <= 100; i++, j++)
      printf("i = %d j = %d\n", i, j);
  }
```

C122 Avoid Changing the Control Variable's Value in a *for* Loop

As you have learned, the *for* statement lets you repeat one or more statements a specific number of times. To perform such processing, the *for* loop uses a *control variable*, which normally works as a counter. As a rule, you should not change the control variable's value within the *for* loop's statement. The only place the control variable's value should change is within the *for* loop's initialization and increment sections. By changing the value of the control variable within the program statements, you run a greater risk of creating an infinite loop, and you make your program's more difficult to understand.

There may be times however, that when the control variable is assigned a specific value, you will want the loop to end or to skip the current iteration. For such cases, you should use C's *break* or *continue* statements, both of which are discussed later in this section.

C123 Repeating One or More Statements Using *while*

As you have learned, the *for* statement lets you repeat one or more statements a specific number of times. In many cases, however, your programs will need to repeat one or more statements until a specific condition, that does not necessarily involve a count, is met. For example, if you write a program that displays the content's of a file on your screen, you will want the program to display each line of the file. In most cases, you will not know in advance, how many lines the file contains. Thus, you can't use a *for* loop to display, for example, 100 lines; the file might contain more or less lines. Instead, you want to the program to read and display lines until the end of the file is reached. For such cases, your programs can use the *while* loop, whose format is as follows:

```
while (condition)
  statement;
```

When C encounters a *while* loop in your program, C will test the condition specified. If the condition is true, C will perform the statements contained within the loop. If the statement is false, C will continue your program's execution at the first statement that follows. A *while* loop can repeat a single statement or a compound statement enclosed between left and right braces:

```
while (condition)
  {
    // Statements
  }
```

The following program, WAIT_YN.C, uses the *while* loop to loop repeatedly until you press the **Y** or **N** key in response to a yes or no question:

```c
#include <stdio.h>
#include <ctype.h>
#include <conio.h>

void main()
  {
    char letter;  // Letter typed by the user

    printf("Do you want to continue? (Y/N): ");

    letter = getch();            // Get the letter
    letter = toupper(letter);    // Convert letter to uppercase

    while ((letter != 'Y') && (letter != 'N'))
      {
        putch(7);                          // Beep the speaker
        letter = getch();                  // Get the letter
        letter = toupper(letter);  // Convert letter to uppercase
      }

    printf("\nYour response was %c\n", letter);
  }
```

The program begins by displaying the message. Next, the program uses *getch* to get the keystroke pressed. To simplify the loop's testing, the program converts the letter to uppercase, so the loop only needs to test for Y or N. Next, the *while* loop tests the letter typed. If the letter is a Y or N, the condition will fail and the loop's statement's will not execute. If the letter pressed is not Y or N, the loop's condition is true, and its statements will execute. Within the loop, the program will beep the computer's built-in speaker to indicate an invalid character. Next, the program will get the new keystroke and convert it to uppercase. The loop will then repeat its test to determine if a Y or N was typed. If not, the loop's statement's repeat. Otherwise, the program's execution continues at the first statement that follows the loop.

Understanding the Parts of a *while* Loop

124

A *while* loop lets you execute one or more commands until a specific condition is met. In Tip 115, you learned that a *for* actually consists of four parts: an initialization, test, statement execution, and an increment. A *while* loop, on the other hand, consists only of a test and the statements you want to repeat:

```
while (condition)
   statement;
```

As you learned in Tip 120, an infinite loop is a loop whose ending condition is never met, and as such, the loop will continue its execution forever. When you write program's that use *while* loops, you can reduce the possibility of an infinite loop by ensuring that your *while* loops perform the same four steps as those performed by a *for* loop. To help you remember, the four steps, you might want to use the acronym *ITEM*:

Initialize	Initialize the loop's control variable
Test	Test the loop's control variable or condition
Execute	Execute the desired statements within the loop
Modify	Modify the control variable's value or perform an operation that affects the condition tested

Unlike the *for* loop that explicitly lets you initialize and increment a control variable, when your program uses a *while* loop, you must include statements within the program that perform these steps for you. The following program, ITEM.C, illustrates how your program may perform these four steps, using a *while* loop to display the numbers 1 through 100:

```c
#include <stdio.h>

void main()
 {
    int counter = 1;  // Initialize the control variable

    while (counter <= 100)  // Test the control variable
      {
        printf("%d ", counter);  // Execute the statements

        counter++;     // Modify the control variable
      }
 }
```

If you write a program that uses the a *while* loop, and the program experiences an infinite loop, one of the ITEM operations is not correct.

C 125 Repeating One or More Statements Using *do*

As you have learned, C's *while* statement lets you repeat one or more statements until a specific condition is true. Likewise, C's *for* statement lets you repeat one or more statements a specific number of times. In addition, C provides the *do* statement, which lets you execute one or more statements at least one time, and then, if necessary, repeat statements. The format of the *do* statement is as follows:

```
do
   statement;
while (condition);
```

The *do* statement is ideal for situations in which you must perform one or more statements at least one time. For example, consider the following code fragment:

```
printf("Do you want to continue? (Y/N): ");

letter = getch();            // Get the letter
letter = toupper(letter);    // Convert letter to uppercase

while ((letter != 'Y') && (letter != 'N'))
   {
      putch(7);                            // Beep the speaker
      letter = getch();                    // Get the letter
      letter = toupper(letter);  // Convert letter to uppercase
   }
```

As you can see, the code prompts the user for a keystrokes, gets the keystroke, and converts the keystroke to uppercase. Then, depending on the key pressed, the fragment starts a *while* loop, which essentially performs the same commands. Note how the statements can be simplified using the *do* statement, as shown here:

```
printf("Do you want to continue? (Y/N): ");

do {
   letter = getch();            // Get the letter
   letter = toupper(letter);    // Convert letter to uppercase

   if ((letter != 'Y') && (letter != 'N'))
      putch(7);    // Sound bell for invalid letter
   }
while ((letter != 'Y') && (letter != 'N'));
```

When C encounters a *do* statement in your program, C executes the statements between the words *do* and *while*. Then C tests the condition specified to determine whether or not the statements should repeat. As such, the statements specified within a *do* loop always execute at least one time. The *do* loop is often used to display and process menu options. The following program, DO_MENU.C, uses the *do* statement to display and process menu options until the user selects the Quit option:

```
#include <stdio.h>
#include <conio.h>
#include <ctype.h>
#include <stdlib.h>

void main()
```

```
{
  char letter;

  do {
    printf("A Display directory listing\n");
    printf("B Display disk information\n");
    printf("C Change system date\n");
    printf("Q Quit\n");
    printf("Choice: ");

    letter = getch();
    letter = toupper(letter);

    if (letter == 'A')
      system("DIR");
    else if (letter == 'B')
      system("CHKDSK");
    else if (letter == 'C')
      system("DATE");
  }
  while (letter != 'Q');
}
```

126 Understanding C's *continue* Statement

As you have learned, the *for, while,* and *do* statements let your programs repeat one or more statements until a specific condition is met. Depending on your program's purpose, there may be times, when based on a specific condition, you will want to skip the current iteration. C's *continue* statement lets you do just that. If C encounters a *continue* statement within a *for* loop, C will immediately execute the loop's increment portion and then perform the ending condition test. If C encounters a *continue* statement within a *while* or *do* loop, C will immediately perform the ending condition test. To better understand the *continue* statement, consider the following program, ODD_EVEN.C, which uses *continue* within a *for* and *while* loop type to display the odd and even values between 1 and 100:

```
#include <stdio.h>

void main()
 {
   int counter;

   printf("\nEven values\n");
   for (counter = 1; counter <= 100; counter++)
```

```
    {
       if (counter % 2)   // Odd
          continue;

       printf("%d ", counter);
     }

  printf("\nOdd values\n");
  counter = 0;
  while (counter <= 100)
     {
        counter++;

        if (! (counter % 2)) // Even
           continue;

        printf("%d ", counter);
     }
  }
```

The program uses the modulo (remainder) operator to determine if a value is even or odd. If you divide a value by 2 and get a remainder of 1, the value is odd. Likewise, if you get a remainder of 0, the value is even.

It's important to note that you can normally eliminate the need to use a *continue* statement by redesigning your program's use of *if* and *else* statements. For example, the following program NO_CONT.C, also displays even and odd values without having to use *continue*:

```
#include <stdio.h>

void main()
  {
    int counter;

    printf("\nEven values\n");
    for (counter = 1; counter <= 100; counter++)
       {
          if (!(counter % 2))   // Even
             printf("%d ", counter);
       }

    printf("\nOdd values\n");
    counter = 0;
    while (counter <= 100)
       {
          counter++;

          if (counter % 2) // Odd
```

```
        printf("%d ", counter);
    }
}
```

Before you place a *continue* statement within your program, examine your code closely to determine if you can write the same statements without using the *continue*. In most cases, the resultant *continue*-less code will be easier to understand.

127 Ending a Loop Using C's *break* Statement

As you have learned, the *for*, *while*, and *do* statements let your programs repeat one or more statements until a specific condition is met. Depending on your program's purpose, there may be times when, based on a specific condition, you will want the loop to end immediately, with your program continuing its processing at the statement that follows the loop. C's *break* statement lets you do just that. When C encounters a break within a loop, the loop's execution will immediately end. The next statement to execute is the statement that immediately follows the loop. In the case of a *for* loop, C will not perform the loop's increment section—instead the loop immediately stops. The following program, USEBREAK.C, illustrates the use of the *break* statement. The program loops through the numbers 1 through 100 and then 100 down to 1. Each time the loop reaches the value 50, the *break* statement immediately ends the loop:

```c
#include <stdio.h>

void main()
  {
    int counter;

    for (counter = 1; counter <= 100; counter++)
      {
        if (counter == 50)
          break;

        printf("%d ", counter);
      }

    printf("\nNext loop\n");

    for (counter = 100; counter >= 1; counter-)
      {
        if (counter == 50)
          break;
```

```
      printf("%d ", counter);
   }
}
```

As was the case with C's *continue* statement, you can normally rewrite your program's *if-else* and looping conditions to eliminate the need for the *break* statement within loops. In most cases, by rewriting your program statements to eliminate *break*, your program will become much easier to understand. As a rule, reserve the *break* statement's use to C's *switch* statement.

Branching with *goto*

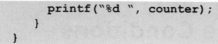

128

If you have previously programmed in BASIC, FORTRAN, or an assembly language, you may be used to implementing *if-else* operations and loops using the GOTO statement. Like most programming languages, C provides a *goto* statement, which lets your program's execution branch to a specific location, called a *label*. The format of the *goto* statement is as follows:

```
goto label;

label:
```

The following C program, GOTO_100.C, uses the *goto* statement to display the numbers 1 through 100:

```
#include <stdio.h>

void main()
  {
    int count = 1;

    label:
      printf("%d ", count++);

      if (count <= 100)
        goto label;
  }
```

When you use the *goto* statement, the label must reside in the current function. In other words, you can't use *goto* to branch from *main* to a label that appears in another function, or vice versa.

Because programmers have misused the *goto* statement in the past, you should restrict your use of the *goto* whenever possible, using instead, constructs such as *if*, *if-else*, and *while*. In most cases, you can rewrite a code fragment that uses *goto* using these constructs to produce code that is more readable.

129 Testing Multiple Conditions

As you have learned, C's *if-else* statements let you test multiple conditions. For example, consider the following test of the variable *letter*:

```
letter = getch();
letter = toupper(letter);

if (letter == 'A')
   system("DIR");
else if (letter == 'B')
   system("CHKDSK");
else if (letter == 'C')
   system("DATE");
```

In cases where you are testing the same variable for multiple possible values, C provides a *switch* statement, whose format is as follows:

```
switch (expression) {
   case Constant_1: statement;
   case Constant_2: statement;
   case Constant_3: statement;
     :     :       :
};
```

Using the previous *if-else* statements, you can use *switch* as follows:

```
switch (letter) {
   case 'A': system("DIR");
             break;
   case 'B': system("CHKDSK");
             break;
   case 'C': system("DATE");
             break;
};
```

When C encounters a *switch* statement in your program, C evaluates the expression that follows to produce a result. C then compares the result to each of the constant values specified that follow the *case* keyword. If C finds a match, it executes the corresponding statements. The *break* statement separates the statements that correspond to one case from another. You will normally place a *break* statement after the last statement that corresponds to an option. Tip 130 discusses the use of the *break* statement within *switch* in detail. The following program, SWT_MENU.C, uses the *switch* statement to process a user's menu selection:

```
#include <stdio.h>
#include <conio.h>
#include <ctype.h>
#include <stdlib.h>

void main()
  {
    char letter;

    do {
      printf("A Display directory listing\n");
      printf("B Display disk information\n");
      printf("C Change system date\n");
      printf("Q Quit\n");
      printf("Choice: ");

      letter = getch();
      letter = toupper(letter);

      switch (letter) {
        case 'A': system("DIR");
                  break;
        case 'B': system("CHKDSK");
                  break;
        case 'C': system("DATE");
                  break;
      };
    }
  while (letter != 'Q');
  }
```

Understanding *break*
Within *switch*

In Tip 129 you learned that C's *switch* statement lets you perform conditional processing. As you learned, you specify one or more possible matching cases using the *switch* statement. For each case, you specify the corresponding statements. At the end of the statements, you normally place a *break* statement to separate one *case* statements from another. If you omit the *break* statement, C will continue to execute all statements that follow, regardless of the case to which the statements belong. For example, consider the following *switch* statement:

```
switch (letter) {
  case 'A': system("DIR");
  case 'B': system("CHKDSK");
  case 'C': system("DATE");
};
```

If the variable *letter* contains the letter A, C will match the first case, executing the DIR command. However, because no *break* statement follows, the program will also execute the CHKDSK and DATE commands. If the variable *letter* contained the letter B, the program will execute the CHKDSK and DATE commands. To prevent the execution of another case's statements, use the *break* statement, as shown here:

```
switch (letter) {
    case 'A': system("DIR");
            break;
    case 'B': system("CHKDSK");
            break;
    case 'C': system("DATE");
            break;
};
```

There may be times when you will want your programs to cascade through *case* options. For example, the following program, VOWELS.C, uses a *switch* statement to count the number of vowels in the alphabet:

```
#include <stdio.h>

void main()
  {
    char letter;

    int vowel_count = 0;

    for (letter = 'A'; letter <= 'Z'; letter++)
      switch (letter) {
        case 'A':
        case 'E':
        case 'I':
        case 'O':
        case 'U': vowel_count++;
      };

    printf("The number of vowels is %d\n", vowel_count);
  }
```

In this case, if the variable *letter* contains the A, E, I, or O, the match occurs and the C falls through to the statement that corresponds to the letter U, which increments the variable *vowel_count*. Because there were no other cases that follow the letter U, the *break* statement was not included.

Using the *switch* Statement *default* Case

As you have learned, C's *switch* statement lets you perform conditional processing. When you use the *switch* statement, you specify one or more cases that you want C to match:

```
switch (letter) {
   case 'A': system("DIR");
             break;
   case 'B': system("CHKDSK");
             break;
   case 'C': system("DATE");
             break;
};
```

As you use the *switch* statement you might find that there are many times when you want C to perform specific statements when none of the other cases match. To do so, you simply include a *default* case with the *switch* statement:

```
switch (expression) {
   case Constant_1: statement;
   case Constant_2: statement;
   case Constant_3: statement;
      :      :          :
   default: statement;
};
```

If C does not match any of the case options that precede the default, C will execute the default statements. The following program, CON_VOWL.C, uses the *default* case to track the number of consonants in the letters of the alphabet:

```
#include <stdio.h>

void main()
  {
   char letter;

   int vowel_count = 0;
   int consonant_count = 0;

   for (letter = 'A'; letter <= 'Z'; letter++)
     switch (letter) {
       case 'A':
```

```
      case 'E':
      case 'I':
      case 'O':
      case 'U': vowel_count++;
                break;
      default: consonant_count++;
    };

  printf("The number of vowels is %d\n", vowel_count);
  printf("The number of vowels is %d\n", consonant_count);
}
```

Macros & Constants

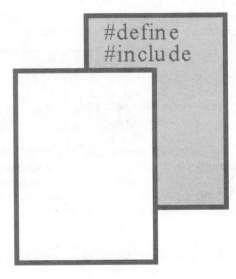

#define
#include

C 132 Defining Constants in Your Programs

As a rule, you can improve your program's readability and portability by replacing references to numbers, such as 512, with a more meaningful constant name. A *constant* is a name the C compiler associates with a value that does not change. To create a constant, you use the #define directive. For example, the following directive creates a constant named LINE_SIZE, and assigns to the constant the value 128:

```
#define LINE_SIZE 128
```

When the C preprocessor later encounters the LINE_SIZE constant name in your program, the preprocessor will replace the constant name with its value. For example, consider the following character string declarations:

```
char line[128];
char text[128];

char current_line[LINE_SIZE];
char user_input[LINE_SIZE];
```

The first two declarations create character strings that contain 128-byte character strings. The second two declarations create character strings based on a constant named LINE_SIZE. When other programmers read your program code, one of the first questions they might ask is why you used 128 in your string declarations. In the case of second declaration, however, the programmer knows that all your strings are declared in terms of a predefined LINE_SIZE. Within your programs, you might include loops similar to the following:

```
for (i = 0; i < 128; i++)
  // statements

for (i = 0; i < LINE_SIZE; i++)
  // statements
```

Not only is the second *for* loop more readable, it makes it easier to change your program. Assume, for example, that your program uses the value 128 throughout to refer to the string size. Should you later need to change the size to 256 characters, you must change every occurrence of the value 128 in your program—a time-consuming process. On the other hand, if you are using a constant such as LINE_SIZE, you only need to change the #define directive—a one-step process, as shown here:

```
#define LINE_SIZE 256
```

Understanding Macro and Constant Expansion

C 133

In Tip 132 you learned that your programs can use the #define directive to define a constant within your program. The following program, for example, uses three constants:

```
#define LINE 128
#define TITLE "Jamsa's 1001 C & C++ Tips"
#define SECTION "Macros"


void main (void)
  {
    char book[LINE];
    char library_name[LINE];

    printf("This book's title is %s\n",
      TITLE);

    printf(SECTION);
  }
```

When you compile a C program, the first program that runs is called a *preprocessor*. The purpose of the preprocessor is to include any specified header files and to expand macros and constants. Before the C compiler actually begins compiling your program, the preprocessor will substitute each constant name with its value, as shown here:

```
void main (void)
  {
    char book[128];
    char library_name[128];

    printf("This book's title is %s\n",
      "Jamsa's 1001 C & C++ Tips");

    printf("Macros");
  }
```

Because the preprocessor is responsible for working with #define, #include, and other # statements, these statements are often called *preprocessor directives*.

C 134 Naming Constants and Macros

A constant is a name the C compiler associates with a value that does not change. Tip 144 introduces C macros. When you use constants and macros within your programs, use meaningful names that accurately describe their use. To help programmers who are reading your code differentiate between constants and variables, you should normally use uppercase letters for your constant and macro names. The following #define directives illustrate several macro definitions:

```
#define TRUE 1
#define FALSE 0
#define PI 3.1415
#define PROGRAMMER "Kris Jamsa"
```

As you can see, constants can contain integer, floating-point, or even character string values.

C 135 Using the __FILE__ Preprocessor Constant

When you work on a large project, there may be times when you want the preprocessor to know the name of the current source file. For example, you might use the filename within a processor directive that includes a message to the user stating the program is still under development, as here:

```
The program PAYROLL.C is still under development and testing.
This is a BETA release only.
```

To help your programs perform such processing, the C preprocessor defines the __FILE__ constant to the name of the current source file. The following program, FILECNST.C, illustrates the use of the __FILE__ constant:

```
#include <stdio.h>

void main ()
  {
    printf("The file %s is under Beta testing\n", __FILE__);
  }
```

When you compile and execute this program, your screen will display the folllowing:

```
C:\> FILECNST  <ENTER>
The file filecnst.c is under Beta testing
```

Using the __LINE__ Preprocessor Constant

136

When you work on a large project, there may be times when you want the preprocessor to know use the current line number of the current source file. For example, if you are debugging a program, you might want the compiler to display messages from various points within your program, as shown here:

```
Successfully reached line 10
Successfully reached line 301
Successfully reached line 213
```

The following program, LINECNST.C, illustrates the use of the __LINE__ preprocessor constant:

```c
#include <stdio.h>

void main ()
  {
    printf("Successfully reached line %d\n", __LINE__);

    // Other statements here

    printf("Successfully reached line %d\n", __LINE__);
  }
```

When you compile and execute this program, your screen will display the following output:

```
C:\> LINECNST    <ENTER>
Successfully reached line 5
Successfully reached line 9
```

Changing the Preprocessors Line Count

137

In Tip 136 you learned how to use the preprocessor's __LINE__ constant within your programs. When you use the __LINE__ constant, there may be times when you want to change the preprocessor's current line number. For example, assume you are using __LINE__ to help you debug your program, as discussed in Tip 136. If you have narrowed down the error to a specific set of instructions, you might want the preprocessor to display line numbers relative to a specific location. To help you perform such processing, the C preprocessor provides the #line directive, which lets you change the current line number. The following directive, for example, directs the preprocessor to set its line number to 100:

```
#line 100
```

You can also use the #line directive to change the name of the source code filename displayed by __FILE__:

```
#line 1 "FILENAME.C"
```

The following program, CHG_LINE.C, illustrates the use of the #line directive:

```c
#include <stdio.h>

void main ()
 {
   printf("File %s: Successfully reached line %d\n",
     __FILE__, __LINE__);

   // Other statements here

#line 100 "FILENAME.C"

   printf("File %s: Successfully reached line %d\n",
     __FILE__, __LINE__);
 }
```

When you compile and execute this program, your screen will display the following:

```
C:\> CHG_LINE  <ENTER>
File chg_line.c: Successfully reached line 6
File FILENAME.C: Successfully reached line 102
```

138 Generating an Unconditional Preprocessor Error

As your programs become complex and use a large number of header files, there may be times when you don't want the program to successfully compile if one or more constants have not been defined. Likewise, if you are working with a group of programmers and you have made a change to the program of which you want them to be aware, you can use the #error preprocessor directive to display an error message and end the compilation. The following directive, for example, ends the compilation, displaying a message to the user about the update:

```
#error The routine string_sort now uses far strings
```

Before the other programmers can successfully compile the program, they must remove the #error directive, therefore becoming aware of change.

Other Preprocessor Constants

C139

Several of the tips in this section have presented preprocessor constants that are supported by most compilers. Many compilers define many other preprocessor constants. The Borland C++ compiler, for example, uses over ten other constants not discussed in this book. Refer to the documentation that accompanied your compiler to determine if there are other preprocessor constants of which your programs can take advantage.

Recording the Preprocessor Date and Time

C140

As you work on large programs, there may be times when you want to preprocessor to work with the current date and time. For example, you might want the program to display a message that states the date and time the program was last compiled, as shown here:

```
Beta Testing: PAYROLL.C Last compiled Jul 4 1993 12:00:00
```

To help you perform such processing, the C preprocessor assigns the constants __DATE__ and __TIME__ to the current date and time. The following program, DATETIME.C, illustrates the use of the __DATE__ and __TIME__ constants:

```c
#include <stdio.h>

void main ()
 {
   printf("Beta Testing: Last compiled %s %s\n", __DATE__,
     __TIME__);
 }
```

C 141 Testing for ANSI C Compliance

Although most C compilers are very similar, every compiler provides unique capabilities. To help you write programs that you can easily move from one system to another, the American National Standards Institute (ANSI) defines standards for operators, constructs, statements, and functions a compiler should support. Compilers that comply with these standards are called *ANSI C compilers*. As you build programs, there may be times when you want to determine whether or not you are using an ANSI compiler. To help you do so, ANSI C compilers define the constant __STDC__ (for STandarD C). If the compiler is compiling for ANSI C compliance, the constant will be defined. Otherwise, the constant is not defined. The following program, CHK_ANSI.C, uses the __STDC__ constant to determine if the current compiler complies to the ANSI standards:

```c
#include <stdio.h>

main ()
 {
#ifdef __STDC__
  printf("ANSI C compliance\n");
#else
  printf("Not in ANSI C mode\n");
#endif
 }
```

Note: *Most compilers provide command-line switches or inline pragmas that direct it to use ANSI compliance.*

C 142 Testing for C++ Versus C

Several of the tips presented in this book can be used for C and C++, while other tips only apply to C++. As you create your own programs, there may be times when you will want the preprocessor to determine if you are using C or C++ and process your statements accordingly. To help you perform such testing, many C++ compilers define the __cplusplus constant. If you are using a standard C compiler, the constant will be undefined. The following program, CHK_CPP.C, uses the __cplusplus constant to determine the compiler's current mode:

```c
#include <stdio.h>

void main ()
```

```
  {
#ifdef __cplusplus
  printf("Using C++\n");
#else
  printf("Using C\n");
#endif
  }
```

If you examine the header files provided by the compiler, you will find many uses of the __cplusplus constant.

Note: *Many C++ compilers provide command-line switches that direct them to compile using C++, as opposed to standard C.*

Undefining a Macro or Constant

Several of the tips presented in this section have discussed constants and macros that are defined by the preprocessor or a header file. Depending on your program, there may be times when you want the preprocessor to undefine or redefine one or more of these constants. For example, the following macro redefines the macro _toupper, which is defined in the header file ctype.h:

```
#define _toupper(c)  ((((c) >= 'a')&&((c)<='z')) ? (c)-'a' + 'A': c)
```

When you compile this program, many preprocessors will display a warning message stating that you have redefined the macro. To avoid the display of this warning message, you can first undefine the macro using the #undef directive, as shown here:

```
#undef _toupper
#define _toupper(c)  ((((c)>='a')&&((c)<='z')) ? (c) - 'a' + 'A': c)
```

Comparing Macros and Functions

New C programmers are often confused as to when they should macros and functions because of their similarity of use. As you have learned, each time the preprocessor encounters a macro reference within your program, the preprocessor replaces the reference with the macro statements. Thus, if your program uses a macro 15 times, the program will have 15 different copies of the macro placed within its statements. As a result, the size of the executable program will grow. When your program uses a function, on the other hand, the program only contains one copy of code, which reduces the program's size. When the program uses the function, the program calls (branches to) the function's code. The disadvantage of using functions, however, is that each function call incurs additional processing that makes the function call take slightly longer than the macro. So, if you want fast performance, use a macro. However, if program size is of greater concern, use a function.

145 Understanding Compiler Pragmas

Several of the tips in this section have presented different preprocessor directives such as #define, #include, and #undef. Depending on your compiler, your preprocessor may support various compiler directives, called *pragmas*. The format of a pragma is as follows:

```
#pragma compiler_directive
```

For example, the Borland C++ compiler provides the startup and exit pragmas that let you specify functions you want your program to automatically execute when it starts or ends:

```
#pragma startup load_data
#pragma exit close_all_files
```

Depending on your compiler, the available pragmas will differ. Refer to the documentation that accompanied your compiler for a complete description of those available for your program use.

146 Learning More About Macros, Constants, and Preprocessor Directives

Several of the tips in this section have discussed macros, constants, and various preprocessor directives. One of the best ways to better understand ways you can use these options is to examine how the C compiler itself uses them. The C compiler places macros and constants within header files that reside in the compiler's INCLUDE subdirectory. Many of the header files present uses of various preprocessor directives. By examining the contents of various header files, you will learn many ways to improve your programs by taking advantage of these preprocessor capabilities.

Creating Your Own Header Files

C 147

As you know, the C compiler provides different header files that contain related macros, constants, and function prototypes. As the number of programs you create increases, you may find that many of your programs use the same constants and macros. Rather than repeatedly typing these macros and constants into your programs, you might consider creating your own header file and placing into the file the corresponding macros and constants. Assuming that you create a header file named my_defs.h, you can include the file at start of you programs using the #include preprocessor directive, as shown here:

```
#include "my_defs.h"
```

By including your macros and constants in a header file in this way, you can quickly change several programs by editing the header file and then recompiling the programs that include the file.

#include <filename.h> Versus #include "filename.h"

C 148

All the programs presented throughout this book have included the header file stdio.h, as shown here:

```
#include <stdio.h>
```

In Tip 147, you learned how to create and include your own header file, my_defs.h:

```
#include <stdio.h>
#include "my_defs.h"
```

As you examine the two *include* statements, the first thing you may note is that the header file stdio.h is enclosed in left and right brackets <>, while my_defs is enclosed in double quotes. When you enclose a header filename within the left and right brackets, the C compiler will first search its directory of header files for the file specified. If the compiler locates the file, the preprocessor will use it. If the file is not found, the compiler will search the current directory or the directory specified. When you enclose a header filename in double quotes, on the other hand, the compiler will only search the current directory for the file.

C 149 Testing Whether a Symbol Is Defined

Several of the tips in this section have presented symbols that are predefined by the C compiler. In addition, tips have discussed how you can define your own constants and macros. Depending on your program, there may be times when you'll want the preprocessor to test whether or not a symbol has been defined and if so, then process a specific set of statements. To help your program test whether or not a symbol is defined, the C preprocessor supports the #ifdef directive. The format of #ifdef directive is as follows:

```
#ifdef symbol
   // statements
#endif
```

When the preprocessor encounters the #ifdef directive, the preprocessor tests if the specified symbol has been defined. If so, the preprocessor processes the statements that follow the directive up to the #endif. In a similar way, there may be times when you want the preprocessor to process statements if a symbol has not been defined. In such cases, you can use the #ifndef directive. The following statements use #ifndef to direct the preprocessor to define the *_toupper* macro if a similar macro is not defined:

```
#ifndef _toupper
#define _toupper(c)  ((((c)>='a')&&((c)<='z')) ? (c) - 'a' + 'A': c)
#endif
```

C 150 Performing *If-Else* Preprocessing

In Tip 149 you learned how to use the #ifdef, #ifndef, and #endif statements to specify a set of statements you want the preprocessor to perform if a symbol is defined (#ifdef) or not defined (#ifndef). There may be times when you want to take such processing one step further by including a set of statements you want the preprocessor to perform when the condition tested is true, and a different set if the condition is false. To perform such processing, you can use the #else directive, as shown here:

```
#ifdef symbol
   // Statements
#else
   // Other statements
#endif
```

Performing More Powerful Preprocessor Condition Testing

151

In Tip 149 you learned how to use #ifdef and #ifndef to direct the preprocessor to test whether a symbol is defined or not defined and then to process the statements that follow. In some cases, you may need the processor to test if several symbols are defined, not defined, or possibly some combination of both. The following directives first test if the symbol MY_LIBRARY is defined. If the symbol is defined, the directives then test whether the symbol MY_FUNCTIONS has not been defined. If MY_FUNCTIONS has not been defined, the preprocessor is directed to include the header file my_code.h:

```
#ifdef MY_LIBRARY
#ifndef MY_ROUTINES
#include "my_code.h"
#endif
#endif
```

Although the directives perform the desired processing, the processing is difficult to follow. As an alternative, your programs can use the #if directive with the *defined* operator to test if a symbol is defined as follows:

```
#if defined(symbol)
   // Statements
#endif
```

The advantage of using the #if directive is that you can combine testing. The following directive performs the same testing as that previously introduced:

```
#if defined(MY_LIBRARY) && !defined(MY_ROUTINES)
#include "my_code.h"
#endif
```

Using #if defined, you can build conditions that use C's logical operators (&&, ||, and !).

Performing *If-Else* and *Else-If* Preprocessing

152

If Tip 151 you learned how to use the #if preprocessor directive to test whether or not a symbol is defined. When you use the #if directive, there may be times when you want the preprocessor to process one set of statements when a symbol is defined and another set if the symbol is undefined. Using the #else directive, you can do just that:

```
#if defined(symbol)
   // Statements
#else
   // Statements
#endif
```

Taking this processing one step further, there may be times when you will want the preprocessor to test the status of other symbols when a specified condition fails. The following directives, for example, direct the preprocessor to process one set of statements if the symbol MY_LIBRARY is defined, another set if MY_LIBRARY is not defined and MY_ROUTINES is, and a third set if neither symbol is defined:

```
#if defined(MY_LIBRRARY)
   // Statements
#elif defined (MY_ROUTINES)
   // Statements
#else
   // Statements
#endif
```

As you can see, using #if and #elif, your preprocessor makes directives very flexible.

C 153 Working with Multiple Line Macros and Constants

Several of the tips presented throughout this section have defined constants and macros. As your constants and macros become more complex, there may be times when a definition will not fit on one line. When you need to wrap a constant or macro definition to the next line, place a backslash character at the end of line, as shown here:

```
#define very_long_character_string "This string constant\
requires two lines"

#define _toupper(c) ((((c) >= 'a') && ((c) <= 'z'))\
 ? (c) - 'a' + 'A': c)
```

C 154 Creating Your Own Macros

As you have learned, macros provide a way for you define constants that the preprocessor substitutes throughout your program before compilation begins. In addition, macros let you create function-like operations that work with *parameters* (values that you pass to the macro). For example, the following macro, *SUM*, returns the sum of the two values that you pass to it:

```
#define SUM(x, y) ((x) + (y))
```

The following program, SHOW_SUM.C, uses the *SUM* macro to add several values:

```
#include <stdio.h>

#define SUM(x, y) ((x) + (y))

void main(void)
  {
    printf("Adding 3 + 5 = %d\n", SUM(3, 5));
    printf("Adding 3.4 + 3.1 = %f\n", SUM(3.4, 3.1));
    printf("Adding -100 + 1000 = %d\n", SUM(-100, 1000));
  }
```

Within the definition of the SUM macro, the *x* and *y* are macro parameters. When you pass two values to the macro, such as *SUM(3, 5)* the preprocessor substitutes the parameters into the macro.

In the case of the program SHOW_SUM.C, the preprocessor's substitutions result in the following code:

```
    printf("Adding 3 + 5 = %d\n", (3) + (5));
    printf("Adding 3.4 + 3.1 = %f\n", (3.4) + (3.1));
    printf("Adding -100 + 1000 = %d\n", (-100) + (1000));
```

Don't Place Semicolons in Macro Defintions

C 155

If you examine the macro definition of the *SUM* macro that follows, you will note that the macro does not include a semicolon:

```
#define SUM(x, y) ((x) + (y))
```

If you include a semicolon within your macro, the preprocessor will place the semicolon at every occurrence of the macro throughout your program. Assume, for example, you placed a semicolon at the end of the *SUM* macro definition:

```
#define SUM(x, y) ((x) + (y));
```

When the preprocessor expands the macro, it will include the semicolon, as shown here:

```
printf("Adding 3 + 5 = %d\n", (3) + (5););
printf("Adding 3.4 + 3.1 = %f\n", (3.4) + (3.1););
printf("Adding -100 + 1000 = %d\n", (-100) + (1000););
```

Because the semicolon now occurs in the middle of the *printf* statement (indicating the end of the statement), the compiler will generate errors.

Note: *Unless you want the preprocessor to include a semicolon in the macro expansion, do not include the semicolon in the macro definition.*

156 Creating *MIN* and *MAX* Macros

In Tip 155 you created the *SUM* macro, which added two values together. The following macros, *MIN* and *MAX* return the minimum and maximum of two values:

```
#define MIN(x, y) (((x) < (y)) ? (x): (y))
#define MAX(x, y) (((x) > (y)) ? (x): (y))
```

The following program, MINMAX.C, illustrates the use of these two macros:

```
#include <stdio.h>
#include <stdlib.h>

void main (void)
  {
    printf("Maximum of %f and %f is %f\n",
      10.0, 25.0, max(10.0, 25.0));
    printf("Minimum of %f and %f is %f\n",
      10.0, 25.0, min(10.0, 25.0));
  }
```

In this case, the preprocessor's substitutions become the following:

```
printf("Minimum of 3 and 5 is %d\n",
  (((3) < (5)) ? (3): (5)));
printf("Maximum of 3.4 and 3.1 is %f\n",
  (((3.4) > (3.1)) ? (3.4): (3.1)));
printf("Minimum of -100 and 1000 is %d\n",
  (((-100) < (1000)) ? (-100): (1000)));
```

Creating *SQUARE* and *CUBE* Macros

157

As you have learned, C lets you define and pass values to macros. The last two macros you will examine the *SQUARE* and *CUBE* macros, which, respectively, return the result of a value squared (x * x) and a value cubed (x * x * x):

```
#define SQUARE(x) ((x) * (x))
#define CUBE(x) ((x) * (x) * (x))
```

The following program, SQR_CUBE.C, illustrates the use of the *SQUARE* and *CUBE* macros:

```
#include <stdio.h>

#define SQUARE(x) ((x) * (x))
#define CUBE(x) ((x) * (x) * (x))

void main(void)
  {
    printf("The square of 2 is %d\n", SQUARE(2));
    printf("The cube of 100 is %f\n", CUBE(100.0));
  }
```

In this case, the preprocessor's substitutions become the following:

```
    printf("The square of 2 is %d\n", (2) * (2));
    printf("The cube of 100 is %f\n", (100.0) * (100.0));
```

Note: *To avoid overflow, the program uses the floating-point value 100.0 within the CUBE macro.*

Be Aware of Spaces in Macro Definitions

158

Several of the previous tips have presented macros that support parameters. When you define such a macro, you need to be careful of white space in the macro definition. Do not place a space between the macro name and its parameters. For example, consider the following definition of the macro *SQUARE*:

```
#define SQUARE (x) ((x) * (x))
```

When the preprocessor examines your program, the space between the macro name cause the preprocessor to assume that each occurrence of the name *SQUARE* should be substituted by **(x)** **((x) * (x))**. In most cases, the substitution will cause the compiler to generate syntax error messages or warnings. To understand this substitution better, experiment with the program SQR_CUBE.C, presented in tip 157, placing a space after each macro name.

C 159 Understanding the Use of Parentheses

Several of the previous tips have presented macros to which you pass values (parameters). If you take a close look at each macro's definitions, you will find that the values are enclosed within parentheses:

```
#define SUM(x, y) ((x) + (y))
#define SQUARE(x) ((x) * (x))
#define CUBE(x) ((x) * (x) * (x))
#define MIN(x, y) (((x) < (y)) ? (x): (y))
#define MAX(x, y) (((x) > (y)) ? (x): (y))
```

The reason the definitions enclose parameters within parentheses is to support expressions. For example, consider the following statement:

```
result = SQUARE(3 + 5);
```

The statement should assign the variable *result* the value 64 (8 * 8). Assume, for example, that you define the SQUARE macro as follows:

```
#define SQUARE(x) (x * x)
```

When the preprocessor substitutes the expression **3 + 5** for *x*, the substitution becomes the following:

```
result = (3 + 5 *  3 + 5);
```

If you will recall C's operator precedence, multiplication has higher precedence than addition. As such, the program would calculate the expression as follows:

```
result = (3 + 5 * 3 + 5);
       = (3 + 15 + 5);
       = 23;
```

By enclosing each parameter within parentheses, however, you ensure that the expression is evaluated correctly:

```
result = SQUARE(3 + 5);
       = ((3 + 5) * (3 + 5));
       = ((8) * (8));
       = (64);
       = 64;
```

Note: *As a rule, you should always enclose your macro parameters within parentheses.*

Macros Are Typeless

C160

In the Functions section of this book, you will learn how to create functions that perform specific operations. As you will learn, C lets you pass parameters to your functions, just as you have passed values to macros. If your function performs an operation and returns a result, you must specify the result's type (such as int, float, and so on). For example, the following function, *add_values*, adds two integer values and returns a result of type *int*:

```
int add_values(int x, int y)
  {
    return(x + y);
  }
```

Within your program, you can only use the *add_values* function to add two values of type *int*. If you try to add two floating-point values, an error will occur. As you have seen, macros let you work with values of any type. The SUM macro that previously created, for example, supported values of type *int* and *float*:

```
printf("Adding 3 + 5 = %d\n", SUM(3, 5));
printf("Adding 3.4 + 3.1 = %f\n", SUM(3.4, 3.1));
```

By using macros for simple arithmetic operations, you eliminate the need to duplicate functions simply because you want to work with values of different types. However, as you will learn in the Functions section of this book, there are other tradeoffs to consider when deciding whether you are going to use macros or functions.

Strings

Abc

Visualizing a C String

161

To store a single ASCII character requires a byte of memory. As you have learned, a *string* is a sequence of ASCII characters. When you declare a string constant, C automatically assigns the NULL character. When your programs create their own strings by reading characters from the keyboard, they must assign the NULL character to the end of the string to indicate the end of string. The best way to visualize a string is simply as a collection of bytes terminated by a NULL, as shown in Figure 161.

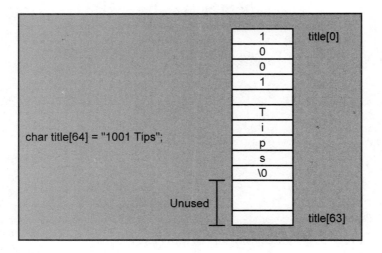

Figure 161 *C stores strings in consectutive byte locations in memory*

When functions work with strings, the functions normally only care about the location at which the string starts. Once the function knows that location, the function can traverse successive memory locations until it encounters the NULL end of string indicator.

How the Compiler Represents
162 a Character String

Several of the tips presented throughout this program will use character string constants enclosed by double quotes:

```
"Jamsa's 1001 C/C++ Tips"
```

When you use a character string contant within your program, the C compiler automatically assigns the NULL ('\0') character at the end of the string. Given the previous string constant, the C compiler will actually store the constant in memory as shown in Figure 162.

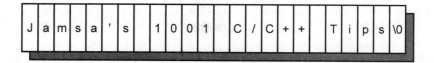

Figure 162 *C automatically appends the NULL character to string contants.*

How C Stores Character Strings

163

Many of the tips presented throughout this book have made extensive use of character strings. For example, programs have used strings to read files, read keyboard input, and perform other operations. In C, a character string is a NULL or zero-terminated array of characters. To create a character string, you simply declare a character array, as shown here:

```
char string[256];
```

In this case, C will create a string capable of storing 256 characters, that is indexed from *string*[0] through *string*[255]. Because the string may contain less than 256 characters, the NULL (ASCII 0) character is *normally* used to represent the string's last character. C does not typically place the NULL character after the last character in the string. Instead, functions such as *fgets* or *gets* place the NULL character at the end of string. As your programs manipulate strings, it is your program's responsibility to ensure that the NULL character is present. The following program BUILDABC.C, defines a 256-character string and then assigns the to the string the uppercase letters of the alphabet:

```
#include <stdio.h>

void main (void)
  {
    char string[256];

    int i;

    for (i = 0; i < 26; i++)
      string[i] = 'A' + i;

    string[i] = NULL;

    printf ("The string contains %s\n", string);
  }
```

The program uses the *for* loop to assign the letters A through Z to the string. The program then places the NULL character after the letter Z to indicate the string's end. The *printf* function then displays each character in the string up to the NULL character. As discussed, the C functions that work with strings use the NULL character to determine the string's end. The following program A_THRU_J.C, also assigns the letters A through Z to a character string. The program then, however, assigns the NULL character to *string*[10], the location that immediately follows the letter J. When *printf* displays the string's contents, it stops at the letter J:

```
#include <stdio.h>

void main (void)
  {
    char string[256];

    int i;

    for (i = 0; i < 26; i++)
      string[i] = 'A' + i;

    string[10] = NULL;

    printf ("The string contains %s\n", string);
  }
```

As you work with strings, you must make sure you correctly include the NULL character to represent the end of string.

C 164 How "A" Differs From 'A'

As you learned in Tip 161, a character string is a sequence of zero or more ASCII characters that is typically terminated by NULL (an ASCII 0). When you work with characters within C, you can use the character's numeric ASCII value, or you can place the character within single quotes, such as 'A'. When you use the double quotes, on the other hand, such as "A", C creates a character string that contains the letter (or letters) specified and is terminated with NULL. Figure 164 illustrates how C stores the constants 'A' and "A".

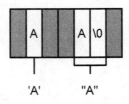

Figure 164 *How C stores the constants 'A' and "A".*

Representing a Quote Within a String Constant

As you have learned, to create a string constant, your program must place the desired characters within double quotes:

```
"This is a string constant"
```

Depending on your programs, there may be times when a string constant must contain a double quote character. For example, assume you need to represent the following string:

```
"Stop!", he said.
```

Because C uses the double quotes to define the string constants, you need a way to tell the compiler that you want to include a quote within the string. To do so, use the escape sequence \" as shown here:

```
"\"Stop!\", he said."
```

The following program, QUOTES.C, uses the \" escape sequence to place quotes within a string constant:

```c
#include <stdio.h>

void main(void)
  {
    char string[] = "\"Stop!\", he said.";

    printf(string);
  }
```

Determining the Length of String

In Tip 163 you learned that C functions normally use the NULL character to represent the end of a string. Functions such as *fgets* and *cgets* automatically assign the NULL character to indicate the end of a string. The following program, SHOW_STR.C, uses the gets function to read a character string from the keyboard. The program then uses a *for* loop to display the string's characters one at a time until the NULL character is found:

Abc

```
#include <stdio.h>

void main (void)
  {
    char string[256];   // String input by user

    int i;              // Index into the string

    printf("Type a string of characters and press Enter:\n");
    gets(string);

    // Display each string character until NULL is found
    for (i = 0; string[i] != NULL; i++)
      putchar(string[i]);

    printf("\nThe number of characters in the string is %d\n", i);
  }
```

C 167 Using the *strlen* Function

As you work with strings within your programs, many of the operations that you perform will be based on the number of characters in the string. To help you determine the number of characters in a string, most C compilers provide a *strlen* function, which returns the number of characters in a string. The format of the *strlen* function is as follows:

```
#include <string.h>

size_t strlen(const char string);
```

The following program, STRLEN.C, illustrates *strlen*'s use:

```
#include <stdio.h>
#include <string.h>

void main(void)
  {
    char book_title[] = "Jamsa's 1001 C/C++ Tips";

    printf("%s contains %d characters\n",
      book_title, strlen(book_title));
  }
```

When you execute this program, your screen will display the following:

Abc

```
C:\> STRLEN <ENTER>
Jamsa's 1001 C/C++ Tips contains 23 characters
```

To better understand how the *strlen* works, consider the following implementation. The function simply counts the characters in a string up to, but not including, the NULL character:

```
size_t strlen(const char string)
  {
     int i = 0;
     while (string[i])
         i++;
     return(i);
  }
```

Copying One String's Characters to Another

168

As your programs work with strings, there will be times when you need to copy the contents of character string to another. To help you perform character string operations, most C compilers provide a *strcpy* function, which copies the characters in one string (called the source string) to another (the destination):

```
#include <string.h>

char *strcpy(char *destination, const char *source);
```

The *strcpy* function returns a pointer to the end of the destination string. The following program, STRCPY.C, illustrates the use of the *strcpy* function:

```
#include <stdio.h>
#include <string.h>

void main(void)
  {
     char title[] = "Jamsa's 1001 C/C++ Tips";
     char book[128];

     strcpy(book, title);
     printf("Book name %s\n", book);
  }
```

To better understand how the *strcpy* function works, consider the following implementation:

```
char *strcpy(char *destination, const char *source)
  {
    while (*destination++ = *source++)
      ;
    return(destination-1);
  }
```

The function simply copies letters from the source string to the destination, up to and including the NULL character.

C 169 Appending One String's Contents to Another

As your programs work with strings, there will be times when you will need to append one string's contents to another. For example, if one string contains a subdirectory name and another contains a filename, you might append the filename to the subdirectory to create a complete pathname. C programmers often refer to the process of appending one string to another as *concatenating* strings. To help you append one string to another, most C compiler provide a function named *strcat*, which concatenates (appends) a source string to a target:

```
#include <string.h>

char *strcat (char target, const char *source);
```

The following program, STRCAT.C, illustrates the use of *strcat* function:

```
#include <stdio.h>
#include <string.h>

void main(void)
  {
    char name[64] = "Triggerhill's I'm so";
    strcat(name, " Happy");
    printf("Happy's full name is %s\n", name);
  }
```

When you compile and execute this program, your screen will display the following:

```
C:\> STRCAT  <Enter>
Happy's full name is Triggerhill's I'm so Happy
```

To help you better understand the *strcat* function, consider the following implementation:

Abc

```
char *strcat(char *target, const char *source)
  {
    char *original = target;

    while (*target)
      target++;        // Find the end of the string

    while (*target++ = *source++)
      ;

    return (original);
  }
```

As you can see, the function loops through the characters of the destination string until the NULL character is found. The function then appends each of the characters in the source string, up to and including the NULL character.

Appending *n* Characters to a String

C 170

In Tip 169 you learned that the *strcat* function lets you append (concatenate) the characters in one string to another. In some cases, you won't want to append all of the characters in a string, but instead, only the first 2, 3, or *n* characters in the string. To help you perform such operations, most C compilers provide a function named *strncat*, which appends the first *n* characters of a source string to a destination string, as shown here:

```
#include <stding.h>

char *strncat(char *destination, const *source, size_t n);
```

If the number of characters specified is greater than the number of characters in the source string, *strncat* will copy characters up to the end of the string and no more. The following program, STRNCAT.C, illustrates the use of the *strncat* function:

```
#include <stdio.h>
#include <string.h>

void main(void)
  {
    char name[64] = "Bill";

    strncat(name, " and Hillary", 4);

    printf("Did you vote for %s?\n", name);
  }
```

When you compile and execute this program, your screen will display the following:

```
C:\> STRNCAT  <ENTER>
Did you vote for Bill and?
```

To help you better understand better understand the *strncat* function, consider the following implementation:

```
char *strncat(char *destination, const char *source, int n)
 {
   char *original = destination;
   int i = 0;

   while (*destination)
     destination++;

   while ((i++ < n) && (*destination++ = *source++))
     ;

   if (i > n)
     *destination = NULL;

   return(original);
 }
```

171 Transforming One String to Another

Several of the tips in this book have shown you ways to copy the contents of one string to another. The *strxfrm* function copies the contents of one string to another (up to the number of characters specified) and then returns the length of the resultant string:

```
#include <string.h>

size_t strxfrm(char *target, char *source, size_t n);
```

The *target* parameter is a pointer to which the source string is copied. The *n* parameter specifies the maximum number of characters to copy. The following program, STRXFRM.C, illustrates the use of the *strxfrm* function:

```
#include <stdio.h>
#include <string.h>

void main(void)
```

Abc

```
{
  char buffer[64] = "Jamsa's 1001 C/C++ Tips";
  char target[64];

  int length;

  length = strxfrm(target, buffer, sizeof(buffer));

  printf("Length %d Target %s Buffer %s\n", length,
    target, buffer);
}
```

Do Not Overwrite a String's Bounds

172

Several of the tips in this section have presented functions that copy or append characters from one string to another. When you perform character string operations, you need to ensure that you do not overwrite a string's memory locations. For example, the following declaration creates a character string capable of storing 10 characters:

```
char string[10];
```

If you assign more than ten characters to the string, your operating system may not detect the error. Instead, the memory locations that correspond to other variables may be overwritten by the characters you intended to assign to the string. Such errors are very difficult. As a rule, declare your strings slightly larger than you anticipate needing. In this way, you will reduce the likelihood of overwriting a string. If your programs experience intermittent errors, examine your program code to determine if a character string may be getting overwritten.

Determining If Two Strings Are the Same

173

As your programs work with strings, you will often need to compare two strings to determine if the strings are the same. To help you determine if two strings contain the same characters, you can use the *streql* function, shown here:

```
int streql(char *str1, char *str2)
{
  while ((*str1 == *str2) && (*str1))
    {
```

```
        str1++;
        str2++;
    }

   return((*str1 == NULL) && (*str2 == NULL));
 }
```

In this case, the function returns the value 1 if the two strings are equal and 0 if the strings are not. The following C program, STREQL.C illustrates the use of *streql* function:

```
#include <stdio.h>

void main(void)
 {
    printf("Testing Abc and Abc %d\n", streql("Abc", "Abc"));
    printf("Testing abc and Abc %d\n", streql("abc", "Abc"));
    printf("Testing abcd and abc %d\n", streql("abcd", "abc"));
 }
```

When you compile and execute this program, your screen will display the following output:

```
C:\> STREQL  <ENTER>
Testing Abc and Abc 1
Testing abc and Abc 0
Testing abcd and abc 0
```

C 174 Ignoring Case When Determining Whether Strings Are Equal

In Tip 173 you created the function *streql*, which lets your programs quickly determine whether two strings are equal. When the *streql* function compares two strings, it considers upper- and lowercase characters as distinct. There may be times when you want to compare two strings without regard for case. To compare strings without regard for case, you can create the function *strieql*, shown here:

```
#include <ctype.h>

int strieql(char *str1, char *str2)
 {
    while ((toupper(*str1) == toupper(*str2)) && (*str1))
      {
        str1++;
        str2++;
```

```
        }
    return((*str1 == NULL) && (*str2 == NULL));
 }
```

As you can see, the function converts each character in a string to uppercase before comparing them. The following program, STRIEQL.C, illustrates use of the *strieql*:

```
#include <stdio.h>
#include <ctype.h>

void main(void)
 {
    printf("Testing Abc and Abc %d\n", strieql("Abc", "Abc"));
    printf("Testing abc and Abc %d\n", strieql("abc", "Abc"));
    printf("Testing abcd and abc %d\n", strieql("abcd", "abc"));
 }
```

When you compile and execute this program, your screen will display the following:

```
C:\> STRIEQL  <ENTER>
Testing Abc and Abc 1
Testing abc and Abc 1
Testing abcd and abc 0
```

Converting a Character String to Upper- or Lowercase

C175

When your programs work with strings, there may be times when you want to covert the string to uppercase. For example, when a user types in a filename or customer name, you may want the program to convert string to uppercase to simplify string compare operations or to ensure that data is stored in a consistent format. To help you perform these conversions, most C compilers provide the functions *strlwr* and *strupr*:

```
#include <string.h>

char *strlwr(char *string);
char *strupr(char *string);
```

The following program, STRCASE.C, illustrates the use of these two functions:

```
#include <stdio.h>
#include <string.h>
```

Abc

```
void main(void)
  {
    printf(strlwr("1001 C/C++ Tips!\n"));
    printf(strupr("1001 C/C++ Tips!\n"));
  }
```

To help you better understand these functions, consider the following implementation of *strlwr*:

```
#include <ctype.h>

char *strlwr(char *string)
  {
    char *original = string;

    while (*string)
      {
        *string = tolower(*string);
        string++;
      }
    return(original);
  }
```

As you can see, both functions simply loop the characters in a string, converting each character to upper- or lowercase.

C 176 Obtaining the First Occurrence of a Character Within a String

As your programs work with strings, there will be times when you need to find the first (leftmost) occurrence of a specific character within a string. For example, if you are working with a string that contains a pathname, you might search the string for the first backslash (\) character. To help you search for the first occurrence of a string, most compilers provide a function named *strchr*, which returns a pointer to the first occurrence of a specific character within a string:

```
#include <string.h>

char *strchr(const char *string, int character);
```

If the character specified is not found within the string, *strchr* returns a pointer to the NULL character that marks the end of the string. The following program, STRCHR.C, illustrates the use of the *strchr* function:

```
#include <stdio.h>
#include <string.h>

void main(void)
  {
    char title[64] = "1001 C/C++ Tips!";
    char *ptr;

    ptr = strchr(title, 'C');
    if (*ptr)
      printf("First occurrence of C is at offset %d\n",
        ptr - title);
    else
      printf("Character not found\n");
  }
```

When you compile and execute this program, your screen will display the following:

```
C:\> STRCHR   <ENTER>
The first occurrence of C is at offset 5
```

It is important to note that *strchr* does not contain an index to the first occurrence of a character, but rather, a pointer to the character. To help you better understand the *strchr* function, consider the following implementation:

```
char *strchr(const char *string, int letter)
  {
    while ((*string != letter) && (*string))
      string++;

    return(string);
  }
```

Returning an Index to the First Occurrence of a String

C 177

In Tip 176 you learned how to use the function *strchr* to obtain a pointer to the first occurrence of a character within a string. If you treat strings as an array, as opposed to a pointer, however, you probably prefer to work with an index to the character, as opposed to a pointer. If you use the *strchr* function, you can obtain an index to the desired character by subtracting the string's starting address from the pointer returned by *strchr*:

```
char_ptr = strchr(string, character);

index = char_ptr - string;
```

If the character was not found in the string, the value assigned to index will be equal to the string's length. In addition to using *strchr* in this way, you can use the function *str_index*, shown here:

```
int str_index(const char *string, int letter)
  {
    char *original = string;

    while ((*string != letter) && (*string))
      string++;

    return(string - original);
  }
```

178 Finding the Last Occurrence of a Character in a String

As your programs work with strings, there will be times when you need to find the last (rightmost) occurrence of a specific character within a string. For example, if you are working with a string that contains a pathname, you might search the string for the last backslash (\) character in order to find the location where the filename begins. To help you search for the last occurrence of a character within a string, most compilers provide a function named *strrchr*, which returns a pointer to the last occurrence of a specific character within a string:

```
#include <string.h>

char *strrchr(const char *string, int character);
```

If the character specified is not found within the string, *strrchr* returns a pointer to the NULL character that marks the end of the string. The following program, STRRCHR.C, illustrates the use of the *strrchr* function:

```
#include <stdio.h>
#include <string.h>

void main(void)
  {
    char title[64] = "1001 C/C++ Tips!";
    char *ptr;
```

```
      if (ptr = strrchr(title, 'C'))
        printf("Rightmost occurrence of C is at offset %d\n",
          ptr - title);
      else
        printf("Character not found\n");
    }
```

It is important to note that *strrchr* does not contain an index to the last occurrence of a character, but rather, a pointer to the character. To help you better understand the *strrchr* function, consider the following implementation:

```
char *strrchr(const char *string, int letter)
  {
    char *ptr = NULL;

    while (*string)
      {
        if (*string == letter)
          ptr = string;
        string++;
      }
    return(ptr);
  }
```

Returning an Index to the Last Occurrence of a String

179

In Tip 178 you learned how to use the function *strrchr* to obtain a pointer to the last occurrence of a character within a string. If you treat a string as an array, as opposed to a pointer, however, you probably prefer to work with an index to the character as opposed to a pointer. If you use the *strrchr* function, you can obtain an index to the desired character by subtracting the string's starting address from the pointer returned by *strrchr*:

```
char_ptr = strrchr(string, character);

index = char_ptr - string;
```

If the character was not found in the string, the value assigned to index will be equal to the string's length. In addition to using *strrchr* in this way, you can use the function *strr_index*, shown here:

```
int strr_index(const char *string, int letter)
  {
    char *original = string;
    char *ptr = NULL;
```

```
  while (*string)
    {
      if (*string == letter)
        ptr = string;

      string++;
    }

  return((*ptr) ? ptr-original: string-original);
}
```

C 180 Working with Far Strings

As discussed in the Memory section of this book, far pointers let DOS programs access data that reside outside of the current 64Kb data segment. When you are working with far pointers, you must also use functions that expect its parameters to be far pointers. Unfortunately, each of the string manipulation routines presented in this section do not expect far pointers to strings. If you pass a far pointer to one of these functions, an error will occur. To support far pointers, however, many compilers provide far-pointer implementations of these functions. For example, to determine the length of a string referenced by a far pointer, you might use the function *_fstrlen*, shown here:

```
#include <string.h>

size_t _fstrlen(const char *string)
```

To determine which far functions your compiler supports, refer to your compiler documentation.

C 181 Writing String Functions for Far Strings

In Tip 180 you learned that several compilers provide functions that support strings that are referenced by far pointers. If your compiler does not provide such functions, you can create the functions yourself by modifying the functions presented in this section. For example, the following function, *fstreql*, illustrates a far pointer based implementation of *streql*:

```
int fstreql(char far *str1, char far *str2)
  {
    while ((*str1 == *str2) && (*str1))
      {
        str1++;
        str2++;
      }
```

Abc

```
        return((*str1 == NULL) && (*str2 == NULL));
   }
```

Counting the Number of Character Occurrences in a String

As your programs work with strings there may be times when you need to know the number of times a character occurs within a string. To help you perform such operations, your programs can use the *chrcnt* function, shown here:

```
int chrcnt(const char *string, int letter)
 {
   int count = 0;

   while (*string)
     if (*string == letter)
       count++;

   return(count);
 }
```

Reversing a String's Contents

As your programs perform different string operations, there may be times when you need to reverse the order of characters within a string. To simplify such operations, most compilers provide a *strrev* function:

```
#include <string.h>

char *strrev(char *string);
```

To better understand the *strrev* function, consider the following implementation:

```
char *strrev(char *string)
 {
   char *original = string;
   char *forward = string;
```

```
    char temp;

    while (*string)
      string++;

    while (forward < string)
      {
        temp = *(—string);
        *string = *forward;
        *forward++ = temp;
      }
   return(original);
}
```

184 Assigning a Specific Character to Every Character of a String

As your programs work with strings, there may be times when you want to set all the characters in a string to a specific character. For example, there may be times when you want to overwrite a string's current value before passing the string to a function. To simplify such operations, most C compilers provide a *strset* function, which assigns every character in the string a specified character:

```
#include <string.h>

char *strset(char *string, int character);
```

The *strset* function assigns the specified character to each string location until the NULL character is encountered. To understand the *strset* function better, consider this implementation:

```
char *strset(char *string, int letter)
  {
    char *original = string;

    while (*string)
      *string++ = letter;

    return(original);
  }
```

As you can see, the function simply loops through a string assigning the specified character until the NULL character is found.

Comparing Two Character Strings

185

In Tip 173 you created the streql function, which let your programs test whether or not two character strings are equal. Depending on the processing your program must perform, there will be times (such as a sort operation) when you need to know if one string is greater than another. To help your programs perform such operations, most C compilers provide a function named *strcmp*, which compares two characters strings:

```
#include <string.h>

int strcmp(const char *str1, const *char str2);
```

If the strings are equal, *strcmp* returns the value 0. If the first string is greater than the first, *strcmp* returns a value less than 0. Likewise, if the second string is greater than the first, *strcmp* returns a value greater than 0. The following program, STRCMP.C, illustrates the use of the *strcmp* function:

```
#include <stdio.h>
#include <string.h>

void main(void)
  {
    printf("Comparing Abc with Abc %d\n", strcmp("Abc", "Abc"));
    printf("Comparing abc with Abc %d\n", strcmp("abc", "Abc"));
    printf("Comparing abcd with abc %d\n", strcmp("abcd", "abc"));
    printf("Comparing Abc with Abcd %d\n", strcmp("Abc", "Abcd"));

    printf("Comparing abcd with abce %d\n", strcmp("abcd", "abce"));
    printf("Comparing Abce with Abcd %d\n", strcmp("Abce", "Abcd"));

  }
```

To understand the *strcmp* function better, consider the following implementation:

```
int strcmp(const char *s1, const char *s2)
  {
    while ((*s1 == *s2) && (*s1))
      {
        s1++;
        s2++;
      }

    if ((*s1 == *s2) && (! *s1))    // Same strings
      return(0);
```

```
   else if ((*s1) && (! *s2))        // Same but s1 longer
      return(-1);
   else if ((*s2) && (! *s1))        // Same but s2 longer
      return(1);
   else
      return((*s1 > *s2) ? -1: 1);
 }
```

C 186 Comparing the First *n* Characters of Two Strings

In Tip 185 you learned how to use the *strcmp* function to compare two strings. Depending on your program's function, there may be times when you only want to compare the first *n* characters of two strings. To make such operations easier to perform, most C compilers provide a function named *strncmp*:

```
#include <string.h>

int strncmp (const char *s1, const char *s2, size_t n);
```

Like *strcmp*, the *strncmp* function returns the value 0 if the strings are equal and a value less than or greater than 0, depending on whether the first or second string is greater. The following program, STRNCMP.C, illustrates the use of the *strncmp* function:

```
#include <stdio.h>
#include <string.h>

void main(void)
  {
   printf("Comparing 3 letters Abc with Abc %d\n",
      strncmp("Abc", "Abc", 3));
   printf("Comparing 3 letters abc with Abc %d\n",
      strncmp("abc", "Abc", 3));
   printf("Comparing 3 letters abcd with abc %d\n",
      strncmp("abcd", "abc", 3));
   printf("Comparing 5 letters Abc with Abcd %d\n",
      strncmp("Abc", "Abcd", 5));

   printf("Comparing 4 letters abcd with abce %d\n",
      strncmp("abcd", "abce", 4));
  }
```

To understand the *strncmp* function better, consider the following implementation:

```
int strncmp(const char *s1, const char *s2, int n)
 {
   int i = 0;

   while ((*s1 == *s2) && (*s1) && i < n)
     {
       s1++;
       s2++;
       i++;
     }

   if (i == n)          // Same strings
     return(0);
   else if ((*s1 == *s2) && (! *s1))    // Same strings
     return(0);
   else if ((*s1) && (! *s2))       // Same but s1 longer
     return(-1);
   else if ((*s2) && (! *s1))       // Same but s2 longer
     return(1);
   else
     return((*s1 > *s2) ? -1: 1);
 }
```

Comparing Strings Without Regard for Case

187

In Tip 185 you learned to use the *strcmp* function to compare two strings. Likewise, in Tip186 you learned how to use the function *strncmp* to compare the first *n* characters of two strings. Both *strcmp* and *strncmp* consider upper and lowercase letters as distinct. Depending on the function your program performs, there may be times when you want the string comparison to ignore case. For such operations, most C compilers provide the functions *stricmp* and *strncmpi*:

```
#include <string.h>

int stricmp(const char s1, const char s2);
int strncmpi(const char *s1, const char *s2, size_t n);
```

The following program, CMPCASE.C, illustrates the use of these two functions:

```
#include <stdio.h>
#include <string.h>

void main(void)
```

```
{
   printf("Comparing Abc with Abc %d\n",
     stricmp("Abc", "Abc"));
   printf("Comparing abc with Abc %d\n",
     stricmp("abc", "Abc"));
   printf("Comparing 3 letters abcd with ABC %d\n",
     strncmpi("abcd", "ABC", 3));
   printf("Comparing 5 letters abc with Abcd %d\n",
     strncmpi("abc", "Abcd", 5));
}
```

When you compile and execute this program, your screen will display the following output:

```
C:\> CMPCASE  <ENTER>
Comparing ABC with ABC 0
Comparing abc with Abc 0
Comparing 3 letters abcd with ABC 0
Comparing 5 letters abc with Abcd -100
```

188 Converting a Character-String Representation of a Number

When your programs work with strings, one of the most common operations you must perform is converting an ASCII representation of a value to a numeric value. For example, if you prompt the user to input his or her salary, you might need to convert the character string input into a floating-point value. To help you perform such operations, most C compilers provide a set of functions that perform ASCII to numeric conversion. Table 188 briefly describes these functions.

Function	Purpose
atof	Converts a character string representation of a floating-point value
atoi	Converts a character string representation of an integer value
atol	Converts a character string representation of a long integer value
strtod	Converts a character string representation of a double precision value
strtol	Converts a character string representation of a long value

Table 188 *Run-time library functions to convert ASCII representations of a numeric value.*

The following program, ASCIINUM.C, illustrates the use of the ASCII to numeric functions:

```
#include <stdio.h>
#include <stdlib.h>
```

Abc

```
void main(void)
  {
    int int_result;
    float float_result;
    long long_result;

    int_result = atoi("1234");
    float_result = atof("12345.678");
    long_result = atol("1234567L");

    printf("%d %f %ld\n", int_result, float_result, long_result);
  }
```

Duplicating a String's Contents

C189

When your program works with strings, there may be times when you want to duplicate a string's contents quickly. If there are times when your program will need to copy the string and others when it might not, you might want the program to allocate the memory *dynamically* to hold the string copy as needed. To let your programs allocate memory on the fly in order to create a copy of a character string, most C compilers provide the *strdup* function:

```
#include <string.h>

char *strdup (const char *some_string);
```

When you invoke *strdup*, the function uses *malloc* to allocate memory and then copies to the memory location the string's contents. When your program has finished using the string copy, it can release the memory using *free*. The following program, STRDUP.C, illustrates the use of the *strdup* function:

```
#include <stdio.h>
#include <string.h>

void main(void)
  {
    char *title;

    if ((title = strdup("Jamsa's 1001 C/C++ Tips")))
      printf("Title: %s\n", title);
    else
      printf("Error duplicating string");
  }
```

To understand the *strdup* function better, consider the following implementation:

```
#include <string.h>
#include <malloc.h>

char *strdup(const char *s1)
  {
    char *ptr;

    if ((ptr = malloc(strlen(s1))))   // Allocate buffer
      strcpy(ptr, s1);

    return(ptr);
  }
```

C 190 Finding the First Occurrence of Any Character from a Given Character Set

In Tip 176 you learned how to use the function *strchr* to find the first occurrence of a specific character. Depending on the function your program performs, there may be times when you want to search a string for the first occurrence of any one of a given set of characters. To help you search a string for any character in a set, most C compilers provide *strspn* function:

```
#include <string.h>

size_t strspn (const char *s1, const char *s2);
```

The function returns the offset within a string of the first character that is not contained somewhere in the second string specified. The following program, STRSPN.C, illustrates the use of the *strcspn* function:

```
#include <stdio.h>
#include <string.h>

void main(void)
  {
    printf("Searching for Abc in AbcDef %d\n",
      strspn("AbcDef", "Abc"));

    printf("Searching for cbA in AbcDef %d\n",
      strspn("AbcDef", "cbA"));

    printf("Searching for Def in AbcAbc %d\n",
      strspn("AbcAbc", "Def"));
  }
```

When you compile and execute this program, your screen will display the following:

```
C:\> STRSPN  <ENTER>
Searching for Abc in AbcDef 3
Searching for cbA in AbcDef 3
Searching for Def in AbcAbc 0
```

To better understand *strspn*, consider the following implementation:

```
size_t strspn(const char *s1, const char *s2)
  {
    int i, j;

    for (i = 0; *s1; i++, s1++)
      {
        for (j = 0; s2[j]; j++)
          if (*s1 == s2[j])
            break;

        if (s2[j] == NULL)
          break;
      }

    return(i);
  }
```

Locating a Substring
Within a String

191

As your programs work with strings, there will be times when you must search a string for a specific substring. To help you search a string for a substring, most C compilers provide a function named *strstr*:

```
#include <string.h>

strstr(string, substring);
```

If the substring exists within the string, *strstr* returns a pointer to the first occurrence of the string. If the substring is not found, the function returns NULL. The following program, STRSTR.C, illustrates the use of *strstr*:

```
#include <stdio.h>
#include <string.h>
```

```
void main(void)
 {
   printf("Looking for Abc in AbcDef %s\n",
     (strstr("AbcDef", "Abc")) ? "Found" : "Not found");
   printf("Looking for Abc in abcDef %s\n",
     (strstr("abcDef", "Abc")) ? "Found" : "Not found");
   printf("Looking for Abc in AbcAbc %s\n",
     (strstr("AbcAbc", "Abc")) ? "Found" : "Not found");
 }
```

To help you understand *strstr* better, consider the following implementation:

```
char *strstr(const char *s1, const char *s2)
 {
   int i, j, k;

   for (i = 0; s1[i]; i++)
     for (j = i, k = 0; s1[j] == s2[k]; j++, k++)
       if (! s2[k+1])
          return(s1 + i);
   return(NULL);
 }
```

C 192 Counting the Number of Substring Occurrences

In Tip 191 you learned how to use the function *strstr* to locate a substring within a string. In some cases you might need to know the number of times a substring appears within a string. The following function, *strstr_cnt* provides that capability:

```
int strstr_cnt(const char *string, const char *substring)
 {
   int i, j, k, count = 0;

   for (i = 0; string[i]; i++)
     for (j = i, k -= 0; string[j] == substring[k]; j++, k++)
       if (! substring[k + 1])
           count++;

   return(count);
 }
```

Abc

Obtaining an Index to a Substring

In Tip 191 you used the function *strstr* to obtain a pointer to a substring within a string. If you treat character strings as arrays, instead of using pointers, there may be times when you want to know the character index at which a substring begins within a string. Using the value returned by *strstr*, you can subtract the string's address to produce an index:

```
index = strstr(string, substr) - string;
```

If the substring is not found, the index value will be equal to the length of the string. In addition, your programs can use the function *substring_index* as shown here:

```
int strstr_index(const char *s1, const char *s2)
  {
    int i, j, k;

    for (i = 0; s1[i]; i++)
      for (j = i, k = 0; s1[j] == s2[k]; j++, k++)
        if (! s2[k+1])
            return(i);
    return(i);
  }
```

Obtaining the Rightmost
Occurrence of a Substring

In Tip 191 you used the function *strstr* to determine the first occurrence of a substring within a string. Depending on your program's function, there may be times when you need to know the last (rightmost) occurrence of a substring within a sting. The following function, *r_strstr* returns a pointer to the rightmost occurrence of a substring within a string or the value NULL if the substring does not exist:

```
char *r_strstr(const char *s1, const char *s2)
  {
    int i, j, k, left = 0;

    for (i = 0; s1[i]; i++)
      for (j = i, k = 0; s1[j] == s2[k]; j++, k++)
        if (! s2[k+1])
            left = i;
    return((left) ? s1+left: NULL);
  }
```

Abc

C195 Displaying a String Without the %s Format Specifier

Several of the tips in this section have used the %s format specifier to display character strings. The following statement, for example, uses *printf* to display the contents of the character string variable named *title*:

```
printf("%s", title);
```

The first argument passed to the *printf* statement is a character string, which may contain one or more format specifiers. When you are using *printf* to display only one character string as just shown, you can omit the character string containing the format specifier, passing to *printf* the character string you want to display, as shown here:

```
printf(title);
```

As you can see, *printf*'s first argument is nothing more than a character string that can contain one or more special symbols.

C196 Removing a Substring From Within a String

In Tip 191 you used the function *strstr* to determine the starting location of substring within a string. In many cases you might need to remove a substring from within a string. To do so, you can use the function *strstr_rem*, shown here, which removes the first occurrence of a substring:

```
char *strstr_rem(char *string, char *substring)
   {
      int i, j, k, loc = -1;

      for (i = 0; string[i] && (loc == -1); i++)
        for (j = i; k = 0; str[j] == substring[k]; j++, k++)
           if (! substring[k + 1])
              loc = i;

      if (loc != -1)  // Substring was found
        {
           for (k = 0; substr[k]; k++)
              ;
```

Abc

```
        for (j = loc, i = loc + k, string[i]; j++, i++)
            string[j] = string[i];

        string[i] == NULL;
    return(string);
}
```

Replacing One Substring with Another

C 197

In Tip 196 you used the function *strstr_rem* to remove a substring from within a string.
In many cases you might need to replace the first occurrence of one substring with another.
The following function *strstr_rep* lets you do just that:

```c
#include <string.h>

char *strstr_rep(char *source, char *old, char *new)
 {
   char *original = source;
   char temp[256];

   int old_length = strlen(old);
   int i, j, k, location = -1;

   for (i = 0; source[i] && (location == -1); ++i)
     for (j = i, k = 0; source[j] == old[k]; j++, k++)
       if (! old[k+1])
         location = i;

   if (location != -1)
     {
       for (j = 0; j < location; j++)
         temp[j] = source[j];

       for (i = 0; new[i]; i++, j++)
         temp[j] = new[i];

       for (k = location + old_length; source[k]; k++, j++)
         temp[j] = source[k];

       temp[j] = NULL;

       for (i = 0; source[i] = temp[i]; i++);    // NULL loop
     }
   return(original);
 }
```

C 198 Converting an ASCII Numeric Representation

When your programs work with character strings, a common operation your programs will need to perform is the conversion of an ASCII representation of a value, such as 1.2345 to the corresponding int, float, double, long, or unsigned value. To help you perform such operations, C provides the functions defined in Table 198.

Function	Purpose
atof	Converts an ASCII representation of a value of type float
atoi	Converts an ASCII representation of a value of type int
atol	Converts an ASCII representation of a value of type long int

Table 198 *C functions that convert ASCII numeric representations.*

The formats of these functions are as follows:

```
#include <stdlib.h>

double atof(char *string);
int atoi(char *string);
int atol(char *string);
```

If a function is unable to convert the character string to a numeric value, the function returns 0. The following program, ASCII_TO.C, illustrates the use of these functions:

```
#include <stdio.h>
#include <stdlib.h>

void main ()
 {
   int int_value;
   float flt_value;
   long long_value;

   int_value = atoi("12345");
   flt_value = atof("33.45");
   long_value =atol("12BAD");

   printf("int %d float %5.2f long %ld\n", int_value,
     flt_value, long_value);
 }
```

Abc

When you compile and execute this program, your screen displays the following output:

```
C:\> ASCII_TO  <ENTER>
int 12345 float 33.45 long 12
```

Note the function call to *atol*. As you can see, when the function encounters the nonnumeric value (the letter B), the function ends the conversion, returning the value that had been converted to that point.

Determining Whether a Character is Alphanumeric

An *alphanumeric* character is either a letter or digit. In other words, an uppercase letter from A through Z, a lowercase letter from a through z, or a digit from 0 through 9. To help your programs determine if a character is alphanumeric, the header file ctype.h contains a macro named *isalnum*. The macro examines a letter and returns the value 0 if the character is not alphanumeric and a nonzero value for alphanumeric characters:

```
if (isalnum(letter))
```

To better understand the macro *isalnum*, consider the following implementation:

```
#define isalnum(c) ((toupper((c)) >= 'A' &&
(toupper((c)) <= 'Z') || ((c) >= '0' && ((c) <= '9'))
```

Determining Whether a Character Is a Letter of the Alphabet

As your programs work with characters within strings, there may be times when you need to test whether a character contains a letter of the alphabet (either lower or uppercase). To help your programs determine whether a character is a letter of the alphabet, the header file ctype.h provides the macro *isalpha*. The macro examines a letter and returns the value 0 if the character does not contain a letter from A through Z or a through z. If the character contains a letter of the alphabet the macro returns a nonzero value:

```
if (isalpha(character))
```

To better understand the *isalpha* macro, consider the following implementation:

```
#define isalpha(c) (toupper((c)) >= 'A' && (toupper((c)) <= 'Z')
```

Abc

C 201 Determining If a Character Contains an ASCII Value

An ASCII value is a value in the range 0 through 127. When your programs work with a string's characters, there may be times when you need to determine if a character contains an ASCII value. To help your programs do so, the header file ctype.h contains the macro *isascii*, which examines a letter and returns the value 0 if the character does not contain an ASCII character and a nonzero value if the character is not:

```
if (isascii(character))
```

To better understand the *isascii* macro, consider the following implementation:

```
#define isascii(ltr) ((unsigned) (ltr) < 128)
```

As you can see, the macro considers a value in the range 0 through 127 as ASCII.

C 202 Determining Whether a Character Is a Control Character

A *control character* is a value from ^A through ^Z or ^a through z. Different applications use control characters differently. For example, DOS uses the Control-Z character to represent the end of a file. Different word processors use control characters to represent boldface or italics. When you work with characters in a string, there may be times when you need to determine whether a character is a control character. To help your programs perform such testing, the header file ctype.h contains the macro *iscntrl*, which returns a nonzero value for a control character and 0 if the letter is not a control character:

```
if (iscntrl(character))
```

C 203 Determining Whether a Character Is a Digit

A *digit* is an ASCII value from 0 through 9. When you work with strings, there may be times when you need to determine if a character is a digit. To help your programs perform such testing, the header file ctype.h provides the macro *isdigit*. The macro examines a letter and returns the value 0 if the character is not digit and a nonzero value for characters in the range 0 through 9:

```
if (isdigit(letter))
```

To better understand the macro *isdigit*, consider the following implementation:

```
#define isdigit(c) ((c) >= '0' && (c) <= '9')
```

Determining Whether a Character Is a Graphics Character

204

A *graphics character* is a printable character (see *isprint*), excluding the space character (ASCII 32). When your programs perform character output operations, there may be times when you want to know if a character is a graphics character. To help your programs perform such testing, the header file ctype.h provides the macro *isgraph*. The macro examines a letter and returns the value 0 if the character is not a graphic and a nonzero value for graphics characters:

```
if (isgraph(letter))
```

To better understand the macro *isgraph*, consider the following implementation:

```
#define isgraph(ltr) ((ltr) >= 33) && ((ltr) <= 127)
```

As you can see, a graphic character is any ASCII character in the range 33 to 127.

Determining Whether a Character Is Upper- or Lowercase

205

As your programs work with characters within a string, there may be times when you need to know whether the character is an upper- or lowercase letter. To help your programs perform such testing, the header file ctype.h provides the macros *islower* and *isupper*. The macros examine a character and return a zero value for characters that are not lower- or uppercase and a nonzero value otherwise:

```
if (islower(character))

if (isupper(character))
```

To better understand the macros, consider these implementations:

```
#define islower(c) ((c) >= 'a' && (c) <= 'z')
#define isupper(c) ((c) >= 'A' && (c) <= 'Z')
```

C 206 Determining Whether a Character Is Printable

When your programs perform character output, you might want to examine each character to ensure that you only output *printable characters*. A printable character is any character in the range 32 (the space character) through 127 (the DEL character). To help your programs test for a printable character, the header file ctype.h provides the macro *isprint*. The macro returns a nonzero value for printable characters and a zero value for characters that are not printable:

```
if (isprint(character))
```

To better understand the *isprint* macro, consider the following implementation:

```
#define isprint(ltr) ((ltr) >= 32) && ((ltr) <= 127)
```

As you can see, the macro considers any ASCII character in the range 32 through 127 as printable.

C 207 Determining Whether a Character Is a Punctuation Symbol

Within a book, punctuation symbols include commas, semicolons, periods, question marks, and so on. To C, however, a punctuation symbol is any graphics ASCII character that is not alphanumeric. As your programs work with characters within a string, there may be times when you need to test whether or not a character contains a punctuation symbol. To help your programs perform such testing, the header file ctype.h defines the macro *ispunct*. The macro examines a character and returns a nonzero value for a character that contains a punctuation symbol and a zero value otherwise:

```
if (ispunct(character))
```

To better understand the *ispunct* macro, consider the following implementation:

```
#define ispunct(c) (isgraph(c)) && ! isalphanum((c)))
```

Abc

Determining Whether a Character Contains White Space

208

Whitespace characters include the space, tab, carriage-return, newline, vertical tab, and formfeed characters. When your programs perform character output, there may be times when you want to test whether or not a character contains a whitespace character. To help your programs perform such testing, the header file ctype.h provides the macro *isspace*. The macro examines a character and returns a nonzero value for whitespace characters and a zero value otherwise:

```
if (isspace(character))
```

To better understand the *isspace* macro, consider the following implementation:

```
#define isspace(c)   (((c) == 32) || ((c) == 9) || ((c) == 13))
```

Determining Whether a Character Is a Hexadecimal Value

209

A *hexadecimal value* is a digit in the range 0–9 or a letter from A–F or a–f. When your programs work with characters within a string, there may be times when you need to determine if a character contains a hexadecimal digit. To help your programs perform such testing, the header file ctype.h defines the macro *isxdigit*. The macro examines a character and returns a nonzero value if the character is a hexadecimal value and a zero otherwise:

```
if (isxdigit(character))
```

To better understand the *isxdigit* macro, consider the following implementation:

```
#define isxdigit(c) (isnum((c)) || (toupper((c)) >= 'A' &&
toupper((c)) <= 'F'))
```

Converting a Character to Uppercase

210

As you work with character strings, a common operation your programs must perform is converting a lowercase character to uppercase. In such cases, your programs have two choices. First, your program can use the macro _toupper that is defined in the header file ctype.h, or you can use the run-time library function *toupper*. The formats of the macro and function are as follows:

```
#include <ctype.h>

int _toupper(int character);

int toupper(int character);
```

Although the macro and function both convert a character to uppercase, they work differently. The macro _toupper does not test to make sure the character being converted is lowercase. If you invoke the macro with a character that is not lowercase, an error will occur. The function *toupper*, on the other hand, only converts lowercase letters, leaving all other characters unchanged. If you are sure that the character contains a lowercase letter, use the _toupper macro; it will execute faster than that the function. If you are not sure if the character is lowercase, however, use the *toupper* function. The following program, TOUPPER.C, illustrates the use of _toupper and *toupper*, as well as the errors that can occur from using the macro with characters that are not lowercase:

```
#include <stdio.h>
#include <ctype.h>

void main (void)
  {
    char string[] = "Jamsa's 1001 C & C++ Tips";

    int i;

    for (i = 0; string[i]; i++)
      putchar(toupper(string[i]));
    putchar('\n');

    for (i = 0; string[i]; i++)
      putchar(_toupper(string[i]));
    putchar('\n');
  }
```

When you compile and execute this program, your screen will display the first string (using *toupper*) in correct uppercase letters. The second string, however, contains errant characters for the conversion of all characters that are not lowercase.

C 211 Converting a Character to Lowercase

As you work with character strings, a common operation your programs must perform is converting an uppercase character to lowercase. In such cases, your programs have two choices. First,

Abc

your program can use the macro *_tolower* that is defined in the header file ctype.h, or you can use the run-time library function *tolower*. The formats of the macro and function are as follows:

```
#include <ctype.h>

int _tolower(int character);

int tolower(int character);
```

Although the macro and function both convert a character to lowercase, they work differently. The macro *_tolower* does not test to make sure the character being converted is uppercase. If you invoke the macro with a character that is not uppercase, an error will occur. The function *tolower*, on the hand, only converts uppercase letters, leaving all other characters unchanged. If you are sure that the character contains an uppercase letter, use the *_tolower* macro; it will execute faster than that the function. If you are not sure if the character is uppercase, however, use the *tolower* function. The following program, TOLOWER.C, illustrates the use of *_tolower* and *tolower*, as well as the errors that can occur from using the macro with characters that are not uppercase:

```
#include <stdio.h>
#include <ctype.h>

void main (void)
 {
   char string[] = "Jamsa's 1001 C & C++ Tips";

   int i;

   for (i = 0; string[i]; i++)
     putchar(tolower(string[i]));
   putchar('\n');

   for (i = 0; string[i]; i++)
     putchar(_tolower(string[i]));
   putchar('\n');
 }
```

When you compile and execute this program, your screen will display the first string (using *tolower*) in correct lowercase letters. The second string, however, contains errant characters for the conversion of all characters that are not uppercase.

Working with ASCII Characters

When you work with character strings and different character functions, there may be times when you need to ensure that a character is a valid ASCII character—whose value is in the range 0 through 127. In such cases, your programs can use the *toascii* macro, defined in the header file ctype.h:

```
#include <ctype.h>

int toascii(int character);
```

To better understand the *toascii* macro, consider the following implementation:

```
#define toascii(character) ((character) & 0x7F)
```

To improve performance, the macro performs a bitwise AND operation that clears the most significant bit of the character's byte value. In this way, the macro ensures that the value falls in the range 0–127.

C 213 Formatted Output to a String Variable

As you know, the *printf* function lets you write formatted output to the screen display. Depending on your program's requirements, there may be times when need to work with a character string that contains formatted output. For example, assume that your employees have a five-digit employee number and a three-character region identifier (such as Sea for Seattle). Assume that you store information about each employee in a file whose name is a combination of the these two values (such as SEA12345). The *sprintf* function lets you write formatted output to a character string. The format of the function is as follows:

```
#include <stdio.h>

int sprintf(char *string, const char *format
    [,arguments...]);
```

The following program, SPRINTF.C, uses the *sprintf* function to create an eight-character employee filename:

```
#include <stdio.h>

void main(void)
  {
    int employee_number = 12345;
    char region[] = "SEA";
    char filename[64];

    sprintf(filename, "%s%d", region, employee_number);

    printf("Employee filename: %s\n", filename);
  }
```

Abc

Reading Input from a Character String

214

As you have learned, the *scanf* function lets you read formatted input from stdin. Depending on your program's processing, there may be times when a character string contains fields that you want to assign to specific variables. The *sscanf* function lets your programs read values from a string, assigning the values to the specified variables. The format of the *sscanf* function is as follows:

```
#include <stdio.h>

int sscanf(const char *string, const char *format
  [,arguments]);
```

The arguments passed to the *sscanf* must be pointers to variable addresses. If *sscanf* successfully assigns fields, it returns the number of fields assigned. If no fields are assigned, the function returns 0, or the EOF if the end of the string was encountered. The following program, SSCANF.C, illustrates the *sscanf* function:

```
#include <stdio.h>

void main(void)
  {
    int age;
    float salary;
    char string[] = "33 25000.00";

    sscanf(string, "%d %f\n", &age, &salary);

    printf("Age: %d Salary %f\n", age, salary);
  }
```

Tokenizing Strings Saves Space

215

Tokenizing strings is the process of using a unique value to represent a string. For example, assume that you have a program that works with a large number of character strings. For example, the program might contain a database by city and state of your customer accounts. Depending on how the program performs its processing, you might end up with many tests such as the following:

```
if (streql(city, "Seattle"))
   // Statement
else if (streql(city, "New York"))
```

```
     // Statement
else if (streql(city, "Chicago"))
   // Statement
```

Within each one of your program's functions that performs such testing, you consume a considerable amount of space for the string constants, as well as a considerable amount of time performing the string comparisons. As an alternative, you can create a function, called *tokenize_string*, that returns a unique token for each string. Within your functions, your testing becomes the following:

```
int city_token;

city_token = tokenize_string(city);

if (city_token == Seattle_token)
   // Statement
else if (city_token == NewYork_token)
   // Statement
else if (city_token == Chicago_token)
   // Statement
```

By using tokens in this way, you eliminate the amount of data space consumed by the string constants, and you improve your program's performance by eliminating the string comparisons.

216 Initializing a String

In the Arrays and Pointers section of this book you will learn how to assign values to arrays during the array's declaration. As you will learn, C represents character strings as an array of bytes. When you declare a string, you can specify an initial value, as shown here:

```
char title[] = "Jamsa's 1001 C/C++ Tips";

char section[64] = "Strings";
```

In the case of the *title* string, the C compiler will allocate an array large enough to hold the characters specified (plus the NULL character). In this case, the *title* string can hold 24 characters. If you later assign more than 24 characters to the string, you will overwrite the memory used to store another variable's value. In the case of the *section* string, the compiler will allocate a string capable of storing 64 characters. The compiler will assign the first seven bytes of the string the letters in the word "Strings" and the eighth byte the NULL character. The remaining 56 characters are normally initialized to NULL.

Abc

Functions

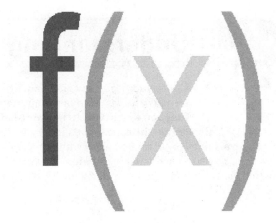

f(x)

C 217 Functions That Don't Return *int*

Several of the functions previously shown have returned values of type *int*. When your function does not return a value type *int* (instead it might return *float, double, char,* and so on), you must tell the compiler the function's return type. The following program, SHOW_AVG.C, uses the function *average_value* to determine the average of three values of type *int.* The function returns the average using a value of type *float*:

```
#include <stdio.h>

float average_value(int a, int b, int c)
  {
    return ((a + b + c) / 3.0);
  }

void main(void)
  {
    printf("The average of 100, 133, and 155 is %f\n",
      average_value(100, 133, 155));
  }
```

As you can see, the function header specifies the function's return type:

```
float average_value(int a, int b, int c)
```

Note: *If you do not tell the compiler otherwise by specifying the function's return type, the C compiler will assume that the function returns the type int.*

C 218 Understanding Local Variables

C lets you declare variables within your functions. Such variables are called *local variables* because their names and values only have meaning in the function within which they were defined. The following program, LOCALERR.C, illustrates the concept of a local variable. The function *local_values* declares three variables, *a, b,* and *c* and assigns to the variables the values 1, 2, and 3. The function *main* tries to print each variable's value. However, because the variable names are local to the function *local_values*, the compiler generates errors stating that the symbols *a, b,* and *c* are undefined:

```
#include <stdio.h>

void local_values(void)
  {
    int a = 1, b = 2, c = 3;

    printf("a contains %d b contains %d c contains %d\n", a, b, c);
  }

void main(void)
  {
    printf("a contains %d b contains %d c contains %d\n", a, b, c);
  }
```

How Functions Use the Stack

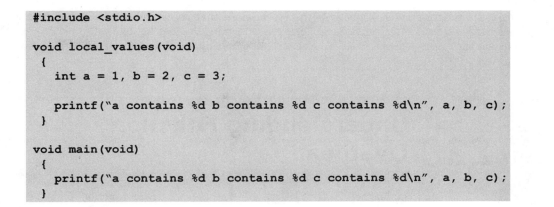

219

The Memory section of this book describes the *stack*, which programs use to temporarily hold information in detail. As you will learn, the stack's primary purpose is to support function invocations. When your program invokes a function, C places onto the stack the address of the instruction that follows the function invocation (called the *return value*). Next, C places on to the stack, from right to left, the function's parameters. Finally, if the function declares local variables, C allocates stack space to hold the variable's value. Figure 219 illustrates the C use of the stack for a simple function call.

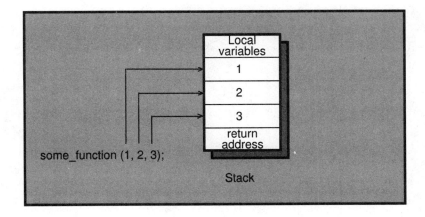

Figure 219 *C's use of the stack for a function call.*

When the function ends, C discards the stack space that contained the local variables and parameters. Next, C uses the return address to determine the instruction that executes next. C removes the return address from the stack, placing the address into the IP (instruction pointer) register.

C 220 Understanding Function Overhead

As you learned in Tip 219, when your program uses a function, C pushes the return address, parameters, and local variables onto the stack. When the function completes, C discards (pops) the stack space that contained the local variables and parameters and then uses the return value to resume the program's execution at the correct location. Although C's use of the stack lets the program invoke and pass information to functions, it also consumes processing time. The amount of time required to push and pop stack information is function overhead. To better understand the impact of function overhead on your program's performance, consider the following program, FUNCTOVR.C. The program first uses a loop to sum the values 1 to 100,000. Next, the program performs the similar processing using a function to add the values:

```c
#include <stdio.h>
#include <time.h>

float add_em(long int a, float b)
  {
    float result;

    result = a + b;

    return(result);
  }

void main(void)
  {
    long int i;
    float result = 0;
    time_t start_time, stop_time;

    printf("Working...\n");
    time(&start_time);

    for (i = 1; i <= 100000L; i++)
      result += i;

    time(&stop_time);
```

f(x)

```
    printf("Using loop %d seconds\n", stop_time - start_time);

    printf("Working...\n");
    time(&start_time);

    for (i = 1; i <= 100000L; i++)
      result = add_em(i, result);

    time(&stop_time);

    printf("Using function %d seconds\n",stop_time - start_time);
}
```

On most systems, the function-based calculations might require almost twice as much processing time. When you use programs within your functions, therefore, you must trade off the benefits the function provides (such as ease of use, reuse of an existing function, reduced testing, ease of understanding, and so on) versus the performance overhead they introduce.

Where C Places Local Variables

C 221

As you have learned, C lets you declare variables within your functions. These variables are *local* to the function, which means their values and existence is known only to the function within which they were declared. The following function, *use_abc*, for example, declares three local variables named *a*, *b*, and *c*:

```
void use_abc(void)
  {
    int a, b, c;

    a = 3;
    b = a + 1;
    c = a + b;

    printf("a contains %d b contains %d c contains %d\n",
      a, b, c);
  }
```

Each time the function is invoked, C allocates stack space to hold the local variables *a*, *b*, and *c*. When the function ends, the stack space is discarded, as are the values that the variables contained. If your function declares many local variables, C stores each variable's value on the stack.

C 222 Declaring Global Variables

In Tip 218 you learned that *local variables* are variables defined within a function whose names and existence are known only to the function. In addition to local variables, C also lets your programs use *global variables*, whose names, values, and existence are known throughout your program. In other words, all of your C programs can use global variables. The following program, GLOBAL.C, illustrates the use of three global variables, *a*, *b*, and *c*:

```c
#include <stdio.h>

int a = 1, b = 2, c = 3;   // Global variables

void global_values(void)
  {
    printf("a contains %d b contains %d c contains %d\n",a, b, c);
  }

void main(void)
  {
    global_values();
    printf("a contains %d b contains %d c contains %d\n",a, b, c);
  }
```

When you compile and execute this program, the functions *global_values* and *main* both display the global variable values. Note that the variables are declared outside of all functions. When you declare global variables in this way, all of your program's functions can use and change the global variable values simply by referring to the global variable name. Although global variables might at first appear convenient, their misuse can lead to errors that are very difficult to debug, as discussed in Tip 223.

C 223 Why Your Program's Should Avoid Global Variables

In Tip 222 you learned how to declare *global variables*, which are known throughout all of your program functions. At first glance, using global variables seems to simplify your programming because it eliminates the need for function parameters and more importantly, the need to understand *call by value* and *call by reference*. Unfortunately, global variables often open the opportunity for more errors than they fix. Because a global variable's value can be changed at virtually any location within your program, it becomes very difficult for another programmer who is reading your program to find each location in your program where the global

f(x)

variable changes. As such, they might make changes to your program without fully understanding the affect the change has on a global variable. As a rule, functions should only change those variables passed to them as parameters. In this way, programmers can study the function prototypes to quickly determine which variables a function changes.

If you find that your program uses global variables, sit back and reconsider your program design. Your goal is to eliminate (definitely minimize) global variable use.

Resolving Global and Local Variable Name Conflicts

 224

As you have learned, local variables are variables declared within a function whose names are known only to that the function. Global variables on the other hand are declared outside of all functions, and their names are known to every function throughout your program. If your program uses global variables, there may be times when the name of a global variable is the same as that of a local variable declared within a function. For example, the following program, CONFLICT.C, uses the global variables *a*, *b*, and *c*. The function *conflict_a* uses a local variable named *a* and the global variables *b* and *c*:

```c
#include <stdio.h>

int a = 1, b = 2, c = 3;   // Global variables

void conflict_a(void)
  {
    int a = 100;

    printf("a contains %d b contains %d c contains %d\n",a, b, c);
  }

void main(void)
  {
    conflict_a();
    printf("a contains %d b contains %d c contains %d\n",a, b, c);
  }
```

When you compile and execute this program, your screen will display the following:

```
C:\> CONFLICT  <ENTER>
a contains 100 b contains 2 c contains 3
a contains 1 b contains 2 c contains 3
```

When the name of a global and local variable conflicts, C will always use the local variable. As you can see, the changes the function *conflict_a* made to the variable *a* only appear within the function.

> **Note:** *Although this program's purpose was to illustrate how C resolves name conflicts, it also illustrates the confusion that can occur through the use of global variables. In this case, a programmer who is reading your code needs to pay close attention to determine that the function does not change the global variable a, but rather a local variable. Because the function combines the use of global and local variables, the code can become difficult to understand.*

225 Better Defining a Global Variable's Scope

In Tip 222 you learned that a *global variable* is a variable that is known to all of the functions throughout your program. Actually, depending on where you define a global variable, you can control which functions are actually able to reference the variable. In other words, you can control the global variable's *scope*. When your program declares a global variable, the variable can be referenced by any functions that follow the variable declaration, up to the end of the source file. Functions whose definitions appear prior to the global variable definition cannot access the global variable. For example, consider the following program, GLOSCOPE.C, which defines the global variable *title*:

```
#include <stdio.h>

void unknown_title(void)
 {
   printf("The book's title is %s\n", title);
 }

char title[] = "Jamsa's 1001 C/C++ Tips";

void main(void)
 {
   printf("Title: %s\n", title);
 }
```

As you can see, the function *unknown_title* tries to display the variable *title*. However, because the global variable declaration occurs after the function definition, the global variable is unknown within the function. When you try to compile this program, your compiler will generate an error. To correct the error, move the global variable declaration before the function.

Understanding Call by Value

As you have learned, your programs pass information to functions using parameters. When you pass a parameter to a function, C uses a technique known as *call by value* to provide the function with a copy of the parameter's value. Using call by value, any changes the function makes to the parameter exist only within the function itself. When the function completes, the value of variables passed to the function are not changed. For example, the following program, NOCHANGE.C, passes three parameters (the variables *a*, *b*, and *c*) to the function *display_and_change*. The function in turn, displays the values, adds 100 to them, and then displays the result. When the function ends, the program displays the variables values. Because C uses call by value, the variable's values are unchanged:

```c
#include <stdio.h>

void display_and_change(int first, int second, int third)
  {
    printf("Original function values %d %d %d\n",
      first, second, third);

    first += 100;
    second += 100;
    third += 100;

    printf("Ending function values %d %d %d\n",
      first, second, third);
  }

void main(void)
  {
    int a = 1, b = 2, c = 3;

    display_and_change(a, b, c);

    printf("Ending values in main %d %d %d\n", a, b ,c);
  }
```

When you compile and execute this program, your screen will display the following:

```
C:\> NOCHANGE  <ENTER>
Original function values 1 2 3
Ending function values 101 102 103
Ending values in main 1 2 3
```

f(x)

As you can see, the changes the function makes to the variables are only visible within the function itself. When the function ends, your variables within *main* are unchanged.

Note: *When using call by reference, a function cannot change a parameter's value so that the change is visible outside of the function.*

C 227 Why Call by Value Prevents Parameter Value Change

In Tip 226 you learned that by default, C uses *call by value* to pass parameters to functions. As a result, any changes to the parameter's value only occur within the function itself. When the function ends, the values of variables passed to the function are unchanged. As discussed in the ABCs section of this book, a variable is essentially a name assigned to a memory location. Every variable therefore, has two attributes of interest—it's current value and its memory address. In the case of the program NOCHANGE.C presented in Tip 226, the variables a, b, c might use the memory addresses shown in Figure 227.1.

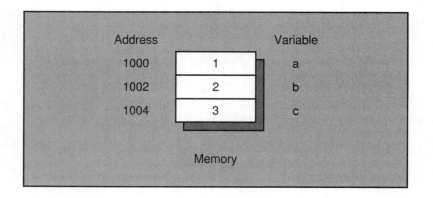

Figure 227.1 *Variables store a value and reside in a specific memory location.*

When you pass parameters to a function, C places the corresponding values on to the stack. In the case of the variables *a, b, c*, the stack contains the values 1, 2, and 3. When the function accesses the variable's values, the function references the stack locations, as shown in Figure 227.2.

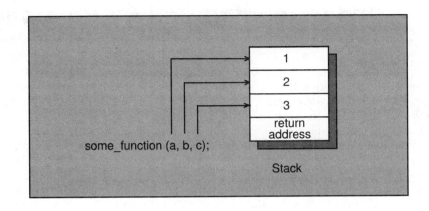

Figure 227.2 *Functions reference parameter values stored on the stack.*

Any changes the function makes to the parameter values actually change the stack values, as shown in Figure 227.3.

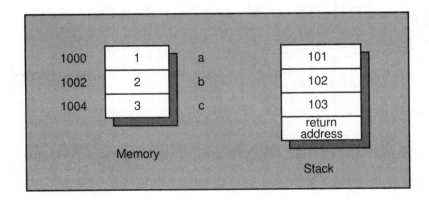

Figure 227.3 *Changes functions make to parameter values affect only those values on the stack.*

When the function ends, C discards the stack and, hence, the changes the function has made to the stack locations. The memory locations that contain each variable's value are never referenced by the function, so using call by value, a function cannot make changes to a variable's value that exists after the function ends.

C 228

Understanding Call By Reference

As you have learned, C, passes parameters to functions using *call by value* by default. Using call by value, functions cannot change the value of a variable passed to a function. In most programs, however, your functions will need to change variables in one way or another. For example, a function that reads information from a file needs to place the information in a character string array. Likewise, a function such as *strupr* (presented in the Strings section of this book) needs to convert the letters in a character string to uppercase. When your functions change value of a parameter, your programs must pass the parameter to the function using *call by reference*. The difference between call by value and call by reference is that using call by value, functions receive a copy of a parameter's value. With call by reference, on the other hand, functions receive the variable's memory address. As such, the functions can make changes to the value stored at a specific memory location, which remains after the function ends. To use call by reference, your program must use *pointers*. The Pointers section of this book discusses pointers in detail. For now, however, think of a pointer as simply a memory address. To assign a variable's address to a pointer you use C's address operator (&). To access the value in the memory location at which the pointer points later, you use C's redirection operator (*). Tips 229 and 230 discuss these operators in detail.

C 229

Getting a Variable's Address

A variable is essentially a name assigned to one or more memory locations. When your program runs, each variable resides in its own memory location. Your program locates variables in memory using the variable's memory *address*. To determine a variable's address, you use C's address operator (&). The following program, SHOWADDR.C, for example uses the address operator to display the addresses (in hexadecimal) of the variable's *a*, *b*, and *c*:

```
#include <stdio.h>

void main(void)
 {
   int a = 1, b = 2, c = 3;

   printf("The address of a is %x the value of a is %d\n",&a, a);
   printf("The address of b is %x the value of b is %d\n",&b, b);
   printf("The address of c is %x the value of c id %d\n",&c, c);
 }
```

When you compile and run this program, your program will display output similar to the following (the actual address values shown may differ):

```
C:\> SHOWADDR  <ENTER>
The address of a is fff4 the value of a is 1
The address of b is fff2 the value of b is 2
The address of c is fff0 the value of c is 3
```

When your programs later pass parameters to functions for variables whose value the function must change, your programs will pass the variables by reference (address), using the address operator, as shown here:

```
some_function(&a, &b, &c);
```

Using a Variable's Address

C 230

In Tip 229 you learned how to use C's address operator to obtain a variable's memory address. When you pass an address to a function, you must tell the C compiler that the function will be using a pointer (the memory address) of a variable, as opposed to the variable's value. To do so, you must declare a *pointer variable*. Declaring a pointer variable is very similar to a standard variable declaration, in that you specify a type and variable name. The difference, however, is that pointer variable names are preceded by an asterisk (*). The following declarations create pointer variables to values of type *int*, *float*, and *char*:

```
int *i_pointer;
float *f_pointer;
char *c_pointer;
```

After you declare a pointer variable, you must assign to the variable a memory address. The following statement, for example, assigns the address of the integer variable *a* to the pointer variable *i_pointer*:

```
i_pointer = &a;
```

Next, to use the value pointed to by pointer variable, your programs must use C's redirection operator—the asterisk (*). For example, the following statement assigns the variable *a* (whose address is contained in the variable *i_pointer*) the value 5:

```
*i_pointer = 5;
```

In a similar way, the following statement assigns the variable *b* the value currently pointed to by the variable *i_pointer*:

```
b = *i_pointer;
```

f(x)

When you want to use the value pointed to by a pointer variable, you use the redirection operator (*). When you want to assign a variable's address to a pointer variable, you use the address operator (&). The following program, USEADDR.C, illustrates the use of a pointer variable. The program assigns the pointer variable *i_pointer* the address of the variable *a*. The program then uses the pointer variable to change, display, and assign the variable's value:

```c
#include <stdio.h>

void main(void)
  {
    int a = 1, b = 2;

    int *i_pointer;

    // Assign an address
    i_pointer = &a;

    // Change the value pointed to by i_pointer to 5
    *i_pointer = 5;

    // Display the value
    printf("Value pointed to by i_pointer %d the variable a %d\n",
      *i_pointer, a);

    // Assign the value
    b = *i_pointer;

    printf("Value of b is %d\n", b);
    printf("Value of i_pointer %x\n", i_pointer);
  }
```

Remember that a pointer is nothing more than a memory address. The value contained in the pointer (the address) must be assigned by your program. In the case of the program USEADDR.C, the program assigned the pointer the address of the variable *a*. The program could have just as easily assigned the address of the variable *b*.

> **Note:** *When you use pointers, you must still keep in mind value types, such as int, float, and char. Your programs should only assign the address of integer values to integer pointers, and so on.*

f(x)

Changing a Parameter's Value

C 231

As you have learned, to change a parameter's value within a function, your programs must use *call by reference*, passing the address of variables. Within the function, you must use pointers. The following program, CHGPARAM.C, uses pointers and addresses (call by reference) to display and then change the parameters passed to the function *display_and_change*:

```c
#include <stdio.h>

void display_and_change(int *first, int *second, int *third)
  {
    printf("Original function values %d %d %d\n",
      *first, *second, *third);

    *first += 100;
    *second += 100;
    *third += 100;

    printf("Ending function values %d %d %d\n",
      *first, *second, *third);
  }

void main(void)
  {
    int a = 1, b = 2, c = 3;

    display_and_change(&a, &b, &c);

    printf("Ending values in main %d %d %d\n", a, b ,c);
  }
```

As you can see, when the program invokes the function, it passes as parameters the addresses of the variables *a*, *b*, and *c*. Within *display_and_change*, the function uses pointer variables and C's redirection operator to change and display the parameter's values. When you compile and execute this program, your screen will display the following output:

```
C:\> CHGPARAM  <ENTER>
Original function values 1 2 3
Ending function values 101 102 103
Ending values in main 101 102 103
```

C 232 Changing Only Specific Parameters

As you have learned, your functions can change a parameter's value using *call by reference*. Tip 231, for example, presented the function *display_and_change*, which used call by reference to change the value of each of its parameters. In many cases, however, your functions may change one parameter's value while leaving a second unchanged. For example, the following program, CHGFIRST.C, uses the function *change_first* to assign the value of the second parameter specified to the first:

```
#include <stdio.h>

void change_first(int *first, int second)
 {
    *first = second;   // Assign value of second to first
 }

void main(void)
 {
    int a = 0, b = 5;

    change_first(&a, b);
    printf("Value of a %d value of b %d\n", a, b);
 }
```

As you can see, the function uses call by reference to change the first parameter's value and call by value for the second parameter. When your functions use both techniques, and they will, you need to keep in mind when to use pointers and when you can directly reference the variable. As a rule, the parameters whose values you want to change will require call by reference. To understand the impact of call by reference versus call by value better, change the function *change_first*, as shown here:

```
void change_first(int *first, int second)
 {
   *first = second;   // Assign the value of second to first
   second = 100;
 }
```

When you compile and execute this program you will see that the value of *first* has changed, but the value of *second* has not. Because the parameter *second* is passed by value, the change to the parameter is not visible outside of the function.

f(x)

Call by Reference Still Uses the Stack

As you have learned, when C passes parameters to functions, C places the parameter's values on the stack. C uses the stack to hold parameters whether you are using call by value or call by reference. When you pass a parameter by value, C places the parameter's *value* on the stack. When you pass a parameter by reference, C places the parameter's *address* on the stack. Tip 232 presented the program CHGFIRST.C, which used the function *change_first* to assign the value of the second parameter to the first. When the program invokes the function, C places the address of the variable *a* and the value of variable *b* on the stack, as shown in Figure 233.

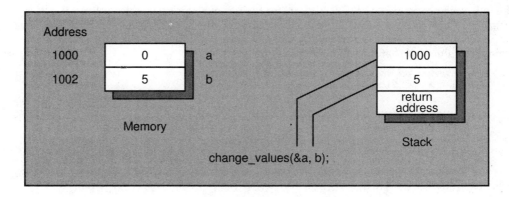

Figure 233 *Using call by reference, C places an address on the stack.*

Because the function *change_values* actually references the memory location containing variable *a*'s value, the changes it makes to the variable exist after the function ends.

Function Variables that Remember

In C, the variables you declare within functions are often called *automatic* because the C compiler automatically creates them as when the function begins and then destroys them when the function ends. The variable's automatic life occurs because the compiler stores function variables temporarily on the stack. As a result, should a function assign a value to a variable during one invocation, the variable's value is lost when the function completes. The next time you invoke the function, the variable's value is not defined. Depending on the processing your function performs, there may be times when you want the function's variables to remember the last value they were assigned. For example, assume that you have written a function called *print_reportcard*, which prints a report card for every student in a school. Your function might use the variable *student_id* to hold the student identification number of the last student whose report card was printed. In this way, the function, without being told, can begin with the next student. For your function's local variables to remember their values in this way, you must declare the variables using the keyword *static*, as shown here:

```
void print_reportcard(int printer_number)
  {
    static int student_id;

    // Other statements
  }
```

The following program, STATIC.C, illustrates the use of a *static* variable within a function. The program, which uses the function *print_reportcard*, begins by assigning the variable *student_id* the value 100. The each time the program invokes the function, the function displays the variable's value and then increments the value by 1:

```
#include <stdio.h>

void print_reportcard(int printer_number)
  {
    static int student_id = 100;

    printf("Printing report card for student %d\n", student_id);
    student_id++;

    // Other statements here
  }

void main(void)
  {
    print_reportcard(1);
    print_reportcard(1);
    print_reportcard(1);
  }
```

When you compile and execute this program, your screen displays the following output:

```
C:\> STATIC  <ENTER>
Printing report card for student 100
Printing report card for student 101
Printing report card for student 102
```

As you can see, the variable *student_id* retains its value from one invocation to the next.

Note: *When you declare static variables, the C compiler does not store the variables on the stack. Instead, the compiler places the variables within the data segment so their values can remain.*

How C Initializes static Variables

In Tip 234 you learned that the *static* keyword directs the compiler to retain a variable's value from one function invocation to the next. When your function declares a static variable, C lets you initialize the variable, as shown here:

```
void print_reportcard(int printer_number)
  {
    static int student_id = 100;  // Initialized once

    // Other statements
  }
```

When you declare a variable as *static*, the C compiler will initialize the variable to the value you specify. When the function is invoked later, the assignment *is not performed*. This function variable initialization is different than the processing that the C would normally perform within a function. In the case of the following function, C will initialize the variable *count* every time the function is called:

```
void some_function(int age, char *name)
  {
    int count = 1;  // Initialized on every call

    // Other statements
  }
```

Using the Pascal Calling Sequence

As you create C programs, you might find that you could really use a function that you have previously created in Pascal. Depending on your compiler, linker, and library type, you might still be able to call the Pascal function from your C program! The steps you must perform to do so, however, will depend on your compiler. Within your program code, however, you simply need to include a function prototype at the start of your program that includes the *pascal* keyword:

```
int pascal some_function(int score, int grade);
```

If you program in the Windows environment, you will find that many of the run-time library functions use the Pascal calling sequence. Functions that use the *pascal* keyword cannot support a variable number of arguments (as can *printf* and *scanf*)

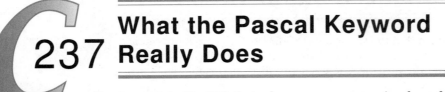

237 What the Pascal Keyword Really Does

You learned in Tip 236 that when your programs invoke a function, C passes parameters to the function using the stack. C places parameters on the stack from right to left. Figure 237.1 illustrates the stack contents for a C function call.

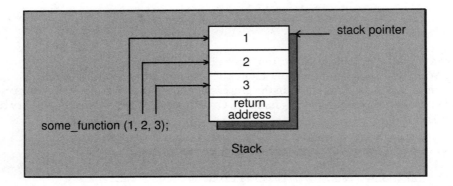

Figure 237.1 *The stack contents for a C function call.*

Pascal, on the other hand, pushes arguments on to the stack from left to right. Figure 237.2 illustrates the stack contents for a Pascal function call.

f(x)

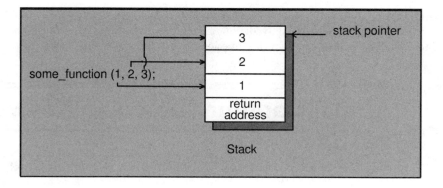

Figure 237.2 *The stack contents for a Pascal function call.*

If you are using a Pascal function from within your C program, using the *pascal* keyword directs the C compiler to place the parameters on the stack from left to right, in the order that Pascal expects.

A Mixed Language Example

C 238

As you have learned, many C compilers let you invoke functions that were written in a different programming language. If you are calling a Pascal function from within your C program, for example, you can precede the function prototype using the *pascal* keyword. As you have learned, the *pascal* keyword directs the compiler to push parameters on to the stack from left to right. To illustrate the processing the *pascal* keyword performs, create the following function, *show_values*, and precede the function with the *pascal* keyword:

```c
#include <stdio.h>

void pascal show_values(int a, int b, int c)
   {
      printf("a %d b %d c %d\n", a, b, c);
   }
```

Next, call the function using the following program code:

```c
void main(void)
   {
      show_values(1, 2, 3);
      show_values(100, 200, 300);
   }
```

Experiment with the show_values function, removing the pascal keyword and note the change in the order of the parameter values displayed. Should your programs later call a Pascal routine, you will need to use the *pascal* keyword in the function prototype.

239 Understanding the *cdecl* Keyword

In Tip 237 you learned that if you are using functions written in Pascal, you can use the *pascal* keyword to inform the compiler so that the compiler places parameters on to the stack in the correct order. When you use functions written with multiple programming languages, you might want to include the keyword *cdecl* within your function prototypes to indicate C functions. For example, the following function prototype informs the compiler that the function *change_values* uses the C calling structure:

```
int cdecl change_values(int *, int *, int *);
```

When the compiler encounters the *cdecl* keyword within a function header, the function will ensure that parameters passed to the function are placed on the stack from right to left. In addition, the compiler will ensure that the function's naming format used by the linker uses the C format.

240 Understanding Recursion

As you have learned, C lets you divide your program into smaller pieces called functions. Using functions, your program becomes easier to understand, program, and test. In addition, the functions you create for one program can often be used by another. As your programs execute, one function may call another, which calls another, which may, in turn, call several other functions—each function to perform a specific operation. As it turns out, C even lets a function call itself! A *recursive function* is a function that calls itself to perform a specific operation. The process of a function calling itself is *recursion*. As the complexity of your programs and functions increases, you might find that many operations are easily defined in terms of themselves. For such cases, you might want to create a recursive function. Many programming books, for example, use the factorial problem to illustrate how recursion works. The factorial of the value 1 is 1. The factorial of the value 2 is 2*1. The factorial of the value 3 is 3*2*1. Likewise, the factorial of the value 4 is 4*3*2*1. This process can essentially go on indefinitely. If you take a close look at the processing that the factorial performs, you will find that factorial of 4, for example, is actually 4 times the factorial of 3 (3*2*1). Likewise, the factorial of 3 is actually 3 times the factorial of 2 (2*1). The factorial of 2 is 2 times the factorial of 1 (1). Table 240 illustrates the factorial processing.

f(x)

Value	Calculation	Result	Factorial
1	1	1	1
2	2*1	2	2 * Factorial(1)
3	3*2*1	6	3 * Factorial(2)
4	4*3*2*1	24	4 * Factorial(3)
5	5*4*3*2*1	120	5 * Factorial(4)

Table 240 *Factorial processing.*

The following program, FACT.C, creates the recursive function *factorial* and then uses the function to return the factorial values for the values 1 through 5:

```c
#include <stdio.h>

int factorial(int value)
{
   if (value == 1)
      return(1);
   else
      return(value * factorial(value-1));
}

void main(void)
{
   int i;

   for (i = 1; i <= 5; i++)
      printf("The factorial of %d is %d\n", i, factorial(i));
}
```

As you can see, the function *factorial*, returns a result that is based on the result of the function itself. Tip 241 examines the *factorial* function in detail.

Understanding the Recursive *factorial* Function

241

In Tip 240 you learned that a recursive function is a function that calls itself to perform a specific task. Tip 240 presented the *factorial* function to illustrate recursion. The *factorial* function receives a specific parameter value. When the function begins, it first checks if the value is 1, which by factorial definition, is 1. If the value is 1, the function returns the value 1. If the value is not 1, the function returns the result of the value times the factorial of the value minus 1. Assume, for example, the function is invoked with the value 3. The function will return the result of 3 . *factorial(3–1)*. When C encounters the function call within the *return* statement, C will invoke the function a second time—this time with the value of 3–1 or 2. Again, because the value is not 1, the function returns the result of the 2 . *factorial(2–1)*. On this invocation of the function, the value is 1. As a result, the function returns the value 1 to the caller. Who in turn returns the result of 2.1 to its caller. Who returns the result of 3.2.1 to its caller. Figure 241 illustrates the chain of recursive function invocations and return values for the factorial(3) function call.

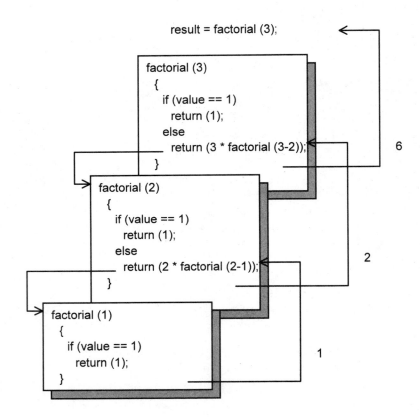

```
result = factorial (3);

factorial (3)
  {
     if (value == 1)
       return (1);
     else
       return (3 * factorial (3-2));
  }

factorial (2)
  {
     if (value == 1)
       return (1);
     else
       return (2 * factorial (2-1));
  }

factorial (1)
  {
     if (value == 1)
       return (1);
  }
```

6

2

1

Figure 241 *The chain of function calls and value returns for the recursive factorial function.*

A recursive function is somewhat like a looping construct in that you must specify an ending condition. If you don't, the function will never end. In the case of the factorial problem, the ending condition is the factorial of 1, which by definition, is 1.

One More Recursive Example

242

In Tip 240 you learned that a recursive function is a function that calls itself in order to perform specific processing. Tip 241, in turn, presented and explained the recursive *factorial* function. Because recursion can be a difficult concept, this tip presents one more recursive function, *display_backward*, which displays the letters of a string in reverse order. Given the letters, ABCDE, the function displays the letters on your screen as *EDCBA*. The following program, BACKWARD.C, uses the *display_backward* function:

```
#include <stdio.h>

void display_backward(char *string)
  {
    if (*string)
      {
        display_backward(string+1);
        putchar(*string);
      }
  }

void main(void)
  {
    display_backward("ABCDE");
  }
```

Display Values to Understand Recursion Better

243

A recursive function is a function that calls itself to perform a specific operation. Tip 241 presented the recursive *factorial* function. To help you understand the process of recursion better, the program SHOWFACT.C has included the *printf* statements within *factorial* that illustrate its processing:

```
#include <stdio.h>

int factorial(int value)
  {
    printf("In factorial with the value %d\n", value);

    if (value == 1)
```

f(x)

```
    {
      printf ("Returning the value 1\n");
      return (1);
    }
  else
    {
      printf ("Returning %d * factorial (%d)\n",
          value, value-1);
      return (value * factorial (value-1));
    }
  }

void main (void)
  {
    printf ("The factorial of 4 is %d\n", factorial (4));
  }
```

When you compile and execute this program, your screen will display the following output:

```
C:\> SHOWFACT   <ENTER>
In factorial the value 4
Returning 4 * factorial (3)
In factorial the value 3
Returning 3 * factorial (2)
In factorial the value 2
Returning 2 * factorial (1)
In factorial the value 1
Returning the value 1
The factorial of 4 is 24
```

By inserting *printf* statements throughout your recursive functions, you can understand better the processing they perform.

244 Direct and Indirect Recursion

A recursive function is a function that calls itself to perform a specific operation. Several of the previous tips have presented recursive functions. When a function invokes itself to perform a task, the function is said to perform *direct recursion*. Once you have examined a few recursive functions, you should be able to understand most functions that use direct recursion. A more difficult form of recursion, *indirect recursion*, occurs when a function (function A) calls another function (function B), which, in turn, calls the original function (function A). As a rule, because it can result in code that is very difficult to understand, you should avoid the use of indirect recursion whenever possible.

To Use or Not to Use Recursion

C 245

A recursive function is a function that calls itself to perform a specific task. When you create functions, you can use recursion to create elegant solutions to many problems. However, you should avoid recursion whenever possible for two reasons. First, recursive functions can be difficult for novice programmers to understand. Second, as a rule, recursive functions are often considerably slower than their nonrecursive counterparts. The following program, NO_RECUR.C, uses invokes the function nonrecursive function *string_length* with the string "Jamsa's 1001 C/C++ Tips" 100,000 times and then displays the amount of time required to perform the processing:

```c
#include <stdio.h>
#include <time.h>

int string_length(const char *str)
  {
    int length = 0;

    while (*str++)
      length++;

    return(length);
  }

void main(void)
  {
    long int counter;

    time_t start_time, end_time;

    time(&start_time);

    for (counter = 0; counter < 100000L; counter++)
      string_length("Jamsa's 1001 C/C++ Tips");

    time(&end_time);

    printf("Processing time %d\n", end_time - start_time);
  }
```

Next, the program OK_RECUR.C uses a recursive implementation of the *string_length* function to perform the same processing:

```
#include <stdio.h>
#include <time.h>

int string_length(const char *str)
  {
    if (*str)
      return(1 + string_length(str+1));
    else
      return(0);
  }

void main(void)
  {
    long int counter;

    time_t start_time, end_time;

    time(&start_time);

    for (counter = 0; counter < 100000L; counter++)
      string_length("Jamsa's 1001 C/C++ Tips");

    time(&end_time);

    printf("Processing time %d\n", end_time - start_time);
  }
```

Experiment with these programs, possibly changing the number of function calls to one or two million. As you will find, the nonrecursive function executes considerable faster than the recursive counterpart. As such, when you design a recursive function, keep in mind that you may be adding considerable overhead to your program's execution time.

C 246 Why Recursive Functions Are Slow

A recursive function is a function that calls itself to perform a specific task. As you learned in Tip 245, one reason to avoid the use of recursion is that recursive functions are normally considerably slower than a nonrecursive counterpart. The reason that recursive functions are slow is due to the function call overhead that occurs with every invocation. As discussed in Tip 219, each time your program calls a function, the C compiler pushes onto the stack the address of the statement that immediately follows the function call (called the *return address*). Next, the compiler pushes the parameter values on to the stack. When the function completes, the return address is popped off of the stack into the CPU's program counter. Although computers can perform these push and pop operations very quickly, the operations still require time. Assume, for example, that you invoke the recursive *factorial* function with the value 50. The function will then invoke itself 49 times. If each function call adds 10 milliseconds to your program, the function will be 1/2 second slower than a nonrecursive counterpart, which only has the overhead of one function invocation. Clearly, 1/2 second of overhead does not seem like much, however, assume that the program calls the function ten times. The half second delay quickly turns into five seconds. If the program uses the function 100 times, the delay becomes 50 seconds, and so on. If you are writing a program that requires maximum performance, you should try to eliminate recursive functions whenever possible.

How to Remove Recursion

A recursive function is a function that calls itself to perform a specific task. As you have learned, you can improve your program's performance by using nonrecursive functions. As a rule, any function you can write recursively, you can write in terms of looping constructs such as a *for* or *while* statement. The following program, LOOPFACT.C, uses a *for* loop to implement the *factorial* function:

```c
#include <stdio.h>

int factorial(int value)
  {
    int result = 1;
    int counter;

    for (counter = 2; counter <= value; counter++)
      result *= counter;

    return(result);
  }

void main(void)
  {
    int i;

    for (i = 1; i <= 5; i++)
      printf("Factorial of %d is %d\n", i, factorial(i));
  }
```

Whenever you can eliminate recursion within your programs using a loop in this way, you will normally improve your program's performance. However, keep in mind that some operations are most easily understood when they are implemented using recursion. Just as there are times when you must make tradeoffs between your programs speed and memory consumption, there may be times when you must trade off between readability and performance.

C 248 Passing Strings to Functions

As you have learned, when you pass parameters to functions, C, by default, passes the parameters *by value*. Therefore, any changes that your function makes to the parameter do not exist outside of the function. To change a parameter's value, you must pass the parameter *by reference*. Many new C programmers are confused, therefore, about why character string arrays seem to violate this rule. After all, when they invoke a function with a character string, they simply pass the string—they don't use the address operator (&).

As discussed in the Strings section of this book, C represents character strings as a byte array. When C passes an array (any type of array—not just a string), C passes the array's starting address to the function. In other words, *C always uses call by reference for arrays*, and you do not need to use the address operator.

C 249 Passing Specific Array Elements

As you learned in Tip 248, C always passes arrays to functions using call by reference. As you work with character strings, there may be times when you want a function to work with specific array elements. For example, the following program, HALFCAPS.C, uses the *strupr* function to convert part of character string to uppercase:

```c
#include <stdio.h>
#include <string.h>

void main(void)
  {
    char alphabet[] = "abcdefghijklmnopqrstuvwxyz";

    strupr(&alphabet[13]);

    printf(alphabet);
  }
```

The *strupr* expects the starting address of a NULL-terminated string as a parameter. In this case, the program passes to *strupr* the address of the letter N, which is then followed by several NULL-terminated characters. By passing the address of a specific array element, your programs can use functions to manipulate specific array elements.

Understanding *const* in Formal Parameters

C 250

If you examine the function prototypes for the string manipulation functions presented in the Strings section of this book, you will find that many of the parameter declarations place the keyword *const* before character string arguments:

```
char *strcpy(char *destination, const char *source);
```

In this case, the *const* keyword specifies that the variable *source* should not be changed within the function. Should your function code try to change the string's value, the compiler will generate an error. The following program, CHKCONST.C, uses the *const* keyword for the parameter *string*:

```c
#include <stdio.h>

void no_change(const char *string)
 {
   while (*string)
     *string++ = toupper(*string);
 }


 void main(void)
  {
    char title[] = "Jamsa's 1001 C/C++ Tips";

    no_change(title);

    printf(title);
  }
```

As you can see, the function *no_change* tries to convert the string's letters to uppercase. However, because the program uses the *const* keyword, the compiler will display an error message, and the code will not successfully compile. You should use the *const* keyword before parameters that are passed by reference when you don't want the parameter's value changed. Because C normally passes other parameters by value, they do not require the *const* keyword.

f(x)

C 251 Using *const* Won't Prevent Parameter Modification

As you learned in Tip 250, the *const* keyword informs the compiler that a specific parameter's value should not be changed. Should a function try to modify such a parameter's value, the compiler will generate an error, and the program will not compile. However, it is important to note that just because a parameter is specified as a constant, does not mean that function cannot change the parameter's value. The following program, CHGCONST.C, uses a pointer to the constant parameter *string* to convert the string's contents to uppercase:

```c
#include <stdio.h>
#include <ctype.h>

void no_change(const char *string)
 {
   char *alias = string;

   while (*alias)
     *alias++ = toupper(*alias);
 }


void main(void)
 {
   char title[] = "Jamsa's 1001 C/C++ Tips";

   no_change(title);

   printf(title);
 }
```

When you compile and execute this program, the function *no_change* will convert the string's characters to uppercase. Because of the use of *pointer aliasing* (referring to a variable's memory locations using a different name), the compiler does not detect the parameter value change. Depending on your compiler type, the compiler may generate a warning message. If you are creating your own functions, do not use aliasing to change a parameter's value in this way. If a parameter is truly a constant, its value should not change. The goal of this tip was to teach you that the *const* keyword cannot actually prevent a parameter's value from changing.

Resolving Name Conflicts

252

As you have learned, most C compilers provide an extensive library of functions that you can call to perform specific tasks. For example, to obtain to the absolute value of an integer expression, you use *abs*. Likewise, to copy one string's contents to another, you use *strcpy*. As you create your own functions, there may be times when one of the function names that you define is the same as the name of a run-time library function. For example, the following program, MYSTRCPY.C, creates and uses a function named *strcpy*:

```c
#include <stdio.h>

char *strcpy(char *destination, const char *source)
  {
    char *start = destination;

    while (*destination++ = *source++)
      ;

    return(start);
  }

void main(void)
  {
    char title[64];

    strcpy(title, "Jamsa's 1001 C/C++ Tips");
    printf(title);
  }
```

When a function name that you declare within your program conflicts with a run-time library function. C uses your program's function, not the run-time library implementation.

Understanding Unbounded String Declarations

253

In C, a character string is an array of character values. You learned in the Strings section of this book that you specify the maximum number of characters the string will ever hold to create a string, as shown here:

```
char name[64];
char title[32];
char buffer[512];
```

When you pass a character string to a function, you actually pass the string's starting address. Because the string is terminated by the NULL character, C functions don't care how many characters the string contains. As a result, many functions declare character string parameters as unbounded arrays (arrays that don't specify a size), as shown here:

```
int strlen(char string[])
```

The declaration **char string[]** tells the compiler that the function will receive a pointer to a NULL-terminated string. The string might contain 64 characters, 1024 characters, or maybe just the NULL character. The following program, STRARRAY.C, uses an unbounded array to implement the *strlen* function:

```
#include <stdio.h>

int strlen(char str[])
  {
    int i = 0;

    while (str[i] != NULL)
      i++;

    return(i);
  }

void main(void)
  {
    printf("Length of ABC is %d\n", strlen("ABC"));
    printf("Length of 1001 C/C++ Tips is %d\n",
      strlen("1001 C/C++ Tips"));
    printf("Length of a NULL string is %d\n", strlen(""));
  }
```

When you compile and execute this program, you will see that the function works for any size string. Like most C functions that work with strings, however, if the string is not terminated by the NULL character, the function will fail.

C 254 Pointers versus String Declarations

As you examine different C functions that manipulate strings, you may find the character strings declared as either unbound arrays or as pointers:

```
char *strcpy(char destination[], char source[]);

char *strcpy(char *destination, char *source);
```

Both of these function declarations inform the compiler that it is working with strings. Both are functionally identical, and both are correct. If you are creating your own functions, the format you choose should depend on how you reference the parameter within the function. If you treat the parameter as a pointer, use the pointer-style declaration. If you instead treat the parameter as an array, use the array. By treating the parameter in a consistent way, you will make your programs easier to understand.

How C Uses the Stack for String Parameters

255

As you have learned, when your programs parameters to functions, C places the parameter's value or address on the stack. When you pass a character string to a function, C places the string's starting address on the stack. For example, Tip 253 presented the program STRARRAY.C, which passed several strings to the function *strlen*. Figure 255 illustrates the parameter value C places on the stack for each function invocation.

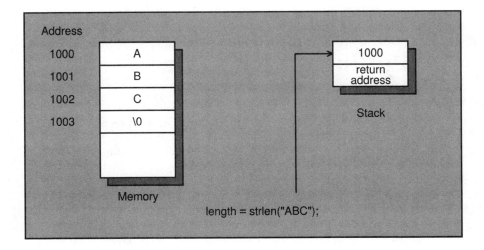

Figure 255 *How C passes string parameters to functions.*

As you can see, C does not place the string's characters on to the stack. Instead, C simply places the address of the NULL-terminated string on the stack. Because the function receives only an address (as opposed to an array of bytes), the function does not care how many characters the string contains.

Understanding External Variables

256

The functions you create for one program can often be used within another. To simplify function reuse, programmers often place functions in object code libraries. The Tools section of this book discusses the use of such libraries. In some cases, a library might define a global variable, such as the *_fmode*, *_psp*, or *errno* variables discussed throughout this book. When a global variable is defined in code outside of the current program and you want to use the global variable within your program, you must declare the variable using the *extern* keyword that tells the compiler the variable is declared *externally* (outside of the current source file). If you examine the header file *dos.h*, for example, you will find several external variable declarations:

```
extern int const _Cdecl _8087;
extern int _Cdecl _argc;
extern char **_Cdecl _argv;
extern char **_Cdecl environ;
```

If you don't use the *extern* keyword word, the compiler will assume that you are creating a variable with the name specified. When you include the *extern* keyword, on the other hand, the compiler will search for the global variable specified.

Putting *extern* to Use

257

Tip 256 introduced the *extern* keyword, which tells the compiler you are using a global variable that is declared outside of the current program. To better understand how the *extern* keyword works, compile the file EXTERNAL.C, which contains the declaration of the variable *tip_count*, as well as the function, *show_title*:

```
#include <stdio.h>

int tip_count = 1001;  // Global variable

void show_title(void)
  {
    printf("Jamsa's 1001 C/C++ Tips");
  }
```

When you compile this program, C will create the object file EXTERNAL.OBJ. Next, the program SHOWEXT.C, uses the external variable *tip_count*:

```
#include <stdio.h>

void main(void)
  {
    extern int tip_count;

    printf("The number of tips is %d\n", tip_count);
  }
```

When you compile this program, use the following command line for Borland's C++ compiler:

```
C:\> BCC SHOWEXT.C EXTERNAL.OBJ   <ENTER>
```

In this case, the program SHOWEXT.C displays the value of the external variable *tip_count*. The program does not use the function *show_title*, although the program could have—simply by invoking *show_title*. The program's goal, however, was to illustrate the use of the *extern* keyword.

Understanding External *static*

258

In Tip 256 you learned that the *extern* keyword tells the C compiler that you are referencing a global variable that is defined in a different file. When your the linker links your program modules, the linker will determine the variable's memory location. In Tip 257 you used the global variable *tip_count*, which was defined in the object file EXTERNAL.OBJ. Because the program SHOWEXT.C referred to the variable using the *extern* keyword, the program could access the variable. Depending on your programs, there may be times when you use global variables in an object file that you don't want functions outside of the object to access. In such cases, you simply precede the variable name with the *static* keyword:

```
static int variable_name;
```

The following file, EXTERN.C, declares two global variables, one named *tip_count* and one named *title*:

```
#include <stdio.h>

int tip_count = 1001;  // Global variable

static char title[] = "Jamsa's 1001 C/C++ Tips";

void show_title(void)
  {
    printf(title);
  }
```

Compile this file to create the object file EXTERN.OBJ. Next, create the following program, NOSTATIC.C, which tries to use both global variables:

```
#include <stdio.h>

void main(void)
  {
    extern int tip_count;
    extern char *title;

    void show_title(void);

    printf("The number of tips is %d\n", tip_count);
    printf("The book's title is %s\n", title);
    show_title();
  }
```

As before, compile and link the program using Borland C++ as follows:

```
C:\> BCC NOSTATIC.C  EXTERN2.OBJ  <ENTER>
```

When you compile and link this program, your linker will probably display a message stating that the variable *title* has not been resolved. Because the declaration of the variable *title* is preceded by the *static* keyword, the variable is only known within the object file EXTERN2.OBJ.

C 259 Understanding the *volatile* Keyword

As the complexity of your programs increase, you might eventually write low-level functions and routines that access the PC's I/O ports or that service interrupts. When your programs perform such operations, you might have variables that correspond to specific memory locations that or port addresses that might get changed by an interrupt or port operation. Because such variables can be changed not only by your program, but also, possibly, by an interrupt, you need to tell the compiler that the variable's value can change at any time. To inform the compiler that operations outside of the program might change a variable's value, use the *volatile* keyword, as shown here:

```
volatile int some_variable;
```

When the compiler encounters the *volatile* keyword, the compiler knows not make assumptions about the variable's value at any time. For example, the compiler will not place the variable's value into a register for quick access because doing so would run the risk that the register value is not the same as the variable's memory contents, which might have been changed (by an interrupt) without the program's knowledge. Instead, when your program needs to access a variable's value, the compiler will specifically reference the variable's memory location.

> **Note:** *Volatile variables are normally declared as global variables. In this way, programs and the outside operations reference memory locations contained within the program's data segment, as opposed to stack locations, which are discarded when the corresponding function ends.*

Understanding the Call Frame and Base Pointer

You have learned that, when your program invokes a function, C pushes the return address, parameters on to the stack. Within the stack, this function call information is referred to as a *call frame*. To help your functions quickly locate the call frame, C assigns the base pointer register (BP), the address of the start of the frame.

C also places the function's local variables on the stack (within the call frame). Figure 260 illustrates the contents of a simple call frame.

```
void some_function (int a, int b, int c)
{
    int d, e;

}
```

Call Frame:
- e, d → Local variables
- BP Register
- a, b, c, return address → Parameters and Return address

Stack

Figure 260 *The information C places onto the stack for a function call constitutes a call frame.*

When you write assembly language functions that are to be called from within your C programs, you need to understand the use and structure of the call frame in order to access the parameter values.

C 261 Calling an Assembly Language Function

In Tip 236 you learned that your programs can call functions that are written in other programming languages such as Pascal. In addition, your programs can call assembly language routines. The following assembly language routine, *swap_values* exchanges the values of two variables passed to the function by reference (by address):

```
        .MODEL  small
        .CODE
        PUBLIC  _swap_values

_swap_values    PROC
        push    bp
        mov     bp,sp
        sub     sp,2
        push    si
        push    di

        mov     si,word ptr [bp+4]          ;Arg1
        mov     di,word ptr [bp+6]          ;Arg2

        mov     ax,word ptr [si]
        mov     word ptr [bp-2],ax

        mov     ax,word ptr [di]
        mov     word ptr [si],ax

        mov     ax,word ptr [bp-2]
        mov     word ptr [di],ax

        pop     di
        pop     si
        mov     sp,bp
        pop     bp
quit:           ret

_swap_values    ENDP
        END
```

The companion disk that accompanies this book contains the file SWAP.ASM. If you are using Borland C++, assemble the file to create the object file SWAP.OBJ, as shown here:

```
C:\> TASM SWAP.ASM  <ENTER>
```

Next, the following C program, USE_SWAP.C, uses the *swap_values* function:

```
#include <stdio.h>

void swap_values(int *, int *);

void main(void)
  {
    int a = 1, b = 2;

    printf("Original values a %d b %d\n", a, b);
    swap_values(&a, &b);

    printf("Swapped values a %d b %d\n", a, b);
  }
```

In this case, the function *swap_values* was written to support near pointers. If you change memory models, you will need to change the assembly language routine.

Returning a Value from an Assembly Language Function

C 262

In Tip 261 you learned how to call an assembly language function from within your C programs. In the example shown, the function did not return a result. The following assembly language routine, *get_maximum*, however, returns the larger of two integer values:

```
            .MODEL small
            .CODE
            PUBLIC _get_maximum

_get_maximum    PROC
        push    bp
        mov     bp,sp

Arg1            equ     [bp+4]
Arg2            equ     [bp+6]

        mov     ax,Arg1       ;Move Arg1 into AX
        cmp     Arg2,ax       ;Compare Arg2 to Arg1
        jg      arg2_bigger   ;Jump if Arg2 is bigger
        jmp     finished

arg2_bigger:    mov     ax,Arg2
```

f(x)

```
finished:        pop    bp
         ret
_get_maximum     ENDP
         END
```

The companion disk that accompanies this book provides the file GET_MAX.ASM, which contains the routine. As you can see, the assembly language routine places its result in the AX register. The following C program, USE_MAX.C, invokes the assembly language function to determine the larger of two values:

```c
#include <stdio.h>

extern int get_maximum(int, int);

void main(void)
  {
    int result;

    result = get_maximum(100, 200);

    printf("The larger value is %d\n", result);
  }
```

When the program calls the function, the C compiler will assign the value of the AX register as the function's result.

263 Functions That Don't Return Values

As the number of functions you create increases, you will eventually create a function that does not return a value. As you learned in Tip 217, the C compiler, unless told otherwise, assumes that a function returns the type *int*. If your function does not return a value, you should declare the function as type *void*, as shown here:

```c
void my_function(int age, char *name);
```

Should the program later try to use the function's return value:

```c
result = my_function(32, "Jamsa");
```

the compiler will generate an error.

f(x)

Functions That Don't Use Parameters

C 264

As the number of programs and, hence, functions that you create increases, you might eventually create a function that does not use any parameters. When you define the function (and the function prototype), you should use the *void* keyword to inform the compiler (and other programmers) that the function does not use parameters:

```
int my_function(void);
```

Should the program later try to invoke the function with parameters, the compiler will generate an error.

Understanding the *auto* Keyword

C 265

As you examine C programs, you might find variable declarations that use the keyword *auto,* as shown here:

```
auto int counter;
auto int flags;
```

The *auto* keyword informs the compiler that the variable is local to the function and should be automatically created and destroyed. The compiler creates automatic variables by allocating stack space. Because variables are automatic by default, most programs omit the *auto* keyword. Within a function, the following variable declarations are identical:

```
auto int counter;
int counter;
```

Understanding C's Categories of Scope

C 266

As you have learned, an identifier's (normally a variable or function name) *scope* is the part of the program within which the identifier has meaning (can be used). C defines five categories of scope: block, function, function prototype, file, and class (for C++). *Block scope* defines the bracketed region within a variable is defined. Normally, block scope refers to a function. Local variables have block scope. As you learned in the Constructs section of this book, however, you can declare variables after any open brace. The variable's scope exists up to the closing brace. Formal parameters have block scope defined by the function for which they are used. *Function scope* defines the region between a function's opening and closing brace. The only item with function scope is a label used by the *goto* statement. *Function prototype scope* specifies the region within the start and end of a function prototype. Identifiers that appear within a function prototype have meaning only within the function prototype:

```
int some_function(int age, char *name);
```

File scope specifies a region from an identifier's declaration to the end of the source file. Global variables have file scope which means they can only be referenced in functions that follow the global variable declaration. In C++, *class scope* defines the named collection of methods and data structures that define the class.

267 Understanding Name Space and Identifiers

As you have learned, *scope* defines the region of a program within which an identifier has meaning. Similarly, *name space* defines a region within which identifier names must be unique. In the simplest sense, an *identifier* is a name. C defines four classes of identifiers.

- *goto* label names   The label names used by a *goto* statement must be unique within a function.

- Structure, union, and enumeration tags   A *tag* is the name of a structure, union, or enumerated type. Tags must be unique within block.

- Structure and union member names   The member names that appear within a structure or union must be unique. Different unions or structures can have the same member names.

- Variables, *typedef* identifiers, functions, and enumerated members   These identifiers must be unique within scope within which they are defined.

268 Understanding Identifier Visibility

As you have learned, *scope* defines the region of a program within which an identifier has meaning. In a similar way, an identifier's *visibility* defines the region of code within which an identifier can be accessed. Normally, an identifier's scope and visibility are the same. However, when an identifier with the same name is declared within a block that appears in an identifier's scope, the outer identifier is temporarily hidden (loses visibility). Consider the following program, VISIBLE.C, which uses two identifiers named *value*:

```c
#include <stdio.h>

void main(void)
  {
    int value = 1001;

    if (value > 1000)
      {
        int value = 1;

        printf("Inner value is %d\n", value);
      }

    printf("Outer value is %d\n", value);
  }
```

When you compile and execute this program, your screen will display the following output:

```
C:\> VISIBLE   <ENTER>
Inner value is 1
Outer value is 1001
```

When the variable *value* is declared within the *if* statement, the variable hides the outer occurrence of the variable with the same name. Outside of the block, however, the outer variable becomes visible once again.

Understanding Duration

C 269

When you discuss variables, duration specifies the time when an identifier has allocated memory. C supports three types of duration: *local*, *static*, and *dynamic*. Local duration corresponds to automatic variables that are created during a function invocation or for variables defined within a block of statements. The program must always initialize local variables. If the variable is not initialized, its contents cannot be predicted. *Static variables* are created as the program execution begins. Static variables normally correspond to global variables. Most C compilers initialize static variables to 0. *Dynamic variables* are allocated from the heap during the program's execution. In most cases, programs must initialize dynamic variables. Some run-time library functions will initialize the dynamic memory locations to 0, while some do not.

C 270 Functions That Support a Variable Number of Parameters

As you have learned, C maps the actual parameters that are passed to a function to the formal parameters defined in the function header. If the function expects three parameters, your function invocation should include three parameter values. If you consider functions such as *printf* or *scanf*, however, you will find that the functions support a variable number of parameters. For example, the following *printf* function calls are all valid:

```
printf("1001 C/C++ Tips");
printf("%d %s", 1001, "C/C++ Tips");
printf("%d %d %d %d %d, 1, 2, 3, 4, 5);
printf("%f %s %s %d %x", salary, name, state, age, id);
```

As you will learn in Tip 272, using the macros *va_arg*, *va_end*, and *va_start* defined in the header file *stdarg.h*, your programs can create their own functions that support a variable number of parameters. The macros essentially pull parameters from the stack, one at a time, until the last parameter is reached. When you use these macros to get parameters, you must know each parameter's type. In the case of *printf*, the function uses the format specifiers such as %d, %s, and %f to track the parameter types.

C 271 Supporting a Variable Number of Parameters

In this tip you will create a function called *add_values*, which adds up all of the integer values it is passed. As shown here, the function supports a variable number of parameters. The last parameter is indicated by the value 0 (which does not affect the sum):

```
result = add_em(3,0);          // Returns 3
result = add_em(3,5,0);        // Returns 8
result = add_em(100,3,4,2,0);  // Returns 109
```

The following program, ADDVALUE.C, contains the *add_values* function:

```
#include <stdio.h>
#include <stdarg.h>

int add_values(int value, ...)
  {
    va_list argument_ptr;
```

```
      int result = 0;

      if (value != 0)
        {
          result += value;
          va_start(argument_ptr, value);

          while ((value = va_arg(argument_ptr, int)) != 0)
            result += value;

          va_end(argument_ptr);
        }
      return(result);
  }

void main(void)
  {
    printf("Sum of 3 is %d\n", add_values(3, 0));
    printf("Sum of 3 + 5 is %d\n", add_values(3, 5, 0));
    printf("Sum of 3 + 5 + 8 is %d\n", add_values(3, 5, 8, 0));
    printf("Sum of 3 + 5 + 8 + 9 is %d\n", add_values(3, 5, 8 , 9,
      0));
  }
```

The function *add_values* begins by assigning a pointer (*argument_ptr*) to the first parameter on the stack using the *va_start* macro. Next, using the *va_arg* macro, the function gets the values one at a time. The *va_arg* macro returns a value of the specified type and then increments the pointer to point to the next argument. When the zero terminator is encountered, the function uses the *va_end* macro to assign a value to the argument pointer that will prevent its future use (without being reinitialized by *va_start*). When you create functions that support a variable number of parameters, your functions must have a way to know the number of parameters and each parameter's type. In the case of *printf*, the format specifier defines the parameters and their types. In the case of *add_values*, the zero terminator marked that last parameter. Likewise, all of the arguments passed to the function where the same type.

Note: *Note the use of the ellipses (...) within the add_values function header to indicate a variable number of parameters.*

How *va_start*, *va_arg*, and *va_end* Work

C272

In Tip 271 you learned that using the *va_start*, *va_arg*, and *va_end* macros that are defined in the header file *stdarg.h*, you can create functions that support a variable number of parameters. To better understand how these macros work, consider the following function call to *add_values*:

```
add_values(10, 20, 30, 0);
```

When the function call is made, the compiler will place the parameters on to the stack from right to left. Within the function, the *va_start* macro assigns a pointer to the first parameter, as shown in Figure 272.

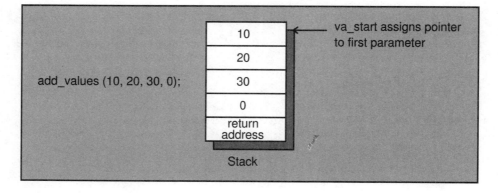

Figure 272 *Using va_start to assign a pointer to the first parameter.*

The *va_arg* macro returns the value pointed to by the argument pointer. To determine the value, the macro must know the parameter's type. A parameter of type *int*, for example, will use 16 bits, whereas a parameter of type *long* will use 32. After the parameter's value is returned, the *va_arg* macro increments the argument pointer so that it points to the next argument. To determine the number of bytes to add to the pointer, *va_arg* again uses the parameter's type. After the last argument has been retrieved, the *va_end* macro nullifies the argument pointer's value.

273 Creating a Function That Supports Multiple Parameters of Multiple Types

In Tip 271 you learned how to create functions that support a variable number of parameters. At that time, the function *add_values* supported only parameters of type *int*. The following program, ALLTYPES.C, changes the function *add_values* to support values of all types.

The function returns a value of type *float*. To help the function determine the parameter types, you pass to the function a format specifier similar to that used by *printf*. For example, to add three integer values, use the following invocation:

```
result = add_values ("%d %d %d", 1, 2, 3);
```

Likewise, to add three floating-point values usethe following :

```
result = add_values ("%f %f %f", 1.1, 2.2, 3.3);
```

Finally, to add integer and floating-point values, use the following:

```
result = add_values ("%f %d %f %d", 1.1, 2, 3.3, 4);
```

Using the format specifier, you eliminate the need to use the zero terminator.

```
#include <stdio.h>
#include <stdarg.h>

double add_values (char *str, ...)
{
    va_list marker;

    double result = 0.0;

    va_start (marker, str);   /* mark first additional argument */

    while (*str)               /* examine each character in the
string */
    {
        if (*str == '%')     /* if not a %_ format specifier,
skip it */
        {
            switch (*(++str)) {
                case 'd' : result += va_arg (marker, int);
                        break;
                case 'f' : result += va_arg (marker, double);
                        break;
            }
        }
        str++;
    }

    va_end (marker);
    return (result);
}
```

f(x)

```
void main(void)
{
  double result;

  printf("Result %f\n", add_values("%f", 3.3));
  printf("Result %f\n", add_values("%f %f", 1.1, 2.2));
  printf("Result %f\n", add_values("%f %d %f", 1.1, 1,2.2));
  printf("Result %f\n", add_values("%f %d %f %d", 1.1, 1,
    2.2, 3));
}
```

C 274 Understanding Functions

Most of the programs presented throughout this book have used only the function *main*. As your programs become larger and more complex, you can simplify your work and improve your understanding by breaking the program into smaller pieces, called *functions*. For example, assume that you are creating an accounting program. You might have a function that performs the general ledger operations, a different function for accounts payable, a third for accounts receivable, and a fourth to generate a balance sheet. If you were to place all of your program's statements within *main*, your program would become very large and very difficult to understand. As a program's size and complexity increases, so too does the chance of program errors. A *function* is a named collection of statements that perform a specific task. For example, the following function, whose name is *hello_world* displays a message using *printf*:

```
void hello_world(void)
{
   printf("Hello, world!\n");
}
```

The keyword *void* tells C that the function does not return a value. In many cases, your functions will *return* the result of a calculation. If the function does not, you should precede its name with *void*. The *void* that appears within the parentheses tell C that the function does not use any parameters. A *parameter* is information passed to the function. When your programs invoke *printf*, for example, the information you specify within the parenthesis are *parameters*. When a function does not use parameters, you should place the word *void* within the parentheses. To use a function, you simply specify the function's name followed by parentheses, much as you have used *printf*. Using a function is often referred to as a *function call*. The following program, USE_FUNC.C, uses the *hello_world* function:

```
#include <stdio.h>

void hello_world(void)
  {
    printf("Hello, world!\n");
  }

void main(void)
  {
    hello_world();
  }
```

When you execute this program, the function *main* is the first to execute. As you can see, the only statement in *main* is the function call to the *hello_world* function. When C encounters the function call, C immediately transfers the program's execution to the function, beginning the program's execution with the first statement within the function. After the last statement in the function completes, C transfers the execution to the statement that immediately follows the function call. To better understand this process, change the function *main* as shown here:

```
void main(void)
  {
    printf("About to call function\n");
    hello_world();
    printf("Back from the function call\n");
  }
```

When you compile and execute this program, your screen will display the following:

```
C:\> USE_FUNC  <ENTER>
About to call function
Hello, world!
Back from the function call
```

Using Variables in Functions

C

275

As you create useful functions, you will need to use variables within the functions. To use a variable within a function, you must declare the variable, just as you have in *main*. For example, the following program THREE_HI.C, calls the function *three_hellos*, which uses the variable *counter* in a *for* loop to display a message three times:

```
#include <stdio.h>

void three_hellos(void)
```

```
{
   int counter; // Variable

   for (counter = 1; counter <= 3; counter++)
     printf("Hello, world!\n");
}

void main (void)
  {
    three_hellos();
  }
```

When you declare variables within a function, the names you use are unique to the function. Thus, if your program uses ten different functions and each function uses a variable named *counter*, C considers each function's variable as distinct. Should your function require many variables, declare the variables at the start of the function, just as you would within *main*.

C 276 *main* Is a Function Too

When you create a C program, C uses the function name *main* to determine the first statement it will execute. Actually *main* is a function, so if you have questions about the types of operations you can perform within your functions, the rule is fairly simple: *Anything you can do in main, you can do within a function.* Just as you can declare variables in *main*, you can also declare variables within your functions. In addition, you can use constructs such as *if, while,* and *for* within your functions. Finally, one function can call (use) another. For example, the following program, CALL_2.C, uses two functions. When the program begins, *main* calls the function *three_hellos*, which in turn, calls the function *hello_world* three times to display messages on your screen:

```
#include <stdio.h>

void hello_world(void)
  {
    printf("Hello, world!\n");
  }

void three_hellos(void)
  {
    int counter;

    for (counter = 1; counter <= 3; counter++)
      hello_world();
  }

void main(void)
```

```
{
   three_hellos();
}
```

Getting Started with Parameters

A *parameter* is a value passed to a function. Most of the programs presented throughout this book have passed parameters to the *printf* function:

```
printf("The value is %d\n", result);
```

As you use functions on a regular basis, you will can improve their usefulness by passing parameters to the function. For example, consider the following *three_hellos* function, which calls the *hello_world* function three times:

```
void three_hellos(void)
{
   int counter;

   for (counter = 1; counter <= 3; counter++)
      hello_world();
}
```

A more useful function might let you specify, as a parameter, the number of times you want the message displayed. To use a parameter, your function must specify the parameter's name and type, as shown here:

```
void hello_count(int message_count)
```

In this case, the function *hello_count* supports one parameter of type *int*, whose name is *message_count*. When another function, such as *main* wants to use *hello_count*, the function must specify the value C is to assign to the parameter *message_count*:

```
hello_count(2);      // Displays the message twice
hello_count(100);    // Displays the message 100 times
hello_count(1);      // Displays the message 1 time
```

The following program, USEPARAM.C, illustrates the use of a function parameter:

```
#include <stdio.h>

void hello_world(void)
{
   printf("Hello, world!\n");
```

```
    }

void hello_count(int message_count)
  {
    int counter;

    for (counter = 1; counter <= message_count; counter++)
      hello_world();
  }

void main(void)
  {
    printf("Display the message twice\n");
    hello_count(2);
    printf("Display the message five times\n");
    hello_count(5);
  }
```

As you can see within *main*, the function call to *hello_count* includes the value that C assigns to the *message_count* parameter.

> **Note:** *When you pass a parameter to a function, the type of value you pass to the parameter (such as int, float, char, and so on), must match the parameter type. Depending on your C compiler, the compiler might detect parameter type mismatches. If your compiler does not, errors that are often difficult to detect and correct can emerge.*

C 278 Using Multiple Parameters

As you have learned, a *parameter* is a value passed to a function. In general, there is no restriction on the number of parameters you can pass to a function. However, research has shown that when the number of parameters exceeds seven, the function becomes more difficult to understand and use correctly, thus making the function more susceptible to errors. When your function uses more than one parameter, you must specify each parameter's type and name, separated by commas, as shown here:

```
void some_function(int age, float salary, int job_number)
  {
    // Function statements
  }
```

When your program wants to call the function, you must specify values for each parameter, as shown here:

```
some_function(33, 40000.00, 534);
```

C, in turn, will assign the values to the parameters, as shown in Figure 278.

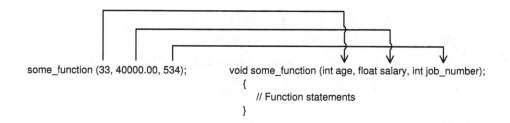

Figure 278 *Mapping parameter values.*

Parameter Declarations in Older C Programs

C 279

When you create a function that uses parameters, you will normally specify each parameter's type and name, separated by commas, within the function header, as shown here:

```
void some_function(int age, float salary, int job_number)
  {
    // Function statements
  }
```

If you work with older C programs, you might find the parameters declared as follows:

```
void some_function(age, salary, job_number)
  int age;
  float salary;
  int job_number;
  {
    // Function statements
  }
```

f(x)

Should you encounter such parameter declarations, understand that although the declaration format differs slightly, the purpose remains the same: to specify the parameter's type and name. If you feel tempted to update the function's format, make sure that your compiler fully supports the new format. Also, remember that the more changes you make to your program, the greater your chances of introducing an error. As a general rule: *If it ain't broke, don't fix it!*

C 280 Returning a Value from a Function

As your functions become more complex, they will normally perform a calculation and return a result. To provide a result to the caller, a function must use the *return* statement, whose format is as follows:

```
return(result);
```

The type of value the function returns (*int, float, char,* and so on) determines the function's type. If a function returns a value of type *int,* for example, you must precede the function name with the type name, as shown here:

```
int some_function(int value)
{
   // Function statements
}
```

The following function, *i_cube,* returns the cube of the integer value specified as a parameter. For example, if the function is passed the value 5, *i_cube* will return the value 5 * 5 * 5 or 125:

```
int i_cube(int value)
{
   return(value * value * value);
}
```

As you can see, the function uses the *return* statement to pass back the result of the calculation to the caller. Within the calling function, the result of the function can be assigned to a variable or used within a function such as *printf,* as shown here:

```
result = i_cube(5);

printf("The cube of 5 is %d\n", i_cube(5));
```

The following program, I_CUBE.C, uses the *i_cube* function to determine several different cube values:

```
#include <stdio.h>

int i_cube(int value)
 {
    return(value * value * value);
 }

void main(void)
 {
   printf("The cube of 3 is %d\n", i_cube(3));
   printf("The cube of 5 is %d\n", i_cube(5));
   printf("The cube of 7 is %d\n", i_cube(7));
 }
```

The values you pass to a function must match the parameter's type. If you want to determine the cube of a floating-point value, for example, you would create a second function called *f_cube*, as shown here:

```
float f_cube(float value)
 {
   return (value * value * value);
 }
```

Understanding the
return Statement

C 281

As you have learned, for a function to provide its caller with a result, the function must use the *return* statement. When C encounters a *return* statement within a function, C immediately ends the function's execution, returning the specified value. Any statements that following the *return* statement are not executed. Instead, the execution resumes within the calling function.

As you examine other C programs, you might encounter functions that contain multiple *return* statements, each of which returns a value for a specific condition. For example, consider the following function, *compare_values*, which examines two integer values and returns one of the values listed in Table 281.

Result	Meaning
0	The values are the same
1	The first value is greater than the second
2	The second value is greater than the first

Table 281 *Values returned by the compare_values function.*

f(x)

```
int compare_values(int first, int second)
  {
    if (first == second)
      return(0);
    else if (first > second)
      return(1);
    else if (first < second)
      return(2);
  }
```

As a rule, you should try to limit your functions to one *return* statement. As your functions become larger and more complex, having multiple *return* statements often makes the functions more difficult to understand. In most cases, you can rewrite your function so that it only uses one *return* statement, as shown here:

```
int compare_values(int first, int second)
  {
    int result;

    if (first == second)
      result = 0;
    else if (first > second)
      result = 1;
    else if (first < second)
      result = 2;

    return(result);
  }
```

In this case, because of the function's simplicity, it is difficult to understand the advantage gained by only using one *return* statement. As your functions become more complex, however, the advantage might become more clear. It is important to note, however, that there may be times when using more than one *return* statement produces more readable code than the single *return* alternative. Your goal is to write the most readable and modifiable code possible, so if using multiple *return* statements achieves that goal, use them.

C 282 Understanding Function Prototypes

If you take a close look at each of the preceding programs, you will find that the calling functions always appear in the program source code following the functions they call. Most new C compilers require knowledge of a function's return and parameter types before the function is called. By placing the functions in front of their callers, the C compiler knows the needed information before the function call. As your programs become more complex, however, it might become impossible for you always to place the functions in the correct order. As such, C lets you place *function prototypes* in your program that describe a function's return and parameter types. For example, consider a program that uses the functions *i_cube* and *f_cube*. Before the functions' first use, the program can include a prototype similar to the following:

```
int i_cube(int);      // Returns an int—one int parameter
int f_cube(float);    // Returns a float—one float parameter
```

As you can see, the function prototype specifies the function's return and parameter types. The following program, USEPROTO.C, uses a function prototype to eliminate the need for function ordering:

```
#include <stdio.h>

int i_cube(int);
float f_cube(float);

void main(void)
  {
    printf("The cube of 3 is %d\n", i_cube(3));
    printf("The cube of 3.7 is %f\n", f_cube(3.7));
  }

int i_cube(int value)
  {
    return(value * value * value);
  }

float f_cube(float value)
  {
    return(value * value * value);
  }
```

If you examine the .h header files, such as stdio.h, you will find that files contain many function prototypes.

Understanding the Run-Time Library

283

As you write your own functions, you will find that a function that you created for one program meets the needs of a second. The ability to reuse functions in more than one program can save you considerable programming and testing time. In the Programming

f(x)

Tools section of this book, you will learn how to place your commonly used functions within a library to make them easier to use within multiple programs. For now, however, you may need to cut and paste the function's statements from one source code file to another.

Before you spend a great deal of time writing a myriad of functions, however, you should examine the functions provided by your compiler. Many compilers refer to these built-in functions as the *run-time library*. Most C compilers provide hundreds of run-time library functions whose purpose range from opening and working with files to accessing disk or directory information or determining the length of a character string. The hour or two you spend reading your compiler's run-time library documentation will save you many programming hours that you would have otherwise spent "reinventing the wheel," so to speak.

C 284 Understanding Formal and Actual Parameters

As you read different books on C, you might encounter the terms *formal* and *actual* parameters. In short, formal parameters are the parameter names that appear in the function definition. For example, the names *age*, *salary*, and *job_number* are the formal parameters for the function *job_information*, shown here:

```
void job_information(int age, float salary, int job_number)
  {
    // Function statements
  }
```

When a function calls another function, the values the calling function passes are the actual parameters. In the case of the following function invocation, the values 30, 42000.00, and 321 are the actual parameters:

```
job_information(30, 42000.00, 321);
```

The actual parameters you pass to a function can be constant values or variables. The only requirement is that the value or variable's type matches that of the formal parameter. For example, the following code fragment illustrates the use of variables as actual parameters:

```
int workers_age = 30;
float workers_salary = 42000.00;
int job_number = 321;

job_information(workers_age, workers_salary, job_number);
```

When you invoke a function with variables as the actual parameters, the variable names used for the actual parameters have no relationship to the names of the formal parameters. Instead, C is concerned only with the values the variables contain.

Understanding Scope

285

Within your programs, function and variables have a *scope*, which defines the areas within the program where their names have meaning. For example, consider the following program, TWOCOUNT.C, which uses two variables named *count*:

```c
#include <stdio.h>

void beeper(int beep_count)
  {
    int count;

    for (count = 1; count <= beep_count; count++)
      putchar(7);
  }

void main(void)
  {
    int count;

    for (count = 1; count <= 3; count++)
      {
        printf("About to beep %d times\n", count);
        beeper(count);
      }
  }
```

As you can see, the functions *beeper* and *main* both use variables named *count*. To C, however, both variables are distinct—each has a different scope. In the case of the function *beeper*, its variable *count* is only known (has a defined scope) while the function is executing. Likewise, in the case of *main*, its variable *count* only has meaning while *main* is executing. As a result, the *for* loop that changes the variable *count* in the function *beeper* has no effect on the variable *count* within *main*.

When you discuss a variable's scope, the terms *local* and *global* variables are often used. A local variable is a variable whose scope is restricted to a specific function. Global variables, on the other hand, can be known throughout the entire program. In the case of the previous program, each occurrence of the variable *count* is local to the function within which it was defined.

Keyboard & Screen I/O

C 286 Reading a Character from the Keyboard

Even the simplest C programs must often read characters from the keyboard. The character read may correspond to a menu option, a yes or no response, or even one of many letters in a name. The most commonly used way to get character input operations is the *getchar* macro, whose format is shown here:

```
#include <stdio.h>

int getchar(void);
```

If successful, *getchar* returns the ASCII value for the character read. If an error occurs or an end of file is encountered (normally for redirected input), *getchar* returns EOF. The following program, GETCHAR.C, uses *getchar* to read a yes or no response from the keyboard:

```
#include <stdio.h>

#include <ctype.h>

void main(void)
 {
   int letter;

   printf("Type Y or N to continue and press Enter\n");

   do {
     letter = toupper(getchar());
   } while ((letter != 'Y') && (letter != 'N'));

   printf("You typed %c\n", ((letter == 'Y') ? 'Y': 'N'));
 }
```

As you can see, the program loops, repeatedly invoking *getchar*, until the user types the **Y** or **N** using a *do while* loop.

Note: *To support I/O redirection, the getchar macro is actually defined in terms of stdin (which by default, corresponds to the keyboard).*

Displaying a Character of Output

287

In Tip 286 you learned how to use the *getchar* macro to read a character from the keyboard. In a similar way, C provides the *putchar* macro that writes a character to the screen (stdout). The format of the *putchar* macro is as follows:

```
#include <stdio.h>

int putchar(int letter);
```

If *putchar* is successful, it returns the character written. If an error occurs, *putchar* returns EOF. The following program, PUTCHAR.C, uses *putchar* to display the letters of the alphabet:

```
#include <stdio.h>

void main(void)
  {
    int letter;

    for (letter = 'A'; letter <= 'Z'; letter++)
      putchar(letter);
  }
```

Note: *Because putchar is defined in terms of stdout, you can use the DOS output redirection operators to redirect the output of the PUTCHAR program to a file or printer.*

Understanding Buffered Input

288

When you perform keyboard input, your program can use buffered or direct input operations. When your program uses buffered input, the letters typed are not actually passed to the program until the user presses **ENTER**. In this way, the user can change characters as he or she types, using the **BACKSPACE** key to rub out characters as needed. When the user presses **ENTER**, all of the characters typed are available to the program. The *getchar* macro uses buffered input. If you use *getchar* to read a single character response, *getchar* does not read a character until the user presses **ENTER**. If the user types multiple characters, all of the characters are available to *getchar* within the input buffer. The following program, BUFFERIO.C, illustrates buffered input. Run the program and then type in a line of text. The characters you type will not be available to the program until you press **ENTER**. After you press **ENTER**, however, the program will read and display characters until the newline character (created when you pressed **ENTER** is encountered):

```
#include <stdio.h>

void main (void)
  {
    int letter;

    do {
      letter = getchar();
      putchar(letter);
    } while (letter != '\n');
  }
```

When you run this program, experiment with the letters you input, using the **BACKSPACE** key to rub out letters, and so on. As you will find, the letters passed to the program correspond your final text.

C 289 Assigning Keyboard Input to a String

The Strings section of this book looks at several different ways to manipulate strings. When you perform keyboard input one of the most common operations you will perform is to assign characters to a string. The following program, FILLSTR.C, uses the *getchar* to assign letters to the variable *string*. To assign characters, the program simply loops, assigning characters to the string elements until the newline character is encountered. The program then assigns the NULL character (end of string) marker to current string position:

```
#include <stdio.h>

void main (void)
  {
    char string[128];

    int index = 0;
    int letter;

    printf("Type in a string and press Enter\n");
    while ((letter = getchar()) != '\n')
      string[index++] = letter;

    string[index] = NULL;

    printf("The string was: %s\n", string);
  }
```

Combining *getchar* and *putchar*

C 290

As you have learned, *getchar* lets you read a letter from the keyboard (stdin), while *putchar* lets you display a letter on the screen (stdout). Depending on your program's function, there may be times when you want to read and display characters. The following *do while* loop, for example, reads and displays characters up to and including the newline character:

```
do {
  letter = getchar();
  putchar(letter);
} while (letter != '\n');
```

Because *getchar* and *putchar* both work with integer values, you can combine the previous statements, as shown here:

```
do
  putchar(letter = getchar());
while (letter != '\n');
```

In this case, *getchar* will assign the character typed to the variable *letter*; *putchar* in turn will display the value assigned to *letter*.

Remember, *getchar* and *putchar* Are Macros

C 291

As you create your programs, remember that *getchar* and *putchar* are macros, not functions. As such, some compilers will not allow you to leave spaces between their names and parenthesis:

```
letter = getchar();

putchar(letter);
```

If you examine the header file *stdio.h* you will find the macro definitions for *getchar* and *putchar*. The I/O Redirection section of this book explains these two macro definitions in detail.

C 292 Reading a Character Using Direct I/O

You learned in Tip 288 that when you perform keyboard input, your programs can perform direct or buffered input. When they use direct input operations, the characters typed at the keyboard are immediately available to the program. In other words, the characters are not buffered. If the user presses the **BACKSPACE** key to rub out a previous character, the program itself must handle the editing operation (erasing the previous character from the screen and removing the character from the buffer). The *getche* function lets your programs read a character from the keyboard using direct input. The format of the *getche* function is as follows:

```
#include <conio.h>

int getche(void);
```

The following program, GETCHE.C, uses the *getche* function to read a yes or no response from the keyboard:

```
#include <stdio.h>
#include <ctype.h>
#include <conio.h>

void main(void)
  {
    int letter;

    printf("Do you want to continue? (Y/N): ");
    do
      {
        letter = getche();
        letter = toupper(letter);
      }
    while ((letter != 'Y') && (letter != 'N'));

    if (letter == 'Y')
      printf("\nYour response was Yes\n");
    else
      printf("\nWhy not?\n");
  }
```

Unlike the program GETCHAR.C, which required the user to press **ENTER** to make the response available to the user, the keys typed by the user with GETCHE.C are immediately available.

Direct Keyboard Input Without Character Display

C 293

In Tip 292 you learned how to use the *getche* function to read characters from the keyboard as the characters are typed (using direct I/O). When you use *getche*, the letters the user types are displayed on the screen. Depending on your program, there may be times when you want to read characters from the keyboard without displaying the characters on the screen. For example, if your program prompts the user for a password, the letters the user types should not appear on the screen for others to see. The *getch* function lets your programs read characters from the keyboard without displaying (echoing) the characters to the screen. The format of the *getch* function is as follows:

```
#include <conio.h>

int getch(void);
```

The following program, GETCH.C, uses the *getch* function to read characters from the keyboard. As the user types, *getch* reads the characters and converts them to uppercase, displaying the uppercase equivalent on the screen. Many database programs, for example, restrict users to working with uppercase letters. The program GETCH.C shows you how you can quickly implement such processing:

```
#include <stdio.h>
#include <conio.h>
#include <ctype.h>

void main(void)
  {
    int letter;

    printf("Type in a string of characters and press Enter\n");

    do {
      letter = getch();
      letter = toupper(letter);
      putch(letter);
    } while (letter != '\r');
  }
```

Knowing When to Use '\r' and '\n'

C 294

As you have learned, C uses the '\r' escape sequence to indicate a carriage-return. Likewise, C uses '\n' to represent a newline (carriage return and line feed). When your programs perform buffered input using *getchar*, C will convert the ENTER key to a carriage-return and linefeed (newline) sequence. When you perform direct I/O using *getch* or *getche* on the other hand, the ENTER key is returned as simply a carriage return ('\r'). Therefore, you need to test for the correct character within your programs, as shown here:

```
do {
  letter = getchar();
  putchar(letter);
} while (letter != '\n');

do {
  letter = getch();
  putchar(letter);
} while (letter != '\r');
```

C 295 Performing Direct Output

As you have learned, the functions *getch* and *getche* let your programs read characters directly from the keyboard, bypassing C's buffered (file-system-based) input streams. In a similar way, your programs can perform fast screen output using the *putch* function:

```
#include <conio.h>

int putch(int letter);
```

If successful, *putch* returns the letter displayed. If an error occurs, *putch* returns EOF. To perform fast output, the *putch* function communicates with the BIOS video services or directly accesses the PC's video memory. Functions such as *putchar*, on the other, use the file system, which in turn calls the BIOS. The *putch* function does not convert a linefeed character into a carriage-return and linefeed sequence. The following program, PUTCH.C, uses *putch* and *putchar* to display the letters of the alphabet 1001 times. The program then displays the amount of time each function required:

```
#include <stdio.h>
#include <conio.h>
#include <time.h>


void main(void)
  {
    int letter;
    int count;

    time_t start_time, stop_time;
```

```
time(&start_time);
for (count = 0; count < 1000; count++)
 for (letter = 'A'; letter <= 'Z'; letter++)
  putchar(letter);
time(&stop_time);

printf("\n\nTime required for putchar %d seconds\n",
   stop_time-start_time);
printf("Press any key...\n");
getch();

time(&start_time);
for (count = 0; count < 1000; count++)
 for (letter = 'A'; letter <= 'Z'; letter++)
  putch(letter);
time(&stop_time);

printf("\n\nTime required for putch %d seconds\n",
   stop_time-start_time);
}
```

Placing a Keystroke Back into the Keyboard Buffer

296

As you have learned, the *getch* function lets your programs read a character from the keyboard. Depending on how you write your program, there may be times when you read keystrokes up to a specific character and then process the keystrokes. When the processing is complete, you read the remaining characters. When you write such code, there may be times when you wish that you could "unread" a character. As it turns out, the *ungetch* function lets your programs do just that:

```
#include <conio.h>

int ungetch(int character);
```

In addition, there may be times when you want to place a character into the keyboard buffer so that it is the next keystroke read. Using *ungetch* your programs can do just that. The following program, UNGETCH.C, uses reads letters from the keyboard until a non-lowercase letter is encountered. The program then displays the letters and then reads and displays any remaining characters on a different line:

```
#include <stdio.h>
#include <ctype.h>
#include <conio.h>
```

```
void main (void)
 {
   int letter;
   int done = 0;
   int uppercase_found = 0;

   do {
     letter = getch ();

     if (islower(letter))
       putchar (letter);
     else
       {
         if (isupper(letter))
           {
             ungetch(letter);
             uppercase_found = 1;
             putchar ('\n');
           }
         done = 1;
       }
   } while (! done);

   if (uppercase_found)
     do {
       letter = getch ();
       putchar (letter);
     } while (letter != '\r');
 }
```

If you are reading characters using *getchar*, you can use the *ungetc* function to unread a character, as shown here:

```
ungetc (letter, stdin);
```

C 297 Fast Formatted Output Using *cprintf*

As you know, the *printf* function lets your programs perform formatted output. The *printf* function is actually defined in terms of the file handle *stdout*. As a result, you can redirect *printf's* output from the screen to a file or device. Because *printf* uses *stdout* in this way, *printf* is written to use the C file system, which in turn uses the DOS functions, which in turn call the BIOS. For faster formatted output, your programs can use the *cprintf* function, which works directly with the BIOS or your computer's video memory:

```
#include <conio.h>

int cprintf(const char *format[,arguments...]);
```

The following program, CPRINTF.C, writes the string "Jamsa's 1001 C/C++ Tips" to your screen 1001 times using *printf* and then *cprintf*. The program then displays a summary of the amount of time both functions required:

```
#include <stdio.h>
#include <conio.h>
#include <time.h>

void main(void)
  {
    int count;

    time_t start_time, stop_time;

    time(&start_time);
    for (count = 0; count < 1001; count++)
      printf("Jamsa's 1001 C/C++ Tips\n");
    time(&stop_time);

    printf("\n\nTime required for printf %d seconds\n",
      stop_time-start_time);
    printf("Press any key...\n");
    getch();

    time(&start_time);
    for (count = 0; count < 1001; count++)
      cprintf("Jamsa's 1001 C/C++ Tips\r\n");

    time(&stop_time);

    printf("\n\nTime required for cprintf %d seconds\n",
      stop_time-start_time);
  }
```

Note: *The cprintf function does not convert the newline character into a carriage-return/linefeed sequence.*

C 298 Fast Formatted Input from the Keyboard

In Tip 297 you learned that the *cprintf* lets your programs bypass the file system to perform fast output to the screen display. In a similar way, the *cscanf* function lets your programs perform fast formatted input from the keyboard:

```
#include <conio.h>

int cscanf(char *format[,arguments]);
```

The following program, CSCANF.C, prompts you for three integer values. The program then reads the values using *cscanf*:

```
#include <conio.h>

void main(void)
  {
    int a, b, c;

    cprintf("Type 3 integer values and press Enter\r\n");
    cscanf("%d %d %d", &a, &b, &c);
    cprintf("The values entered were %d %d %d\r\n", a, b, c);
  }
```

C 299 Writing a Character String

As you have learned, the *printf* function lets your programs write formatted output to the screen display. Using *printf*, your programs can write strings, integer, floating-point, or combinations of different values. When your programs only need to write a character string, however, you may be able to improve your program's performance by using the *puts* function instead of *printf*:

```
#include <stdio.h>

int puts(const char *string);
```

The *puts* function writes the NULL-terminated string to the screen (actually to stdout). If it is successful, *puts* returns a nonnegative value. If an error occurs, *puts* returns EOF. The *puts* function automatically writes a newline character at the end of the string. The following program, PUTS.C, uses *printf* and *puts* to output the string "Jamsa's 1001 C/C++ Tips" 1001 times. The program displays the amount of time each function required:

```
#include <stdio.h>
#include <conio.h>
#include <time.h>

void main(void)
  {
    int count;

    time_t start_time, stop_time;

    time(&start_time);
    for (count = 0; count < 1001; count++)
      printf("Jamsa's 1001 C/C++ Tips\n");
    time(&stop_time);

    printf("\n\nTime required for printf %d seconds\n",
      stop_time-start_time);
    printf("Press any key...\n");
    getch();

    time(&start_time);
    for (count = 0; count < 1001; count++)
      puts("Jamsa's 1001 C/C++ Tips");

    time(&stop_time);

    printf("\n\nTime required for puts %d seconds\n",
      stop_time-start_time);
  }
```

Note: *Because the puts function automatically appends a new line character, the character string displayed by puts did not include the character.*

Faster String Output
Using Direct I/O

C300

In Tip 299 you learned that the *puts* function lets your programs quickly output a
character string. However, because the *puts* function is defined in terms of stdout (so it can
support redirection), the function must use the file system. For faster string output to the screen, your programs
might want to use the *cputs* function:

```
#include <conio.h>

int cputs (const char string);
```

Like, *puts*, the *cputs* function outputs a NULL terminated string. Unlike *puts*, however, cputs does not automatically append a newline character. The following program, CPUTS.C, uses the *puts* and *cputs* functions to display the string "Jamsa's 1001 C/C++ Tips" 1001 times. The program displays the amount of time each function required:

```
#include <stdio.h>
#include <conio.h>
#include <time.h>

void main(void)
 {
   int count;

   time_t start_time, stop_time;

   time(&start_time);
   for (count = 0; count < 1001; count++)
     puts("Jamsa's 1001 C/C++ Tips");
   time(&stop_time);

   printf("\n\nTime required for puts %d seconds\n",
     stop_time-start_time);
   printf("Press any key...\n");
   getch();

   time(&start_time);
   for (count = 0; count < 1001; count++)
     cputs("Jamsa's 1001 C/C++ Tips\r\n");

   time(&stop_time);

   printf("\n\nTime required for cputs %d seconds\n",
     stop_time-start_time);
 }
```

C 301 Reading a Character String from the Keyboard

In Tip 299 you learned that C provides the *puts* function, which lets you write a character string to the screen display. In a similar way, the *gets* function lets your programs read a character string from the keyboard:

```
#include <stdio.h>

char *gets(char *string);
```

If *gets* is successful, it returns a pointer to the character string. If an error occurs or end of file is encountered, *gets* returns the NULL value. The *gets* function reads characters up to and including the newline character. However, *gets* replaces the newline character with NULL. The following program, GETS.C, uses the *gets* function to read a string of characters from the keyboard:

```c
#include <stdio.h>

void main(void)
  {
    char string[256];

    printf("Type in a string of characters and press Enter\n");
    gets(string);

    printf("The string was %s\n", string);
  }
```

Note: *The gets function is actually defined in terms of stdin (which by default is the keyboard), which lets the function fully support I/O redirection.*

Faster Keyboard String Input

302

In Tip 301 you learned how your programs can use the *gets* function to read a character string from the keyboard. Because *gets* is defined in terms of stdin, *gets* must use the file system to perform its input operations. If you don't need support for I/O redirection, you can improve your program's performance by using the *cgets* function to read characters from the keyboard:

```
#include <conio.h>

char *cgets(char *string);
```

If successful, *cgets* returns a pointer to *string[2]*. If an error occurs, *cgets* returns NULL. The *cgets* function behaves differently than *gets*. Before you call *cgets* with a character string, you must first assign the maximum number of characters to be read to *string[0]*. When *cgets* returns, *string[1]* contains a count of the number of characters read. The NULL-terminated character string actually begins at *string[2]*. The following program, CGETS.C, illustrates the use of the *cgets* function:

```
#include <stdio.h>
#include <conio.h>

void main(void)
 {
    char buffer[256];
    buffer[0] = 253;   // Number of characters that can be read

    printf("Type in a string and press Enter\n");
    cgets(buffer);

    printf("\n\nThe number of characters read was %d\n",
      buffer[1]);

    printf("The string read: %s\n", &buffer[2]);
 }
```

Experiment with this program, reducing to say ten, the number of characters *cgets* can read. If the user tries to type more than ten characters, the function will ignore the extra characters.

303 Displaying Output in Color

Using the ANSI.SYS device driver, your programs can display screen output in color. In addition, many C compilers provide text-based output functions that let you display color output. If you are using Borland C++ or Microsoft C++, the *outtext* (called *_outtext* for Microsoft C++) function lets you display colored output. If you are using Borland C++, you can only use the *outtext* function in graphics mode. The Microsoft *_outtext* function, on the other hand, works in either text or graphics mode. If you need to perform colored output, refer to the documentation that accompanied your compiler for specifics on these functions. As you will find, the compilers provide functions that set the text position, colors, and graphics modes. Because the routines tend to be compiler dependent, they will not be covered as tips within this book.

304 Clearing the Screen Display

Most C compilers do not provide a function that lets you clear the screen display. If you are using Borland or Microsoft C, however, you can use the *clrscr* function to clear the contents of a text mode window:

```
#include <conio.h>

void clrscr(void);
```

The following program, CLRSCR.C, uses the *clrscr* function to clear the screen display:

```c
#include <conio.h>

void main(void)
  {
    clrscr();
  }
```

Erasing to the End of the Current Line

305

As your programs perform screen I/O, there may be times when you want to erase the contents of the current line from the current cursor position to the end of the line. To do so, your programs can use the *clreol* function:

```c
#include <conio.h>

void clreol(void);
```

The function erases the current line contents without moving the cursor.

Deleting the Current Screen Line

306

As your programs perform screen-based I/O, there may be times when you want to delete the current line's contents, moving up one line all of the output that follows. In such cases, your program's can use the *delline* function:

```c
#include <conio.h>

void delline(void);
```

The following program, DELLINE.C, fills the screen with 24 lines the text. When you press **ENTER**, the program uses *delline* to erase lines 12, 13, and 14:

```c
#include <conio.h>

void main(void)
  {
    int line;
```

```
   clrscr();

   for (line = 1; line < 25; line++)
    cprintf("This is line %d\r\n", line);
   cprintf("Press a key to Continue: ");
   getch();

   gotoxy(1, 12);

   for (line = 12; line < 15; line++)
     delline();

   gotoxy(1, 25);
}
```

C 307 Positioning the Cursor for Screen Output

As you have learned, you can use the ANSI.SYS device driver to position the cursor for screen output operations. If you are working in a DOS environment, many C compilers provide the *gotoxy* function, which lets you position the cursor at a specific column and row position:

```
#include <conio.h>

void gotoxy(int column, int row);
```

The column parameter specifies a column (x) position from 1 though 80. The row parameter specifies a row position from 1 through 25. If either values are invalid, the *gotoxy* operation is ignored. The following program, GOTOXY.C, uses the *gotoxy* function to display screen output at specific locations:

```
#include <conio.h>

void main(void)
 {
   clrscr();

   gotoxy(1, 5);
   cprintf("Output at row 5 column 1\n");

   gotoxy(20, 10);
   cprintf("Output at row 10 column 20\n");
 }
```

Determining the Row and Column Position

In Tip 307 you learned how to use *gotoxy* to place the cursor at a specific row and column position. In many cases, your programs will want to know the current cursor position before performing a screen I/O operation. The functions *wherex* and *wherey* return the cursor's column and row:

```
#include <conio.h>

int wherex(void);
int wherey(void);
```

The following program, WHEREXY.C, clears the screen, writes three lines of output, and then uses the *wherex* and *wherey* functions to determine the current cursor position:

```
#include <conio.h>

void main(void)
  {
    int row, column;

    clrscr();

    cprintf("This is line 1\r\n");
    cprintf("Line 2 is a little longer\r\n");
    cprintf("This is the last line");

    row = wherey();
    column = wherex();

    cprintf("\r\nThe cursor position was row %d column %d\n",
      row, column);
  }
```

Inserting a Blank Line on the Screen

As your programs perform screen-based I/O operations, there may be times when you want to insert a blank line on the screen so that you can insert text in the middle of existing text. To do so, your programs can use the *insline* function:

```
#include <conio.h>

void insline(void);
```

When you invoke the *insline* function, all text below the current cursor position are moved down one line. The line at the bottom of the screen will scroll off the window. The following program, INSLINE.C, writes a screenful of information on the screen. The program then uses the *insline* function to insert text at line 12:

```
#include <conio.h>

void main(void)
  {
    int line;

    clrscr();

    for (line = 1; line < 25; line++)
     cprintf("This is line %d\r\n", line);

    cprintf("Press a key to Continue: ");
    getch();

    gotoxy(1, 12);

    insline();
    cprintf("This is new text!!!");
    gotoxy(1, 25);
  }
```

C 310 Copying Screen Text to a Buffer

When your programs perform extensive screen I/O, there may be times when the program needs to copy the current screen contents to a buffer. To copy screen text, your programs can use the *gettext* function:

```
#include <conio.h>

int gettext(int left, int top, int right, int bottom,
    void *buffer);
```

The left and top parameters specify the column and row positions of the upper-left text-box corner of the screen region you want to copy. Likewise, the right and bottom parameters specify the box's lower-right corner. The *buffer* parameter is the buffer into which the text and its attributes are placed. The PC uses an attribute byte for every letter of text displayed on your screen. If you want to buffer ten characters, for example, your buffer must be large enough to hold the ten ASCII characters plus the ten attribute bytes (20 bytes in length). The following program, SAVESCR.C, saves the current text mode screen contents to the file SAVESCR.DAT:

```c
#include <conio.h>
#include <io.h>
#include <fcntl.h>
#include <sys\stat.h>

void main(void)
 {
    char buffer[8000];
    int handle;

    if ((handle = creat("SAVESCR.DAT", S_IWRITE)) == -1)
     cprintf("Error opening SAVESCRN.DAT\r\n");
    else
      {
        gettext(1, 1, 80, 25, buffer);
        write(handle, buffer, sizeof(buffer));
        close(handle);
      }
 }
```

Note: *In most cases, the current text attribute is 7. If you try to display the contents of the file SAVESCR.DAT using the TYPE command, your system will beep for every attribute value.*

Writing a Text Buffer at a Specific Screen Location

As you have learned, many DOS-based compilers provide functions that your programs can use to control video output. In Tip 310 you learned that your programs can use the *gettext* function to copy a range of screen characters (and their attributes) to a buffer. After you copy a text buffer, you can later copy it back to the screen using the *puttext* function:

```c
#include <conio.h>

int puttext(int left, int top, int right, int bottom,
  void *buffer);
```

The left, top, right, and bottom parameters specify the screen location at which you want the buffer's contents written. The buffer parameter contains the characters and attributes previously stored by *gettext*. The following program, PUTTEXT.C, moves the text "Jamsa's 1001 C/C++ Tips" around your screen until you press any key:

```c
#include <conio.h>
#include <io.h>
#include <fcntl.h>
#include <sys\stat.h>
#include <stdlib.h>
#include <dos.h>

void main(void)
 {
    char buffer[128];
    int row, column;

    clrscr();
    cprintf("Jamsa's 1001 C/C++ Tips\r\n");
    gettext(1, 1, 23, 1, buffer);

    while (! kbhit())
     {
        clrscr();
        row = 1 + random(24);
        column = 1 + random(58);
        puttext(column, row, column+22, row, buffer);
        delay(2000);
     }
 }
```

C 312 Determining Text Mode Settings

As you have learned, many C compilers provide several text-based functions that your programs can use to control screen output operations. To help your programs determine the current screen settings, your programs can use the *gettextinfo* function:

```c
#include <conio.h>

void gettextinfo(struct text_info *data);
```

The data parameter is a pointer to a structure of type *text_info*, as shown here:

```c
struct text_info {
  unsigned char winleft;    // Left column
  unsigned char wintop;     // Top row
```

```
  unsigned char winright;   // Right column
  unsigned char winbottom;  // Bottom row
  unsigned char attribute;  // Text attribute
  unsigned char normattr;   // Normal attribute
  unsigned char currmode;   // Current text mode
  unsigned char screenheight;  // In rows
  unsigned char screenwidth;   // In columns
  unsigned char curx;       // Cursor column
  unsigned char cury;       // Cursor row;
};
```

The following program, TEXTINFO.C, uses the *gettextinfo* function to display the current text settings:

```
#include <conio.h>

void main(void)
  {
    struct text_info text;

    gettextinfo(&text);

    cprintf("Screen coordinates %d,%d to %d,%d\r\n",
      text.wintop, text.winleft, text.winbottom, text.winright);

    cprintf("Text attribute %d Normal attribute %d\r\n",
      text.attribute, text.normattr);

    cprintf("Screen height %d width %d\r\n", text.screenheight,
      text.screenwidth);

    cprintf("Cursor position was row %d column %d\r\n",
      text.cury, text.curx);
  }
```

Controlling Screen Colors

As you have learned, using the ANSI.SYS device driver, your programs can display screen output in color. In addition, many DOS-based compilers provide the *textattr* function, which lets you select the foreground and background text colors:

```
#include <conio.h>

void textattr(int attribute);
```

The attribute parameter contains eight bits that specify the desired colors. The least significant four bits specify the foreground color. The three bits that follow specify the background color, and the most significant bit controls blinking. To select a color, you must assign the desired color value to the correct bits. Table 313 pecifies the color values:

Color Constant	Value	Use
BLACK	0	Foreground/background
BLUE	1	Foreground/background
GREEN	2	Foreground/background
CYAN	3	Foreground/background
RED	4	Foreground/background
MAGENTA	5	Foreground/background
BROWN	6	Foreground/background
LIGHTGRAY	7	Foreground/background
DARKGRAY	8	Foreground
LIGHTBLUE	9	Foreground
LIGHTGREEN	10	Foreground
LIGHTCYAN	11	Foreground
LIGHTRED	12	Foreground
LIGHTMAGENTA	13	Foreground
YELLOW	14	Foreground
WHITE	15	Foreground
BLINK	128	Foreground

Table 313 *Color attribute parameters.*

The following program, TEXTATTR.C, illustrates the available foreground colors:

```
#include <conio.h>

void main(void)
 {
  int color;

  for (color = 1; color < 16; color++)
   {
     textattr(color);
     cprintf("This is color %d\r\n", color);
   }

  textattr(128 + 15);
  cprintf("This is blinking\r\n");
 }
```

Assigning a Background Color

314

As you learned in Tip 313, the *textattr* function lets your programs select foreground and background colors. To set the background color using *textattr*, your program must assign the desired color value to bits 4 through 6 of the color value. To do so, your programs can use bitwise shift operations, or you can declare a structure with bit fields as shown here:

```
struct TextColor {
   unsigned char foreground:4;
   unsigned char background:3;
   unsinged char blinking:1;
};
```

The following program, SETBACK.C uses the TextColor structure to set the current screen colors:

```
#include <conio.h>

void main(void)
 {
   union TextColor {
     struct {
       unsigned char foreground:4;
       unsigned char background:3;
       unsigned char blinking:1;
     } color_bits;
     unsigned char value;
   } colors;
   colors.color_bits.foreground = BLUE;
   colors.color_bits.background = RED;
   colors.color_bits.blinking = 1;

   textattr(colors.value);

   clrscr();
   cprintf("This is the new text colors\n");
 }
```

C 315 Setting the Foreground Color Using *textcolor*

As you have learned, many DOS-based compilers provide the *textattr* function, which lets you select the desired foreground and background colors for text display. To simplify the process of assigning a foreground color, you might want to use the *textcolor* function, shown here:

```
#include <conio.h>

void textcolor(int foregroundcolor);
```

The *foregroundcolor* parameter specifies one of the color values listed in Table 315.

Color Constant	Value
BLACK	0
BLUE	1
GREEN	2
CYAN	3
RED	4
MAGENTA	5
BROWN	6
LIGHTGRAY	7
DARKGRAY	8
LIGHTBLUE	9
LIGHTGREEN	10
LIGHTCYAN	11
LIGHTRED	12
LIGHTMAGENTA	13
YELLOW	14
WHITE	15
BLINK	128

Table 315 *Valid foreground color values for textcolor.*

The following program, TXTCOLOR.C, illustrates the use of the *textcolor* function to set the foreground color:

```
#include <conio.h>

void main(void)
  {
  int color;

  for (color = 1; color < 16; color++)
```

```
  {
    textcolor(color);
    cprintf("This is color %d\r\n", color);
  }

  textcolor(128 + 15);
  cprintf("This is blinking\r\n");
}
```

Setting the Background Color Using *textbackground*

C 316

As you have learned, many DOS-based compilers provide the *textattr* function, which lets you select the desired foreground and background colors for text display. To simplify the process of assigning a background color, you might want to use the *textbackground* function, shown here:

```
#include <conio.h>

void textbackground(int backgroundcolor);
```

The *backgroundcolor* parameter specifies one of the color values listed in Table 316.

Color Constant	Value
BLACK	0
BLUE	1
GREEN	2
CYAN	3
RED	4
MAGENTA	5
BROWN	6
LIGHTGRAY	7

Table 316 *Valid background color values.*

The following program, BACKGRND.C, uses the *textbackground* function to display the different background colors:

```
#include <conio.h>

void main(void)
  {
    int color;
```

```
for (color = 0; color < 8; color++)
  {
    textbackground(color);
    cprintf("This is color %d\r\n", color);
    cprintf("Press any key to continue\r\n");
    getch();
  }
}
```

C 317 Controlling Text Intensity

As you have learned, many DOS-based compilers provides functions that let you control your screen output. When you use these functions to write text to the screen, there may bay be times when you want to control the intensity of information written to the screen. In such cases, you can use one of three functions to select the text output intensity:

```
#include <conio.h>

void highvideo(void);
void lowvideo(void);
void normvideo(void);
```

The functions control the intensity with which text is displayed on your screen. The following program, NTENSITY.C, illustrates the use of these three functions:

```
#include <conio.h>

void main(void)
  {
    clrscr();

    highvideo();
    cprintf("This text is high video\r\n");

    lowvideo();
    cprintf("This text is low video\r\n");

    normvideo();
    cprintf("This text is normal video\r\n");
  }
```

Determining the Current Text Mode

C 318

As you have learned, many DOS-based compilers provide functions that your programs can use to control text-based output. When your programs perform screen output, they need to know and possibly change the PC's current text mode. For example, a program that expects 80 columns will display inconsistent results on a screen that is in 40-column mode. To help your programs change the current text mode, your programs can use the *textmode* function, shown here:

```
#include <conio.h>

void textmode(int desired_mode);
```

The desired_mode parameter specifies the text mode you desire. Table 318 lists the valid text modes.

Constant	Value	Text Mode
LASTMODE	-1	Previous mode
BW40	0	Black and white 40 column
C40	1	Color 40 column
BW80	2	Black and white 80 column
C80	3	Color 80 column
MONO	7	Monochrome 80 column
C4350	64	EGA 43 line or VGA 50 line

Table 318 *Valid text mode operations.*

The following statement, for example, would select 43 or 50 line mode on an EGA or VGA monitor:

```
textmode(C4350);
```

Note: *If you use textmode to change the current text mode, the change remains in effect after your program ends.*

Moving Screen Text from One Location to Another

C 319

As you have learned, many DOS-based compilers provide functions that let you control your screen's text output. If your program performs extensive screen output, there may be times when you want to copy or move the text that appears in one part of your screen to another. To copy screen text, your programs can use the *movetext* function, shown here:

```
#include <conio.h>

int movetext(int left, int top, int right, int bottom,
  int destination_left, int destination_top);
```

The left, top, right, and bottom parameters box the region of text that you want to move. The *destination_left* and *destination_top* parameters specify the desired location of the box's upper-left corner. The following program, MOVETEXT.C, writes five lines of text to the screen and then asks you to press a key. When you do, the program will then copy the text to a new location:

```
#include <conio.h>

void main(void)
  {
    int i;

    clrscr();
    for (i = 1; i <= 5; i++)
      cprintf("This is line %d\r\n", i);

    cprintf("Press any key\n\r");
    getch();

    movetext(1, 1, 30, 6, 45, 18);
    gotoxy(1, 24);
  }
```

To move the text, as opposed to copying it, you must delete the copied text after *movetext* completes.

C 320 Defining a Text Window

As you have learned, many DOS-based compilers provide functions your programs can use to control screen output better. By default, these functions write their output to the entire screen. Depending on your program's purpose, there may be times when you want to restrict the program's output to a specific screen region. To do so, your programs can use the *window* function:

```
#include <conio.h>

void window(int left, int top, int right, int bottom);
```

The left, top, right, and bottom parameters define the upper-left and lower-right corners of a screen region within which you want output written. The following program, WINDOW.C, restricts the program's output to the top-left quarter of the screen:

```c
#include <conio.h>

void main(void)
 {
   int i, j;

   window(1, 1, 40, 12);

   for (i = 0; i < 15; i++)
     {
       for (j = 0; j < 50; j++)
        cprintf("%d", j);
       cprintf("\r\n");
     }
 }
```

When program output reaches the right edge of window, it wraps to the next line. After the program ends, the full screen is used for output operations.

C 321 Using the Absolute Value of an Integer Expression

The *absolute value* specifies the number-line distance of the value from zero. Absolute values are always positive. For example, the absolute value of 5 is 5. Likewise, the absolute value of –5 is 5. To help your programs determine an absolute value, C provides the *abs* function. As shown here, *abs* returns the absolute value for an integer expression:

```
#include <stdlib.h>

int abs(int expression);
```

The following program, SHOW_ABS.C, illustrates the use of the *abs* function:

```
#include <stdio.h>
#include <stdlib.h>

void main (void)
 {
   printf("The absolute value of %d is %d\n", 5, abs(5));
   printf("The absolute value of %d is %d\n", 0, abs(0));
   printf("The absolute value of %d is %d\n", -5, abs(-5));
 }
```

When you compile and execute this program, your screen will display the following:

```
C:\> SHOW_ABS  <ENTER>
The absolute value of 5 is 5
The absolute value of 0 is 0
The absolute value of -5 is 5
```

Note: *Many C compilers also provide the function labs, which returns the absolute value for an expression of type long int.*

C 322 Using the Arccosine

The arccosine is the ratio between the hypotenuse of a right triangle and the leg adjacent to a given acute angle; the inverse of the cosine of an angle. If *y* is the cosine of θ, then θ is the arccosine of *y*. To help your programs determine the arccosine, C provides the *acos* function. The function returns the arccosine (0 through pi) of an angle specified in radians (as type double):

```
+ −
× ÷
```

```
#include <math.h>

double acos(double expression);
```

If the expression specified is not in the range −1.0 through 1.0, *acos* sets the global variable *errno* to EDOM and displays an DOMAIN error to standard error. The following program, SHOWACOS.C, illustrates the use of the *acos* function:

```
#include <stdio.h>
#include <math.h>

void main (void)
 {
   double radians;

   for (radians = -0.5; radians <= 0.5; radians += 0.2)
     printf("%f %f\n", radians, acos(radians));
 }
```

Note: *Many C compilers also provide the function acosl, which returns the arccosine value for a long double expression.*

Using the Arcsine

C **323**

The arcsine is the ratio between the hypoteneuse of a right triangle and the leg opposite a given acute angle; the inverse of the sine of an angle. If *y* is the sine of θ, then θ is the arcsine of *y*. To help your programs determine the arcsine, C provides the *acos* function. The function returns the arcsine (−pi/2 through pi/2) of an angle specified in radians (as type double):

```
#include <math.h>

double asin(double expression);
```

If the expression specified is not in the range −1.0 through 1.0, *asin* sets the global variable *errno* to NAN and displays an DOMAIN error to stderr. The following program, SHOWASIN.C, illustrates the use of the *asin* function:

```
#include <stdio.h>
#include <math.h>

void main (void)
 {
   double radians;
```

```
for (radians = -0.5; radians <= 0.5; radians += 0.2)
   printf("%f %f\n", radians, asin(radians));
}
```

Note: *Many C compilers also provide the function asinl, which returns the arcsine value for a long double expression.*

324 Using the Arctangent

The arctangent is the ratio between the leg adjacent to a given acute angle and the leg opposite it in a right triangle; the inverse of the tangent of an angle. If *y* is the tangent of θ, then θ is the arctangent of *y*. To help your programs determine the arcsine, C provides the *acos* function. To help your programs determine the arctangent, C provides the *atan* function. The function returns the arcsine (–pi/2 through pi/2) of an angle specified in radians (as type double):

```
#include <math.h>

double atan(double expression);
```

The following program, SHOWATAN.C, illustrates the use of the *atan* function:

```
#include <stdio.h>
#include <math.h>

void main (void)
  {
    double radians;

    for (radians = -0.5; radians <= 0.5; radians += 0.2)
      printf("%f %f\n", radians, atan(radians));
  }
```

Note: *Many C compilers also provide the function atanl, which returns the arctangent value for a long double expression. Also, C provides the functions atan2 and atan2l, which return the arctangent of y/x.*

325 Using the Absolute Value of a Complex Value

A complex number contains a real and imaginary part. C functions represent complex numbers as a structure with an x and y member, as shown here:

```
struct complex {
  double x, y;
};
```

When you work with complex numbers, there may be times when you need to calculate the value's absolute value (positive distance from zero). To let your program calculate the absolute value for a complex number, C provides the *cabs* function:

```
#include <math.h>

double cabs(struct complex value);
```

The *cabs* function is similar to taking the square root of the sum of the squares of each complex number. The following program, SHOWCABS.C, illustrates the use of the *cabs* function:

```
#include <stdio.h>
#include <math.h>

void main (void)
  {
    struct complex complex_number;

    complex_number.x = 10;
    complex_number.y = 5;

    printf("Absolute value of 10,5 is %f\n",
      cabs(complex_number));
  }
```

When you compile and execute this program, your screen will display the following output:

```
C:\> SHOWCABS  <ENTER>
Absolute value of 10,5 is 11.180340
```

Note: *Many C compilers also provide the cabls function, which returns absolute value for long double complex numbers.*

Rounding a Floating-Point Value Up

326

When you work with floating-point numbers, there may be times when you need to round up the value to the next higher integer. For such cases, C provides the *ceil* function:

```
#include <math.h>

double ceil (double value);
```

As you can see, *ceil* receives a parameter of type double and returns a value of type double. The following program, SHOWCEIL.C, illustrates the use of the *ceil* function:

```
#include <stdio.h>
#include <math.h>

void main (void)
  {
    printf("The value %f ceil %f\n", 1.9, ceil(1.9));
    printf("The value %f ceil %f\n", 2.1, ceil(2.1));
  }
```

When you compile and execute this program, your program displays the following output:

```
C:\> SHOWCEIL   <ENTER>
The value 1.900000 ceil 2.000000
The value 2.100000 ceil 3.000000
```

Note: *Many C compilers also provide the function ceill, which rounds up a value of type long double.*

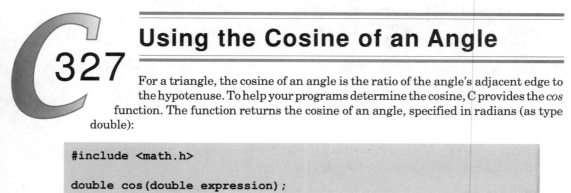

Using the Cosine of an Angle

327

For a triangle, the cosine of an angle is the ratio of the angle's adjacent edge to the hypotenuse. To help your programs determine the cosine, C provides the *cos* function. The function returns the cosine of an angle, specified in radians (as type double):

```
#include <math.h>

double cos (double expression);
```

The *cos* function returns a value in the range −1.0 through 1.0. The following program, SHOW_COS.C, illustrates the use of the *cos* function:

```
#include <stdio.h>
#include <math.h>
```

```
void main (void)
  {
    printf("cosine of pi/2 is %6.4f\n", cos(3.14159/2.0));
    printf("cosine of pi is %6.4f\n", cos(3.14159));
  }
```

When you compile and execute this program, your screen will display the following output:

```
C:\> SHOW_COS  <ENTER>
cosine of pi/2 is 0.0000
cosine of pi is -1.0000
```

Note: *Many C compilers also provide the function cosl, which returns the cosine value for a long double expression.*

Using the Hyperbolic Cosine of an Angle

 **328**

The hyperbolic cosine of an angle is the cosine of a "circular-like" angle, that is defined using ratios of hyperbolic radians. To help your programs determine the hyperbolic cosine, C provides the *cosh* function. The function returns the hyperbolic cosine of an angle, specified in radians (as type double):

```
#include <math.h>

double cosh(double expression);
```

If overflow occurs, *cosh* returns the value HUGE_VAL (or _LHUGE_VAL for coshl) and sets the global variable *errno* to ERANGE. The following program, SHOWCOSH.C, illustrates the use of the *cosh* function:

```
#include <stdio.h>
#include <math.h>

void main (void)
  {
    double radians;

    for (radians = -0.5; radians <= 0.5; radians += 0.2)
      printf("%f %f\n", radians, cosh(radians));
  }
```

Note: *Many C compilers also provide the function coshl, which returns the hyperbolic cosine value for a long double expression.*

```
+ -
x ÷
```

Performing Integer Division

C 329

As you have learned, C provides the division (/) and modulo (%) operators, which let your programs perform a division or determine the remainder of a division operation. In a similar way, C provides the function *div*, which divides a numerator value by a denominator, returning a structure of type *div_t* that contains the quotient and remainder, as shown here:

```
struct div_t {
   int quot;
   int rem;
} div_t;
```

The *div* function works with integer values, as shown here:

```
#include <stdlib.h>

div_t div(int numerator, int denominator);
```

The following program, DIV_REM.C, illustrates the use of the *div* function:

```
#include <stdio.h>
#include <stdlib.h>

void main (void)
  {
    div_t result;

    result = div(11, 3);

    printf("11 divided by 3 is %d Remainder %d\n",
       result.quot, result.rem);
  }
```

When you compile and execute this program, your screen will display the following output:

```
C:\> DIV_REM  <ENTER>
11 divided by 3 is 3 Remainder 2
```

Note: *Many C compilers also provide the function ldiv, which returns the quotient and remainder for long values.*

$$\begin{array}{c} + - \\ \times \div \end{array}$$

Working With an Exponential

When your programs perform complex mathematical operations, they might need to calculate the exponential of e^x. In such cases, your programs can use the *exp* function, which returns a value of type double, as shown here:

```
#include <math.h>

double exp(double x);
```

The following program, SHOW_EXP.C, illustrates the use of the *exp* function:

```
#include <stdio.h>
#include <math.h>

void main (void)
  {
    double value;

    for (value = 0.0; value <= 1.0; value += 0.1)
      printf("exp(%f) is %f\n", value, exp(value));
  }
```

Note: *Many C compilers also provide the function expl, which works with values of type long double.*

Using the Absolute Value of a Floating-Point Expression

The *absolute value* specifies the number line distance of the value from zero. Absolute values are always positive. For example, the absolute value of 2.5 is 2.5. Likewise, the absolute –2.5 is 2.5. When you work with absolute values, there may be times when you need to calculate the absolute value of a floating-point expression. For such cases, C provides the *fabs* function. As shown here, *fabs* returns the absolute value for a floating-point number:

```
#include <math.h>

float fabs(float expression);
```

The following program, SHOWFABS.C, illustrates the use of the *fabs* function:

```
#include <stdio.h>
#include <math.h>

void main (void)
  {
    float value;

    for (value = -1.0; value <= 1.0; value += 0.1)
      printf ("Value %f fabs %f\n", value, fabs (value));
  }
```

Note: *Many C compilers also provide the function fabsl, which returns the absolute value for an expression of type long double.*

C 332 Using the Floating-Point Remainder

In Tip 82 you learned how to use C's modulo operator (%) to get the remainder of an integer division. Depending on your program, there may be times when you want to know the remainder of a floating-point division. In such cases, C provides the *fmod* function to divide two floating-point values, returning the remainder as a floating-point value:

```
#include <math.h>

double fmod(double x, double y);
```

For example, if you invoke *fmod* with the values 10.0 and 3.0, *fmod* would return the value 1.0 (10 divided by 3 is 3 remainder 1). The following program, SHOWFMOD.C, illustrates the use of the *fmod* function:

```
#include <stdio.h>
#include <math.h>

void main (void)
  {
    double numerator = 10.0;
    double denominator = 3.0;

    printf ("fmod(10, 3) is %f\n", fmod (numerator,
      denominator));
  }
```

+ −
× ÷

When you compile and execute this program, your screen will display the following output:

```
C:\> SHOWFMOD  <ENTER>
fmod(10, 3) is 1.000000
```

> **Note:** *Many C compilers also provide the function fmodl, which returns fractional remainder of a long double value.*

Using a Floating-Point Value's Mantissa and Exponent

When your programs work with floating-point values, the computer stores the values using a mantissa (whose value is between 0.5 and 1.0) and exponent, as shown in Figure 333.

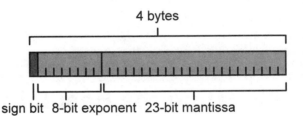

Figure 333 *The computer stores floating-point values using an exponent and mantissa format.*

To determine the value, the computer combines the mantissa and exponent, as shown here:

```
value = mantissa * 2^exponent;
```

Normally, you don't need to be aware of the fact that the computer is using the mantissa and exponent. Depending on your program, there may be times when you want to know the mantissa and exponent values. For such cases, C provides the *frexp* function, which returns the mantissa and assigns the exponent to the variable passed to function by reference:

```
#include <math.h>

double frexp(double value, int *exponent);
```

The following program, FREXP.C, illustrates the use of the *frexp* function:

```
#include <stdio.h>
#include <math.h>

void main (void)
 {
   double value = 1.2345;

   double mantissa;
   int exponent;

   mantissa = frexp(value, &exponent);

   printf("Mantissa %f Exponent %d Value %f\n",
     mantissa, exponent, mantissa * pow(2.0, 1.0 * exponent));
 }
```

When you compile and execute this program, your screen displays the following output:

```
C:\> FREXP  <ENTER>
Mantissa 0.617250 Exponent 1 Value 1.234500
```

> **Note:** *Many C compilers also provide the function frexpl, which returns the exponent and mantissa of a long double value.*

Calculating the Result of $x * 2^e$

In Tip 330 you learned how to use C's *exp* function to obtain the result e^x. Depending on your programs, there may be times when you need to calculate $x * 2^e$. For such cases, you can use C's *ldexp* function:

```
#include <math.h>

double ldexp(double value, int exponent);
```

The following program, LDEXP.C, illustrates the use of the *ldexp* function:

```
#include <stdio.h>
#include <math.h>

void main (void)
 {
   printf("3 * 2 raised to the 4 is %f\n",
     ldexp(3.0, 4));
 }
```

When you compile and execute this program, your screen displays the following output:

```
C:\> LDEXP <ENTER>
3 * 2 raised to the 4 is 48.000000
```

Note: *Many C compilers also provide the function ldexpl to support long double values.*

Calculating the Natural Log

C 335

The natural logarithm of a number is the power to which *e* must be raised to equal the given number. To help your programs determine the natural log, C provides the *log* function, which returns the natural logarithm of a floating-point value:

```
#include <math.h>

double log(double value);
```

If the value of the parameter is less than 0, log sets the global variable *errno* to ERANGE and returns the value HUGE_VAL (or _LHUGE_VAL for *logl*). The following program, SHOW_LOG.C, illustrates the use of *log* function:

```
#include <stdio.h>
#include <math.h>

void main (void)
  {
    printf("Natural log of 256.0 is %f\n", log(256.0));
  }
```

When you compile and execute this program, your screen will display the following output:

```
C:\> SHOW_LOG <ENTER>
Natural log of 256.0 is 5.545177
```

Note: *Many C compilers also provide the function logl, which returns the natural logarithm of a long double expression.*

```
+ −
× ÷
```

C 336 Calculating the Result of $\log_{10}x$

In Tip 335 you learned how to use C's log function to calculate a natural logarithm. As your programs perform mathematical operations, there may be times when you need to determine the log-to-the-base-10 of a value, $\log_{10}x$. For such cases, C provides the *log10* function:

```
#include <math.h>

double log10(double value);
```

If the parameter value is 0, log10 sets the global variable *errno* to EDOM and returns the value HUGE_VAL (or _LHUGE_VAL for log10l). The following program, LOG_10.C, illustrates the use of C's *log10* function:

```
#include <stdio.h>
#include <math.h>

void main (void)
  {
    printf("Log10 of 100 is %f\n", log10(100.0));
    printf("Log10 of 10000 is %f\n", log10(10000.0));
  }
```

When you compile and execute this program, your screen displays the following output:

```
C:\> LOG_10  <ENTER>
Log10 of 100 is 2.000000
Log10 of 10000 is 4.000000
```

Note: *Many C compilers also provide the function log10l, which supports long double values.*

C 337 Determining Maximum and Minimum Values

When your programs compare two numbers, there will be times when you will want to know the minimum or maximum of two values. For such cases, the header file stdlib.h provides the macros *min* and *max*. The following program, MIN_MAX.C, illustrates the use of these two macros:

```
#include <stdio.h>
#include <stdlib.h>

void main (void)
 {
   printf("Maximum of %f and %f is %f\n",
     10.0, 25.0, max(10.0, 25.0));
   printf("Minimum of %f and %f is %f\n",
     10.0, 25.0, min(10.0, 25.0));
 }
```

To better understand these two macros, consider the following implementations:

```
#define max(x,y)   (((x) > (y)) ? (x) : (y))
#define min(x,y)   (((x) < (y)) ? (x) : (y))
```

Breaking a Floating-Point Value into Its Integer and Fractional Components

 338

A floating-point value consists of two parts, an *integer* portion and a *fraction* part. For example, given the number 12.345, the value 12 is the integer portion and 0.345 is the fractional part. Depending on your program, there may be times when you will want to work with a value's integer or fractional component, or both. For such cases, C provides the *modf* function, shown here:

```
#include <math.h>

double modf(double value, double *integer_part);
```

The *modf* function returns the fractional part of the value and assigns the integer portion to the specified variable. The following program, INT_FRAC.C, illustrates the use of the *modf* function:

```
#include <stdio.h>
#include <math.h>

void main (void)
 {
   double value = 1.2345;
   double int_part;
   double fraction;

   fraction = modf(value, &int_part);
```

```
    printf("Value %f Integer part %f Fraction %f\n",
      value, int_part, fraction);
}
```

When you compile and execute this program, your screen will display the following output:

```
C:\> INT_FRAC  <ENTER>
Value 1.234500 Integer part 1.000000 Fraction 0.234500
```

Note: *Many C compilers also provide the function modfl, which returns the integer and fractional parts of a long double expression.*

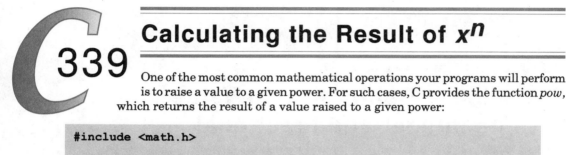

Calculating the Result of x^n

C 339

One of the most common mathematical operations your programs will perform is to raise a value to a given power. For such cases, C provides the function *pow*, which returns the result of a value raised to a given power:

```
#include <math.h>

double pow(double value, double power);
```

If the result of the value raised to the given power results in overflow, *pow* assigns the global variable *errno* the value ERANGE and returns HUGE_VAL (or _LHUGE_VAL for *powl*). If the value passed to *pow* is less than 0 and the power is not a whole number, *pow* sets the global variable *errno* to EDOM. The following program, SHOW_POW.C, illustrates the use of C's *pow* function:

```
#include <stdio.h>
#include <math.h>

void main (void)
  {
    int power;

    for (power = -2; power <= 2; power++)
      printf("10 raised to %d is %f\n", power,
        pow(10.0, power));
  }
```

When you compile and execute this program, your screen will display the following output:

```
C:\> SHOW_POW  <ENTER>
10 raised to -2 is 0.010000
10 raised to -1 is 0.100000
```

```
10 raised to 0 is 1.000000
10 raised to 1 is 10.000000
10 raised to 2 is 100.000000
```

> **Note:** *Many C compilers also provide the function powl, which supports values of type long double. Likewise, if you are working with complex values, the header file complex.h defines a function prototype for pow that works with complex numbers.*

Calculating the Result of 10^X

In Tip 339 you learned how to use the *pow* function to determine the result of a value raised to a given power. There may be times when your programs need to calculate the result of 10^X. In such cases, you can use the *pow* function, or if your compiler supports it, you can use C's *pow10*, shown here:

```
#include <math.h>

double pow10(int power);
```

The following program, POW10.C, illustrates the use of the *pow10* function:

```
#include <stdio.h>
#include <math.h>

void main (void)
  {
    printf("10 raised to -1 is %f\n", pow10(-1));
    printf("10 raised to 0 is %f\n", pow10(0));
    printf("10 raised to 1 is %f\n", pow10(1));
    printf("10 raised to 2 is %f\n", pow10(2));
  }
```

When you compile and execute this program, your screen displays the following output:

```
C:\> POW10  <ENTER>
10 raised to -1 is 0.100000
10 raised to 0 is 1.000000
10 raised to 1 is 10.000000
10 raised to 2 is 100.000000
```

> **Note:** *Many C compilers also provide the function pow10l, which supports values of type long double.*

```
+ −
× ÷
```

C 341 Generating a Random Number

Depending on your program, there may be times when you need to generate one or more random numbers. For such cases, C provides two functions *rand* and *random*, both of which return integer random numbers:

```
#include <stdlib.h>

int rand(void);
int random(int ceiling);
```

The first function, *rand*, returns an integer random number in the range 0 through RAND_MAX (defined in stdlib.h). The second function, *random*, returns a random number in the range 0 through *ceiling*, where ceiling is a parameter passed to the random function. The following program, RANDOM.C, illustrates the use of both random-number generators:

```
#include <stdio.h>
#include <stdlib.h>

void main(void)
 {
   int i;

   printf("Values from rand\n");
   for (i = 0; i < 100; i++)
     printf("%d ", rand());

   printf("Values from random(100))\n");
   for (i = 0; i < 100; i++)
     printf("%d ", random(100));
 }
```

C 342 Mapping Random Values to a Specific Range

In Tip 341 you learned that the C functions *rand* and *random* return random numbers. When your program generates random numbers, there may be times when you need the program to map the values to a specific range. If you are working with integer values, you can use the *random* function, using a parameter to specify the highest value in the range of random numbers. If you are working with floating-point values, however, such as values in the range 0.0 through 1.0, you can divide the number as needed. The following program, MAP_RAND.C, maps random numbers to the range 0.0 through 1.0 and integer values to the range –5 though 5:

```c
include <stdio.h>
#include <stdlib.h>

void main(void)
 {
   int i;

   printf("Values from rand\n");
   for (i = 0; i < 100; i++)
     printf("%d ", rand());

   printf("Values from random(100))\n");
   for (i = 0; i < 100; i++)
     printf("%d ", random(100));
 }
```

Seeding the Random Number Generator

C 343

Tip 341 presented C's *rand* and *random* functions that generate random numbers. When you work with random numbers, there will be times when you want to control the series of numbers the random number generator creates (so you can test your program's processing with the same set of numbers), and times when you want the generator to create actual numbers at random. The process of assigning the random number generators starting number is *seeding the generator*. To help you seed the random number generators, C provides two functions, *randomize* and *srand*:

```c
#include <stdlib.h>

void randomize(void);
void srand(unsigned seed);
```

The first function, *randomize*, uses the PC's clock to produce an random seed. The second function, *srand*, on the other hand, lets you specify the random number generator's starting value. Using *srand*, your programs can control the range of numbers the random number generator creates. The following program, RANDSEED.C, illustrates the use of the *srand* and *randomize* functions:

```
#include <stdio.h>
#include <time.h>
#include <stdlib.h>

void main(void)
 {
   int i;

   srand(100);
   printf("Values from rand\n");
   for (i = 0; i < 5; i++)
     printf("%d ", rand());

   printf("\nSame 5 numbers\n");
   srand(100);
   for (i = 0; i < 5; i++)
     printf("%d ", rand());

   randomize();
   printf("\nDifferent 5 numbers\n");
   for (i = 0; i < 5; i++)
     printf("%d ", rand());
 }
```

C 344   Using the Sine of an Angle

In a triangle, the sine of an angle is the ratio of the angles opposite edge to the hypotenuse. To help your programs determine the sine, C provides the *sin* function. The function returns the sine of an angle specified in radians (as type double):

```
#include <math.h>

double sin(double expression);
```

The following program, SHOW_SIN.C, illustrates the use of the *sin* function:

```
#include <stdio.h>
#include <math.h>

void main(void)
 {
   double radians;
```

```
    for (radians = 0.0; radians < 3.1; radians += 0.1)
      printf("Sine of %f is %f\n", radians, sin(radians));
}
```

Note: *Many C compilers also provide the function sinl, which returns the sine value for a long double expression.*

Using the Hyperbolic Sine of an Angle

The hyperbolic sine of an angle is the sine of a "circular-like" angle, that is defined using ratios of hyperbolic radians.. To help your programs determine the hyperbolic sine, C provides the *sinh* function. The function returns the hyperbolic sine of an angle specified in radians (as type double):

```
#include <math.h>

double sinh(double expression);
```

If overflow occurs, *sinh* returns the value HUGE_VAL (or _LHUGE_VAL for *sinhl*) and sets the global variable *errno* to ERANGE. The following program, SHOWSINH.C, illustrates the use of the *sinh* function:

```
#include <stdio.h>
#include <stdlib.h>
#include <math.h>

void main(void)
 {
   double radians;
   double result;

   for (radians = 0.0; radians < 3.1; radians += 0.1)
     if (((result = sinh(radians)) == HUGE_VAL) &&
       (errno == ERANGE))
       printf("Overflow error\n");
     else
       printf("Sine of %f is %f\n", radians, result);
 }
```

Note: *Many C compilers also provide the function sinhl, which returns the hyperbolic sine value for a long double expression.*

C 346 Calculating a Value's Square Root

When your programs calculate mathematical expressions, they will often need to perform square root operations. To help your programs perform square root operations, C provides the *sqrt* function:

```
#include <math.h>

double sqrt(double value);
```

The *sqrt* function only works with positive values. If your program invokes *sqrt* with a negative value, *sqrt* sets the global variable *errno* to EDOM. The following program, SQRT.C, illustrates the use of the *sqrt* function:

```
#include <stdio.h>
#include <math.h>

void main(void)
  {
    double value;

    for (value = 0.0; value < 10.0; value += 0.1)
      printf("Value %f sqrt %f\n", value, sqrt(value));
  }
```

Note: *Many C compilers also provide the function sqrtl, which returns the square root of a long double value.*

C 347 Using the Tangent of an Angle

In a triangle, the tangent of an angle is the ratio the angle's opposite edge to the adjacent edge. To help your programs determine the tangent, C provides the *tan* function. The function returns the tangent of an angle, specified in radians (as type double):

```
#include <math.h>

double tan(double expression);
```

The following program, SHOW_TAN.C, illustrates the use of the *tan* function:

```c
#include <stdio.h>
#include <math.h>

void main(void)
 {
    double pi = 3.14159265;

    printf("Tangent of pi is %f\n", tan(pi));
    printf("Tangent of pi/4 is %f\n", tan(pi / 4.0));
 }
```

When you compile and execute this program, your screen will display the following output:

```
C:\> SHOW_TAN   <ENTER>
Tangent of pi is -0.000000
Tangent of pi/4 is 1.000000
```

Note: *Many C compilers also provide the function tanl, which returns the tangent value for a long double expression.*

Using the Hyperbolic Tangent of an Angle

C 348

The hyperbolic tangent of an angle is the tangent of a "circular-like" angle that is expressed in ratios whose units are hyperbolic radians. To help your programs determine the hyperbolic tangent, C provides the *tanh* function. The function returns the hyperbolic tangent of an angle specified in radians (as type double):

```c
#include <math.h>

double tanh(double expression);
```

Note: *Many C compilers also provide the function tanhl, which returns the hyperbolic tangent value for a long double expression.*

```
+ −
× ÷
```

C 349 Creating a Customized Math Error Handler

Several of the functions presented in this section detect range and overflow errors. By default, when such errors occur, the functions invoke a special function named *matherr*, which performs additional processing, such as assigning the global variable *errno* a specific error number. As it turns out, if your programs define their own *matherr* function, the C math routines will invoke your custom handler. When the math routines invoke your *matherr* function, they will pass to it a pointer to a variable of type exception:

```
struct exception {
  int type;
  char *function;
  double arg1, arg2, retval;
};
```

The *type* member contains a constant that describe the error's type. Table 349 describes the error values:

Error Value	Meaning
DOMAIN	An argument is not in the domain of values the function supports
OVERFLOW	An argument produces a result that overflows the resulting type
SING	An argument produces a result in a singularity
TLOSS	An argument produces a result in which all the digits of precision are lost
UNDERFLOW	An argument produces a result that overflows the resulting type

Table 349 *C constants that describe mathematical errors.*

The *function* member contains the name of the routine that experienced the error. The members *arg1* and *arg2* contain the parameters that were passed to the function, while *retval* contains default return value (which you can you assign). If you return the value 0 from *matherr*, it will display an error message on the screen. The following program, MATHERR.C, illustrates the use of a custom error handler:

```
#include <stdio.h>
#include <math.h>

void main(void)
 {
   printf("Sqrt of -1 is %f\n", sqrt(-1.0));
 }
```

+ −
× ÷

```
int matherr(struct exception *error)
 {
   switch (error->type) {
     case DOMAIN: printf("Domain error\n");
                 break;
     case PLOSS: printf("Partial precision loss error\n");
                 break;
     case OVERFLOW: printf("Overflow error\n");
                   break;
     case SING:  printf("Error in singularity\n");
                 break;
     case TLOSS: printf("Total precision loss error\n");
                 break;
     case UNDERFLOW: printf("Underflow error\n");
                    break;
   };
   printf("Error occurred in %s values %f\n",
     error->name, error->arg1);
   error->retval = 1;
   return(1);
 }
```

Note: *The matherr function only catches domain and overflow errors. To detect divide-by-zero errors, use signal. Many C compilers also support the function matherrl, which supports arguments of type long double.*

Files, Directories, & Disks

C 350 Determining the Current Disk Drive

If your programs work in the DOS environment, there will be many times when they need to determine the current disk drive. In such cases, your programs can use the _dos_getdrive function, shown here:

```
#include <dos.h>

void _dos_getdrive(unsigned *disk_drive);
```

The function returns a disk drive number, where 1 is drive A, 2 is drive B, and so on. The following program, GETDRIVE.C, uses the _dos_getdrive function to display the current disk drive letter:

```
#include <stdio.h>
#include <dos.h>

void main (void)
  {
    unsigned drive_number;

    _dos_getdrive(&drive_number);

    printf("The current drive is %c\n", drive_number - 1 + 'A');
  }
```

C 351 Selecting the Current Drive

In Tip 350 you learned how to use the _dos_getdrive function to determine the current disk drive in a DOS-based environment. Just as there may be times when your programs need to determine the current disk drive, there may be times when you need to select a specific disk drive. In such cases, your programs can use the function _dos_setdrive:

```
#include <dos.h>

void _dos_setdrive(unsigned drive, unsigned *drive_count);
```

The drive parameter is an integer value that specifies the desired drive, where 1 is drive A, 2 is B, and so on. The function assigns the *drive_count* parameter the number of disk drives present in the system. The following program, SELECT_C.C, uses the _dos_setdrive function to select drive C as the current drive. The program also displays a count of the number of available drives (as set by the CONFIG.SYS LASTDRIVE entry):

```
#include <stdio.h>
#include <dos.h>

void main (void)
  {
    unsigned drive_count;

    _dos_setdrive(3, &drive_count);
    printf("The number of available drives is %d\n",
      drive_count);
  }
```

In addition to the *_dos_setdrive* function, your programs can use the *_chdrive* function, which also uses a drive number, beginning with 1 for drive A to select the current drive. If *_chdrive* is successful, it returns the value 0. If an error occurs, *_chdrive* will return −1:

```
#include <direct.h>

int _chdrive(int drive);
```

Determining Available Disk Space

C 352

When your programs store considerable information on disk, the programs should keep track of the available disk space to reduce the possibility of the disk running out of space during a critical disk operation. If you are working in a DOS-based system, your programs can use the *_dos_getdiskfree* function. The function returns a structure of type *diskfree_t*, shown here:

```
struct diskfree_t {
  unsigned avail_clusters;
  unsigned total_clusters;
  unsigned bytes_per_sector;
  unsigned sectors_per_cluster;
};
```

The format of the *_dos_getdiskfree* function is as follows:

```
#include <dos.h>

unsigned _dos_getdiskfree(unsigned char drive_number,
    struct diskfree_t *diskinfo);
```

The *drive_number* parameter specifies the desired drive, where 0 is the current drive, 1 is drive A, 2 is B, and so on. If *_dos_getdiskfree* is successful, the function returns the value 0. If an error occurs, *_dos_getdiskfree* returns the value –1 and assigns the global variable error the value EINVAL (for an invalid drive). The following program, DISKFREE.C, uses the *_dos_getdiskfree* function to obtain specifics about the current disk drive:

```c
#include <stdio.h>
#include <dos.h>

void main (void)
 {
   struct diskfree_t diskinfo;
   long disk_space;

   if (_dos_getdiskfree(0, &diskinfo))
     printf("Error accessing drive C:\n");
   else
     {
       disk_space = (long) diskinfo.avail_clusters *
                    (long) diskinfo.bytes_per_sector *
                    (long) diskinfo.sectors_per_cluster;

       printf("Available disk space %ld\n", disk_space);
     }
 }
```

C 353 Be Aware of DBLSPACE

Some of the tips presented in this section show you ways to perform absolute disk read and write operations that work with a disk's sectors. Before your programs perform low-level disk I/O operations, make sure that the disk you are going to read is not a compressed disk whose contents have been compressed by DBLSPACE or another third-party disk utility. Compressed disks do store information in a sector-by-sector basis. If you write a compressed disk sector, you run considerable risk of corrupting the compressed disk—losing the information it contains. As a rule, most programs do not need to perform such low-level disk read and write operations. If you are writing a disk utility program such as UNDELETE, make sure that know how to test for and work with compressed disks.

Reading File Allocation Table Information

C 354

If you are working in a DOS-based system, the file allocation table tracks which parts of your disk are in use, damaged, and available for use. If your programs perform low-level disk operations, there may be times when you will need to know information such as the disk's type, bytes per sector, number of clusters, and sectors per cluster. In such cases, your programs can use the *getfat* or *getfatd* functions:

```
#include <dos.h>

void getfat(unsigned char drive, struct fatinfo *fat);
void getfatd(struct fatinfo *fat);
```

The difference between the two functions is that the *getfat* function lets you specify the desired drive, whereas *getfatd* returns the information for the current drive. To specify a disk drive letter to the *getfat* function, specify a number value where 1 is drive A, 2 is B, 3 is C, and so on. The functions assign the information to a structure of type *fatinfo*, shown here:

```
struct fatinfo {
  char fi_sclus;     // sectors per cluster
  char fi_fatid;     // disk type
  unsigned fi_nclus; // clusters per disk
  int fi_bysec;      // bytes per sector
};
```

The following program, GETFATD.C, uses the *getfatd* function to display information about the current disk drive:

```
#include <stdio.h>
#include <dos.h>

void main(void)
 {
   struct fatinfo fat;

   getfatd(&fat);

   printf("Sectors per cluster %d\n", fat.fi_sclus);
   printf("Clusters per disk %u\n", fat.fi_nclus);
   printf("Bytes per cluster %d\n", fat.fi_bysec);
   printf("Disk type %x\n", fat.fi_fatid & 0xFF);
 }
```

355 Understanding the Disk ID

In Tip 354 you used the *getfat* and *getfatd* functions to get information about the current disk drive. As you found, these functions returned a byte called the disk ID. Table 355 specifies the possible disk ID values.

Value	Disk Type
FOH	3 1/2 inch 1.44Mb or 2.88Mb
F8H	Hard disk
F9H	3 1/2 inch 720Kb or 5 1/4 inch 1.2Mb
FAH	5 1/4 inch 320Kb
FCH	5 1/4 inch 180Kb
FDH	5 1/4 inch 360Kb
FEH	5 1/4 inch 160Kb
FFH	5 1/4 inch 320Kb

Table 355 *Disk ID values returned by DOS.*

356 Performing an Absolute Sector Read or Write

If you work in a DOS-based environment, DOS lets you perform absolute disk read and write operations, at the sector level. Normally, your programs use the DOS services to perform these operations. However, to make these operations easier to perform, many C compilers provide the *absread* and *abswrite* functions, shown here:

```
#include <dos.h>

int absread(int drive, int number_of_sectors,
   long starting_sector, void *buffer);
int abswrite(int drive, int number_of_sectors,
   long starting_sector, void *buffer);
```

The *drive* parameter specifies the disk drive you want to read, where 0 is drive A, 1 is B, and so on. The *number_of_sectors* parameters specifies the number of sectors you want to read or write, beginning at the sector specified in the *starting_sector* parameter. Finally, the *buffer* parameter is a pointer to the buffer into which information is read or the output is written. If the functions are successful, they return the value 0. If an error occurs, the functions return the value –1. The following program, CHK_DISK.C, reads every sector on drive C. If the program experiences errors reading a sector, it displays the sector number:

```
#include <stdio.h>
#include <dos.h>
#include <malloc.h>

void main(void)
  {
    struct fatinfo fat;
    long sector, total_sectors;
    void *buffer;

    getfat(3, &fat);
    total_sectors = fat.fi_nclus * fat.fi_sclus;

    if ((buffer = malloc(fat.fi_bysec)) == NULL)
      printf("Error allocating sector buffer\n");
    else
      for (sector = 0; sector < total_sectors; sector++)
        if (absread(2, 1, sector, buffer) == -1)
          {
            printf("\n\007Error reading sector %ld press Enter\n",
              sector);
            getchar();
          }
        else
          printf("Reading sector %ld\r", sector);
  }
```

Performing BIOS-Based Disk I/O

357

When your programs perform file operations, they use the DOS system services to manipulate files. The DOS services in turn, call other DOS services to read and write logical disk sectors. To perform the actual disk I/O operations, the DOS services then call BIOS disk services. If you are writing disk utility programs, there may be times when your programs need to perform low-level disk I/O operations. In such cases, your programs can use the *biosdisk* function:

```
#include <bios.h>

int biosdisk(int operation, int drive, int head,
  int track, int sector, int sector_count,
  void *buffer);
```

The *operation* parameter specifies the desired function. Table 357.1 lists the valid operations. The *drive* parameter specifies the drive number, where 0 is drive A, 1 is drive B, and so on. For a hard disk, 0x80 is the first hard drive, 0x81 is the second drive, and so on. The *head, track, sector,* and *sector_count* parameters specify the physical disk sectors that you want to read or write. The *buffer* parameter is a pointer to the buffer into which data is read or from which the data is written.

Operation	Function
0	Reset the disk system
1	Return the status of the last disk operation
2	Read the specified number of sectors
3	Write the specified number of sectors
4	Verify the specified number of sectors
5	Format the specified track—buffer contains a table of bad locations
6	Format the specified track, setting bad sectors
7	Format the drive beginning at the specified track
8	Return the drive parameters in the first 4 bytes of buffer
9	Initialize the drive
10	Perform a long read—512 sector bytes plus 4 extra
11	Perform a long write—512 sector bytes plus 4 extra
12	Perform a disk seek
13	Alternate disk reset
14	Read sector buffer
15	Write sector buffer
16	Test drive ready
17	Recalibrate the drive
18	Perform the controller RAM diagnostic
19	Perform the drive diagnostic
20	Perform the controller internal diagnostic

Table 357.1 *Valid biosdisk operations.*

If successful, the function returns the value 0. If an error occurs, the return value specifies the error. Table 357.2 lists the error values.

Error Value	Error
0	Successful
1	Invalid command
2	Address mark not found
3	Write-protected disk
4	Sector not found
5	Hard disk reset failed
6	Disk change line
7	Drive parameter activity failed
8	DMA overrun
9	DMA across 64Kb boundary

Table 357.2 *Error status values returned by biosdisk.*

10	Bad sector
11	Bad track
12	Unsupported track
16	CRC/ECC read error
17	CRC/ECC corrected data
32	Controller failure
64	Seek failed
128	No response
170	Hard disk not ready
187	Undefined error
204	Write fault
224	Status error
255	Sense operation failed

Table 357.2 *Error status values returned by biosdisk. (continued)*

Note: *Many compilers also provide a function named _bios_disk, which performs identical processing, exception that your programs pass to the function a structure of type diskinfo_t, which contains the drive, head, track, sector, and sector count values.*

Testing a Floppy Drive's Readiness

358

In Tip 357 you learned how to use the *biosdisk* function to invoke BIOS disk services. A useful operation of the *biosdisk* function is to test whether or not a floppy disk contains a disk and is ready. The following program, TEST_A.C, uses the *biosdisk* function to do just that:

```c
#include <stdio.h>
#include <bios.h>

void main(void)
  {
    char buffer[8192];

    // Try reading head 1, track 1, sector 1
    if (biosdisk(2, 0, 1, 1, 1, 1, buffer))
      printf("Error accessing drive\n");
    else
      printf("Drive ready\n");
  }
```

Performing Formatted File Output

359

Several of the tips in this section present ways that your programs can write output to a file. In many cases, your programs will need to perform formatted file output. For example, if you are creating an inventory report, you will want to line up columns, work with text and numbers, and so on. In the Getting Started section of this book you learned how to use the *printf* function to perform formatted I/O to the screen display. In a similar way, C provides the *fprintf*, which uses format specifiers to write formatted file output:

```c
#include <stdio.h>

int fprintf(FILE *file_pointer, const char
  *format_specifier, [argument[,...]]);
```

The following program, FPRINTF.C, uses *fprintf* to write formatted output to a file named FPRINTF.DAT:

```c
#include <stdio.h>

void main (void)
  {
    FILE *fp;

    int pages = 892;
    float price = 39.95;

    if (fp = fopen("FPRINTF.DAT", "w"))
      {
        fprintf(fp, "Book Title: Jamsa's 1001 C & C++ Tips\n");
        fprintf(fp, "Pages: %d\n", pages);
        fprintf(fp, "Price: $%5.2f\n", price);
        fclose(fp);
      }
    else
      printf("Error opening FPRINTF.DAT\n");
}
```

Renaming a File

360

As your programs work with files, there may be times when you need to rename or move a file. For such cases, C provides the *rename* function. The format of the *rename* function is as follows:

```
#include <stdio.h>

int rename(const char *old_name, const char *new_name);
```

If *rename* successfully renames or moves a file, the function will return the value 0. If an error occurs, *rename* will return a nonzero value and assign the global variable *errno* one of the following error status values:

Value	Meaning
EACCES	Access denied
ENOENT	File not found
EXDEV	Cannot move from one disk to another

The following program, MY_REN.C, uses the *rename* function to create a program that can rename or move a file specified in the command line:

```
#include <stdio.h>

void main(int argc, char *argv[])
  {
  if (argc < 3)
    printf("Must specify a source and target filename\n");
  else if (rename(argv[1], argv[2]))
    printf("Error renaming file\n");
  }
```

Deleting a File

C 361

When your programs work with files, there will be many times when you may need to delete one or more files. In such cases, your programs can use C's *remove* function. The format of the *remove* function is as follows:

```
#include <stdio.h>

int remove(const char *filename);
```

If the function successfully removes the file, it returns the value 0. If an error occurs, *remove* returns the value –1 and assigns the global value *errno* one of the following values:

Value	Meaning
EACCES	Access denied
ENOENT	File not found

The following program, MY_DEL.C, uses the *remove* function to delete all of the files specified in the command line:

```
#include <stdio.h>

void main(int argc, char *argv[])
  {
    while (*++argv)
      if (remove(*argv))
        printf("Error removing %s\n", *argv);
  }
```

In addition to the *remove* function, most C compilers support the *unlink* function, which also deletes a file:

```
#include <io.h>

int unlink(const char *filename);
```

If *unlink* successfully deletes the file, it returns the value 0. If an error occurs, *unlink* returns the error status –1, assigning to the global variable *errno* the error status constants just listed. The following program, UNLINK.C, uses the *unlink* function to delete the files specified in the program's command line:

```
#include <stdio.h>

void main(int argc, char *argv[])
  {
    while (*++argv)
      if (unlink(*argv))
        printf("Error removing %s\n", *argv);
  }
```

C 362 Determining How a Program Can Access a File

When your program works with files, there may be times when you need to determine if your program can access a specific file as required. The C function *access* checks whether a file exists as specified and if you can open the file as required. The format of the *access* function is as follows:

```
#include <io.h>

int access(const char *filename, int access_mode);
```

The *access_mode* specifies how your program needs to use the file, as shown here:

Value	Meaning
0	Check if file exists
2	Check if file can be written to
4	Check if file can be read
6	Check for read and write permission

If the program can access the file as specified, *access* returns the value 0. If an error occurs, *access* returns the value −1 and assigns the global variable *errno* one of the following error values:

Value	Meaning
EACCES	Access denied
ENOENT	File not found

The following program, ACCESS.C, uses the *access* function to determine how your program can access the file specified in the program's command line:

```c
#include <stdio.h>
#include <io.h>

void main (int argc, char *argv[])
  {
    int access_mode;

    access_mode = access(argv[1], 0);

    if (access_mode)
      printf("File %s does not exist\n");
    else
      {
        access_mode = access(argv[1], 2);

        if (access_mode)
          printf("File cannot be written\n");
        else
          printf("File can be written\n");

        access_mode = access(argv[1], 4);

        if (access_mode)
          printf("File cannot be read\n");
        else
          printf("File can be read\n");

        access_mode = access(argv[1], 6);
```

```
    if (access_mode)
       printf("File cannot be read/write\n");
    else
       printf("File can be read/write\n");
  }
}
```

C 363 Setting a File's Access Mode

When your programs work with files, there will be times when you will want to change a program's read/write access. For example, assume that you have an important data file. To protect the file when the program is not in use, you might set the file to read-only access. In this way, the user cannot accidentally delete the file. When the program starts, you can change the file to read/write access as required. For such cases, your programs can use C's *chmod* function, shown here:

```
#include <sys\stat.h>
#include <io.h>

int chmod(const char *filename, int access_mode);
```

The file header file sys\stat.h defines the following access mode constants:

Value	Meaning
S_IWRITE	Write permission is authorized
S_IREAD	Read permission is authorized

To provide read/write access, perform a bitwise OR of the two constants (S_IWRITE | S_IREAD). If *chmod* successfully changes the file's attributes, it returns the value 0. If an error occurs, *chmod* returns the value –1 and sets the global variable *errno* to one of the following error status values:

Value	Meaning
ENOENT	File not found
EACCES	Permission denied

The following program, READONLY.C, sets the file specified in the command line to read-only access:

```
#include <stdio.h>
#include <sys\stat.h>
#include <io.h>
```

```
void main(int argc, char *argv[])
  {
    if (chmod(argv[1], S_IREAD))
      printf("Error setting %s\n", argv[1]);
  }
```

Better Control of File Attributes

In Tip 363 you learned how to use C's *chmod* function to set a file's read and write attributes. When you use the DOS operating system, you can work with the following attributes:

Value	Meaning
FA_ARCH	Archive attribute
FA_DIREC	Directory attribute
FA_HIDDEN	Hidden attribute
FA_LABEL	Disk volume label
FA_RDONLY	Read-only attribute
FA_SYSTEM	System attribute

Note: *Some compilers name these constants slightly differently. Examine the include file dos.h, provided with your compiler, for the correct constant names.*

To help you work with these attributes, some C compilers provide the *_chmod* function, whose format is shown here:

```
#include <dos.h>
#include <io.h>

int _chmod(const char *filename, int operation
   [,int attribute]);
```

The *operation* tells *_chmod* if you want to set or get the attribute's setting. If operation is set to 0, *_chmod* returns the file's current attributes. If operation is set to 1, *_chmod* sets the attribute specified. The left and right brackets, therefore, indicate that the attributes parameter is optional. If *_chmod* is successful, it returns the file's current attributes. If an error occurs, *_chmod* returns the value –1 and assigns the global variable *errno* one of the following values:

Value	Meaning
ENOENT	File not found
EACCES	Permission denied

The following program, TELLATTR.C, uses *_chmod* to display a file's current attributes:

```
#include <stdio.h>
#include <dos.h>
#include <io.h>

void main(int argc, char *argv[])
 {
   int attributes;

   if ((attributes = _chmod(argv[1], 0)) == -1)
     printf("Error accessing %s\n", argv[1]);
   else
     {
        if (attributes & FA_ARCH)
          printf("Archive ");

        if (attributes & FA_DIREC)
          printf("Directory ");

        if (attributes & FA_HIDDEN)
          printf("Hidden ");

        if (attributes & FA_LABEL)
          printf("Volume label ");

        if (attributes & FA_RDONLY)
          printf("Readonly ");

        if (attributes & FA_SYSTEM)
          printf("System ");
     }
 }
```

Many C compilers also provide the functions _dos_getilefattr_ and _dos_setfileattr_, which let you get or set a file's DOS attributes:

```
#include <dos.h>

int _dos_getfileattr(const char *filename,
  unsigned *attributes);

int _dos_setfileattr(const char *filename,
  unsigned attributes);
```

The function uses the following attribute constants:

Value	Meaning
_A_ARCH	Archive attribute
_A_HIDDEN	Hidden attribute

_A_NORMAL	Normal attribute
_A_RDONLY	Read-only attribute
_A_SUBDIR	Directory attribute
_A_SYSTEM	System attribute
_A_VOLID	Disk volume label

If the *_dos_getfileattr* and *_dos_setfileattr* functions are successful, the functions return the value 0. If an error occurs, the functions return the value –1 and assign the global variable *errno* the value ENOENT (file not found).

As a rule, your programs should only manipulate the archive, read-only, and hidden file attributes, reserving the other attributes for use by DOS. If you are only changing the read-only attribute, use the *chmod* function presented in Tip 363 to increase your program's portability.

Testing for a File Stream Error

C 365

When your programs perform file I/O operations, they should always test the return values of functions such as *fopen*, *fputs*, *fgets*, and so on to verify that the operations were successful. To help your programs perform such testing, C provides the *ferror* macro, which examines an I/O stream for a read or write error. If an error has occurred, *ferror* returns a true value. If no error has occurred, ferror returns false:

```
#include <stdio.h>

int ferror(FILE *stream);
```

Once a file I/O error occurs, the *ferror* macro will remain true until your programs invoke the *clearerr* macro for the given stream:

```
#include <stdio.h>

void clearerr(FILE *stream);
```

The following program, FERROR.C, reads and displays a file's contents to the screen. After each I/O operation, the program tests for an error. If an error occurs, the program ends, displaying an error message to stderr:

```
#include <stdio.h>
#include <stdlib.h>

void main (int argc, char *argv[])
  {
    FILE *fp;

    char line[256];
```

```
     if (fp = fopen(argv[1], "r"))
       {
         while (fgets(line, sizeof(line), fp))
           {
             if (ferror(fp))
               {
                 fprintf(stderr, "Error reading from %s\n",argv[1]);
                 exit(1);
               }
             else
               {
                 fputs(line, stdout);
                 if (ferror(fp))
                   {
                     fprintf(stderr, "Error writing to stdout\n");
                     exit(1);
                   }
               }
           }
       }
     else
       printf("Error opening %s\n", argv[1]);
}
```

C 366 Determining a File's Size

As your programs perform file I/O operations, there may be times when you need to determine a file's size in bytes. For such cases, you can use C's *filelength* function. The *filelength* function returns a long value. You must pass the program a file handle, not a file pointer:

```
#include <io.h>

long filelength(int file_handle);
```

If *filelength* is successful, it returns the file size in bytes. If an error occurs, *filelength* will return the value −1 and set the global variable *errno* to EBADF (bad file number). The following program, FILELEN.C, displays the size of a given file to the screen display:

```
#include <stdio.h>
#include <io.h>
#include <fcntl.h>
#include <sys\stat.h>

void main (int argc, char *argv[])
```

```
{
  int file_handle;

  long file_size;

  if ((file_handle = open(argv[1], O_RDONLY)) == -1)
    printf("Error opening the file %d\n", argv[1]);
  else
    {
      file_size = filelength(file_handle);
      printf("The file size in bytes is %ld\n", file_size);
      close(file_handle);
    }
}
```

Flushing an I/O Stream

C 367

To improve your program performance, the C run-time library normally buffers your file output until it has a complete buffer (normally a disk sector) to write to disk, or until you close the file. In this way, the run-time library reduces the number of slow disk I/O operations. Unfortunately, when your programs perform such a buffer, they leave open the door for losing data. When your program performs a function such as *fputs* to write output and the function does not return an error, the program assumes the data has been correctly recorded to disk. In actuality, however, the data still may reside in your computer's memory. If the user should turn off the computer, the data will be lost! If you have a program for which you must ensure that data is actually written to disk, you can use *fflush* to direct the run-time library to write the data from its buffer in memory to disk. The format of the *fflush* function is as follows:

```
#include <stdio.h>

int fflush(FILE *file_stream);
```

If *fflush* is successful, it returns the value 0. If an error occurs, *fflush* returns the constant EOF. The following statements illustrate how you can use *fflush* to empty the file buffer to disk following each output operation:

```
while (fgets(line, sizeof(line), input_file))
  {
    fputs(line, output_file);
    fflush(output_file);
  }
```

Note: *When you use the fflush function, you direct the C run-time library to invoke an operating system service to write the data to disk. If the operating system performs its own buffering (called a disk cache), the operating system may place your data into its memory buffer, as opposed to disk. Depending on the disk-caching software, you may be able to invoke another system service to flush the output.*

C 368 Closing All Open Files in One Step

Before your programs end, you should use the *fclose* function to close your open files. Assume that you have a function that performs a critical operation. If the function experiences an error, the program should immediately end. Unfortunately, the function might not be aware of the open files. In such cases, your program can use C's *fcloseall* function to close all open functions:

```
#include <stdio.h>

int fcloseall(void);
```

If *fcloseall* is successful, it returns the number of files it successfully closed. If an error occurs, *fcloseall* returns the EOF constant. The following statements illustrate how you might use *fcloseall*:

```
if (error_status == CRITICAL)
  {
    fprintf(stderr, "Critical device error\n");
    fcloseall();
    exit(1);
  }
```

C 369 Getting a File Stream's File Handle

When your programs perform file operations, they can perform high-level operations using file streams (FILE *stream). You can also use low-level file handles (int handle). As you have learned, several of C's run-time library functions require file handles. If your program is using file streams, you can close the file and reopen it using a file handle, or you can obtain a file handle using C's *fileno* function:

```
#include <stdio.h>

int fileno(FILE *stream);
```

The following program, FILENO.C, uses the *fileno* function to get the file handle for an open file stream:

```
#include <stdio.h>
#include <io.h>

void main (int argc, char *argv[])
  {
    FILE *stream;

    int handle;

    long file_length;

    if (stream = fopen(argv[1], "r"))
      {
        // Some statements
        handle = fileno(stream);
        file_length = filelength(handle);
        printf("The file length is %ld\n", file_length);
        fclose(stream);
      }
    else
      printf("Error opening %s\n", argv[1]);
  }
```

Creating a Temporary Filename Using *P_tmpdir*

370

As your programs perform file I/O operations, there may be many times when your programs will need open one or more temporary files or write output to a nonexistent file on disk. In such cases, the difficulty often becomes determining a unique filename, so that the program does not overwrite an existing file. To help your programs generate a unique filename, you can use the *tmpnam* function:

```
#include <stdio.h>

char *tmpnam(char *buffer);
```

If your program passes a buffer to *tmpnam*, the function will assign the temporary name to the buffer. If you invoke *tmpnam* with NULL, *tmpnam* will allocate memory for the filename, returning to the program a pointer to the start of the filename. The *tmpnam* function examines the *P_tmpdir* entry in the stdio.h header file. If *P_tmpdir* is defined, *tmpnam* will create the unique filename in the corresponding directory. Otherwise, *tmpnam* will create the file in the current directory. Note that *tmpnam* does actually create the file, but rather, it returns a filename that your program can use with *fopen* or *open*. The following program, TMPNAM.C, illustrates the use of the *tmpname* function:

```
#include <stdio.h>

void main (void)
  {
    char buffer[64];

    int counter;

    for (counter = 0; counter < 5; counter++)
      printf("Temporary filename %s\n", tmpnam(buffer));
  }
```

C 371 Creating a Temporary Filename Using TMP or TEMP

As your programs perform file I/O operations, there may be many times when your programs will need open one or more temporary files or write output to a nonexistent file on disk. In such cases, the difficulty often becomes determining a unique filename, so that the program does not overwrite an existing file. To help your programs generate a unique filename, you can use the *tempnam* function:

```
#include <stdio.h>

char *tempnam(char *buffer, char *prefix);
```

If your program passes a buffer to *tempnam*, the function will assign the temporary name to the buffer. If you invoke *tempnam* with NULL, *tempnam* will allocate memory for the filename, returning to the program a pointer to the start of the filename. The *prefix* parameter lets you define a set of characters that you want *tempnam* to place at the start of each filename. The *tempnam* function examines the environment entries to determine if a TMP or TEMP entry exists. If TMP or TEMP is defined, *tempnam* will create the unique filename in the corresponding directory. Otherwise, *tempnam* will create the file in the current directory. Note that *tempnam* does actually create the file, but rather, it returns a filename that your program can use with *fopen* or *open*. The following program, TEMPNAM.C, illustrates the use of the *tempnam* function:

```
#include <stdio.h>

void main (void)
  {
    char buffer[64];

    int counter;

    printf("Temporary filename %s\n", tempnam(buffer, "1001"));
  }
```

Creating a Truly Temporary File

C 372

In Tips 370 and 371 you learned how to use the *tmpnam* and *tempnam* functions to generate temporary filenames. As you learned, *tmpnam* and *tempnam* do not actually create a file, but rather they simply return a filename that is not currently in use. As it turns out, C also provides a function named *tmpfile* that determines a unique filename and then opens the file, returning a file pointer to the program:

```
#include <stdio.h>

FILE *tmpfile(void);
```

If it is successful, *tmpfile* opens the file in read/write mode, returning a file pointer. If an error occurs, *tmpfile* returns NULL. The file *tmpfile* returns is truly a temporary file. When your program ends (or calls *rmtmp*), the file is deleted, and its contents discarded. The following statements illustrate how your program might use the *tmpfile* function:

```
FILE *temp_file;

if (temp_file = tmpfile())
  {
    // Temporary file successfully opened
    // Statements that use the file
  }
else
  printf("Error opening temporary file\n");
```

373 Removing Temporary Files

In Tip 372 you learned that the *tmpfile* function lets your programs create a temporary file, whose contents exist only for the duration of the program's execution. Depending on your programs, there may be times when you want to discard temporary files before the program ends. In such cases, your program can use the *rmtmp* function, whose format is shown here:

```
#include <stdio.h>

int rmtmp(void);
```

If *rmtmp* is successful, it returns the number of files it successfully closed and deleted.

374 Searching the Command Path for a File

When you work within the DOS environment, the PATH command defines the directories that DOS searches for EXE, COM, and BAT files when you execute an external command. Because the subdirectories defined in the PATH normally contain your most commonly used commands, there may be times when you want a program to search the PATH subdirectory entries for a data file. For such cases, some compilers provide the *searchpath* function. You invoke the function with the desired filename. If *searchpath* successfully locates the file, it returns a complete pathname to the file that your programs can use within *fopen*. If the file is not found, *searchpath* returns NULL:

```
#include <dir.h>

char *searchpath(const char *filename);
```

The following program, SRCHPATH.C, illustrates the use of the *searchpath* function to search for the specified filename:

```
#include <stdio.h>
#include <dir.h>

void main (int argc, char *argv[])
 {
   char *path;

   if (path = searchpath(argv[1]))
     printf("Pathname: %s\n", path);
```

```
    else
      printf("File not found\n");
  }
```

Note: *The searchpath function searches the current directory for the specified file before searching the command path subdirectories.*

Searching an Environment Entry's Subdirectory List for a File

C 375

In Tip 374 you used the *searchpath* function to search directories in the command path for a specified file. In a similar way, there may be times when you want to search the directories specified in a different environment entry for a file. For example, many C compilers define LIB and INCLUDE entries that specify the location of library files (with the lib extension) and header files (with the h extension). To search the directories such entries specify, you can use the *_searchenv* function:

```
#include <dos.h>

char *_searchenv(const char *filename, const char
  *environment_entry, *pathname);
```

The *_searchenv* function searches the directories specified in the *environment_entry* for the specified filename. If the filename is found, *_searchenv* assigns the file's pathname to the pathname character string buffer, returning a pointer to the pathname. If the file is not found, *_searchenv* returns NULL. The following program, SRCH_ENV.C, uses the *_searchenv* function to search the subdirectories specified in the LIB entry for a specified file:

```
#include <stdio.h>
#include <stdlib.h>

void main (int argc, char *argv[])
  {
    char path[128];

    _searchenv(argv[1], "LIB", path);

    if (path[0])
      printf("Pathname: %s\n", path);
    else
      printf("File not found\n");
  }
```

Note: *The _searchenv function searches the current directory for the specified file before searching the environment entry's subdirectories.*

C 376 Opening Files in the TEMP Directory

As you know, many programs create their temporary files in the subdirectory specified in by the TEMP environment entry. Within your programs you can easily create your own files within the TEMP directory (if it is defined) by using the *getenv* function. The following statements illustrate how your programs can open a file named TEMPDATA.DAT within the TEMP directory:

```
char pathname[_MAX_PATH];

strcpy(pathname, getenv("TEMP"));

if (pathname[0])
  strcat(pathname, "\\TEMPDATA.DAT");
else
  strcat(pathname, "TEMPDATA.DAT");

if (fp = fopen(pathname, "w"))
```

In this case, if the TEMP entry exists, the program opens the file in the corresponding subdirectory. If the entry is not defined, the program opens the file in the current directory. Note that the code fragment assumes that the TEMP variable does not contain a value that ends with a backslash.. Ideally, your programs will test TEMP's current value and process accordingly.

C 377 Minimize File I/O Operations

Compared to the fast electronic speed of your computer's CPU and memory, the mechanical disk is very slow. As a result, you should try to minimize the number of disk I/O operations your programs must perform. With respect to file operations, the file open is probably the most time consuming. Therefore, you should always examine your programs to make sure you don't open and close a file unnecessarily or repeatedly open a file from within a loop. For example, consider the following statements:

```
while (menu_choice != QUIT)
  {
    if (fp = fopen("DATABASE.DAT", "r"))
      {
        // Get customer name
        get_customer(name);
```

```
            // Search file for customer info
            search_customer_info(name, fp, data_buffer);

            fclose(fp);
        }
    else
        {
            file_open_error("Aborting...");
        }

    menu_choice = get_menu_choice();
    }
```

The statements repeatedly loop, getting customer information until the user selects the QUIT option. Note that the *fopen* function call occurs within the loop. As such, the program repeatedly performs the slow disk I/O operation. To improve the system's performance, the program should pull the fopen outside of the loop. If the *search_customer* function needs to start at the beginning of the file, the program can rewind the file, as shown here:

```
if (fp = fopen("DATABASE.DAT", "r"))
    file_open_error("Aborting...");

while (menu_choice != QUIT)
    {
        // Get customer name
        get_customer(name);

        rewind(fp);

        // Search file for customer info
        search_customer_info(name, fp, data_buffer);

        menu_choice = get_menu_choice();
    }

fclose(fp);
```

Be Aware of Backslashes (\) in Directory Names

C378

Several of the tips presented in this section work with directory names. For example, the *chdir* function lets your programs select a specific directory. When your program specifies a directory name as a constant value, make sure you use double backslashes (\\) within pathnames as required. The following *chdir* function call, for example, tries to select the subdirectory DOS:

```
status = chdir("\DOS");
```

When you use a backslash character within a C string, remember that C treats the backslash character as a special symbol. When the C compiler encounters the backslash, it checks the character that follows to determine if it character is a special symbol and, if so, replaces the characters with the correct ASCII counterparts. If the character that follows the backslash is not a special symbol, the C compiler ignores the backslash character. As such, the previous *chdir* function would try to select the directory DOS as opposed to \\DOS. The correct function invocation in this case would be as follows:

```
status = chdir("\\DOS");
```

C 379 Changing the Current Directory

As your programs execute, there may be times when they need to change the current directory. To help you perform such operations, most C compilers provide the *chdir* function. The *chdir* function is very similar to the DOS CHDIR command, if you invoke the function with a string that does not contain a disk drive letter, *chdir* looks for the directory on the current drive. The following function call, for example, selects the directory DATA on drive C:

```
status = chdir("C:\\DATA");   // Note the use of \\
```

In a similar way, the following command selects the directory BORLANDC on the current drive:

```
status = chdir("\\BORLANDC");
```

If the *chdir* function is successful, it returns the value 0. If the directory does not exist, *chdir* returns the value −1 and sets the global variable *errno* to the constant ENOENT. The following program, NEWCHDIR.C, implements the DOS CHDIR command:

```
#include <stdio.h>
#include <stdlib.h>
#include <dir.h>
#include <errno.h>

void main (int argc, char *argv[])
  {
    char directory[MAXPATH];

    if (argc == 1)  // Display the current directory
```

```
    {
      getcwd(directory, MAXPATH);
      puts(directory);
    }
  else if ((chdir(argv[1])) && (errno == ENOENT))
    puts("Invalid directory");
}
```

Note: *Some compilers define the symbol _MAX_PATH in the include file direct.h, as opposed to using MAX_PATH.*

Creating a Directory

As your programs execute, there may be times when they need to create a directory. To help your programs do so, most C compilers provide a *mkdir* function. The *mkdir* function is very similar to the DOS MKDIR command, if you invoke the function with a string that does not contain a disk drive letter, mkdir creates the directory on the current drive. The following function call, for example, creates the directory DATA on drive C:

```
status = mkdir("C:\\DATA");  // Note the use of \\
```

In a similar way, the following command creates the directory TEMPDATA on the current drive, in the current directory:

```
status = mkdir("TEMPDATA");
```

If the *mkdir* function is successful, it returns the value 0. If the directory cannot be created, *mkdir* returns the value −1.

Removing a Directory

As your programs execute, there may be times when they need to create or remove a directory. To help your programs remove a directory, most C compilers provide a *rmdir* function. The *rmdir* function is very similar to the DOS RMDIR command; if you invoke the function with a string that does not contain a disk drive letter, *rmdir* creates the directory on the current drive. The following function call, for example, removes the directory DATA from drive C:

```
status = rmdir("C:\\DATA");  // Note the use of \\
```

In a similar way, the following command removes the directory TEMPDATA from the current drive and directory:

```
status = rmdir ("TEMPDATA");
```

If the *mkdir* function is successful, it returns the value 0. If the directory does not exist or cannot be removed, *mkdir* returns the value –1 and assigns the global variable *errno* one of the following values:

Value	Meaning
EACCES	Access denied
ENOENT	No such directory

C 382 Removing a Directory Tree

Beginning with version 6, DOS introduces DELTREE command, which lets you delete a directory, its files, and any subdirectories within the directory in one step. If you are not using DOS 6, you can create your own DELTREE command using the program DELTREE.C, shown here:

```
#include <dos.h>
#include <stdio.h>
#include <stdlib.h>
#include <direct.h>
#include <malloc.h>
#include <string.h>

void main (int argc, char **argv)
 {
   void delete_tree(void);

   char buffer[128];

   char drive[_MAX_DRIVE], directory[_MAX_DIR],
     filename[_MAX_FNAME], ext[_MAX_EXT];

   if (argc < 2)
     {
       printf ("Syntax error\n");
       exit(0);
```

```
   _splitpath (argv[1], drive, directory, filename, ext)
   getcwd (buffer, sizeof(buffer));

   if (drive[0] == NULL)
     {
       _splitpath (buffer, drive, directory, filename, ext);
       strcpy (buffer, directory);
       strcat (buffer, filename);
       strcat (buffer, ext);
     }
   else
     {
       printf ("Do not specify drive letter\n");
       exit (1);
     }

   if (strcmpi(buffer, argv[1]) == 0)
     {
       printf ("Cannot delete current directory\n");
       exit (1);
     }

   getcwd (directory, 64);

   if (chdir (argv[1]))
     printf ("Invalid directory %s\n", argv[1]);
   else
     delete_tree ();

   chdir (directory);
   rmdir (argv[1]);
 }

union REGS inregs, outregs;
struct SREGS segs;

void delete_tree(void)
 {
   struct find_t fileinfo;

   int result;

   char far *buffer;
```

```c
   unsigned dta_seg, dta_ofs;

    result = _dos_findfirst("*.*", 16, &fileinfo);

 inregs.h.ah = 0x2f;
 intdosx (&inregs, &outregs, &segs);
 dta_seg = segs.es;
 dta_ofs = outregs.x.bx;

 while (! result)
   {
     if ((fileinfo.attrib & 16) && (fileinfo.name[0] != '.'))
       {
          buffer = _fmalloc (256);
          if (buffer == NULL)
            {
               printf ("Insufficient memory\n");
               exit(1);
            }
          inregs.h.ah = 0x1A;
          inregs.x.dx = FP_SEG(buffer);
          segread(&segs);
          intdosx (&inregs, &outregs, &segs);

          chdir (fileinfo.name);
          delete_tree();
            chdir ("..");

          inregs.h.ah = 0x1A;
          inregs.x.dx = dta_ofs;
          segs.ds = dta_seg;
          _ffree (buffer);
          rmdir (fileinfo.name);
       }
     else if (fileinfo.name[0] != '.')
       {
          _dos_setfileattr(fileinfo.name, 0);
          remove (fileinfo.name);
       }

      result = _dos_findnext (&fileinfo);
   }
}
```

Building a Full Pathname

C 383

When your programs work with files and directories, there may be times when you need to know the file's complete (full) pathname. For example, if the current directory is DATA and the current drive is C, the full name of the file REPORT.DAT is C:\DATA\REPORT.DAT. To help you resolve a file's full name, some C compilers provide a function named *fullpath*. The function uses three parameters, a buffer into which the full pathname is placed, the name to resolve, and the maximum number of characters the buffer can hold:

```
name_ptr = _fullpath (buffer, filename, _MAX_PATH);
```

If the value of buffer parameter is NULL, *fullpath* will allocate the memory used to hold the full pathname. If *fullpath* can successfully resolve the filename, it will return a pointer to the buffer. If an error occurs, the function returns NULL. The following program, FULLNAME.C, illustrates the use of the *fullname* function:

```c
#include <stdio.h>
#include <stdlib.h>

void main (void)
 {
   char *file = "FILENAME.EXT";

   char *full_name = NULL;

   if (full_name = _fullpath(NULL, file, _MAX_PATH))
     {
       printf ("Full name for %s is %s\n", file, full_name);
       free (full_name);
     }
   else
     {
       printf("Unable to allocate memory for the full name\n");
       exit (1);
     }
 }
```

Note: *Some compilers use the include file direct.h, as opposed to dir.h.*

C 384 Parsing a Directory Path

As your programs work with files and directories, there may be times when you need to parse a pathname into a disk drive letter, subdirectory path, filename and extension. To help you parse a pathname, some C compilers provide *_splitpath* function. The format of the function call is as follows:

```
_splitpath (path, drive, subdirectory, filename, ext);
```

The following program, SPLIT.C, illustrates the use of the *_splitpath* function:

```c
#include <stdio.h>
#include <dir.h>
#include <stdlib.h>

void main (void)
  {
    char *path_1 = "C:\\SUBDIR\\FILENAME.EXT";
    char *path_2 = "SUBDIR\\FILENAME.EXT";
    char *path_3 = "FILENAME.EXE";

    char subdir[_MAX_DIR];
    char drive[_MAX_DRIVE];
    char filename[_MAX_FNAME];
    char extension[_MAX_EXT];

    _splitpath (path_1, drive, subdir, filename, extension);
    printf ("Splitting %s\n", path_1);
    printf ("Drive %s Subdir %s Filename %s Extension %s\n",
      drive, subdir, filename, extension);

    _splitpath (path_2, drive, subdir, filename, extension);
    printf ("Splitting %s\n", path_2);
    printf ("Drive %s Subdir %s Filename %s Extension %s\n",
      drive, subdir, filename, extension);

    _splitpath (path_3, drive, subdir, filename, extension);
    printf ("Splitting %s\n", path_3);
    printf ("Drive %s Subdir %s Filename %s Extension %s\n",
      drive, subdir, filename, extension);

  }
```

Note the use of the constants to define the proper buffer sizes. When you compile and execute this program, your screen will display the following:

```
Splitting C:\SUBDIR\FILENAME.EXT
Drive C: Subdir \SUBDIR\ Filename FILENAME Extension .EXT
Splitting SUBDIR\FILENAME.EXT
Drive  Subdir SUBDIR\ Filename FILENAME Extension .EXT
Splitting FILENAME.EXE
Drive  Subdir  Filename FILENAME Extension .EXE
```

Building a Pathname

C 385

As you work with files and directories within your programs, there may be times when you need to combine a disk drive letter, subdirectory, filename, and extension into a complete pathname. To help you perform such operations, some C compilers provide the _makepath_ function. The format of the _makepath_ function is as follows:

```
_makepath(pathname, drive, subdir, filename, ext);
```

The following program, MAKEPATH.C, illustrates the use of the _makepath_ function:

```c
#include <stdio.h>
#include <stdlib.h>

void main (void)
 {
   char pathname[_MAX_PATH];

   char *drive = "C:";
   char *subdir = "\\SUBDIR";
   char *filename = "FILENAME";
   char *extension = "EXT";

   _makepath(pathname, drive, subdir, filename, extension);

   printf("The complete pathname is %s\n", pathname);
 }
```

When you compile and execute this program, your screen will display the following output:

```
The complete pathname is C:\SUBDIR\FILENAME.EXT
```

C 386 Opening and Closing a File Using Low-Level Functions

C supports high-level file I/O operations that work with file streams and low-level operations that work with byte ranges. When you perform low-level I/O, you open an existing file using the *open* function. To close the file later, you use *close*:

```
#include <fcntl.h>
#include <sys\stat.h>

int open(const char *path, int access_mode
  [,creation_mode]);

int close(int handle);
```

If *open* successfully opens the file, it returns a handle to the file. If an error occurs, *open* returns −1 and sets the global variable *errno* to one of the values listed in Table 386.1:

Value	Meaning
ENOENT	No such file or directory entry
EMFILE	Too many open files
EACCES	Access permission denied
EINVACC	Invalid access code

Table 386.1 *Error status codes assigned to errno by open.*

The *path* parameter is a character string that contains the name of the desired file. The *access_mode* parameter specifies how you want the file to be used. The access_mode value can be a combination (by ORing) of the values listed in Table 386.2.

Access Mode	Meaning
O_RDONLY	Read-only access
O_WRONLY	Write-only access
O_RDWR	Read and write access
O_NDELAY	Delay value used by UNIX
O_APPEND	Positions pointer for append operations
O_TRUNC	Truncates an existing file's contents
O_EXCL	If O_CREAT is specified and the file already exists, an error is returned
O_BINARY	Open file in binary mode
O_TEXT	Open file in text mode

Table 386.2 *Access mode values used by open.*

By default, *open* will not create an output file if the file does not exist. If you want *open* to create files, you must include the *O_CREAT* flag in the desired access modes. If you specify *O_CREAT*, the *creation_mode* parameter lets you specify the mode with which you want the file created. The *creation_mode* parameter can use a combination of the values specified in Table 386.3.

Creation Mode	Meaning
S_IWRITE	Create for write operations
S_IREAD	Create for read operations

Table 386.3 *Creation mode values used by open.*

The following statement illustrates how to use *open* to open the root directory file CONFIG.SYS for read-only operations:

```
if ((handle = open("\\CONFIG.SYS", O_RDONLY)) == -1)
    printf("Error opening the file \\CONFIG.SYS\n");
else
    // Statements
```

If you want to open the file OUTPUT.DAT for write operations and you want *open* to create the file if it does not exist, use *open* as follows:

```
if ((handle = open("\\CONFIG.SYS", O_RDONLY |
    O_CREAT, S_IWRITE)) == -1)
    printf("Error opening the file \\CONFIG.SYS\n");
else
    // Statements
```

When you have finished using a file, you should close it using the *close* function, as shown here:

```
close(handle);
```

Creating a File

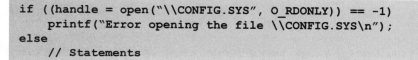

In Tip 386 you learned that by default, the *open* function does not create a file if the file does not exist. As you learned, however, by specifying *O_CREAT* in the access mode, you can direct *open* to create a file. If you are using an older compiler, the *open* function might not support *O_CREAT*. As a result, you may need to use the *creat* function:

```
#include <sys\stat.h>

int creat(const char *path, int creation_mode);
```

As before, the path parameter specifies the file you want to create. The *creation_mode* parameter can contain a combination of the following values:

Mode	Meaning
S_IWRITE	Create for write operations
S_IREAD	Create for read operations

If *creat* is successful, it will return a handle to the file. If an error occurs, *creat* will return the value −1 and assign an error status value to the global variable *errno*. The mode of translation (binary or text) that *creat* uses depends on the setting of the *_fmode* global variable. If a file with the name specified already exists, *creat* will truncate the file's contents. The following statement illustrates how to use *creat* to create the file OUTPUT.DAT:

```
if ((handle = creat("OUTPUT.DAT", S_IWRITE)) == -1)
    printf("Error creating file\n");
else
    // Statements
```

Note: *If you want it to be obvious to another programmer that you are creating a file, you might want to use the creat function, as opposed to opening with the O_CREAT flag.*

388 Performing Low-Level Read and Write Operations

When you perform low-level file I/O operations using file handles, you open and close files using the *open* and *close* functions. In a similar way, you read and write files using *read* and *write*:

```
#include <io.h>

int read(int handle, void *buffer, unsigned length);
int write(int handle, void *buffer, unsigned length);
```

The *handle* parameter is the handle returned from the *open* or *creat* functions. The *buffer* parameter is the data buffer into which information is read or from which data is written. The *length* parameter specifies the number of bytes to be read or written (the maximum is 65,534). If *read* is successful, it returns the number of bytes read. If the end of file is encountered, *read* returns 0, and on an error, *read* returns −1 and sets the global variable *errno* to one of the following:

Value	Meaning
EACCES	Invalid access
EBADF	Invalid file handle

If *write* is successful, it returns the number of bytes written. If an error occurs, *write* returns the value −1 and assigns the global variable *errno* one of the values previously shown. The following loop illustrates how you might use *read* and *write* to copy the contents of one file to another:

```
while ((bytes_read = read(input, buffer, sizeof(buffer))
   write(output, buffer, bytes_read);
```

Testing for the End of a File

389

In Tip 388 you learned that the *read* function returns the value 0 when it encounters EOF. Depending on your program, there may be times when you want to test for the end of file before performing a specific operation. When you use file handles, the *eof* function returns the value 1 if the end of the file has been reached, 0 if the pointer is not at the end of the file, and −1 if the file handle is invalid:

```
#include <io.h.

int eof(int handle);
```

The following statements modify the code shown in Tip 388 to use *eof* to test for the end of the input file:

```
while (! eof(input))
  {
     bytes_read = read(input, buffer, sizeof(buffer));
       write(output, buffer, bytes_read);
  }
```

Putting the Low-Level File Routines to Work

390

Several of the tips in this section have discussed C's low-level file I/O routines. To help you better understand each routine's use, consider the following program, LOWCOPY.C, which uses the functions to copy the contents of the first file specified in the command line to the second:

```
#include <stdio.h>
#include <io.h>
#include <fcntl.h>
#include <sys\types.h>
#include <sys\stat.h>
```

```
void main(int argc, char *argv[])
 {
    int source, target; // file handles
    char buffer[1024];   // I/O buffer
    int bytes_read;

    if (argc < 3)
      fprintf(stderr, "Must specify source and target files\n");
    else if ((source = open(argv[1], O_BINARY | O_RDONLY))==-1)
      fprintf(stderr, "Error opening %s\n", argv[1]);
    else if ((target = open(argv[2], O_WRONLY | O_BINARY |
          O_TRUNC | O_CREAT, S_IWRITE)) == -1)
        fprintf(stderr, "Error opening %s\n", argv[2]);
    else
      {
        while (!eof(source))
         {
            if ((bytes_read = read(source, buffer,
                sizeof(buffer))) <= 0)
              fprintf(stderr, "Error reading from source file");
            else if (write(target, buffer, bytes_read) !=
                bytes_read)
              fprintf(stderr, "Error writing to target file");
         }

        close(source);
        close(target);
      }
 }
```

C 391   Specifying the Mode for a File-Handle Translation

As you have learned, C translates a file's contents using either binary or text translation. Unless you specify otherwise, C uses the setting in the *_fmode* global variable to determine the translation type: *O_BINARY* or *O_TEXT*. When you open or create a file using C's low-level routines, you can specify the file's translation mode. In some cases, there may be times when your program needs to specify the translation mode after a file has been opened. To specify the mode, you can use the *setmode* function:

```
#include <fcntl.h>

int setmode(int handle, int translation_mode);
```

If *setmode* is successful, it returns the previous translation mode. If an error occurs, *setmode* returns −1 and sets the global variable *errno* to *EINVAL* (invalid argument). The following statement, for example, sets the file associated with the handle *output* to text translation:

```
if ((old_mode = setmode(output, O_TEXT)) == -1)
    printf("Error changing file mode\n");
```

Positioning the File Pointer Using *lseek*

392

As you work with C's low-level file I/O functions, there may be times when you want to position the file pointer to a specific location within the file before you perform a read or write operation. To do so, you can use the *lseek* function:

```
#include <io.h>

long lseek(int handle, long offset, int relative_to)
```

The *handle* parameter specifies the file pointer you want to position. The *offset* and *relative_to* parameters combine to specify the desired position. The *offset* contains the a byte offset into the file. The *relative_to* parameter specifies the location in the file from which the offset should be applied. Table 392 specifies the values you can use for the *relative_to* parameter.

Constant	Meaning
SEEK_CUR	From current file position
SEEK_SET	From the beginning of the file
SEEK_END	From the end of the file

Table 392 *File positions from which an offset can be applied.*

To position the file pointer at the end of a file, for example, you can use *lseek* as follows:

```
lseek(handle, 0, SEEK_END);  // At end of file
```

If successful, *lseek* returns the value 0. If an error occurs, *lseek* returns a nonzero value.

C 393 Opening More Than 20 Files

As you have learned, a file handle is an integer value that identifies an open file. Actually, a file handle is an index into the process file table, which contains entries for up to 20 files. If your program needs to open more than 20 files, the easiest way to do is to use the DOS file services. To begin, your program must request support for more than 20 files. To do so, use the DOS INT 21H function 67H to increase the number of file handles. When you do so, DOS will allocate a table large enough to hold the number of handles specified (up to 255—the number of handles currently in use). Next, your program should open the files using the DOS services, as opposed to the C run-time library. In this way, your program can bypass the compiler's file limit. The following code fragment increases the number of file handles to 75:

```
inregs.h.ah = 0x67;
inregs.x.bx = 75;    // Number of handles
intdos(&inregs, &outregs);

if (outregs.x.ax)
  printf("Error allocating handles\n");
```

C 394 Using DOS-Based File Services

As discussed in the DOS and BIOS section of this book, DOS provides a collection of services that let you open, read, write, and close files. To make these services easier to use from within C, many C compilers provide the functions listed in Table 394.

Function	Purpose
_dos_creat	Creates a file returning a file handle
_dos_close	Closes a specified file
_dos_open	Opens a file, returing a file handle
_dos_read	Reads the specified number of bytes from a file
_dos_write	Writes the specified number of bytes to a file

Table 394 *Functions that use the DOS file system services.*

To help you better understand these services, consider the following program, DOSCOPY.C, which copies the contents of the first file specified in the command line to the second:

```
#include <stdio.h>
#include <dos.h>
#include <fcntl.h>
void main(int argc, char *argv[])
{
   char buffer[1024];

   int input, output;                   /* file handles */
   unsigned bytes_read, bytes_written;  /* actual number of bytes
                                           transferred */

   if (argc < 3)
     fprintf(stderr, "Must specify source and target file\n");
   else if (_dos_open (argv[1], O_RDONLY, &input))
     fprintf(stderr, "Error opening source file\n");
   else if (_dos_creat (argv[2], 0, &output))
     fprintf(stderr, "Error opening target file\n");
   else
     {
        while (!_dos_read(input, buffer, sizeof(buffer),
          &bytes_read))
          {
            if (bytes_read == 0)
                break;
            _dos_write(output, buffer, bytes_read, &bytes_written);
          }

        _dos_close(input);
        _dos_close(output);
     }
}
```

Note: *Although the DOS-based file routines are very similar to C's low-level file functions, you will increase your programs' portability by using the C's open, read, and write functions, as opposed to the DOS-based functions. Most C compilers, support C's low-level functions.*

Obtaining a File's Date and Time Stamp

C 395

When you perform a directory listing, the DOS DIR command displays each file's name, extension, size, and the date and time the file was created or last changed. The date and time DOS stores for the file is called the file's *date and time stamp*. DOS only changes the date and time stamp when you make changes to the file. Some operating systems, on the other hand, track the date and time the file was created or last modified, as well as the date and time the file was last used (read). The operating systems refer to this second date and time stamp as the *last access time*. Depending on your program's purpose, there may be times when you need to know a file's date and time stamp. Therefore, most compilers provide the *_dos_getftime* function:

```
#include <dos.h>

unsigned _dos_getftime(int handle, unsigned *datefield,
    unsigned *timefield);
```

If the function successfully sets the file's date and time stamp, the function returns the value 0. If an error occurs, the function returns a nonzero value and assigns the global variable *errno* the value EBADF (invalid handle). The *handle* parameter is an open file handle to the desired file. The *datefield* and *timefield* parameters are pointers to unsigned integer values whose bits mean the following:

Date Bits	Meaning
0–4	Day from 1 through 31
5–8	Month from 1 through 12
9–15	Years since 1980

Time Bits	Meaning
0–4	Seconds divided by 2 (1 through 30)
5–10	Minutes from 1 through 60
11–15	Hours from 1 through 12

The following program, FILEDT.C, uses the *_dos_getftime* function to display the date and time stamp of the file specified in the command line:

```
#include <stdio.h>
#include <dos.h>
#include <fcntl.h>

void main(int argc, char *argv[])
{
    unsigned date, time;
    int handle;

    if (_dos_open(argv[1], O_RDONLY, &handle))
        fprintf(stderr, "Error opening source file\n");
    else
       {
        if (_dos_getftime(handle, &date, &time))
          printf("Error getting date/time stamp\n");
```

```
        else
          printf("%s last modified %02d-%02d-%d %02d:%02d:%02d\n",
                argv[1],
                (date & 0x1E0) >> 5,   /* month */
                (date & 0x1F),         /* day */
                (date >> 9) + 1980,    /* year */
                (time >> 11),          /* hours */
                (time & 0x7E0) >> 5,   /* minutes */
                (time & 0x1F) * 2);    /* seconds */
        _dos_close(handle);
    }
}
```

As you can see, the program uses C's bitwise operators to extract the date and time fields. In Tip 396 you will learn how to perform similar processing using structure bit fields.

Obtaining a File's Date and Time Using Bit Fields

C 396

In Tip 395 you used the function *_dos_getftime* to obtain a file's date and time stamp. As you learned, the function encodes the date and time fields as bits within two unsigned values. To extract the field values, the program FILEDT.C, used C's bitwise operators. To make your program easier to understand, you might consider using bit fields within a structure. The following program, DTBITS.C, does just that:

```
#include <stdio.h>
#include <dos.h>
#include <fcntl.h>

void main(int argc, char *argv[])
{
    struct Date {
      unsigned int day:5;
      unsigned int month:4;
      unsigned int years:7;
    } date;

    struct Time {
      unsigned seconds:5;
      unsigned minutes:6;
      unsigned hours:5;
    } time;

    int handle;
```

```
    if (_dos_open(argv[1], O_RDONLY, &handle))
        fprintf(stderr, "Error opening source file\n");
    else
     {
        if (_dos_getftime(handle, &date, &time))
          printf("Error getting date and time stamp\n");
        else
          printf("%s last modified %02d-%02d-%d %02d:%02d:%02d\n",
            argv[1],
            date.month,             /* month */
            date.day,               /* day */
            date.years + 1980,      /* year */
            time.hours,             /* hours */
            time.minutes,           /* minutes */
            time.seconds * 2);      /* seconds */
        _dos_close(handle);
     }
}
```

By using bit fields, the program eliminates the need for other programmers to understand the complicated bitwise operations that occurred in the program FILEDT.C.

C 397 Setting a File's Date and Time Stamp

In Tip 395 you used the function _dos_getftime to obtain a file's date and time stamp. Depending on your program, there may be times when you need to set a file's date and time stamp. For such cases, many C compilers provide the _dos_setftime function:

```
#include <dos.h>

unsigned _dos_setftime(int handle, unsigned date,
    unsigned time);
```

If the function is successful, it returns the value 0. If an error occurs, the function returns a nonzero value. The *handle* parameter is a handle to an open file. The date and *time* parameters contain the bit-encoded date and time values (similar to those shown in Tip 396). The following program, JULY4_94.C, sets the date and time stamp of the file specified in the command line to noon, July 4, 1994:

```
#include <stdio.h>
#include <dos.h>
#include <fcntl.h>
```

```
void main(int argc, char *argv[])
{
    union {
      struct Date {
        unsigned int day:5;
        unsigned int month:4;
        unsigned int years:7;
      } bits;
      unsigned value;
    } date;

    union {
      struct Time {
        unsigned seconds:5;
        unsigned minutes:6;
        unsigned hours:5;
      } bits;
      unsigned value;
    } time;

    int handle;

    if (_dos_open(argv[1], O_RDONLY, &handle))
        fprintf(stderr, "Error opening source file\n");
    else
      {
        date.bits.day = 4;
        date.bits.month = 7;
        date.bits.years = 14;   // 1980 + 14
        time.bits.hours = 12;
        time.bits.minutes = 0;
        time.bits.seconds = 0;

        if (_dos_setftime(handle, date.value, time.value))
          printf("Error setting date/time stamp\n");

        _dos_close(handle);
      }
}
```

The program uses bit fields to simplify the assignment of the date and time bits. However, the function requires parameters of type *unsigned int*. Because the bits need to be viewed in two different ways, they are an excellent candidate for a *union*.

C 398 Setting a File Date and Time Stamp to the Current Date and Time

Several of the tips in this book have shown ways to set a file's date and time stamp. When you want to set a file's date and time stamp to the current date and time, a quick way to do so is with the *utime* function:

```
#include <utime.h>

int utime(char *path, struct utimbuf *date_time);
```

The *path* parameter is a character string that specifies the name and directory of the desired file. The *date_time* parameter is a structure that contains the date and time the file was last changed and last accessed:

```
struct utimbuf {
   time_t actime;    // Last access
   time_t modtime;   // Last modification
};
```

If you working in the DOS environment, only the modification time is used. If you invoke the *utime* function with the times set to NULL, the function sets the date and time stamp to the current date and time. If the function is successful, it returns 0. If an error occurs, the function returns –1 and sets the global variable *errno*. The following program, UTIME.C, uses the *utime* function to set the date and time stamp of the file specified to the current date and time:

```
#include <stdio.h>
#include <utime.h>

void main(int argc, char **argv)
  {
   if (utime(argv[1], (struct utimbuf *) NULL))
     printf("Error setting date and time\n");
   else
     printf("Date and time stamp set\n");
  }
```

Reading and Writing Data a Word at a Time

As you have learned, the *getc* and *putc* functions let you read and write file information a byte at a time. Depending on your file's contents, there may be times when you want to read and write data a word at a time. To help you do so, most C compilers provide the *getw* and *putw* functions:

```
#include <stdio.h>

int getw(FILE *stream);
int putw(int word, FILE *stream);
```

If it is successful, the *getw* function returns the integer value read from the file. If an error occurs or the end of file is encountered, *getw* returns *EOF*. If it is successful, the *putw* function returns the integer value written to the file. If an error occurs, *putw* returns *EOF*. The following program, PUTWGETW.C, uses the function *putw* to write the values 1 to 100 to a file. The program then opens the same file and reads the values using *getw*:

```
#include <stdio.h>
#include <stdlib.h>

void main(void)
  {
    FILE *fp;

    int word;

    if ((fp = fopen("DATA.DAT", "wb")) == NULL)
      {
        printf("Error opening DATA.DAT for output\n");
        exit(1);
      }
    else
      {
        for (word = 1; word <= 100; word++)
          putw(word, fp);
        fclose(fp);
      }

    if ((fp = fopen("DATA.DAT", "rb")) == NULL)
      {
        printf("Error opening DATA.DAT for input\n");
        exit(1);
      }
```

```
    else
      {
        do {
          word = getw(fp);
          if ((word == EOF) && (feof(fp)))
            break;
          else
            printf("%d ", word);
        } while (1);
        fclose(fp);
      }
  }
```

C 400 Changing a File's Size

As you work with files, there may be times when you need to allocate a large amount of disk space for a file or when you want to truncate a file's size. For such cases, your programs can use the *chsize* function:

```
#include <io.h>

int chsize(int handle, long size);
```

The *handle* parameter is the file handle returned by *open* or *creat*. The *size* parameter specifies the desired file size. If *chsize* is successful, it returns the value 0. If an error occurs, *chsize* returns the value −1 and sets the global variable *errno* to one of the following:

Value	Meaning
EACCES	Invalid access
EBADF	Invalid file handle
ENOSPC	Insufficient space (UNIX)

If you increase a file's size, *chsize* will fill the new file space will NULL characters. The following program, CHSIZE.C, creates file named 100ZEROS.DAT and then uses the *chsize* function to zero-fill the file's first 100 bytes:

```
#include <stdio.h>
#include <io.h>
#include <fcntl.h>
#include <sys\types.h>
#include <sys\stat.h>

void main(void)
  {
    int handle;
```

```
    if ((handle = creat("100ZEROS.DAT", S_IWRITE)) == -1)
        fprintf(stderr, "Error opening 100ZEROS.DAT");
    else
      {
        if (chsize(handle, 100L))
          printf("Error changing file size\n");
        close(handle);
      }
}
```

Controlling Read/Write File-Open Operations

401

As you have learned, when you open a file, whether you are using *open, creat,* or *fopen,* you must specify whether you want to access the file in read, write, or read/write mode. The *umask* function lets you control how the program can open files later. The format of the function is as follows:

```
#include <io.h>

unsigned umask(unsigned access_mode);
```

The *access_mode* parameter specifies the modes you want to prevent files from using. Valid values for the *access_mode* parameter are as follows:

Access Mode	Meaning
S_IWRITE	Prevents write access
S_IREAD	Prevents read access
S_IWRITE | S_IREAD	Prevents read/write access

For example, if you wanted to prevent the program from opening files with write access, you would use *umask* as follows:

```
old_mode = umask(S_IWRITE);
```

As shown, the function returns the previous setting. The following program, UMASK.C, uses the *umask* function to set the access mode to *S_IWRITE*, which will clear a file's write-access bit (making the file read-only). The program then creates and writes output to the file OUTPUT.DAT. After the program closes the file, it tries to open OUTPUT.DAT for write access. Because the file has been set to read-only, the open operation fails:

```
#include <stdio.h>
#include <io.h>
#include <fcntl.h>
```

```
#include <sys\stat.h>
#include <stdlib.h>

void main (void)
 {
   int output;

   int old_setting;

   old_setting = umask(S_IWRITE);

   if ((output = creat("OUTPUT.DAT", S_IWRITE)) == -1)
     {
       fprintf(stderr, "Error creating OUTPUT.DAT\n");
       exit(1);
     }
   else
     {
       if (write(output, "Test", 4) == -1)
         fprintf(stderr, "Cannot write to file\n");
       else
         printf("File successfully written to\n");

       close(output);
     }

   if ((output = open("OUTPUT.DAT", O_WRONLY)) == -1)
     fprintf(stderr, "Error opening OUTPUT.DAT for output\n");
   else
     printf("File successfully opened for write access\n");
 }
```

Note: *To remove the file OUTPUT.DAT from your disk, you must issue the command **ATTRIB -R OUTPUT.DAT** and then delete the file.*

C 402 Assigning a File Buffer

In the Keyboard section of this book you will learn that C provides I/O functions that perform buffered and direct I/O. For buffered I/O operations, data is first written to or read into a buffer before being made available to your program. File operations, for example, use buffered I/O. When your programs perform direct I/O, on the other hand, the data is immediately available to your programs, without being placed in an intermediate buffer. Direct I/O is often used to gain direct access to the keyboard. Normally, C automatically allocates a buffer for file streams. Using the *setbuf* function however, you can specify your own buffer:

```
#include <stdio.h>

void setbuf(FILE *stream, char *buffer);
```

The *stream* parameter corresponds to the open file for which you want to assign the new buffer. The *buffer* parameter is a pointer to the desired buffer. If the *buffer* parameter contains NULL, data will not be buffered. The following program, SETBUF.C, uses the *setbuf* function to change the buffer assigned to the *stdout* file handle. The program then writes output to *stdout*. However, because the data is being placed in a large buffer, it will not appear on your screen until a three-second delay passes. The program then fills the buffer a character at a time, delaying ten milliseconds between characters. When the buffer becomes full, it is flushed (written) to the screen:

```c
#include <stdio.h>
#include <dos.h>
#include <conio.h>

void main(void)
  {
    char buffer[512];
    int letter;

    setbuf(stdout, buffer);

    puts("First line of output");
    puts("Second line of output");
    puts("Third line of output");

    delay(3000);

    printf("About to fill buffer\n");
    fflush(stdout);

    for (letter = 0; letter < 513; letter++)
      {
      putchar('A');
      delay(10);
      }
  }
```

C 403 Allocating a File Buffer

In Tip 402 you learned how to use the *setbuf* function to assign a buffer to a file. When you use *setbuf*, you must specify the desired buffer. In a similar way, many C compilers provide the *setvbuf* function, which allocates a buffer (using *malloc*) of the size desired and then assigns the buffer to the specified file. In addition, the function lets you specify the desired buffering:

```
#include <stdio.h>

int setvbuf(FILE *stream, char *buffer,
   int buffer_type, size_t buffer_size);
```

The *stream* parameter is a pointer to an open file. The *buffer* parameter is a pointer to the buffer into which your data is buffered. If the *buffer* parameter is NULL, the *setvbuf* function will allocate the buffer for you. Type *buffer_type* parameter lets you control the buffer type. Table 403 lists the valid values for the *buffer_type* parameter. Finally, the *buffer_size* parameter lets you specify a buffer size up to 32,767 bytes. If the function is successful it returns 0. If an error occurs (such as insufficient memory), a nonzero value is returned.

Buffer Type	Buffering
_IOFBF	Full buffering. When the buffer is empty, the next read operation will try to fill the buffer. For output, the buffer must be full before data is written to the disk.
_IOLBF	Line buffering. When the buffer is empty, the next read operation will try to fill the buffer. For output, the buffer is written to disk when full or the newline character is encountered.
_IONBF	Unbuffered. The program will perform direct I/O.

Table 403 *Valid buffering types used by _setvbuf.*

The following program, SETVBUF.C, uses *_setvbuf* to allocated an 8Kb buffer for full buffering:

```
#include <stdio.h>
#include <dos.h>
#include <conio.h>

void main(void)
 {
   char line[512];
   char *buffer;

   FILE *input;
```

```
if ((input = fopen("\\AUTOEXEC.BAT", "r")) == NULL)
  printf("Error opening \\AUTOEXEC.BAT\n");
else
  {
    if (setvbuf(input, buffer, _IOFBF, 8192))
      printf("Error changing file buffer\n");
    else
      while (fgets(line, sizeof(line), input))
        fputs(line, stdout);
    fclose(input);
  }
}
```

Creating a Unique Filename Using *mktemp*

C404

As you work with files, the ability to create a unique filename for temporary files is very important. Some of the tips in this section have shown you ways to create random filenames. In many cases, you will want to create a unique filename, but you will want the filename to follow a specific format that relates it to the application. For example, for an accounting program, you might want all of your filenames to begin with the letters *ACCNTG*. To help you control the creation of unique filenames, many C compilers provide the *mktemp* function:

```
#include <dir.h>

char *mktemp(char *template);
```

The *template* is a pointer to a character string that contains six characters followed by six Xs and a NULL. In the case of the accounting example, the template would be a pointer to "ACCNTGXXXXXX". The *mktemp* function replaces the Xs with two filename characters, a period, and three characters for the extension. If *mktemp* is successful, it returns a pointer to the template string. If an error occurs, the function returns NULL. Because *mktemp* appends letters to the *template* parameter, you must ensure that you allocate 13 or more character positions within the string. The following program MKTEMP.C illustrates the use of the *mktemp* function:

```
#include <stdio.h>
#include <dir.h>

void main(void)
  {
    char name_a[13] = "ACCTNGXXXXXX";
    char name_b[13] = "COMPUTXXXXXX";
    char name_c[13] = "PCCHIPXXXXXX";
```

```
    if (mktemp(name_a))
      puts(name_a);

    if (mktemp(name_b))
      puts(name_b);

    if (mktemp(name_c))
      puts(name_c);
}
```

When you compile and execute this program, your screen will display the following:

```
C:\> MKTEMP  <ENTER>
ACCTNGAA.AAA
COMPUTAA.AAA
PCCHIPAA.AAA
```

C 405 Reading and Writing Structures

The Structures section of this book presents many programs that work with structures. When your programs work with structures, there will be many times when you programs will need to store the structure data in disk and then later read the data. As a rule, when you need to read or write a structure, you can treat the structure as a long byte range. The following program, DTOUT.C, for example, uses C's *write* function to write the current system date and time to the file DATETIME.DAT:

```
#include <stdio.h>
#include <dos.h>
#include <io.h>
#include <sys\stat.h>

void main (void)
 {
    struct date curr_date;
    struct time curr_time;

    int handle;

    getdate(&curr_date);
    gettime(&curr_time);

    if ((handle = creat("DATETIME.OUT", S_IWRITE)) == -1)
      fprintf(stderr, "Error opening file DATETIME.OUT\n");
    else
      {
```

```
        write(handle, &curr_date, sizeof(curr_date));
        write(handle, &curr_time, sizeof(curr_time));
        close(handle);
    }
}
```

As you can see, to write the structure, the program simply passes the structure's address. In a similar way, the following program, DTIN.C, uses the *read* function to read the date and time structures:

```
#include <stdio.h>
#include <dos.h>
#include <io.h>
#include <fcntl.h>

void main (void)
 {
    struct date curr_date;
    struct time curr_time;

    int handle;

    if ((handle = open("DATETIME.OUT", O_RDONLY)) == -1)
      fprintf(stderr, "Error opening file DATETIME.OUT\n");
    else
      {
        read(handle, &curr_date, sizeof(curr_date));
        read(handle, &curr_time, sizeof(curr_time));
        close(handle);

        printf("Date: %02d-%02d-%02d\n", curr_date.da_mon,
          curr_date.da_day, curr_date.da_year);
        printf("Time: %02d:%02d\n", curr_time.ti_hour,
          curr_time.ti_min);
      }
 }
```

Reading Structure Data from a File Stream

C406

In Tip 405 you learned how to use C's *read* and *write* functions to perform file I/O operations using structures. If your programs use file streams, as opposed to file handles, for file I/O, you can perform similar processing using the *fread* and *fwrite* functions:

```
#include <stdio.h>

size_t fread(void *buffer, size_t buffer_size,
  size_t element_count, FILE *stream);

size_t fwrite(void *buffer, size_t buffer_size,
  size_t element_count, FILE *stream);
```

The *buffer* parameter contains a pointer to the data you want to output. The *buffer_size* parameter specifies the data's size in bytes. The *element_count* parameter specifies the number of structures you are writing, and the *stream* parameter is a pointer to an open file stream. If the functions are successful, they return the number of items read or written. If an error occurs or the end of file is encountered, the functions return 0. The following program DTOUTF.C, uses the *fwrite* function to write the current date and time structures to a file:

```
#include <stdio.h>
#include <dos.h>

void main (void)
  {
    struct date curr_date;
    struct time curr_time;

    FILE *output;

    getdate(&curr_date);
    gettime(&curr_time);

    if ((output = fopen("DATETIME.OUT", "w")) == NULL)
      fprintf(stderr, "Error opening file DATETIME.OUT\n");
    else
      {
        fwrite(&curr_date, sizeof(curr_date), 1, output);
        fwrite(&curr_time, sizeof(curr_time), 1, output);
        fclose(output);
      }
  }
```

Likewise, the program DTINF.C, uses the *fread* function to read the structure values:

```
#include <stdio.h>
#include <dos.h>

void main (void)
  {
    struct date curr_date;
    struct time curr_time;
```

```
  FILE *input;

  if ((input = fopen("DATETIME.OUT", "r")) == NULL)
    fprintf(stderr, "Error opening file DATETIME.OUT\n");
  else
    {
      fread(&curr_date, sizeof(curr_date), 1, input);
      fread(&curr_time, sizeof(curr_time), 1, input);
      fclose(input);

      printf("Date: %02d-%02d-%02d\n", curr_date.da_mon,
        curr_date.da_day, curr_date.da_year);
      printf("Time: %02d:%02d\n", curr_time.ti_hour,
        curr_time.ti_min);
    }
}
```

Duplicating a File Handle

C 407

Several of the tips in this section have presented functions that work with file handles. Depending on your programs, there may be times when you want to duplicate a handle's value. For example, if your program performs critical I/O operations, you might want to duplicate a file handle and then close the new copied handle in order to flush the file's output to disk. Because the first file handle remains open, you don't have the overhead of reopening the file after the flush operation:

```
#include <io.h>

int dup(int handle);
```

The *handle* parameter is the open file handle that you want to duplicate. If *dup* successfully duplicates the handle, it returns a nonnegative value. If an error occurs, *dup* returns –1. The following program, DUP.C, illustrates how you might use the *dup* function to flush a file's buffers:

```
#include <stdio.h>
#include <fcntl.h>
#include <io.h>
#include <sys\stat.h>

void main(void)
  {
    int handle;
    int duplicate_handle;

    char title[] = "Jamsa's 1001 C/C++ Tips!";
```

```
  char section[] = "Files";

  if ((handle = open("OUTPUT.TST", O_WRONLY | O_CREAT,
      S_IWRITE)) == -1)
    printf("Error opening OUTPUT.TST\n");
  else
   {
     if ((duplicate_handle = dup(handle)) == -1)
       printf("Error duplicating handle\n");
     else
      {
        write(handle, title, sizeof(title));
        close(duplicate_handle);  // Flush the buffer
        write(handle, section, sizeof(section));
        close(handle);
      }
   }
}
```

C 408 Forcing a File Handle's Setting

In Tip 407 you learned how to use the *dup* command to make a duplicate copy of a file handle's contents. There may be times when you want to change an open file handle's setting, assigning the value of a different handle. In such cases, you can use *dup2*:

```
#include <io.h>

int dup2(int source_handle, int target_handle);
```

The *target_handle* parameter is the file handle whose value you want to update. If the function successfully assigns the handle, it returns the value 0. If an error occurs, the function returns –1. The *source_handle* parameter is the file handle whose value you want to assign to the target. The following program, DUP2.C, uses the *dup2* function to assign the value of the *stderr* function to stdout. In this way, the program's output cannot be redirected from the screen display:

```
#include <stdio.h>
#include <io.h>

void main(void)
 {
   dup2(2, 1);  // stdout is handle 1 stderr is handle 2

   printf("This message cannot be redircted!\n");
 }
```

Associating a File Handle with a Stream

409

Many of the tips in this section have presented functions that work with either file streams or file handles. Depending on your program, there may be times when you are working with a file handle and want to use a function that corresponds to a file stream. In such cases, your programs can use the *fdopen* function to associate a file handle with a file stream:

```
#include <stdio.h>

FILE *fdopen(int handle, char *access_mode);
```

The *handle* parameter is the handle of an open file that you want to associate with a file stream. The *access_mode* parameter is a pointer to a character string that specifies how you plan to use the file stream. The *access_mode* value must be one of the mode values you would normally use with *fopen*. If the function is successful, it returns the stream pointer. If an error occurs, the function returns NULL. The following statement, for example, associates the file handle *input* with the file pointer *fpin* for read access:

```
if ((fp = fdopen(input, "r")) == NULL)
  printf("Error associating file\n");
else
  {
    gets(string, sizeof(string), fpin);
    fclose(fpin);
  }
```

Understanding File Sharing

410

If you are working in a network environment and have installed the DOS SHARE command, you can write programs that let more than one program access different parts of the same file at the same time! For example, consider a program that lets multiple users assign the seats in an airplane. When one user wants to assign a specific seat, the program locks that seat so another user won't assign it too. After the seat has been assigned, the user unlocks the seat. When you share files in this way, you must first open the file for sharing using the *sopen* function. Next, when your program wants to access a range of bytes in the file, the program tries to lock the data. If no one else is currently using the data (has it locked for their own use), the program's lock succeeds. After the program has finished with the data it, can unlock the range of bytes in the file. When a program locks a range of bytes within a file, the program can assign a lock that allows other users to access the data in specific ways. For example, the program might let another file read the locked range or it might allow other programs to read and write the same byte range. Several of the tips that follow discuss C run-time library functions that support file sharing and locking.

411 Opening a File for Shared Access

In Tip 410 you learned that if you are using the DOS SHARE command, you can open file for use by multiple programs at the same time. To open a file for shared use, your programs must use the *sopen* function:

```
#include <share.h>

int sopen(char *pathname, int access_mode,
  int share_flag[, int create_mode]);
```

The *pathname, access_mode,* and *create_mode* parameters are similar to those used by the *open* function. The *share_flag* parameter specifies how the file can be shared. Table 411 lists the valid values for the *share_flag* parameter. If *sopen* successfully opens the file, it returns a file handle. If an error occurs, *sopen* returns −1.

Share Flag	Sharing Allowed
SH_COMPAT	Allows compatible sharing
SH_DENYRW	Prevents read/write access
SH_DENYWR	Prevents write access
SH_DENYRD	Prevents read access
SH_DENYNONE	Allows all access (read/write)
SH_DENYNO	Allows all access (read/write)

Table 411 *Shared access modes supported by sopen.*

The following program, SOPEN.C, opens the file specified in the command line for shared read access. The file then waits for you to press a key before reading and displaying the file's contents:

```
#include <stdio.h>
#include <share.h>
#include <io.h>
#include <fcntl.h>

void main(int argc, char *argv[])
  {
    int handle, bytes_read;

    char buffer[256];
```

```
if ((handle = sopen(argv[1], O_RDONLY, SH_DENYWR)) == -1)
  printf("Error opening the file %s\n", argv[1]);
else
  {
    printf("Press Enter to continue\n");
    getchar();

    while (bytes_read = read(handle, buffer, sizeof(buffer)))
      write(1, buffer, bytes_read);  // 1 is stdout

    close(handle);
  }
}
```

To better understand how this program works, invoke the SHARE command. Next, start Windows and create a DOS window within which your run the program using the filename SOPEN.C as the shared file. When the program prompts you to press a key, open a second DOS window and use TYPE to display the file's contents. As TYPE displays the file SOPEN.C's contents, two programs have the file open at the same time. Close the window and return to the first window. Press **ENTER** to display the file's contents. Next experiment with this program, chaining the allowed shared modes. Repeat the process of trying to access the file using two programs.

Locking a File's Contents

C 412

As you have learned when you share a file's contents, there may be times when you want to lock a range of bytes within a file to prevent another program from changing them. To lock a specific range of bytes within a file, your programs can use the *lock* function:

```
#include <io.h>

int lock(int handle, long start_position, long byte_count);
```

The *handle* parameter is a handle that corresponds to a file opened for sharing by *sopen*. The *start_position* parameter specifies the starting offset within the file of the range of bytes you want to lock. The *byte_count* parameter specifies the number of bytes you want to lock. If the *lock* function successfully locks the range of bytes, it returns the value 0. If an error occurs, the function returns −1. You must have the DOS SHARE command installed for the *lock* function to work.

After you lock a range of bytes, other programs that try to read or write the locked range will make three attempts. If, after the third try the program cannot read the data, the *read* or *write* function will return an error. The following program, LOCKAUTO.C, locks the first five bytes of the root directory file AUTOEXEC.BAT and the waits for you to press a key:

```
#include <stdio.h>
#include <io.h>
#include <share.h>
#include <fcntl.h>

void main(void)
 {
   int handle;

   if ((handle = sopen("\\AUTOEXEC.BAT",O_RDONLY,SH_DENYNO))==-1)
     printf("Error opening AUTOEXEC.BAT\n");
   else
    {
      lock(handle, 0L, 5L);
      printf("File locked—press Enter to continue\n");
      getchar();
      close(handle);
    }
 }
```

Next, the following program TRYAUTO.C, tries to read the file AUTOEXEC.BAT a byte at a time. If an error occurs while reading the file, the program displays an error message:

```
#include <stdio.h>
#include <io.h>
#include <share.h>
#include <fcntl.h>

void main(void)
 {
   int handle;
   int offset = 0;
   int bytes_read;
   char buffer[128];

   if ((handle = sopen("\\AUTOEXEC.BAT", O_BINARY | O_RDONLY,
        SH_DENYNO)) == -1)
     printf("Error opening AUTOEXEC.BAT\n");
   else
    {
      while (bytes_read = read(handle, buffer, 1))
       {
         if (bytes_read == -1)
           printf("Error reading offset %d\n", offset);
         else
           write(1, buffer, bytes_read);
         offset++;
         lseek(handle, offset, SEEK_SET);
```

```
        }
    close(handle);
    }
}
```

Finer File-Locking Control

C 413

In Tip 412 you learned how to use the *lock* function to lock a range of bytes within a file. When you use the *lock* function, the operation is either successful or immediately fails. If you want finer control of the lock operation, you can use the *locking* function, shown here:

```
#include <io.h>
#include <sys\locking.h>

int locking(int handle, int lock_command,
    long byte_count);
```

The *handle* parameter is the handle associated with the file you want to lock. The *lock_command* specifies the desired locking operation. Table 413.1 specifies the desired values. The *byte_count* specifies the number of bytes you want to lock. The start of the region depends on the file's current position pointer. If you want to lock a specific region, you can use the *lseek* function first to position the file pointer.

Lock Command	Meaning
LK_LOCK	Locks the specified region. If the lock is unsuccessful, *locking* will try once every second for ten seconds to apply the lock.
LK_RLCK	Same as LK_LOCK.
LK_NBLCK	Locks the specified region. If the lock is unsuccessful, *locking* will immediately return an error.
LK_NBRLCK	Same as LK_NBLCK.
LK_UNLCK	Unlocks a previously locked region.

Table 413.1 *Commands used by the locking function.*

If *locking* successfully locks the file, it returns the value 0. If an error occurs, *locking* returns the value −1 and sets the global variable *errno* to one of the values specified in Table 413.2.

Error Status	Meaning
EBADF	Invalid file handle
EACCESS	File already locked/unlocked
EDEADLOCK	File cannot be locked after ten tries
EINVAL	Invalid command specified

Table 413.2 *Error status values returned by locking.*

The following program, LOCKING.C, changes the program LOCKAUTO.C, presented in Tip 412 to lock the first 5 bytes of AUTOEXEC.BAT using *locking*:

```c
#include <stdio.h>
#include <io.h>
#include <share.h>
#include <fcntl.h>
#include <sys\locking.h>

void main(void)
  {
    int handle;

    if ((handle = sopen("\\AUTOEXEC.BAT",O_RDONLY,SH_DENYNO))==-1)
      printf("Error opening AUTOEXEC.BAT\n");
    else
      {
        printf("Trying to lock file\n");
        if (locking(handle, LK_LOCK, 5L))
          printf("Error locking file\n");
        else
          {
            printf("File locked—press Enter to continue\n");
            getchar();
            close(handle);
          }
      }
  }
```

As before, if you have Windows available, try running this program from within two DOS windows at the same time.

Note: *Before you can use the locking function, you must have the DOS SHARE command installed.*

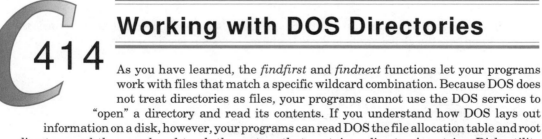

Working with DOS Directories

414

As you have learned, the *findfirst* and *findnext* functions let your programs work with files that match a specific wildcard combination. Because DOS does not treat directories as files, your programs cannot use the DOS services to "open" a directory and read its contents. If you understand how DOS lays out information on a disk, however, your programs can read DOS the file allocation table and root directory and then read and track the sectors that contain a directory's entries. Disk utility commands such as UNDELETE and a directory sort tool perform these low-level disk I/O operations. To simplify the task of reading a directory, some C compilers provide the functions listed in Table 414. Several of the tips that follow illustrate how your programs can use these directory I/O functions.

Function	Purpose
closedir	Closes a directory stream
opendir	Opens a directory stream for read operations
readdir	Reads the next entry in a directory stream
rewinddir	Moves the directory stream pointer back to the start of the directory

Table 414 *Directory I/O functions and their purposes.*

When you read a directory entry, the run-time library function *readdir* returns the name of the next directory entry.

Opening a Directory

C 415

In Tip 414 you learned that many C compilers provide functions that let you open and read the names of files that reside in a specific directory. To open a directory for read operations, your programs can use the *opendir* function:

```
#include <dirent.h>

DIR *opendir(char *directory_name);
```

The *directory_name* parameter is pointer to a character string that contains the desired directory name. If the directory name is NULL, *opendir* opens the current directory. If the *opendir* function is successful, it returns a pointer to a structure of type *DIR*. If an error occurs, the function returns NULL. The following statement, for example, illustrates how you would open the DOS directory for read operations:

```
struct DIR *input_directory;

if ((input_directory = opendir("\\DOS")) == NULL)
  printf("Error opening directory\n");
else
  // Statements
```

After you have performed your directory read operations, you should close the directory stream using the *closedir* function:

```
#include <dirent.h>

void closedir(DIR *directory);
```

C 416 Reading a Directory Entry

In Tip 415 you learned how to use the *opendir* function to open a directory listing. After you open a directory, you can use the *readdir* function to read the name of the next entry in the directory list:

```
#include <dirent.h>

struct dirent readdir(DIR *directory_pointer);
```

The *directory_pointer* parameter is pointer returned by the *opendir* function. If *readdir* successfully reads a directory entry, it returns the entry read. If an error occurs or the end of directory is reached, the function returns NULL. The *readdir* function reads all of the entries in the directory list, including the . and .. entries.

C 417 Putting It All Together—Reading C:\DOS

In Tip 415 you learned how to open and close a directory listing. In Tip 416 you learned how to use the *readdir* function to read the next entry in the directory list. The following program, SHOWDIR.C, uses the run-time library directory entries to open, read, and then close the directory specified in the command line:

```
#include <stdio.h>
#include <dirent.h>

void main(int argc, char *argv[])
  {
    DIR *directory_pointer;
    struct dirent *entry;

    if ((directory_pointer = opendir(argv[1])) == NULL)
      printf("Error opening %s\n", argv[1]);
    else
      {
        while (entry = readdir(directory_pointer))
          printf("%s\n", entry);
        closedir(directory_pointer);
      }
  }
```

The following command, for example, uses the SHOWDIR program to display the names of the files in the directory C:\DOS.

```
C:\> SHOWDIR C:\DOS  <ENTER>
```

Rewinding a Directory

In Tip 414 you learned that C provides run-time library functions that let you open and read the names of files in a specified directory. As you read directories, there may be times when you want to start reading files at the start of the directory list for a second time. One way to perform this operation is to close the directory list and reopen it. Second, your programs can use the *rewinddir* function, shown here:

```
#include <dirent.h>

void rewinddir(DIR *directory_pointer);
```

The *directory_pointer* parameter is the pointer to the directory list that you want to reset. If you experiment with the *rewinddir* function, you will find that it is much faster than closing and reopening the directory list.

Reading a Disk's Files Recursively

In Tip 417 you used the SHOWDIR program to display the files in a directory list. The following program ALLFILES.C, uses the run-time library functions to display the names of every file on your disk. To do so, the program uses the recursive function *show_directory* to display filenames:

```
#include <stdio.h>
#include <dirent.h>
#include <dos.h>
#include <io.h>
#include <direct.h>
#include <string.h>

void show_directory(char *directory_name)
  {
    DIR *directory_pointer;
```

```
   struct dirent *entry;

 unsigned attributes;

 if ((directory_pointer = opendir(directory_name)) == NULL)
   printf("Error opening %s\n", directory_name);
 else
    {
       chdir(directory_name);
       while (entry = readdir(directory_pointer))
         {
           attributes = _chmod(entry, 0);

           // Check if entry is for a subdirectory
           // and is not . or ..

           if ((attributes & FA_DIREC) &&
              (strncmp(entry, ".", 1) != 0))
            {
              printf("\n\n—%s—\n", entry);
              show_directory(entry);
            }
           else
            printf("%s\n", entry);
         }

       closedir(directory_pointer);
       chdir("..");
    }
}

void main(void)
  {
    char buffer[MAXPATH];

    // Save current directory so we can restore it later
    getcwd(buffer, sizeof(buffer));
    show_directory("\\");
    chdir(buffer);
  }
```

Determining the Current File Position

C 420

Using a file pointer, C tracks the current position in files open for input or output operations. Depending on your program, there may be times when you need to determine the position pointer's value. If you are working with file streams, you can use the *ftell* function to determine the file pointer position. If you are working with file handles, however, your programs can use the *tell* function:

```
#include <stdio.h>

long tell(int handle);
```

The *tell* function returns a long value that specifies the byte offset of the current position in the specified file. The following program, TELL.C, uses the *tell* to display position pointer information. The program begins by opening the root directory file CONFIG.SYS in read mode. The program then uses *tell* to display the current position. Next, the program reads and displays the file's contents. After the end of file is found, the program again uses *tell* to display the current position:

```c
#include <stdio.h>
#include <io.h>
#include <fcntl.h>

void main(void)
  {
    int handle;
    char buffer[512];
    int bytes_read;

    if ((handle = open("\\CONFIG.SYS", O_RDONLY)) == -1)
      printf("Error opening \\CONFIG.SYS\n");
    else
      {
        printf("Current file position %ld\n", tell(handle));

        while (bytes_read = read(handle, buffer, sizeof(buffer)))
          write(1, buffer, bytes_read);

        printf("Current file position %ld\n", tell(handle));
        close(handle);
      }
  }
```

C421 Opening a Shared File Stream

Several of the tips in this section have presented ways to share and lock files using file handles. If you normally work with file streams, your programs can use the *_fsopen* function, shown here:

```
#include <stdio.h>
#include <share.h>

FILE * _fsopen(const char *filename,
    const *access_mode, int share_flag);
```

The *filename* and *access_mode* parameters contain character-string pointers to the desired filename and access mode that you would normally use with *fopen*. The *share_flag* specifies the sharing mode. Table 421 lists the valid values you can assign to *share_flag*. If the function is successful, it returns a file pointer. If an error occurs, the function returns NULL.

Share Flag	Sharing Allowed
SH_COMPAT	Allows compatible sharing
SH_DENYRW	Prevents read/write access
SH_DENYWR	Prevents write access
SH_DENYRD	Prevents read access
SH_DENYNONE	Allows all access (read/write)
SH_DENYNO	Allows all access (read/write)

Table 421 *Valid values for the access_mode parameter.*

The following statements, for example, open the root directory file AUTOEXEC.BAT for shared read operations:

```
if ((fp = _fsopen("\\AUTOEXEC.BAT", "r", SH_DENYWR))==NULL)
  printf("Error opening \\AUTOEXEC.BAT\n");
else
  // Statements
```

C422 Creating a Unique File in a Specific Directory

Several of the tips in this section have shown ways that your programs can create temporary files. If you normally work with file handles, you can use the function *creattemp*, which returns a handle, as shown here:

```
#include <dos.h>

int creattemp(char *path, int attribute);
```

The *path* parameter specifies the name of the directory within which you want the file created. The name must end with backslash characters ('\\'). The function will append the filename to the string to produce a complete pathname. The *attribute* function specifies the desired file attributes (or 0 for none):

FA_RDONLY	Read-only file
FA_HIDDEN	Hidden file
FA_SYSTEM	System file

If the function is successful, it returns a file handle. If an error occurs, the function returns −1. The following program, CREATTMP.C, uses the *creattemp* function to create a unique file in the TEMP directory:

```
#include <stdio.h>
#include <dos.h>
#include <io.h>

void main(void)
  {
    char path[64] = "C:\\TEMP\\";

    int handle;


    if ((handle = creattemp(path, 0)) == -1)
      printf("Error creating file\n");
    else
      {
        printf("Complete path: %s\n", path);
        close(handle);
      }
  }
```

Creating a New File

C 423

Several of the tips in this section have shown ways to create files. In many cases, if a file with the name specified in the function already exists, the file's contents are truncated. In many cases, however, you might only want a file to be created if a file with the same name does not already exist. For such cases, your programs can use the *creatnew* function:

```
#include <dos.h>

int creatnew(const char *pathname, int attribute);
```

The *pathname* parameter specifies the complete path of the file you want to create. The *attribute* function specifies the desired file attributes (or 0 for none):

FA_RDONLY	Read-only file
FA_HIDDEN	Hidden file
FA_SYSTEM	System file

If the function is successful, it returns a file handle. If an error occurs, the function returns the value −1 and sets the global variable *errno* to one of the following:

Error	Meaning
EXISTS	File already exists
ENOENT	Path not found
EMFILE	Too many open files
EACCES	Access violation

The following program, CREATNEW.C, uses the *creatnew* function to create a file named NEW.DAT in the current directory. Experiment with this program, trying to create the file more than once:

```
#include <stdio.h>
#include <dos.h>
#include <io.h>

void main(void)
  {
    int handle;

    if ((handle = creatnew("NEW.DAT", 0)) == -1)
      printf("Error creating NEW.DAT\n");
    else
      {
        printf("File successfully created\n");
        close(handle);
      }
  }
```

Opening a File Using *fopen*

C424

Many of the C programs you create will store and retrieve information in a file. Before your programs can read information from or write information to a file, the program must *open* the file. The *fopen* function lets your programs do just that. The format of *fopen* is as follows:

```
#include <stdio.h>

FILE *fopen(const char *filename, const char mode);
```

The *filename* parameter is a character string that contains the name of the desired file, such as "C:\DATAFILE.DAT". The *mode* parameter specifies how you want to use the file: read, write, or append. Table 424 describes the mode values *fopen* supports.

Mode	Meaning
a	Opens the file for append operations—if the file does not exist, it is created
r	Opens an existing file for read operations
w	Opens a new file for output—if a file with the same name exists, it is overwritten
r+	Opens an existing file for reading and writing
w+	Opens a new file for reading and writing—if a file with the same name exists, it is overwritten
a+	Opens a file for append and read operations—if the file does not exist, it is created

Table 424 *Mode values supported by fopen.*

The *fopen* function returns a pointer (called a *file pointer*) to a structure of type *FILE*, which is defined in the header file stdio.h. Your program will use the file pointer for its input and output operations. If the *fopen* function cannot open the file specified, it returns the value NULL. Your programs should always test *fopen*'s return value to make sure it successfully opened the file:

```
if ((fp = fopen("FILENAME.EXT", "r")) != NULL)
   {
     // File successfully opened
   }
else
   {
     // Error opening the file
   }
```

Within your program, you must declare the file pointer variable as follows:

```
void main(void)
  {
    FILE *fp;  // Pointer to a structure of type FILE
```

Many programs open one file for input and another for output. In such cases, you would declare two file pointers, as shown here:

```
FILE *input, *output;
```

Many of the tips in this section use *fopen* to open a file for read, write, or append operations.

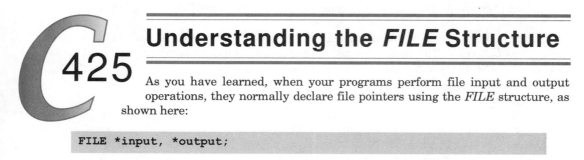

425 Understanding the *FILE* Structure

As you have learned, when your programs perform file input and output operations, they normally declare file pointers using the *FILE* structure, as shown here:

```
FILE *input, *output;
```

If you examine the header file stdio.h, you will find the defintion of the *FILE* structure. In the case of Borland C++, the structure takes the following form:

```
typedef struct  {
  int level;                    /* fill/empty level of buffer */
  unsigned flags;               /* File status flags          */
  char fd;                      /* File descriptor            */
  unsigned char hold;           /* Ungetc char if no buffer   */
  int bsize;                    /* Buffer size                */
  unsigned char _FAR *buffer;   /* Data transfer buffer       */
  unsigned char _FAR *curp;     /* Current active pointer      */
  unsigned istemp;              /* Temporary file indicator   */
  short token;                  /* Used for validity checking */
} FILE;                         /* This is the FILE object    */
```

The *FILE* contains the low-level *file descriptor* used by the operating system to access the file, the file's buffer size and location, the character buffer used by *unget*, a flag that indicates the file is a temporary file, and other flag variables. In addition, the *FILE* stores the file pointer which keeps track of your current location within the file.

If you are working in the DOS environment, most compilers define an fixed size (normally 20) array of file pointers that hold the information for each file your program opens. If your program needs to open more than 20 files, you must refer to the documentation that accompanied your compiler for the steps you must perform to change the file pointer array size.

Closing an Open File

C 426

Just as your programs must open a file before they use it, your programs should close the file when it is no longer needed. Closing a file directs the operating system to flush all of the disk buffers associated with the file and to free up system resources the file consumed, such as the file pointer data. The C *fclose* function closes the file associated with the specified file pointer:

```
#include <stdio.h>

int fclose(FILE *file_pointer);
```

If *fclose* is successful, it will return the value 0. If an error occurs, *fclose* returns the constant *EOF*:

```
if (fclose(fp) == EOF)
  printf("Error closing the data file\n");
```

As you examine C programs, you will find that most programs do not test *fopen*'s return status value:

```
fclose(fp);
```

In most cases, should a file close operation experience an error, there is little the program can do to correct the situation. However, if you are working with critical data files, you should display an error message to the user so he or she can examine the file's contents.

Note: *If you do invoke the fclose function, C will close your open files when the program ends.*

Reading and Writing File Information a Character at a Time

C 427

When your programs perform file input and output operations, your programs can read and write data a character at a time or a line at a time. For character input and output operations, your programs can use the *fgetc* and *fputc* functions, whose formats are shown here:

```
#include <stdio.h>

int fgetc(FILE *input_pointer);
int fputc(int character, FILE *output_pointer);
```

The *fgetc* function reads and the current character from the input file specified. If the end of the file has been reached, *fgetc* returns the constant *EOF*. The *fputc* function writes a character to the current location of the output file specified. If an error occurs, *fputc* returns the constant *EOF*. The following program, CONFCOPY.C, uses *fgetc* and *fputc* to copy the contents of the root directory file CONFIG.SYS to a file named CONFIG.TST:

```c
#include <stdio.h>

void main(void)
 {
   FILE *input, *output;

   int letter;

   if ((input = fopen("\\CONFIG.SYS", "r")) == NULL)
     printf("Error opening \\CONFIG.SYS\n");
   else if ((output = fopen("\\CONFIG.TST", "w")) == NULL)
     printf("Error opening \\CONFIG.TST\n");
   else
     {
       // Read and write each character in the file
       while ((letter = fgetc(input)) != EOF)
         fputc(letter, output);

       fclose(input);      // Close the input file
       fclose(output);     // Close the output file
     }
 }
```

C 428 Understanding the File Pointer's Position Pointer

Tip 425 presented the *FILE* structure. As you learned, one of the structure's fields holds a *position pointer* to the current location within the file. When you first open a file for read or write operations, the position pointer is set to the start of the file. Each time you read or write a character, the position pointer advances one character. If you read a line of text from the file, the position pointer advances to the start of the next line. Using the position pointer, the file input and output functions can always keep track of the current location within the file. When you open a file in append mode, the position pointer is placed at the very end of the file. In later tips you will learn how to change the position pointer to specific file locations using the *fseek* and *fsetpos* functions. Table 428 specifies the location at which *fopen* places the position pointer when you open the file in read, write, and append modes.

Open Mode	File Pointer Position
a	Immediately after the last character in the file
r	At the start of the file
w	At the start of the file

Table 428 *File position pointer settings by fopen.*

Determining the Current File Position

C429

Using a file pointer, C tracks the current position in files open for input or output operations. Depending on your program, there may be times when you need to determine the position pointer's value. In such cases, your programs can use the *ftell* function:

```
#include <stdio.h>

long int ftell(FILE *file_pointer);
```

The *ftell* function returns a long integer value that specifies the byte offset of the current position in the specified file. The following program, SHOW_POS.C, uses the *ftell* to display position pointer information. The program begins by opening the root directory file CONFIG.SYS in read mode. The program then uses *ftell* to display the current position. Next, the program reads and displays the file's contents. After the end of file is found, the program again uses *ftell* to display the current position:

```
#include <stdio.h>

void main(void)
  {
    FILE *input;

    int letter;

    if ((input = fopen("\\CONFIG.SYS", "r")) == NULL)
      printf("Error opening \\CONFIG.SYS\n");
    else
      {
        printf("Current position is byte %d\n\n", ftell(input));

        // Read and write each character in the file
        while ((letter = fgetc(input)) != EOF)
```

```
        fputc(letter, stdout);

      printf("\nCurrent position is byte %d\n", ftell(input));

      fclose(input);      // Close the input file
    }
  }
```

C 430 Understanding File Streams

Many books and magazines refer to C's file pointers as *pointers to file streams*. Unlike other programming languages that assume files contain information in a specific format, C does not. Instead, C considers all files as nothing more than a collection of bytes. When you read a file for example, you read one byte after another, in other words, a *stream* of bytes. It is up to your programs or functions, such *fgets*, to interpret the bytes. For example, *fgets* considers the linefeed character the end of one line and the start of another. The *fgets* function makes this character interpretation, C itself does not. As you write programs and functions that manipulate files, think of the files as nothing more than a collection of bytes.

C 431 Understanding File Translations

The C file manipulation functions such as *fgets* and *fputs* can interpret files in one of two ways: *text* and *binary* mode. By default, the functions use text mode. In text mode, functions such as *fputs*, which write information to a file, convert the linefeed character to a carriage-return/linefeed combination. During an input operation, on the other hand, functions such as *fgets* convert the carriage-return/linefeed combination to a single linefeed character. In binary mode, on the other hand, the functions do not perform these character translations. To help you determine the current translation mode, many DOS-based compilers provide the global variable *_fmode*, which contains one of the following values:

O_TEXT   Text mode translations
O_BINARY   Binary mode translations

The following program, FMODE.C, displays the current value of the *_fmode* variable:

```
#include <stdio.h>
#include <fcntl.h>  // Contains the _fmode declaration

void main(void)
  {
    if (_fmode == O_TEXT)
```

```
        printf("Text mode translations\n");
    else
        printf("Binary mode translations\n");
}
```

Understanding the CONFIG.SYS FILES= Entry

432

If you are working in a DOS-based environment, the CONFIG.SYS FILES entry specifies the number of files that the system can open at one time. As briefly discussed in the I/O Redirection section of this book, DOS uses the first five file handles for stdin, stdout, stderr, stdaux, and stdprn. By default, DOS provides support for eight file handles. Because this number is too few for all but the simplest programs, most users increase the number of available handles to 20 or 30, as shown here:

```
FILES=30
```

The FILES entry defines the number of files DOS can open—not the number each program running under DOS can open. If you are running memory-resident programs for example, the programs can have open files of which you are not aware. If you set the FILES entry to a large number of handles (DOS supports up to 255 handles), it doesn't mean that your C programs can open that many files. As it turns out, there are two problems. First, most C compilers restrict the size of the file pointer array to 20. Before you can open more than 20 files, you will need to change the array size. Second, as you will learn, DOS restricts the number of files a program can open to 20. Before you can open more than 20 files, you must use a DOS system service to request DOS to support more than 20 open files for the current program.

Low-Level and High-Level File I/O

433

When your C programs work with files, they can perform two types of input and output operations: *low-level* and *high-level* file I/O. All of the tips presented to this point have used C's high-level (or stream-based) capabilities, such as *fopen*, *fgets*, and *fputs*. When you use C's high-level file I/O functions, they in turn use operating system services that are based on *file handles*. The C run-time library provides low-level functions that your programs can use. Instead of working with a stream pointer, the low-level functions use *file descriptors*. Table 433 briefly describes several of C's most commonly used low-level functions.

Function Name	Purpose
close	Closes the file associated with the specified file handle, flushing the file's buffers
creat	Creates a file for output operations, returning a file handle
open	Opens an existing file for input or output, returing a file handle
read	Reads a specified number of bytes from the file associated with a given file handle
write	Writes a specified number of bytes to the file associated with a given handle

Table 433 *C's common low level file functions.*

When you write your programs, your choice of using low-level or high-level functions is primarily your personal preference. However, keep in mind that most programmers have a better understanding of C's high-level file manipulation functions. As a result, if you use the high-level functions such as *fopen* and *fgets*, more programmers will readily understand your program code.

C434 Understanding File Handles

As you know, the CONFIG.SYS FILES entry lets you specify the number of file handles DOS supports. In short, a *file handle* is a unique integer value that uniquely defines an open file. When you use C's low-level file I/O functions you will declare your program's file handles as type *int*, as shown here:

```
int input_handle, output_handle;
```

The functions *open* and *creat* return file descriptors or the value −1 if the file cannot be opened:

```
int new_file, old_file;

// Create a new file for output
new_file = creat("FILENAME.NEW", S_IWRITE);

// Open an existing file for reading
old_file = open("FILENAME.OLD", O_RDONLY);
```

Each file you open or create is assigned a unique file handle. As it turns out, the handle's value is actually an index into the process file table, within which DOS keeps track of the program's open files. Tip 435 discuses the *process file table* in detail.

Understanding the Process File Table

When you run a program in the DOS environment, DOS keeps track of the program's open files using a *process file table*. Within the program segment prefix, DOS stores a far pointer to a table that describes the program's open files. Actually, the table contains entries into a second table, the *system file table*, within which DOS tracks all open files. Figure 435 illustrates the relationship between the file handle, process file table, and system file table.

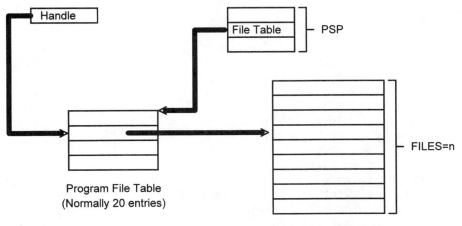

Figure 435 *The relationship between a file handle, process file table, and system file table.*

Viewing the Process File Table Entries

As Tip 435 describes, DOS keeps track of a program's open files using a process file table. At offset 18H within the program segment prefix is an array of integer values. These values specify indexes into the DOS system file table or are set to FFH if they are not in use. The following program, FILETABL.C, displays the values in the process file table. Remember, the table contains integer values that serve as indexes into the system file table:

```c
#include <stdio.h>
#include <dos.h>
#include <stdlib.h>

void main (void)
  {
    struct fcbs {
      char drive;
      char filename[8];
      char extension[3];
      int current_block;
      int record_size;
    };

    typedef struct fcbs fcb;

    struct program_segment_prefix {
      char near *int20;
      char near *next_paragraph_segment;
      char reserved_1;
      char dos_dispatcher[5];
      char far *terminate_vector;
      char far *ctrlc_vector;
      char far *critical_error_vector;
      char near *parent_psp;
      unsigned char file_table[20];
      char near *environment_block_segment;
      char far *stack_storage;
      int  handles_available;
      char far *file_table_address;
      char far *shares_previous_psp;
      char reserved_2[20];
      char dos_int21_retf[3];
      char reserved_3[9];
      fcb fcb1;
      fcb fcb2;
      char reserved_4[4];
      char command_tail[128];
    } far *psp;

    int i;

    psp = (struct program_segment_prefix far *)
          ((long) _psp << 16);

    for (i = 0; i < 20; i++)
      printf("Entry %d contains %x\n", i, psp->file_table[i]);
  }
```

When you compile and execute this program, you will find that the first five entries in the process file table are in use. These entries correspond to stdin, stdout, stderr, stdaux, and stdprn. Edit this program and open one or more files before displaying the file table entries.

Understanding the System File Table

File handles are index values into the process file table, which in turn points to the system file table. The system file table stores information about every file that DOS, a device driver, a memory-resident program, or your program has open. Figure 437 illustrates the contents of the system file table.

00H	Far pointer to next table
04H	Number of entries in this table
06H	Handles to this entry
08H	File open mode
0AH	File attribute
0BH	Device local / remote
0DH	Driver header or DPB
12H	Starting cluster
14H	Time stamp
16H	Date stamp
18H	File size
1CH	Current pointer offset
20H	Relative cluster
22H	Directory entry sector
26H	Directory entry offset
27H	Filename.ext
34H	Reserved
44H	

Figure 437 *The contents of the DOS system file table.*

DOS actually divides the system table into two parts. The first part contains five entries. The second part provides enough space for the number of entries specified by your CONFIG.SYS FILES entry (minus five—the entries that reside in the first part of the table).

C 438 Displaying the System File Table

DOS stores information about every open file within the system file table. Using the DOS list of lists, discussed in the DOS and BIOS section of this book, the following program, SYSTABLE.C, displays the system file table entries:

```c
#include <stdio.h>
#include <dos.h>
#include <stdlib.h>

void main (void)
  {
    union REGS inregs, outregs;
    struct SREGS segs;

    int i, j;

    int structure_size;

    struct SystemTableEntry {
      struct SystemTableEntry far *next; // Next SFT entry
      unsigned file_count;      // Files in table
      unsigned handle_count;    // Handles to this file
      unsigned open_mode;       // File open mode
      char file_attribute;      // Attribute byte
      unsigned local_remote;    // Bit 15 set means remote
      unsigned far *DPD;        // Drive parameter block
      unsigned starting_cluster;
      unsigned time_stamp;
      unsigned date_stamp;
      long file_size;
      long current_offset;
      unsigned relative_cluster;
      long directory_sector_number;
      char directory_entry_offset;
      char filename_ext[11];    // No period, space padded
      // Ignore SHARE fields for example
    } far *table_ptr, far *file;

    long far *system_table;

    // Get DOS version
    inregs.x.ax = 0x3001;
    intdos (&inregs, &outregs);
    if (outregs.h.al < 3)
      {
```

```
          printf ("This program requires DOS version 3 or later\n");
          exit (1);
       }
    else if (outregs.h.al == 3)
      structure_size = 0x35;
    else if (outregs.h.al >= 4)
      structure_size = 0x3B;

    // Get the list of lists pointer
    inregs.h.ah = 0x52;
    intdosx (&inregs, &outregs, &segs);

    // The pointer to the system file table is at offset 4
    system_table = MK_FP(segs.es, outregs.x.bx + 4);
    table_ptr = (struct SystemTableEntry far *) *system_table;

    do {
       printf ("%d entries in table\n", table_ptr->file_count);
       for (i = 0; i < table_ptr->file_count; i++)
         {
           file = MK_FP(FP_SEG(table_ptr), FP_OFF(table_ptr) +
             (i * structure_size));

           if (file->handle_count)
             {
                for (j = 0; j < 8; j++)
                  if (file->filename_ext[j] != ' ')
                    putchar(file->filename_ext[j]);
                  else
                    break;

                if (file->filename_ext[8] != ' ')
                  putchar('.');

                for (j = 8; j < 11; j++)
                  if (file->filename_ext[j] != ' ')
                    putchar(file->filename_ext[j]);

                printf ("  %ld bytes %x attribute %d references\n",
                  file->file_size, file->file_attribute,
                  file->handle_count);
             }
         }
       table_ptr = table_ptr->next;
    } while (FP_OFF(table_ptr) != 0xFFFF);
}
```

When you run this program from the DOS prompt, its output probably isn't very exciting. However, if you have Windows available, start Windows and use the MSDOS icon to open a DOS window. From within the DOS window run the SYSTABLE program. You might also want to edit the program and use *fopen* to open one or more files before displaying the system file table contents.

C 439 Understanding the Relationship Between Stream Pointers and File Handles

Tip 425 presented the FILE structure defined in the header file stdio.h. You have read that, when you perform high-level file operations using *fopen* or *fgets*, you declare stream pointers in terms of the *FILE* structure:

```
FILE *input, *output;
```

The C functions later convert the stream pointers to file handles to perform the actual I/O operation. To understand better the relationship between stream pointers and file handles, consider the following program, HANDLES.C, which opens the root directory file CONFIG.SYS and then displays the file descriptor for the file, as well as the predefined file handles stdin, stdout, stderr, stdaux, and stdprn:

```c
#include <stdio.h>

void main(void)
 {
   FILE *input;

   if ((input = fopen("\\CONFIG.SYS", "r")) == NULL)
     printf("Error opening \\CONFIG.SYS\n");
   else
     {
       printf("Handle for CONFIG.SYS %d\n", input->fd);
       printf("Handle for stdin %d\n", stdin->fd);
       printf("Handle for stdout %d\n", stdout->fd);
       printf("Handle for stderr %d\n", stderr->fd);
       printf("Handle for stdaux %d\n", stdaux->fd);
       printf("Handle for stdprn %d\n", stdprn->fd);

       fclose(input);
     }
 }
```

When you compile and execute this program, your screen will display the handle values 0 through 5.

Opening More Than 20 Files

C 440

As you have learned, a *file handle* is an integer value that identifies an open file. Actually, a file handle is an index into the process file table, which contains entries for up to 20 files. If your program needs to open more than 20 files, the easiest way to do is to use the DOS file services. To begin, your program must request support for more than 20 files. To do so, use the DOS INT 21H function 67H to increase the number of file handles. When you do so, DOS will allocate a table large enough to hold the number of handles specified (up to 255—the number of handles currently in use). Next, your program should open the files using the DOS services, as opposed to the C run-time library. In this way, your program can bypass the compiler's file limit. The following code fragment increases the number of file handles to 75:

```
inregs.h.ah = 0x67;
inregs.x.bx = 75;    // Number of handles
intdos(&inregs, &outregs);
if (outregs.x.ax)
  printf("Error allocating handles\n");
```

Using the DOS Services to Access a File

C 441

In Tip 440 you learned that when your programs need to access more than 20 files, you might want to use the DOS services, bypassing the C run-time library routines. The following program, COPYDOS.C, uses the DOS services to copy the contents of the first file specified in the command line to the second:

```
#include <stdio.h>
#include <dos.h>

void main (int argc, char **argv)
  {
    union REGS inregs, outregs;
    struct SREGS segs;

    char buffer[256];

    unsigned source_handle, target_handle;

    if (*argv[1] && *argv[2])
      {
```

```
           // Open the file to copy
inregs.h.ah = 0x3D;
inregs.h.al = 0;        // Open for read access
inregs.x.dx = (unsigned) argv[1];
segread (&segs);
intdosx(&inregs, &outregs, &segs);

if (outregs.x.cflag)
  printf ("Error opening source file %s\n", argv[1]);
else
  {
     source_handle = outregs.x.ax;

     // Create the target file, truncating an
     // existing file with the same name
     inregs.h.ah = 0x3C;
     inregs.x.cx = 0;       // Open with normal attribute
     inregs.x.dx = (unsigned) argv[2];
     intdosx (&inregs, &outregs, &segs);

     if (outregs.x.cflag)
       printf ("Error creating target file %s\n",
       argv[2]);
     else
        {
           target_handle = outregs.x.ax;

           do {
              // Read the source data
              inregs.h.ah = 0x3F;
              inregs.x.bx = source_handle;
              inregs.x.cx = sizeof(buffer);
              inregs.x.dx = (unsigned) buffer;
              intdosx (&inregs, &outregs, &segs);

              if (outregs.x.cflag)
                {
                   printf ("Error reading source file\n");
                   break;
                }
              else if (outregs.x.ax)  // Not end of file
                {
                   // Write the data
                   inregs.h.ah = 0x40;
                   inregs.x.bx = target_handle;
                   inregs.x.cx = outregs.x.ax;
                   inregs.x.dx = (unsigned) buffer;
                   intdosx (&inregs, &outregs, &segs);
```

```
                         if (outregs.x.cflag)
                           {
                               printf ("Error writing target file\n");
                               break;
                           }
                       }
                  } while (outregs.x.ax != 0);

                  // Close the files
                  inregs.h.ah = 0x3E;
                  inregs.x.bx = source_handle;
                  intdos (&inregs, &outregs);
                  inregs.x.bx = target_handle;
                  intdos (&inregs, &outregs);
              }
          }
      }
    else
       printf ("Specify source and target filenames\n");
}
```

Forcing a Binary or Text File Open

C 442

Many C compilers use the global variable *fmode* to determine whether a file
is opened in text or binary mode. When you use the *fopen* function, you can control
which mode is used by placing the letter t or b immediately after the desired mode, as shown in
Table 442.

Access Specifier	Access Mode
ab	Append access binary mode
at	Append access text mode
rb	Read access binary mode
rt	Read access text mode
wb	Write access binary mode
wt	Write access text mode

Table 442 *File mode specifiers for fopen.*

The following *fopen* statement, for example, opens the file FILENAME.EXT for read access in
binary mode:

```
if ((fp = fopen ("FILENAME.EXT", "rb")))
```

C 443 Reading and Writing Lines of Text

When your programs read and write text files, they will normally do so a line at a time. To read a line from a file, your programs can use the *fgets* function, whose format is shown here:

```
#include <stdio.h>

char *fgets(char string, int limit, FILE *stream);
```

The *string* parameter is the character buffer into which the file data is read. Normally, your programs will declare an array of 128 or 256 bytes to hold the data. The *limit* parameter specifies number of characters the buffer can hold. When *fgets* reads characters from the file, *fgets* will read up to *limit*–1 or to the first newline character (\n), whichever comes first. The function will then place a NULL character in the buffer to indicate the end of the string.

Many programs will use the *sizeof* to specify the buffer size, such as *sizeof(string)*. Finally, the *stream* parameter specifies the file from which the string is to be read. You must have previously opened the stream using *fopen* or use a predefined handle such as *stdin*. If *fgets* successfully reads information from the file, *fgets* will return a pointer to the string. If an error occurs or the end of file is reached, *fgets* will return NULL.

To write a string to a file, your programs can use the *fputs* function:

```
#include <stdio.h>

int fputs(const char *string, FILE *stream);
```

The *fputs* function writes the characters in specified string up to the NULL termination character. If *fputs* successfully writes the string, it returns the a positive value. If an error occurs, *fputs* returns the constant EOF.

C 444 Putting *fgets* and *fputs* to Use

In Tip 443 you learned that your programs can use the functions *fgets* and *fputs* to read and write file data. The following program, TEXTCOPY.C, uses *fgets* and *fputs* to copy the contents of the first file specified in the command line to the second:

```
#include <stdio.h>

void main(int argc, char **argv)
  {
    FILE *input, *output;

    char string[256];

    if ((input = fopen(argv[1], "r")) == NULL)
      printf("Error opening %s\n", argv[1]);
    else if ((output = fopen(argv[2], "w")) == NULL)
      {
        printf("Error opening %s\n", argv[2]);
        fclose(input);
      }
    else
      {
        while (fgets(string, sizeof(string), input))
          fputs(string, output);

        fclose(input);
        fclose(output);
      }
  }
```

As you can see, the program opens an input file and output file and then reads and write text until the end of file is encountered (*fgets* returns NULL). To copy the contents of the file TEST.DAT to TEST.SAV, for example, you would use the TEXTCOPY program as follows:

```
C:\> TEXTCOPY TEST.DAT TEST.SAV  <ENTER>
```

Forcing Binary File Translation

C 445

Many compilers use the global variable *_fmode* to determine text or binary file access. In text mode, the C run-time library functions translate linefeed characters into carriage-return/linefeed combinations and vice versa. As you learned, by setting the *_fmode* variable to *O_TEXT* or *O_BINARY*, you can control the access mode. In addition, by placing a t or b within the access mode specified in *fopen*, you can for text or binary mode access. The following *fopen* function call, for example, opens the file FILENAME.EXT for read access in binary mode:

```
if ((fp = fopen("FILENAME.EXT", "rb")) == NULL)
```

C446 Why TEXTCOPY Can't Copy Binary Files

Tip 444 presented the program TEXTCOPY.C, which copied the contents of the first file specified in the command line to the second. If you try to use TEXTCOPY to copy a binary file such as an EXE file, the copy operation will fail. When the *fgets* function reads a text file, *fgets* considers the **Ctrl-Z** character the ASCII character 26 as the end of file. Because a binary file is likely to contain one or more occurrences of the ASCII 26, *fgets* will end its copy operation at the first occurrence. If you want to copy an executable or other binary file, you must use C's low-level I/O routines.

C447 Testing for the End of File

As you have learned, when the *fgets* function encounters the end of a file, it returns NULL. Likewise, when *fgetc* reaches the end of a file, it returns EOF. There may be times when your programs need to determine if a file pointer is at the end of the file before it performs a specific operation. In such cases, your programs can call *feof*:

```
#include <stdio.h>

int feof(FILE *stream);
```

If the file pointer specified is at the end of the file, *feof* returns a nonzero value (true). If the end of file has not yet been reached, the *feof* returns 0 (false). The following loop reads and displays the characters in the file that corresponds to the file pointer *input*:

```
while (! feof(input))
  fputc(fgetc(input), stdout);
```

Note: *Once the end-of-file indicator for a file has been set, it remains set until the file is closed or rewind is called.*

Ungetting a Character

Many programs, such as a compiler, for example, often read characters from a file one at a time until a specific character (a delimeter or token) is found. Once the character is found, the program performs specific processing, after which it continues reading from the file. Depending on how the file your program is reading is structured, there may be times when it would be convenient for the program to "unread" a character. In such cases, the program can use the *ungetc* function, whose format is shown here:

```
#include <stdio.h>

int ungetc(int character, FILE *stream);
```

The *ungetc* function places the character specified back into the file buffer. You can only "unget" one character. If you call *ungetc* two times in succession, the first character you unget will be overwritten by the second. The *ungetc* function places the specified character in the *FILE* structure *hold* member. The next file read operation will include the character.

Reading Formatted File Data

As you have learned, the *fprintf* function lets you write formatted output to a file. In a similar way, the *fscanf* function lets you read formatted file data, just as the *scanf* function lets you read formatted data from the keyboard. The format of the *fscanf* function is as follows:

```
#include <stdio.h>

int fscanf(FILE *stream, const char *format[,
  variable_address...]);
```

The *stream* parameter is a pointer to the file from which you want *fscanf* to read. The *format* parameter specifies the data format—using the same control character as *scanf*. Finally, the *variable_address* parameter specifies an address into which you want the data read. The ellipses (...) that follow the *variable_address* parameter indicate that you can have multiple addresses separated by commas. Upon completion, *fscanf* returns the number of fields read. If the end of file is encountered, *fscanf* returns the constant *EOF*. The following program, FSCANF.C, opens the file DATA.DAT for output, writes formatted output to the file using *fprintf*, closes the file, and then reopens it for input, reading its contents with *fscanf*:

```
#include <stdio.h>

void main(void)
 {
    FILE *fp;

    int age;
    float salary;
    char name[64];

    if ((fp = fopen("DATA.DAT", "w")) == NULL)
      printf("Error opening DATA.DAT for output\n");
    else
      {
        fprintf(fp, "33 35000.0 Kris");
        fclose(fp);

        if ((fp = fopen("DATA.DAT", "r")) == NULL)
          printf("Error opening DATA.DAT for input\n");
        else
          {
            fscanf(fp, "%d %f %s", &age, &salary, name);
            printf("Age %d Salary %f Name %s\n", age, salary, name);
            fclose(fp);
          }
      }
 }
```

C 450 Relative Positioning of the File Pointer

You have learned that, to track your current position within the file, the file pointer contains a position pointer. When you know the format of your file, there may be times when you want to advance the position pointer to a specific location before you start reading the file. For example, the first 256 bytes of your file can contain header information that you don't want to read. In such cases, your programs can use the *fseek* function to position the file pointer:

```
#include <stdio.h>

int fseek(FILE *stream, long offset, int relative_to);
```

The *stream* parameter specifies the file pointer you want to position. The *offset* and *relative_to* parameters combine to specify the desired position. The *offset* contains the a byte offset into the file. The *relative_to* parameter specifies the location in the file from which the offset should be applied. Table 450 specifies the values you can use for the *relative_to* parameter.

Constant	Meaning
SEEK_CUR	From current file position
SEEK_SET	From the beginning of the file
SEEK_END	From the end of the file

Table 450 *File positions from which an offset can be applied.*

To position the file pointer immediately after the first 256 bytes of header information in a file, for example, you would use *fseek* as follows:

```
fseek(fp, 256, SEEK_SET);   // Offset 0 is the start
```

If successful, *fseek* returns the value 0. If an error occurs, *fseek* returns a nonzero value.

Getting File Handle Information

C 451

When you work with a file handle, there may be times when you need to know specifics about the corresponding file, such as the disk drive on which the file is stored. In such cases, your programs can use the *fstat* function, whose format is as follows:

```
#include <sys\stat.h>

int fstat(int handle, struct stat *buffer);
```

The function assigns specifics about the file to a structure of type *stat*, which is defined as follows within the *include* file stat.h:

```
struct stat {
   short st_dev;      // Drive number of disk
   short st_ino;      // Not used by DOS
   short st_mode;     // File open mode
   short st_nlink;    // Always 1
   short st_uid;      // User id—Not used
   short st_gid;      // Group id—Not used
   short st_rdev;     // Same as st_dev
   long st_size;      // File size in bytes
   long st_atime;     // Time file was last opened
   long st_mtime;     // Same as st_atime
   long st_ctime;     // Same as st_atime
};
```

If *fstat* is successful, it returns the value 0. If an error occurs, *fstat* returns the value –1 and sets the global variable *errno* to EBADF (for a bad file handle). The following program, AUTOINFO.C, uses the *fstat* function to display the size of and date and time the root directory file AUTOEXEC.BAT was last modified:

```
#include <stdio.h>
#include <io.h>
#include <fcntl.h>
#include <sys\stat.h>
#include <time.h>

void main(void)
  {
    int handle;

    struct stat buffer;

    if ((handle = open("\\AUTOEXEC.BAT", O_RDONLY)) == -1)
     printf("Error opening \\AUTOEXEC.BAT\n");
    else
      {
        if (fstat(handle, &buffer))
          printf("Error getting file information\n");
        else
          printf("AUTOEXEC.BAT is %ld bytes Last used %s\n",
            buffer.st_size, ctime(&buffer.st_atime));
        close(handle);
      }
  }
```

C 452 Reopening a File Stream

As your program work with files, there may be times when you want to override an open file pointer. For example, DOS does not provide a way to redirect the output of the *stderr* file handle from the command line. However, from within your program, you can override the destination of the *stderr* file pointer by reopening it using the *freopen* function:

```
#include <stdio.h>

FILE *freopen(const char *filename, const char
   access_mode, FILE *stream);
```

The *freopen* function is very similar to *fopen*, except that you pass to the function a file pointer whose value you want to overwrite. If the function is successful, it returns a pointer to the file original file stream. If an error occurs, *freopen* returns NULL. The following program, NOSTDERR.C, for example, redirects *stderr*'s to the file STANDARD.ERR, as opposed to the screen:

```c
#include <stdio.h>

void main(void)
  {
    if (freopen("STANDARD.ERR", "w", stderr))
      fputs("stderr has been redirected", stderr);
    else
      printf("Error in reopen\n");
  }
```

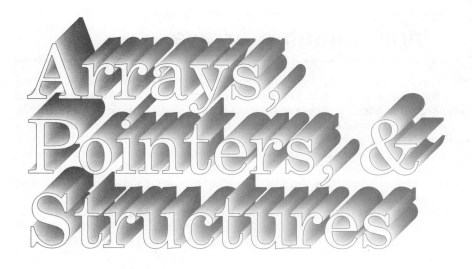

Arrays, Pointers, & Structures

C453 Understanding Arrays

As you have learned, a type describes the set of values a variable can hold and the set of operations that can be performed on the variable. With the exception of character strings, all of the types you have examined to this point can hold only one value. As your programs begin to perform more useful work, there will be times when you will want a variable to hold many values. For example, the variable *scores* might keep track of 100 students' test scores. Likewise, the variable *salaries* might hold the different salary for each company employee. An *array* is a data structure that can store multiple values of the same type. For example, you can create an array that can hold 100 values of type *int* and a second array that can hold 25 values of type *float*. Every value you assign to an array must be the same type as that of the array. In this section you will learn how to create and work with arrays in your programs. Once you work with one or two arrays, you will find their use very straightforward. If you already feel comfortable with strings, you are in great shape. A character string is simply an array of characters.

C454 Declaring an Array

An *array* is a variable capable of storing multiple values of the same type. To declare an array, you must specify the desired type (such as *int*, *float*, or *double*), as well as the array size. To specify an array size, you place the number of values the array can store within brackets that follow the array name. The following declaration, for example, creates an array named *scores* that is capable of storing 100 test scores of type *int*:

```
int scores[100];
```

In a similar way, the following declaration creates an array of type *float* that contains 50 salaries:

```
float salaries[50];
```

When you declare an array, C allocates enough memory to hold the all of the elements. The first entry resides at location 0. For example, given the arrays *scores* and *salaries*, the first statements assign the values 80 and 35000 to the first array elements:

```
scores[0] = 80;

salaries[0] = 35000.0;
```

Because the first array element begins at offset 0, the array's last element occurs one location before the array's size. Given the previous array's *scores* and *salaries*, the following statements assign values to the arrays last elements:

```
scores[99] = 75;

salaries[49] = 24000.0;
```

Visualizing an Array

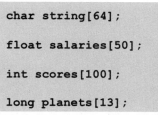

As you have learned, an *array* is variable that can store multiple values of the same type. To help you better understand how an array stores information, consider the following array declarations:

```
char string[64];

float salaries[50];

int scores[100];

long planets[13];
```

After you assign values to each array, the arrays will reside in memory similar to those shown in Figure 455.

Figure 455 *Storing values in arrays.*

As you can see, each array's first value is resides at offset 0. In the ABCs section of this book, a variable was described as a name assigned to one or memory locations. In the case of an array, the number of memory locations that correspond to an array can be quite large.

C456 Understanding an Array's Storage Requirements

As you have learned, an *array* is a named collection of values of the same type. When you declare an array, the C compiler allocates enough memory to hold the number of values specified. The actual amount of memory allocated depends on the array type. For example, an array of 100 elements of type int will normally require 100 * 2 or 200 bytes of memory. An array of 100 elements of type float on the other hand, would consume 100 * 4 bytes or 400 bytes. The following program, ARRAYSIZ.C, uses C's *sizeof* operator to display the amount of memory consumed by different array types:

```
#include <stdio.h>

void main(void)
  {
    int scores[100];
    float salaries[100];
    char string[100];

    printf("Bytes used to hold int scores[100] is %d bytes\n",
      sizeof(scores));

    printf("Bytes used to hold int salaries[100] is %d bytes\n",
      sizeof(salaries));

    printf("Bytes used to hold char string[100] is %d bytes\n",
      sizeof(string));
  }
```

When you compile and execute this program, your screen will display the following output:

```
C:\> ARRAYSIZ  <ENTER>
Bytes used to hold int scores[100] is 200 bytes
Bytes used to hold float salaries[100] is 400 bytes
Bytes used to hold char string[100] is 100 bytes
```

C457 Initializing an Array

Throughout this book, many of the programs have initialized character strings as follows:

```
char title[] = "Jamsa's 1001 C/C++ Tips";
char section[64] = "Arrays";
```

In the first case, the C compiler will allocate 24 bytes to hold the string. In the second case, the compiler will allocate an array of 64 bytes, initializing the first seven characters to the letters "Arrays" and the NULL character. Most compilers will also initialize the remaining byte locations to NULL. When you declare arrays of other types, you can initialize them in this same way. For example, the following statement initializes the integer array *scores* to the values 80, 70, 90, 85, and 80:

```
int scores[5] = {80, 70, 90, 85, 80};
```

When you assign initial values to an array, you must enclose the values within right and left braces {}. In this case, the array size matches the number of values assigned to the array. The following statement, however, assigns four floating-point values to an array that can store 64 values:

```
float salaries[64] = {25000.0, 32000.0,
    44000.0, 23000.0};
```

Depending on your compiler, the values assigned to the elements that are not explicitly assigned, may be assigned to 0. As a rule, you should not make assumptions that the compiler will initialize the other elements. If you don't specify an array size, the compiler will allocate enough memory to hold only the specified values. The following array declaration, for example, creates an array large enough to hold three values of type *long*:

```
long planets[] = {1234567L, 654321L, 1221311L};
```

Accessing Array Elements

C458

The values stored in an array are called *array elements*. To access an array element, you specify the array name and the desired element. The following program, ELEMENTS.C, initializes the array *scores* and then uses *printf* to display the element values:

```
#include <stdio.h>

void main(void)
 {
   int scores[5] = {80, 70, 90, 85, 80};

   printf("Array Values\n");
   printf("scores[0] %d\n", scores[0]);
   printf("scores[1] %d\n", scores[1]);
```

```
      printf("scores[2] %d\n", scores[2]);
      printf("scores[3] %d\n", scores[3]);
      printf("scores[4] %d\n", scores[4]);
 }
```

When you compile and execute this program, your screen will display the following output:

```
C:\> ELEMENTS  <ENTER>
Array Values
scores[0] = 80
scores[1] = 70
scores[2] = 90
scores[3] = 85
scores[4] = 80
```

As you can see, to access a specific array element, you specify the desired element number within the left and right braces that follow the array name.

C 459 Looping Through Array Elements

In Tip 458 you used the values 0 through 4 to display the values of the array *scores*. When you reference array elements, specifying numbers for each array element in this way can become very cumbersome. As an alternative, your programs can use a variable to reference array elements. For example, assuming the variable i contains the value 2, the following statement would assign *array[2]* the value 80:

```
i = 2;

array[i] = 80;
```

The following program, SHOWARRA.C, uses the variable i and a *for* loop to display the elements of the array *scores*:

```
#include <stdio.h>

void main(void)
 {
   int scores[5] = {80, 70, 90, 85, 80};
   int i;

   printf("Array Values\n");
```

```
    for (i = 0; i < 5; i++)
      printf("scores[%d] %d\n", i, scores[i]);
  }
```

Use Constants to Define Arrays

As you have learned, when your programs work with arrays, you must specify the array size. For example, the following program 5_VALUES.C, declares an array of five values and then uses a *for* loop to display the array's values:

```
#include <stdio.h>

void main(void)
  {
    int values[5] = {80, 70, 90, 85, 80};
    int i;

    for (i = 0; i < 5; i++)
      printf("values[%d] %d\n", i, values[i]);
  }
```

Assume, for example, that you later want to change this program so that it supports ten values, you must change not only the array declaration, but also the *for* loop. The more changes you must make to a program, the greater your chance of error. As an alternative, your programs should declare arrays using constants. The following program, 5_CONST.C, declares an array based on the constant *ARRAY_SIZE*. As you can see, the program not only uses the constant to declare the array, but also within the *for* loop:

```
#include <stdio.h>

#define ARRAY_SIZE 5

void main(void)
  {
    int values[ARRAY_SIZE] = {80, 70, 90, 85, 80};
    int i;

    for (i = 0; i < ARRAY_SIZE; i++)
      printf("values[%d] %d\n", i, values[i]);
  }
```

Should you later need to change the array size, you can simply change the value assigned to the *ARRAY_SIZE* constant, and loops that control the array are automatically updated, as well as the array size.

Passing an Array to a Function

461

As you have learned, an array is a variable capable of storing multiple values of the same type. Like all variables, your programs can pass arrays to functions. When you declare a function that works with an array parameter, you must tell the compiler. The following program, ARRFUNCT.C, for example, uses the function *show_array* to display the values in an array. As you can see, the program passes to the function the array and the number of elements it contains:

```c
#include <stdio.h>

void show_array(int values[], int number_of_elements)
  {
    int i;

    for (i = 0; i < number_of_elements; i++)
     printf("%d\n", values[i]);
  }

void main(void)
  {
    int scores[5] = {70, 80, 90, 100, 90};

    show_array(scores, 5);
  }
```

When a function receives an array as a parameter, the compiler does not have to specify the array size in the parameter declaration. In the case of the function *show_values*, the brackets the follow the variable name *value* inform the compiler that the parameter is an array. Other than knowing that the parameter is an array, the compiler does not care about the size of an array passed to the function.

Revisiting Arrays as Functions

462

In Tip 461 you learned that when you declare the formal parameter for an array, you don't need to declare an array size. Instead, you need only specify the left and right brackets. The following program, ARRPARAM.C, passes three different arrays (of different sizes) to the function *show_values*:

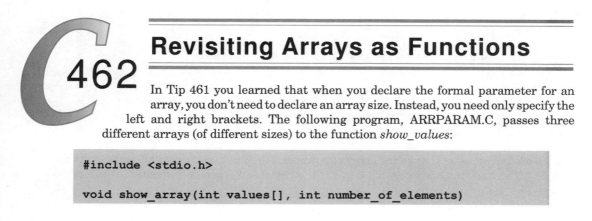

```c
#include <stdio.h>

void show_array(int values[], int number_of_elements)
```

```
{
  int i;

  printf("About to display %d values\n", number_of_elements);
  for (i = 0; i < number_of_elements; i++)
   printf("%d\n", values[i]);
}

void main(void)
  {
    int scores[5] = {70, 80, 90, 100, 90};
    int count[10] = {1, 2, 3, 4, 5, 6, 7, 8, 9, 10};
    int small[2] = {-33, -44};

    show_array(scores, 5);
    show_array(count, 10);
    show_array(small, 2);
  }
```

When you compile and execute this program, your screen will display each array's values. The function does not care about the array size. However, note that the arrays passed to the function are all type *int*. If you tried to pass an array of type *float* to the function, the compiler would generate an error.

How String Arrays Differ

C463

Many of the tips presented throughout this book have passed strings to the functions. In most cases, the functions did not specify the string size. For example, the following statement uses the *strupr* function to convert a string to uppercase:

```
char title[64] = "Jamsa's 1001 C/C++ Tips";

strupr(title);
```

As you have learned, in C, the end of a character string is represented by the NULL character. As such, functions can search the array elements for the NULL to determine where the array ends. Arrays of other types, such as *int*, *float*, or *long*, however, do not have an equivalent "ending" character. Therefore, you must normally pass to functions that work with arrays the number of elements the array contains.

C 464 Passing Arrays On the Stack

Several of the previous tips have discussed passing arrays as parameters to functions. When you pass an array to a function, C only places the address of the array's first element on the stack. Figure 464, for example, illustrates the array *scores* and a function call to *show_array* using *scores*. As you can see, C places only the array's starting address on the stack.

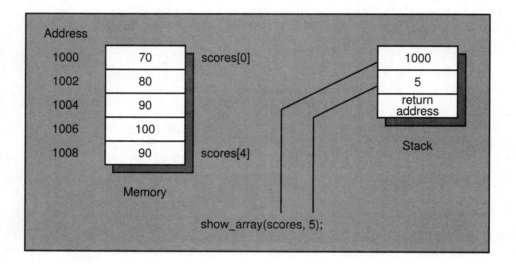

Figure 464 *When you pass an array parameter, C places an array's starting address on the stack.*

As you can see from Figure 464, the function receives no information from C regarding the size of the array.

C 465 How Many Elements Can an Array Hold

As you have learned, depending on your array type, the actual amount of memory an array can consume will differ. If you are working in the DOS environment, the amount of memory your arrays can consume will depend on the current memory model. In general, an array cannot consume more than 64Kb. The following program, TOO_BIG.C, for example, may fail to compile because the arrays simply consume too much memory:

```
void main (void)
  {
    char string[66000L];    // 66,000 bytes

    int values[33000L];     // 33,000 * 2 = 66,000 bytes

    float numbers[17000];   // 17,000 * 4 = 68,000 bytes
  }
```

Using the Huge Memory Model for Big Arrays

C 466

If the amount of memory an array consumes exceeds 64Kb, you can direct many DOS-based compilers to use the *huge memory model* by treating the array as a pointer and including the word *huge* within the declaration, as shown here:

```
float huge values[17000];
```

The following program, HUGE_FLT.C, creates a huge floating-point array:

```
#include <stdio.h>
#include <malloc.h>

void main (void)
  {
    int i;

    float huge *values;

    if ((values = (float huge *) halloc (17000,
        sizeof(float))) == NULL)
      printf ("Error allocating huge array\n");
    else
      {
        printf("Filling the array\n");

        for (i = 0; i < 17000; i++)
          values[i] = i * 1.0;

        for (i = 0; i < 17000; i++)
          printf ("%8.1f ", values[i]);

        hfree(values);
      }
  }
```

C 467 Arrays versus Dynamic Memory—Tradeoffs

As you become more comfortable with C and the use of pointers within C, you may start to use arrays less often and instead allocate memory dynamically as you need it. There are several tradeoffs you need to consider when you determine whether to use dynamic memory or an array. To begin, many users find arrays simpler to understand and use. As a result, your program itself might be easier for other programmers to follow. Second, because the compiler allocates space for arrays, your programs do not experience the run-time overhead associated with dynamic memory allocation. As a result, an array based program might execute slightly faster.

As you have learned however, when you declare an array, you must specify the array size. If you do know the size you will need, there might be a tendency to allocate a larger array than you need. As a result, memory might be wasted. If the array size is too small, you will need to edit your program, change the array sizes, and recompile.

When you declare an array within your programs, keep in mind that you can perform identical processing by allocating memory dynamically. As you will learn in the Pointer section of this book, you can reference dynamically allocated memory using array indexes and eliminate the pointer confusion that often frustrates new C programmers. Because most operating systems allow programs to allocate memory very quickly, your programs might prefer the flexibility and improved memory management opportunities provided by dynamic memory allocation over the slight system overhead it incurs.

C 468 Understanding Multidimensional Arrays

As you have learned, an array is a variable capable of storing multiple values of the same type. In all of the examples presented to this point, the arrays have consisted of a single row of data. However, C supports 2, 3, and multidimensional arrays, as shown in Figure 468.

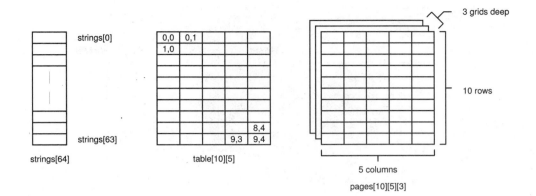

Figure 468 *Multidimensional arrays.*

The best way to visualize a two-dimensional array is as a table with rows and columns. If array contains three dimensions, visualize the array as several pages, each of which contains a two-dimensional table. The following array declarations create the arrays shown in Figure 468.

```
char strings[64];

int table[10][5];

float pages[10][5][3];
```

Understanding
Rows and Columns

C469

As you have learned, C supports multidimensional arrays are similar to tables of values. When you work with a two-dimensional array, think of the array as a table of rows and columns. The rows of the table go from left to right while columns go up and down the page, as shown in Figure 469.

Figure 469 *Array rows and columns.*

When you declare a two-dimensional array, the first value you specify states the number of rows and the second value the number of columns:

```
int table [2][3];
```

C 470 Accessing Elements in a Two-Dimensional Array

As you have learned, a two-dimensional array is best visualized as a table consisting of rows and columns. To reference a specific array element, you must specify the corresponding row and column position. Figure 470, illustrates statements that access specific elements within the array *table*.

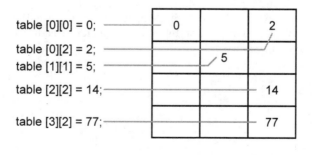

table [4][3];

Figure 470 *To access elements in a two-dimensional array, you must specify row and column position.*

Initializing Elements in a Two-Dimensional Array

In Tip 457 you learned that you can initialize array elements by placing the element values within left and right braces following the array declaration. The following statement uses this same technique to initialize a two-dimensional array. However, in this case, the values for each array row are specified within their own braces:

```
int table[2][3] = {{1, 2, 3},
                    {4, 5, 6}};
```

The C compiler will initialize the array elements as shown in Figure 471.

1	2	3
4	5	6

table [2][3];

Figure 471 *Initializing the elements of a two-dimensional array.*

In a similar manner, the following statement initializes the elements of a larger array:

```
int sales[4][5] {{1, 2, 3, 4, 5},
                 {6, 7, 8, 9, 10},
                 {11, 12, 13, 14, 15},
                 {16, 17, 18, 19, 20}};
```

C 472 Determining the Amount of Memory a Multidimensional Array Consumes

In Tip 456 you learned to determine an array's memory consumption by multiplying the number of elements in the array by the number of bytes required to represent the array's type (such as 2 for *int*, 4 for *char*, and so on). To determine the memory consumed by a multidimensional array, you perform identical processing. To determine the number of elements in a multidimensional array, simply multiply the number of rows by the number of columns. The following expressions illustrate the amount of memory consumed by different array declarations:

```
int a[5][10];          // 2 * 5 * 10 == 100 bytes
float b[5][8];         // 4 * 5 * 8 == 160 bytes
int c[3][4][5];        // 2 * 3 * 4 * 5 = 120 bytes
```

The following program MD_SIZE.C, uses the *sizeof* operator to determine the number of bytes consumed by different array declarations:

```c
#include <stdio.h>

void main(void)
  {
    int box[3][3];

    float year_sales[52][5];

    char pages[40][60][20];

    printf("Bytes to hold int box[3][3] %d bytes\n", sizeof(box));
    printf("Bytes to hold float year_sales[52][5] %d bytes\n",
      sizeof(year_sales));
    printf("Bytes to hold char pages[40][60][20] %ld bytes\n",
      sizeof(pages));
  }
```

When you compile and execute this program, your screen will display the following:

```
C:\> MD_SIZE  <ENTER>
Bytes to hold int box[3][3] 18 bytes
Bytes to hold float year_sales[52][5] 1040 bytes
Bytes to hold char pages[40][60][20] 48000 bytes
```

Looping Through a Two-Dimensional Array

In Tip 458 you learned how to use a variable to index elements in an array. When your programs work with two-dimensional arrays, you will normally use two variables to access array elements. The following program, SHOW_2D.C, uses the variables *row* and *column* to display the values of the array *table*:

```c
#include <stdio.h>

void main(void)
{
   int row, column;

   float table[3][5] = {{1.0, 2.0, 3.0, 4.0, 5.0},
                        {6.0, 7.0, 8.0, 9.0, 10.0},
                        {11.0, 12.0, 13.0, 14.0, 15.0}};

   for (row = 0; row < 3; row++)
    for (column = 0; column < 5; column++)
     printf("table[%d][%d] = %f\n", row, column,
       table[row][column]);
}
```

By nesting the *for* loops as shown, the program displays the elements contained in the arrays first row (1.0 through 5.0) and then moves to the second and then the third row, repeating this process.

Traversing a Three-Dimensional Array

In Tip 473 you learned how to traverse a two-dimensional array using two variables named *row* and *column*. The following program, SHOW_3D.C, uses the variables *row*, *column*, and *table* to traverse a three-dimensional array:

```c
#include <stdio.h>

void main(void)
{
   int row, column, table;
```

```
   float values[2][3][5] = {
                          {{1.0, 2.0, 3.0, 4.0, 5.0},
                           {6.0, 7.0, 8.0, 9.0, 10.0},
                           {11.0, 12.0, 13.0, 14.0, 15.0}},

                          {{16.0, 17.0, 18.0, 19.0, 20.0},
                           {21.0, 22.0, 23.0, 24.0, 25.0},
                           {26.0, 27.0, 28.0, 29.0, 30.0}}
                          };

      for (row = 0; row < 2; row++)
        for (column = 0; column < 3; column++)
          for (table = 0; table < 5; table++)
            printf("values[%d][%d][%d] = %f\n", row, column, table,
              values[row][column][table]);
   }
```

C 475 Initializing Multidimensional Arrays

In Tip 474 you learned to how display the contents of a three-dimensional array using three variables, row, column, and table. At that time, the program initialized the three-dimensional array values:

```
   float values[2][3][5] = {
                          {{1.0, 2.0, 3.0, 4.0, 5.0},
                           {6.0, 7.0, 8.0, 9.0, 10.0},
                           {11.0, 12.0, 13.0, 14.0, 15.0}},

                          {{16.0, 17.0, 18.0, 19.0, 20.0},
                           {21.0, 22.0, 23.0, 24.0, 25.0},
                           {26.0, 27.0, 28.0, 29.0, 30.0}}
                          };
```

At first glance, intializing a multidimensional array can be confusing at best. To understand better how to initialize such arrays, this tip presents several sample initializations. As you examine the initializations, perform the initializations from right to left:

```
int a[1][2][3] = {
                { {1, 2, 3}, {4, 5, 6} }
              };  // Array braces

int b[2][3][4] = {
          { {1, 2, 3, 4}, {5, 6, 7, 8}, {9, 10, 11, 12} },
```

```
                    { {13, 14, 15, 16}, {17, 18, 19, 20}, {21, 22, 23, 24} }
                  };  // Array braces

int c[3][2][4] = {
                    { {1, 2, 3, 4}, {5, 6, 7, 8} },
                    { {9, 10, 11, 12}, {13, 14, 15, 16}},
                    { {17, 18, 19, 20}, {21, 22, 23, 24}}
                  };  // Array braces


int d[1][2][3][4] = {
                  {{{1, 2, 3, 4}, {5, 6, 7, 8}, {9, 10, 11, 12}},
                   {{13, 14, 15, 16}, {17, 18, 19, 20}, {21, 22, 23, 24}}}
                  }; // Array braces
```

Each array initialization gets a set of outer braces. Within those braces, you then define, within additional braces, the different array elements.

Passing a Two-Dimensional Array to a Function

476

As you programs work with multidimensional arrays, there will be times when you need to write functions that work with the arrays. In Tip 461 you learned that when you pass arrays to a function, you don't need to specify the number of array elements. When you work with two-dimensional arrays, you don't need to specify the number of rows in the array, but you do need to specify the number of columns. The following program, FUNCT_2D.C, uses the function *show_2d_array* to display the contents of several two-dimensional arrays:

```
#include <stdio.h>

void show_2d_array(int array[][10], int rows)
  {
    int i, j;

    for (i = 0; i < rows; i++)
      for (j = 0; j < 10; j++)
        printf("array[%d][%d] = %d\n", i, j, array[i][j]);
  }


void main(void)
  {
    int a[1][10] = {{1, 2, 3, 4, 5, 6, 7, 8, 9, 10}};
```

```
   int b[2][10] = {{1, 2, 3, 4, 5, 6, 7, 8, 9, 10},
                   {11, I2, 13, 14, 15, 16, 17, 18, 19, 20}};
   int c[3][10] = {{1, 2, 3, 4, 5, 6, 7, 8, 9, 10},
                   {11, 12, 13, 14, 15, 16, 17, 18, 19, 20},
                   {21, 22, 23, 24, 25, 26, 27, 28, 29, 30}};

   show_2d_array(a, 1);
   show_2d_array(b, 2);
   show_2d_array(c, 3);
}
```

C 477 Treating a Multidimensional Arrays as One Dimensional

In Tip 476 you learned that when you pass a two-dimensional array to a function and you want to access the array's row and column positions, you must specify the number of columns, as shown here:

```
void show_2d_array(int array[][10], int rows)
```

If you want to work with the elements of a multidimensional array, but you don't need to access the elements in their row or column positions, your functions can treat the multidimensional array is if it were one dimensional. The following program, SUM_2D.C, returns the sum of the values in a two-dimensional array:

```
#include <stdio.h>

long sum_array(int array[], int elements)
 {
    long sum = 0;

    int i;

    for (i = 0; i < elements; i++)
      sum += array[i];

    return(sum);
 }


void main(void)
 {
   int a[10] = {1, 2, 3, 4, 5, 6, 7, 8, 9, 10};
   int b[2][10] = {{1, 2, 3, 4, 5, 6, 7, 8, 9, 10},
```

```
                   {11, 12, 13, 14, 15, 16, 17, 18, 19, 20}};
    int c[3][10] = {{1, 2, 3, 4, 5, 6, 7, 8, 9, 10},
                   {11, 12, 13, 14, 15, 16, 17, 18, 19, 20},
                   {21, 22, 23, 24, 25, 26, 27, 28, 29, 30}};

    printf("Sum of first array elements %d\n", sum_array(a, 10));
    printf("Sum of second array elements %d\n", sum_array(b, 20));
    printf("Sum of third array elements %d\n", sum_array(c, 30));
}
```

As you can see, the function *sum_array* supports arrays of one, two, or more dimensions. The secret to understanding how the function works is to understand how C stores multidimensional arrays in memory. Tip 478 discusses array storage in detail.

Understanding How C Stores Multidimensional Arrays

C 478

In Tip 454 you learned that when you declare an array, such as *int scores[100];* C allocates a memory to hold each array element. When you allocate a multidimensional array, the same is true. Although conceptually, multidimensional arrays consist of rows and columns, to the compiler, a multidimensional array is one long byte range. For example, assume that your program declares the following array:

```
#include table[3][5];
```

Figure 478 illustrates the array's conceptual appearance and actual memory use.

☞

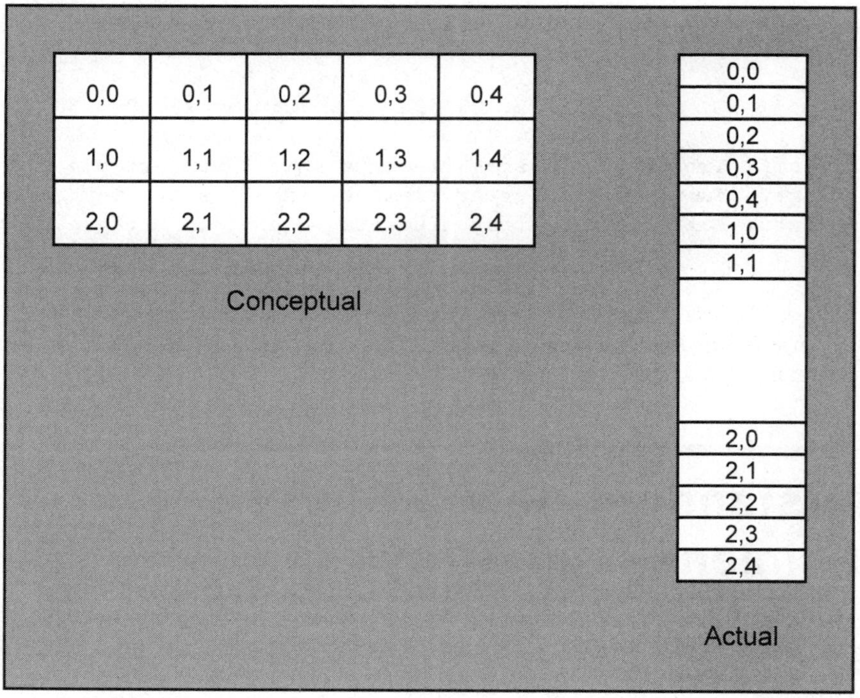

0,0	0,1	0,2	0,3	0,4
1,0	1,1	1,2	1,3	1,4
2,0	2,1	2,2	2,3	2,4

Conceptual

0,0
0,1
0,2
0,3
0,4
1,0
1,1
2,0
2,1
2,2
2,3
2,4

Actual

Figure 478 *Mapping a multidimensional array to memory.*

In Tip 477 you created a function that added up the values in a multidimensional array by treating the array as one dimensional. Because the C compiler actually maps the multidimensional array to a one-dimensional memory range, treating the array as one dimensional is valid.

C479 Row-Major Order versus Column-Major Order

In Tip 478 you learned that the C compiler maps multidimensional arrays to one-dimensional memory. When the compiler maps a multidimensional array to a memory, the compiler has two options. As shown in Figure 479, the compiler can place the array's row elements in memory before the column values, or the compiler can place the column elements first.

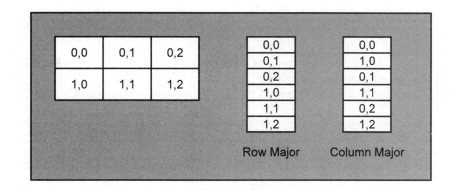

Figure 479 *Mapping array elements to memory.*

When the compiler places the array's row elements in memory before the column elements, the compiler is performing *row-major ordering*. Likewise, when the compiler places the column elements first, the compiler performs *column-major ordering*. C compilers store multidimensional arrays in row-major order.

Arrays of Structures
of Arrays (...)

480

Arrays and structures let you group related information. As you have learned, C lets you create arrays of structures or use arrays as structure members.

In general, C does not place a limit on the depth to which your programs can go with respect to nested data structures. For example, the declaration creates an array of 100 employee structures. Within each structure is an array of *Date* structures that correspond to the employee's hiring, first review, and last review:

```
struct Employee {
    char name[64];
    int age;
    char ssan[11];    // Social security number
    int pay_grade;
    float salary;
    unsigned employee_number;
    struct Date {
        int month;
        int day;
        int year;
    } emp_dates[3];
} staff[100];
```

To access members and arrays elements, you simply work from left to right, starting from the outside and working in. For example, the following statements assign an employee's hiring date:

```
staff[10].emp_dates[0].month = 7;
staff[10].emp_dates[0].day = 7;
staff[10].emp_dates[0].year = 7;
```

Although nesting structures and arrays in this way can be very convenient, keep in mind that the deeper your structures nest such data structures, the more difficult the structure will become for other programmers to understand.

C481 Understanding Unions

As you have learned, structures let your programs store related information. Depending on your program's purpose, there may be times when the information you store in a structure will be either one value or another. For example, assume that your program tracks two special date values for each employee. For current employees, the program tracks the number of days the employee has worked. For employees who no longer work for the company, the program tracks the date of the employee's last employment. One way to track this information is be to use a structure:

```
struct EmpDates {
  int days_worked;
  struct LastDate {
    int month;
    int day;
    int year;
  } last_day;
};
```

Because the program will either use the *days_worked* or *last_day* members, the memory to hold unused value is wasted for each employee. As an alternative, C lets your programs use a *union*, which allocates only the memory required to hold the union's largest member:

```
union EmpDates {
  int days_worked;
  struct LastDate {
    int month;
    int day;
    int year;
  } last_day;
};
```

To access the union members, you use the dot operator, just as you would with a structure. Unlike the structure, however, the union is only capable of storing one member's value. Figure 481 illustrates how C allocates memory for the structure and member.

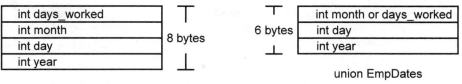

Figure 481 *Allocating memory for a similar structure and union.*

As you will learn, using unions not only saves memory, but also provides your programs with the ability to interpret memory values in a different way.

Saving Memory with Unions

C482

In Tip 481 you learned that C lets you store information within a *union*. When you use a union, C allocates the amount of memory required to hold the union's largest member. The following program, UNIONSIZ.C, uses the *sizeof* operator to display the amount of memory consumed by different unions:

```c
#include <stdio.h>

void main(void)
  {
    union EmployeeDates {
      int days_worked;
      struct Date {
        int month;
        int day;
        int year;
      } last_day;
    } emp_info;

    union Numbers {
      int a;
      float b;
      long c;
      double d;  // Largest—requires 8 bytes
    } value;
```

```
        printf("Size of EmployeeDates %d bytes\n", sizeof(emp_info));
        printf("Size of Numbers %d bytes\n", sizeof(value));
    }
```

When you compile and execute this program, your screen will display the following output:

```
C:\> UNIONSIZ   <ENTER>
Size of EmployeeDates 6 bytes
Size of Numbers 8 bytes
```

C 483 Using *REGS*—A Classic Union

As you have learned, unions let your programs reduce their memory requirements and view information in different ways. In the DOS & BIOS section of
this book, you will learn that to access the DOS and BIOS services, your programs
normally assign parameters (at the assembly language level) to specific PC registers. To
make the services available to your C programs, most C compilers provides access to the DOS and
BIOS services through run-time library routines that use a union of type *REGS*:

```
struct WORDREGS {
  unsigned int ax, bx, cx, dx, si, di, cflag, flags;
};

struct BYTEREGS {
  unsigned char al, ah, bl, ah, cl, ch, dl, dh;
};

union REGS {
  struct WORDREGS x;
  struct BYTEREGS h;
};
```

When your programs access the PC's general purpose registers (AX, BX, CX, and DX), the PC lets
you refer to the register in a 16-bit (word) format or you can refer to the register's high and low
bytes (AL, AH, BL, BH, CL, CH, DL, and DH). Because either method refers to the same register,
you have two ways of looking at the same storage location. Using a union, your programs have
two ways to access the general purpose registers. Figure 483 illustrates how C stores variables
of the *REGS* union in memory.

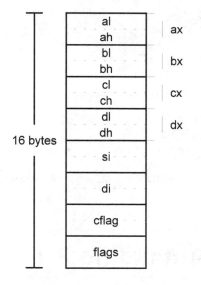

Figure 483 *How C stores variables of the union REGS.*

Putting the *REGS* Union to Use

C484

In Tip 483 you learned that one of the most frequently used unions in DOS-based programs is the *REGS* union. The following program, GET_VERX.C, uses the *REGS* union to display the current DOS version, accessing the general-purpose registers in their word form:

```
#include <stdio.h>
#include <dos.h>

void main(void)
  {
    union REGS inregs, outregs;

    inregs.x.ax = 0x3000;
    intdos(&inregs, &outregs);

    printf("Current version %d.%d\n", outregs.x.ax & 0xFF,
        outregs.x.ax >> 8);
  }
```

The following program, GET_VERH.C, uses the union's byte registers to display the current DOS version:

```
#include <stdio.h>
#include <dos.h>

void main(void)
  {
    union REGS inregs, outregs;

    inregs.h.ah = 0x30;
    inregs.h.al = 0;
    intdos(&inregs, &outregs);

    printf("Current version %d.%d\n", outregs.h.al, outregs.h.ah);
  }
```

C 485 Understanding Bit Fields

Many of the functions in this book reduce the number of variables (and hence the amount of allocated memory) your programs must use by returning values whose bits have specific meanings. When a value's bits have specific meanings, your programs can use C's bitwise operators to extract the values (the specific bits). Assume, for example that your program needs to track 100,000 dates. One way to track the dates is to create a structure of type Date, as shown here:

```
struct Date {
   int month; // 1 through 12
   int day;   // 1 through 31
   int year;  // last two digits
};
```

As an alternative, your programs can use specific bits within an *unsigned int* value to hold the date fields, as shown in Figure 485.

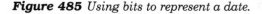

Figure 485 *Using bits to represent a date.*

Then, each time your program needs to assign a date, it can perform the correct bitwise operations, as shown here:

```
unsigned date;

date = month;
date = date | (day << 4);
date = date | (year << 9);

printf("Month %d Day %d Year %d\n", date & 0xF,
  (date >> 4) & 0x1F, (date >> 9));
```

However, to make your programs easier to understand, C lets you create a *bit-field structure*. When you declare a bit-field structure, you define a structure that specifies the meaning of the corresponding bits:

```
struct Date {
   unsigned month:4;
   unsigned day:5;
   unsigned year:7;
} date;
```

Your programs reference the bit fields, as shown here:

```
date.month = 12;
date.day = 31;
date.year = 94;

printf("Month %d Day %d Year %d\n", date.month,
  date.day, date.year);
```

Note: *When you declare a bit-field structure, the structure's members must each be unsigned int values.*

Visualizing a Bit-Field Structure

C486

In Tip 485 you learned that C lets you represent bits within a value using a bit field structure. When you declare a bit field structure, C allocates enough bytes of memory to hold the structure's bits. If the structure does not use all of the bits in the last byte, most C compilers will initialize the bits to 0. To help you better visualize how C stores a bit field structure, Figure 486 illustrates how the C compiler will represent the bit field structure *Date,* shown here:

```
struct Date {
   unsigned month:4;
   unsigned day:5;
   unsigned year:7;
} date;
```

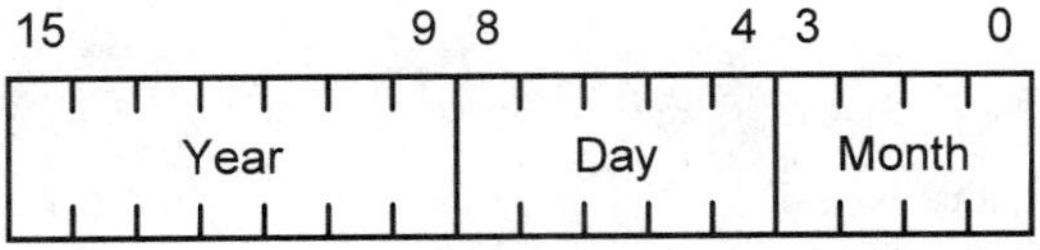

```
 15            9 8      4 3      0
 ┌─┬─┬─┬─┬─┬─┬─┬─┬─┬─┬─┬─┬─┬─┬─┬─┐
 │     Year      │   Day   │  Month  │
 └─┴─┴─┴─┴─┴─┴─┴─┴─┴─┴─┴─┴─┴─┴─┴─┘
```

Figure 486 *How C represents the Date bit-field structure.*

487 Understanding the Range of Values a Bitwise Structure Can Hold

In Tip 486 you learned that C lets you represent bits within a value using a bit-field structure. When you create a bit field structure, you must allocate enough bits to hold each member's desired value. To help you determine the number of bits you require, Table 487 specifies the range of values that can be represented using a given number of bits.

Size of Field	Range of Values
1	0–1
2	0–3
3	0–7
4	0–15
5	0–31
6	0–63
7	0–127
8	0–255
9	0–511
10	0–1023
11	0–2047
12	0–4095
13	0–8191
14	0–16383
15	0–32767
16	0–65535

Table 487 *The range of values representable with a given number of bits.*

Searching an Array for a Specific Value

488

As you have learned, arrays let you store related values of the same type. A common operation when you work with arrays is searching an array for a specific value. There are two common ways to search an array: a *sequential search* and a *binary search*. To perform a sequential search, your program starts at the array's first element and searches one element at a time until the desired value is found or the array runs out of elements. For example, the following *while* loop illustrates how your programs might search an array for the value 1001:

```
found = 0;
i = 0;

while ((i < ARRAY_ELEMENTS) && (! found))
  if (array[i] == 1001)
    found = true;
  else
    i++;

if (i < ARRAY_ELEMENTS)
  printf("Value found at element %d\n", i);
else
  printf("Value not found\n");
```

If the array of values is sorted from lowest to highest, your programs can perform a binary search, which Tip 489 describes in detail.

Understanding a Binary Search

489

As you have learned, one way of locating a value within an array is simply to search through every array element. Although such a sequential search is probably acceptable when your array size is small, looping through a large array can be very time consuming. If the array of values is sorted, your programs can use a *binary search* to locate the value. The binary search is so named because with each operation, the search divides the number of values it needs to examine by two. The best way to conceptualize the binary search is to think of how you look up a word in the dictionary. Assume you want to find the word "Dalmatian." To begin, you may open the dictionary to the middle and examine the words shown. Assuming that you open to the letter M, you know that "Dalmatian" appears before the current page, so you have just eliminated half the words in the dictionary. If you turn to the middle of the remaining pages, you will very likely display words beginning with the letter F. Once again, you can discard half the possible choices, continuing your search in the pages that precede the current page. This time when you turn to the middle page, you will probably turn to the letter C. The word "Dalmatian" appears somewhere in the pages between C and F. When you select the middle page, you will very like be in the D words. By repeatedly discarding a pages and selecting the middle page, you can quickly close in the page containing a the word "Dalmatian."

Note: *To perform a binary search, the values in the array must be sorted from lowest to highest.*

C490 Using a Binary Search

As you learned in Tip 489, a binary search provides a quick way to search a sorted array for a specific value. The following program, BINARY.C, uses a binary search to search for several values in the array *count*, which contains the values 1 to 100. To help you better understand the processing the binary search performs, the function *binary_search* prints out messages that describe its processing:

```
#include <stdio.h>

int binary_search(int array[], int value, int size)
  {
    int found = 0;
    int high = size, low = 0, mid;

    mid = (high + low) / 2;

    printf("\n\nLooking for %d\n", value);

    while ((! found) && (high >= low))
      {
        printf("Low %d Mid %d High %d\n", low, mid, high);

        if (value == array[mid])
          found = 1;
        else if (value < array[mid])
          high = mid - 1;
        else
          low = mid + 1;

        mid = (high + low) / 2;
      }
    return((found) ? mid: -1);
  }
```

```
void main(void)
{
   int array[100], i;

   for (i = 0; i < 100; i++)
     array[i] = i;

   printf("Result of search %d\n", binary_search(array,33, 100));
   printf("Result of search %d\n", binary_search(array,75, 100));
   printf("Result of search %d\n", binary_search(array,1, 100));
   printf("Result of search %d\n", binary_search(array,1001,100));
}
```

Compile and execute this program and observe the number of operations the search must perform to find each value. The program uses the variables *high, mid,* and *low* to keep track of the range of values it is currently searching.

Sorting an Array

491

As you have learned, arrays let you store related values of the same type. As your programs work with arrays, there will be times when your programs need to sort the array's values, either from lowest to highest (ascending order) or from highest to lowest (descending order). There are several different sorting algorithms your programs can use to sort arrays: bubble sort, selection sort, Shell sort, and the quick sort. Several of the tips that follow discuss each of these sorting methods.

Understanding the Bubble Sort

492

The *bubble sort* algorithm is a simple array-sorting technique that is normally the first method most programmers learn. Because of its simplicity, the bubble sort is not very efficient and will consume more processor time than other sorting techniques. However, if you are sorting small arrays with 30 or less elements, using the bubble sort is fine. Assuming that you sort values from lowest to highest, the bubble sort loops through the values in an array comparing and moving the largest array value to the top of the array (like a bubble in water rises to the surface). Figure 492 illustrates a two iterations of a bubble sort. The first iteration moves the array's largest value to the top of the array. The second iteration moves the array's second largest value to the second-to-the-top position. The third iteration moves the third-largest value, and so on.

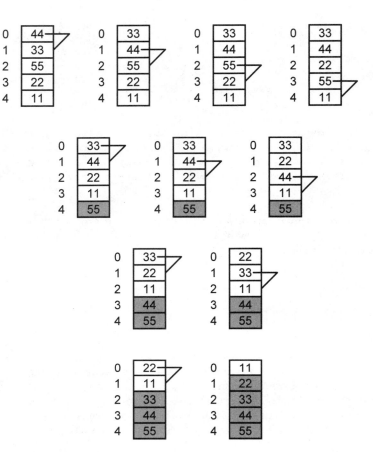

Figure 492 *Iterations of a bubble sort.*

Putting a Bubble Sort to Use

C 493

Tip 492 briefly illustrated the bubble sort's functioning. The following program, BUBBLE.C, uses the bubble sort to sort an array containing 30 random values:

```c
#include <stdio.h>
#include <stdlib.h>

void bubble_sort(int array[], int size)
  {
    int temp, i, j;
```

```
    for (i = 0; i < size; i++)
      for (j = 0; j < size; j++)
        if (array[i] < array[j])
          {
            temp = array[i];
            array[i] = array[j];
            array[j] = temp;
          }
  }

void main(void)
  {
    int values[30], i;

    for (i = 0; i < 30; i++)
      values[i] = rand() % 100;

    bubble_sort(values, 30);

    for (i = 0; i < 30; i++)
      printf("%d ", values[i]);
  }
```

Note: *The bubble_sort function sorts values from lowest to highest. To reverse the sort order, simply change the comparison to* **if (array[i] > array[j]).**

Understanding the Selection Sort

494

Like the bubble sort presented in Tip 493, the *selection sort* is a simple sorting algorithm. Like the bubble sort, your programs should only use the selection to sort arrays that are small (such as 30 elements). The selection sort begins by selecting an array element (such as the first element). The sort then searches the entire array until it finds the minimum value. The sort places the minimum value in the element, selects the second element, and searches for the second-smallest element. Figure 494 illustrates two iterations of a the selection sort on an array of values.

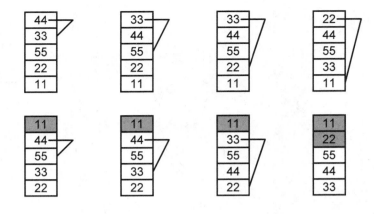

Figure 494 *Sorting values with the selection sort.*

Putting a Selection Sort to Use

C 495

Tip 494 briefly illustrated the selection sort's functioning. The following program, SELECT.C, uses the selection sort to sort an array containing 30 random values:

```c
#include <stdio.h>
#include <stdlib.h>

void selection_sort(int array[], int size)
 {
   int temp, current, j;

   for (current = 0; current < size; current++)
    for (j = current + 1; j < size; j++)
     if (array[current] > array[j])
       {
         temp = array[current];
         array[current] = array[j];
         array[j] = temp;
       }
  }
```

```
void main(void)
  {
    int values[30], i;

    for (i = 0; i < 30; i++)
      values[i] = rand() % 100;

    selection_sort(values, 30);

    for (i = 0; i < 30; i++)
      printf("%d ", values[i]);
  }
```

Note: *The selection_sort function sorts values from lowest to highest. To reverse the sort order, simply change the comparison to* **if (array[current] < array[j]).**

Understanding the Shell Sort

The *Shell sort* is named after its creator, Donald Shell. The sort technique works by comparing array elements that are separated by a specific distance (gap) until the elements compared with the current gap are in order. The gap is then divided by two, and the processes continues. When the gap is finally 1 and no changes occur, the array is sorted. Figure 496 illustrates how the Shell sort might sort an array.

☞

Figure 496 *Sorting an array with the Shell sort.*

Putting a Shell Sort to Use

C 497

Tip 496 briefly illustrated the Shell sort's functioning. The following program, SHELL.C, uses the Shell sort to sort an array containing 50 random values:

```c
#include <stdio.h>
#include <stdlib.h>

void shell_sort(int array[], int size)
  {
    int temp, gap, i, exchange_occurred;

    gap = size / 2;

    do {
     do {
       exchange_occurred = 0;

       for (i = 0; i < size - gap; i++)
        if (array[i] > array[i + gap])
          {
            temp = array[i];
            array[i] = array[i + gap];
            array[i + gap] = temp;
            exchange_occurred = 1;
          }
     } while (exchange_occurred);
    } while (gap = gap / 2);
  }

void main(void)
  {
    int values[50], i;

    for (i = 0; i < 50; i++)
      values[i] = rand() % 100;

    shell_sort(values, 50);

    for (i = 0; i < 50; i++)
      printf("%d ", values[i]);
  }
```

Note: *The shell_sort function sorts values from lowest to highest. To reverse the sort order, simply change the comparison to* **if (array[i] < array[i + gap]).**

Understanding the Quick Sort

498

As the number of elements in your arrays increase, the *quick sort* is one of the fastest sorting techniques your programs can use. The quick sort considers your array as a list of values. When the sort begins, it selects the list's middle value as the *list separator*. The sort then divides the list into two lists, one with values that are less than the list separator and a second list whose values are greater than or equal to the list separator. The sort then recursively invokes itself with both lists. Each time the sort is invoked, it further divides the elements into smaller lists. Figure 498 illustrates how the quick sort might sort an array of ten values.

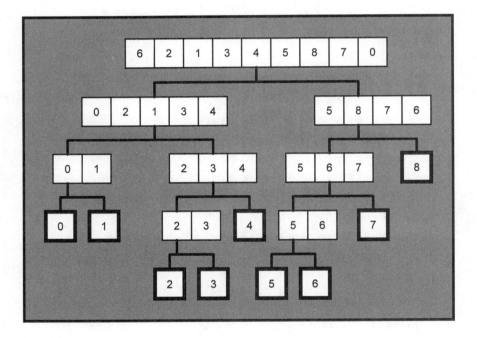

Figure 498 *Sorting values with the quick sort.*

Putting a Quick Sort to Use

499

Tip 498 briefly illustrated the quick sort's functioning. The following program, QUICK.C, uses the quick sort to sort an array containing 100 random values:

```
#include <stdio.h>
#include <stdlib.h>

void quick_sort(int array[], int first, int last)
 {
    int temp, low, high, list_separator;

    low = first;
    high = last;
    list_separator = array[(first + last) / 2];

    do {
      while (array[low] < list_separator)
        low++;

      while (array[high] > list_separator)
        high--;

      if (low <= high)
        {
          temp = array[low];
          array[low++] = array[high];
          array[high--] = temp;
        }
    } while (low <= high);

  if (first < high)
    quick_sort(array, first, high);
  if (low < last)
    quick_sort(array, low, last);
 }

void main(void)
 {
    int values[100], i;

    for (i = 0; i < 100; i++)
      values[i] = rand() % 100;

    quick_sort(values, 0, 99);

    for (i = 0; i < 100; i++)
      printf("%d ", values[i]);
 }
```

Note: *The quick_sort function sorts values from lowest to highest. To reverse the sort order, simply change the comparisons in the two while statements to:*

```
while (array[low] > list_separator)
  low++;

while (array[high] < list_separator)
  high++;
```

500 Problems with Previous Sorting Solutions

Several of the previous tips have shown different sorting techniques your programs can use to sort arrays. Unfortunately, each of the tips presented worked with arrays of type *int*. If your programs need to sort a different array type, you must create new functions. For example, to sort an array of type *float*, your programs must change the *quick_sort* function, as shown here:

```
void quick_sort(float array[], int first, int last)
  {
    float temp, list_separator;
    int low, high;
```

If you need to sort an array of *long* values later, you will need to create a different function. As you will learn, however, using the C run-time library *qsort* function, your programs can use the same function to sort different array types. The function succeeds through the use of memory indirection.

501 Sorting an Array of Character Strings

As you have learned, C lets you create an array of character strings:

```
char *days[] = {"Monday", "Tuesday", "Wednesday" };
```

Just as there may be times when your programs need to sort arrays of other types, the same is true for sorting character-string arrays. The following program, STR_SORT.C, uses a bubble sort to sort an array of character strings:

```
#include <stdio.h>
#include <stdlib.h>
#include <string.h>
```

```
void bubble_sort(char *array[], int size)
  {
    char *temp;
    int i, j;

    for (i = 0; i < size; i++)
     for (j = 0; j < size; j++)
       if (strcmp(array[i], array[j]) < 0)
         {
           temp = array[i];
           array[i] = array[j];
           array[j] = temp;
         }
  }

void main(void)
  {
    char *values[] = {"AAA", "CCC", "BBB", "EEE", "DDD"};
    int i;

    bubble_sort(values, 5);

    for (i = 0; i < 5; i++)
     printf("%s ", values[i]);
  }
```

When the function sorts the array, it does not change the string contents to rearrange the array, but rather, it arranges the character string pointers so the character strings are in order.

Searching an Array with *lfind*

C 502

As you have learned, a sequential search operation searches the elements of an array in order until a specific value is found. To help your programs search arrays of any type, the C run-time library provides the *lfind* function:

```
#include <stdlib.h>

void *lfind(const void *element, void *base,
    size_t *number_of_entries, size_t element_width,
    int (*compare)(const void *, const void *));
```

As you can see, the function makes tremendous use of pointers. The *element* parameter is a pointer to the desired value. The *base* parameter is a pointer to the start of the array. The *number_of_entries* parameter is a pointer to the number elements in the array. The *element_width* parameter specifies the number of bytes required for each array element. Finally, the *compare* parameter is a pointer to a second function that compares two array elements. Unlike the functions previously shown, which returned an array index to the desired value, the *lfind* function returns a pointer to the desired or the value 0 if the element was not found. The following program, LFIND.C, uses the *lfind* function to search for a value of type *int* and a value of type *float*:

```c
#include <stdlib.h>
#include <stdio.h>

int compare_int(int *a, int *b)
 {
   return(*a - *b);
 }

int compare_float(float *a, float *b)
 {
   return((*a == *b) ? 0: 1);
 }


void main(void)
 {
   int int_values[] = {1, 3, 2, 4, 5};
   float float_values[] = {1.1, 3.3, 2.2, 4.4, 5.5};

   int *int_ptr, int_value = 2, elements = 5;
   float *float_ptr, float_value = 33.3;

   int_ptr = lfind(&int_value, int_values,
      &elements, sizeof(int),
      (int (*) (const void *, const void *)) compare_int);

   if (*int_ptr)
     printf("Value %d found\n", int_value);
   else
     printf("Value %d not found\n", int_value);

   float_ptr = lfind(&float_value, float_values,
      &elements, sizeof(float),
      (int (*) (const void *, const void *)) compare_float);


   if (*float_ptr)
     printf("Value %3.1f found\n", float_value);
   else
     printf("Value %3.1f not found\n", float_value);

 }
```

Using pointers, the function is able to eliminate type conflicts that affected the searching and sorting functions previously discussed.

Searching for Values with *lsearch*

C 503

In Tip 502 you learned how to use the *lfind* function to search an array of values for a specific element. If the element was found, the function returned a pointer to it. If the value was not found, the function returned 0. Depending on your programs, there may be times when you will want to add the value to the array if it was not found. In such cases, your programs can use the *lsearch* function:

```
#include <stdlib.h>

void *lsearch(const void *element, void *base,
    size_t *number_of_entries, size_t element_width,
    int (*compare)(const void *, const void *));
```

The following program, LSEARCH.C, uses the *lsearch* function to search for the value 1001. If the value is not found, the *lsearch* function appends the value to the array:

```
#include <stdlib.h>
#include <stdio.h>

int compare_int(int *a, int *b)
 {
   return(*a - *b);
 }

int compare_float(float *a, float *b)
 {
   return((*a == *b) ? 0: 1);
 }


void main(void)
 {
   int int_values[10] = {1, 3, 2, 4, 5};
   int *int_ptr, int_value = 1001, elements = 5, i;

   printf("Array contents before search\n");
   for (i = 0; i < elements; i++)
     printf("%d ", int_values[i]);
```

```
    int_ptr = lsearch(&int_value, int_values,
      &elements, sizeof(int),
      (int (*) (const void *, const void *)) compare_int);

  printf("\nArray contents after search\n");
  for (i = 0; i < elements; i++)
    printf("%d ", int_values[i]);

}
```

As you can see, when the function adds the array value, it also updates the value parameter that specifies the number of array elements.

Note: *When your programs use the lsearch function, you must include additional space within the array into which values can be appended.*

C 504 Searching a Sorted Array with *bsearch*

In Tip 489 you learned that a binary search locates a value in a sorted array by repeatedly reducing the number of array elements it will continue by a factor of two with each iteration. To help your programs perform binary search operations, the C runtime library provides the *bsearch* function:

```
#include <stdlib.h>

void *lfind(const void *element, void *base,
    size_t *number_of_entries, size_t element_width,
    int (*compare)(const void *, const void *));
```

As you can see, the function makes tremendous use of pointers. The *element* parameter is a pointer to the desired value. The *base* parameter is a pointer to the start of the array. The *number_of_entries* parameter specifies the number elements in the array. The *element_width* parameter specifies the number of bytes required for each array element. Finally, the *compare* parameter is a pointer to a second function, which compares two array elements. Unlike the functions previously shown, which returned an array index to the desired value, the *bsearch* function returns a pointer to the desired or the value 0 if the element was not found. The following program, BSEARCH.C, uses the *bsearch* function to search for a value of type *int* and a value of type *float*:

```
#include <stdlib.h>
#include <stdio.h>

int compare_int(int *a, int *b)
```

```
  {
    return(*a - *b);
  }

int compare_float(float *a, float *b)
  {
    return((*a == *b) ? 0: 1);
  }


void main(void)
  {
    int int_values[] = {1, 3, 2, 4, 5};
    float float_values[] = {1.1, 3.3, 2.2, 4.4, 5.5};

    int *int_ptr, int_value = 2, elements = 5;
    float *float_ptr, float_value = 33.3;

    int_ptr = bsearch(&int_value, int_values,
        elements, sizeof(int),
        (int (*) (const void *, const void *)) compare_int);

    if (*int_ptr)
      printf("Value %d found\n", int_value);
    else
      printf("Value %d not found\n", int_value);

    float_ptr = bsearch(&float_value, float_values,
      elements, sizeof(float),
      (int (*) (const void *, const void *)) compare_float);


    if (*float_ptr)
      printf("Value %3.1f found\n", float_value);
    else
      printf("Value %3.1f not found\n", float_value);

  }
```

Note: *To use the bsearch function, the array values must be sorted from lowest to highest.*

Sorting Arrays with *qsort*

C 505

In Tip 498 you learned that a quick sort operation sorts array elements by treating an array as a list. By repeating separating elements into smaller sorted list, the quick sort is very efficient. To help your programs sort arrays of all types using a quick sort, the C run-time library provides the *qsort* function:

```
#include <stdlib.h>

void *qsort(void *base, size_t number_of_entries,
    size_t element_width,
    int (*compare)(const void *, const void *));
```

As you can see, the function makes tremendous use of pointers. The *base* parameter is a pointer to the start of the array. The *number_of_entries* parameter specifies the number elements in the array. The *element_width* parameter specifies the number of bytes required for each array element. Finally, the *compare* parameter is a pointer to a second function, which compares two array elements returning a value, as follows:

```
*a < *b  // Return value < 0
*a == *a // Return 0
*a > *b  // Value > 0
```

The following program, QSORT.C, uses the *qsort* function to search for a value of type *int* and a value of type *float*:

```
#include <stdlib.h>
#include <stdio.h>

int compare_int(int *a, int *b)
 {
   return(*a - *b);
 }

int compare_float(float *a, float *b)
 {
   if (*a < *b)
     return(-1);
   else if (*a == *b)
     return(0);
   else
     return(1);
 }
```

```
void main (void)
 {
   int int_values[] = {51, 23, 2, 44, 45};
   float float_values[] = {21.1, 13.3, 22.2, 34.4, 15.5};

   int elements = 5, i;

   qsort(int_values, elements, sizeof(int),
      (int (*) (const void *, const void *)) compare_int);

   for (i = 0; i < elements; i++)
     printf("%d ", int_values[i]);

   putchar('\n');

   qsort(float_values, elements, sizeof(float),
      (int (*) (const void *, const void *)) compare_float);

   for (i = 0; i < elements; i++)
     printf("%4.1f ", float_values[i]);
 }
```

Determining the Number of Array Elements

506

Several of the previous tips have included the number of array elements as a function parameter. If the number of elements in your array might change, you can reduce the number of changes you must make to your program by using a constant value, such as

```
#define NUM_ELEMENTS 5
```

Second, your programs can use the *sizeof* operator, as shown here, to determine the number of elements in an array:

```
elements = sizeof(array) / sizeof(array[0]);
```

The following program, NUM_ELS.C, uses this technique to display the number of elements in two different arrays:

```
#include <stdio.h>

void main (void)
```

```
{
  int int_values[] = {51, 23, 2, 44, 45};
  float float_values[] = {21.1, 13.3, 22.2, 34.4, 15.5};

  printf("Number of elements in int_values %d\n",
    sizeof(int_values) / sizeof(int_values[0]));

  printf("Number of elements in float_values %d\n",
    sizeof(float_values) / sizeof(float_values[0]));
}
```

507 A Pointer is an Address

As you learned in the ABCs section of this book, a *variable* is the name of a location in memory that is capable of storing a value of a specific type. Each location in memory is located using a unique *address*. A *pointer* is variable or value that contains an address. The C programming language makes extensive use of pointers. When you pass arrays or strings to functions, the C compiler passes a pointer. Likewise, when a function must change a parameter's value, the program must pass to the function a pointer to the variable's memory address. Several of the tips that follow examine pointers in detail.

508 Determining a Variable's Address

A *pointer* is an address to a location in memory. When your program works with arrays (and strings), the program works with a pointer to the array's first element. When your programs need to determine a variable's address, your programs must use C address operator (&). For example, the following program, ADDRESS.C, uses the address operator to display the address of several different variables:

```
#include <stdio.h>

void main(void)
  {
    int count = 1;
    float salary = 40000.0;
    long distance = 1234567L;

    printf("Address of count is %x\n", &count);
    printf("Address of salary is %x\n", &salary);
    printf("Address of distance is %x\n", &distance);
  }
```

When you compile and execute this program, your screen will display the following output:

```
C:\> ADDRESS   <ENTER>
Address of count is fff4
Address of salary is fff0
Address of distance is ffec
```

C Treats Arrays as Pointers

509

As discussed, the C compiler treats arrays as pointers. When your program passes an array to a function, for example, the compiler passes the arrays starting address. The following program, ARRAYADD.C, displays the starting address of several different arrays:

```c
#include <stdio.h>

void main(void)
  {
    int count[10];
    float salaries[5];
    long distances[10];

    printf("Address of the array count is %x\n", count);
    printf("Address of the array salaries is %x\n", salaries);
    printf("Address of the array distances is %x\n", distances);
  }
```

When you compile and execute this program, your screen will display the following:

```
C:\> ARRAYADD   <ENTER>
Address of the array count is ffe2
Address of the array salaries is ffce
Address of the array distances is ffa6
```

Applying the Address Operator (&) to An Array

510

As you have learned, the C compiler treats arrays as a pointer to the array's first element. In Tip 508 you learned that C uses the address operator & to return a variable's address. If you apply the address operator to an array, C will return the value's starting address. Therefore, applying the address operator to the an array is redundant. The following program, ARRAYTWO.C, displays an array's starting address, followed by the pointer returned by C's address operator:

```
#include <stdio.h>

void main(void)
  {
   int count[10];
   float salaries[5];
   long distances[10];

   printf("Address of the array count is %x &count is %x\n",
      count, &count);
   printf("Address of the array salaries is %x &count is %x\n",
      salaries, &salaries);
   printf("Address of the array distances is %x &distances is %x\n",
      distances, &distances);
  }
```

When you compile and execute this program, your screen will display the following output:

```
C:\> ARRAYTWO  <ENTER>
Address of the array count is ffe2 &count is ffe2
Address of the array salaries is ffce &count is ffce
Address of the array distances is ffa6 &distances is ffa6
```

511 Declaring Pointer Variables

As your programs become more complex, you will find that you work with pointers on a regular basis. In order to store pointers, your program must declare pointer variables. To declare a pointer you must specify the type of value to which the pointer points (such as int, float, char and so on), and an asterisk (*) before the variable name. For example, the following statement declares a pointer to a value of type *int*:

```
int *iptr;
```

Like any variable, you must assign a value to a pointer variable before you can use it. When you assign a value to a pointer, you really assign an address. Assuming that you have previously declared *int count;* the following statement assigns the address of the variable *count* to the pointer *iptr*:

```
iptr = &count;   // Assign count's address to iptr
```

The following program, IPTR.C, declares the pointer variable *iptr* and assigns to the pointer the address of the variable *count*. The program then displays the pointer variable's value, along with the address of *count*:

```
#include <stdio.h>

void main(void)
  {
    int *iptr;          // Declare pointer variable
    int count = 1;

    iptr = &count;

    printf("Value of iptr %x Value of count %d Address of count
%x\n",
       iptr, count, &count);
  }
```

When you compile and execute this program, your screen will display the following output:

```
C:\> IPTR  <ENTER>
Value of iptr fff2 Value of count 1 Address of count fff2
```

Dereferencing a Pointer

As you have learned, a pointer contains an address that points to a value of a specific type. Using the address a pointer contains, you can determine the value in memory at which the pointer points. The process of accessing the value at a specific memory location is called *dereferencing a pointer*. To dereference a pointer's value, you use the asterisk (*) indirection operator. For example, the following *printf* statement displays the value pointed to by integer pointer *iptr*:

```
printf("Value pointed to by iptr is %d\n", *iptr);
```

Likewise, the following statement assigns the value pointed to by the variable *iptr* to the variable *count*:

```
count = *iptr;
```

Finally, the following statement assigns the value 7 to the memory location pointed to by *iptr*:

```
*iptr = 7;
```

Note: *To use the value stored in the memory location pointed to by a pointer, you must dereference the pointer's value using the asterisk (*) indirection operator.*

513 Using Pointer Values

In Tip 512 you learned that you can assign an address to a pointer variable using the ampersand (&) address operator. In Tip 512 you learned that to access the value stored in memory at the memory location pointed to by a pointer, you must use the asterisk (*) indirection operator. The following program, PTR_DEMO.C, assigns the *int* pointer *iptr* the address of the variable *counter*. The program then displays the pointer's value and the value stored in the location at which the pointer points (*counter's* value). The program then changes the value pointed to by the pointer:

```c
#include <stdio.h>

void main(void)
  {
    int counter = 10;
    int *iptr;             // Declare pointer value

    iptr = &counter;       // Assign the address
    printf("Address in iptr %x Value at *iptr %d\n", iptr, *iptr);

    *iptr = 25;            // Change the value in memory

    printf("Value of counter %d\n", counter);
  }
```

514 Using Pointers with Function Parameters

The Functions section of this book examines the process of passing parameters to functions in detail. As you will learn, when you need to change the value of a parameter, you must pass to the function a pointer to parameter. The following program, SWAPVALS.C, uses the pointers to two parameters of type *int* to exchange (swap) the variable's values:

```c
#include <stdio.h>

void swap_values(int *a, int *b)
 {
   int temp;

   temp = *a;   // Temporarily hold the value pointed to by a
   *a = *b;     // Assign b's value to a
   *b = temp;   // Assign a's value to b
 }

void main(void)
 {
   int one = 1, two = 2;

   swap_values(&one, &two);

   printf("one contains %d two contains %d\n", one, two);
 }
```

As you can see, within the function, the pointers are dereferenced using the indirection operator (*). The program passes each variable's address to the function using the address operator (&).

Pointer Arithmetic

C 515

A pointer is an address that points to a value of a specific type in memory. In the simplest sense, a pointer is value that points to a specific memory location. If you add the value one to a pointer, the pointer will point to the next location in memory. If you add 5 to a pointer's value, the pointer will point to the memory location five locations ahead of the current address. Pointer arithmetic is not quite as simple as you might guess. Assume, for example, that a pointer contains the address 1000. If you add 1 to the pointer, you would expect the result to be the address 1001. However, the resulting address depends the on the pointer's type. For example, if you add 1 to a pointer variable of type *char* (which contains 1000), the result would be 1001. If you add 1 to a pointer of type *int* (which requires two bytes of memory), the resulting address is 1002. Likewise, if you add one to a pointer of type *float* (which requires four bytes), the resulting address is 1004. When you perform pointer arithmetic, keep the pointer's type in mind. In addition to adding values to pointers, your programs can subtract values, or add and subtract two pointers. Several of the tips in this section present pointer various pointer arithmetic operations.

516 Incrementing and Decrementing a Pointer

As your programs work with pointers, one of the most common operations they will perform is incrementing and decrementing a pointer's value to point to the next or previous memory location. The following program, PTRARRAY.C, assigns the starting address of an array of integer values to the pointer *iptr*. The program then increments the pointer's value to display the five elements the array contains:

```c
#include <stdio.h>

void main(void)
  {
    int values[5] = {1, 2, 3, 4, 5};
    int counter;
    int *iptr;

    iptr = values;

    for (counter = 0; counter < 5; counter++)
      {
        printf("%d\n", *iptr);
        iptr++;
      }
  }
```

When you compile and execute this program, your screen will display the values 1 through 5. The pointer is initially assigned the array's starting address. The program then increments the pointer to point at each element.

517 Combining a Pointer Reference and Increment

In Tip 516 you used the pointer *iptr* to display the contents of an array. To display the array contents, the pointer used a *for* loop, as shown here:

```c
for (counter = 0; counter < 5; counter++)
  {
    printf("%d\n", *iptr);
    iptr++;
  }
```

As you can see, the *for* loop accesses the pointer's value on one line and then increments the pointer on the next. As you have learned, using C's postfix increment operator, you can use a variable's value and then increment the value. Using the postfix increment operator, the following *for* loop references the value pointed to the by the pointer variable and then increments the pointer's value:

```
for (counter = 0; counter < 5; counter++)
  printf("%d\n", *iptr++);
```

Looping Through a String Using a Pointer

C 518

The Strings section of this book makes extensive use of pointers. As you have learned, a string is a NULL-terminated character array. The following program, STR_PTR.C, uses the function *show_string* to display a character using a pointer:

```
#include <stdio.h>

void show_string(char *string)
  {
    while (*string)
      putchar(*string++);
  }

void main(void)
  {
    show_string("Jamsa's 1001 C/C++ Tips");
  }
```

As you can see, the function declares the *string* variable as a pointer. Using the pointer, the function simply loops through the string's characters until the NULL character is encountered. To display the character, the function first dereferences the pointer's address (getting the character). Next, the function increments the pointer to point to the next character in the string.

Functions That Return Pointers

C 519

As you have learned, functions can return a value to your programs. The values that a function returns is always the same type, such as *int*, *float*, or *char*. In addition to returning these basic types, functions can declare pointers to values. For example, the function *fopen*, which most C programs use to open a file stream, returns a pointer to a structure of type FILE:

```
FILE *fopen(const char *pathname, const char *mode);
```

In a similar way, many of the functions presented in the Strings section of this book return pointers to character strings. As you examine the function prototypes presented in this book, note the functions that return a *pointer to a value*, as opposed to a value of a basic type.

C 520 Creating a Function That Returns a Pointer

In Tip 519 you learned that many of C's run-time library functions return pointers. As your programs become more complex, you will create functions that return pointers to specific types. For example, the following program, PTR_UPR.C, creates a function named *string_uppercase* that converts each character of a string to uppercase and then returns a pointer to the string:

```
#include <stdio.h>
#include <ctype.h>

char *string_uppercase(char *string)
  {
    char *starting_address;

    starting_address = string;

    while (*string)
      toupper(*string++);

    return(starting_address);
  }

void main(void)
  {
    char *title = "Jamsa's 1001 C/C++ Tips";
    char *string;

    string = string_uppercase(title);
    printf("%s\n", string);

    printf("%s\n", string_uppercase("Arrays and Pointers"));
  }
```

As you can see, to create a function that returns a pointer, you simply place the asterisk before the function name as shown here:

```
char *string_uppercase(char *string);
```

Understanding an Array of Pointers

Several of the tips presented in this section have discussed arrays in detail. To this point, all of the arrays presented have used C's basic types (such as *int*, *float*, or *char*). C does not restrict arrays to such simple types. Just you can create functions that return pointers, you can create arrays of pointers. The most common use of arrays of pointers is to hold characters strings. For example, the following declaration creates an array, named *weekdays*, that contains pointers to character strings:

```
char *weekdays[7] = {"Sunday", "Monday", "Tuesday",
                     "Wednesday", "Thursday", "Friday",
                     "Saturday" };
```

If you examine the array's type from right to left, you will note that the array contain seven elements. The asterisk before the variable name specifies a pointer. If you combine the type name *char* that precedes the variable name, the declaration becomes *an array of pointers to seven character strings*. One of the most widely used arrays of pointers to character strings is *argv*, which as discussed in the Command Line section of this book contains your program's command line.

> **Note:** *When you declare an array of character strings, the C compiler does not append a NULL entry to indicate the end of the array as it does for character strings.*

Visualizing an Array of Character Strings

As you have learned, C treats arrays as a pointer to the array's starting location in memory. In Tip 521 you created a character string array, named *weekdays*, that contained the days of the week. When you create an array of character strings, the C compiler stores pointers to the array's strings. Figure 522 illustrates how the C compiler would store the array *letters*, shown here:

```
char *letters[4] = {"AAA", "BBB", "CCC", "DDD"};
```

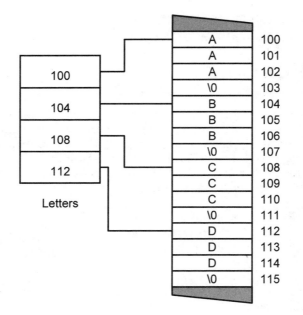

Figure 522 *C stores character string arrays as an array of pointers.*

Note: *When you declare an array of character strings, the C compiler does not append a NULL entry to indicate the end of the array as it does for character strings.*

523 Looping Through an Array of Character Strings

As you have learned, when you create an array of character strings, C stores pointers to each string within the array elements. The following program, WEEKDAYS.C, loops through the array *weekdays*, which contains pointers to strings that contain the names of the days of the week:

```
#include <stdio.h>

void main(void)
  {
    char *weekdays[7] = {"Sunday","Monday","Tuesday","Wednesday",
                         "Thursday", "Friday", "Saturday"};

    int i;
```

```
    for (i = 0; i < 7; i++)
      printf("weekdays[%d] contains %s\n", i, weekdays[i]);
  }
```

As you can see, the program simply loops through the array elements, using *printf*'s %s format specifier.

Treating a Character String Array as a Pointer

As you have learned, C treats an array as a pointer to the array's starting element in memory. Several of the tips presented in Strings section of this book access character string arrays using a pointer similar to the following:

```
char *string;
```

As you have learned, C lets you create arrays of character strings. The following declaration, for example, creates an array, named *workdays*, that is capable of storing the pointers to five character strings:

```
char *workdays[5];
```

Because the declaration creates an array, C lets you access the array using a pointer. To access the array using a pointer, you must declare a pointer variable that points to an array of character strings. In this case, the declaration would become the following:

```
char **work_day_ptr;
```

The double asterisks, in this case, state that *work_day_ptr* is *a pointer to a pointer of character strings*. Several of the tips presented in this books Command Line section work with a pointer to a pointer to character strings.

Using a Pointer to a Pointer to Character Strings

In Tip 524 you learned that following declaration creates a pointer to a pointer to character strings:

```
char **work_day_ptr;
```

The following C program, WORKDAYS.C, uses the pointer to the pointer to character strings to display the contents of the array *workdays*:

```c
#include <stdio.h>

void main(void)
 {
    char *workdays[] = {"Monday", "Tuesday", "Wednesday",
                        "Thursday", "Friday", "" };
    char **work_day;

    work_day = workdays;

    while (*work_day)
      printf("%s\n", *work_day++);
 }
```

When the program begins, it assigns the pointer *week_day* the starting address of the array *workdays* (the address of the string Monday). The program then loops until the pointer to the NULL string is encountered (the ending condition).

Note: *When you declare an array of character strings, the C compiler does not append a NULL entry to indicate the end of the array as it does for character strings. As such, the declaration of the workdays arrays explicitly included a NULL string for which the program can test for within the loop.*

C 526 Declaring a String Constant Using a Pointer

Several of the tips presented throughout this book have initialized character strings at declaration as shown here:

```c
char title[] = "Jamsa's 1001 C/C++ Tips";
```

When you declare an array in this way, the C compiler allocates enough memory to hold the characters specified (and the NULL terminator), assigning to the variable *title* a pointer to the first character. Because the C compiler automatically allocates the necessary memory and then works with a pointer to the memory, your programs can use a character string pointer, as opposed to an array, as shown here:

```c
char *title = "Jamsa's 1001 C/C++ Tips";
```

Understanding the *void* Pointer

As you have learned, when you declare a pointer variable, you must specify the type of value to which the pointer points (such as *int*, *float*, or *char*). By specifying the type of value to which the pointer points, the compiler can later correctly perform pointer arithmetic, adding the correct offset values when you increment or decrement the pointer. In some cases, however, your programs will not manipulate a pointer's value in any way. Instead, your programs only want to obtain a pointer to memory with which the program will determine the pointer's usage. In such cases, your programs can create a pointer to the type *void*:

```
void *memory_pointer;
```

As you examine the C run-time library functions presented in the Memory section of this book, you will find that several of the functions return pointers to the type *void*. Such functions essentially tell you that they return a pointer to a memory location with which no assumptions (by the compiler) have be made to the memory's contents or access.

Pointers to Functions

As you have learned, C lets you create pointers to all data types (such as *int*, *char*, *float*, and even character strings). In addition, C lets your programs create and use pointers to functions. The most common use of pointers to functions is to let your programs pass a function as parameter to another function. The following declarations create pointers to functions:

```
int (*min) ();
int (*max) ();
float (*average) ();
```

Note the use of the parentheses around the variable names. If the parentheses were removed, the declarations would serve as function prototypes for functions that return pointers to a specific type:

```
int *min ();
int *max ();
float *average;
```

When you read a variable declaration, begin with the innermost declaration that appears within parentheses and then work right to left:

```
int (*min) ();
```

Using a Pointer to a Function

C 529

In Tip 528 you learned that C lets you create pointers to functions. The most common use of a pointer to a function is to pass a function as a parameter to another function. Later in this section you will examine C's run-time library sorting and searching functions. As you will learn, if you want to sort values in from smallest to largest, you will pass a specific function to the run-time library routine. If you want to sort values from highest to lowest, you will pass a different function. The following program, PASSFUNC.C, passes either the function *min* or *max* to the function *get_result*. Depending on the function passed, the value *get_result* returns will differ:

```c
#include <stdio.h>

int get_result(int a, int b, int (*compare)())
 {
   return(compare(a, b));   // Invoke the function passed
 }


int max(int a, int b)
 {
   printf("In max\n");
   return((a > b) ? a: b);
 }

int min(int a, int b)
 {
   printf("In min\n");
   return((a < b) ? a: b);
 }

void main(void)
 {
   int result;

   result = get_result(1, 2, &max);
   printf("Max of 1 and 2 is %d\n", result);

   result = get_result(1, 2, &min);
   printf("Min of 1 and 2 is %d\n", result);
 }
```

A Pointer to a Pointer to a Pointer...

C 530

As you have learned, C lets you create variables that are pointers to other pointers. In general, there is no limit on the number of indirections (pointers to pointers) your programs can use. However, for most C programmers, using more than a *pointer to a pointer* will result in considerable confusion and will make your program very difficult to understand. For example, the following program, PTRTOPTR.C, uses three levels of pointers to a value of type *int*. Spend some time with this program drawing the levels of indirection on a piece of paper until you understand the processing it performs:

```c
#include <stdio.h>

int what_is_the_value(int ***ptr)
  {
    return(***ptr);
  }

void main(void)
  {
    int *level_1, **level_2, ***level_3, value = 1001;

    level_1 = &value;
    level_2 = &level_1;
    level_3 = &level_2;

    printf("The value is %d\n", what_is_the_value(level_3));
  }
```

Understanding Structures

C 531

As you have learned, an *array* is a variable that lets your programs store multiple values of the same type. In other words, an array lets your programs group related information into a single variable, such as 100 test scores or 50 employee salaries. As your programs become more complex, there will be times when you will want to group related information whose types differ. For example, assume that you have a program that works with employee information. You might need to track the following information for each employee:

```
char name[64];
int age;
char ssan[11];     // Social security number
int pay_grade;
float salary;
unsigned employee_number;
```

Assume that you have several different functions in your program that works with this information. Each time your program invokes such a function, you must ensure that you have specified all of the parameters and in the correct order. As discussed in the Functions section of this book, the more parameters that your programs pass to functions, the harder your programs become to understand and the greater the chance of error. To reduce such complexity, your programs can create a *structure*, which groups the related information into one variable. For example, the following structure declaration creates a structure, named *Employee*, that contains the employee fields previously shown:

```
struct Employee {
  char name[64];
  int age;
  char ssan[11];     // Social security number
  int pay_grade;
  float salary;
  unsigned employee_number;
} ;
```

As you will learn in the following tips, this declaration creates a structure of type *Employee*.

532 A Structure is a Template for Variable Declarations

In Tip 531 you learned that C lets you group related information into a structure. By itself, a structure definition does not create any variables. Instead, the definition specifies a template that your programs can later use to declare variables. As such, a structure definition does not allocate any memory. Instead, the compiler simply makes a note of the definition in case your program later declares a variable of the structure type.

533 A Structure Tag is the Structure's Name

In Tip 531 you learned that C lets you group related variables in a structure. Using the *struct* keyword, your programs can declare a structure as shown here:

```
struct Employee {
  char name[64];
  int age;
  char ssan[11];    // Social security number
  int pay_grade;
  float salary;
  unsigned employee_number;
} ;
```

In this case, the structure name is *Employee*. C programmers refer to the structure name as the structure's *tag*. As you will learn in Tip 534, your programs can use the structure tag to declare variables of a specific type. The following declaration creates a structure named *Shape*:

```
struct Shape {
  int type;      // 0 = circle, 1 = square, 2 = triangle
  int color;
  float radius;
  float area;
  float perimeter;
};
```

Different Ways to Declare a Structure Variable

534

In Tip 531 you learned that C lets you group related information into a structure. As you have learned, a structure definition on its own does not create a usable variable. Instead, the definition simply serves as a template for future variable declarations. C provides two ways to declare variables of a specific structure type. First, assume that your program declares a structure of type *Employee*, as shown here:

```
struct Employee {
  char name[64];
  int age;
  char ssan[11];    // Social security number
  int pay_grade;
  float salary;
  unsigned employee_number;
} ;
```

Following the structure definition, your programs can declare variables of type *Employee*, as shown here:

```
struct Employee employee_info;
struct Employee new_employee, terminated_employee;
```

Second, C lets you declare variables of a structure type following the structure definition, as shown here:

```
struct Employee {
  char name[64];
  int age;
  char ssan[11];    // Social security number
  int pay_grade;
  float salary;
  unsigned employee_number;
} employee_info, new_employee, terminated_employee;
```

C 535 Understanding Structure Members

As you have learned, C lets you group related information within structures. For example, the following statement creates a variable called *triangle* of using the structure *Shape*:

```
struct Shape {
  int type;       // 0 = circle, 1 = square, 2 = triangle
  int color;
  float radius;
  float area;
  float perimeter;
} triangle;
```

Each piece of information in the structure is a *member*. In the case of the *Shape* structure, there are five members: *type, color, radius, area,* and *perimeter*. To access a specific member, you use C's dot (.) operator. For example, the following statements assign values to different members of the *triangle* variable:

```
triangle.type = 2;
triangle.perimeter = 30.0;
triangle.area = 45.0;
```

Visualizing a Structure

C 536

As you have learned, C lets you group related information in structures. When you declare a variable of a specific structure type, C allocates enough memory to hold the values for each structure member. For example, if you declare a structure of type *Employee*, C will allocate memory as shown in Figure 536.

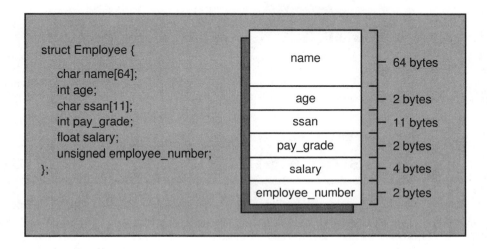

```
struct Employee {
    char name[64];
    int age;
    char ssan[11];
    int pay_grade;
    float salary;
    unsigned employee_number;
};
```

name	64 bytes
age	2 bytes
ssan	11 bytes
pay_grade	2 bytes
salary	4 bytes
employee_number	2 bytes

Figure 536 *Visualizing the memory allocated to hold a structure.*

Putting a Structure to Use

C 537

As you have learned, C lets you group related information in a structure. In the Date and Time section of this book you will use the *getdate* function to determine the current system date. The function assigns the current date to members of a structure of type *date*, which is shown here:

```
struct date {
  int da_year;   // Current year
  char da_day;   // Day of month
  char da_mon;   // Month of year
};
```

The following program, DOSDATE.C, uses the *getdate* function to assign the date to the variable *curr_date*:

```
#include <stdio.h>
#include <dos.h>

void main (void)
  {
    struct date curr_date;

    getdate(&curr_date);

    printf("Current date: %d-%d-%d\n", curr_date.da_mon,
      curr_date.da_day, curr_date.da_year);
  }
```

Because the function must change the parameter's value, the program passes the structure variable to the function by reference (by address).

C 538 Passing a Structure to a Function

As you have learned, C lets you group related information within a structure. Like all variables, C lets you pass variables to a function. The following program, STRUFUNC.C, passes a structure of type *Shape* to the function *show_structure*, which in turn, displays each of the structure's members:

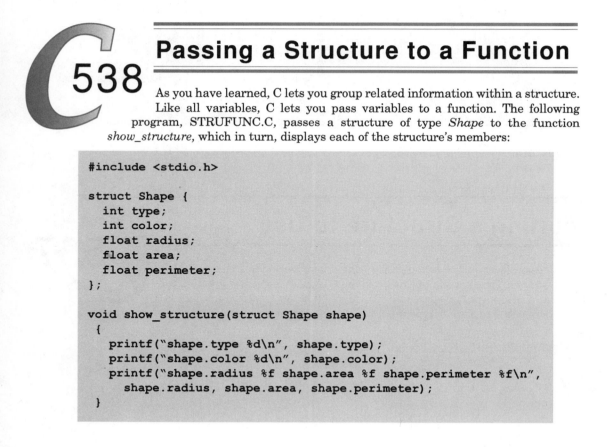

```
#include <stdio.h>

struct Shape {
  int type;
  int color;
  float radius;
  float area;
  float perimeter;
};

void show_structure(struct Shape shape)
  {
    printf("shape.type %d\n", shape.type);
    printf("shape.color %d\n", shape.color);
    printf("shape.radius %f shape.area %f shape.perimeter %f\n",
      shape.radius, shape.area, shape.perimeter);
  }
```

```
void main(void)
  {
    struct Shape circle;

    circle.type = 0;
    circle.color = 1;
    circle.radius = 5.0;
    circle.area = 22.0 / 7.0 * circle.radius * circle.radius;
    circle.perimeter = 2.0 * 22.0 / 7.0 * circle.radius;

    show_structure(circle);
  }
```

Changing a Structure Within a Function

In Tip 538 you learned that you can pass structures to functions just as you can variables of all types. To change a structure's members within a function, you must pass the structure by address (just as you would pass a variable, whose value you want to change). The following program, CHGSTRUC.C, invokes the function *change_structure* that changes the values contained in a structure of type *Shape*:

```
#include <stdio.h>

struct Shape {
  int type;
  int color;
  float radius;
  float area;
  float perimeter;
};

void change_structure(struct Shape *shape)
  {
    (*shape).type = 0;
    (*shape).color = 1;
    (*shape).radius = 5.0;
    (*shape).area = 22.0 / 7.0 * (*shape).radius * (*shape).radius;
    (*shape).perimeter = 2.0 * 22.0 / 7.0 * (*shape).radius;
  }

void main(void)
  {
    struct Shape circle;
```

```
        change_structure(&circle);

    printf("circle.type %d\n", circle.type);
    printf("circle.color %d\n", circle.color);
   printf("circle.radius %f circle.area %f circle.perimeter %f\n",
       circle.radius, circle.area, circle.perimeter);
 }
```

To change the structure's members, the program passes to the function a pointer to the structure. Within the function, the pointer's members are dereferenced using the asterisk indirection operator:

```
(*pointer).member = value;
```

Tip 540 examines this pointer indirection.

C 540 Understanding (*pointer).member Indirection

To change a structure member within a function, the program must pass a pointer to the structure. Within the function, the pointer is dereferenced using the asterisk indirection operator:

```
(*pointer).member = value;
```

To resolve the pointer, C starts within the parentheses, first obtaining the location of the structure. Next, C adds to the address the offset of the specified member. If you omit the parentheses

```
*pointer.member = value;
```

C assumes that the member itself is a pointer and uses the asterisk indirection operator to resolve it. This syntax would be correct for a structure having a member that was a pointer, such as the following:

```
struct Planet {
  char name[48];
  int *some_pointer;
} planet;
```

As you can see, the second member is a pointer to a value of type *int*. Assuming the pointer has been assigned to a memory location, the following statement places the value 5 in the memory location:

```
*planet.some_pointer = 5;
```

Using the *pointer->member* Format

In Tip 540 you learned that to change a structure member within a function, the program must pass a pointer to the structure. To dereference the pointer within the function, C provides two formats. First, as you have seen, you can refer to a structure member in the following form:

```
(*pointer).member = value;
some_value = (*pointer).member;
```

Second, C lets you use the following format:

```
pointer->member = value;
some_value = pointer->member;
```

The following program, CHMEMBER.C, uses the second format within the function *change_structure* to reference members of a structure passed to the function by address:

```
#include <stdio.h>

struct Shape {
   int type;
   int color;
   float radius;
   float area;
   float perimeter;
};

void change_structure(struct Shape *shape)
  {
     shape->type = 0;
     shape->color = 1;
     shape->radius = 5.0;
     shape->area = 22.0 / 7.0 * shape->radius * shape->radius;
     shape->perimeter = 2.0 * 22.0 / 7.0 * shape->radius;
  }

void main(void)
  {
     struct Shape circle;

     change_structure(&circle);
```

```
    printf("circle.type %d\n", circle.type);
    printf("circle.color %d\n", circle.color);
    printf("circle.radius %f circle.area %f circle.perimeter %f\n",
        circle.radius, circle.area, circle.perimeter);
}
```

542 Using a Tagless Structure

As you have learned, a structure *tag* is the structure's name. Using the tag, your programs can declare variables of a specific structure type. When you declare variables of structure types, however, it is not necessary that you specify a structure tag. For example, the following declaration creates two variables of a structure:

```
struct {
    int type;       // 0 = circle, 1 = square, 2 = triangle
    int color;
    float radius;
    float area;
    float perimeter;
} triangle, circle;
```

If your program will not later refer to a structure by name (such as in a function prototype or formal parameters), you can omit the structure tag, as just shown. However, including the tag provides other programmers who are reading your program with insight into the structure's purpose. By including meaningful tag names, your programs may become more readable.

543 Structure Definitions Have Scope

In the Functions section of this book you will learn that *scope* defines the region of program within which an identifier (such as a variable or function) is defined. When you define a structure, you need to consider the structure's scope. If you examine the previous programs that work with structures within functions, you will find that the structure is defined outside of and before the functions that use it. As a result, the structure definitions have a *global scope*, which lets all of the functions that follow make reference to them. Had the structures instead been defined within *main*, the only function that would be aware of the structure's existence is *main*. If you need several of your program's functions to use a structure definition, define the structure outside of your functions in this way.

Initializing a Structure

C 544

As you have learned, C lets you initialize arrays when you declare them. In a similar way, your programs can also initialize a structure at declaration. The following program, INITSTRU.C, declares and initializes a structure of type *Shape*:

```
#include <stdio.h>

void main(void)
  {
    struct Shape {
     int type;
     int color;
     float radius;
     float area;
     float perimeter;
    } circle = {0, 1, 5.0, 78.37, 31.42};

    printf("circle.type %d\n", circle.type);
    printf("circle.color %d\n", circle.color);
   printf("circle.radius %f circle.area %f circle.perimeter %f\n",
      circle.radius, circle.area, circle.perimeter);
  }
```

Because the structure is only used within *main*, the program defines structure within *main*.

Performing Structure I/O

C 545

Several of the tips presented throughout this section have used *printf* to display the value of one or more structure members. When you perform screen or keyboard I/O operations that affect structure members, you must perform you I/O a member at a time. When you read or write structures from/to a file, however, your programs can work with the entire structure. If your program uses file streams, you can use the *fwrite* and *fread* functions to write and read structures. The Files section of this book illustrates how to use these functions to perform structure I/O. To better understand this process, refer to the companion disk program DTOUTF.C and DTINF.C. If your programs use file handles, you can use the *read* and *write* functions to perform structure I/O. When C stores a structure in memory, the structure is really just a range of bytes. The companion disk DTOUT.C and DTIN.C illustrate how your programs can use *write* and *read* to perform structure I/O. Each of the I/O functions just discussed read or write a byte range. To use a structure with these functions, simply pass a pointer to the structure, as shown in the sample programs.

546 Using a Nested Structure

As you have learned, C lets you store related information within structures. Within a structure, you can include members of any type (*int, float,* and so on), as well as members that are themselves structures. For example, the following structure declaration includes the structure type of type *date* that contains the date an employee was hired:

```
struct Employee {
  char name[64];
  int age;
  char ssan[11];    // Social security number
  struct Date {
    int day;
    int month;
    int year;
  } hire_date;
  int pay_grade;
  float salary;
  unsigned employee_number;
} new_employee;
```

To access a member of a nested structure, you use the dot operator, first to specify the nested structure and then to specify the desired member:

```
new_employee.hire_date.month = 12;
```

547 Structures That Contain Arrays

As you have learned, structure members can be any type, including structures or arrays. When a structure member is an array, your programs reference the array member just as it would any array, with the exception that the variable name and dot operator precede the array name. The following program, STRUARRA.C, for example, initializes several structure fields, including an array. The program then loops through the array elements, displaying their value:

```
#include <stdio.h>

void main(void)
 {
   struct Date {
     char month_name[64];
```

```
    int   month;
    int   day;
    int   year;
  } current_date = { "July", 7, 4, 1994 };

  int i;

  for (i = 0; current_date.month_name[i]; i++)
    putchar(current_date.month_name[i]);
}
```

Creating an Array of Structures

C 548

As you have learned, an array lets your programs store multiple values of the same type. Throughout this section, most of the arrays presented in this section have been the type *int, float,* or *char.* However, C also lets you declare arrays of a specific structure type. For example, the following declaration creates an array capable of storing 100 employees:

```
struct Employee {
  char name[64];
  int age;
  char ssan[11];    // Social security number
  int pay_grade;
  float salary;
  unsigned employee_number;
} staff[100];
```

Assuming that the program has assigned values to each employee, the following *for* loop displays each employee's name and number:

```
for (emp = 0; emp < 100; emp++)
  printf("Employee: %s Number: %d\n",
    staff[emp].name, staff[emp].employee_number);
```

When you use an array of structures, you simply add the dot operator to each array element.

DOS & BIOS Services

C549 Understanding DOS System Services

As you know, DOS is the operating system for the IBM PC and PC compatibles. DOS lets you run programs and store information on disk. In addition DOS provides services that let programs allocate memory, access devices such as the printer, and manage other system resources. To help your programs take advantage of capabilities built into DOS, such as determining the amount of free disk space, creating or selecting a directory, or even capturing keystrokes, DOS provides a set of services your programs can use. Unlike the functions provided by the C run-time library, your programs don't access the DOS services using a simple function-call interface. Instead, the services were written to be accessed at the assembly language level using registers and interrupts. However, as you will learn in this section, C actually makes it easy for your programs to take advantage of the DOS services without forcing you to use assembly language. In addition, the C run-time library might actually provide an interface to many of the DOS services through a function.

When you create your programs, there may be times when you have a choice of using a C run-time library function or a DOS service. As a rule, you should use the run-time library functions whenever possible, instead of the DOS services. Using the run-time library functions will increase your program's portability. In some cases, C run-time library functions provided in the UNIX environment might match those provided by your DOS compiler. By using the C run-time library function, as opposed to the DOS service, you don't need to change your program for it to run under UNIX. Instead, you simply need to recompile.

C550 Understanding the BIOS Services

BIOS stands for *Basic Input/Output Services*. In short, the BIOS is a chip within your computer that contains the instructions your computer uses to write to the screen or printer, to read characters from the keyboard, or to read and write to your disk. As was the case with the DOS services, your programs can use the BIOS services to perform different operations. For example, you might use a BIOS service to determine the number of parallel or serial ports, the video display type, or the number of available disk drives. Like the DOS services, the BIOS routines are designed for use by assembly language programs. However, most C compilers provide run-time library functions that let your programs use these services without the need for assembly language. Many programs confuse the DOS and BIOS services. As in Figure 550 shows, the BIOS resides directly above your computer's hardware. Next, the DOS services sit on top of the BIOS, and your programs then sit on top of DOS.

Programs
DOS
BIOS
Hardware

Figure 550 The relationship between the BIOS, DOS, and programs.

As Figure 550 shows, however, there are times when DOS, and even programs, can bypass the BIOS and directly access the computer's hardware. An application that must provide very fast video, for example, might bypass DOS and the BIOS to work directly with video memory. As a rule, however, bypassing DOS and BIOS should be done only by experienced programmers. The DOS and BIOS perform considerable error checking that simplify your programming tasks.

Understanding Registers

C 551

When your program executes, the program must reside in your computer's memory. Your computer's central processing unit (the CPU) will get your program's instruction and data from memory as they are needed. To improve performance, the CPU contains several temporary storage locations called *registers*. Because these registers reside within the CPU itself, the CPU can access their contents very quickly. In general, the CPU uses four types of registers: segment, offset, general-purpose, and the flags register. Table 551 briefly describes each register type's use.

Register Type	Use
Segment	Holds the starting memory address of a block of memory, such as the start of your program's code or data
Offset	Holds the 16-byte offset into a block of memory—such as the location of a specific variable within your program's data segment
General-Purpose	Temporarily stores program data
Flags	Contains processor status and error information

Table 551 The PC's register types.

The PC uses a segment and offset value to locate items in memory. When you use the DOS services, you might need to assign the segment and offset address of one or more variables to different segment registers. The PC provides four general purpose registers, named AX, BX, CX, and DX. Each of the general-purpose registers can hold 16 bits of data (2 bytes). In some cases, you might only need to store a byte of information within a register. To help you do so, the PC lets you access the upper and lower byte of each register using the names shown in Figure 551.1.

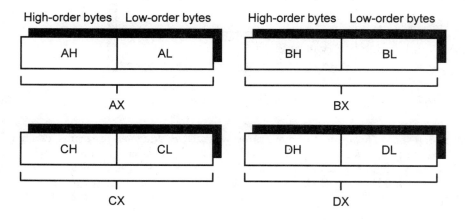

Figure 551.1 The PC's general purpose registers.

When you use the DOS and BIOS services, you will place parameters for the service within the general-purpose registers. When the service completes, DOS or the BIOS may place their result in one of the general purpose registers. Finally, the flags register stores the CPU's state and possible error status values. When DOS and BIOS services complete, they often set or clear different bits within the flags register to indicate success or an error. Figure 551.2 illustrates the bits within the flags register.

Figure 551.2 Bit within the PC's flags register.

Several of the tips presented throughout this section discuss segments, offsets, and registers in greater detail.

Understanding the Flags Register

552

As you have learned, the flags register contains CPU status and error information. After the PC completes different operations, such as an add or subtract, or compare, it sets different bits in the flags register. Likewise, many of the BIOS and DOS services set the carry flag to indicate an error. Table 552 describes the bits used within the flags register:

Bit	Flag	Meaning
0	Carry	Indicates an arithmetic carry
2	Parity	Indicates an arithmetic operation resulted in an even number of bits set to 1
4	Auxiliary	Indicates an adjustment is required following a BCD (binary coded decimal) arithmetic operation
6	Zero	Indicates a zero result from a comparison or arithmetic operation
7	Sign	Indicates a negative result
8	Trap	Used for debugger trapping
10	Direction	Controls the direction of string instructions
11	Overflow	Indicates an arithmetic overflow

Table 552 Bits within the flags register.

When you use a DOS or BIOS service within your program, make sure that your program tests the flag bit set by the service to determine success or failure.

Understanding Software Interrupts

553

An *interrupt* occurs when the CPU must temporarily stop what it is doing so that it can perform a different operation. When the operation is finished, the CPU can resume its original work as if it had never stopped. There are two types of interrupts: hardware and software interrupts. Hardware interrupts are caused by devices connected to or inside of your computer, such as the clock, disk drive, or keyboard. When the PC was designed, the developers provided support for up to 256 interrupts that are numbered 0 through 255. Because your computer's hardware only needs a small number of these interrupts, many are available for use by software. The BIOS services, for example, make use of interrupts 5 and 10H through 1FH. Likewise, DOS uses interrupts 21H through 28H and 2FH.

When you write programs in assembly language, you assign parameters to the PC registers and then invoke the interrupt that corresponds to the desired system service. For example, the BIOS uses interrupt 10H to access the video. To display a letter on the screen, for example, you assign the desired letter to the AL register, assign the value 9H to the AH, directing the BIOS to perform a video write operation, assign the desired attribute (bold, blinking, normal, and so on) to the BX register, and then invoke INT 10H, as shown here:

```
MOV AL,41        ; A is the ASCII 41H
MOV AH,9         ; Request a video write
MOV BX,7         ; Character attribute
MOV CX,1         ; Number of characters to write
INT 10           ; Perform the video service
```

As you will learn, most of the DOS services use INT 21H. Fortunately, you don't have to work with assembly language within your C programs to invoke a service.

554 Using the BIOS to Access the Printer

Several of the tips presented throughout this book have written output to the printer using the stdprn file handle. Before your programs perform printer I/O, however, you might want the program to verify that the printer is on line and has paper. To do so, your programs can use the *biosprint* function, whose format is as follows:

```
#include <bios.h>

int biosprint(int command, int byte, int port_number);
```

The *command* specifies one of the following operations:

Command	Meaning
0	Print the byte specified
1	Initialize the printer port
2	Read the printer status

If you are printing a character, the *byte* specifies the desired character's ASCII or extended ASCII value. Finally, *port_number* specifies the desired printer, where 0 is LPT1, 1 is LPT2 and so on.

To access a printer connected to a serial port, you must use *_bios_serialcom*. The function returns an integer value in the range 0 through 255, whose bits are defined in Table 554.

Bit	Meaning if Set
0	Device timeout
3	I/O error
4	Printer selected
5	Out of paper
6	Device acknowledgment
7	Device not busy

Table 554 Status bits returned by biosprint.

The following program, PRINTCHK.C, uses the *biosprint* function to test your printer status repeatedly until you press a key. Run this program and experiment with your printer, taking it off line, removing the paper, and so on. As you do so, the program should display different messages on your screen:

```c
#include <bios.h>
#include <conio.h>
#include <stdio.h>

void main (void)
  {
    int status = 0;
    int old_status = 0;

    do
      {
        status = biosprint(2, 0, 0);   // Read LPT1

        if (status != old_status)
          {
            if (status & 1)
              printf ("Time-out\t");

            if (status & 8)
              printf ("Output Error\t");

            if (status & 16)
              printf ("Printer Selected\t");

            if (status & 32)
              printf ("Out of Paper\t");

            if (status & 64)
              printf ("Acknowledge\t");
```

```
        if (status & 128)
          printf ("Printer Not Busy");

        printf ("\n");

        old_status = status;
      }
    }
  while (! kbhit());
}
```

Note: *Many compilers provide a function named _bios_printer that is similar to biosprint.*

C 555 Control-Break Information

When you work within the DOS environment, the DOS BREAK command lets you enable and disable extended **Ctrl-Break** checking. When extended checking is enabled, DOS increases the number of operations after which it checks for a user entered **Ctrl-C** or **Ctrl-Break**. When **Ctrl-Break** is disabled, DOS only checks for a **Ctrl-Break** after performing keyboard, screen, or printer I/O. Many C compilers provide two functions that your programs can use to obtain and set the state of **Ctrl-Break** checking: *getcbrk* and *setcbrk*:

```
#include <dos.h>

int getcbrk(void);
int setcbrk(int setting);
```

The *getcbrk* function returns the value 0 if extended **Ctrl-Break** checking is disabled and 1 if it is active. Likewise, the *setcbrk* function uses the values 0 and 1 to disable and enable extended checking. The *setcbrk* function returns the value 0 or 1, depending on the state of extended checking selected. The following program, CTRLBRK.C, uses the *setcbrk* function to disable extended **Ctrl-Break** checking. The program uses the *getcbrk* function's return value to display the previous setting:

```
#include <stdio.h>
#include <dos.h>

void main(void)
  {
    printf("Previous extended Ctrl-Break status %s\n",
      (getcbrk()) ? "On": "Off");

    setcbrk(0);  // Turn if off
  }
```

Note: *The setcbrk function sets state of* **Ctrl-Break** *checking for the system, not just for the current program. When the program ends, the selected state remains in effect.*

Be Aware of DOS Side Effects

556

In Tip 557 you learned how to use the *setcbrk* function to change the state of extended **Ctrl-Break** checking. Likewise, in the Disk and Files section you learned how to change the state of disk verification. Several other tips have presented ways your programs can change the current drive or directory. When your programs perform these operations, they should save the original settings when they begin so they can restore the settings before they end. Unless it is the program's explicit purpose to change one or more of these settings, the program should not leave the setting changed after it ends. Such changes in settings are called *side effects*, and should be avoided. When a user runs your budget program, for example, the user's default drive and directory should not have changed after the program ends. Likewise, changes that are even more subtle, such as disabling disk verification or extended **Ctrl-Break** checking should not occur. As you create your program, include the additional statements required to restore original environment settings.

Temporarily Suspending a Program

557

In the Date and Time section you used the *delay* function to pause your program for a specific number of milliseconds. In a similar way, your programs can use the *sleep* function to specify the pausing interval in seconds:

```
#include <dos.h>

void sleep(unsigned seconds);
```

Because the *delay* function works with milliseconds, it is more accurate than *sleep*. However, by using the *sleep* function, you might increase your program's portability to other operating systems. Most operating systems provide a *sleep* function, which lets programs enter an inactive state until a time interval has expired or a specific event has occurred. The following program, SLEEP_5.C, uses the *sleep* function to pause for five seconds:

```
#include <stdio.h>
#include <dos.h>

void main(void)
```

```
{
  printf("About to sleep for 5 seconds\n");
  sleep(5);
  printf("Awake\n");
}
```

558 Having Some Fun with Sound

Within the PC is a small (low-quality) speaker that programs normally use to generate beeps. However, using the *sound* function provided with many C compilers, your programs can generate sounds that use different frequencies through the speaker. The *sound* function lets your programs turn on the speaker to display a specific frequency sound. The *nosound* function turns off the speaker:

```
#include <dos.h>

void sound(unsigned frequency);
void nosound(void);
```

The following program, SIREN.C, uses the *sound* function to generate a siren-like sound. When you press a key, the program turns off the speaker using *nosound*:

```
#include <dos.h>
#include <conio.h>

void main(void)
  {
    unsigned frequency;

    do {
      for (frequency = 500; frequency <= 1000; frequency += 50)
        {
          sound(frequency);
          delay(50);
        }
      for (frequency = 1000; frequency >= 500; frequency -= 50)
        {
          sound(frequency);
          delay(50);
        }
    } while (! kbhit());

    nosound();
  }
```

Obtaining Country-Specific Information

As you know, the DOS operating system is used worldwide. To support international users, DOS supports different keyboard templates, code pages, and country-specific information. To help your programs determine the current country settings, your programs can use the *country* function:

```
#include <dos.h>

struct COUNTRY *country(int code,
   struct COUNTRY *info);
```

If successful, the function returns a pointer a structure of type COUNTRY, shown here:

```
struct COUNTRY {
   int  co_date;        // Date format
   char co_curr[5];     // Currency symbol
   char co_thsep[2];    // Thousands separator
   char co_desep[2];    // Decimal separator
   char co_dtsep[2];    // Date separator
   char co_tmsep[2];    // Time separator
   char co_currstyle;   // Currency style
   char co_digits;      // Currency significant digits
   char co_time;        // Time format
   long co_case;        // Pointer to case map
   char co_dasep;       // Data separator
   char co_fill[10];    // Filler
};
```

The *code* value specifies a country code you want to select. If the value of the *info* parameter is −1, the current country code is set to the specified code. If the value of *info* is not −1, the buffer is assigned the settings for the current country code. The following program, COUNTRY.C, displays the current country settings:

```
#include <stdio.h>
#include <dos.h>

void main(void)
  {
    struct COUNTRY info;

    country(0, &info);
```

```
     if (info.co_date == 0)
       printf("Date format: mm/dd/yy\n");
     else if (info.co_date == 1)
       printf("Date format: dd/mm/yy\n");
     else if (info.co_date == 2)
       printf("Date format: yy/mm/dd\n");

     printf("Currency symbol %s\n", info.co_curr);
     printf("Decimal separator %s\n", info.co_thsep);
     printf("Date separator %s Time separator %s\n",
       info.co_dtsep, info.co_tmsep);

     if (info.co_currstyle == 0)
       printf("Currency symbol precedes with no leading spaces\n");
     else if (info.co_currstyle == 1)
       printf("Currency symbol follows with no spaces\n");
     else if (info.co_currstyle == 2)
       printf("Currency symbol precedes with leading space\n");
     if (info.co_currstyle == 4)
       printf("Currency symbol follows with space\n");

     printf("Currency significant digits %d\n", info.co_digits);

     if (info.co_time)
       printf("24 hour time\n");
     else
       printf("12 hour time\n");

     printf("Data separator %s\n", info.co_dasep);
   }
```

C 560 Understanding the Disk Transfer Address

Prior to DOS 3.0, programs performed file operations using file control blocks (FCBs). By default, when DOS read or wrote information, DOS would do so through an area in memory called the *disk transfer area*. By default, DOS used a 128-byte disk transfer area. The address of the area's first byte is called the *disk transfer address* (DTA). By default, DOS used offset 80H of the program segment prefix as the disk transfer address. As you learned in the Command Line section of this book, offset 80H of the program segment prefix also contains the program's command line. Because most programs don't use file control block disk operations, many programmers assume they can ignore the DTA. Unfortunately, routines such as *findnext* and *findfirst*, discussed in the Files section of this book, place their results in the DTA, overwriting your program's command line. To prevent operations that used the DTA from overwriting the command line, many programs assign the DTA to point to a different memory buffer using a DOS service. As you will learn in Tip 561, your programs can change and determine the DTA using run-time library functions.

Accessing and Controlling the DTA

In Tip 560 you learned that the disk transfer area is a 128-byte region used by DOS for file control block-based I/O services or *findfirst* and *findnext* opera-tions. To help you control the disk transfer area, most C compilers support the *getdta* and *setdta* functions:

```
#include <dos.h>

char *far getdta(void);
void setdta(char far *disk_transfer_address);
```

The *getdta* function returns a far (32-bit) pointer to the current disk transfer area. Likewise, the *setdta* function lets you assign the program's disk transfer address to the far address specified. The following program, DTA.C, illustrates the use of the *getdta* and *setdta* functions:

```
#include <stdio.h>
#include <dos.h>
#include <malloc.h>

void main(void)
 {
   char far *dta;

   dta = getdta();

   printf("Current DTA is %lX\n", dta);

   if (MK_FP(_psp, 0x80) == dta)
     printf("DTA is at same location as command line\n");

   dta = _fmalloc(128);
   setdta(dta);

   printf("New DTA is %lX\n", getdta());
 }
```

C 562 Using the BIOS Keyboard Services

DOS, the BIOS, and the C run-time library all provide services that let your programs access the keyboard. As a rule, you should try to use the C run-time library functions, followed next by the DOS functions, and finally, the BIOS services. In this way, your programs remain more portable. To help your programs access the BIOS keyboard services, the C run-time library provides the *_bios_keybrd* function:

```
#include <bios.h>

unsigned _bios_keybrd(unsigned command);
```

The *command* parameter specifies the desired operation. Table 562 lists the possible values you can pass for *command*.

Value	Meaning
_KEYBRD_READ	Directs _bios_keybrd to read a character from the keyboard buffer. If the lower byte of the return value is 0, the upper byte contains an extended keyboard code.
_KEYBRD_READY	Directs _bios_keybrd to determine if a character is present in the keyboard buffer. If _bios_keybrd returns 0, no keystroke is present. If the return value is 0xFFFF, the user has pressed CTRL-C.
_KEYBRD_SHIFTSTATUS	Directs _bios_keybrd to return the keyboard's shift state: Bit 7 Set INS is on Bit 6 Set CAPSLOCK is on Bit 5 Set NUMLOCK is on Bit 4 Set SCROLLLOCK is on Bit 3 Set ALT key pressed Bit 2 Set Left SHIFT key pressed Bit 1 Set Right SHIFT key pressed
_NKEYBRD_READ	Directs _bios_keybrd to read a character from the keyboard buffer. If the lower byte of the return value is 0, the upper byte contains an extended keyboard code.
_NKEYBRD_READ	directs _bios_keybrd to read enhanced keys such as the cursor arrow keys.
_NKEYBRD_READY	Directs _bios_keybrd to determine if a character is present in the keyboard buffer. If _bios_keybrd returns 0, no keystroke is present. If the return value is 0xFFFF, the

user has pressed **Ctrl-C**. The _NKEYBRD_READY value directs _bios_keybrd to support enhanced keys such as the cursor arrow keys.

_NKEYBRD_SHIFTSTATUS   Directs _bios_keybrd to return the keyboard's shift state, including enhanced keys:

Bit 15 Set	**Sysreq** key pressed
Bit 14 Set	**Capslock** pressed
Bit 13 Set	**Numlock** pressed
Bit 12 Set	**Scrolllock** pressed
Bit 11 Set	Right **Alt** pressed
Bit 10 Set	Right **Ctrl** pressed
Bit 9 Set	Left **Alt** pressed
Bit 8 Set	Right **Alt** pressed

The following program, KEYSTATE.C, loops displaying changes in the keyboard state until you press any key other than **Shift**, **Alt**, **Ctrl**, **NumLock**, and so on. The program only reads the nonenhanced keys:

```c
#include <stdio.h>
#include <bios.h>

void main(void)
 {
   unsigned int state, old_state = 0;

   do {
     state = _bios_keybrd(_KEYBRD_SHIFTSTATUS);

     if (state != old_state)
       {
         old_state = state;

         if (state & 0x80)
           printf("Ins On ");
         if (state & 0x40)
           printf("Caps On ");
         if (state & 0x20)
           printf("Num Lock On ");
         if (state & 0x10)
           printf("Scroll Lock On ");
         if (state & 0x08)
           Printf("Alt pressed ");
         if (state & 0x04)
           Printf("Ctrl pressed ");
         if (state & 0x02)
           printf("Left shift pressed ");
         if (state & 0x01)
```

```
        printf("Right shift pressed ");
        printf("\n");
      }
   } while (! _bios_keybrd(_KEYBRD_READY));
 }
```

Note: *Many C compilers provide a function named bioskey, which performs similar processing. Refer to the documentation that accompanied your compiler.*

C 563 Obtaining the BIOS Equipment List

As your they increase in complexity, there may be times when your programs must determine specifics about the computer's hardware. In such cases, your programs can use the *_bios_equiplist* function:

```
#include <bios.h>

unsigned _bios_equiplist(void);
```

The function returns an unsigned integer value whose bits have the following meaning:

```
struct Equip {
  unsigned floppy_available:1;       // 1 if present
  unsigned coprocessor_available:1;  // 1 if present
  unsigned system_memory:2;          // Original PC
  unsigned video_mode:2;             // 01 = 40 x 25 mono
                                     // 10 = 80 x 25 color
                                     // 11 = 80 x 25 mono
  unsigned floppy_disk_count:2;      // Add 1
  unsigned serial_port_count:2;
  unsigned game_adapter_available:1; // 1 if present
  unsigned printer_count:2;
};
```

The following program, SHOWEQUP.C, uses the *_bios_equiplist* to display the system equipment list:

```
#include <stdio.h>
#include <bios.h>
```

```
void main(void)
 {
   struct Equip {
     unsigned floppy_available:1;
     unsigned coprocessor_available:1;
     unsigned system_memory:2;
     unsigned video_memory:2;
     unsigned floppy_disk_count:2;
     unsigned unused_1:1;
     unsigned serial_port_count:3;
     unsigned game_adapter_available:1;
     unsigned unused_2:1;
     unsigned printer_count:2;
   } ;

   union Equipment {
     unsigned list;
     struct Equip list_bits;
   } equip;

   equip.list = _bios_equiplist();

   if (equip.list_bits.coprocessor_available)
     printf("Math coprocessor available\n");
   else
     printf("No math coprocessor\n");

   printf("System board memory %d\n",
       (equip.list_bits.system_memory + 1) * 16);

   printf("Number of floppies %d\n",
       equip.list_bits.floppy_disk_count + 1);

   printf("Number of printers %d\n",
       equip.list_bits.printer_count);

   printf("Number of serial ports %d\n",
       equip.list_bits.serial_port_count);
 }
```

Note: *Some C compilers provide a function named biosequip, which performs similar processing.*

Serial Port I/O

564

To help your programs perform I/O operations to a serial port, such as COM1, many DOS-based compilers provide the *_bios_serialcom* function:

```
#include <bios.h>

unsigned _bios_serialcom(int command, int port,
  char byte);
```

The *command* parameter specifies the desired operation and must be one of the following values:

_COM_INIT	Sets the port's communication settings
_COM_RECEIVE	Receives a byte from the port
_COM_SEND	Sends a byte to the port
_COM_STATUS	Returns the port settings

The *port* parameter specifies the desired serial port, where 0 corresponds to COM1, 1 to COM2, and so on. The *byte* parameter specifies a byte to output or the desired communications settings. The value can be a combination of the following:

_COM_CHR7	7-bit data
_COM_CHR8	8-bit data
_COM_STOP1	1 stop bit
_COM_STOP2	2 stop bits
_COM_NOPARITY	Parity none
_COM_ODDPARITY	Parity odd
_COM_EVENPARITY	Parity even
_COM_110	110 baud
_COM_150	150 baud
_COM_300	300 baud
_COM_600	600 baud
_COM_1200	1200 baud
_COM_2400	2400 baud
_COM_4800	4800 baud
_COM_9600	9600 baud

Regardless of the command, the most significant byte of the return value has the following bit meanings:

Bit	**Meaning If Set**
8	Data ready
9	Overrun error
10	Parity error

11	Framing error
12	Break detect
13	Transmit holding register empty
14	Transmit shift register empty
15	Time out

For _COM_INIT and _COM_STATUS, the least significant byte of the return value is defined as follows:

Bit	Meaning If Set
0	Change in clear to send
1	Change in data set ready
2	Trailing-edge ring detector
3	Change in receive line signal detector
4	Clear to send
5	Data set ready
6	Ring indicator
7	Received line signal detect

The following program, SETCOM1.C, sets the data communications for COM1 to 9600 baud, 8 data bits, 1 stop bit, and no parity:

```c
#include <stdio.h>
#include <bios.h>

void main(void)
 {
   char i = 0, title[] = "Jamsa's 1001 C/C++ Tips";

   unsigned status;

   status = _bios_serialcom(_COM_INIT, 0, _COM_9600 |
        _COM_CHR8 | _COM_STOP1 | _COM_NOPARITY);

   if (status & 0x100) // Data ready
     while (title[i])
       {
         _bios_serialcom(_COM_SEND, 0, title[i]);
         putchar(title[i]);
         i++;
       }
 }
```

Note: *Some C compilers provide a bioscom function, which provides similar processing.*

C 565 Accessing DOS Services Using *bdos*

As you have learned, the *intdos* function lets your programs access the DOS services. Some DOS services only use the AX and DX registers. For such services, your programs can use the *bdos* function:

```
#include <dos.h>

int bdos(int dos_function, unsigned dx_register,
  unsigned al_register);
```

The *dos_function* parameter specifies the desired service. The *dx_register* and *al_register* specify the values the service expects in the DX and AL registers. Upon return, the function returns the value of the AX register upon the service's termination. The following program, BDOS.C, uses the *bdos* function to display the current disk drive:

```
#include <stdio.h>
#include <dos.h>

void main(void)
  {
    int drive;

    drive = bdos(0x19, 0, 0);

    printf("Current drive is %c\n", 'A' + drive);
  }
```

Note: *The bdos function passes an unsigned value for DX register. If you are using a DOS service that requires a pointer, you can use the bdosptr function. If you use the small memory model, the second parameter corresponds to DX. In the large memory model, the value corresponds to DS:DX.*

C 566 Getting Extended DOS Error Information

When a DOS system service fails, your programs can request additional error information from DOS to determine the source and cause of the error. To help you request extended error information, many C compilers provide the *dosexterr* function:

```
#include <dos.h>

int dosexterr(struct DOSERROR *error_info);
```

The *error_info* parameter is a pointer to a structure of type *DOSERROR* that contains the extended error information:

```
struct DOSERROR {
   int de_exterror;   // Extended error
   int de_class;      // Error class
   int de_action;     // Recommended action
   int de_locus;      // Error locus
};
```

If the *dosexterr* function returns 0, the previous DOS service call did not experience an error. The extended error value provides a specific error. The error class describes the category of the error:

Value	Meaning	Value	Meaning
01H	Out of resource	02H	Temporary error
03H	Authorization error	04H	System error
05H	Hardware failure	06H	System error not due to current program
07H	Application error	08H	Item not found
09H	Invalid format	0AH	Item locked
0BH	Media error	0CH	Item exists
0DH	Unknown error		

The recommended action tells your program how to respond to the error:

Value	Action
01H	Retry first and then prompt user
02H	Retry after delay and then prompt user
03H	Prompt user for solution
04H	Abort with cleanup
05H	Abort without cleanup
06H	Ignore error
07H	Retry after user intervention

Finally, the locus specifies source of the error:

Value	Location
01H	Unknown locus
02H	Block device error
03H	Network error
04H	Serial device error
05H	Memory error

When your programs must respond to errors in a thoughtful way, you should use the *dosexterr* to obtain additional information.

Memory Management

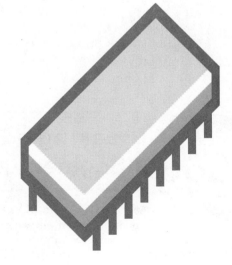

C 567 Determing the BIOS Conventional Memory Amount

Many older programs do not take advantage of extended and expanded memory. Instead, the programs only use the PC's 640Kb conventional memory. As you examine such programs, you may find calls to the *biosmemory* function, which returns the amount of conventional memory (in Kb) that was reported by the BIOS during your system startup. The memory amount *biosmemory* returns does not include extended, expanded, or upper memory:

```
#include <bios.h>

int biosmemory(void);
```

In addition to the *biosmemory* function, you may encounter the *_bios_memsize* function, which performs identical processing:

```
#include <bios.h>

int _bios_memsize(void);
```

The following program, BIOSMEM.C, displays the amount of memory reported by BIOS using *biosmemory* and *_bios_memsize*:

```
#include <stdio.h>
#include <bios.h>

void main (void)
 {
   printf("BIOS Memory report %dKb\n", biosmemory());
   printf("BIOS Memory report %dKb\n", _bios_memsize());
 }
```

C 568 Breaking a Far Address into a Segment and Offset

As discussed in Tip 569, a far pointer consists of a 16-bit segment and a 16-bit offset address. When you work with far pointers, there will be times when you need to break a far address into its segment and offset counterparts. In such cases, your programs can use the *FP_SEG* and *FP_OFF* macros:

```
#include <dos.h>

unsigned FP_OFF(void far *pointer);
unsigned FP_SEG(void far *pointer);
```

The following statements illustrate the use of the *FP_SEG* and *FP_OFF* macros:

```
char far *title = "Jamsa's 1001 C & C++ Tips";

unsigned segment, offset;

segment = FP_SEG(title);
offset = FP_OFF(title);
```

Building a Far Pointer

C 569

A *far pointer* consists of a 16-bit segment and a 16-bit offset address. When you work with far pointers, there may be times when you need to break the pointer into its segment and offset counterparts. Likewise, there may be times when you need to build a far pointer from a segment and offset address. To help you build a far pointer, C provides the *MK_FP* macro:

```
#include <dos.h>

void far *MK_FP(unsigned segment, unsigned offset);
```

The following program uses *MK_FP* to build a far pointer out of a near variable's address:

```
long far *fptr;
long variable;

struct SREGS segs;

  // Get the current data segment
segread(&segs);

fptr = MK_FP(segs.ds, &variable);
```

To better understand the *MK_FP* macro, consider the following implementation:

```
#define MK_FP(s, o) ((void far *) (((long) s << 16) | (o)))
```

To create the 32-bit far address, the macro creates a long value and shifts the segment address bits into the value's upper 16 bits. Next, the macro uses a bitwise OR operation to assign the offset address to the lower 16 bits.

C 570 Determining Free Core Memory

As your programs allocate memory, you can use the *coreleft* function to estimate the amount of (conventional) memory currently available for allocation. The *coreleft* function does not provide an exact report of the unused memory. Instead, if you are using a small memory model, *coreleft* returns the amount of unused memory between the top of the heap and the stack. If you are using a larger memory model, *coreleft* returns the amount of memory between the highest allocated memory and the end of conventional memory. The *coreleft* function returns the unused memory in bytes. In the case of the small memory model, *coreleft* returns an unsigned value:

```
#include <alloc.h>

unsigned coreleft(void);
```

If you are using a larger memory model, *coreleft* returns a value of type long:

```
#include <alloc.h>

long coreleft(void);
```

The following program, CORELEFT.C, displays the amount of available memory. The model uses the memory model constants supported by many compilers to determine the current memory model:

```
#include <stdio.h>
#include <alloc.h>

void main (void)
  {
#if defined(__SMALL__)
    unsigned result;
#else
    long result;
#endif

    result = coreleft();
```

```
    printf("The amount of available memory is %dKb\n",
      result / 1024);
}
```

Note: *If your compiler does not support the coreleft function, check whether it provides the functions _memavl and _memmax.*

Reading the Segment Register Settings

571

When you work within the DOS environment, the compiler keeps track of your program code, data, and stack using four segment registers:

CS	Code segment register
DS	Data segment register
SS	Stack segment register
ES	Extra segment register

Depending on your program's memory model, each segment register may point to a unique 64Kb segment, or two or more segment registers may share the same segment. When your programs use the DOS and BIOS services, there may be times when you need to know a segment register's value. For such cases, you can use the *segread* function:

```
#include <dos.h>

void segread(struct SREGS *segs);
```

The header file dos.h defines the SREGS structure, as shown here:

```
struct SREGS {
  unsigned int es;
  unsigned int cs;
  unsigned int ss;
  unsigned int ds;
};
```

The following program, SHOWSEGS.C, uses the *segread* function to display the current segment register contents:

```
#include <stdio.h>
#include <dos.h>
```

```
void main (void)
 {
   struct SREGS segs;

   segread(&segs);

   printf("CS %X DS %X SS %X ES %X\n", segs.cs,
     segs.ds, segs.ss, segs.es);
 }
```

C 572 Understanding Memory Types

The PC can hold three types of memory: conventional, extended, and expanded. Several of the tips that follow discuss these memory types in detail. As you program, it is important that you understand the different memory types and their characteristics. The steps you must perform to allocate and use the different memory types will differ. In addition, each memory type has a different access speed, which will affect your program's performance. To determine the amount and types of memory installed your PC use the DOS 5 (or later) MEM /CLASSIFY command:

```
C:\> MEM /CLASSIFY   <ENTER>
```

If you are not using DOS 5 or later, you should upgrade your system. DOS 5 provides several memory management capabilities that let you maximize your PC's memory use.

C 573 Understanding Conventional Memory

When the PC was first released in 1981, it normally came with 64 to 256Kb of RAM! At the time, that was more than enough memory. This memory became known as the PC's *conventional memory*. Today, the PC's conventional memory is the first 1Mb of RAM. DOS programs typically run within the first 640Kb of conventional memory. The PC uses the 384Kb of memory (called *reserved* or *upper memory*) that resides between 640Kb and 1Mb for your computer's video memory, device drivers, other memory-mapped hardware devices and the BIOS. For years, however, large sections of this reserved memory were unused. Beginning with version 5, DOS provides ways that your programs and device drivers can reside in these unused regions as they run. By taking advantage of this upper memory, you can free up more of the 640Kb conventional memory for use by DOS. For information on how to take advantage of this upper memory region, refer to the CONFIG.SYS DOS=UMB (UMB stands for *upper memory block*) entry in your DOS documentation.

Understanding the Conventional Memory Layout

In Tip 573 you learned that *conventional memory* is your computer's first 1Mb of RAM. Your programs and DOS normally reside in the first 640Kb of conventional memory. To help you better understand how conventional memory is used, Figure 574 resents a conventional memory map.

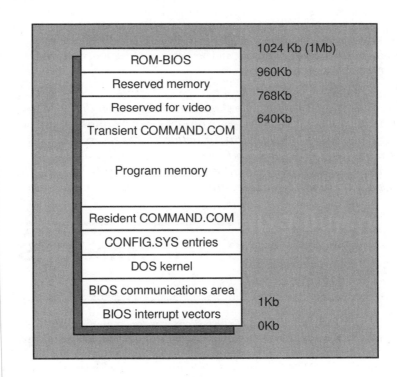

Figure 574 *map of the PC's conventional memory.*

The DOS and BIOS section of this book explains the BIOS interrupt vectors and BIOS communication area. The DOS kernel is the software, IO.SYS and MSDOS.SYS, that DOS loads into memory during the system startup. The CONFIG.SYS entries is the region of memory that DOS allocates for device drivers, disk buffers, and so on. COMMAND.COM is the software responsible for displaying the DOS prompt and processing the commands you type. To make more memory available to programs, DOS divides COMMAND.COM into a resident part, which always remains in memory and a transient part, which can be overwritten by each command. After the command completes, the resident portion of COMMAND.COM reloads the transient section from disk. The 384Kb of memory between 640Kb and 1Mb is your computer's upper memory, which contains the video memory, upper memory blocks, and the ROM-based BIOS services, discussed in the DOS & BIOS section of this book.

575 Accessing Conventional Memory

In short, your program's *memory model* defines the program's conventional memory use. Depending on the memory model in use, the compiler will allocate one or more 64Kb segments to store your program code and data. When your program needs to allocate memory dynamically, your program can use C functions such as *malloc* to allocate memory from the near heap, or *_fmalloc* to allocate memory from the far heap. Tips 597 and 598 discuss the near and far heaps. In addition, your programs can use the DOS system services to allocate memory.

Note: *As a rule, your programs should use only one method to allocate and deallocate memory. To improve your program's portability, your programs should try to use C run-time library functions for memory management. Do not mix the C memory allocation functions with those provided by DOS. By combining DOS and C memory allocation functions, you increase the possibility of errors and make your program more difficult to understand.*

576 Why the PC, and Hence DOS, is Restricted to 1Mb

Many people often refer to the *640Kb barrier* when they discuss DOS. In short, this barrier refers to the conventional memory region within which your programs must run. As you have learned, however, DOS programs actually use the BIOS services and video memory, which reside in the memory range 640K to 1Mb. In addition, beginning with DOS 5, your programs and device drivers can actually reside in the upper memory area, so the DOS memory restriction actually occurs at 1Mb.

The 1Mb memory limit is more of a PC limit than a limit of DOS. The original PC (which used the 8088 processor) used a 16-bit segment address and a 16-bit offset within the segment. Within the PC's memory, segments occur at 16-byte intervals. The 65,536 unique segment addresses allow 65,536 * 16 byte (or 1,048,576) memory locations. Because DOS must run within this environment, DOS receives the "bum rap" for restricting your program memory.

How the PC Combines Segments and Offsets to Produce an Address

To manage address specific memory locations, the PC uses a 16-bit *segment* and *offset* address. The segment address normally identifies the start of a 64Kb region. The offset address identifies a specific byte within the region. As briefly discussed in Tip 576, segments can begin at 16-byte intervals called *paragraphs*. To address memory, the PC combines the segment and offset address to produce a 20-bit address—which can address 1,048,576 unique memory locations (1Mb). To create the 20-bit address, the PC shifts the 16-bit segment address left by four bit locations and then adds to the result the offset address. For example, assume that the segment address is 1234H. When the PC shifts the address to the left, the result becomes 12340H. Next, if the offset address is 5, the result is 12340H + 5H or 12345H. The following equation better illustrates the processing involved:

```
1234H Segment shifted becomes    12340H
            Add the offset of     0005H
                       Yields    12345H
```

If you examine the operation in binary, the result becomes

```
      0001 0010 0011 0100         Segment
 0001 0010 0011 0100 0000         Shifted
                     0101         Offset
==========================
 0001 0010 0011 0100 0101         Result (20-bit address)
```

Understanding Expanded Memory

As you have learned, DOS programs normally run within your computer's 640Kb conventional memory. Many larger programs, however, such as a spreadsheet, require more than 640Kb. The original IBM PC (8088) could not address memory beyond 1Mb. To allow the PC to access more than 1Mb of memory, the companies Lotus, Intel, and Microsoft created an *expanded memory specification* (EMS), which combines software and a special expanded memory board to trick the PC into accessing large amounts of memory. To use expanded memory, your computer must contain an expanded memory board. The EMS software begins by allocating a 64Kb block of upper memory (the 384Kb region between 640Kb and 1Mb). Next, the software divides the region into four 16Kb sections called *pages*. When your program starts, it uses special EMS functions to allocate and load expanded memory. To do so, your program defines logical (16Kb) pages within the expanded memory region. For example, if you have a 128Kb spreadsheet, you divide the data into eight 16Kb logical pages. When your program needs to access a specific logical page, the program uses an EMS function to *map* the logical page into one of the EMS pages in your computer's upper memory, which your DOS program can then directly access. As your program needs to use other logical pages, it maps pages in and out of the EMS area as needed.

The expanded memory mapping is required only because the 8088 processor cannot access memory locations beyond 1Mb. Although the expanded memory provides a way for the 8088 to access large amounts of data, the continual mapping of data introduces considerable overhead, which decreases your system performance. If you are using an 80286 or greater, your computer can access memory beyond 1Mb (called extended memory), which is a much faster process.

Note: *When a program uses expanded memory, the program code remains in the 640Kb conventional memory region. Only the program's data can reside in the expanded memory area.*

C 579 Using Expanded Memory

Tip 578 introduced the PC's use of expanded memory. As a rule, to improve performance, your programs should *extended memory* (see Tip 580) instead of expanded memory. However, if you are forced to write a program that must run on an older 8088-based PC, your programs access the EMS services using INT 67H, using the *int86* function, discussed in the DOS and BIOS section of this book. There are many EMS services that let you allocate, map, deallocate, and manipulate expanded memory. For a complete description and example programs that use these services, refer to the book *DOS Programming: The Complete Reference* (Osborne/McGraw-Hill, 1991). The companion disk that accompanies this book, however, provides the sample program, SHOWEMS.C, that illustrates use the expanded memory.

C 580 Understanding Extended Memory

The original IBM PC (8088) used 20-bit addressing, which restricted it to 1Mb. Beginning with the IBM PC AT (the 80286), the PC gained the ability to use 24-bit addressing, which let it address up to 16Mb. 386- and 486-based machines increased the addressing to 32-bit, which lets the PC address up to 4Gb of memory! When the PC first gained the ability to access memory beyond 1Mb, the memory beyond 1Mb was termed *extended memory*. Because the original IBM PC cannot access beyond 1Mb, it cannot use extended memory.

To access extended memory, you must load an extended memory device driver. In the case of DOS, the driver is normally HIMEM.SYS. When your DOS-based programs use extended memory, only the program's data can reside in extended memory. The program's code must reside in the 640Kb conventional memory. When your programs use extended memory, however, the system services that provide access to the memory must change your CPU's mode of execution from real mode to protected mode and back again. This changing of CPU modes requires some processing time, which introduces overhead. However, the overhead is less than that of expanded memory— making extended memory more desirable.

Understanding Real and Protected Modes

581

DOS is a single-tasking operating system, which means (with the exception of device drivers and memory-resident programs) that there is normally only one program running at a time. Because DOS is not required to protect one program from another, DOS lets programs access memory in any way they desire. In other words, a DOS-based program can change any conventional memory location's value. DOS does not care. When you run multiple programs at the same time, one program cannot indiscriminately change memory in this way— because they would likely overwrite the contents of an another program in memory. In a multiprogram environment, one program's memory must be protected from another's. To protect programs in memory, the operating system relies on hardware-based memory protection. Beginning with the 80286, the CPU can run in one of two modes: *real* or *protected*. Real mode exists for compatibility with the original 8088-based IBM PC. Real mode is the mode used by DOS. There is no memory protection within real mode. Other operating systems such as Unix, OS/2, or Windows can run in protected mode. In protected mode, one program cannot access the memory of another. In addition, within protected mode, the PC changes from its segment and offset addressing scheme to one that allows the CPU to use 24-bit addressing within the 80286 and 32-bit addressing within 386-based machines and higher. In this way, protected mode lets the PC address extended memory for code and data.

When your DOS-based programs use extended memory, the software they use to access the extended memory transparently switches the CPU from real mode (which was running DOS) to protected mode (which can access the extended memory) and then back to real mode again.

Accessing Extended Memory

582

Before your programs can use extended memory, an extended memory device driver (normally HIMEM.SYS) must be installed. Next, using the DOS multiplex interrupt, INT 2FH service 4300H, your programs can obtain an entry point in memory of the extended memory services. The extended memory driver provides functions that let your programs allocate, deallocate, and manipulate extended memory. To access the services, you assign different parameters to PC registers and then branch to the specified entry point. For a complete description of the extended memory services, refer to the book *DOS Programming: The Complete Reference* (Osborne/McGraw-Hill, 1991). To help you better understand the extended memory services, the companion disk that accompanies this book includes the file XMSDEMO.C.

583 Understanding the High Memory Area

As you have learned, extended memory is your computer's memory above 1Mb. When DOS programs access extended memory, the CPU changes from real mode to protected mode and back again. If you are using a 386 and DOS 5 or later, your can take advantage of a "glitch" in the 286 processors design that lets you access the first 64Kb of extended memory from within real mode. As shown in Figure 583 this 64Kb region is called the *high memory area*.

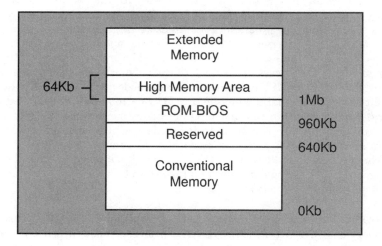

Figure 583 *The high memory area is the first 64Kb of extended memory.*

The best way to use the high memory area is to load the DOS kernel into it, freeing up memory within the 640Kb conventional memory. However, if DOS is not using the high memory area, your program can allocate it using a extended memory service. To load DOS into the high memory area, you must have installed the HIMEM.SYS driver and then use the CONFIG.SYS DOS=HIGH entry.

Understanding the Stack

584

The *stack* is a region of memory within which your programs temporarily store data as they execute. For example, when your programs pass parameters to functions, C places the parameters on the stack. When the function completes, C removes the items from the stack. Likewise, when your functions declare local variables, C stores the variable's values on the stack during the function's execution. When the function completes, the variables are discarded.

The stack is so named because programs *push* values on to the stack, much as you would stack the cafeteria trays one on top of another, and later *pop* the top value off the stack, just as you would remove the top cafeteria tray. Depending on the program's memory model, the amount of stack space the compiler provides will differ. Depending on your program's use of functions and parameters, the amount of stack space your program will require will differ. As a minimum the compiler will allocate 4Kb of stack space. If your program needs more or less stack space, you can use compiler and linker directives to control the amount of stack space allocated. The PC uses two registers to locate the stack. The stack segment register (SS) points to the start of the stack and the stack pointer register (SP) points to the top of the stack.

Understanding Different Stack Configurations

585

In Tip 584 you learned that your program uses the stack to temporarily store information—primarily during function calls. Depending on your program's use of functions and the number and size of parameters your programs pass to those functions, the amount of stack space your program requires will vary from one program to the next. When you use the small memory model, C allocates the stack space from the top of the data segment, as shown in Figure 585.

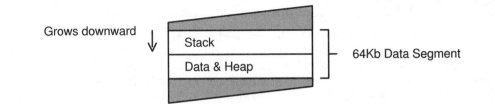

Figure 585 *C's small memory model stack space allocation.*

When you use the large or compact memory model on the other hand, C will allocate an entire 64Kb segment for the stack. If your program places more information on to the stack than the stack can hold, a *stack overflow error* will occur. If your program has disabled stack checking (See the Optimization section of this book), you will be unaware of the error and the data placed on to the stack may overwrite your program data. Tip 586 presents ways you can determine your program's current stack size.

586 Determining Your Program's Current Stack Size

Depending on your program's function and parameter use, the amount of stack space your program requires will differ. Using compiler and linker directives, your programs can allocate a specific stack size. As your program's execute, there may be times when you want to know the current stack size. If you are using Borland C++, you can use the *_stklen* global variable. The following program, STK_LEN.C, uses the *_stklen* global variable to display the current stack size:

```
#include <stdio.h>
#include <dos.h>

void main(void)
  {
    printf("The current stack size %d bytes\n", _stklen);
  }
```

If you are using Microsoft C, the *stackavail* function returns the amount of available stack space.

587 Controlling the Stack Space with _stklen

In Tip 586 you learned that the *_stklen* global variable lets your programs determine the current stack size. In addition, your programs can use the *_stklen* variable to control the amount of stack space the compiler allocates. To specify a stack size using *_stklen* your programs must declare the variable as a external global variable. The following program 8KBSTACK.C, using *_stklen* global variable to allocate an 8Kb stack:

```
#include <stdio.h>
#include <dos.h>
```

```
extern unsigned _stklen = 8096;

void main(void)
  {
    printf("The current stack size %d bytes\n", _stklen);
```

Assigning a Value to a Memory Range

When your programs work with arrays and pointers to memory ranges, there may be times when you will want to initialize the memory to a specific value. To do so, your programs can use the *memset* function:

```
#include <mem.h>

void *memset(void *ptr, int character, size_t num_bytes);
```

The *ptr* parameter is a pointer to the first byte in the memory range. The *character* parameter is the byte value you want to assign to the range of memory. Finally, the *num_bytes* parameter specifies the number of bytes in the memory range. The function returns a pointer to the start of the memory range. The following statement uses *memset* to initialize a character string array to NULL:

```
char string[128];

memset(string, NULL, sizeof(string));
```

Copying One Memory Range to Another

When your programs work with character strings, they can use the *strcpy* function to copy one string's contents to another. When you need to copy an array of integer or floating-point values, however, your programs can perform similar processing using the *memmove* or *memcpy* functions:

```
#include <mem.h>

void *memmove(void *target, const void *source,
```

```
       size_t num_bytes);

void *memcpy(void *target, const void *source,
       size_t num_bytes);
```

The *target* and *source* parameters are pointers to the array into which the data is being copied (*target*) and from which the copy is being made (*source*). The *num_bytes* parameter specifies the number of bytes to copy. The primary difference between the two functions is that *memmove* correctly copies data between two bytes ranges that happen to overlap in memory while *memcpy* might not. The following program, MEMMOVE.C, uses the *memmove* function to copy the contents of a floating-point array:

```
#include <stdio.h>
#include <mem.h>

void main(void)
 {
    float values[] = { 1.1, 2.2, 3.3, 4.4, 5.5 };
    float empty[5];

    int i;

    memmove(empty, values, sizeof(values));

    for (i = 0; i < 5; i++)
      printf("%3.1f ", empty[i]);
 }
```

C 590 Copying a Memory Range up to and Including a Specific Byte

When your programs work with arrays, there may be times when you will need to copy the contents of one array to another. Depending on the contents of the array, you might want the copy to move up to *n* bytes, or immediately end if a specific character is copied. To perform such processing, your programs can use the *memccpy* function:

```
#include <mem.h>

void *memccpy(void *target, const void *source,
  int character, size_t num_bytes);
```

The *target* and *source* parameters are pointers to the array into which the data is being copied (*target*) and from which the copy is being made (*source*). The *character* parameter specifies the character that, if copied, immediately ends the copy operation. The *num_bytes* parameter specifies the number of bytes to copy. If the function copies *num_bytes*, it returns the value NULL. If the specified character was encountered, the function returns a pointer to byte in the target that immediately follows the character. The following program, MEMCCPY.C, uses the *memccpy* function to copy the letters A–K to the array *target*:

```c
#include <stdio.h>
#include <mem.h>

void main(void)
 {
   char alphabet[27] = "ABCDEFGHIJKLMNOPQRSTUVWXYZ";
   char target[27];
   char *result;

   result = memccpy(target, alphabet, 'K', sizeof(alphabet));

   if (result)
     *result = NULL;

   printf(target);
 }
```

Comparing Two Arrays of *unsigned char*

591

When your programs work with arrays (most likely a character string in this case), there may be times when you want to compare two memory ranges. To do so, your programs can use the *memcmp* or *memicmp* functions:

```c
#include <mem.h>

int memcmp(const void *block_1, const void *block_2,
   size_t num_bytes);

int memicmp(const void *block_1, const void *block_2,
   size_t num_bytes);
```

The difference between the two functions is that *memicmp* ignores the case of characters. The *block_1* and *block_2* parameters are pointers to the start of each memory range. The *num_bytes* parameter specifies the number of bytes to compare. The function returns one of the following values:

Value less than 0	block_1 is less than block_2
0	blocks are the same
Value greater than 0	block_1 is greater than block_2

The following program MEMCMP.C uses these two functions to compare two character strings:

```
#include <stdio.h>
#include <mem.h>

void main(void)
 {
   char *a = "AAA";
   char *b = "BBB";
   char *c = "aaa";

   printf("Comparing %s and %s with memcmp %d\n",
     a, b, memcmp(a, b, sizeof(a)));

   printf("Comparing %s and %s with memicmp %d\n",
     a, c, memicmp(a, c, sizeof(a)));
 }
```

C 592 Swapping Adjacent Character String Bytes

When you work with different types of computers, there may be times when you need swap adjacent bytes of memory. To do so, your programs can use the *swab* function:

```
#include <stdlib.h>

void swab(char *source, char *target, int num_bytes);
```

The *source* parameter is a pointer to a string whose bytes you want to swap. The *target* parameter is a pointer to a string to which the swapped bytes are assigned. The *num_bytes* parameter specifies the number of bytes to swap. The following program SWAB.C, illustrates the *swab* function:

```
#include <stdio.h>
#include <stdlib.h>
#include <string.h>
#include <mem.h>

void main(void)
 {
   char *source = "AJSM'A S0110T pi!s";
   char target[64];

   memset(target, NULL, sizeof(target));
```

```
    swab(source, target, strlen(source));

    printf("Source: %s Target %s\n", source, target);
  }
```

Allocating Dynamic Memory

593

When your programs declare an array, the C compiler allocates memory to hold the array. Should your program requirements change and the array size need to increase or decrease, you must edit and recompile the program. To reduce the number of changes you must make to your programs for changes in array sizes, your programs can allocate their own memory during run-time. When you allocate memory in this way, the C run-time library returns a pointer to the start of the memory range. Your programs can then work with the memory using an array or pointer format, whichever you prefer. When you allocate memory during run time, your program can use the *malloc* run-time library function:

```
#include <alloc.h>

void *malloc(size_t number_of_bytes);
```

The *number_of_bytes* parameter specifies the number of bytes desired. If the *malloc* successfully allocates the byte range, *malloc* returns a pointer to the start of the range. If an error occurs, *malloc* returns NULL. The following program, MALLOC.C, uses *malloc* to allocate memory for a character-string array, and array of integer values, and a floating-point array:

```
#include <stdio.h>
#include <alloc.h>

void main(void)
  {
    char *string;
    int *int_values;
    float *float_values;

    if ((string = (char *) malloc(50)))
      printf("Successfully allocated a 50 byte string\n");
    else
      printf("Error allocating string\n");

    if ((int_values = (int *) malloc(100 * sizeof(int))) != NULL)
      printf("Successfully allocated int_values[100]\n");
    else
      printf("Error allocating int_values[100]\n");
```

```
   if ((float_values = (float *) malloc(25 * sizeof(float))) !=
      NULL)
     printf("Successfully allocated float_values[25]\n");
   else
     printf("Error allocating float_values[25]\n");
 }
```

As you can see, the program invokes *malloc* with the required number of bytes. If *malloc* returns NULL, the program displays an error message.

594 Casts Revisited

In Tip 593 you learned that, using the *malloc* run-time library function, your programs could allocate memory during run time. As you learned, the *malloc* function returns a *void* pointer:

```
void *malloc(size_t number_of_bytes);
```

When you use *malloc* to allocate memory, your programs should cast *malloc's* result to a pointer of the desired type. For example, the following statement uses *malloc* to allocate a pointer to 100 values of type *int*:

```
int *int_values;

int_values = (int *) malloc(100 * sizeof(int));
```

If you are allocating memory to hold 50 floating-point values, your statements become the following:

```
float *float_values;

float_values = (float *) malloc(50 * sizeof(float));
```

By casting the *malloc's* return value in this way, you can eliminate compiler warning messages.

595 Releasing Memory When It Is No Longer Needed

As you have learned, using the *malloc* function, your programs can allocate memory during execution to hold arrays or other items. When your program no longer needs the memory, your program should release the memory so it can be reused (allocated by *malloc* for a different purpose). To release allocated memory, your programs can use the *free* function:

```
#include <alloc.h>

void free(void *ptr);
```

The *ptr* parameter is a pointer to the start of the memory range you want to release. The following program, FREE.C, uses *malloc* to allocate an integer array. The program then uses the array. When the program no longer needs the array, it releases the corresponding memory using *free*:

```
#include <stdio.h>
#include <alloc.h>

void main(void)
  {
    int *int_values;

    int i;

    if ((int_values = malloc(100 * sizeof(int))) == NULL)
      printf("Error allocating the array\n");
    else
      {
        for (i = 0; i < 100; i++)
          int_values[i] = i;

        for (i = 0; i < 100; i++)
          printf("%d ", int_values[i]);

        free(int_values);
      }
  }
```

Note: *If your programs do not use free to release memory, the memory is automatically released when the program ends. As a rule, however, your programs should release memory as soon as the memory is no longer needed.*

Allocating Memory Using *calloc*

C596

As you have learned, using the *malloc* function lets your programs allocate memory dynamically during run time. When you use *malloc*, you specify the desired number of bytes. In addition to using *malloc*, C lets your programs allocate memory using *calloc*. The difference between the two functions is that *malloc* directs you to specify the desired number of bytes, whereas *calloc* directs you to specify the number of elements of a specific size:

```
#include <alloc.h>

void *calloc(size_t number_of_items, size_t item_size);
```

The *number_of_items* parameter specifies how many elements for which *calloc* must allocate memory. The *item_size* parameter specifies the size of each element in bytes. If *calloc* successfully allocates the memory, *calloc* returns a pointer to the start of the memory range. If an error occurs, *calloc* returns NULL. The following program, CALLOC.C, uses *calloc* to allocate several different types of arrays:

```
#include <stdio.h>
#include <alloc.h>

void main(void)
 {
   char *string;
   int *int_values;
   float *float_values;

   if ((string = (char *) calloc(50, sizeof(char))))
     printf("Successfully allocated a 50 byte string\n");
   else
     printf("Error allocating string\n");

   if ((int_values = (int *) calloc(100, sizeof(int))) != NULL)
     printf("Successfully allocated int_values[100]\n");
   else
     printf("Error allocating int_values[100]\n");

   if ((float_values = (float *)
        calloc(25, sizeof(float))) != NULL)
     printf("Successfully allocated float_values[25]\n");
   else
     printf("Error allocating float_values[25]\n");
 }
```

Note: *When your program has finished using the memory allocated by calloc, your program should release the memory using free.*

Understanding the Heap

When your programs allocate memory dynamically, the C run-time library gets the memory from a collection of unused memory called the *heap*. As shown in Figure 597, when you compile programs using the small memory model, the heap is the area of memory between the top of your program's data area and the stack.

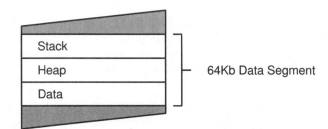

Figure 597 *The heap resides between the program's data area and stack.*

As you can see, the heap resides in your program's data segment. Therefore, the amount of heap space available to your program is fixed, and can vary from one program to the next. When you use *calloc* or *malloc* to allocate memory, the most memory the functions can allocate is 64Kb (assuming no data and stack). The following program, NO_SPACE.C, tries to allocate three 30Kb arrays. Because the heap does not have 90Kb available, the memory allocation fails:

```c
#include <stdio.h>
#include <alloc.h>

void main(void)
 {
   char *one, *two, *three;

   if ((one = (char *) malloc(30000)) == NULL)
     printf("Error allocating array one\n");
   else if ((two = (char *) malloc(30000)) == NULL)
     printf("Error allocating array two\n");
   else if ((three = (char *) malloc(30000)) == NULL)
     printf("Error allocating array three\n");
   else
     printf("All arrays successfully allocated\n");
 }
```

In the large memory model, the total heap size is not restricted to 64Kb; however the largest value you can allocate at any one time is still restricted to a 64Kb segment. To allocate a value larger than 64Kb, you must use the huge model. Try compiling the NO_SPACE.C program using the large memory model. The program should then be able to satisfy the memory allocation.

598 Getting Around the 64Kb Heap Limit

As you have learned, when your DOS-based programs allocate memory from the heap, your programs can allocate, at most, 64Kb of memory. Because the 64Kb limit is a DOS (PC real mode) restriction, many DOS-based compilers provide functions named *farmalloc* and *farcalloc* that let your program's allocate memory from a *far heap*, which resides outside of the current data segment:

```
#include <alloc.h>

void far *farcalloc(unsigned long number_of_items,
    unsigned long element_size);

void far *farmalloc(unsigned long number_of_bytes);
```

The parameters are identical in function to those passed to *calloc* and *malloc*. When you allocate memory from the far heap, you use a far pointer to the data. The following program, FMALLOC.C, allocates several arrays from the far heap:

```
#include <stdio.h>
#include <alloc.h>

void main(void)
  {
    char far *string;
    int far *int_values;
    float far *float_values;

    if ((string = (char *) farmalloc(50)))
      printf("Successfully allocated a 50 byte string\n");
    else
      printf("Error allocating string\n");

    if ((int_values = (int *)
        farmalloc(100 * sizeof(int))) != NULL)
      printf("Successfully allocated int_values[100]\n");
    else
      printf("Error allocating int_values[100]\n");
```

```
    if ((float_values = (float *)
        farmalloc(25 * sizeof(float))) != NULL)
      printf("Successfully allocated float_values[25]\n");
    else
      printf("Error allocating float_values[25]\n");
  }
```

In the large memory model, all pointers are treated as far pointers. However, the use of the far pointer is transparent within your application.

> **Note:** *When your programs allocate memory from the far heap using farcalloc or farmalloc, you should release the memory when it is no longer needed using the farfree function. If you are using a different compiler, the names of these functions might differ. Refer to far heap in your compiler documentation.*

Allocating Memory from the Stack

C 599

As you have learned, the *malloc* and *calloc* functions let you allocate memory from the heap. When you have finished with the memory, you should release it using *free*. Depending on your program, there may be times when you need to allocate memory that only exists for the duration of a specific function call. To do so, your programs can allocate the memory from the stack using *alloca*:

```
#include <malloc.h>

void *alloca(size_t number_of_bytes);
```

The *number_of_bytes* parameter specifies the size of memory range. If *alloca* is successful, it returns a pointer to the start of the memory block. If an error occurs, the function returns NULL. Do not use *free* to release memory allocated using *alloca*—*free* works with the heap, while *alloca* works with the stack. When the function within which the memory was allocated ends, the memory is released.

> **Note:** *For the stack pointer to be correctly restored, the function must contain local variables. To ensure a correct stack frame, declare a local variable after the pointer to which alloca assigns its result as shown here:*

```
char *pointer;
char stack_fix[1];

stack_fix[0] = NULL;
```

The following program, ALLOCA.C, illustrates the use of the *alloca* function:

```
#include <stdio.h>
#include <malloc.h>

void some_function(size_t size)
  {
    int i;

    char *pointer;

    char stack_fix[1];
    stack_fix[0] = NULL;

    if ((pointer = alloca(size)) == NULL)
      printf("Error allocating %u bytes from the stack\n", size);
    else
      {
        for (i = 0; i < size; i++)
          pointer[i] = i;
        printf("Allocated and used a buffer of %u bytes\n", size);
      }
  }
void main(void)
  {
    some_function(1000);
    some_function(32000);
    some_function(65000);
  }
```

C 600 Allocating Huge Data

As you have learned, the largest array size you can create is 64Kb. If your applications need a larger array, you can allocate a memory for a *huge* array. To help your programs work with huge data structures, many DOS-based C compilers provide the *halloc* and *hfree* functions:

```
void huge *halloc(long number_of_elements, size_t size);

void hfree(void huge *pointer);
```

The *number_of_elements* parameter specifies the number of array elements. The *size* parameter specifies each element's size in bytes. If *halloc* is successful, it returns a pointer to the start of the memory area. If an error occurs, *halloc* returns NULL. The following program, HUGEINT.C, uses *halloc* to allocate an array of (400,000 bytes):

```c
#include <stdio.h>
#include <malloc.h>

void main (void)
  {
    long int i;

    int huge *big_array;

    if ((big_array = (int huge *) halloc (100000L,
      sizeof(long int))) == NULL)
      printf ("Error allocating huge array\n");
    else
      {
        printf("Filling the array\n");

        for (i = 0; i < 100000L; i++)
          big_array[i] = i % 32768;

        for (i = 0; i < 100000L; i++)
          printf ("%d ", big_array[i]);

        hfree(big_array);
      }
  }
```

Changing the Size of an Allocated Block

As you have learned, C lets your programs dynamically allocate memory during execution. After you allocate a block of memory, there may be times when you later need to change the block's size. In such cases, your programs can use *realloc*:

```c
#include <stdlib.h>

void *realloc(void *block, size_t desired_bytes);
```

The *block* parameter is a pointer to the previously allocated memory. The *desired_bytes* parameter is the size required for the new block. The *realloc* function can shrink or expand a block. If *realloc* is successful, it returns a pointer to the block, which may be a different pointer from the original. In other words, *realloc* may move the block to find space (copying the data as necessary). If an error occurs, *realloc* returns NULL. The following program, REALLOC.C, uses *realloc* to increase the size of a block from 100 bytes to 1000 bytes:

```
#include <stdio.h>
#include <alloc.h>

void main(void)
  {
    char *string, *new_string;

    if ((string = (char *) malloc(100)))
      {
        printf("Successfully allocated a 100 byte string\n");
        if ((new_string = (char *) realloc(string, 1000)))
          printf("String size increased to 1000\n");
        else
          printf("Error reallocating the string\n");
      }
    else
      printf("Error allocating the 100 byte string\n");
  }
```

C 602 Understanding *brk*

As you have learned, the heap starts at the byte location that immediately follows the last byte in the data segment. The address at which the heap starts is called the *break value*. The *brk* function lets your programs change the break value, assigning it to a specific address:

```
#include <alloc.h>

int brk(void *address);
```

If the *brk* function is successful, it returns the value 0. If an error occurs, brk returns −1. The following program uses *brk* to set the break value 512 bytes above its current location. The program uses the *coreleft* function to display the amount of available heap before and after the *brk* operation:

```
#include <stdio.h>
#include <alloc.h>
```

```
void main(void)
 {
   char *ptr;

   printf("Starting heap available %u\n", coreleft());


   ptr = malloc(1);  // Get pointer to current break value

   if (brk(ptr + 512) == 0)
   printf("Ending heap available %u\n", coreleft());
 }
```

Validating the Heap

C 603

If you are experiencing errors in a program that allocates memory dynamically and you can't locate the source of the error, you might consider performing *heap validations*. To help you test the state of the heap, many compilers provide a collection of run-time library routines such as *heapwalk* and *heapcheck*. Several of the tips that follow present ways your programs can test the heap.

Performing a Fast Heap Check

C 604

As you have learned, to help you locate errors in your programs that perform dynamic memory allocation, you might want to check the state of the heap. One routine your programs can use to do just that is *heapcheck*:

```
#include <alloc.h>

int heapcheck(void);
```

The *heapcheck* function walks through and examines each of the heap entries. The function returns one of the following values:

_HEAPEMPTY	No heap
_HEAPOK	Heap is verified
_HEAPCORRUPT	One or more corrupted entries

The following program, HEAPCHK.C, uses the *heapcheck* function to test the state of the heap:

```c
#include <stdio.h>
#include <alloc.h>

void main(void)
  {
    char *buffer, *second_buffer;
    int i, state;

    buffer = malloc(100);
    second_buffer = malloc(100);

    state = heapcheck();

    if (state == _HEAPOK)
      printf("Heap is ok\n");
    else if (state == _HEAPCORRUPT)
      printf("Heap is corrupt\n");


    for (i = 0; i <= 100; i++)
      buffer[i] = i;


    state = heapcheck();

    if (state == _HEAPOK)
      printf("Heap is ok\n");
    else if (state == _HEAPCORRUPT)
      printf("Heap is corrupt\n");
  }
```

When the program first allocates the memory, *heapcheck* returns a status value stating that the heap is OK. After the program assigns values to *buffer*, however, the heap is corrupted. If you examine the *for* loop closely, you will find that it assigns 101 values to a 100-byte buffer (corrupting the entry). Using *heapcheck*, you can detect such errors very quickly.

C605 Filling Free Heap Space

One way to detect memory-use errors in programs that work with dynamic memory is to fill all of the free heap space with a specific value. Then, as you perform your memory operations, you can test if the value has changed. To help you fill and test free heap space, many C compilers provide the following functions:

```
#include <alloc.h>

int heapcheckfree(unsigned int value);
int heapfillfree(unsigned int value);
```

The *value* parameter is the value you want to assign to the free heap space. The functions return one of the following values:

_HEAPEMPTY	No heap
_HEAPOK	Heap is verified
_HEAPCORRUPT	One or more corrupted entries
_BADVALUE	A different value was encountered

The following program, FILLHEAP.C, uses these two functions to detect a programming error:

```
#include <stdio.h>
#include <alloc.h>

void main(void)
  {
    char *buffer1, *buffer2, *buffer3;
    int i, state;

    buffer1 = malloc(100);
    buffer2 = malloc(200);
    buffer3 = malloc(300);
    free(buffer2);              // Free space in the middle

    state = heapfillfree('A');

    if (state == _HEAPOK)
      printf("Heap is ok\n");
    else if (state == _HEAPCORRUPT)
      printf("Heap is corrupt\n");


    for (i = 0; i <= 150; i++)
      buffer1[i] = i;


    state = heapcheckfree('A');

    if (state == _HEAPOK)
      printf("Heap is ok\n");
    else if (state == _HEAPCORRUPT)
      printf("Heap is corrupt\n");
    else if (state == _BADVALUE)
      printf("Value has been changed in free space\n");
  }
```

C 606 Checking a Specific Heap Entry

In Tip 604 you learned how to use the *heapcheck* function to test the status of the entire heap. As you hunt down errors, it may be convenient to test the state of individual heap entries. To do so, your programs can use the *heapchecknode* function:

```
#include <alloc.h>

int heapchecknode(void *block);
```

The *block* parameter is a pointer to a dynamically allocated block of memory. The function will return one of the following values:

_HEAPEMPTY	No heap
_HEAPOK	Heap is verified
_HEAPCORRUPT	One or more corrupted entries
_BADNODE	Block was not found
_FREEENTRY	Block is free
_USEDENTRY	Block is in use

The following program, HEAPNODE.C, illustrates the use of the *heapchecknode* function:

```c
#include <stdio.h>
#include <alloc.h>

void main(void)
  {
    char *buffer, *second_buffer;
    int i, state;

    buffer = malloc(100);
    second_buffer = malloc(100);

    state = heapchecknode(buffer);

    if (state == _USEDENTRY)
      printf("buffer is ok\n");
    else
      printf("buffer is not ok\n");

    state = heapchecknode(second_buffer);

    if (state == _USEDENTRY)
      printf("second_buffer is ok\n");
```

```
  else
    printf("second_buffer is not ok\n");

  for (i = 0; i <= 100; i++)
    buffer[i] = i;

  state = heapchecknode(buffer);

  if (state == _USEDENTRY)
    printf("buffer is ok\n");
  else
    printf("buffer is not ok\n");

  state = heapchecknode(second_buffer);

  if (state == _USEDENTRY)
    printf("second_buffer is ok\n");
  printf("second_buffer is not ok\n");
}
```

Walking the Heap Entries

C 607

To help you examine the individual heap entries, many C compilers provide a function named *heapwalk*, which lets you display the size and state (in use or free) of each heap entry:

```
#include <alloc.h>

int heapwalk(struct heapinfo *info)
```

The *info* parameter is a pointer to a structure of type *heapinfo*:

```
struct heapinfo {
  void *pointer;
  unsigned int size;
  int in_use;
};
```

Before the first call to *heapwalk*, you need to set the *ptr* member to NULL. The function returns one of the following values:

_HEAPEMPTY	No heap
_HEAPOK	Heap is verified
_HEAPEND	Last heap entry

The following program, HEAPWALK.C, walks the heap entries using *heapwalk*:

```c
#include <stdio.h>
#include <alloc.h>

void main(void)
 {
   char *buffer1, *buffer2, *buffer3;

   struct heapinfo node = { NULL, 0, 0};

   buffer1 = malloc(100);
   buffer2 = malloc(200);
   buffer3 = malloc(300);
   free(buffer2);

   while (heapwalk(&node) == _HEAPOK)
     printf("Size %u bytes State %s\n", node.size,
       (node.in_use) ? "In use": "Free");

 }
```

C 608 Peeking into a Specific Memory Location

Depending on your program's function, there may be times when you want the program to access specific segment and offset locations in memory. If you are working with far pointers, you can combine a segment and offset address using *MK_FP*. In addition, your programs can use the *peekb* and *peek* functions:

```c
#include <dos.h>

char peekb(unsigned segment, unsigned offset);
int peek(unsigned segment, unsigned offset);
```

The *segment* and *offset* parameters combine to specify the desired memory location. The following program, FILE_SCR.C, uses the *peekb* function to capture the contents of the current (text mode) screen display the file SAVE_SCR.DAT. The program peeks at the character and attribute byte. As such, the program must peek 4000 characters and 4000 attributes:

```c
#include <stdio.h>
#include <dos.h>

#define VIDEO 0xB800    // CGA base
```

```
void main(void)
 {
   FILE *fp;
   int offset;

   if ((fp = fopen("SAVE_SCR.DAT", "wb")) == NULL)
     printf("Error opening file\n");
   else
     {
       for (offset = 0; offset < 8000; offset++)
         fprintf(fp, "%c", peekb(VIDEO, offset));
       fclose(fp);
     }
 }
```

Note: *This program uses the CGA video base address of B800H. If you are using a CGA, VGA, or other video adapter, you might need to change this base address.*

Poking Values into Memory

C 609

In Tip 608 you learned how to use the *peekb* and *peek* functions to read values from specific segment and offset addresses in memory. In a similar way, most C compilers provide *poke* and *pokeb* functions, which let your programs place values at specific memory locations:

```
#include <dos.h>

void pokeb(unsigned segment, unsigned offset, char value);

void poke(unsigned segment, unsigned offset, int value);
```

The following program, SCR_POKE.C, uses the *pokeb* function to restore the screen contents previously saved by the FILE_SCR.C program:

```
#include <stdio.h>
#include <dos.h>

#define VIDEO 0xB800    // CGA base

void main(void)
 {
   FILE *fp;
   int offset;
   char value;
```

```
if ((fp = fopen("SAVE_SCR.DAT", "rb")) == NULL)
  printf("Error opening file\n");
else
  {
    for (offset = 0; offset < 8000; offset++)
     {
       fscanf(fp, "%c", &value);
       pokeb(VIDEO, offset, value);
     }
    fclose(fp);
  }
}
```

610 Understanding PC Ports

The PC uses two techniques to communicate with internal hardware devices. First, the PC can reference memory locations that have been reserved for the device. Input and output operations that occur through such memory locations are called *memory-mapped I/O*. The PC uses memory mapped I/O to perform video output. Second, the PC can communicate to hardware devices using *ports*. A port is best viewed as a register into which the PC or the device can place specific values. Table 610 lists the port addresses used by different devices in an EISA system.

Port	Device	Port	Device
00H-1FH	DMA controller	20H-3FH	Interrupt controller
40H-5FH	System timer	60H-6FH	Keyboard
70H-7FH	Real-time clock	80H-9FH	DMA page registers
A0H-BFH	Int controller 2	C0H-DFH	DMA controller 2
F0H-FFH	Math coprocessor	1F0H-1FFH	Hard disk
200H-220H	Game adapter	270H-27FH	LPT2
2B0H-2DFH	Alternate EGA	2E0H-2E7H	COM4
2E8H-2EFH	COM3	2EFH-2FFH	COM2
300H-31FH	Network cards	378H-37FH	LPT1
380H-38FH	SDLC	390H-39FH	Cluster adapter
3B0H-3BFH	Monochrome	3C0H-3CFH	EGA
3D0H-3DFH	CGA	3FOH-3F7H	Floppy disk
3F8H-3FFH	COM1	400H-4FFH	DMA
500H-7FFH	Aliases 100H-3FFH	800H-8FFH	CMOS
900H-9FFH	Reserved	9FFH-FFFFH	Reserved

Table 610 *PC port addresses.*

The meaning of each port depends on the corresponding device. To obtain port specific meanings refer to the technical documentation for your PC or device.

Accessing Port Values

C611

If your programs perform low-level hardware control, there may be times when they will need to read or write a port value. To help your programs do so, most DOS-based C compilers provide the following functions:

```
#include <dos.h>

int inport(int port_address);
char inportb(int port_address);
void outport(int port_address, int value);
void outportb(int port_address, unsigned char value);
```

The *port_address* specifies the address of the desired port, as listed in Tip 610. The *value* parameter specifies the word or byte value your program wants to output to the port. Tip 612 illustrates the use of the *inportb* function to read and contents of the PC's CMOS memory.

Understanding the CMOS

C612

As you know, the PC stores system configuration information such as your drive types, system date, and so on in CMOS memory. The PC does not access the CMOS using standard segment and offset addressing. Instead, the PC uses PC port addresses to communicate with the CMOS. As you learned in Tip 611, the functions such as *inport* and *outport* let your programs access the PC ports. The following program, SHOWCMOS.C, uses the *inportb* function to obtain and display CMOS information:

```
#include <stdio.h>
#include <stdlib.h>
#include <dos.h>

void main (void)
 {
   struct CMOS {
     unsigned char current_second;
     unsigned char alarm_second;
     unsigned char current_minute;
     unsigned char alarm_minute;
     unsigned char current_hour;
     unsigned char alarm_hour;
     unsigned char current_day_of_week;
     unsigned char current_day;
     unsigned char current_month;
```

```
    unsigned char current_year;
    unsigned char status_registers[4];
    unsigned char diagnostic_status;
    unsigned char shutdown_code;
    unsigned char drive_types;
    unsigned char reserved_x;
    unsigned char disk_1_type;
    unsigned char reserved;
    unsigned char equipment;
    unsigned char lo_mem_base;
    unsigned char hi_mem_base;
    unsigned char hi_exp_base;
    unsigned char lo_exp_base;
    unsigned char fdisk_0_type;
    unsigned char fdisk_1_type;
    unsigned char reserved_2[19];
    unsigned char hi_check_sum;
    unsigned char lo_check_sum;
    unsigned char lo_actual_exp;
    unsigned char hi_actual_exp;
    unsigned char century;
    unsigned char information;
    unsigned char reserved3[12];
  } cmos;

  char i;

  char *pointer;
  char byte;

  pointer = (char *) &cmos;

  for (i = 0; i < 0x34; i++)
   {
     outportb(0x70, i);
     byte = inportb(0x71);
     *pointer++ = byte;
   }

  printf("Current date %d/%d/%d\n", cmos.current_month,
    cmos.current_day, cmos.current_year);
  printf("Current time %d:%d:%d\n", cmos.current_hour,
    cmos.current_minute, cmos.current_second);
  printf("Hard disk type %d\n", cmos.fdisk_0_type);
}
```

Understanding Memory Models

When you create programs in the PC environment, the compiler uses a *memory model* to determine how much memory is allocated to your program. As you have learned, the PC divides memory into 64Kb blocks called *segments*. Normally, your program uses one segment for code (the program instructions) and a second segment for data. If your program is very large or uses large amounts of data, there will be times when the compiler must provide multiple code and/or data segments. A memory model defines the number of segments the compiler can use for each. The reason memory models are important to you is that, if you use the wrong memory model, your program might not have enough memory to execute. Normally, the compiler will select a memory model large enough for your program. However, as you will learn, the larger the memory model, the slower your program execution. Therefore, your goal is always to use the smallest memory model that satisfies your program needs. Most compilers support a tiny, small, medium, compact, large, and huge memory models. Several of the tips that follow describe these memory models in detail. To select a specific memory model, you normally include a switch within the compiler's command line. Refer to the documentation that accompanied your compiler to determine the memory model switches.

Understanding the Tiny Memory Model

A *memory model* describes the number of 64Kb memory segments the compiler allocates for a program. The smallest and fastest memory model is the *tiny* model. As Figure 614 shows, the tiny memory model combines your program code and data into one 64Kb segment. Because of its compact nature, the tiny memory model consumes the least amount of memory and loads faster than other models.

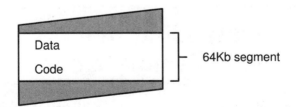

Figure 614 *The tiny memory model places program code and data into one 64Kb segment.*

If you are creating small programs, such as many of the example programs presented throughout this book, you should direct the compiler to use the tiny memory model.

615 Understanding the Small Memory Model

A *memory model* describes the number of 64Kb memory segments the compiler allocates for a program. The most common memory model is the *small* model. As Figure 615 shows, the small memory model uses one 64Kb segment for your program code and a second for your program data.

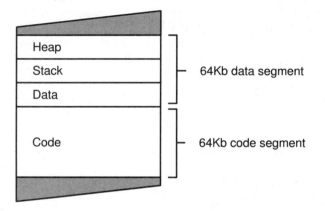

Figure 615 *The small memory model uses one 64Kb segment for program code and another for data.*

The advantage of using the small memory model is that all function calls and all data references use near 16-bit addresses. Such a program will execute faster than those using other larger memory models.

616 Understanding the Medium Memory Model

A *memory model* describes the number of 64Kb memory segments the compiler allocates for a program. If your program requires more than 64Kb of memory for code, but only 64Kb (or less) for data, your programs can use the *medium* memory model. As Figure 616 shows, the medium memory model allocates multiple code segments and only one data segment.

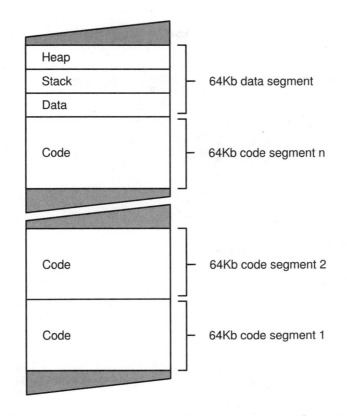

Figure 616 *The medium memory model allocates multiple code segments and one data segment.*

If your program contains a large number of instructions, the medium memory model provides fast data access because all data references use near addresses. Because multiple code segments are used, however, all function calls require 32-bit far addresses. The pushing and popping of the additional segment address for function calls will slightly decrease program performance.

Understanding the Compact Memory Model

A *memory model* describes the number of 64Kb memory segments the compiler allocates for a program. If your program uses a large amount of data but limited instructions, your programs can use the *compact* memory model. As Figure 617 shows, the compact memory model allocates one 64Kb segment for your program code and multiple segments for data.

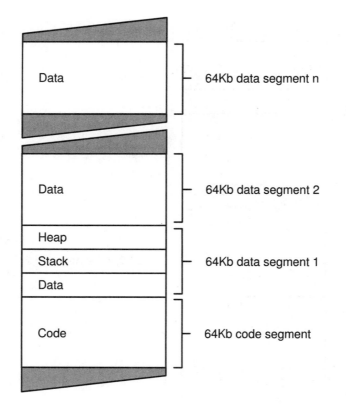

Figure 617 *The compact memory model allocates one 64Kb segment for code and multiple data segments.*

Because the compact memory model only uses one code segment, all function calls use 16-bit near addresses. As a result, they are fast. Data references, one the other hand require a segment and offset address (a 32-bit far address). The overhead required to work with segment and offset address for each data reference will decrease your program's performance.

618 Understanding the Large Memory Model

A *memory model* describes the number of 64Kb memory segments the compiler allocates for a program. If your program contains a large amount of code and data, your program can use the *large* memory model. As Figure 618 shows, the large memory model allocates multiple code and data segments.

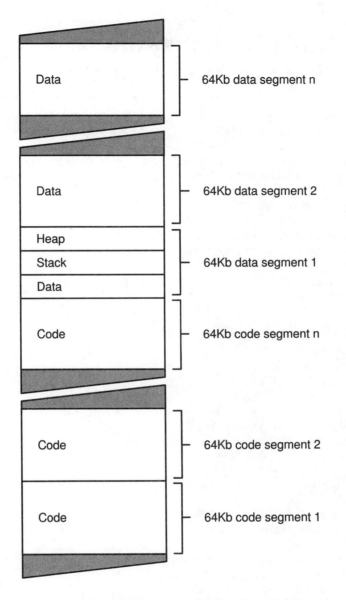

Figure 618 *The large memory model allocates multiple code and data segments. .*

You should use the large memory model only as a last resort. Because the large memory model uses multiple code and data segments, each function call and each data reference requires a 32-bit far address. The overhead associated with the constant segment and offset manipulation makes the large memory model the slowest of the models described so far.

C 619 Understanding the Huge Memory Model

A *memory model* describes the number of 64Kb memory segments the compiler allocates for a program. As you have learned, most PC-based C compilers provide many different memory models to satisfy your program's data and code requirements. A special condition arises, however, when your program uses an array larger than 64Kb. To allocate such an array, your program must use the *huge* keyword to create a pointer, as shown here:

```
int huge *big_array;
```

Next, your program must use the *halloc* function to allocate the memory. The following program, HUGEINT.C, for example, uses the *halloc* to allocate a 400,000-byte array:

```
#include <stdio.h>
#include <malloc.h>

void main (void)
  {
    long int i;

    int huge *big_array;

    if ((big_array = (int huge *) halloc (100000L,
      sizeof(long int))) == NULL)
      printf ("Error allocating huge array\n");
    else
      {
        printf("Filling the array\n");

        for (i = 0; i < 100000L; i++)
          big_array[i] = i % 32768;

        for (i = 0; i < 100000L; i++)
          printf ("%d ", big_array[i]);

        hfree(big_array);
      }
  }
```

When you compile an execute a program using the huge memory model, most compilers will use 32-bit far addresses for both code and data, similar to the large memory model. As such, the model's execution might be slower than you would desire.

Determining the Current Memory Model

C 620

Depending on your program's processing, there may be times when the program might need to be compiled using a specific memory model. To to help your programs determine the current memory model, most C compilers predefine a specific constant. Table 620, for example, lists the constants defined by the Microsoft and Borland C compilers for different memory models.

Memory Model	Microsoft Constant	Borland Constant
Small	M_I86SM	__SMALL__
Medium	M_I86MM	__MEDIUM__
Compact	M_I86CM	__COMPACT__
Large	M_I86LM	__LARGE__

Table 620 *Constants defined by Microsoft C and Borland C++ to indicate the current memory model.*

Should your program require a specific memory model, the program can test for the model, as shown here:

```
#ifndef __MEDIUM__
  printf("Program requires Medium memory model\n");
  exit(1);
#endif
```

C 621 Obtaining the Current Date and Time as Seconds Since 1/1/1970

As your programs become more functional, they will often need to know the current date and time. Most C compilers provide several functions that return the date and time in different formats. One such function is *time*, which returns the current date and time as seconds since 00:00 January 1, 1970. The function returns a value of type *time_t*, as shown here:

```
#include <time.h>

time_t time(time_t *date_time);
```

If you don't want to pass a parameter to *time*, you can invoke the function with NULL:

```
current_time = time(NULL);
```

The following program, DELAY_5.C, uses the *time* function to implement a 5-second delay:

```
#include <stdio.h>
#include <time.h>

void main (void)
 {
    time_t current_time;
    time_t start_time;

    printf("About to delay 5 seconds\n");

    time(&start_time);  // Get starting time in seconds

    do {
      time(&current_time);
    } while ((current_time - start_time) < 5);

    printf("Done\n");
 }
```

Converting a Date and Time from Seconds to ASCII

622

Tip 621 introduced the *time* function, which returns the current time as seconds since 00:00 January 1, 1970. Using the *ctime* function, your programs can covert the seconds to an character string in the following format:

```
"Wed Dec 8 11:30:00 1993\n"
```

The following program, CTIME.C, illustrates the use of the *ctime* function:

```c
#include <stdio.h>
#include <time.h>

void main (void)
  {
    time_t current_time;

    time(&current_time);  // Get the time in seconds;

    printf("The current date and time: %s",
      ctime(&current_time));
  }
```

Daylight Savings Adjustment

623

Several functions presented in this section take daylight savings into account. To perform such processing, many C compilers declare a global variable named *daylight*. If daylight savings is in effect, the variable contains the value 1. If daylight savings is not in effect, the variable is set to 0. The functions *tzset*, *localtime*, and *ftime* control the variable's value. The following code fragment uses daylight variable to determine whether or not daylight or standard time is in effect:

```c
if (daylight)
  printf("Daylight savings is active\n");
else
  printf("Daylight savings is not active\n");
```

Note: *The function tzset assigns the value to the daylight variable.*

C 624 Delaying a Specific Number of Milliseconds

Depending on your program, there may be times when you need the program to delay a specific number of milliseconds (1/1000 second). For example, you may want to display a message on your screen for a few seconds, continuing the program's execution without forcing the user to press a key. For such cases, many C compilers provide the *delay* function. The function will delay the number of milliseconds specified, as shown here:

```
#include <dos.h>

void delay(unsigned milliseconds);
```

Using the *delay* function, your programs can specify a delay period up to 65,535 milliseconds. The following program, USEDELAY.C, uses the *delay* function to delay 5 seconds (5000 milliseconds):

```
#include <stdio.h>
#include <dos.h>

void main (void)
  {
     printf("About to delay 5 seconds\n");

     delay(5000);

     printf("Done\n");
  }
```

C 625 Determining Your Program's Processing Time

When you perform different steps to improve your program's performance, you might want to measure the amount of time different parts of your program consume. In this way, you can determine which parts of your program are the most time consuming. As a rule, you should start your optimizing at the part of your program that consumes the most processor time. To help you determine your program's processing time, C provides the *clock* function, which returns the number of clock ticks (which normally occur 18.2 times per second), as shown here:

```
#include <time.h>

clock_t clock(void);
```

The *clock* function returns the program's processing time in clock ticks. To convert the time to seconds, you can divide the result by the constant CLK_TCK, which is defined in the header file time.h. The following program, CLOCK.C, uses the clock function to display the program's processor time in seconds:

```
#include <stdio.h>
#include <time.h>
#include <dos.h>        // Contains the delay prototype

void main (void)
  {
    clock_t processor_time;

    printf("Processor time consumed %ld\n",
      clock() / (long) CLK_TCK);

    delay(2000);

    printf("Processor time consumed %ld\n",
      (long) clock() / (long) CLK_TCK);

    delay(3000);

    printf("Processor time consumed %ld\n",
      clock() / (long) CLK_TCK);
  }
```

Note: *If your compiler does not provide the delay function, you can use one or more for loops to implement a delay.*

Comparing Two Times

C 626

In Tip 621 you learned how to use the *time* function to obtain the number of seconds since January 1, 1970. When you work with such times, your programs might need to compare two or more times. In such cases, your programs can use C's *difftime* function, which returns the difference between two times has a floating-point value:

```
float difftime(time_t later_time, time_t start_time);
```

The following program, DIFFTIME.C, uses the *difftime* function to delay until 5 seconds have passed:

```
#include <stdio.h>
#include <time.h>

void main (void)
 {
   time_t start_time;
   time_t current_time;

   time(&start_time);

   printf("About to delay 5 seconds\n");

   do {
     time(&current_time);
   } while (difftime(current_time, start_time) < 5.0);

   printf("Done\n");
 }
```

C 627 Obtaining a Date String

Many C compilers provide the *asctime* function to create a character string that contains the date and time. To use the *asctime* function, you must first invoke the *time* function to obtain the number of seconds since January 1, 1970. If you are only interested in obtaining the current date, your programs can use _strdate function, shown here:

```
#include <dos.h>

char *_strdate(char *date_buffer);
```

The character string buffer you pass to the _strdate function must be large enough to hold 9 characters (the eight character date and NULL). The _strdate function places the date in the form *mm/dd/yy*. The following program, STRDATE.C, uses the _strdate function to display the current date:

```
#include <stdio.h>
#include <time.h>

void main (void)
 {
   char date[9];

   _strdate(date);

   printf("The current date is %s\n", date);
 }
```

Obtaining a the Time String

C
628

Many C compilers provide the *asctime* function to create a character string that contains the date and time. To use the *asctime* function, you must first invoke the *time* function to obtain the number of seconds since January 1, 1970. If you are only interested in obtaining the current time, your programs can use *_strtime* function, shown here:

```
#include <dos.h>

char *_strtime(char *time_buffer);
```

The character string buffer you pass to the *_strtime* function must be large enough to hold nine characters (the eight-character date and NULL). The *_strtime* function places the time in the form *hh:mm:nn*. The following program, STRTIME.C, uses the *_strtime* function to display the current time:

```
#include <stdio.h>
#include <time.h>

void main (void)
  {
    char time[9];

    _strtime(time);

    printf("The current time is %s\n", time);
  }
```

Reading the BIOS Timer

C
629

The PC BIOS has a built-in timer that ticks 18.2 times per second. Within memory, the BIOS stores the number of ticks that have occurred since midnight. In the past, many programs have used the BIOS timer to delay their programs until a specific number of ticks have occurred. As previously discussed, however, your programs can specify a much finer time interval (at the millisecond level) using the *delay* function. The BIOS timer remains useful for generating a seed for a random number generator. Many C compiler's provide two functions that let you control the BIOS timer: *biostime* and *_bios_timeofday*. The function *biostime* lets your programs access the number of clock ticks that have occurred since midnight. The format of the *biostime* function is as follows:

```
#include <bios.h>

long biostime(int operation, long newtime);
```

The *operation* parameter lets you specify whether you want to read or set the BIOS timer:

Value	Meaning
0	Read the timer's current value
1	Set the timer's value to the value in *newtime*

The function returns the current number of clock ticks.

The *_bios_timeofday* function also lets you read or set the BIOS timer:

```
#include <bios.h>

long _bios_timeofday(int operation, long *ticks);
```

The *operation* parameter again specifies whether you want to read or set the timer:

Value	Meaning
_TIME_GETCLOCK	Read the timer's current value
_TIME_SETCLOCK	Set the timer's value to the value in ticks

The *_bios_timeofday* function returns the value returned in the AX register by the BIOS timer service. The following program, BIOSTIME.C, uses both of these functions to read the current BIOS clock ticks:

```
#include <stdio.h>
#include <bios.h>

void main (void)
  {
    long ticks;

    ticks = biostime(0, ticks);

    printf("Ticks since midnight %ld\n", ticks);

    _bios_timeofday(_TIME_GETCLOCK, &ticks);

    printf("Seconds since midnight %f\n", ticks / 18.2);
  }
```

Working With the Local Time

In Tip 621 you learned that the *time* function returns the current time in seconds since midnight, January 1, 1970. To make the system time easier for your programs to use, the C compiler provides the *localtime* function, which converts the time in seconds to a structure of type *tm* shown here:

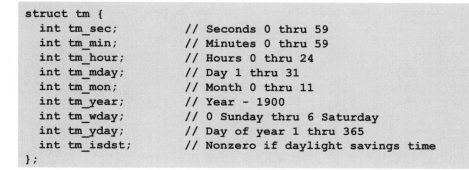

```
struct tm {
   int tm_sec;              // Seconds 0 thru 59
   int tm_min;              // Minutes 0 thru 59
   int tm_hour;             // Hours 0 thru 24
   int tm_mday;             // Day 1 thru 31
   int tm_mon;              // Month 0 thru 11
   int tm_year;             // Year - 1900
   int tm_wday;             // 0 Sunday thru 6 Saturday
   int tm_yday;             // Day of year 1 thru 365
   int tm_isdst;            // Nonzero if daylight savings time
};
```

The format of the *localtime* function is as follows:

```
#include <time.h>

struct tm *localtime(const time_t *timer);
```

The *localtime* function uses the global variables *timezone* and *daylight* to adjust the time for your current time zone and to take daylight savings into account. The following program, LOCALTIM.C, illustrates the use of the *localtime* function:

```
#include <stdio.h>
#include <time.h>

void main (void)
 {
   struct tm *current_date;

   time_t seconds;

   time(&seconds);

   current_date = localtime(&seconds);

   printf("Current date: %d-%d-%d\n", current_date->tm_mon+1,
     current_date->tm_mday, current_date->tm_year);
   printf("Current time: %02d:%02d\n", current_date->tm_hour,
     current_date->tm_min);
 }
```

C 631 Working With Greenwich Mean Time

In Tip 621 you learned that the *time* function returns the current time in seconds since midnight, January 1, 1970. If you work with other international users, there may be times when you need to work in terms of Greenwich Mean Time. For such times, the C compiler provides the *gmtime* function, shown here, which converts the time in seconds to a structure of type *tm*:

```
struct tm {
    int tm_sec;          // Seconds 0 thru 59
    int tm_min;          // Minutes 0 thru 59
    int tm_hour;         // Hours 0 thru 24
    int tm_mday;         // Day 1 thru 31
    int tm_mon;          // Month 0 thru 11
    int tm_year;         // Year - 1900
    int tm_wday;         // 0 Sunday thru 6 Saturday
    int tm_yday;         // Day of year 1 thru 365
    int tm_isdst;        // Nonzero if daylight savings time
};
```

The format of the *gmtime* function is as follows:

```
#include <time.h>

struct tm *gmtime(const time_t *timer);
```

The *gmtime* function uses the global variables *timezone* and *daylight* to adjust the time for your current time zone and to take daylight savings into account. The following program, GMTIME.C, illustrates the use of the *gmtime* function:

```
#include <stdio.h>
#include <time.h>

void main (void)
  {
    struct tm *gm_date;

    time_t seconds;

    time(&seconds);

    gm_date = gmtime(&seconds);
```

```
    printf("Current date: %d-%d-%d\n", gm_date->tm_mon+1,
      gm_date->tm_mday, gm_date->tm_year);
    printf("Current time: %02d:%02d\n", gm_date->tm_hour,
      gm_date->tm_min);
  }
```

Getting the DOS System Time

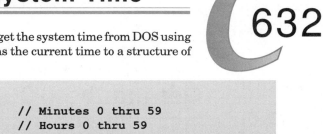

If you are using DOS, your programs can get the system time from DOS using the *gettime* function. The function assigns the current time to a structure of type *time,* as shown here:

```
struct time {
  unsigned char ti_min;        // Minutes 0 thru 59
  unsigned char ti_hour;       // Hours 0 thru 59
  unsigned char ti_hund;       // Hundreds of seconds 0 thru 99
  unsigned char ti_sec;        // Seconds 0 thru 59
};
```

The format of the *gettime* function is as follows:

```
#include <dos.h>

void gettime(struct time *current_time);
```

The following program, DOSTIME.C, uses the *gettime* function to display get the current system time:

```
#include <stdio.h>
#include <dos.h>

void main (void)
  {
    struct time curr_time;

    gettime(&curr_time);

    printf("Current time %02d:%02d:%02d.%d\n", curr_time.ti_hour,
      curr_time.ti_min, curr_time.ti_sec, curr_time.ti_hund);
  }
```

Note: *Many DOS-based C compilers also provide the _dos_gettime function, which returns a structure of type dostime_t, shown here:*

```
struct dostime_t {
  unsigned char hour;          // 0 thru 23
  unsigned char minute;        // 0 thru 59
  unsigned char second;        // 0 thru 59
  unsigned char hsecond;       // 0 thru 99
};
```

The format of the _dos_gettime function is as follows:

```
#include <dos.h>

void _dos_gettime(struct dostime_t *current_time);
```

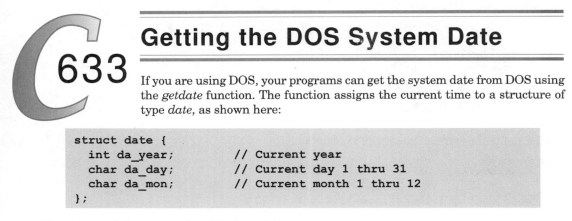

C633 Getting the DOS System Date

If you are using DOS, your programs can get the system date from DOS using the *getdate* function. The function assigns the current time to a structure of type *date*, as shown here:

```
struct date {
  int da_year;         // Current year
  char da_day;         // Current day 1 thru 31
  char da_mon;         // Current month 1 thru 12
};
```

The format of the *getdate* function is as follows:

```
#include <dos.h>

void getdate(struct date *current_date);
```

The following program, DOSDATE.C, uses the *getdate* function to display get the current system date:

```
#include <stdio.h>
#include <dos.h>

void main (void)
  {
    struct date curr_date;

    getdate(&curr_date);

    printf("Current date: %d-%d-%d\n", curr_date.da_mon,
      curr_date.da_day, curr_date.da_year);
  }
```

Note: *Many DOS-based C compilers also provide the _dos_getdate function, whicht returns a structure of type dosdate_t, as shown here:*

```
struct dosdate_t {
  unsigned char day;                    // 1 thru 31
  unsigned char month;                  // 1 thru 12
  unsigned int year;                    // 1980-2099
  unsigned char dayofweek;              // 0 Sunday thru 6 Saturday
};
```

The format of the *_dos_getdate* function is as follows:

```
#include <dos.h>

void _dos_getdate(struct dosdate_t *current_date);
```

Setting the DOS System Time

C634

If you are using DOS, your programs can set the DOS system time using the *settime* function, just as if you issued the DOS TIME command. To use settime, you assign the desired time to a structure of type *time* as shown here:

```
struct time {
  unsigned char ti_min;      // Minutes 0 thru 59
  unsigned char ti_hour;     // Hours 0 thru 59
  unsigned char ti_hund;     // Hundreds of seconds 0 thru 99
  unsigned char ti_sec;      // Seconds 0 thru 59
};
```

The format of the *settime* function is as follows:

```
#include <dos.h>

void settime(struct time *current_time);
```

The following program, SETTIME.C, uses the *settime* function to set the current system time to 12:30:

```
#include <stdio.h>
#include <dos.h>

void main (void)
  {
    struct time desired_time;
```

```
   desired_time.ti_hour = 12;
   desired_time.ti_min = 30;

   settime(&desired_time);
}
```

Note: *Many DOS-based C compilers also provide the _dos_settime function, which sets the system time using a structure of type dostime_t, shown here:*

```
struct dostime_t {
   unsigned char hour;        // 0 thru 23
   unsigned char minute;      // 0 thru 59
   unsigned char second;      // 0 thru 59
   unsigned char hsecond;     // 0 thru 99
};
```

The format of the *_dos_settime* function is as follows:

```
#include <dos.h>

void _dos_settime(struct dostime_t *current_time);
```

C 635 Setting the DOS System Date

If you are using DOS, your programs can get the system date from DOS using the *setdate* function. The function assigns the current time to a structure of type *date*, as shown here:

```
struct date {
   int da_year;        // Current year
   char da_day;        // Current day 1 thru 31
   char da_mon;        // Current month 1 thru 12
};
```

The format of the *setdate* function is as follows:

```
#include <dos.h>

void setdate(struct date *current_date);
```

The following program, SETDATE.C, uses the *setdate* function to set the current system date to December 8, 1993:

```
#include <stdio.h>
#include <dos.h>

void main (void)
  {
    struct date desired_date;

    desired_date.da_mon = 12;
    desired_date.da_day = 8;
    desired_date.da_year = 1993;

    setdate(&desired_date);
  }
```

Note: *many DOS-based compilers also provide the _dos_setdate function, which sets the system date using a structure of type dosdate_t, as shown here:*

```
struct dosdate_t {
  unsigned char day;
  unsigned char month;
  unsinged in year;
  unsigned char dayofweek;
}
```

The format of the *_dos_setdate* function is as follows:

```
#include <dos.h>

unsigned _dos_setdate(struct dosdate_t *date);
```

Converting a DOS Date to UNIX Format

636

In Tip 633 you learned how to use the *getdate* function to get the DOS system date. Likewise, in Tip 632 you learned how to use the *gettime* function to get the DOS system time. If you are working in an environment where both DOS and UNIX are used, there may be times when you need to convert a DOS-based date and time format to that used by UNIX. In such cases, your programs can use the *dostounix* function to perform the conversion. The function converts structures of type date and time to seconds since midnight, January 1, 1970, as shown here:

```
#include <dos.h>

long dostounix(struct date *DOS_date,
    struct time *DOS_time);
```

The following program, DOSUNIX.C, uses the *dostounix* function to convert the current DOS system date and time to the corresponding UNIX format:

```
#include <stdio.h>
#include <dos.h>
#include <time.h>

void main (void)
 {
    struct time dostime;
    struct date dosdate;

    time_t unix_format;
    struct tm *local;

    getdate(&dosdate);
    gettime(&dostime);

    unix_format = dostounix(&dosdate, &dostime);
    local = localtime(&unix_format);
    printf("UNIX time: %s\n", asctime(local));
 }
```

C 637 Determining the Difference Between Local and Greenwich Mean Time

As you have learned, the C run-time library provides several functions that convert between local and Greenwich mean time. To help your programs quickly determine the time difference between the two times, many C compilers provide the *timezone* function, which contains the number of seconds between the two times. The following program, TIMEZONE.C, uses the *timezone* global variable to display the time difference:

```
#include <stdio.h>
#include <time.h>
```

```
void main(void)
  {
    tzset();
    printf("Difference between local and GMT is %d hours\n",
      timezone / 3600);
  }
```

Note: *The tzset function uses the environment entry TZ to determine the current time zone.*

Determining the Current Time Zone

C638

Several of the tips in this section have presented functions that calculate times based on the current time zone. To help your programs determine the current time zone, many compilers provide the *tzname* global variable. The variable contains two pointers: *tzname[0]* points to the three-character time zone name, and *tzname[1]* points to the three-character daylight savings zone name. The following program, TZNAME.C, uses the *tzname* global variable to display the current time zone names:

```
#include <stdio.h>
#include <time.h>

void main(void)
  {
    tzset();

    printf("Current time zone is %s\n", tzname[0]);

    if (tzname[1])
      printf("Daylight savings zone is %s\n", tzname[1]);
    else
      printf("Daylight savings zone is not defined\n");
  }
```

Note: *The tzset function uses the environment entry TZ to determine the current time zone.*

C 639 Setting Time Zone Fields with *tzset*

Several of the functions and global variables in this section return information about the current time zone. To determine the time zone information, many functions call the *tzset* function, shown here:

```
#include <time.h>

void tzset(void);
```

The *tzset* function uses the TZ environment entry to determine the current time zone settings. The function then assigns appropriate values to the *timezone*, *daylight*, and *tzname* global variables. The program TZNAME.C presented in Tip 638 illustrates the use of the *tzset* function.

C 640 Using the TZ Environment Entry

Many of the tips presented throughout this section rely on the *tzset* function to provide time zone information. The *tzset* function examines your environment entries for the TZ entry and then assigns the *daylight*, *timezone*, and *tzname* variables, based on the entry's value. Use the DOS SET command to assign a value to the TZ set entry. The entry's format is as follows:

```
TZ=SSS[+/-]h[h][DDD]
```

Where *SSS* contains the standard time zone name (such EST or PST), the *[+/–]h[h]* specifes the difference in hours between the standard time zone and GMT, and *DDD* specifies the name of the daylight savings time zone (such as PDT). The following entry sets the time zone for the West Coast when daylight savings time is active:

```
C:\> SET TZ=PST8PDT   <ENTER>
```

When daylight savings time is not active, omit the time zone name, as shown here:

```
C:\> SET TZ=PST8   <ENTER>
```

Experiment with the *TZ* environment entry and the time zone programs presented in this section.

Note: *If you do not specify a TZ entry, the default is EST5EDT.*

Setting the TZ Environment Entry from Within Your Program

C 641

As you have learned, several of the C run-time library functions use *tzset* to determine the local time zone. As discussed in Tip 639, the *tzset* function uses the *TZ* environment entry to determine time zone. In most cases, expecting end users to correctly set the *TZ* environment entry is probably unreasonable. If you know the correct setting for a specific user, however, you can use the *putenv* function within the program to create the correct entry for that user:

```
putenv("TZ=PST8PDT");
```

The following program, SET_TZ.C, uses the *putenv* function to set the correct time zone. The program then displays the time zone settings using the *tzname* global variable:

```c
#include <stdio.h>
#include <stdlib.h>
#include <time.h>

void main(void)
  {
    putenv("TZ=PST8PDT");

    tzset();

    printf("Current time zone is %s\n", tzname[0]);

    if (tzname[1])
      printf("Daylight savings zone is %s\n", tzname[1]);
    else
      printf("Daylight savings zone is not defined\n");
  }
```

Getting Time Zone Information

C 642

Several of the tips presented throughout this section have presented ways for your programs to determine time zone information. One of the most useful functions your programs can use to obtain time zone information is *ftime*:

```
#include <sys\timeb.h>

void ftime(struct timeb *timezone);
```

The *timezone* parameter is a pointer to a structure of type *timeb*, shown here:

```
struct timeb {
  long time;
  short millitm;
  short timezone;
  short dstflag;
};
```

The *time* field contains the number of seconds since January 1, 1970 (GMT). The *millitm* field contains the fractional part of the seconds in milliseconds. The *timezone* field contains the difference between the local time zone and GMT in minutes. Finally, the *dstflag* specifies whether daylight savings is active (if set to 1) or inactive (0). The following program, FTIME.C, uses the *ftime* function to display the current time zone information:

```
#include <stdio.h>
#include <time.h>
#include <sys\timeb.h>

void main(void)
 {
   struct timeb timezone;

   tzset();

   ftime(&timezone);

   printf("Seconds since 1 January 1970 (GMT) %ld\n",
     timezone.time);
   printf("Fractional seconds %d\n", timezone.millitm);
   printf("Hours difference between GMT and local zone %d\n",
     timezone.timezone / 60);
   if (timezone.dstflag)
     printf("Daylight savings time active\n");
   else
     printf("Daylight savings time inactive\n");
 }
```

Setting the System Time Using Seconds Since Midnight 1/1/70

C643

Several of the tips throughout this section have shown you ways to set the system time using DOS or the BIOS. In addition, your programs can use the *stime* function to set the system time using seconds since midnight January 1, 1970:

```
#include <time.h>

int stime(time_t *seconds);
```

The *stime* function always returns 0. The following program, STIME.C, uses the *stime* function to set the date exactly one day ahead of the current date and time:

```
#include <time.h>

void main(void)
  {
    time_t seconds;

    time(&seconds);  // Get current time

    seconds += (time_t) 60 * 60 * 24;

    stime(&seconds);
  }
```

Converting Calendar Time to Seconds Since Midnight 1/1/70

C644

Several of the tips throughout this book have presented run-time library functions that use or return seconds since midnight 1/1/1970. To help you determine the seconds for a specific date, your programs can use the *mktime* function:

```
#include <time.h>

time_t mktime(struct tm *time_fields);
```

If the time fields are valid, the function returns the number of seconds for the specified time. If an error occurs, the function returns −1. The *time_fields* parameter is a pointer to a structure of type *tm*, shown here:

```
struct tm {
   int tm_sec;
   int tm_min;
   int tm_hour;
   int tm_mday;
   int tm_mon;
   int tm_year;
   int tm_wday;
   int tm_yday;
   int tm_isdst;
};
```

The following program, MKTIME.C, uses the *mktime* function to determine the number of seconds between midnight 1/1/70 and midnight 7/4/94:

```
#include <stdio.h>
#include <time.h>

void main(void)
  {
    time_t seconds;

    struct tm time_fields;

    time_fields.tm_mday = 4;
    time_fields.tm_mon = 7;
    time_fields.tm_year = 94;
    time_fields.tm_hour = 0;
    time_fields.tm_min = 0;
    time_fields.tm_sec = 0;

    seconds = mktime(&time_fields);

    printf("The number of seconds between 7-4-94 and 1-1-70 is
       %ld\n", seconds);
  }
```

Note: *When you pass a partial tm structure to the mktime function, the function will fill in the fields that are not correct. The mktime function supports dates in the range of January 1 1970 through January 19, 2028.*

Determining a Date's Julian Date

645

In Tip 644 you used the *mktime* function to determine the number of seconds between a specific date and midnight January 1, 1970. As you learned, the *mktime* function uses a structure of type *tm* to hold the date components. If one or more of the components are not complete, the *mktime* function fills them in. If you examine the *tm* structure, you will see the *tm_yday* member. When you invoke *mktime*, the function will assign to this member the Julian date for the day specified. The following program, JULIAN.C, uses the *mktime* function to determine the Julian date for July 4, 1994:

```c
#include <stdio.h>
#include <time.h>

void main(void)
  {
    time_t seconds;

    struct tm time_fields;

    time_fields.tm_mday = 4;
    time_fields.tm_mon = 7;
    time_fields.tm_year = 94;

    if (mktime(&time_fields) == -1)
      printf("Error converting fields\n");
    else
      printf("Julian date for July 4, 1994 is %d\n",
        time_fields.tm_yday);
  }
```

Creating a Formatted Date and Time String

646

As you have learned, the *_strdate* and *_strtime* functions return the current date and time in a character string format. To provide you with better control of a formatted date and time string, many compilers provide the *strftime* function:

```c
#include <time.h>

size_t strftime(char *string, size_t max_length,
    const char *format, const struct tm *datetime);
```

The *string* parameter is the character string to which the formatted date and time string is written. The *max_length* parameter specifies the maximum number of characters that can be placed into the string. The *format* string specifies your desired format using %*letter* formatting characters similar to *printf*. Table 646 lists the valid characters you can place in the formatted string. Finally, the *datetime* parameter is a pointer to a structure of type *tm* that contains the date and time fields. The function returns a count of the number of characters assigned to the buffer or 0 if the buffer was overflowed.

Format Specifier	Meaning
%%	% character
%a	Abbreviated weekday name
%A	Complete weekday name
%b	Abbreviated month name
%B	Complete month name
%c	Date and time
%d	Two-digit day of month 01 thru 31
%H	Two-digit hour 00 thru 23
%I	Two-digit hour 01 thru 12
%j	Three-digit Julian day
%m	Decimal month 1 thru 12
%M	Two-digit minute 00 thru 59
%p	AM or PM characters
%S	Two-digit second 00 thru 59
%U	Two-digit week number 00 thru 53 with Sunday first day of week
%w	Day of week (0 = Sunday 6 = Sat)
%W	Two-digit week number 00 thru 53 with Monday first day of week
%x	Date
%X	Time
%y	Two-digit year 00 thru 99
%Y	Four-digit year
%Z	Time zone name

Table 646 *Format specifiers for strftime.*

The following program, STRFTIME.C, illustrates the *strftime* function:

```
#include <stdio.h>
#include <time.h>

void main(void)
  {
    char buffer[128];

    struct tm *datetime;
    time_t current_time;
```

```
        tzset();

        time(&current_time);
        datetime = localtime(&current_time);

        strftime(buffer, sizeof(buffer), "%x %X", datetime);
        printf("Using %%x %%X: %s\n", buffer);

        strftime(buffer, sizeof(buffer), "%A %B %m, %Y", datetime);
        printf("Using %%A %%B %%m %%Y: %s\n", buffer);

        strftime(buffer, sizeof(buffer), "%I:%M%p", datetime);
        printf("Using %%I:%%M%%p: %s\n", buffer);
    }
```

When you compile and execute this program, your screen will display the following output:

```
C:\> STRFTIME  <ENTER>
Using %x %X: Fri Jun 18, 1993 22:03:13
Using %A %B %m %Y: Friday June 06, 1993
Using %I:%M%p: 10:03PM
```

Understanding PC Clock Types

C647

Several of the tips in this section discuss PC dates and times. To understand these functions better, you need to know that the PC uses four basic clock types: the CPU clock, timers, the real-time clock, and the CMOS clock. The CPU clock controls how fast your programs execute. When a user states they are using a 66MHz system, they are referring to the CPU clock. The timer clock is a chip inside the PC that generates an interrupt 18.2 times per second. Each time the clock tick occurs, the PC generates interrupt 8. By capturing this interrupt, memory resident programs can activate themselves at specific time intervals. The real time clock tracks the current date and time. In most cases, the real time clock contains the same value as the CMOS clock.

I/O Redirection & Command Line Processing

C 648 Waiting for a Keypress

When many programs display messages to the user, the programs will wait for the user to press any key before removing the message and continuing. To help your programs perform such processing, you can use the *kbhit* function, which returns true if a key has been pressed or false otherwise:

```
#include <conio.h>

int kbhit(void);
```

The following program, KBHIT.C, displays a message on the screen prompting the user to press any key to continue. The program then uses *kbhit* to wait for the keystroke:

```
#include <stdio.h>
#include <conio.h>

void main (void)
  {
    printf("Press any key to continue...");

    while (! kbhit());
      ;

    printf("Done\n");
  }
```

C 649 Prompting the User for a Password

Depending on your programs, there may be times when you will need to prompt the user for a password. When the user types in the password, the keystrokes the user types should not appear on the screen. To help your programs perform such processing, your programs can use the *getpass* function:

```
#include <conio.h>

char *getpass(const char *prompt);
```

The function displays the specified prompt and then waits for the user type in keystrokes and press **ENTER**. The function then returns a pointer to the password typed. The following program, GETPASS.C, uses *getpass* to prompt the user for a password.

```c
#include <stdio.h>
#include <conio.h>
#include <string.h>

void main (void)
 {
   char *password;

   password = getpass ("Enter Password:");

   if (strcmp(password, "1001"))
     printf("Password Incorrect\n");
   else
     printf("Password OK\n");
 }
```

Note: *If your compiler does not provide the getpass function, you can use the function get_pasword, shown in Tip 650.*

Writing Your Own Password Function

650

In Tip 649 you learned how to use the *getpass* function to prompt the user for a password. As you learned, *getpass* does not display keystrokes as the user types. Some new users will have difficulty typing a password if no keystrokes are shown, so some programs choose to display an asterisk (*) each time a keystroke is pressed. To perform such processing, you can use the function *get_password*, shown here:

```c
#include <stdio.h>
#include <conio.h>
#include <string.h>

#define BACKSPACE 8
char *get_password(const char *prompt)
 {
   static char buffer[128];

   int i = 0;
```

```
   char letter = NULL;

   printf(prompt);

   while ((i < 127) && (letter != '\r'))
     {
        letter = getch();

        if (letter == BACKSPACE)
          {
             if (i > 0)
               {
                  buffer[-i] = NULL;   // Erase previous *
                  putchar(BACKSPACE);
                  putchar(' ');
                  putchar(BACKSPACE);
               }
             else
                putchar(7);   // BELL
          }
        else if (letter != '\r')
           {
              buffer[i++] = letter;
              putchar('*');
           }
     }
   buffer[i] = NULL;
   return (buffer);
}


void main (void)
 {
   char *password;

   password = get_password("Enter Password: ");

   if (strcmp(password, "1001"))
      printf("\nPassword Incorrect\n");
   else
      printf("\nPassword OK\n");
 }
```

Understanding Output Redirection

651

Each time you execute a command, the operating system associates the default input device with your keyboard. The operating system refers to the monitor as the standard output device or *stdout* for short. Using the output redirection operator (>), you can direct the operating system to route a program's output to a file or some other device. The following command, for example, directs DOS to redirect the output of the DIR command from the screen display to the printer:

```
C:\> DIR > PRN   <ENTER>
```

In a similar way, this command directs DOS to redirect the output of the CHKDSK command to the file DISKINFO.DAT:

```
C:\> CHKDSK > DISKINFO.DAT   <ENTER>
```

To help you write programs that support output redirection, the header file stdio.h defines the constant stdout, to which file output operations can direct their output. Several of the tips presented in this book write their output to *stdout*.

Understanding Input Redirection

652

Each time you execute a command, the operating system associates the default output device with your computer screen. The operating system refers to the keyboard as the standard input device or *stdin* for short. Using the input redirection operator (<), you can direct the operating system to route a program's input from keyboard to a file or some other device. The following command, for example, directs DOS to redirect the input of the MORE command from the keyboard to the file CONFIG.SYS:

```
C:\> MORE < CONFIG.SYS   <ENTER>
```

In a similar way, this command directs DOS to redirect the input of the SORT command from the keyboard to the file AUTOEXEC.BAT:

```
C:\> SORT < AUTOEXEC.BAT   <ENTER>
```

To help you write programs that support input redirection, the header file stdio.h defines the constant stdin, from which file input operations can obtain their input. Several of the tips presented in this book read their input from *stdin*.

C 653 Combining Input and Output Redirection

As discussed in Tips 651 and 652, you can change a program's default input and output source from the keyboard and monitor using the input (<) and output (>) redirection operators. As you create a collection of programs that support input and output redirection, there may be times when you will want to redirect a program's input and output sources in the same command. For example, the following command directs DOS to sort the contents of the file CONFIG.SYS, writing the sorted output to the printer:

```
C:\> SORT < CONFIG.SYS > PRN   <ENTER>
```

To understand the processing the operating system performs, read the command from left to right. In this case, the input redirection operator (<) directs SORT to obtain its input from the file CONFIG.SYS. Likewise, the output redirection operator (>) directs SORT's output from the monitor to the printer.

C 654 Using stdout and stdin

In Tips 651 and 652 you learned that C defines the file handles stdin and stdout that allow you to write programs that support I/O redirection. The following program, UPPER.C, reads a line of text from the stdin file handle, converting the text to uppercase. The program then writes its output to stdout. The program continues this processing until an end-of-file is detected:

```c
#include <stdio.h>
#include <string.h>

void main (void)
  {
    char line[255];   // Line of text read

    while (fgets(line, sizeof(line), stdin))
      fputs(strupr(line), stdout);
  }
```

Using the UPPER command, you can display the contents of the file AUTOEXEC.BAT, as shown here:

```
C:\> UPPER < AUTOEXEC.BAT   <ENTER>
```

By using the output redirection operator, the following command prints the contents of the file CONFIG.SYS in uppercase:

```
C:\> UPPER < CONFIG.SYS > PRN   <Enter>
```

If you invoke UPPER without using an I/O redirection operator, as shown here,

```
C:\> UPPER   <Enter>
```

the UPPER command will read its input from the keyboard and write its output to the screen display. Each time you type a line of text and press **Enter**, UPPER will display the corresponding text in uppercase. To end the program, you must press the end-of-file key combination **Ctrl-Z** (under DOS) or **Ctrl-D** (under UNIX).

Understanding the Pipe Operator

C655

In Tips 651 and 652 you learned how to use the input and output redirection operators to change a program's source of input from the keyboard to a file or device or to route a program's output from the screen display to a file or device. DOS and UNIX provide a third redirection operator, called the *pipe* that lets you redirect one program's output to become another program's input. For example, the following command directs DOS to redirect the output of the DIR command to become the SORT command's input:

```
C:\> DIR | SORT   <Enter>
```

Programs that get their input from another command or file and change the input in some way are called *filters*. The following command, for example, uses the FIND command to filter the DIR command's output to only display subdirectory entries:

```
C:\> DIR | FIND "<DIR>"   <Enter>
```

Just as you can use multiple input and output redirection operators in the same command line, you can also place two or more pipe operators in the same command. The following command, for example, uses three pipe operators to display the names of subdirectories in sorted order, one screenful at a time:

```
C:\> DIR | FIND "<DIR>" | SORT | MORE   <Enter>
```

C 656 Understanding getchar and putchar

Many programs use the *getchar* and *putchar* macros for character input and output. For example, the following program, LOWER.C, converts each line of input to lowercase before displaying the character on the screen:

```
#include <stdio.h>
#include <ctype.h>   // Contains the tolower prototype

void main (void)
  {
    int letter;

    for (letter = getchar(); ! feof(stdin); letter = getchar())
      putchar(tolower(letter));
  }
```

Using LOWER, the following command prints the contents of the AUTOEXEC.BAT file in lowercase:

```
C:\> LOWER < AUTOEXEC.BAT > PRN   <ENTER>
```

When you use the *getchar* and *putchar* macros, your programs automatically support I/O redirection. The key to understanding how such redirection occurs is to examine the header file stdio.h, in which you will find that *getchar* and *putchar* are macros that define their source of input and output in terms of stdin and stdout, as shown here:

```
#define getchar()  getc(stdin)
#define putchar(c) putc((c), stdout)
```

C 657 Numbering Redirected Input

Depending on the contents of a file or a program's output, there may be times when you want to file or print the data preceded by a line number. The following program, NUMBER.C, filters its input to precede each line with its corresponding line number:

```
#include <stdio.h>

void main (void)
```

```
{
   char line[255];  // Line of input

   long line_number = 0;  // Current line number

   while (fgets(line, sizeof(line), stdin))
     printf("%ld %s", ++line_number, line);
}
```

The following command, for example, prints a copy of the file NUMBER.C, with each line preceded by its line number:

```
C:\> NUMBER < NUMBER.C > PRN  <ENTER>
```

Ensuring That a Message Appears on the Screen

C 658

Using the output and pipe redirection operators, its is possible to redirect a program's output from the screen to a file, device, or to the input of another program. Although such output redirection can be a powerful tool, it can cause users to miss an error message if they don't closely watch their work. For example, the following program, NEW_TYPE.C displays a file's contents on the screen:

```
#include <stdio.h>
#include <stdlib.h>

void main (int argc, char *argv[])
  {
    char line[255];  // Line read from the file

    FILE *fp;

    if (fp = fopen(argv[1], "r"))
      {
        while (fgets(line, sizeof(line), fp))

          fputs(line, stdout);
        fclose(fp);
        exit(0);  // Successful
      }
    else
      {
        printf("Cannot open %s\n", argv[1]);
        exit (1);
      }
  }
```

Using the output redirection operator, you can redirect the program's output to a device or file. The following command, for example, redirects NEW_TYPE's output to print the file AUTOEXEC.BAT:

```
C:\> NEW_TYPE AUTOEXEC.BAT > PRN   <ENTER>
```

If NEW_TYPE successfully opens AUTOEXEC.BAT, it will write the file's contents to stdout, which, based on output redirection, causes the file to print. If NEW_TYPE cannot open the file specified, it uses the *printf* function to display an error message stating the file could not be opened. Unfortunately, due to the output redirection, the message does not appear on the screen, but rather, it is sent to the printer. Unless the user immediately checks the printout, he or she might mistakenly believe the command was successful. To prevent error messages from being redirected from the screen, C defines the *stderr* file handle, which cannot be redirected from the screen display. When your program must display an error message on the screen, your program should use *fprintf* to write the message to stderr, as shown here:

```
fprintf (stderr, "Cannot open %s\n", argv[1]);
```

659 Writing Your Own MORE Command

One of the best known filters provided by DOS and UNIX is the MORE command, which displays its input one screenful at a time. Each time MORE displays a screenful of output, MORE pauses, displaying the following the message and waiting for the user to press a key:

```
— More —
```

When the user presses a key, MORE repeats this process, displaying the next screenful of output. The following program, MORE.C implements the MORE command:

```c
#include <stdio.h>
#include <dos.h>

void main (void)
  {
    char buffer[256];

    long row_count = 0;
    union REGS inregs, outregs;

    int Ctrl_Key_Pressed, scancode;
```

```
    while (fgets (buffer, sizeof(buffer), stdin))
  {
    fputs (buffer, stdout);

    if ((++row_count % 24) == 0)
      {
          printf ("— More —");
        // get the scancode of the key pressed
        inregs.h.ah = 0;
        int86 (0x16, &inregs, &outregs);
        scancode = outregs.h.ah;

        // get keyboard state in case of Ctrl-C
        Ctrl_Key_Pressed = 0;
        inregs.h.ah = 2;
        int86 (0x16, &inregs, &outregs);

        // Ctrl key flag is bit 2
        Ctrl_Key_Pressed = (outregs.h.al & 4);

        // scancode for C is 0x2E
        if ((Ctrl_Key_Pressed) && (scancode == 0x2E))
          break;      // Ctrl-C pressed
        printf ("\r");
      }
  }
}
```

Each time MORE pauses for the user to press a key, it invokes the BIOS keyboard interrupt (INT 16H) to get the keystroke. Because DOS defines its input operations in terms of stdin, you cannot use *getchar*, *getch*, or *kbhit* to read the keystroke. Such functions use the next redirected input, treating the next redirected character as the user keystroke. The BIOS services, however, are not defined in terms of stdin, and hence are not redirected.

Displaying a Count of Redirected Lines

C660

Several of the tips presented in this section have created filter commands you can use with the input and pipe redirection operators. The following program, LINECNT.C, displays a count of the number of lines of redirected input:

```
#include <stdio.h>

void main (void)
```

```
{
  char line[256];  // Line of redirected input

  long line_count = 0;

  while (fgets(line, sizeof(line), stdin))
    line_count++;

  printf("The number of redirected lines: %ld\n", line_count);
}
```

C 661 Displaying a Count of Redirected Characters

Several of the tips presented in this section have created filter commands you can use with the DOS input and pipe redirection operators. In a similar way, the following program, CHARCNT.C, displays a count of the number of characters in the redirected input:

```
#include <stdio.h>

void main (void)
  {
    long character_count = 0;

    getchar();

    while (! feof(stdin))
      {
        getchar();
        character_count++;
      }

    printf("The number of redirected characters is %ld\n",
      character_count);
  }
```

A Timed MORE Command

C 662

Several of the tips presented in this section have created filter commands you can use with the DOS input and pipe redirection operator. In a similar way, the following program, MORE15.C, changes the DOS MORE command to display a screenful of redirected input with each keystroke or every 15 seconds, whichever comes first:

```c
#include <stdio.h>
#include <time.h>
#include <dos.h>

void main (void)
  {
    char buffer[256];

    char key_pressed = 0;

    long int counter = 1;

    union REGS inregs, outregs;

    time_t start_time, current_time, end_time;

    while (fgets(buffer, sizeof(buffer), stdin))
      {
        fputs (buffer, stdout);

        if ((++counter % 25) == 0)

          {
            time (&start_time);

            end_time = start_time + 15;

            do
              {
                key_pressed = 0;
                time (&current_time);

                inregs.h.ah = 1;
                int86 (0x16, &inregs, &outregs);

                if ((outregs.x.flags & 64) == 0)
                  {
                    key_pressed = 1;
```

```
        do {
          inregs.h.ah = 0;
          int86 (0x16, &inregs, &outregs);
          inregs.h.ah = 1;
          int86 (0x16, &inregs, &outregs);
         } while (! (outregs.x.flags & 64));
       }
     }

    while ((current_time != end_time) && (! key_pressed));
   }
  }
}
```

To view the contents of a long program a screenful at a time, you would use MORE15 as follows:

```
C:\> MORE15 < FILENAME.C  <Enter>
```

C663 Preventing I/O Redirection

As you have learned, creating programs that support I/O redirection lets you build a library of powerful filter commands. However, many programs you will create will not support I/O redirection. Depending on the function that your program performs, allowing redirection to occur can result in a severe error. The following program, NO_REDIR.C, tests the file handles stdin and stdout to ensure that they have not been redirected. The program uses the DOS service INT 21H function 4400H to examine the file handle. If the handle points to a device, the service sets bit 7 of the DX registers to 1. If the bit 7 and bit 2 are set, the handle refers to stdout. If bit 7 and bit 1 are set, the handle refers to stdin. If bit 7 is not set, the handle has been redirected to a file. If bit 1 or 2 is not set, the handle has been redirected to a device other than stdin or stdout:

```
#include <stdio.h>
#include <dos.h>

void main (void)
  {
    union REGS inregs, outregs;

    // check the stdin handle first
    inregs.x.ax = 0x4400;
    inregs.x.bx = 0;       // stdin is handle 0
    intdos (&inregs, &outregs);

    if ((outregs.x.dx & 1) && (outregs.x.dx & 128))
```

```
        fprintf (stderr, "stdin has not been redirected\n");
    else
        fprintf (stderr, "stdin is redirected\n");

    // Now check stdout
    inregs.x.ax = 0x4400;
    inregs.x.bx = 1;        // stdout is handle 1
    intdos (&inregs, &outregs);

    if ((outregs.x.dx & 2) && (outregs.x.dx & 128))
        fprintf (stderr, "stdout has not been redirected\n");
    else
        fprintf (stderr, "stdout is redirected\n");
}
```

Using INT 21H service 4400H, your programs can determine if a program's input or output has been redirected and then process accordingly.

Using the stdprn File Handle

As you have learned, the header file stdio.h defines the file handles stdin, which (by default) points to the keyboard, and stdout, which points to the screen. By writing input and output operations in terms of stdin and stdout, your programs will automatically support I/O redirection. In a similar way, stdio.h defines the file handle stdprn, which points to standard printer device (PRN or LPT1). Unlike stdin and stdout, you cannot redirect stdprn. The following program, PRT_ECHO.C, uses the stdprn file to print redirected input as the program displays the output to the screen using stdout:

```c
#include <stdio.h>
#include <string.h>

void main (void)
  {
    char line[255];  // Line of text read

    while (fgets(line, sizeof(line), stdin))
      {
        fputs(line, stdout);
        strcat(line, "\r");
        fputs(line, stdprn);
      }
}
```

The following command line uses PRT_ECHO to print and display a directory listing:

```
C:\> DIR | PRT_ECHO  <ENTER>
```

C 665 Splitting Redirected Output to a File

When you use the DOS pipe to redirect the output of one program to become the input of another, there may be times when you want to save an intermediate copy of a program's output to a file. The following program, TEE.C, lets you do just that:

```c
#include <stdio.h>

void main(void)
  {
    char buffer[256];

    while (fgets(buffer, sizeof(buffer), stdin))
      {
        fputs(buffer, stdout);
        fputs(buffer, stderr);
      }
  }
```

The TEE command writes its redirected input to a specified file and to stdout so the output can be redirected to another program. The following command, for example, uses TEE to print an unsorted directory list before the SORT command displays the sorted directory listing on your screen:

```
C:\> DIR | TEE PRN | SORT  <ENTER>
```

C 666 Using the stdaux File Handle

As you have learned, the header file stdio.h defines the file handles stdin, which (by default) points to the keyboard, and stdout, which points to the screen. By writing input and output operations in terms of stdin and stdout, your programs will automatically support I/O redirection. In a similar way, stdio.h defines the file handle stdaux, which points to standard auxiliary device (AUX or COM1). Unlike stdin and stdout, you cannot redirect stdaux. The following program, AUX_ECHO.C, uses the stdaux file to send redirected input to COM1 as the program displays the output to the screen using stdout:

```
#include <stdio.h>
#include <string.h>

void main (void)
 {
   char line[255];   // Line of text read

   while (fgets(line, sizeof(line), stdin))
     {
       fputs(line, stdout);
       strcat(line, "\r");
       fputs(line, stdaux);
     }
 }
```

The following command line uses AUX_ECHO to print (to a printer attached to COM1) and display a directory listing:

```
C:\> DIR | AUX_ECHO   <ENTER>
```

Finding Each Occurrence of a
String Within Redirected Input

C 667

Several of the tips presented in this section have created filter commands you can use with the DOS input and pipe redirection operators. The following program, IO_FIND.C, displays each occurrence of a word or phrase within its redirected input:

```
#include <stdio.h>
#include <string.h>

void main (int argc, char *argv[])
 {
   char string[256];

   while (fgets(string, sizeof(string), stdin))
     if (strstr(string, argv[1]))
       fputs(string, stdout);
 }
```

To display each occurrence of the word #*include* within the file TEST.C, you can invoke IO_FIND as follows:

```
C:\> IO_FIND #include < TEST.C   <ENTER>
```

To search for a two or more words, simply place the words within quotes, as shown here:

```
C:\> IO_FIND "We the people" < CONSTITU.DAT  <ENTER>
```

C 668 Displaying the First *n* Lines of Redirected Input

Several of the tips presented in this section have created filter commands you can use the input and pipe redirection operators. The following program, SHOFIRST.C, displays specified the number of lines of redirected input. By default, unless told to do otherwise, the program displays the first ten lines of redirected input. The following command, on the other hand, directs SHOFIRST to display the first 25 lines of redirected directory listing:

```
C:\> DIR | SHOFIRST 25  <ENTER>
```

C 669 Understanding Command-Line Arguments

When you execute commands, the characters you type after the command line and before you press the **ENTER** key become the program's command line. For example, the following command line invokes a program named FIRST with two arguments, the number of lines to display and the desired filename:

```
C:\> FIRST 15 FILENAME.EXT  <ENTER>
```

Support for command-line arguments increases the number of applications for which your programs can be used. In the case of the program FIRST, you can use the program to display the contents of an unlimited number of files without having to change your program code. As it turns out, C makes it very easy for your programs to support command-line arguments. Each time you invoke a C program, each of the command-line arguments are passed to the program—as parameters to the function *main*. To access the command-line arguments, you must declare *main* as follows:

```
void main (int argc, char *argv[])
  {
    // program statements
  }
```

The first parameter, *argc*, contains a count of the number of distinct command-line entries. Given the command line

```
C:\> FIRST 10 FILENAME.EXT   <ENTER>
```

the parameter *argc* would contain the value 3. Because the value assigned to *argc* includes the command name, *argc* will always contain a value greater than or equal to 1. The second parameter, *argv*, is an array of pointers to character strings that point to each command-line argument. Given the previous command line, the elements of the *argv* array would be pointers to the following:

```
argv[0] contains a pointer to "FIRST.EXE"
argv[1] contains a pointer to "10"
argv[2] contains a pointer to "FILENAME.EXT"
argv[3] contains NULL
```

Many of the programs presented throughout this book make extensive use of the command-line arguments.

Displaying a Count of Command-Line Arguments

Each time you invoke a C program, the number of command-line arguments, as well as pointers to the actual elements, are passed to the function *main*. The following C program, CMD_CNT.C, uses the *argc* parameter to display a count of the number of command-line arguments passed to the program:

```c
#include <stdio.h>

void main (int argc, char *argv[])
  {
    printf("The number of command line entries is %d\n", argc);
  }
```

Assuming you invoke CMD_CNT with no parameters, CMD_CNT will display the following:

```
C:\> CMD_CNT   <ENTER>
The number of command line entries is 1
```

If you include the command-line arguments A, B, and C, CMD_CNT will display the following:

```
C:\> CMD_CNT A B C   <ENTER>
The number of command line entries is 4
```

C 671 Displaying the Command Line

Each time you invoke a C program, the number of command-line entries, as well as an array of pointers to the actual entries, are passed to *main* as parameters. The following program, SHOW_CMD.C, uses the parameter count within a *for* loop to display each of the command-line entries:

```
#include <stdio.h>

void main (int argc, char *argv[])
  {
    int i;

    for (i = 0; i < argc; ++i)
      printf("argv[%d] points to %s\n", i, argv[i]);
  }
```

If you invoke SHOW_CMD with no parameters, SHOW_CMD will display the following:

```
C:\> SHOW_CMD   <ENTER>
argv[0] points to C:\SHOW_CMD.EXE
```

Likewise, if you invoke SHOW_CMD with the command-line arguments A, B, and C, SHOW_CMD will display the following:

```
C:\> SHOW_CMD A B C   <ENTER>
argv[0] points to C:\SHOW_CMD.EXE
argv[1] points to A
argv[2] points to B
argv[3] points to C
```

C 672 Working with Quoted Command-Line Arguments

Each time you invoke a C program, the number of command-line entries and an array of pointers to the actual entries are passed to *main* as parameters. There may be times when your programs need to work with parameters that are passed within quotes. For example, assume that a program named FINDTEXT searches the file specified for specific text, as shown here:

```
C:\> FINDTEXT "We the people" FILENAME.EXT   <ENTER>
```

Most C compilers treat quoted parameters as a single argument. Experiment with the program SHOW_CMD presented in Tip 671 to determine how your compiler treats quoted parameters:

```
C:\> SHOW_CMD "We the people" FILENAME.EXT  <ENTER>
argv[0] points to SHOWCMD.EXE
argv[1] points to We the people
argv[2] points to FILENAME.EXT
```

Using Command-Line Arguments to Display a File's Contents

C 673

Several of the previous tips have shown you how to use the parameters *argc* and *argv* to access command-line parameters. The following program, SHOWFILE.C, uses *argv* to display the contents of the file specified in the command line:

```c
#include <stdio.h>

void main (int argc, char *argv[])
  {
    FILE *fp;         // File pointer

    char line[255];  // Line from file

    if ((fp = fopen(argv[1], "r")) == NULL)
      printf("Error opening %s\n", argv[1]);
    else
      {
        // Read and display each line of the file
        while (fgets(line, sizeof(line), fp))
          fputs(line, stdout);
        fclose (fp);   // Close the file
      }
  }
```

To display the contents of a file, invoke SHOWFILE with the desired filename, as shown here:

```
C:\> SHOWFILE FILENAME.EXT  <ENTER>
```

Note the if statement that opens the specified file. The *fopen* function call within the if statement tries to open the file specified by *argv*[1]. If the file does not exist, *fopen* will return NULL, causing the program to display a message stating the file could not be opened. If the user does not specify a filename, *argv*[1] will contain NULL, which also causes *fopen* to return NULL. If *fopen* successfully opens the file, the program uses a *while* loop to read and display the file's contents.

674 Treating *argv* as a Pointer

Several of the previous tips have used the array of pointers *argv* to access command-line arguments. Because *argv* is an array, your programs can access its elements using a pointer. In this case, *argv* becomes a pointer to an array of pointers. The following program, ARGV_PTR.C, displays the command by treating *argv* as pointer to a pointer:

```c
#include <stdio.h>

void main (int argc, char **argv)
  {
    while (*argv)
      printf ("%s\n", *argv++);
  }
```

To begin, note the declaration of *argv* as a pointer to pointer to a character string. Using a *while* statement, the program loops through the command-line arguments until the value pointed at by *argv* is NULL. As you will recall, C uses NULL to indicate the last command-line argument. Within the *while* loop, the *printf* statement displays string pointed to by *argv*. The *printf* statement then increments the value in *argv* so that it points to the next command-line argument.

675 How C Knows About the Command Line

Each time you execute a program, the operating system loads the program into memory. In the case of the DOS operating system, DOS first loads 256 bytes into memory called the *program segment prefix*, which contains such information as the program's file table, environment segment, and command line. Figure 675 illustrates the format of the DOS program segment prefix.

As you can see, beginning at offset 80H, DOS stores up to 128 bytes of command-line information. When you compile a C program, the C compiler embeds additional code that parses the command, assigning it to the argv array, making the arguments easily accessible within your C programs.

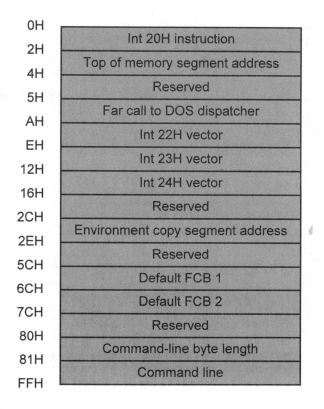

0H	Int 20H instruction
2H	Top of memory segment address
4H	Reserved
5H	Far call to DOS dispatcher
AH	Int 22H vector
EH	Int 23H vector
12H	Int 24H vector
16H	Reserved
2CH	Environment copy segment address
2EH	Reserved
5CH	Default FCB 1
6CH	Default FCB 2
7CH	Reserved
80H	Command-line byte length
81H	Command line
FFH	

Figure 675 *The DOS program segment prefix.*

Understanding the Environment

C 676

As you know, DOS (and UNIX) store information in a memory region called the environment. Using the SET command, you can display, add, or change environment entries. Depending on your program's function, there may be times when you need to access information contained within the environment. For example, many programs use the environment entry TEMP to determine the disk drive and subdirectory within which they should create temporary files. As it turns out, C makes it very easy to access the contents of the environment entries. One way to access the environment is to declare *main* as follows:

```
void main (int argc, char *argv[], char *env[])
```

Just as C lets you access a program's command-line arguments using an array of character string pointers, you can access the environment entries in a similar way. The following program, SHOW_ENV.C, uses the *env* array to display the current environment entries:

```
#include <stdio.h>

void main (int argc, char *argv[], char *env[])
  {
    int i;

    for (i = 0; env[i] != NULL; i++)
      printf("env[%d] points to %s\n", i, env[i]);
  }
```

As you can see, the program loops through the *env* array's entries until the NULL value, which indicates that the end of the environment is found.

C677 Treating *env* as a Pointer

In Tip 676 you learned that C lets you access the environment contents using the *env* array of pointers to character strings. Because *env* is an array, you can treat *env* as a pointer. The following program, ENV_PTR.C, displays the environment's contents by treating *env* as a pointer to a pointer to a character string:

```
#include <stdio.h>

void main (int argc, char **argv, char **env)
  {
    while (*env)
      printf("%s\n", *env++);
  }
```

As you can see, the program loops until *env* points to NULL, which indicates the end of the environment. Within the loop, the *printf* statement prints the string pointed to by *env* and then increments *env* to point to the next entry.

C678 Use *void* for *main*'s Parameters

When your program does not use command-line parameters and you do not need to use *argc* and *argv*, you can omit the parameters, declaring *main* as follows:

```
void main ()
```

However, when a function does not receive parameters, you should use the *void* keyword to make explicit the fact that no parameters are used, as shown here:

```
void main (void)
```

Working with Command-Line Numbers

C 679

As you create programs that use command-line arguments, you will eventually need to work with numbers in the command line. For example, the following command line directs the program FIRST to display the first 15 lines of the file AUTOEXEC.BAT:

```
C:\> FIRST 15 AUTOEXEC.BAT  <ENTER>
```

When the command line contains numbers, the *argv* stores the numbers in their ASCII format. To use the number, you must first convert the number from ASCII to an integer or floating-point value. To do so, use the functions *atoi*, *atol*, and *atof*, discussed in the Math Functions section of this book. The following program, BEEPS.C, sounds the computer's built-in speaker the number of times specified in the command line. For example, the following command line directs BEEPS to sound the speaker three times:

```
C:\> BEEPS 3  <ENTER>
```

```c
#include <stdio.h>
#include <stdlib.h>

void main (int argc, char *argv[])
  {
    int count; // The number of times to sound the speaker
    int i;     // The number of times the speaker has been sounded

    // Determine the number of times to ring the bell
    count = atoi (argv[1]);

    for (i = 0; i < count; i++)
      putchar(7);    // ASCII 7 sounds the speaker
  }
```

If the user specifies a command-line parameter that is not a valid integer, the *atoi* function returns the value 0.

C 680 Understanding Exit Status Values

Many DOS commands support exit status values that you can test from within your batch files to determine the command's success. For example, the DOS XCOPY command supports the following exit status values:

Exit Value	Meaning
0	Successful file copy operation
1	No files found to copy
2	File copy terminated by user Ctrl-C
4	Initialization error
5	Disk write error

Using the IF ERRORLEVEL command, your batch files can test a program's exit status to determine if the command was successful and then continue its processing in an appropriate manner. As you create programs, you may want to provide exit status value support. The easiest way to return an exit status value is to use the *exit* function, as shown here:

```
exit(exit_status_value);
```

The following function call, for example, returns the exit status value 1:

```
exit (1);
```

When your program invokes the *exit* function, the program immediately ends, returning to the operating system, the exit status value specified. The following program, NEW_TYPE.C, displays a file's contents. If the file specified cannot be opened, the program returns the exit status value 1. If NEW_TYPE successfully displays the file's contents, it returns the exit status value 0:

```
#include <stdio.h>
#include <stdlib.h>

void main (int argc, char *argv[])
  {
    char line[255];  // Line read from the file

    FILE *fp;

    if (fp = fopen(argv[1], "r"))
      {
        while (fgets(line, sizeof(line), fp))
          fputs(line, stdout);
        fclose(fp);

        exit(0);  // Successful
```

```
    }
  else
    {
      printf("Cannot open %s\n", argv[1]);
      exit (1);
    }
}
```

Note: *Many C compilers provide a function named _exit, which like exit, immediately ends a program returning an exit status value. However, unlike exit which first closes open files and flushes output buffers, the _exit function does not close open files, possibly resulting in lost data.*

Using *return* for Exit Status Processing

681

Within a C function, the *return* statement ends the function's execution returning the value specified to the caller. Within the C function *main*, the *return* statement behaves in a similar way, ending your program's execution, returning the value specified to the operating system (the program's caller). The following program, RET_EXIT.C, displays a file's contents on your screen. If the file cannot be opened, RET_EXIT returns the exit status 1. If RET_EXIT successfully displays the file's contents, it returns the exit status value 0:

```c
#include <stdio.h>
#include <stdlib.h>

int main (int argc, char *argv[])
  {
    char line[255];  // Line read from the file

    FILE *fp;

    if (fp = fopen(argv[1], "r"))
      {
        while (fgets(line, sizeof(line), fp))
          fputs(line, stdout);
        fclose(fp);

        return(0);  // Successful
      }
    else
      {
        printf("Cannot open %s\n", argv[1]);
```

```
        return(1);
    }
}
```

Note that program has changed the defination of *main* to indicate that the function returns an integer exit status value.

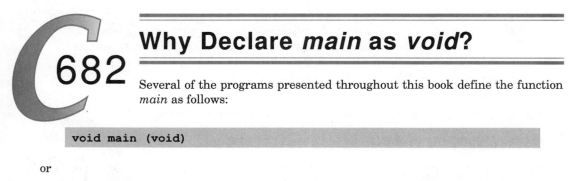

C 682 Why Declare *main* as *void*?

Several of the programs presented throughout this book define the function *main* as follows:

```
void main (void)
```

or

```
void main (int argc, char *argv[])
```

The keyword *void*, which appears in front of *main*, tells the C compiler (and programmers that are reading your code) that the function main does not use a *return* statement to return an exit status value to the operating system. The keyword *void* does not, however, prevent your program from returning an exit status value using the exit function. As a rule, however, if *main* does not use the *return* statement, precede the function name using the keyword *void*. If you do not, some compilers may display a warning message similar to the following:

```
Warning Function should return a value in function main
```

C 683 Searching the Environment for a Specific Entry

In Tip 676 you learned how to access a program's environment copy using the *env* array of character string pointers:

```
void main (int argc, char *argv[], char *env[])
```

When your programs need to search the environment for a specific entry, you might find it convenient to use the *getenv* function:

```
#include <stdlib.h>

char *getenv(const char *entry_name);
```

The *getenv* function searches the environment entries for a specific entry, such as "TEMP". The entry name does not include an equal sign. If the specified entry is in the environment, *getenv* returns a pointer to entry's value. If the entry is not found, *getenv* returns NULL. The following program, SHOWPATH.C, searches the environment for the PATH entry, displaying entry's value if it is found:

```c
#include <stdio.h>
#include <stdlib.h>

void main (void)
  {
    char *entry;

    entry = getenv("PATH");

    if (*entry)
      printf("PATH=%s\n", entry);
    else
      printf("PATH is not defined\n");
  }
```

How DOS Treats the Environment

C 684

When you work with DOS, the environment provides a region in memory in which you can place configuration information, such as your command path or system prompt. The SET command lets you display, add, or change environment entries:

```
C:\> SET  <Enter>
COMSPEC=C:\DOS\COMMAND.COM
PROMPT=$P$G
PATH=C:\DOS;C:\WINDOWS;C:\BORLANDC\BIN
```

DOS maintains one master copy of the environment that can only be changed using SET. When you invoke a program, DOS makes a copy of the environment's current contents and passes the copy to your programs, as shown in Figure 684.

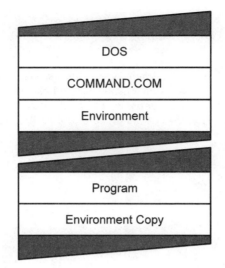

Figure 684 *DOS passes each program its own environment copy.*

Because your programs receive a copy of the environment, changes the programs make to environment entries do not affect the master environment. Several of the tips presented throughout this section present functions that get or set environment entries. In each case, these functions only access the program's environment copy.

C 685 Using the *environ* Global Variable

In Tip 676 you learned that your programs can access their environment copy using the array of character string pointers passed to main:

```
void main (int argc, char *argv[], char *env[])
```

In addition to letting you use *env*, C defines a global variable, named *environ*, that contains your environment copy. The following program, ENVIRON.C, uses the *environ* global variable to display the environment entries:

```
#include <stdlib.h>
#include <stdio.h>
#include <dos.h>

void main (void)
 {
```

```
  int i;
  for (i = 0; environ[i]; i++)
    printf("%s\n", environ[i]);
}
```

When your programs use the *putenv* function to add or change an environment entry, you should later access your environment entries using the *getenv* function or by accessing the *environ* global variable. To place an entry in environment, *putenv* may need to move the program's environment copy, which invalidates the *env* pointer passed to *main*.

Adding an Entry to the Current Environment

686

In Tip 684 you learned that DOS keeps one master environment copy whose contents it copies and passes to each program you invoke. As a result, your programs normally can't change entries in the master environment. Instead, any changes your programs make to their environment are made only to the program's environment copy. Regardless, there may be times when your programs need to store an entry in their own environment copy. For example, assume that a program spawns a child process that needs to know the name of a specific file. The program can first place the filename into its environment copy. When the program spawns the child process, the child receives a copy of the program's environment and, hence, has access to the filename. For such cases, your programs can use the *putenv* function:

```
#include <stdlib.h>

int putenv(const char *entry);
```

If *putenv* successfully adds the entry to the program's environment copy, *putenv* returns the value 0. If an error occurs (the environment is full), *putenv* returns –1. The following program, PUTENV.C, illustrates the use of the *putenv* function:

```
#include <stdio.h>
#include <stdlib.h>

void main (void)
  {
    if (putenv("BOOK=Jamsa's 1001 C & C++ Tips"))
      printf("Error writing to environment\n");
    else
      {
        int i;

        for (i = 0; environ[i]; ++i)
```

```
        printf("%s\n", environ[i]);
    }
}
```

Note: *Do not invoke putenv with an automatic character string variable or with a string pointer that may later be freed. Also, if your program uses the array of character string pointers that is passed to main, be aware that the putenv function may move the program's environment copy, invalidating the env pointer. To access the environment entries, use getenv or the environ global variable.*

C687 Adding Elements to the DOS Environment

You have learned that, when you run a program, DOS makes a copy of the current environment entries and passes the copy to the program. Because the program does not have access to the master copy of the environment entries, DOS cannot change the entries maintained by DOS. Because DOS does not provide memory protection that prevents one program from accessing the memory of another, you can write a program that locates and finds the DOS master environment copy. Once you know the location of the environment, you can change or delete existing entries or you can add entries. Because the environment has a fixed size, there may be times when the entries you want to add will not fit in the environment. In some cases, you may be able to change the environment's size, allocating more memory. The process of locating and sizing the DOS master environment is very complex. If you have an application that must change the entries, however, you can learn how to do so. In the book *DOS Programming: The Complete Reference* (Osborne/McGraw-Hill 1991), I devote an entire chapter to working with the environment. Because the discussion and sample programs would require 20 to 30 pages, I will instead tell you that it is possible for your programs to update the master environment copy, but to do so, you should refer to the examples in the book discussed.

C688 Aborting the Current Program

As your programs become more complex, there may be times that should a critical error occur, you want the program to immediately terminate, displaying an error message to stderr. For such cases, your programs can use the *abort* function:

```
#include <stdlib.h>

void abort(void);
```

When your program invokes the abort function, abort displays the following message to stderr and then invokes the *DOS _exit* function with an exit status value of 3:

```
Abnormal program termination
```

The best way to understand the *abort* function is to consider the following implementation:

```
void abort(void)
  {
    fputs("Abnormal program termination", stderr);
    _exit(3);
  }
```

It is important to note that *abort* invokes *_exit* and not *exit*. As discussed in Tip 680, the *_exit* function does not close any files or flush output.

Defining Functions That Execute at Program Termination

C 689

Depending on your programs, there may be times when you want your program to automatically execute one or more functions when the program ends. For such cases, your programs can use the *atexit* function, which lets your program specify up to 32 functions that your program automatically executes when it ends:

```
#include <stdlib.h>

int atexit(void (*function(void));
```

The functions *atexit* invokes cannot use parameters. If the functions need to access specific data, you must declare the data as global variables. When you define an at-termination-function list, your program will execute the functions in order, beginning with the last function registered, to the first. The following program, ATEXIT.C, uses the *atexit* function to *register* two at-termination functions:

```
#include <stdio.h>
#include <stdlib.h>

void first(void)
  {
    printf("First function registered\n");
  }

void second(void)
```

```
    {
      printf("Second function registered\n");
    }

void main (void)
    {
      atexit(first);
      atexit(second);
    }
```

When you compile and execute this program, your screen will display the following output:

```
C:\> ATEXIT  <ENTER>
Second function registered
First function registered
```

As you can see, functions in the at-termination list execute in the opposite order they are registed (last registered is the first executed).

> **Note:** *If your program invokes the exit function, functions in the the at-termination list are executed. However, if the program invokes _exit, the functions are not executed.*

Programming Tools

690 Understanding Libraries

Throughout this book, many of tips have discussed C run-time library functions. When you use a run-time library function in your program, the linker loads the corresponding code from a library file into your executable program. The obvious advantage of using run-time library functions is that you don't have to write the corresponding code. If you examine the files that accompany your compiler, you will find many files with the LIB extension. These files contain object libraries. When you compile and link your programs the linker knows to examine these files to resolve function references.

As you create useful functions, you can build your own libraries. In this way, you can quickly use a function that you created for one program within another. Most compilers provide a librarian program that lets you build and change libraries. In the case of Borland C++, the library program is called TLIB. If you are using Microsoft C/C++, the librarian is LIB. Several of the tips that follow discuss library operations.

691 Reusing Object Code

As you create functions, you will often find that a function you wrote for one program solves a requirement of a second program. For example, the companion disk file STR_LEN.C, contains the function *string_length*, shown here:

```
int string_length(char *str)
  {
    int length = 0;

    while (*str++)
      length++;

    return(length);
  }
```

Compile the file to create the object file STR_LEN.OBJ. Next, the program FIND_LEN.C, uses the function to display the length of several different strings:

```
#include <stdio.h>

int string_length(char *);

void main(void)
  {
    char *title= "Jamsa's 1001 C/C++ Tips";
```

```
char *section = "Tools";

printf("Length of %s is %d\n", title, string_length(title));
printf("Length of %s is %d\n",section,string_length(section));
}
```

If you are using Borland C++, compile the program as follows so that it uses the contents of the object file STR_LEN.OBJ:

```
C:\> BCC FIND_LEN.C STR_LEN.OBJ    <ENTER>
```

In this case, by combining the function's object code with your program, you can resolve and use the function. As you will learn in Tip 692, however, compiling object files in this way has limited usefulness.

Problems with Compiling C and OBJ Files

692

In Tip 691 you learned that to reuse functions, you can compile the function separately to create an OBJ file and later compile the program's C code and the function's OBJ file to produce an executable program:

```
C:\> BCC SOMEFILE.C  FUNCTION.OBJ  <ENTER>
```

Although this technique lets you resolve and use the function code, it restricts the number of functions you can resolve to the length of your command line. For example, assume that your program uses ten functions that reside in separate object files. Remembering which files you need to compile—even just fitting all the filenames in the command line will become very difficult. One solution would be to group all of your functions into a single object file. A better solution, however is to create a library file that contains the object code for each function. The library file is preferred, because as you will learn, most librarian programs let you quickly update the library (replacing, adding, or deleting object files).

Creating a Library File

693

Depending on your compiler, the name of your librarian and the command-line switches the program supports will differ. However, the operations the librarian supports will be essentially the same:

Create a library

Add one or more object files to the library

Replace an object code file with another

Delete one or more object files from the library

List the routines contained in the library

Using Borland's TLIB librarian, the following command creates a library named MY_STUFF.LIB, inserting into the library, the object code for the *string_length* function contained in STR_LEN.OBJ:

```
C:\> TLIB MY_STUFF.LIB +STR_LEN.OBJ  <ENTER>
```

After the library file exists, you can compile and link the program FIND_LEN.C using the library as follows:

```
C:\> BCC FIND_LEN.C  MY_STUFF.LIB  <ENTER>
```

694 Common Library Operations

Depending on your compiler, the operations your librarian supports may differ. However, most librarians let you add and remove object code files using the plus symbol (+) to add a file and the minus symbol (–) to remove an object file. Table 694 lists several library operations using the library file MY_STUFF.LIB.

Command	Operation
MY_STUFF.LIB +STRCPY.OBJ	Adds the object file STRCPY.OBJ to the library
MY_STUFF.LIB +STRLEN.OBJ+STRUPR.OBJ	Adds the object files STRLEN.OBJ and STRUPR.OBJ to the library
MY_STUFF.LIB -STRLWR.OBJ	Removes the object file STRLWR.OBJ from the library
MY_STUFF.LIB -STRLWR.OBJ+STRSIZ.OBJ	Removes the object file STRLWR.OBJ from the library while adding the object file STRSIZ.OBJ
MY_STUFF.LIB +-STRLWR.OBJ	Replaces the object file STRLWR.OBJ in the library with the current disk file
MY_STUFF.LIB * STRUPR.OBJ	Extracts the code for the object file STRUPR.OBJ from the library to a file with the same name

Table 694 *Common library operations.*

Listing the Routines in a Library File

C 695

As you have learned, library files provide a convenient storage locations for functions you may want to use in other programs. Depending on your compiler, the operations your librarian supports may differ. However, most librarians will let you view the routines a library file contains. Using the Borland C++ TLIB librarian, the following command lists the routines contained in the library file GRAPHICS.LIB:

```
C:\> TLIB  \BORLANDC\LIB\GRAPHICS.LIB, CON  <ENTER>
```

To print the names of the functions the library contains, replace *CON* with *PRN* in the previous command line.

Use Libraries to Reduce Your Compilation Time

C 696

As your programs increase in size, so too will the program's compilation time. One way you can reduce your program's compilation time is to extract the program's working functions into a library. In this way, when you later compile your program, you will not spend time recompiling the functions. Depending on the number of functions your program contains, removing the functions in this way can speed up your compilation time significantly. In addition, by removing the function code from your program, your program becomes smaller, more manageable, and possibly easier to understand.

Learning More About Your Librarian's Capabilities

C 697

The librarian tips just presented have provided only an introduction to libraries. The documentation that accompanies your compiler will discuss the librarian's capabilities in detail. If you are using the Borland TLIB librarian, you can display the program's switches by invoking TLIB without a command line as shown here:

```
C:\> TLIB  <ENTER>
```

If you are using Microsoft's LIB command, use the following command to display the available command-line switches:

```
C:\> LIB /?   <ENTER>
```

698 Understanding the Linker

As you have learned, the compiler converts your C file to machine language. If your programs calls functions that are contained in library or other object files, the linker resolves the calls to the functions by loading the corresponding code to produce the executable file. Assume, for example, your program contains the following:

```
void main(void)
{
    printf("Jamsa's 1001 C/C++ Tips");
}
```

When the compiler compiles the program, it notes that the function *printf* was called but not defined. The linker, in turn, locates the *printf* function in the run-time library, loads the code into your executable file, and then updates the function call to reference the correct address of the function within your program. If the linker is unable to locate a function, it will display an error message on your screen stating that it encountered an *unresolved external*. The linker's primary function, therefore, is to pull (link) together all of the pieces of your program code. However, depending on your linker, you may be able to use it to produce a *link map* that describes the layout of your executable file, to specify a stack size, or control the program's underlying segment use. For specifics on your linker's capabilities, refer to the documentation that accompanied your compiler.

699 Viewing Linker Capabilities

As you learned in Tip 698, the primary role of the linker is to pull together all of the functions used by a program into the executable file. Depending on your compiler, your linker may have additional capabilities. If you are using Borland C++, you can list the command-line options for the TLINK linker by invoking TLINK without any parameters, as shown here:

```
C:\> TLINK   <ENTER>
```

If you are using Microsoft C/C++, you can display the command-line switches for LINK as follows:

```
C:\> LINK /?   <ENTER>
```

Using a Link Map

As you have learned, the linker locates external functions within your program, loads the functions into the executable file, and updates the addresses of each function reference. When you debug a program, there may be times when you know the program has an error at a specific memory location. Using a *link map*, which shows where the linker has loaded each function, you may be able to determine the location of the error. Depending on your linker, the steps you must perform to produce a link map can differ. The following command line creates the link map file FIND_LEN.MAP using the Borland C/C++ BCC command:

```
C:\> BCC  -lm FILE_LEN.C STR_LEN.OBJ  <ENTER>
```

The link map is an ASCII file whose contents you can display or print.

Using Linker Response Files

When you use Borland's TLINK or Microsoft's LINK commands, the general formats of the commands are as follows:

```
TLINK [switches] object_files, exe_file,  map_file,
         library_files, def_file

 LINK [switches] object_files, exe_file, map_file,
         library_files, def_file
```

Depending on the number of files you are linking, your command lines may become quite long. To prevent you from having to remember all of the filenames, as well as the command format, both linkers support *response files*. In short, a response file is an ASCII file that contains the filenames you want the linker to use for each option. The filenames for each file type must appear in the command-line order, with each file type on its own line. For example, consider the following TLINK command:

```
C:\> TLINK FIND_STR.OBJ STR_LEN.OBJ, FIND_STR.EXE, FIND_STR.MAP,
SOMELIB.LIB
```

Your response file in this case would contain the following:

```
FIND_STR.OBJ STR_LEN.OBJ
FIND_STR.EXE
FIND_STR.MAP
SOMELIB.LIB
```

Assuming you name the response file FIND_STR.LNK, you can invoke TLINK as follows:

```
C:\> TLINK @FIND_STR.LNK  <ENTER>
```

If you are linking multiple object files that cannot fit on one line, your response file can continue on to a second line. To indicate the continuation, place a plus sign at the end of the first line.

702 Simplifying Application Building with MAKE

As your programs become more complex, they will normally require specific header files, source code modules, object code files, and libraries. When you make a change to your program, there may be times when it becomes difficult to remember which files the change affects. To simplify your task of rebuilding an executable file after you make changes to your programs, many C compilers provide a MAKE utility. In short, MAKE works with an application-specific file that specifies the different files used to build an application and the steps that must be performed when a change occurs. MAKE is a very powerful programming tool. As you will learn, the files you provide to MAKE are almost like programs themselves (they contain conditions and instructions that MAKE evaluates and possibly executes). There are two common ways to use MAKE. First, you can place the operations you want MAKE to perform in a file named MAKEFILE. Next, you simply invoke MAKE, as shown here:

```
C:\> MAKE  <ENTER>
```

In this case, MAKE will read the file's contents and process accordingly. If you are working on several different programs, however, you will probably want to create MAKE files that use the application's name. For example, you might have a file named FIND_LEN.MAK. When you want to invoke MAKE with a specific file, you must include the -f switch as shown here:

```
C:\> MAKE  -f  FIND_LEN.MAK  <ENTER>
```

Several of the following tips describe MAKE operations in detail.

703 Creating a Simple MAKE File

MAKE is tool that helps you build executable files or libraries after changes have been made to a file from which the program or library was originally built. You invoke MAKE with a file that contains specifics about an application, such as the files used to create the application and their dependencies. MAKE files follow a specific format. To begin, you specify a target file and the files used to create the target. For example, assume you want to build the program BUDGET.EXE from the source file BUDGET.C. Within your MAKE file you would specify the dependency as follows:

```
BUDGET.EXE:BUDGET.C
```

On the line that immediately follows the dependency, you specify the command MAKE must perform to build the target file. In this case, the two lines of the MAKE file become the following:

```
BUDGET.EXE:      BUDGET.C
                 BCC BUDGET.C
```

When you execute MAKE with this file, MAKE first examines the dependancy line. If the file specified (in this case BUDGET.EXE) does not exist, or if the file is older than any one of the files upon which it is dependent (meaning a change has occurred), MAKE executes the command that follows, which in this case, compiles the program. To better understand this process, create the following C file TIPS.C:

```c
#include <stdio.h>

void main(void)
 {
    printf("Jamsa's 1001 C/C++ Tips");
 }
```

Next, create the file TIPS.MAK that contains the following:

```
TIPS.EXE:      TIPS.C
               BCC TIPS.C
```

Invoke MAKE, using the -f switch as follows:

```
C:\> MAKE   -f   TIPS.MAK   <ENTER>
```

Because the file TIPS.EXE does not exist, MAKE performs the corresponding command to build the file. After MAKE ends, invoke MAKE a second time using the same command. In this case, because the file exists and because the file is older than TIPS.C, MAKE does not execute the command. Edit the file TIPS.C and change the *printf* statement in some way. Repeat the MAKE command. In this case, because the file TIPS.C is older than TIPS.EXE, MAKE builds a new EXE file.

C 704 Multiple Dependency Files and MAKE

As you have learned, MAKE is a tool that helps you build applications after a file with which an application is built changes. When you use MAKE, there will be many times when a target file is dependent on several files. For example, assume that the program BUDGET.EXE is dependent on the C file BUDGET.C, the header file BUDGET.H, and the library file BUDGET.LIB. Within MAKE, you can specify the dependencies as follows:

```
BUDGET.EXE:     BUDGET.C BUDGET.H BUDGET.LIB
                BCC BUDGET.C BUDGET.LIB
```

C 705 Commenting Your MAKE Files

All of the MAKE files presented to this point have been small and fairly straightforward. As the complexity of your MAKE files increases, you will want to add comments that explain the processing the files perform. To place a comment within a MAKE file, simply place the pound sign (#) anywhere in your file. MAKE will consider any text that follows (on the current line) as a comment. The following MAKE file illustrates the use of comments:

```
# Build the Budget program BUDGET.EXE

# Make file created: 12-25-93 by Kris Jamsa

BUDGET.EXE:     BUDGET.C BUDGET.H BUDGET.LIB
                BCC BUDGET.C BUDGET.LIB     # BUDGET.LIB contains
                                            # General Ledger functions
```

C 706 Command Lines and MAKE

As you have learned, if a target file is older than a file from which it is built, MAKE executes a specific command. In the examples shown thus far, MAKE has simply invoked the BCC command to compile and link the corresponding files. As it turns out, however, MAKE can issue any command. In addition, MAKE fully supports the DOS input (<), output (>), and append (>>) redirection operators. The following command for example, directs MAKE to compile a specific program, redirecting the compiler's output to the printer:

```
BUDGET.EXE:        BUDGET.C BUDGET.H BUDGET.LIB
                   BCC BUDGET.C BUDGET.LIB > PRN
```

In addition to supporting the DOS redirection operators, MAKE supports two special operators, << and &&. The double less-than signs (<<) direct MAKE to redirect the command's standard input source. Rather that directing the input source to file, however, MAKE uses the text that immediately follows, up to a specified delimiter as the redirected input. For example, the following MAKE file directs MAKE to redirect the text "Jamsa's 1001 C/C++ Tips" to the command SHOWMSG:

```
SOMEFILE.EXE:      SOMEFILE.C
                   SHOWMSG << ^Jamsa's 1001 C/C++ Tips
   ^
```

In this case, the command uses the caret (^) as the input delimiter. MAKE lets you use any character except the pound sign (#) or backslash (\) as the delimiter. The first line that begins with the specified delimiter marks the end of the redirected text. The && operator is similar but it does not cause a redirection. Instead, it creates a temporary file that contains the text that appears between the specified delimeters. During the command's execution, the operator itself is replaced by the temporary filename. The most common use of the && operator is to create an on-the-fly linker response file:

```
SOMEFILE.EXE:      SOMEFILE.C
                   TLINK &&^
                   SOMEFILE.C
                   SOMEFILE.EXE
                   SOMEFILE.MAP
                   SOMEFILE.LIB
   ^
```

As before, the first line that begins with the specified delimeter marks the end of the temporary file.

Placing Multiple Dependencies in a MAKE File

707

If you are building a large system, you can actually have several different executable files. Rather than having to manage several different MAKE files, you can create one file and include in the file, all of the related dependencies. For example, the following MAKE file contains the rules needed to build the programs BUDGET.EXE, PAYROLL.EXE, and TAXES.EXE:

```
BUDGET.EXE:          BUDGET.C BUDGET.H
                     BCC BUDGET.C

PAYROLL.EXE:         PAYROLL.C PAYROLL.C
                     BCC PAYROLL.C

TAXES.EXE:           TAXES.C TAXES.H
                     BCC TAXES.C
```

When you execute MAKE with this file, MAKE will begin at the first entry in the file. If the target file needs to be built, MAKE will execute the corresponding command. MAKE will then continue this process with the second and third files specified.

708 Explicit and Implicit MAKE Rules

When you create a MAKE file, the entries you place in the file that tell MAKE file dependencies and the corresponding file operations are called *rules*. MAKE supports *explicit* and *implicit* rules. An explicit rule is a rule that defines one or more target names, zero or more dependent files, and zero or more commands. Filenames within explicit rules can be complete DOS pathnames or wildcards. All of the example MAKE files presented to this point have used explicit rules. Implicit rules on the other hand, on the other hand are more general. An implicit rule corresponds to all files with a specific extension. MAKE uses an implicit rule when no explicit rule is provided for a target file. For example, you might specify that an OBJ file is dependent on a C file. The following implicit rule directs MAKE to compile all C files whose C source code files are newer than the corresponding OBJ file:

```
.C.OBJ:
     BCC $<
```

The syntax for an implicit rule is the dependent file type (C) followed by the target file type (OBJ). The rule uses a special macro ($<) that, as you will learn, directs MAKE to use the complete name of the corresponding C file. Placing only an implicit rule within a MAKE file by itself has no effect when MAKE runs. The only time the implicit rule is used is when make encounters a target file for which no explicit rule has been provided.

709 Using MAKE Macros

A *MAKE macro* is a symbol that MAKE replaces with a specific value. You can use macros within MAKE for many purposes. For example, the following macro, MEM_MODEL, defines the switches required to select the small memory model:

```
MEM_MODEL = -ms
```

To use a macro's value within your MAKE file, you place the macro name within parentheses that are preceded by a dollar sign. For example, the following command line uses the *MEM_MODEL* macro:

```
FILENAME.EXE:     FILENAME.C
                  BCC $(MEM_MODEL) FILENAME.C
```

Predefined MAKE Macros

C 710

As you have learned, a MAKE macro is a symbol that MAKE replaces with a specific value. Make provides several predefined macros you can use within your MAKE files. Depending on whether you are using the macro within an explicit or implicit rule, the value MAKE substitutes for the symbol will differ. Table 710.1 discusses the use of MAKE's predefined macros in explicit rules. Likewise, Table 710.2 discusses the macro use in implicit rules.

Macro Name	Value Returned
$*	Dependent basename with path
$&	Dependent basename without path
$.	Dependent fullname without path
$**	Dependent fullname with path
$<	Dependent fullname with path
$?	Dependent fullname with path

Table 710.1 *MAKE predefined macro values for explicit rules.*

Macro Name	Value Returned
$*	Target basename with path
$&	Target basename without path
$.	Target fullname without path
$**	All dependent filenames
$<	Target fullname with path
$?	All out of date dependents

Table 710.2 *MAKE predefined macro values for implicit rules.*

The following MAKE file, for example, creates an implicit rule that tells MAKE the relationship between files with the OBJ and C extensions:

```
.C.OBJ:
    BCC $<
```

In this case, MAKE will expand the $< macro into the target filename and path (using the implicit rule expansion).

711 Performing Conditional Processing with MAKE

In the Macros section of this book you learned how to use preprocessor directives such as *#if*, *#elif*, *#else*, and *#endf*. In a similar way, MAKE provides conditional processing statements that begin with an exclamation point (!), such as *!if*, *!else*, *!elif*, and *!endif*. You can also use the directives *!ifdef*, *!ifndef*, and *!undef* to test for defined macros and to undefine a macro. If a conditional directive evaluates as true, MAKE will perform the rules that follow. If the directive is false, MAKE will not process the corresponding rules. The following statements illustrate several different conditional statements:

```
!ifdef  macro_name        # Test if the macro macro_name is defined
    # statements
!endif

!if  $(Value) > 5         # Test if the value of the macro Value is > 5
    # statements
!endif

!if   ! $d(Macro_name)    # Test if the macro Macro_name is not defined
    # statements
!endif
```

712 Testing for a MAKE Macro

As you have learned, MAKE lets you define your own macros. Depending on the processing your MAKE file performs, there may be times when you want to test if a specific macro is defined. To do so, you can use the $d(*macro*) test. If the macro is defined, the test returns the value 1. If the macro is not defined, the result is 0. The following statements use MAKE's !if conditional operator to determine if the macro *MEM_MODEL* has been defined. If the macro is undefined, the statements assign it the value of the small memory model:

```
!if  ! $d(MEM_MODEL)
MEM_MODEL = -ms
!endif
```

In addition to using the $d(*macro*) test, your macros can perform equivalent processing using the !*ifdef* and !*ifndef* conditional statements. Should you later want to undefine a macro, you can do so using the !*undef* statement, as shown here:

```
!undef macro_name
```

Including a Second MAKE File

C713

If your MAKE files typically take the same form, you might find it convenient to place your commonly used implicit rules into a MAKE file named IMPLICIT.MAK. At the start of each of your MAKE files, you can include the file using MAKE's !*include* directive, shown here:

```
!include "IMPLICIT.MAK"
```

Using MAKE's Macro Modifiers

C714

As you learned in Tip 710, MAKE predefines several different macros that your MAKE files can use to obtain the target or dependent file. To provide your MAKE files with greater control over the filenames these macros return, MAKE lets you use the *B*, *D*, *F*, and *R* modifiers, described here:

$(macroB)	Returns the basename only
$(macroD)	Returns the drive and directory
$(macroF)	Returns the basename and extension
$(macroR)	Returns the drive, directory, and base

The following statement, for example, uses the D modifier with the $< to copy files from the target file directory to a backup directory:

```
C:\SUBDIR\TIPS.EXE:      TIPS.C
                         COPY $(<D)*.C   C:\BACKUP
                         BCC TIPS.C
```

Note: *This MAKE file executes two commands within the rule. The first command copies files with the C extension to a directory named BACKUP and the second command compiles the source file.*

715 Ending a MAKE File with an Error

Depending on the processing your MAKE file performs, there may be times when you want MAKE to end its processing and display an error message to the user. In such cases, you can use the *!error* directive. The following statements, for example, test if the macro *MEM_MODEL* is undefined. If the macro is not defined, MAKE ends its processing displaying an error message to the user:

```
!ifndef MEM_MODEL
!error Ending program build—define the macro MEM_MODEL
!endif
```

716 Disabling Command Name Display

By default, MAKE displays each command before the command executes. To disable the command display, simply precede the command name with an at symbol (@). For example, the following statements use the @ symbol to disable the display of the BCC command:

```
TIPS.EXE:       TIPS.C
                @BCC TIPS.C
```

If you want to disable the display of the command's output as well, simply redirect the output to the NUL device, as shown here:

```
TEST.EXE:       TIPS.C
                @BCC TIPS.C > NUL
```

717 Using the File BUILTINS.MAK

As you have learned, there may be many implicit rules that you use on a regular basis. One way to ensure that the rules are available to all of your MAKE files is to place them in a special file named BUILTINS.MAK. Each time you invoke MAKE, it looks for BUILTINS.MAK. If the file exists, MAKE immediately processes the information that it contains. If the file does not exist, MAKE continues its processing using MAKEFILE or the file that you specified in the command line. The following BUILTINS.MAK file contains the implicit rule for converting C files to OBJ files:

```
.C.OBJ:
    BCC $<
```

Performing Exit Status Processing in Make

718

When MAKE executes a command, there may be times when you want MAKE to evaluate the command's exit status value and then either continue or end. If you precede a command name with a hyphen followed by a value, MAKE will compare the command's exit status value to the value specified. If the exit status is *greater than* the value, MAKE aborts the current program build. For example, the following statement compares the exit status of the SHOWFILE command to 3. If exit status is greater than 3, MAKE aborts the build:

```
TEST.EXE:       TIPS.C
                -3  SHOWFILE $?
```

If you want MAKE to ignore a command's exit status, precede the command name with a hyphen and no corresponding value:

```
-   CC  TEST.C
```

Invoking and Changing a Macro at the Same Time

719

As you have learned, MAKE lets you define your own macros. Depending on the processing your MAKE file performs, there may be times when you will want to change and immediately use a macro. For example, assume you define macro INPUT_FILE as follows:

```
INPUT_FILE = BUDGET.C
```

You can then use the macro as follows:

```
BUDGET.EXE:          $(INPUT_FILE)
                     BCC $(INPUT_FILE)
```

Next assume that you want to copy the input file to a file with the same name but the SAV extension. You can change the macro, replacing the .C with .SAV and immediately use the new definition. The following command illustrates how.

```
COPY $(INPUT_FILE)     $(INPUT_FILE:.C=.SAV)
```

The first part of the COPY command uses the filename BUDGET.C. The second part of the command replaces the .C with .SAV to create the filename BUDGET.SAV.

C 720 Executing a MAKE Command for Multiple Dependent Files

As you have learned, there may be times when a target file is dependent on two or more files. Depending on the processing your MAKE file performs, you might want MAKE to execute a specific command for each file. To do so, simply precede the command name with an ampersand (&). The following rule, for example, directs MAKE to individually compile each of the out-of-date dependent files:

```
BUDGET.EXE:     BUDGET.C ACCOUNT.C PAYROLL.C
                & BCC $?
```

Advanced C

721 Determining Whether a Math Coprocessor Is Present

If your programs perform complex mathematical operations, there may be times when you can improve their performance by using the computer's math coprocessor. To help your programs take advantage of the math coprocessor, several third-party libraries have been written that provide commonly used functions. Before your programs use such functions, however, your program should verify that a math coprocessor is present. For such cases, many C compilers define the global variable *_8087* which contains the value 1 if a coprocessor is present and 0 otherwise. The following program, CHK_MATH.C, illustrates the use of the global variable *_8087*:

```c
#include <stdio.h>
#include <dos.h>

void main(void)
  {
    if (_8087)
      printf("Math coprocessor found\n");
    else
      printf("No math coprocessor\n");
  }
```

You can control the value the C compiler assigns to the _8087 variable by using the 87 environment entry. To set the variable's value to 1, assign 87 the value Yes, as shown here:

```
C:\> SET 87=Yes   <ENTER>
```

Likewise, to set the variable to 0, assign the environment entry the value No.

722 Understanding the ctype.h istype Macros

The Macros section of this book presents several macros that test if a character is uppercase, lowercase, and so on. If you examine the header file, ctype.h, you find macro definitions similar to the following:

```c
#define isalpha(c)  (_ctype[(c) + 1] & (_IS_UPP | _IS_LOW))
#define isascii(c)  ((unsigned)(c) < 128)
#define iscntrl(c)  (_ctype[(c) + 1] & _IS_CTL)
```

```
#define isdigit(c)    (_ctype[(c) + 1] & _IS_DIG)
#define isgraph(c)    ((c) >= 0x21 && (c) <= 0x7e)
#define islower(c)    (_ctype[(c) + 1] & _IS_LOW)
```

To decrease the processing time that such tests require, many C compilers define a global variable named *ctype*, which contains settings that define each ASCII character. Using these settings, the macros can perform fast bitwise operations to perform the necessary testing. The following program, CTYPE.C, displays the settings the compiler uses for each ASCII character:

```c
#include <stdio.h>
#include <ctype.h>

void main (void)
  {
    int ascii_char;

    for (ascii_char = 0; ascii_char < 128; ascii_char++)
      if (isprint(ascii_char))
        printf("ASCII value %d setting (hex) %x ASCII %c\n",
          ascii_char, _ctype[ascii_char], ascii_char);
      else
        printf("ASCII value %d setting (hex) %x ASCII %c\n",
          ascii_char, _ctype[ascii_char], ascii_char);
  }
```

Controlling Direct Video

C723

The header file conio.h defines prototypes for functions that perform console I/O, such as *cputs*. To improve the performance of these functions, most PC compilers bypass DOS and the BIOS, writing the output directly to your PC's video memory. Although most video operations are standard from one PC to the next, you may encounter a video board for which the direct video operations are not supported. If you experience such errors, you can use the global variable *directvideo* to control whether or not the PC uses BIOS video routines to perform their output, if they perform direct I/O. If you set the variable's value to 1, the routines will perform direct video output. If the value is 0, the routines will perform their output using the BIOS.

724

Detecting System and Math Errors

Several of C's run-time library functions presented throughout this book assign values to the global variable *errno* when an error occurs. When your programs use these functions, you should test the return value and *errno*'s value. Table 724 defines the constants functions assign to *errno*.

Constant	Meaning
E2BIG	The argument list is too long
EACCES	Permission denied
EBADF	Bad file handle
ECONTRL	Error in memory control blocks
ECURDIR	Attempt to remove current directory
EDOM	An argument violates the domain of supported values
EEXIST	File already exists
EFAULT	Unknown error
EINVACC	Invalid access specifier
EINVAL	Invalid argument value
EINVDAT	Invalid argument data
EINVDRV	Invalid drive specifier
EINVENV	Invalid environment
EINVFMT	Invalid argument format
EINVFNC	Invalid function number
EINVMEM	Invalid memory block specified
ENFILE	Too many open files
ENMFILE	No more files
ENODEV	No such device
ENOENT	Invalid entry (file or directory)
ENOEXEC	Format error in EXEC
ENOFILE	No such file or directory
ENOMEM	Insufficient memory
ENOPATH	Path not found
ENOTSAM	Not same device
ERANGE	Function result is out of range of valid values
EXDEV	Cross linked device
EZERO	Error zero

Table 724 *Constant values functions assign to errno.*

Displaying Predefined Error Messages

725

Tip 724 introduced the *errno* global variable, to which various math and system functions assign status values that provide your program with more information about the cause of the error. Depending on your program's processing, you might want to display a predefined message when such errors occur. To help your program perform such processing, the C compiler provides a global variable named *sys_errlist*, which contains character string error messages for most errors. In addition, to increase the portability of your programs, the array contains error messages from the UNIX environment.

The compiler also assigns the global variable *sys_nerr* the number of error messages in the array. The following program, ERR_MSG.C, uses the *sys_errlist* array to display the predefined error messages:

```c
#include <stdio.h>
#include <stdlib.h>

void main (void)
  {
    int error;

    for (error = 0; error < sys_nerr; error++)
        printf("Error %d %s\n", error, sys_errlist[error]);
  }
```

Determining the Operating System Version Number

726

If you are developing applications for the DOS environment, there may be times when your programs need to know the current operating system version number. In such cases, your programs can use the predefined global variables *_osmajor* and *_osminor*, which contain the operating system's major and minor version numbers. In addition, some compilers provide the variable *_version*, whose low byte contains the major version number and high byte the minor. Given DOS 6.0, for example, the variable *_osmajor* will contain the value 6, while the variable *_osminor* will be 0. The following program, OS_VER.C, uses these global variables to display the operating system version number:

```
#include <stdio.h>
#include <dos.h>

void main (void)
 {
   printf("Operating system version number %d.%d\n",
    _osmajor, _osminor);

   printf("Operating system version number %d.%d\n",
    _version & 255, _version >> 8);
 }
```

Note: *If the previous program does not compile on your system, comment out the statements that use _version, and include the header file STDLIB.H.*

727 Understanding Portability

Portability is a measure of the ease with which you can move your program from one system to the next. For example, when you write a program using assembly language for the PC, it is very difficult to move that program to a workstation that uses a different assembly language. If the same program were written in C, however, you might need only to make a few small changes to the program before it would compile and run on the new system. As you program, you should keep portability in mind. The code that you write for one program can often be used in another, and you can save considerable programming and testing time if you focus on writing portable code. To improve your program's portability, consider the following as you code:

- Avoid operating system services whenever possible, relying instead on C runtime library routines.

- Avoid functions and global variables that are specific to your compiler. In most cases, the compiler will precede such function and variable names with an underscore, such as _8087.

- Do not make assumptions about the machine's word size. For example, on the PC, a variable of type *int* typically holds 16 bits, but on other machines it might hold 32.

- Do not access hardware-specific locations or rely on specific interrupts unless your program's performance absolutely requires it.

- Always try to correct and eliminate compiler warning messages.

- Do not make memory model assumptions that might not exist in a UNIX-based environment.

- Restrict hardware- or operating system-dependent code to as few functions as possible.

Performing a Nonlocal Goto

In the Constructs section of this book you learned that the *goto* statement lets your program execution branch from one location to another. As you learned, the label to which you want to "goto" must reside in the current function. Depending on your programs, there may be times when you need to branch to a label outside of the current function (called a *nonlocal goto*). To perform a nonlocal goto, your programs can use the *setjmp* and *longjmp* functions:

```
#include <setjmp.h>

void longjmp(jmp_buf location, int return_value);
void setjmp(jmp_buf location);
```

To begin, your program stores the current location (task state) in the buffer *location*. Later, your programs can jump to that location using *longjmp*. The first time your program invokes *setjmp*, the function returns 0. When the program later calls *longjmp*, it returns to the location stored by *setjmp* with the return value specified by *longjmp return_value* parameter. The following program, LONGJMP.C, illustrates a nonlocal goto:

```
#include <stdio.h>
#include <setjmp.h>
#include <stdlib.h>

jmp_buf location;    // Global variable

void function(void)
  {
    printf("About to longjmp\n");
    longjmp(location, 1);  // Return 1
  }

void main(void)
  {

    if (setjmp(location) != 0)  // Save the current location
      {
        printf("Returning from longjmp\n");
        exit(1);
      }

    function();
  }
```

Getting the Process Id (PID)

729

In a multitasking environment, the operating system assigns each program a unique identifier, called a process ID or PID. The UNIX operating system provides a function named *getpid*, which returns a program's process ID. Many DOS-based compilers provide a similar *getpid* function:

```
#include <process.h>

unsigned getpid(void);
```

Within DOS, the process ID is actually the segment address of the program's program segment prefix or PSP. If you have two or more memory-resident programs active, each program would have a unique process ID, because each has a unique PSP segment address. The following program, GETPID.C, displays the program's process ID:

```
#include <stdio.h>
#include <process.h>

void main (void)
  {
    printf("Process id: %X\n", getpid());
  }
```

Invoking an Internal DOS Command

730

Several of the tips presented in this section have shown you ways your programs can invoke executable (EXE and COM) files. Depending on your program, there may be times when you will need to invoke an internal DOS command or a batch file. In such cases, your programs can use the *system* function:

```
#include <stdlib.h>

int system(const char *command);
```

The *command parameter* is a character string containing the name of the desired internal or external DOS command or batch file. If system successfully executes the command it returns the value 0. If an error occurs, system returns the value −1 and assigns the global variable *errno* on of the following values:

Value	Meaning
ENOENT	No such file
ENOMEM	Not enough memory
E2BIG	Argument list too long
ENOEXEC	Error in exec format

The system function spawns a copy of COMMAND.COM to execute the specified command. The function uses the COMSPEC environment entry to locate the command processor. The following program, SYSTEM.C, uses the system function to display a directory listing using the DOS DIR command:

```c
#include <stdlib.h>

void main (void)
  {
    if (system("DIR"))
      printf("Error invoking DIR\n");
  }
```

Using the *_psp* Global Variable

731

Each time you execute a program, DOS loads in the program into memory immediately following a 256-byte buffer called the program segment prefix (PSP). The program segment prefix contains information about the command line, a pointer to the program's environment copy, file table information and so on. Figure 731 illustrates the contents of the program segment prefix.

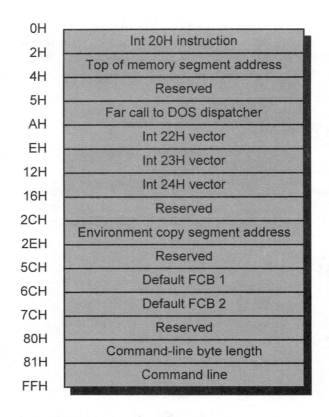

0H	Int 20H instruction
2H	Top of memory segment address
4H	Reserved
5H	Far call to DOS dispatcher
AH	Int 22H vector
EH	Int 23H vector
12H	Int 24H vector
16H	Reserved
2CH	Environment copy segment address
2EH	Reserved
5CH	Default FCB 1
6CH	Default FCB 2
7CH	Reserved
80H	Command-line byte length
81H	Command line
FFH	

Figure 731 *The contents of the program segment prefix.*

As you begin to do program work with DOS internal commands, there may be times when your programs access information contained in a program's PSP. Therefore, DOS provides a system service that returns the address of the PSP. To simplify such programs, some C compilers define a global variable _psp, which contains the segment address of the program's PSP. The following program, PSP_ADDR.C, uses the _psp global variable to display the program's PSP address:

```
#include <stdio.h>
#include <dos.h>

void main (void)
  {
    printf("The Program Segment Prefix begins at %X\n", _psp);
  }
```

Note: *Some C compilers also provide the function getpsp, which returns the segment address of the program's PSP:*

```
#include <dos.h>

unsigned getpsp(void);
```

Using the *const* Modifier in Variable Declarations

732

Several of the function prototypes presented throughout this book use the *const* keyword before parameter names:

```
char *strcpy(char *target, const char *source);
```

When you use the *const* keyword before a parameter name, you tell the compiler that the parameter should not be changed within the function. If a statement tries to change the parameter, the compiler will generate an error message. C also lets you use the *const* keyword when you declare variables. When you declare a variable as a constant, the C compiler performs a one-time initialization of variable; following the initialization, the compiler will generate an error for any attempts to change the constant. The following statements create several different constants:

```
const int number = 1001;
const float price = 39.95;
```

The advantage of using a constant over a macro created with #define is that using the constant, you can specify the value's type explicitly.

> **Note:** *When you declare a constant, the variable's value can still be changed using a pointer alias.*

Using Enumerated Types

733

As you have learned, using meaningful variable names can significantly improve your program's readability. In addition, replacing constant values such as 1, 2, 3, and so on and replacing them with meaningful names that correspond to the values they represent (such as Monday, Tuesday, and Wednesday) can improve your program's readability. To help your programs work with such constants, C supports *enumerated types*. In general, an enumerated type is a list of items, each of which has a unique value. For example, the following declaration creates an enumerated type called *weekdays*:

```
enum weekdays { Monday, Tuesday, Wednesday,
   Thursday, Friday };
```

In this case, the enumerated type is similar to a structure definition, in that you can declare variables of the type immediately, or you can refer to the type name later:

```
enum weekdays { Monday, Tuesday, Wednesday,
   Thursday, Friday } work_day;

enum weekdays day_off;
```

After you declare an enumerated variable, you can assign the variable a value by referring to a member name:

```
day_off = Friday;
work_day = Tuesday;
```

Using enumerated types, you can improve your program's readability.

734 Putting an Enumerated Type to Use

In Tip 733 you learned that your programs can use enumerated types to improve their readability. The following program, WHICHDAY.C, illustrates how your programs might use an enumerated type to improve their readability:

```
#include <stdio.h>

void main(void)
  {
    enum { Monday, Tuesday, Wednesday, Thursday, Friday } day;

    for (day = Monday; day <= Friday; day++)
     if (day == Monday)
       printf("No fun—meetings all day Monday\n");
     else if (day == Tuesday)
       printf("No fun—do Monday's work today\n");
     else if (day == Wednesday)
       printf("Hump day...");
     else if (day == Thursday)
       printf("Schedule meetings for next Monday\n");
     else
       printf("Meet everyone at happy hour!\n");
  }
```

Understanding an Enumerated Value

As you learned in Tip 734, each member within an enumerated type has a unique value. By default, the C compiler assigns the first member the value 0, the second the value 1, and so on. The following program, SHOWENUM.C, displays the values that correspond to the enumerated days of the week:

```c
#include <stdio.h>

void main(void)
  {
    enum weekdays { Monday, Tuesday, Wednesday, Thursday,
        Friday };

    printf("%d %d %d %d %d\n", Monday, Tuesday, Wednesday,
      Thursday, Friday);
  }
```

When you compile and execute this program, your screen will display the values 0 through 4.

Assigning a Specific Value to an Enumerated Type

In Tip 735 you learned that the C compiler assigns unique values to each member of an enumerated type. Depending on the function your program performs, there may be times when you want to specify each member's value. The following declaration, for example, assigns the values 10, 20, 30, 40, and 50 to days of the week:

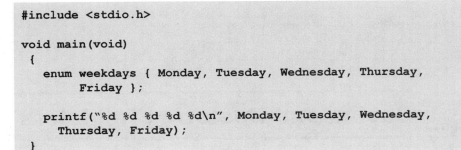

```c
enum weekdays { Monday = 10, Tuesday = 20,
                Wednesday = 30, Thursday = 40,
                Friday = 50 };
```

The following program, SETENUM.C, assigns these values to the members of the enumerated type and then displays their values:

```c
#include <stdio.h>

void main(void)
  {
```

```
enum weekdays { Monday = 10, Tuesday = 20,
               Wednesday = 30, Thursday = 40,
               Friday = 50 };

printf("%d %d %d %d %d\n", Monday, Tuesday, Wednesday,
   Thursday, Friday);
}
```

In addition to assigning each member a value, you can assign a value to a specific member, and the C compiler will later increment the members' values by 1. The following declaration, for example, assigns the values 10, 11, 12, 13, and 14:

```
enum weekdays { Monday = 10, Tuesday,
               Wednesday, Thursday,
               Friday};
```

C737 Saving and Restoring Registers

Many compilers let you access register values from within your C programs. Programs that perform such operations often push register values onto the stack before they change the register and later pop the value to restore. If you have function that performs such low-level operations, you can direct the C compiler to insert PUSH and POP instructions in the object code that automatically save all registers when the function is called and later restore the registers before the function ends. To direct the compiler to perform such operations, simply include the _*saveregs* modifier the function header, as shown here:

```
int _saveregs some_function(int parameter);
```

To better understand the processing the _*saveregs* modifier directs the compiler to perform, create a simple function that uses the _*saveregs* modifier and then generate an assembly language listing of the source code.

C738 Getting Started with Dynamic Lists

In the Structures section of this book you learned how to group related information into a single variable. If your program needs to work with a fixed number of occurrences of a structure, your program can create an array of structures. As your programs become more complex, however, there will be many times when you won't know in advance how many structure entries you will need. In such cases, you have two choices. First, your program can allocate memory dynamically for an array structures. Second, your programs can create a *linked list* of structures, where one entry points to the next. Figure 738 illustrates a linked list of filenames.

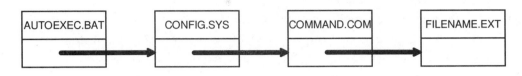

Figure 738 *A linked list of file names.*

In general, the program maintains a pointer to the start of the list. The last entry is the list is indicated by a pointer to NULL.

Declaring a Linked-List Structure

739

To create a linked list, one of the structure members is a pointer to a structure of the same type. For example, consider the following structure:

```
struct FileList {
   char filename[64];
   struct FileList *next;
};
```

The *filename* member contains a filename. The *next* member is a pointer to the next entry in the list. To create and later traverse a linked list, your programs will normally use at least two variables. The variable *start* is a structure whose member *next* will contain a pointer to the start of the list or NULL if the list is empty. The variable *node* will be a pointer to the current node.

```
struct FileList start, *node;
```

Building a Linked List

740

To create a linked list, your programs should perform the following steps:

1. Declare the structure that defines the list entries
2. Declare the variables *start* and **node*
3. Assign *start.next* NULL to signify an empty list

4. For each list entry

    a. Find the end of the list so that *node->next* is NULL

    b. Allocate memory for the new entry assigning it to *node->next*

    c. Assign node the value of *node->next*

    d. Assign the member values to *node*

    e. Assign *node->next* the value NULL to indicate the end of the list

C741

Simple Linked-List Example

Tip 740 discussed the steps your programs must perform to create a linked list. The following program, 1_10LIST.C, uses creates a linked list whose entries contain the numbers 1 through 10:

```c
#include <stdio.h>
#include <alloc.h>

void main (void)
  {
    int i;

    struct ListEntry {
      int number;
      struct ListEntry *next;
    } start, *node;

    start.next = NULL;   // Empty list

    node = &start;       // Point to the start of the list

    for (i = 1; i <= 10; i++)
      {
        node->next = (struct ListEntry *)
            malloc (sizeof (struct ListEntry));
        node = node->next;
        node->number = i;
        node->next = NULL;
      }

    // Display the list
    node = start.next;

    while (node)
      {
```

```
        printf("%d ", node->number);
        node = node->next;
    }
}
```

Understanding the
Linked-List Traversal

Tip 741 presented the program 1_10LIST.C that created a simple linked list whose entries contained the numbers 1 through 10. The program used the following loop to display the list entries:

```
// Display the list
node = start.next;

while (node)
   {
     printf("%d ", node->number);
     node = node->next;
   }
```

As you will recall, the variable *start.next* points to the first entry in the list. As you can see, the code assigns the address of the first entry to *node*. Likewise, as you will recall, the end of the list is indicated by NULL; the loop simply tests the current value of *node* to see if it is NULL. If *node* is not NULL, the loop displays the entry's value and assigns *node* the address of the next list entry.

Building a More Interesting List

In Tip 741 you created a simple linked list that contained the numbers 1 though 10. The following program, FILELIST.C, creates a linked list that contains the names of current directory files:

```
#include <stdio.h>
#include <dirent.h>
#include <alloc.h>
#include <string.h>

void main(int argc, char *argv[])
  {
    DIR *directory_pointer;
```

```
   struct dirent *entry;

   struct FileList {
     char filename[64];
     struct FileList *next;
   } start, *node;


   if ((directory_pointer = opendir(argv[1])) == NULL)
     printf("Error opening %s\n", argv[1]);
   else
     {
       start.next = NULL;
       node = &start;

       while (entry = readdir(directory_pointer))
         {
           node->next = (struct FileList *)
                   malloc(sizeof(struct FileList));
           node = node->next;
           strcpy(node->filename, entry);
           node->next = NULL;
         }

       closedir(directory_pointer);


       node = start.next;

       while (node)
         {
           printf("%s\n", node->filename);
           node = node->next;
         }

     }
}
```

As you can see, the program uses the *readdir* function to read directory entries. The program then allocates memory to hold and entry and copies to the list entry the corresponding filename. After all the files have been added to the list, the program loops through the list, displaying each entry.

Appending a List Entry

744

Each of the linked-list programs presented thus far have built the linked list at one time, normally within a *while* or *for* loop. Depending on your program, you will, at some point, probably need to add entries to the list at different times. The easiest way to add an entry is to append it. To append an item to a linked list, you loop through the list until you find the element whose *next* member points to NULL:

```
node = &start;

while (node->next)
  node = node->next;
```

When *node->next* points to NULL, you have found the end of the list, so you can allocate memory for the entry as shown here:

```
node->next = malloc(required_size);
```

Next, you assign the desired entry values and assign the new entry's next field to point to NULL:

```
node = node->next;
node->member = some_value;
node->next = NULL;
```

In some cases, you might want your programs to place elements at specific locations in a list. To perform such processing see Tip 745.

Inserting a List Entry

745

In Tip 744 you learned how to append items to a linked list. Depending on your program's function, there will be times when you will want to place items at specific locations in a list. For example, if you want to create a linked list that contains the sorted names of files in the current directory, your program must place each filename into the list at the correct position. To insert an item at a specific location in a list, your programs will normally track the starting node, current node, and the previous node. When your program needs to insert a new element, it will perform the following processing:

```
struct ListMember start, *node, *previous, *new;

// Code that performs insert of an entry between
// the elements pointed to by node and previous
```

```
new = malloc(sizeof(struct ListMember);
new->next = node;
previous->next = new;
new->member = some_value;
```

C 746 Displaying a Sorted Directory

In Tip 745 you learned that to insert an element in a singly linked list (where each element contains a pointer to the next element), your programs must track the current and previous nodes (list elements). The following program, SORTLIST.C, inserts elements into a list to create a list containing the sorted current directory filenames:

```
#include <stdio.h>
#include <dirent.h>
#include <alloc.h>
#include <string.h>
#include <stdlib.h>

void main(int argc, char *argv[])
 {
   DIR *directory_pointer;
   struct dirent *entry;

   struct FileList {
     char filename[64];
     struct FileList *next;
   } start, *node, *previous, *new;


   if ((directory_pointer = opendir(argv[1])) == NULL)
     printf("Error opening %s\n", argv[1]);
   else
     {
        start.next = NULL;

        while (entry = readdir(directory_pointer))
          {
            // Find the correct location
            previous = &start;
            node = start.next;
            while ((node) && (strcmp(entry, node->filename) > 0))
              {
                node = node->next;
                previous = previous->next;
```

```
          }

      new = (struct FileList *)
          malloc(sizeof(struct FileList));
      if (new == NULL)
        {
          printf("Insufficient memory to store list\n");
          exit(1);
        }
      new->next = node;
      previous->next = new;
      strcpy(new->filename, entry);
    }

  closedir(directory_pointer);


  node = start.next;

  while (node)
    {
      printf("%s\n", node->filename);
      node = node->next;
    }

  }
}
```

Deleting an Element from a List

747

In Tip 745 you learned how to insert items into a linked list. As your programs manipulate linked lists, there will be times when you need to delete an element from a list. Removing an element from a singly linked list is very similar to an insertion operation, in that you must track pointers to the current and previous nodes. Once your program locates the list element it wants to delete, it can use code similar to the following to remove the node:

```
previous->next = node->next;
free(node);
```

The following program, REMOVE5.C, creates a linked list containing the numbers 1 through 10. The program then searches the list for the element containing the number 5. The program then removes the element:

```c
#include <stdio.h>
#include <alloc.h>

void main(void)
 {
   int i;

   struct ListEntry {
     int number;
     struct ListEntry *next;
   } start, *node, *previous;

   start.next = NULL;   // Empty list
   node = &start;       // Point to the start of the list

   for (i = 1; i <= 10; i++)
     {
       node->next = (struct ListEntry *)
         malloc(sizeof(struct ListEntry));
       node = node->next;
       node->number = i;
       node->next = NULL;
     }

   // Remove the number 5
   node = start.next;
   previous = &start;

   while (node)
     if (node->number == 5)
       {
         previous->next = node->next;
         free(node);
         break;          // End the loop
       }
     else
       {
         node = node->next;
         previous = previous->next;
       }

   // Display the list
   node = start.next;
   while (node)
     {
       printf("%d ", node->number);
       node = node->next;
     }
 }
```

Using a Doubly Linked List

A *singly linked list* is so named because each list element contains a pointer to the next element. You have learned that, to insert elements in a singly linked list, your programs have to maintain pointers the current and previous elements. To simplify the process of the inserting and removing list elements, your programs can use a *doubly linked list*, for which each element maintains a pointer each to the next and previous list elements. Figure 748 illustrates a doubly linked list.

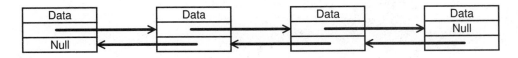

Figure 748 *A doubly linked list maintains two pointers.*

The following structure illustrates a doubly-linked list structure:

```
struct FileList {
   char filename[64];
   struct FileList *next;
   struct FileList *previous;
};
```

When your programs use a doubly-linked list, the program can traverse the list from left to right or right to left. Therefore, two NULL pointers are maintained. When traversing the list from left to right, your programs knows it has reached the end of the list when *node->next* is NULL. Likewise, when traversing the list from right to left, the end of the list is indicated when *node->previous* is NULL.

Building a Simple
Doubly Linked List

749

In Tip 748 you learned that a doubly linked list simplifies the process of inserting and removing list elements. The following program DBL_1_10.C, uses a doubly linked list to display the numbers 1 to 10 forward and backward:

```
#include <stdio.h>
#include <alloc.h>
```

```c
void main(void)
 {
   int i;

   struct ListEntry {
     int number;
     struct ListEntry *next;
     struct ListEntry *previous;
   } start, *node;

   start.next = NULL;  // Empty list
   start.previous = NULL;
   node = &start;        // Point to the start of the list

   for (i = 1; i <= 10; i++)
     {
       node->next = (struct ListEntry *)
         malloc(sizeof(struct ListEntry));
       node->next->previous = node;
       node = node->next;
       node->number = i;
       node->next = NULL;
     }

   // Display the list

   node = start.next;

   do {
       printf("%d ", node->number);
       node = node->next;
   } while (node->next);  // Show 10 only one time

   do {
       printf("%d ", node->number);
       node = node->previous;
   } while (node->previous);
 }
```

Understanding
node->previous->next

C 750

As you have learned, working with doubly linked list simplifies element insert and delete operations. As you examine programs that work with doubly linked lists, you might encounter statements such as the following:

```
node->previous->next = new_node;
```

As you examine such statements, work from left to right. Figure 750 illustrates how the C compiler resolves the pointer.

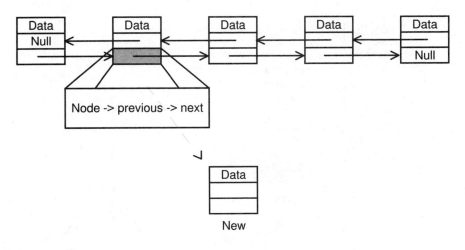

Figure 750 *Resolving a complex pointer operation.*

Removing an Element from
a Doubly Linked List

C 751

A doubly linked list simplifies the process of inserting and removing list elements. The following program, REMOVE_7.C, builds a doubly linked list that contains the numbers 1 through 10. The program then searches the list for the entry containing the number 7 and removes the entry:

```c
#include <stdio.h>
#include <alloc.h>

void main(void)
 {
   int i, found;

   struct ListEntry {
     int number;
     struct ListEntry *next;
     struct ListEntry *previous;
   } start, *node;

   start.next = NULL;   // Empty list
   start.previous = NULL;
   node = &start;        // Point to the start of the list

   for (i = 1; i <= 10; i++)
     {
       node->next = (struct ListEntry *)
         malloc(sizeof(struct ListEntry));
       node->next->previous = node;
       node = node->next;
       node->number = i;
       node->next = NULL;
     }

   // Remove the entry
   node = start.next;
   found = 0;
   do {
       if (node->number == 7)
         {
           found = 1;
           node->previous->next = node->next;
           node->next->previous = node->previous;
           free(node);
         }
       else
         node = node->next;
   } while ((node) && (! found));  // Show 10 only one time

   node = start.next;
   do {
       printf("%d ", node->number);
       node = node->next;
   } while (node);
 }
```

Inserting an Element into a Doubly Linked List

As you have learned, doubly linked lists exist to simplify the insertion and deletion of list elements. The following program, BLD_1_10.C, builds a list containing the numbers 1, 3, 5, 7, and 9. The program then inserts the numbers 2, 4, 6, 8, and 10 in their correct locations:

```c
#include <stdio.h>
#include <alloc.h>

void main(void)
 {
   int i;

   struct ListEntry {
     int number;
     struct ListEntry *next;
     struct ListEntry *previous;
   } start, *node, *new;

   start.next = NULL;   // Empty list
   start.previous = NULL;
   node = &start;       // Point to the start of the list

   for (i = 1; i < 10; i += 2)
     {
       node->next = (struct ListEntry *)
         malloc(sizeof(struct ListEntry));
       node->next->previous = node;
       node = node->next;
       node->number = i;
       node->next = NULL;
     }


   for (i = 2; i <= 10; i += 2)
     {
       int found = 0;

       new = (struct ListEntry *)
         malloc(sizeof(struct ListEntry));
       new->number = i;
       node = start.next;
```

```
    do {
      if (node->number > new->number)
        {
          new->next = node;
          new->previous = node->previous;
          node->previous->next = new;
          node->previous = new;
          found = 1;
        }
      else
        node = node->next;
    } while ((node->next) && (! found));

    if (! found)
      if (node->number > new->number)
        {
          new->next = node;
          new->previous = node->previous;
          node->previous->next = new;
          node->previous = new;
        }
      else
        {
          new->next = NULL;
          new->previous = node;
          node->next = new;
        }
  }

// Display the list
node = start.next;
do {
    printf("%d ", node->number);
    node = node->next;
} while (node);
}
```

753 Understanding Child Processes

When you run a program, that program can run a second program, called a *child process*. The program that runs the second program is called the *parent*. Depending on your needs, the child process can run to completion and the parent can continue, or the child can take the parent's place, overwriting the parent in memory. When the child program runs to completion and the parent continues, the child's execution is called *spawning*. When the child process replaces the parent in memory, the child has be *execed*.

To help your programs perform such processing, the C run-time library provides two different types of run-time library functions: *spawn* and *exec*. Tips 754 and 757 discuss these run-time library routines in detail.

Spawning a Child Process

As Tip 753 describes, when a program spawns a child task, the parent program suspends its processing while the child process runs, and then later continues. To spawn a child process, your programs can use the *spawnl* function, shown here:

```
#include <process.h>
#include <stdio.h>

int spawnl(int mode, char *child, char *arg0,
    ...,char *argn, NULL);
```

The *mode* parameter specifies how the child process is run. Table 754 lists the possible mode values. The *child* parameter is a pointer to a character string that specifies the name of the executable file containing the child process. The parameters *arg0* through *argn* specify the child process's command-line arguments.

Value	Mode of Execution
P_NOWAIT	Parent process continues to run in parallel with the child. Not available for DOS-based programs.
P_OVERLAY	The child process overwrites the parent in memory.
P_WAIT	The parent process resumes after the child ends.

Table 754 *Modes of child process execution.*

If the *spawnl* function is successful, it returns the value 0. If an error occurs, the function returns the value −1 and sets the global variable *errno* to one of the following:

E2BIG	Argument list too long
EINVAL	Invalid argument
ENOENT	Child program not found
ENOEXEC	Format error
ENOMEM	Insufficient memory

To understand child processes better, create the program CHILD.C, which displays its command-line arguments and environment entries:

```
#include <stdlib.h>
#include <stdio.h>

void main(int argc, char *argv[], char *env[])
 {
   printf("Command line\n");
   while (*argv)
     puts(*argv++);

   printf("Environment entries\n");
   while (*env)
     puts(*env++);
 }
```

Compile the program. Next, create the program SPAWNL.C that uses *spawnl* function to execute the child process:

```
#include <process.h>
#include <stdio.h>

void main(void)
 {
   printf("About to call child process\n\n");
   spawnl(P_WAIT, "CHILD.EXE", "CHILD.EXE",
     "AAA", "BBB", "CCC", NULL);
   printf("\n\nBack from child process\n");
 }
```

When you execute the SPAWNL program, your screen will display a message stating that it is about to call the child process. Next, the child process will run displaying its command-line arguments and environment entries. After the child process ends, the program displays a message stating that it has returned from the child process.

C 755 Using Other *spawnlxx* Functions

In Tip 754 you learned that the *spawnl* function lets you run a child process. If you examine the C run-time library, you will find several other *spawnlxx* functions, as shown here:

```
#include <stdio.h>
#include <process.h>

int spawnle(int mode, char *child, char *arg0,
   ..., char *argn, NULL, char *environ);
```

```
int spawnlp(int mode, char *child, char *arg0,
   ..., char *argn, NULL);

int spawnlpe(int mode, char *child, char *arg0,
   ..., char *argn, NULL, char *environ);
```

If the *spawnlxx* functionx are successful, it return the value 0. If an error occurs, the functions return the value –1 and set the global variable *errno* to one of the following:

E2BIG	Argument list too long
EINVAL	Invalid argument
ENOENT	Child program not found
ENOEXEC	Format error
ENOMEM	Insufficient memory

The parameters to these functions are similar to those used by *spawnl*, described in Tip 754, with the exception of the *environ* parameter, which contains a pointer to the child's environment entries. The difference between *spawnl* and *spawnlp* is that functions containing the letter p will search the command path for the child process. The following program, SPAWNLXX.C, illustrates the use of these functions:

```
#include <process.h>
#include <stdio.h>

void main(void)
  {
    char *env[] = { "FILE=SPAWNLXX.C", "LANGUAGE=C",
                    "OS=DOS", NULL};

    spawnle(P_WAIT, "CHILD.EXE", "CHILD.EXE",
        "Using-spawnle", "BBB", NULL, env);

    spawnlp(P_WAIT, "CHILD.EXE", "CHILD.EXE", "Using-spawnlp",
        "BBB", NULL);
    spawnlpe(P_WAIT, "CHILD.EXE", "CHILD.EXE", "Using-spawnlpe",
        "BBB", NULL, env);
  }
```

Using the *spawnvxx* Functions

C 756

In Tip 754 you learned how to use the *spawnl* function to create a child process. Likewise, in Tip 755 you used the different *spawnlxx* functions, which let you pass an array of environment entries to the child process and also let you use the command path to locate the child process. When you use the *spawnl* functions, you pass the command-line arguments as a list of NULL-terminated parameters. In addition to the *spawnlxx* functions, C provides a collection of *spawnvxx* functions that let you pass the command-line parameters as array of character strings:

```
#include <stdio.h>
#include <process.h>

int spawnv(int mode, char *child, char *argv[]);
int spawnve(int mode, char *child, char *argv[],
   char *env[]);
int spawnvp(int mode, char *child, char *argvp[]);
int spawnvpe(int mode, char *child, char *argv[],
   char *env[]);
```

If the *spawnvxx* functions are successful, they return the value 0. If an error occurs, the functions return the value −1 and set the global variable *errno* to one of the following:

E2BIG	Argument list too long
EINVAL	Invalid argument
ENOENT	Child program not found
ENOEXEC	Format error
ENOMEM	Insufficient memory

The parameters to the *spawnvxx* functions are similar to those passed to the *spawnlxx* functions, except that the command-line arguments are passed as an array of character strings. The following program, SPAWNVXX.C, illustrates the *spawnvxx* functions:

```
#include <stdio.h>
#include <process.h>

void main(void)
 {
   char *env[] = { "FILENAME=SPAWNVXX.C", "OS=DOS",
                   "ROUTINES=SPAWNVXX", NULL };

   char *argv[] = { "CHILD.EXE", "AAA", "BBB", NULL };

   spawnv(P_WAIT, "CHILD.EXE", argv);
   spawnve(P_WAIT, "CHILD.EXE", argv, env);
   spawnvp(P_WAIT, "CHILD.EXE", argv);
   spawnvpe(P_WAIT, "CHILD.EXE", argv, env);
 }
```

Execing a Child Process

C 757

As discussed in Tip 753, when a program execs a child task, the parent program is overwritten in memory by the child process. Because the child overwrites the parent, the parent process never resumes. To exec a child process, your programs can use the *execl* function, shown here:

```
#include <process.h>
#include <stdio.h>

int execl(char *child, char *arg0,
    ...,char *argn, NULL);
```

The *child* parameter is a pointer to a character string that specifies the name of the executable file containing the child process. The parameters *arg0* through *argn* specify the child process's command-line arguments.

If the *execl* function is successful, it does not return. If an error occurs, the function returns the value –1 and sets the global variable *errno* to one of the following:

E2BIG	Argument list too long
EINVAL	Invalid argument
ENOENT	Child program not found
ENOEXEC	Format error
ENOMEM	Insufficient memory

To better understand child processes, create the program CHILD.C that displays its command-line arguments and environment entries:

```
#include <stdlib.h>
#include <stdio.h>

void main(int argc, char *argv[], char *env[])
  {
    printf("Command line\n");
    while (*argv)
      puts(*argv++);

    printf("Environment entries\n");
    while (*env)
      puts(*env++);
  }
```

Compile the program. Next, create the program EXECL.C, which uses *execl* function to execute the child process:

```
#include <process.h>
#include <stdio.h>

void main(void)
  {
    printf("About to call child process\n\n");
    execl("CHILD.EXE", "CHILD.EXE",
      "AAA", "BBB", "CCC", NULL);
    printf("\n\nBack from child process—SHOULD NOT APPEAR\n");
  }
```

When you execute the EXECL program, your screen will display a message stating that it is about to call the child process. Next, the child process will run, displaying its command-line arguments and environment entries. After the child process ends, the parent process has been overwritten, so no addition processing occurs.

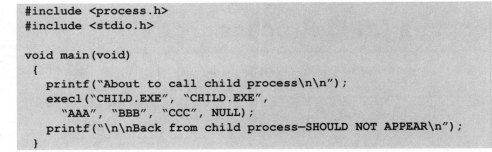

Using Other *execlxx* Functions

758

In Tip 752 you learned that the *execl* function lets you run a child process. If you examine the C run-time library you, will find several other *execlxx* functions, as shown here:

```
#include <stdio.h>
#include <process.h>

int execle(char *child, char *arg0,
    ..., char *argn, NULL, char *environ);

int execlp(char *child, char *arg0,
    ..., char *argn, NULL);

int execlpe(char *child, char *arg0,
    ..., char *argn, NULL, char *environ);
```

If the *execlxx* functionx are successful, they do not return. If an error occurs, the functions return the value −1 and set the global variable *errno* to one of the following:

E2BIG	Argument list too long
EINVAL	Invalid argument
ENOENT	Child program not found
ENOEXEC	Format error
ENOMEM	Insufficient memory

The parameters to these functions are similar to those used by *spawnl*, described in Tip 754, with the exception of the *environ* parameter, which contains a pointer to the child's environment entries. The difference between *execl* and *execlp* is that functions containing the letter p will search the command path for the child process. The following program, EXECLPE.C, illustrate the use of the *execlpe* function:

```c
#include <process.h>
#include <stdio.h>

void main(void)
{
   char *env[] = { "FILE=EXECLPE.C", "LANGUAGE=C",
                   "OS=DOS", NULL};

   execlpe("CHILD.EXE", "CHILD.EXE", "Using-spawnlpe",
      "BBB", NULL, env);
}
```

Using the *execvxx* Functions

In Tip 757 you learned how to use the *execl* function to create a child process. Likewise, in Tip 758 you used the different *execlxx* functions, which let you pass an array of environment entries to the child process and also let you use the command path to locate the child process. When you use the *execl* functions, you pass the command-line arguments as a list of NULL-terminated parameters. In addition to the *execlxx* functions, C provides a collection of *execvxx* functions, which let you pass the command-line parameters as array of character strings:

```c
#include <stdio.h>
#include <process.h>

int execv(char *child, char *argv[]);
int execve(char *child, char *argv[], char *env[]);
int execvp(char *child, char *argvp[]);
int execvpe(char *child, char *argv[], char *env[]);
```

If the *execvxx* functions are successful, they do not return. If an error occurs, the functions return the value −1 and set the global variable *errno* to one of the following:

E2BIG	Argument list too long
EINVAL	Invalid argument
ENOENT	Child program not found
ENOEXEC	Format error
ENOMEM	Insufficient memory

The parameters to the *execvxx* functions are similar to those passed to the *execlxx* functions, except that the command-line arguments are passed as an array of character strings. The following program, EXECVPE.C, illustrates the *execvpe* function:

```
#include <stdio.h>
#include <process.h>

void main(void)
  {
    char *env[] = { "FILENAME=SPAWNVXX.C", "OS=DOS",
                    "ROUTINE=EXECVPE", NULL };

    char *argv[] = { "CHILD.EXE", "AAA", "BBB", NULL };

    execvpe("CHILD.EXE", argv, env);
  }
```

760 Understanding Overlays

As you learned in the Memory section of this book, DOS-based programs are restricted to 640Kb. To support larger programs, older programs divided their code into fixed areas called *overlays*. As the program ran, it loaded different overlay sections as needed. Although overlays let programs be very large, they required the program to keep track of which overlays were currently loaded, as well as which overlays contained the desired functions. As you can guess, such processing could be difficult, requiring application programs to provide the memory management operations often provided by an operating system. To help your programs load and execute overlays, DOS provides a system service that loads an overlay file and then transfers control to the start of the file. For specifics on using DOS to load and execute overlays, refer to the book *DOS Programming: The Complete Reference* (Osborne/McGraw-Hill, 1991). Using DOS to manage overlays can become very difficult. If you are using Borland C++, however, your programs can perform overlay management using VROOOM, Borland's Virtual Run-time Object-Oriented Memory Manager to perform overlay management. For more information on VROOOMM, refer to the documentation that accompanied your compiler.

761 Understanding Interrupts

An *interrupt* is an event that causes the computer to temporarily stop the task it is currently performing so that it can work on a second task. When the interrupt's processing is complete, the computer resumes the original task as if the interrupt had never occurred. The PC supports *hardware* and *software* interrupts. The

DOS and BIOS section of this book discusses the use of software interrupts to access the DOS and BIOS interrupts. Hardware interrupts, on the other hand are generated by devices such as the disk drive or the PC's system clock. An *interrupt handler* is software that responds to a specific interrupt. Normally, interrupt handlers are written by experienced programmers who work in assembly language. However, newer C compilers let you write handlers within C. The first 1024 bytes of the PC's memory contain the segment and offset addresses (called *interrupt vectors*) for the PC's 256 interrupts. When a specific interrupt occurs, the PC pushes onto the stack the current instruction pointer (IP), code segment, and the flags register (machine state). The PC then finds the address of the corresponding interrupt handler using the interrupt vector. The interrupt handler then pushes the PC registers and begins its processing. After the interrupt handler's processing is complete, it pops the registers from the stack and then performs an IRET instruction, which pops the flags register, CS and IP. The following assembly language statements, for example, illustrate the layout of a typical interrupt handler:

```
; Save the registers on the stack
PUSH AX
PUSH BX
PUSH CX
PUSH DX
PUSH SI
PUSH DI
PUSH DS
PUSH ES

; Perform the interrupt handling instructions

; Pop the registers from the stack
POP ES
POP DS
POP DI
POP SI
POP DX
POP CX
POP BX
POP AX

; Return the previous task
IRET
```

When you define your own interrupt handler in this way, you then update the interrupt vector to point your own interrupt routine. Before your program ends, you must restore the interrupt vector to its original setting.

The PC Interrupts

C762

Within the PC, the first 1024 bytes of your computer's memory contain the addresses (vectors) of PC's 256 interrupts. Many of interrupts are not used and are available to your programs for custom purposes. Table 762 lists the PC interrupt vectors and their uses.

Interrupt	Purpose	Interrupt	Purpose
00H	Hardware divide by 0	01H	Hardware single-step trap
02H	Nonmaskable interrupt	03H	Debuggger breakpoint set
04H	Arithmetic overflow	05H	BIOS print screen
08H	IRQ0 clock tick	09H	IRQ1 keyboard
0AH	IRQ2	0BH	IRQ3 COM2
OCH	IRQ4 COM2	0DH	IRQ5 PC/AT LPT1
OEH	IRQ6 Diskette	0FH	IRQ7 LPT1
10H	BIOS video services	11H	BIOS equipment list
12H	BIOS memory size	13H	BIOS disk services
14H	BIOS comm services	15H	BIOS misc services
16H	BIOS keyboard services	17H	BIOS printer services
18H	Invoke ROM-BASIC	19H	System reboot
1AH	BIOS time of day	1BH	Ctrl-Break handler
1CH	Called by 08 handler	1DH	Video parameter table
1EH	Disk parameter table	1FH	Graphics character table
20H	DOS terminate program	21H	DOS system services
22H	Program terminate	23H	DOS Ctrl-Break
24h	DOS critical error	25H	DOS disk read
26H	DOS disk write	27H	DOS terminate resident
28H	DOS idle	29H	DOS fast putchar
2AH	MS-Net services	2EH	DOS primary loader
2FH	MS-DOS multiplex	33H	Mouse services
40H	Diskette vector	41H	Hard disk parameter table
42H	EGA BIOS redirection	43H	EGA parameter table
44H	EGA character table	4AH	PC/AT Int 70H alarm
5CH	NetBIOS services	67H	EMS services
70H	IRQ8 PC/AT real-time	71H	IRQ9 PC/AT redirect of INT 0AH
75H	IRQ13 PC/AT math coprocessor		

Table 762 *The PC's interrupt vector use.*

Using the *interrupt* Keyword

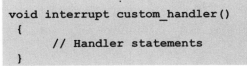

As you have learned, DOS lets you create your own interrupt handlers. If you are using Borland C++, the *interrupt* keyword makes it very easy to create an interrupt handler:

```
void interrupt custom_handler()
  {
       // Handler statements
  }
```

When the compiler encounters the *interrupt* keyword, the compiler inserts statements to push and pop registers as required and then later to return from the handler using an IRET. To understand the processing the *interrupt* keyword produces, create a program that contains the *custom_handler* shown above using the -S switch, as shown here:

```
C:\> BCC  -S  PROGRAM.C  <ENTER>
```

The –S switch directs the compiler to produce an assembly language output. If you examine the assembly language source file, you will see machine instructions similar to those shown in Tip 761.

Determining an Interrupt's Vector

As you have learned, an *interrupt vector* is the segment and offset address of the code that handles the interrupt. To help your programs determine an interrupt vector, many DOS-based compilers provide the *_dos_getvect* function:

```
#include <dos.h>

void interrupt(*_dos_getvect(unsigned interrupt_number))();
```

The *interrupt_number* specifies the desired interrupt (from 0 through 255). The function returns a pointer to an interrupt handler. The following program, GET_VECT.C, displays the vectors for all of the PC's interrupts:

```
#include <stdio.h>
#include <dos.h>

void main(void)
 {
   int i;

   for (i = 0; i <= 255; i++)
     printf("Interrupt: %x Vector: %lx\n",
       i, _dos_getvect(i));
 }
```

765 Setting an Interrupt Vector

When your programs create their own interrupt handlers, the program must assign the interrupt vector to point to their handler. To help your program's assign interrupt vectors, most DOS-based compilers provide the *_dos_setvect* function:

```
#include <dos.h>

void _dos_setvect(unsigned interrupt_number,
        void interrupt(*handler)());
```

The *interrupt_number* parameter specifies the interrupt whose vector you want to change. The *handler* parameter is a pointer to the interrupt handler. Tip 762 illustrates the use of the *_dos_setvect* function. When your program change an interrupt vector, it needs to save the vector's original settings so it can restore the original vector before ending. If a program ends without restoring the interrupt vector, your system can behave erratically.

766 Enabling and Disabling Interrupts

When your programs perform interrupt handling, there will be times when your programs will want to enable and disable interrupts. To help you control interrupts in this way, many DOS-based compilers provide the *_disable* and *_enable* macros:

```
#include <dos.h>

void _disable(void);
void _enable(void);
```

To run, the PC must generate key interrupts on a regular basis, so if your programs disable interrupts, they should minimize the amount of time for which interrupt are disabled. A common use of the *_disable* and *_enable* macros is when your programs change an interrupt vector using *_dos_setvect:*

```
_disable();
_dos_setvect(interrupt_number, handler);
_enable();
```

Creating a Simple Interrupt Handler

C767

As you have learned, creating interrupt handlers with the Borland C++ *interrupt* keyword becomes much easier. The following program, NOPRTSCR.C, creates an interrupt handler that replaces the BIOS print-screen interrupt handler, which prints the screen contents when you press the **SHIFT-PRTSC** keyboard combination. The program uses the *_dos_getvect* function to determine the original vector setting so it can restore the vector before the program ends. When you press **SHIFT-PRTSC** when the program is active, your interrupt handler gets invoked, which in turn displays a screen message stating that **SHIFT-PRTSC** was pressed. When you press **SHIFT-PRTSC** three times, the program will end:

```
#include <stdio.h>
#include <dos.h>
#include <conio.h>

int count = 0;

void interrupt handler(void)
  {
    count++;
  }

void main(void)
  {
    void interrupt (*original_handler)();

    int old_count = 0;

    original_handler = _dos_getvect(5);

    _disable();  // Turn off interrupts during _dos_setvect
    _dos_setvect(5, handler);
    _enable();
```

```
    printf("Press Shift-PrtSc three times or any key to end\n");

    while (count < 3)
      if (count != old_count)
        {
          printf("Shift-PrtSc pressed\n");
          old_count = count;
        }

    _disable();
    _dos_setvect(5, original_handler);
    _enable();
}
```

C 768 Chaining a Second Interrupt

In Tip 767 you learned how to write an interrupt handler for the BIOS print-screen operation. Depending on the function your program performs, there may be times when you want to execute the original interrupt handler after your handler completes its processing. In such instances, your programs can use the *_chain_interrupt* function:

```
#include <dos.h>

void _chain_interrupt(void (interrupt far *handler)());
```

The following program, COUNTDOS.C, for example, keeps a counter of the number of times your programs call specific DOS interrupts (by examining the AH register for INT 21). After the program ends, the program displays a count of the number services called:

```
#include <stdio.h>
#include <dos.h>
#include <dir.h>

int function[255];  // DOS services

void interrupt far (*original_handler)();

void interrupt far handler(void)
  {
    char i;

    asm { mov i, ah }
```

```
    function[i]++;
    _chain_intr(original_handler);
  }

void main(void)
  {
    int i;

    // Zero the function counts
    for (i = 0; i < 255; i++)
      function[i] = 0;

    original_handler = _dos_getvect(0x21);
    _disable();
    _dos_setvect(0x21, handler);
    _enable();

    printf("This is a message\n");
    fprintf(stdout, "This is a second message\n");
    printf("Current disk is %c\n", getdisk() + 'A');

    _disable();
    _dos_setvect(0x21, original_handler);
    _enable();

    for (i = 0; i <= 255; i++)
      if (function[i])
        printf("Function %x called %d times\n", i, function[i]);
  }
```

Generating an Interrupt

C 769

As you learned in the DOS & BIOS section of this book, the C run-time library provides the *intdos* and *int86* functions, which let your programs access the DOS and BIOS services. As your programs handle specific interrupts, there may be times when you want to generate an interrupt to test your handlers, or times when your programs need to invoke a specific interrupt. To do so, your programs can use the *geninterrupt* function:

```
#include <dos.h>

void geninterrupt(int interrupt);
```

The *interrupt* parameter specifies the desired interrupt. The following program, GENINTR.C, invokes the normally unused interrupt 0xFF to notify the program of a specific event:

```c
#include <stdio.h>
#include <dos.h>
#include <stdlib.h>

void interrupt far (*original_handler)();

void interrupt far handler(void)
 {
   printf("Some event just happened\n");
   _disable();
   _dos_setvect(0xFF, original_handler);
   _enable();

   exit(0);
 }

void main(void)
 {
  int i = 0;

  original_handler = _dos_getvect(0xFF);

  _disable();
  _dos_setvect(0xFF, handler);
  _enable();

  while (i++ < 100)
    ;
  geninterrupt(0xFF);
 }
```

C 770 Trapping the PC Timer

Many devices inside and outside of the PC have to perform operations at specific intervals. To accomplish this, the PC provides a timer chip that generates a signal 18.2 times per second. Each time the signal occurs, the PC generates interrupt 8, which updates the time-of-day clock, and interrupt 1CH, which your programs can trap. The following program, TIMER.C, traps interrupt 1CH each time it occurs. The interrupt handler counts the number of occurrences and after 15 seconds, toggles the value of the global variable *alphanum*. If the value of *alphanum* is 1, the program repeatedly displays the letters of the alphabet. If the value of *alphanum* is 0, the program displays the numbers 1 to 100:

```c
#include <stdio.h>
#include <dos.h>
#include <conio.h>

int alphanum = 0;
int counter = 0;

void interrupt far handler(void)
  {
    if (++counter == 273)   // 15 seconds
      {
        alphanum = !alphanum;   // Toggle
        counter = 0;
      }
  }

void main(void)
  {
    int i;

    void interrupt far (*original_handler)();

    original_handler = _dos_getvect(0x1C);


    _disable();
    _dos_setvect(0x1c, handler);
    _enable();

    while (! kbhit())
      if (alphanum)
        for (i = 'A'; i <= 'Z'; i++)
            printf("%c\n", i);
      else
        for (i = 0; i <= 100; i++)
            printf("%d\n", i);

    _disable();
    _dos_setvect(0x1c, original_handler);
    _enable();
  }
```

Understanding Critical Errors

771

As you know, when you try to use a floppy drive that does not contain a formatted disk, DOS displays an error message followed by the familiar:

```
Abort, Retry, Fail?
```

Such errors are called *critical errors* because DOS cannot resolve them without user help. When a critical error occurs, DOS invokes interrupt 24H. By trapping interrupt 24H, your programs can perform their own critical-error handling, possibly displaying an error message that is more meaningful or instructional to the user. When DOS invokes INT 24H, DOS places considerable information on the stack that describes the cause and source of the error. For a complete discussion of the stack contents and the operations your programs should perform if handling critical errors, refer to the book *DOS Programming: The Complete Reference*. As you will learn in Tip 772, most DOS-based C compilers provide run-time library functions that simplify critical-error handling.

Critical-Error Handling in C

772

As Tip 771 describes, a *critical error* is an error from which DOS cannot continue without user intervention. To help your C programs perform their own critical-error handling, most C compilers provide the following run-time library functions:

```
#include <dos.h>

void _harderr(int (*handler)());
void _hardresume(int ax_register);
void _hardreturn(int handler_value);
```

The *_harderr* function lets you specify the name of the function that will handle critical errors. The *_hardresume* function lets your programs return a status value to DOS. The value must be one of those listed in Table 772. The *_hardreturn* function, on the other hand, lets you return a value (any value) to your program.

Constant	Meaning
_HARDERR_ABORT	End the current program
_HARDERR_RETRY	Retry service causing the error
_HARDERR_FAIL	Fail the service causing the error
_HARDERR_IGNORE	Ignore the error

Table 772 *Constants used with _hardresume.*

The following program, ERSIMPLE.C, provides a simple critical-error handler that displays a message on the screen and then uses the *_hardresume* function to abort the program:

```c
#include <stdio.h>
#include <dos.h>
#include <conio.h>

void far handler(unsigned device_error, unsigned error_code,
  unsigned far *device_header)
 {
   cputs("Critical error ending program\n");
   _hardresume(_HARDERR_ABORT);    // Abort
 }

void main(void)
 {
   FILE *fp;

   _harderr(handler);

   fp = fopen("A:SOMEFILE.EXT", "r");

   printf("Program message...\n");
   fclose(fp);
 }
```

A More Complete Critical-Error Handler

773

In Tip 772 you created a simple critical-error handler that displayed a message and then ended the program causing the error. If you take a close look at the critical-error handler, you will find that it supports three parameters:

```c
void far handler(unsigned device_error, unsigned error_code,
    unsigned far *device_header)
```

When DOS invokes the critical-error handler, DOS places information about the error on to the stack. The *device_error* parameter contains a error value that DOS would normally pass to a critical-error handler in the AX register. If bit 7 of the *device_error* parameter is set, the error is a disk error. Table 773.1 lists the values that may be assigned to *device_error*. The *error_code* parameter contains the error information DOS would normally pass to the critical-error handler in the DI register. Table 773.2 lists the values DOS passes in DI for disk errors. Finally, the *device_header* parameter is a pointer to the device driver header for the device generating the error.

Bit(s)	Value	Meaning
0	0	Read error
	1	Write error
1–2	00	DOS error
	01	FAT error
	10	Directory error
	11	File error
3	0	Fail operation not allowed
	1	Fail operation allowed
4	0	Retry operation not allowed
	1	Retry operation allowed
5	0	Ignore operation not allowed
	1	Ignore operation allowed
7	0	Disk error
	1	Not disk error

Table 773.1 *Error values in the error_code variable.*

Value	Meaning	Value	Meaning
0	Write protected	1	Unknown drive
2	Drive not ready	3	Unknown command
4	CRC data error	5	Invalid request structure
6	Seek error	7	Unknown media type
8	Sector not found	9	Printer out of paper
10	Write fault	11	Read fault
12	General failure	15	Invalid disk change

Table 773.2 *Disk error values passed in the DI register.*

To help you better understand how your programs can use these values, the companion disk that accompanies this book contains the program CRITERR.C, which displays the values these variables contain.

Restoring Altered Interrupts

774

When your programs exit, DOS automatically restores the CTRL-BREAK interrupt handler, the program termination handler, and the critical error handlers to their original settings (before the program was run). Depending on your programs, there may be times when you want DOS to restore these settings before your program ends. For such cases, many compilers provide the _cexit function:

```
#include <process.h>

void _cexit(void);
```

The *_cexit* function does not terminate your program. Instead, it simply directs DOS to restore the interrupt vectors discussed. The function will not close files or flush disk buffers. If your compiler does not provide the *_cexit* function, you can write such a function yourself that restores the interrupts using the original settings (your program saved before changing the interrupt vectors).

Creating a Ctrl-Break Handler

By default, when the users presses the **CTRL-BREAK** keyboard combination, your program will end. In many cases you will not want the user to have the ability to end the program at any time by pressing **CTRL-BREAK**. As a solution, your programs can define their own interrupt handler using the *ctrlbrk* function:

```
#include <dos.h>

void ctrlbrk(int (*handler)(void));
```

To create your own interrupt handler, you define a function that you want invoked each time the user presses **CTRL-BREAK** and then pass the name of the function to the *ctrlbrk* function. The following program, CTRLBRK.C, creates a custom **CTRL-BREAK** handler:

```
#include <stdio.h>
#include <dos.h>

int Ctrl_Handler(Void)
  {
    printf("\007Press Enter to end the program\n");
    return(1);
  }

void main(void)
  {
    Ctrlbrk(Ctrl_Handler);

    printf("Press Enter to end the program\n");

    while (getchar() != '\n');
      ;
  }
```

The program loops until the user presses **ENTER**. Each time the user presses **CTRL-BREAK**, the function **CTRL_HANDLER** is invoked, which beeps and displays a message that directs the user to press **ENTER** to end the program. In this case, the function returns the value 1. If the handler returns any value other than 0, the program continues. If the handler returns 0, the program ends.

C776 Things Your Critical-Error Handler Can Do

When DOS invokes a critical-error handler, you need to understand that your system is somewhat unstable—an operating system service has abruptly ended. Within your critical-error handler, you should restrict your use of DOS services to the services listed in Table 776.

Service	Function	Service	Function
01H	Character input	02H	Character output
03H	Aux port input	04H	Aux port output
05H	Printer output	06H	Direct console I/O
07H	Character input	08H	Character input
09H	String output	0AH	Buffered keyboard input
0BH	Test input state	0CH	Flush buffer and input
3300H	Get Ctrl-C state	3301H	Set Ctrl-C state
3305H	Get startup disk	3306H	Get DOS version
50H	Set PSP	51H	Get PSP
59H	Get extended error	62H	Get PSP

Table 776 *Usable DOS services in a critical-error handler.*

If your programs must perform I/O within a critical-error handler, consider using the I/O functions in conio.h.

C777 Improving Performance Using Instruction Set Selection

By default, most DOS-based compilers generate programs that can run on all Intel-based systems, from the 8088 through the Pentium. If you know in advance that a program will only be run on a specific machine, you can improve the program's performance by using the instruction set of a more advanced machine. For example, the 80386 provides instructions that simply aren't available on an 8088. Using one of these 80386-based instructions might replace several equivalent 8088 instructions. However, when you take advantage of such instructions, your programs will no longer run on the older machines. To generate executable code for a specific machine, refer to your compiler's command-line switches. For example, the –1 switch directs the Borland C++ compiler to generate instructions for the 80186 and 80286:

```
C:\> BCC -1 FILENAME.C  <ENTER>
```

Inlining Intrinsic Functions

778

To improve performance, many C compilers let you replace functions with *inline code*. In addition to letting you use the *inline* keyword before the functions you create, many C compilers let you replace intrinsic run-time library functions with an inline counterpart. The intrinsic functions that you can inline will differ from one compiler to the next. Refer to your compiler documentation to determine the available functions. In the case of the Borland C++ compiler, the following intrinsic functions can be placed inline:

memchr	memcmp	memcpy	memset	stpcpy
strcat	strchr	strcmp	strcpy	strlen
strncat	strncmp	strncpy	strnset	strrchr
rotl	rotr	fabs	alloc	

To direct your compiler to place these functions inline, you can use the –Oi compiler switch or the *#pragma* intrinsic, discussed in Tip 779.

Enabling and Disabling Intrinsic Functions

779

In Tip 778 you learned that many C compilers let you replace specific intrinsic functions with inline code. Using compiler command-line switches, you can direct the compiler to place intrinsic functions inline. In addition, many preprocessors support the *intrinsic pragma*, which lets you enable or disable intrinsic inlining:

```
#pragma    intrinsic  function      // Enables inlining
#pragma    intrinsic -function      // Disables inlining
```

The following statement, for example, directs the compiler to generate inline code for the *strlen* function:

```
#pragma    intrinsic  strlen
```

When you use the intrinsic pragma, you must precede the pragma with a function prototype. The compiler encounters the pragma, the compiler will replace the function name with an equivalent name that begins and ends with an underscore. In the case of the *strlen* function, the compiler will generate the constant *_strlen_*, as shown here:

```
#define strlen _strlen_
```

C 780 Understanding Fast Function Calls

When your program invokes a function, C passes parameters to functions on the stack. As discussed in the Functions section of this book, this stack use is responsible for most of the overhead that corresponds to a function call. In an attempt to make function invocations faster, some C compilers provide a *_fastcall* modifier, which you can place before a function name:

```
int _fastcall some_function(int a, int b);
```

The following program, FASTCALL.C, illustrates the use of the *_fastcall* modifier:

```
#include <stdio.h>
#include <time.h>

int _fastcall add_fast(int a, int b)
 {
   return(a + b);
 }

int add_slow(int a, int b)
 {
   return(a + b);
 }

void main(void)
 {
   unsigned long int i, result;

   clock_t start_time, stop_time;

   printf("Processing...\n");
   start_time = clock();

   for (i = 0; i < 2000000L; i++)
     result = add_fast(i, -i);
```

```
stop_time = clock();
printf("Processing time for fast call %d ticks\n",
  stop_time - start_time);

start_time = clock();

for (i = 0; i < 2000000L; i++)
  result = add_slow(i, -i);

stop_time = clock();
printf("Processing time for normal call %d ticks\n",
  stop_time - start_time);
}
```

Rules for _fastcall Parameter Passing

781

In Tip 780 you learned that many compilers support *fastcall* function modifier, which directs the compiler to pass parameters to the function using registers. Depending on the target machine, the number of registers available for parameters will differ. In the case of Borland's C++ compiler, your programs can only pass three parameters via registers. Table 781 specifies how parameters are passed to functions when the *fastcall* modifier is used for Borland's C++ compiler.

Parameter Type	Registers Used
char (signed and unsigned)	AL, DL, BL
int (signed and unsigned)	AX, DX, BX
long (signed and unsigned)	DX:AX
near pointer	AX, DX, BX
Others	Passed on the stack

Table 781 *Registers used for parameter passing with the _fastcall modifier.*

Understanding Invariant Code

782

As you examine compiler directives that affect optimization, you may encounter the term *invariant code*. In general, invariant code refers to statements that appear within a loop whose values do not change. For example, the following *for* loop assigns the result of the multiplication $a * b * c$ to each element of an array:

```
for (i = 0; i < 100; i++)
    array[i] = a * b * c;
```

Because the values of *a*, *b*, and *c* do not change within the loop, the result of the multiplication is *invariant* (it does not change). As you program, you should watch for invariant code. When you find it, you can normally improve your program's performance by changing your program in some way. In the case of the previous *for* loop, you can improve your program's performance by replacing the multiplication with its result, as shown here:

```
result = a * b * c;
for (i = 0; i < 100; i++)
    array[i] = result;
```

To improve program performance, many compilers will test for invariant code, replacing it within the target object code with a noninvariant equivalent. Ideally, you should find and correct invariant code yourself. However, using command-line switches, you may be able to direct your compiler to perform such substitutions for you during compilation.

783 Understanding Redundent Load Suppression

As you have learned, to improve performance, the C compiler often loads values into registers. When the compiler performs *redundant load suppression*, it keeps track of the values it is has already placed into registers and refers to the registers, as opposed to loading the value a second time. Using redundant load suppression the compiler prevents duplicate load operations, which improves your program's performance. The disadvantage of using load suppression is that your programs may slightly longer to compile. As a rule, however, you should always direct the compiler to perform load suppression.

784 Understanding Code Compaction

When you examine your compiler documentation, you might encounter the term *code compaction*. In general, code compaction eliminates redundant statements by branching to the previous code. For example, consider the following program, COMPACT.C:

```
#include <stdio.h>

void main(void)
  {
    int a = 1, b, c, d;
```

```
    switch (a) {
     case 1: a = 5;
             b = 6;
             c = 7;
             d = 8;
             break;
     case 2: b = 6;
             c = 7;
             d = 8;
             break;
     };
    }
```

If you examine the *switch* statement, you will find that the statements the program performs for each case are very similar. Rather than duplicating the assignment statements in both locations, the compiler might place a JMP instruction that branches back to the statement **b = 6**, which occurs in the first case at the start of the second case.

Understanding Loop Compaction

785

If you examine the *for* loops that occur throughout your programs, you may find that most loops manipulate a strings or other arrays. When your program assigns the same value to every element in an array, the C compiler can optimize your program's performance by replacing the loop with one of the 80x86 ST*xxx* instructions. For example, the following *for* loop initializes the array *null_string* to NULL:

```
    for (i = 0; i < sizeof(null_string); i++)
        null_string[i] = NULL;
```

If you examine the assembly language output produced by the compiler, you will find that the compiler has eliminated the loop, using the STOSW instruction. Such compiler substitutions are called *loop compaction*.

Understanding Loop Induction and Strength Reduction

786

Loop induction and strength reduction are techniques used to optimize loops within a program. The compiler normally performs such operations when arrays are manipulated within a loop. For example, consider the following loop, which assigns values to array elements:

```
for (i = 0; i < 128; i++)
   array[i] = 0;
```

For each reference to the array, the compiler must perform a multiplication operation in order to determine the correct element (*base* + *i* * *sizeof*(*array_type*)). As an alternative to using the array, the compiler may instead use a pointer, as shown here:

```
end = &array[128];

for (ptr = array; ptr < end; ptr++)
   *ptr = 0;
```

By eliminating the slow multiplication, the compiler improves the program's performance. The process of creating new variables out of loop variables is called *loop induction*. Because the inducted variables are normally less complex than the variables they are replacing, the newly created loop has introduced a *strength reduction*.

C 787 Understanding Common Subexpression Elimination

If your programs work with arrays, there may be times when you can improve your program's performance by eliminating common subexpressions. For example, consider the following *if* statement, which tests whether an array element contains an upper or lowercase A:

```
if ((array[i] == 'A') || (array[i] == 'a'))
```

For each test, the compiler must resolve the array element by performing a multiplication (*base* + *i* * *sizeof*(*array_type*)). A faster implementation, however, would replace the array reference with a pointer, as shown here:

```
ptr = &array[i];
if ((*ptr == 'A') || (*ptr == 'a'))
```

By replacing the common subexpression with a faster alternative, the program's performance is improved. In some cases, however, trying to eliminate common subexpressions can make your program more difficult to understand. Many C compilers will detect opportunities for subexpression elimination and perform the operations for you within the resulting code. As you work with compound conditions, be aware that you might be able to improve your program performance by eliminating or reducing subexpressions.

Understanding Standard Conversions

C788

When you perform arithmetic operation on different value types, the C compiler often *promotes* the lower type value. To help you understand the standard C conversions, consider the following rules. C applies the rules from top to bottom:

- With the exception of *unsigned short*, all small integer values are promoted to int—unsigned short is promoted to *unsigned int*.
- If either operand is *long double*, the other is promoted to *long double*.
- If either operand is *double*, the other is promoted to *double*.
- If either operand is *float*, the other is promoted to *float*.
- If either operand is *unsigned long*, the other is promoted to *unsigned long*.
- If either operand is *long*, the other is promoted to *long*.
- If either operand is *unsigned*, the other is promoted to *unsigned*.
- Otherwise, both operands are treated as type *int*.

Understanding C's Four Basic Types

C789

As you examine complex declarations in C, keep in mind that C supports four basic types: *void, scalar, function,* and *aggregate.* The type *void* specifies the absence of values. For example, *void* in a parameter list states that a function does not receive any parameters. Likewise, *void* in front of a function name specifies that a function does not return a value. *Scalar* values include arithmetic, enumerated, pointer, and reference values. A *function* type specifies a function that returns a specific type. Finally, a an *aggregate* type specifies an array, union, structure, or C++ class. As you examine complex declarations, try to map the declaration to one of this four supported types.

C 790 Fundamental versus Derived Types

As you examine complex declarations in C, understand that C supports *fundamental* and *derived* types. C's fundamental data types include the following: *void*, *char*, *double*, *float*, and *int*. In addition, C lets you apply the modifiers *long*, *short*, *signed* and *unsigned* to the fundamental types. Derived types, on the other hand, include arrays, classes, functions, pointers, structures, and unions to other types. The types *char*, *int*, *long* and *short* are integral types. As you examine declarations, the following integral types are equivalent:

```
char, signed char       // Normally a compiler default
int, signed int
unsigned, unsigned int
short, short int, signed short int
unsigned short, unsigned short int
long, long int, signed long int
unsigned long, unsigned long int
```

C 791 Understanding Initializers

Initializers are the values assigned to variables at declaration. When you use initializers, keep the following rules in mind:

- If an arithmetic type is not explicitly initialized, most compilers will initialize the variable with 0.

- If a pointer type is not explicitly initialized, most compilers will initialize the pointer with NULL.

- If the number of initializers exceeds the number of variable to be initialized, the compiler will generate an error.

- All expressions used to initialize a variable must be constants (not required for C++) if the initializers are for a static object, array, structure, or union.

- If the variable declared has block scope and has not been declared as external, the declaration cannot have an initializer.

- If fewer initializers are provided than are required, the remainder of the values are initialized following the compiler's default initialization technique.

Understanding Linkage

792

As you have learned, the linker combines code from your programs, object files, and libraries. Depending on the files used, there may be times when two or more functions in the linked files have the same name. *Linkage* is the process of determining which function is applied to a reference. In C, identifiers have one of three possible linkage attributes: *external*, *internal*, and *none*. An identifier with *external linkage* represents the same object throughout all the files that make up a program. An identifier with *internal linkage* represents the same object within one file. An identifier with *no linkage* is unique throughout the files. The linker uses an identifier's linkage to determine to which function an identifier is associated. The linker uses the following linkage rules:

- If an identifier is declared as *static*, the identifier will have *internal linkage*.
- If an identifier appears with internal and external linkage, C will use *internal linkage*, and C++ will use *external linkage*.
- If an identifier is declared as *extern*, the identifier has the same linkage as any visible declaration with file scope—if no such declaration exists, the identifier has *external linkage*.
- If a function identifier does not have a storage class specifier, the identifier has the same linkage as if *extern* was used.
- If an object identifier is declared without a storage class specifier, the identifier has external linkage.
- If an identifier declared to be other than an object or function has no linkage.
- Function parameters have no linkage.
- Identifiers having block scope declared without a storage class *extern* have no linkage.

Understanding Tentative Declarations

793

A *tentative declaration* is an external data declaration that has no storage class specifier and no initialization. For example, assume the compiler encounters the following declaration:

```
int value;
```

If the compiler later encounters a definition for the variable, the compiler treats the variable as if it were preceded by *extern*. If the compiler reaches the end of the translation unit without encountering a definition, the compiler allocates memory for the variable. The following program, TENTATVE.C, creates a tentative variable declaration for the variable *value*:

```
#include <stdio.h>

int value;

void main(void)
  {
    printf("%d\n", value);
  }

int value = 1001;
```

When the compiler encounters the definition of the variable *value* that initializes the variable to 1001, the compiler converts the first declaration of value from tentative to a full definition.

C 794 Contrasting Declarations and Definitions

Many of the tips presented throughout this book use the terms "declaration" and "definition." In general, a *declaration* introduces one or more identifiers within a program. A *definition*, on the other hand, directs the compiler to actually allocate memory for the object. For example, you can consider a function prototype as a declaration and the function header and code as a definition. C classifies declarations as *defining* or *referencing*. A *defining* declaration both declares one or more identifiers and defines the amount of memory allocated to the object. A *referencing* declaration on the other hand, simply introduces an identifier. Within C, the following objects can be declared:

arrays	classes	class members
enumerated	enumerated tags	constants
functions	labels	macros
structures	structure members	types
unions	union members	variables

Understanding lvalues

When your program works with pointers, you may encounter compiler error messages that state *an lvalue is required.* An lvalue is an expression that the compiler can use to locate an object. You can consider lvalues as expressions that would be valid on the left side of the assignment operator. The following are valid lvalues:

```
variable = value;

*variable = value;

variable[i] = value;
```

It is important to note, however, that each of the lvalues just shown could have been on the right side of the assignment operator as well. An lvalue simply provides a value the compiler can use to locate an object in memory. C supports *modifiable* and *nonmodifiable* lvalues. A *modifiable* lvalue is a pointer value that can be changed to point to a different value—such as a pointer. A *nonmodifiable* lvalue, on the other hand, cannot be changed. A constant pointer, for example, is a nonmodifiable lvalue.

Understanding rvalues

When you compile your programs, you might encounter a compiler error message that states that an unexpected *rvalue* was encountered. An rvalue is an expression that appears on the right side of an equal sign. The following expressions are examples of rvalues:

```
result = value;

result = 1001;

result = value + 1001;
```

The following statements, however, are invalid because they do not specify a memory location to which C can assign a value:

```
1001 = result;

value + 1001 = result;
```

Such errors normally appear when users are trying to create pointers:

```
*(value + 1001) = result;
```

797 Using Segment Register Keywords

As you have learned, the PC uses four specific registers to locate your program's code, data, and stack. Using the *segread* run-time library function, your programs can determine the register settings. In addition, many DOS-based compilers provide the following keywords:

Keyword	Meaning
_cs	Creates a pointer to code segment
_ds	Creates a pointer to data segment
_es	Creates a pointer to extra segment
_ss	Creates a pointer to stack segment

The following declaration, for example, creates a pointer to the stack segment:

```
char _ss *my_stack_pointer;
```

Depending on the current memory model, the pointers will contain near or far pointers as required.

798 Be Aware of Far Pointers

In the Pointers section of this book you learned that a far pointer is a 32-bit pointer that contains a 16-bit segment and a 16-bit offset address. Far pointers let your programs access the PC's 1Mb conventional memory range. When you use far pointers, however, you need to understand how the pointer value wraps when the offset value exceeds its 16-bit limit. For example, assume the far *char* pointer *location* contains the following value:

```
location = 0x1000FFFE;    // Segment 0x1000 Offset FFFE
```

If you increment the pointer, its value becomes the following:

```
location = 0x1000FFFF;    // Segment 0x1000 Offset FFFF
```

If the pointer is incremented once more, the possible error results:

```
location = 0x10000000;    // Segment 0x1000 Offset 0000
```

Note that the offset value has wrapped back to 0, but the segment value has not changed. In this way, the pointer has wrapped back to the start of the 64Kb segment address. If you need the pointer to move the start of the next segment, use a *huge* pointer instead.

Understanding Normalized Pointers

As you know, the PC addresses memory locations using segment and offset addresses. The PC supports up to 65,636 segment addresses. Each segment address starts at a 16-byte address 0, 16, 32, 48, and so on. If you multiply the 16 bytes times the 65,536 segments, the result is a 1Mb address space. Given a segment address, an offset address lets you choose one of 65,536 possibly locations within the segment. When you use segment and offset addresses, every location in memory can be addressed using different segment and offset combinations. For example, assume you want to address location 48 in memory. You can use any one of the following segment/offset combinations:

> Segment 0 Offset 48
>
> Segment 1 Offset 32
>
> Segment 2 Offset 16
>
> Segment 3 Offset 0

Because each memory location can be referenced differently, it is possible for two far pointers to reference the same memory location, but contain different values. Consider the following pointer assignments:

```
char far *ptr1 = 0x00000030;   // Seg 0 offset 48
char far *ptr2 = 0x00030000;   // Segment 3 offset 0
```

Both pointers will reference the same memory location. However if your program compares the pointer values, the values are not equal. A *normalized* pointer eliminates such disparity by always storing values such that a 16-byte offset is used. In this way, segment addresses are always stored using the segment nearest to the value. In the previous case, the normalized pointer would contain segment 3 offset 0.

C 800

Math Coprocessor Statements

A floating-point (or math) processor is a specialized chip that contains instructions that can perform arithmetic operations such as division, multiplication, and even square-root calculations very quickly using floating-point values. If you are using an 8088, 80286, or 80386, you need to purchase a floating-point coprocessor (an 8087, 80287, or 80387). If you are using a 80846DX, the floating-point processor is built into the chip. Because they only perform floating-point operations, the math coprocessors can perform the operations very quickly. If your computer has a math coprocessor, you should direct your compiler to generate instructions that use the coprocessor. Depending on your compiler, the switches you must use to generate instructions for a floating-point coprocessor will differ. To allow programs to run on systems that don't have a math coprocessor, most compilers do not, by default, generate floating-point instructions. If you are using Borland C++, the compiler supports several /FP*x* switches that let you direct the compiler to always use floating-point instructions, to never use floating-point instructions, or to insert instructions that use the floating-point processor if one is present and if not, to perform the operations using software. The floating-point switches you select will affect your program size and speed. Refer to your compiler documentation for more information on your compiler's floating-point switches.

C 801

Understanding *cdecl* and *pascal* in Variables

As you examine programs that use mixed-language modules such as Pascal and C, you might encounter variables declared with the *pascal* and *cdecl* modifiers. To maintain compatibility with Pascal identifiers, the *pascal* modifier directs the compiler to ignore case insensitivity and not to precede the identifier with a leading underscore. The *cdecl* modifier, on the other hand, directs compiler to ensure case sensitivity and include leading underscores. The following program, for example, declares an external variable named *number* that is defined within a Pascal program:

```
#include <stdio.h>

extern int pascal number;

void main(void)
  {
    printf("The value is %d\n", number);
  }
```

Preventing Circular Includes

C 802

As your programs make more extensive use of header files (C++ programs often define classes in header files), there may be times when a file that you include includes a second header file, which in turn includes the same header file. As the preprocessor performs the inclusions, it can end up in a circular operation. To reduce the possibility of such operations, your header files can declare a macro when they are processed that prevents them from being processed a second time. For example, the following header file uses the macro *MY_STUFF_DEFINED* to determine whether its contents have already been processed:

```
#ifndef MY_STUFF_DEFINED
#define MY_STUFF_DEFINED 1

 // Other include statements

#endif
```

In this case, the first time the header file is processed, the macro is defined. If the header file is included a second time, its contents will not be processed, due to the *#ifndef* directive.

Getting Started with C++

C++ 803 What Is C++?

C++ is a programming language developed by Dr. Bjarne Stroustrup at AT&T Bell Labs that builds upon the C programming language to add object-oriented capabilities and other enhancements. C++ can be called a superset of C because the features of the C programming language that you have learned throughout this book are supported by C++. As you will learn, however, C++ is more than just an "object-oriented C." The language adds many new features that improve your capabilities. If you are using a C++ compiler, most of the programs presented in the first part of this book should successfully compile and execute with no changes. The tips presented in this section start with the C++ basics and then build on your knowledge of C. By the time your reach Tip 1001, you should be very proficient in C and C++.

C++ 804 How Do C++ Source Files Differ?

In general, there are no differences between C and C++ source files. The compiler directives such as *#include* and *#define* are fully supported by both languages. With respect to naming, many programmers use the CPP extension to differentiate C and C++ source files. Everything you learned in the first part of this book still applies as you begin to create C++ programs. You can include header files, you can link object code libraries, and so on.

C++ 805 Getting Started with a Simple C++ Program

In Tip 3 you created your first C program, which used *printf* to display a message on the screen:

```
#include <stdio.h>

void main(void)
  {
    printf("Jamsa's 1001 C/C++ Tips!");
  }
```

The following C++ program, SIMPLE.CPP, performs identical processing:

```
#include <iostream.h>

void main(void)
  {
    cout << "Jamsa's 1001 C/C++ Tips!";
  }
```

This program uses the C++ *cout* I/O stream, discussed in Tip 806. If you are using Borland C++, compile this program as follows:

```
C:\> BCC SIMPLE.CPP  <ENTER>
```

Understanding the *cout* I/O Stream

In Tip 805 the sample program used the *cout* I/O stream to write a character string to the screen display:

```
cout << "Jamsa's 1001 C/C++ Tips!"
```

Redirecting output to the *cout* I/O stream is the same as using *printf* to write output to stdout. The double less-than symbols is not the bitwise left-shift operator. Instead, the symbols are the output operator that specifies to which stream the data is being sent. The following program, COUT.CPP, uses the C++ output operator to display several different messages:

```
#include <iostream.h>

void main(void)
  {
    cout << "This is line one.\n";
    cout << "This text is on ";
    cout << "line two.\n";
    cout << "This is the last line.";
  }
```

When you compile and execute this program, your screen will display the following:

```
C:\> COUT  <ENTER>
This is line one.
This text is on line two.
This is the last line.
```

C++ 807 Writing Values and Variables with *cout*

As you have learned, the *cout* output stream lets your program display output to the screen display. The previous programs have used *cout* to display character strings. The following program, COUT_NUM.CPP, uses *cout* to display character strings and numbers:

```
#include <iostream.h>

void main(void)
  {
    cout << "cout lets you display strings, ints, and floats\n";
    cout << 1001;
    cout << "\n";
    cout << 1.2345;
  }
```

When you compile and execute this program, your screen will display the following output:

```
C:\> COUT_NUM    <ENTER>
cout lets display strings, ints, and floats
1001
1.2345
```

C++ 808 Combining Different Value Types with *cout*

In Tip 807 you learned that the *cout* I/O stream lets your programs display all types of values. The program presented used several statements to display its output:

```
    cout << "cout lets you display strings, ints, and floats\n";
    cout << 1001;
    cout << "\n";
    cout << 1.2345;
```

As it turns out, *cout* lets you place different value types in the output stream in one statement, as shown in the following program, COUT_ONE.CPP:

```
#include <iostream.h>

void main(void)
  {
      cout << "cout displays strings " << 1001 << "\n" << 1.2345;
  }
```

Displaying Hexadecimal and Octal Values

As you have learned, the *cout* I/O stream lets your programs display values type *int* and *float*. When you use *printf* to display integer values, you can use the *%x* and *%o* format specifiers to display the values in hexadecimal and octal. When your programs use *cout* to display output, they can use the dec, oct, and hex modifiers, as shown in the following program, COUT_HEX.C:

```
#include <iostream.h>

void main(void)
  {
    cout << "Decimal value " << dec << 0xFF;
    cout << "\nOctal value " << oct << 10;
    cout << "\nHexadecimal value " << hex << 255;
  }
```

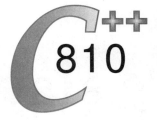

Redirecting *cout*

As you have learned, your programs can use the *cout* I/O stream to display output, just as if the output had been written to *stdout*. Therefore, if you have a program that uses *cout*, you can redirect the program's output to a file or to some other device. The following program, 1_TO_100.CPP, uses *cout* to display the numbers 1 to 100:

```
#include <iostream.h>

void main(void)
  {
    int i;
```

```
    for (i = 1; i <= 100; i++)
      cout << i  << '\n';
  }
```

Using the DOS output redirection operator, you can redirect the program's output to a file, as shown here:

```
C:\> 1_TO_100 >> FILENAME.EXT  <ENTER>
```

811 If You Like *printf*, Use *printf*

Several of the previous tips have performed their output using the *cout* I/O stream. If you feel more comfortable using the *printf* function, use *printf*. In later tips you will learn how to format output your program displays better with *cout*. At that time, you might choose to use *cout* for all your output. The following program, USE_BOTH.CPP, displays output using *cout* and *printf*. As a rule, however, to make your programs easier to understand, you should pick one technique and stick with it.

```cpp
#include <iostream.h>
#include <stdio.h>

void main(void)
  {
    cout << "Jamsa's ";
    printf("1001 ");
    cout << "C/C++ Tips!";
  }
```

812 Writing Output to *cerr*

As you know, when your programs write output to the stderr file handle, the output cannot be redirected from the screen. If you are using C++ I/O streams to perform your input and output, your programs can write output to *cerr*. The following program, USE_CERR.CPP, uses the *cerr* I/O stream to prevent the program's output from being redirected:

```cpp
#include <iostream.h>
#include <stdio.h>

void main(void)
  {
```

```
  cout << "Jamsa's ";
  printf("1001 ");
  cout << "C/C++ Tips!";
}
```

Getting Input with *cin*

As you have learned, the *cout* I/O stream lets your programs display output to *stdout*. In a similar way, your C++ programs can get input using the *cin* I/O stream. The following program, USE_CIN.CPP, uses *cin* to get input for several different variable types:

```
#include <iostream.h>

void main(void)
  {
    int age;
    float salary;
    char name[128];

    cout << "Enter your first name age salary: ";
    cin >> name >> age >> salary;

    cout << name << ' ' << age << ' ' << salary;
  }
```

How *cin* Selects Data Fields

In Tip 813 you used the *cin* I/O stream to read the user's name, age, and salary on one line:

```
    cin >> name >> age >> salary;
```

When your programs use *cin* to read input, you need to understand how *cin* parses input. Unless told otherwise, *cin* uses white space (a blank, tab, or newline) to delimit input fields. As such, if the user were to type his full name (such as John Smith) in the previous operation, *cin* would use the first name for the *name* variable and the last name for the *age* variable, and the I/O operation would be in error. In later tips, you will learn how to perform formatted input using *cin*.

815 How *cin*, *cout*, *cerr* Know Value Types

As you have learned, your programs can use the *cin, cout,* and *cerr* I/O streams to perform I/O operations to stdin, stdout, and stderr. Using these I/O streams, you can perform I/O operations with character strings, integers, and floating-point values. When your C programs perform I/O operations using *printf* and *scanf,* the functions use the format specifiers to determine the value types (such as *string, int,* and so on). When you perform input and output operations with the C++ I/O streams, the compiler provides information about each value's type, so there is no need for a format specifier. An interesting exercise is to generate and examine an assembly language listing for a file such as USE_CIN.CPP that uses *cin* and *cout*:

```
C:\> BCC -S USE_CIN.CPP  <ENTER>
```

816 Performing Output Using *clog*

As you have learned, C++ provides the *cin, cout,* and *cerr* I/O streams that correspond to stdin, stdout, and stderr. In addition, C++ provides a fourth I/O stream called *clog*. The *clog* I/O stream is similar to *cerr*, except that it performs buffered output. The following program, CLOG.CPP uses the *clog* I/O stream to display a message:

```cpp
#include <iostream.h>

void main(void)
  {
    clog << "Some strange processing error";
  }
```

817 *cin*, *cout*, *cerr* and *clog* Are Class Instances

Several of the preceding tips have performed I/O operations using *cin, cout, cerr,* and *clog*. It is important to know that these I/O stream identifiers are not magic operators that are built into C++. Instead, they are instances of an *I/O class*.

In later tips, you will learn that a *class* defines a template that contains data and methods (functions or operations that work on the data). The class, therefore, is the C++ fundamental mechanism for object-oriented programming. When you start creating your own classes, you can relax, knowing you have been using several classes since the time your compiled your first program. The double less-than (<<) and double greater-than (>>) symbols are simply class operators. If these terms seem confusing, relax—we'll cover them in detail later. For now, however, you can tell people you've been using C++ classes and objects!

Flushing Output with *flush*

As you have learned, your programs can use the *cout* I/O stream to output data to *stdout* and the *clog* I/O stream to perform buffered output to *stderr*. When you perform buffered output, the output might not appear on the screen as soon as you would like. Normally, output is not flushed until a carriage return is encountered or an input operation occurs. In such cases, your programs can use *flush* to immediately flush the output from the buffer. The following program, FLUSH.CPP, illustrates the use of *flush* to flush data to *stdout* and *stderr*:

```cpp
#include <iostream.h>

void main(void)
  {
    cout << "This immediately appears" << flush;
    clog << "\nSo does this..." << flush;
  }
```

What's In iostream.h?

All of the C++ programs presented thus far have included the header file iostream.h instead of the file stdio.h. The I/O streams *cin, cout, cerr,* and *clog* are actually class instances. The file iostream.h defines the corresponding stream class and these four identifiers. Do not look in the file iostream.h yet! Its contents are complicated and might scare you back into programming with BASIC! By the time you finish this book's tips, however, you will be able to traverse the file's contents with ease and understanding. For now, however, if anyone asks, tell them that the file iostream.h defines the class library for screen and keyboard I/O.

820 C++ Requires Function Prototypes

In the Functions section of this book you learned that a *function prototype* specifies the type of parameters a function receives, as well as the type of value the function returns. When you don't specify a function prototype for a function within C, the compiler will generate and display a warning message. In C++, however, you must specify function prototypes, if you do not, the program will not compile. The following program, NOPROTO.CPP tries to use the *printf* function without providing a function type (that's contained in the header file stdio.h):

```
void main(void)
{
    printf("This won't compile under C++\n");
}
```

If you try to compile the program, C++ will generate an error message, and the compilation will end.

821 C++ Adds New Keywords

A *keyword* is an identifier that has special meaning to the compiler, such as *for, while, if,* and so on. In addition to the keywords defined by the C compiler, C++ adds the following keywords:

asm	catch	class
delete	friend	inline
new	operator	private
protected	public	template
this	virtual	

As was the case with keywords in C, you cannot use C++ keywords for variable, type, or function names.

C++ Supports Anonymous Unions

As you have learned, a *union* is a special data structure for which C maps two or more members to the same memory location. When you declare a union in C, you must declare a variable of the *union* type, as shown here:

```
union Values {
   unsigned my_data;
   float his_data;
} solution;
```

When you later want to store data within the union, you must specify the variable name and member, as shown here:

```
solution.my_data = 3;
```

C++, however, lets your programs use anonymous (or unnamed) unions. For example, the following program ANONYM.CPP, uses a union similar to the one just shown:

```
#include <iostream.h>

void main(void)
  {
    union {
      int my_data;
      float his_data;
    };

    my_data = 3;

    cout << "Value of my_data is " << my_data;

    his_data = 1.2345;

    cout << "\nValue of his_data is " << his_data;
  }
```

By using the anonymous union in this way, programs can eliminate the programming overhead of working a union name and member names. However, the member names of an anonymous union must be unique from any other variables within the current scope.

823 Resolving Global Scope

As you have learned, a global variable is known from its declaration to the end of your program. When you use global variables, there may be times when a global variable has the same name as a local variable. In such cases, the local variable is used. There may be times, however, when you want to refer to the global variable within a function that has a similarly named local variable. For such cases, C++ lets you precede the global variable name with two colons, such as *::variable*. The following program, GLOBAL.CPP, illustrates the use of the C++ *global resolution operator*:

```cpp
#include <iostream.h>

int global_name = 1001;

void main(void)
  {
    int global_name = 1;  // Local variable

    cout << "Local variable value " << global_name << '\n';
    cout << "Global variable value " << ::global_name << '\n';
  }
```

824 Providing Default Parameter Values

As you have learned, parameters are the values passed to functions. The primary difference between C and C++ function parameters is that C++ lets your program's provide default values for parameters. Should your program invoke a function without specifying one or more parameters, the program will use the default values. For example, the following program, DEFAULT.CPP, uses the function *show_values* to display three parameters. If the user invokes the function with less than three parameters, the program uses the default values 1, 2, and 3:

```cpp
#include <iostream.h>

void show_values(int one=1, int two = 2, int three = 3)
  {
    cout << one << ' ' << two << ' ' << three << '\n';
  }
```

```
void main(void)
  {
    show_values(1, 2, 3);
    show_values(100, 200);
    show_values(1000);
    show_values();
  }
```

Note: *When you omit parameters, you cannot skip a parameter. In other words, when you omit a parameter, you must omit all the parameters to the right of the parameter.*

Controlling *cout*'s Output Width

C++ 825

Several of the tips in this section have used the *cout* I/O stream to display output. When you use *cout*, you can use the *cout width* member to specify the minimum number of characters used to display output. For example, the following program, SETWIDTH.CPP, uses the *width* member to select a minimum output width of five characters:

```
#include <iostream.h>

void main(void)
  {
    int i;

    for (i = 0; i < 3; i++)
      {
        cout.width(5);
        cout << i << '\n';
      }
  }
```

When you compile and execute this program, your screen will display the following:

```
C:\> SETWIDTH  <ENTER>
    0
    1
    2
```

Note: *When you use the width member, you must specify the desired width for each value you output.*

Using *setw* to Set *cout* Width

826

In Tip 825 you used the *cout* width member to specify the minimum number of characters used to display a value. In addition, your programs can use the *setw* manipulator to specify the desired width:

```
#include <iomanip.h>

smanip_int      _Cdecl _FARFUNC setw(int _desired_width);
```

For now, don't worry about fully understanding the *setw* prototype. The following program, SETW.CPP, uses *setw* to select different widths:

```
#include <iostream.h>
#include <iomanip.h>

void main(void)
  {
    cout << setw(5) << 1 << '\n' << setw(6) << 2;
    cout << '\n' << setw(7) << 3;
  }
```

When you compile and execute this program, your screen will display the following output:

```
C:\> SETW   <ENTER>
    1
     2
      3
```

Note: *When you use the setw manipulator, you must specify the desired width for each value you output.*

Specifying a cout Fill Character

827

By default, when you use the *cout* width member or the *setw* manipulator to specify character padding, the space character is used. Using the *cout* fill member, your programs can specify a different fill character. For example, the following program, COUTDOTS.CPP, uses a period as a fill character:

```
#include <iostream.h>

void main(void)
  {
    int i;

    for (i = 0; i < 3; i++)
      {
       cout.fill('.');
       cout.width(5 + i);
       cout << i << '\n';
      }
  }
```

When you compile and execute this program, your screen will display the following output:

```
C:\> COUTDOTS   <ENTER>
....1
......2
.......3
```

Right- and Left-Justifying
cout Output

C++
828

You have learned that, using the *setw* manipulator or *cout width* member, your programs can specify the minimum width used to output a specific value. When you specify an output, your programs can select right or left justification using the *setiosflags* manipulator and the *ios* class members:

```
#include <iomanip.h>

smanip_long      _Cdecl _FARFUNC setiosflags(long flags);
```

The to select right justification, place the following manipulator in the *cout* stream:

```
setioflags(ios::right)
```

Likewise, to select left justification, use the following:

```
setioflags(ios::left)
```

For now, do not try to understand the format used. Instead, you can use the flags within your programs as shown next. In later tips, you will understand the *ios* class use. The following program, RGHTLEFT.CPP, uses these flags to select right and left justification:

```cpp
#include <iostream.h>
#include <iomanip.h>

void main (void)
  {
    int i;

    cout << "Right justification\n";
    for (i = 0; i < 3; i++)
      {
        cout.width(5);
        cout << setiosflags(ios::right) << i;
      }

    cout << "\nLeft justification\n";
    for (i = 0; i < 3; i++)
      {
        cout.width(5);
        cout << setiosflags(ios::left) << i;
      }
  }
```

When you compile and execute this program, your screen will display the following output:

```
C:\> RGHTLEFT  <ENTER>
Right justification
      1    2    3
Left justification
1    2    3
```

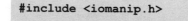

C++ 829 Controlling the Number of Floating-Point Digits Displayed

As you have learned, the *cout* I/O stream lets your programs display floating-point values. When you display such values, you can use the *setprecision* manipulator to specify the desired number of digits to the right of the decimal point:

```cpp
#include <iomanip.h>

smanip_int   _Cdecl _FARFUNC setprecision(int number_of_digits);
```

The following program, SETPREC.CPP, uses the *setprecision* manipulator to change the number of digits displayed to the right of the decimal point:

```
#include <iostream.h>
#include <iomanip.h>

void main(void)
  {
    int i;

    float value = 1.2345;

    for (i = 0; i < 4; i++)
      cout << setprecision(i) << value << '\n';
  }
```

When you compile and execute this program, your screen will display the following output:

```
C:\> SETPREC   <ENTER>
1.2345
1.2
1.23
1.235
```

As you can see, if you specify a precision of 0, *cout* will display all the value's digits.

Displaying Values in Fixed or Scientific Format

As you have learned, the *cout* I/O stream lets your programs display floating-point values. When you use *cout*, you can select fixed or scientific (exponential) format to display the values. To control the value's display format, your programs can use the *setioflags* manipulator's *ios::fixed* and *ios::scientific* flags:

```
#include <iomanip.h>

smanip_long      _Cdecl _FARFUNC setiosflags(long flags);
```

The following program, FIXED.CPP, uses the *setioflags* manipulator to display values in fixed and scientific formats:

```
#include <iostream.h>
#include <iomanip.h>
```

```
void main(void)
  {
    float value = 0.000123;

    cout << setiosflags(ios::fixed) << value << '\n';
    cout << setiosflags(ios::scientific) << value << '\n';
  }
```

When you compile and execute this program, your screen will display the following output:

```
C:\> FIXED   <ENTER>
0.000123
1.23e-04
```

Restoring *cout* Default

Several of the tips in this section have used the *setiosflags* manipulator to control different *cout* formatting options. To quickly restore *cout's* default settings, you can use the *resetiosflags* manipulator:

```
#include <iomanip.h>

smanip_long    _Cdecl _FARFUNC resetiosflags(long flag);
```

The *flag* parameter specifies the option you want to set. For example, the following program uses the *resetiosflags* modifier to turn off right justification:

```
#include <iostream.h>
#include <iomanip.h>

void main(void)
  {
    cout.width(5);
    cout << setiosflags(ios::left) << 5 << '\n';
    cout.width(5);
    cout << 5 << '\n' << resetiosflags(ios::left);
    cout.width(5);
    cout << 1;
  }
```

When you compile and execute this program, your screen will display the following output:

```
C:\> RESETIO   <ENTER>
5
5
    1
```

Setting the I/O Base

C++ 832

You have learned that, using the *dec, oct,* and *hex* modifiers, you can select decimal, octal, and hexadecimal values. If your program needs to output several values using a specific base, your programs can use the *setbase* modifier. The following program, SETBASE.CPP, uses the *setbase* modifier to display the value 255 using different bases:

```
#include <iostream.h>
#include <iomanip.h>

void main(void)
  {
    cout << setbase(8) << 255 << '\n';
    cout << setbase(10) << 255 << '\n';
    cout << setbase(16) << 255 << '\n';
  }
```

When you compile and execute this program, your screen will display the following output:

```
C:\> SETBASE    <ENTER>
377
255
ff
```

Declaring Variables Where You Need Them

C++ 833

In C, your programs can declare variables following any opening brace. In C++, however, your programs can declare variables at any location in your program. The advantage of such declarations is that your programs can declare variables closer to their use. For example, the following program, DEC_INT.CPP, declares the *int* variable *count* within the *for* loop within which the variable is used:

```
#include <iostream.h>

void main(void)
  {
    cout << "About to start the loop\n";

    for (int count = 0; count < 10; count++)
```

```
    cout << count << '\n';

  cout << "count's ending value " << count;
}
```

When your program declares a variable in this way, the variable's scope begins at the point of declaration to the end of the current block and all blocks that appear within the current block.

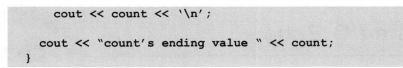

834 Placing Default Parameter Values in Function Prototypes

As you have learned, C++ lets you specify default value for function parameters. Normally, such default values appear in the function header, as shown here:

```
void some_function(int a = 1, int b = 2, int c = 3)
  {
     cout << a << b << c;
  }
```

In addition to placing the default parameter values in the function *header*, however, your programs can specify the defaults within the function *prototype*, as shown here:

```
void some_function(int a = 1, int b = 2, int c = 3);

void main(void)
  {
     // Statements
  }
```

If the function for which you want to specify default parameters does not reside in the current source file, you can direct the compiler to include the correct defaults by specifying the values in the function prototype, as just shown.

835 Using Bitwise Operators and *cout*

As you have learned, to output data using the *cout* I/O stream, your program use operators identical to C's bitwise left-shift operator (<<). The following program BITSCOUT.CPP, uses both the bitwise operator and *cout*. As you will see, the compiler can tell which operation should be performed by the way in which the operator is used:

```cpp
#include <iostream.h>

void main(void)
 {
   unsigned int value, one = 1;

   value = one << 1;
   cout << "Value: " << value << '\n';
   cout << "Result: " << (one << 1) << '\n';
 }
```

When you compile and execute this program, your screen will display the following:

```
C:\> BITSCOUT   <ENTER>
Value: 2
Result: 2
```

By grouping the bitwise operation within parentheses, the compiler associates the operator with the bitwise left shift. If you were to remove the surrounding parentheses, the program would produce the following result:

```
C:\> BITSCOUT   <ENTER>
Value: 2
Result: 11
```

Understanding Lazy (or Short-Circuit) Evaluation

Many of the programs presented throughout this book combine conditions within *if* and *while* constructs, as shown here:

```cpp
if  ((a > 1) && (b < 3))

while ((letter >= 'A') && (letter <= 'Z'))
```

When your programs combine conditions in this way, you need to understand that C++ compiler generates code that performs *lazy* or *short-circuit* evaluation. What that means is that if the outcome of a one of the conditions will make the entire condition true or false, the program stops performing the remainder of the condition. For example, given the previous *if* statement, the program will not compare the variable *b* to the value 3 if the first part of the *if* condition has failed.

Performing the comparison would unnecessarily consume processor time. Likewise, given the previous *while* statement, the program would not compare the variable *letter* to 'Z' if the letter is not greater than or equal to 'A'. By performing short-circuit evaluation, programs can save processor time. However, if you are not aware of the fact that such processing is being performed, your programs can experience errors. For example, consider the following *if* statement:

```
if ((value < 10) && ((letter = getchar()) != 'Q'))
```

In this case, if the variable *value* is not less than 10, the program will not perform the second comparison, which uses the *getchar* macro to assign a value to the variable *letter*. As a result, there are times when the *if* statement will assign a value to *letter* and times when it won't.

837 The *const* Keyword in C++

As you have learned, the *const* keyword informs the compiler that the variable that follows should not be changed during the program's execution. When you use the *const* keyword in C++ programs, you can use the corresponding variable in any way that you could normally use a constant expression. For example, the following statements use a the constant *array_size* to specify the size of a character string array:

```
const int array_size = 64;

char string[array_size];
```

The advantage of using constants over macros created with #define is that constants let you specify type information.

838 The *enum* Keyword in C++

As you have learned, the *enum* keyword lets your programs define enumerated types. The *enum* keyword in C++ is very similar to that used by C except that when you declare an enumerated type in C++, the type's tag can later be used as a type. For example, the following statements declare a variable named *day* in C:

```
enum Days { Monday, Tuesday, Wednesday, Thursday, Friday };

enum Days day;
```

In C++, the declaration becomes the following:

```
enum Days { Monday, Tuesday, Wednesday, Thursday, Friday };

Days day;
```

As you can see, the second declaration does not require the use of the *enum* keyword before the type name *Days*.

Understanding Free Space

As you learned in the Memory section of this book, your programs can dynamically allocate memory from the heap during run time. As you read C++ documentation, you will find references to the *free space*. The heap and free space are the same. To allocate memory from the free space, C++ programs use *new* and *delete*. It is important to note that unlike *malloc* and *free*, which are functions, *new* and *delete* are operators. Tip 840 shows you how allocate memory with *new*.

Allocating Memory with *new*

As you have learned, C++ programs allocate dynamic memory from the free space using the *new* operator. To use *new*, a program must specify the desired number of bytes. The following program NEWARRAY.CPP, allocates memory for a 256 byte array. The program then fills the array with the letter A and then displays the array's contents:

```
#include <iostream.h>

void main(void)
  {
    char *array = new char[256];
    int i;

    for (i = 0; i < 256; i++)
      array[i] = 'A';

    for (i = 0; i < 256; i++)
      cout << array[i] << ' ';
  }
```

Allocating Multiple Arrays

In Tip 840 you used the *new* operator to dynamically allocate a 256-byte character string. At that time, the program allocated the memory when the pointer variable was declared:

```
char *array = new char[256];
```

When your programs use the *new* operator to allocate memory, however, your programs can do so from any location. The following program, NEW_COPY.CPP, uses the *new* operator to allocate three character strings—each at different locations throughout the program:

```
#include <iostream.h>

void main(void)
  {
    char *array = new char[256];
    char *target, *destination;

    int i;

    target = new char[256];
    for (i = 0; i < 256; i++)
      {
        array[i] = 'A';
        target[i] = 'B';
      }

    destination = new char[256];
    for (i = 0; i < 256; i++)
      {
        destination[i] = target[i];
        cout << destination[i] << ' ';
      }
  }
```

Testing for No Free Space

You learned in the Memory section of this book that, when the heap cannot satisfy a request, the functions *calloc* and *malloc* return NULL. The same is true for the *new* operator and the free space. The following program, NO_FREE.CPP, uses the *new* operator to allocate memory until the free space is empty:

```
#include <iostream.h>

void main(void)
 {
   char *pointer;

   do {
     pointer = new char[10000];

     if (pointer)
       cout << "Allocated 10,000 bytes\n";
     else
       cout << "Allocation failed\n";
   } while (pointer);
 }
```

Understanding Near and Far Free Space

As you have learned, C++ refers to the heap as the free space. Depending on your memory model, the amount of available heap space will differ. Using the –ml command-line switch, the following command directs the Borland C++ to compile the program NO_FREE.CPP using the large memory model:

C:\> BCC -ml NO_FREE.CPP <ENTER>

When you execute the NO_FREE program compiled with the large memory model, the program can allocate considerably more heap space before failing.

Using Far Pointers and the *new* Operator

As you have learned the *new* operator lets your programs allocate memory from the free space. If you are using the small memory model, the free space corresponds to the near heap. If your programs need to allocate more memory than the near heap provides, your programs can allocate far pointers. The following program, NEW_FAR.CPP, allocates far pointers from the free space until the far heap runs out of memory:

```
#include <iostream.h>

void main(void)
 {
   char far *pointer;

   do {
     pointer = new far char[10000];

     if (pointer)
       cout << "Allocated 10,000 bytes\n";
     else
       cout << "Allocation failed\n";
   } while (pointer);
 }
```

C++ 845 Releasing Memory Back to the Free Space

As you have learned, when your programs allocate memory dynamically, the programs should release the memory as soon as they no longer need it. When your C programs allocated memory using *calloc* and *malloc*, your programs released the memory using *free*. When your C++ programs allocate memory using *new*, your programs should later free the memory using *delete*. The following program, DELETE.CPP, uses the *delete* operator to release three dynamically allocated arrays back to the free space:

```
#include <iostream.h>

void main(void)
 {
   char *array = new char[256];
   char *target, *destination;

   int i;

   target = new char[256];
   for (i = 0; i < 256; i++)
    {
     array[i] = 'A';
     target[i] = 'B';
    }

   delete array;
```

```
   destination = new char[256];
   for (i = 0; i < 256; i++)
     {
      destination[i] = target[i];
      cout << destination[i] << ' ';
     }

   delete target;
   delete destination;
 }
```

Understanding C++ References

C++
846

An *alias* is a second name for a variable. In C, your programs can create aliases using pointers. C++ simplifies the creation of aliases using references. To create a reference, you use the reference operator (&), as shown here:

```
int variable;
int& alias = variable;
```

The reference operator is similar to C's address operator. However, note the operator's positioning. The reference operator immediately follows a type, such as *int*, *float*, or *char*. The following program, ALIAS.CPP, creates two aliases, using them to display the address of a specific variables. Each alias can correspond to only one variable throughout its lifetime:

```
#include <iostream.h>

void main(void)
  {
    int a = 1001;
    int& a_alias = a;

    float price = 39.95;
    float& price_alias = price;

    cout << "The value of a is "<< a << " the alias is "<< a_alias;
    cout << "\nThe price is " << price << " the alias is " <<
      price_alias;

    a_alias++;
    cout << "\nThe value of a is " << a << " the alias is " <<
    a_alias;
  }
```

The program uses the reference variable *a_alias* to increment the value of *a*. When a program refers to a reference, any operations correspond directly to the aliased variable.

C++ 847 Passing a Reference to a Function

As you have learned, to change a variable within a function, your programs must pass a pointer to the variable. When you use C++, you can simplify the changing of a variable within a function by using a *reference*. Using a reference, you eliminate the need for the pointer operator (->). The following program, FUNCTREF.CPP, passes a reference to the variable *value* to the function *change_value*, which assigns the value 1001 to the variable:

```
#include <iostream.h>

void change_value(int& reference_value)
  {
    reference_value = 1001;
  }

void main(void)
  {
    int value = 10;
    int& alias = value;

    cout << "Value before function: " << value << '\n';

    change_value(alias);

    cout << "Value after function: " << value << '\n';
  }
```

As you can see, using a reference simplifies a the process of changing a value within a function.

C++ 848 Be Aware of Hidden Objects

As you have learned, a reference creates a second name for a variable—an alias. When you create references, you need to ensure that the reference type is identical to the type it is to reference. For example, the following statement creates a reference to a variable of type *int*:

```
int value;
int& alias = value;
```

If the reference type and variable type differ, C++ will create a *hidden object* that does not alias the specified value, but instead, holds the value for an unnamed variable of the reference type. For example, the following statement creates a hidden object of type *float*:

```
int value;
float& alias = value;
```

As you can see, the reference and variable types differ. As such, the compiler will not alias the variable *value*, but rather, will allocate memory for a floating-point value, aliasing the memory with the given reference. The reason you need to be aware of hidden objects is that they can lead to errors that are very difficult to detect. If you change the type of a variable, make sure you also change the type of the corresponding reference, if a reference exists.

Three Ways to Pass Parameters

In C, your programs can pass parameters to functions using *call by value* or *call by pointer reference*. In C++, as you have learned, your programs can use a third technique, *call by reference*. The following program, CALL_3.CPP, illustrates the use of all three calling techniques:

```cpp
#include <iostream.h>
#include <iomanip.h>

void call_by_value(int a, int b, int c)
  {
    a = 3; b = 2; c = 1;
  }

void call_by_pointer_reference(int *a, int *b, int *c)
  {
    *a = 3; *b = 2; *c = 1;
  }

void call_by_reference(int& a, int& b, int& c)
  {
    a = 1; b = 2; c = 3;
  }

void main(void)
  {
    int a = 1, b = 2, c = 3;
    int& a_alias = a;
```

```
    int& b_alias = b;
    int& c_alias = c;

    call_by_value(a, b, c);
    cout << "By value: " << a << b << c << '\n';

    call_by_pointer_reference(&a, &b, &c);
    cout << "By pointer: " << a << b << c << '\n';

    call_by_reference(a_alias, b_alias, c_alias);
    cout << "By reference: " << a << b << c << '\n';
}
```

C++ 850 Rules for Working with References

In C++, a reference lets you create an alias for a variable. When you use references, keep the following rules in mind:

- Once initialized, a reference value cannot be changed.
- The reference type and variable type should be the same.
- You cannot create a pointer to a reference.
- You cannot compare the value of two references—the comparisons would compare the values of the referenced variables.
- You cannot increment, decrement, or change a reference value—the operations will apply to the value of the referenced variable.
- You can distinguish the reference operator from the address operator because the reference operator always follows as type *int&*.

C++ 851 Functions Can Return References

In C++, a reference is an alias for a variable. As you have learned, references can simplify parameter passing by eliminating the need to perform pointer operations. All of the tips presented to this point have initialized reference variables at declaration, near the top of *main*. As it turns out, C++ lets functions return references. Because C++ lets your programs declare variables at any location, your programs can create an initialize a reference at any location in your program by returning a reference from a function. The following program, RTN_REF.CPP, invokes the function *get_book*, which returns a reference to a variable of type *book*:

```cpp
#include <iostream.h>

struct book {
  char author[64];
  char title[64];
  float price;
};

book library[3] = {
  {"Jamsa", "Jamsa's 1001 C/C++ Tips", 39.95},
  {"Wyatt", "1001 Word for Windows Tips", 39.95},
  {"Jamsa", "Jamsa's 1001 Windows Tips", 39.95}};

book& get_book(int i)
  {
    if ((i >= 0) && (i < 3))
      return(library[i]);
    else
      return(library[0]);
  }

void main(void)
  {
    cout << "About to get book 0\n";
    book& this_book = get_book(0);
    cout << this_book.author << ' ' << this_book.title;
    cout << ' ' << this_book.price;
  }
```

Using C++ *inline* Keyword

C++
852

As you have learned, programs pass parameters to functions using the stack. Each time your program invokes a function, therefore, the parameters (and return address) must be pushed onto and later popped off of the stack. These push and pop operations lead to overhead that makes using functions slightly slower than using inline code. If your programs have one or two critical functions that must execute very quickly, you should use the *inline* keyword to direct the compiler not to create the function code, but rather, to place the corresponding code inline in the program at each function call. If your programs call the function from five different locations, the compiler will insert the corresponding function in the program five times. If your programs call the functions from 50 different locations, the compiler inserts the code 50 times. As such, inline code has the time/space tradeoff. Using inline code is creates a faster program, but also makes the program code larger (which, in theory, can slow the program down). The following program, INLINE.CPP, uses two similar functions, placing one inline and calling the second. The program displays the amount of time required to call each function 30,000 times:

```cpp
#include <iostream.h>
#include <time.h>

inline void swap_inline(int *a, int *b, int *c, int *d)
  {
    int temp;

    temp = *a;
    *a = *b;
    *b = temp;

    temp = *c;
    *c = *d;
    *d = temp;
  }

void swap_call(int *a, int *b, int *c, int *d)
  {
    int temp;

    temp = *a;
    *a = *b;
    *b = temp;

    temp = *c;
    *c = *d;
    *d = temp;
  }


void main(void)
  {
    clock_t start, stop;
    long int i;
    int a = 1, b = 2, c = 3, d = 4;

    start = clock();
    for (i = 0; i < 300000L; i++)
      swap_inline(&a, &b, &c, &d);
    stop = clock();
    cout << "Time for inline: " << stop - start;

    start = clock();
```

```
    for (i = 0; i < 300000L; i++)
      swap_call(&a, &b, &c, &d);
    stop = clock();

    cout << "\nTime for called function: " << stop - start;
  }
```

Using C++ *asm* Keyword

Depending on your program's purpose, there may be times when it is necessary to perform low-level assembly language programming. At such times, you can create an assembly language function and link the function to your program, or you can use the *asm* keyword to insert assembly language statements into your C++ code. The following program, ASM_DEMO.CPP, uses the *asm* keyword to include the assembly language statements required to sound the computer's built-in speaker:

```
#include <iostream.h>

void main(void)
  {
    cout << "About to sound the speaker...\n";

    asm {
      MOV AX,0x0200
      MOV DL,7
      INT 0x21
    };

    cout << "Done...\n";
  }
```

Reading a Character Using *cin*

Several of the preceding tips have used the *cin* I/O stream to read input from the keyboard. To improve your control over keyboard or redirected input, your programs can use *cin.get* to read input a character at a time:

```
character = cin.get();
```

The following program, CIN_GET.CPP, uses *cin.get* to assign characters, up to, but not including, the newline character of the character string *str*:

```
#include <iostream.h>
#include <stdio.h>


void main(void)
  {
    char str[256];
    int i = 0;

    while ((str[i] = cin.get()) != '\n')
      i++;

    str[i] = NULL;

    cout << "The string was: " <<  str;
  }
```

C++ 855 Writing a Character with *cout*

In Tip 854 you learned that your programs can input characters one at a time using *cin.get*. In a similar way, your programs can use *cout.put* to write one character:

```
cout.put(character);
```

The following program, COUT_PUT.CPP, uses *cout* to output a character string one character at a time:

```
#include <iostream.h>

void main(void)
  {
    char *title = "Jamsa's 1001 C/C++ Tips";

    while (*title)
      cout.put(*title++);
  }
```

A Simple Filter Program

C++ 856

As you have learned, *cout.put* and *cin.get* let your programs perform character I/O. The following program, TO_UPPER.CPP, converts redirected input to uppercase. To perform the conversion, the program simply loops until *cin.get* returns –1 indicating the end of file:

```cpp
#include <iostream.h>
#include <ctype.h>

void main(void)
  {
    char letter;

    while ((letter = cin.get()) != -1)
      cout.put(toupper(letter));
  }
```

A Simple Tee Command

C++ 857

As you have learned, C++ lets you redirect the output of the *cout* I/O stream. The following program, TEE.CPP, writes its redirected input to the *cout* and *cerr* I/O streams. In this way, you can view the program's input on the screen while still redirecting the output to a different source:

```cpp
#include <iostream.h>

void main(void)
  {
    char letter;

    while ((letter = cin.get()) != -1)
      {
        cout.put(letter);
        cerr.put(letter);
      }
  }
```

C++ 858

A Simple First Command

As you have learned, the *cin* and *cout* I/O streams support I/O redirection. The following program, SIMP1ST.CPP, uses these input streams to write the first ten lines of redirected input to the screen:

```
#include <iostream.h>

void main(void)
  {
    char letter;
    int count = 0;

    while ((letter = cin.get()) != -1)
      {
        cout.put(letter);
        if ((letter == '\n') && (++count == 10))
          break;
      }
  }
```

C++ 859

A Better First Command

In Tip 858 you created the program SIMP1ST.CPP that displayed the first ten lines of redirected input. A more flexible command would allow the user to specify, as a command-line argument, the number of lines desired. The following program, FIRST.CPP lets the user do just that:

```
#include <iostream.h>
#include <stdlib.h>

void main(int argc, char **argv)
  {
    char letter;
    int count = 0;
    int line_limit;

    line_limit = atoi(argv[1]);

    while ((letter = cin.get()) != -1)
      {
        cout.put(letter);
```

```
      if ((letter == '\n') && (++count == line_limit))
        break;
    }
}
```

If the user does not specify the desired number of lines, or if the user specifies an invalid line count, the program displays all the redirected input.

Testing for End of File

C++ 860

Several of the previous tips have used *cin.get* as follows to determine the end of the end of the redirected input:

```
while ((letter = cin.get()) != -1)
```

In addition to testing cin.get in this way, your programs can test *cin.eof* as follows:

```
while (! cin.eof())
```

The following program, FIRSTEOF.CPP, changes the program FIRST.CPP to test for an end of file in this way:

```
#include <iostream.h>
#include <stdlib.h>

void main(int argc, char **argv)
  {
    char letter;
    int count = 0;
    int line_limit;

    line_limit = atoi(argv[1]);

    while (! cin.eof())
      {
        letter = cin.get();
        cout.put(letter);
        if ((letter == '\n') && (++count == line_limit))
          break;
      }
  }
```

Generating a Newline with *endl*

Many of the preceding tips have placed the newline character (\n) in the *cout* output stream to generate a carriage return and line feed. In addition to using the newline character, your programs can use *endl*:

```
cout << "Hello, world!" << endl;
```

The following program, ENDL.CPP, uses *endl* several times to generate a carriage return and line feed:

```
#include <iostream.h>

void main(void)
  {
    cout << "This is line one" << endl;
    cout << "This is line two" << endl;
    cout << "This is line three—";
    cout << "It is the last line" << endl;
  }
```

When you compile and execute this program, your screen will display the following:

```
C:\> ENDL <ENTER>
This is line one
This is line two
This is line three—It is the last line
```

Understanding Linkage Specifications

As you have learned, C++ requires function prototypes for every function your program uses. The C++ compiler uses the prototypes to verify parameter and return value types. During compilation, the C++ compiler changes the names of functions and their parameters in the resulting object code. The linker in turn, uses these new names to resolve external references. Unfortunately, if you are linking to code compiled by a C compiler, the function names in the object code will not be in this same "C++ function name format". To prevent the C++ compiler from changing the names of C functions, you can use a *linkage specifier*. In short, the linkage specifier tells the C++ compiler the correct format it should use for naming functions in the object file. Assume, for example, that you have a function named *calculate_payroll* that is written in C. To direct the C++ compiler not to change the function name format, you would use the following linkage specifier:

```
extern "C" {
 float calculate_payroll (int employee_count,char *employee_file);
} ;
```

Note: *If you examine the header files provided by your compiler, you will find several linkage specifiers in the files that are similar to the one shown here.*

Understanding Overloading

Overloading is the process of assigning more than one operation to an operator or providing more two or more functions with the same name. For example, C and C++ use the plus symbol (+) as the addition operator. Using overloading, you can direct C++ to also use the plus symbol to concatenate strings:

```
pathname = directory_name + filename;
```

Depending on how your program uses the plus symbol, the C++ compiler will determine if addition or string concatenation is being performed. Likewise, as you have learnedthere are times, when using C, when you have to create differently named functions that work with values of different types. For example, if you have created a function that returns the sum of values in an integer array, you must create a differently named function if you want to sum values in an array of type *float*. As you will learn, C++ lets you overload functions and operators, which simplifies many operations.

Overloading Functions

As you learned, C++ lets you have multiple functions with the same name. During compilation, the C++ compiler determines which function to call, based on the number and types of parameters passed. For example, the following program, OVERLOAD.CPP, creates two functions named *sum* that return the sum of the number of elements in an array. The first function supports arrays of type *float*, while the second supports arrays of type *int*:

```
#include <iostream.h>

int sum(int *array, int element_count)
  {
    int result = 0;
```

```
    int count;

    for (count = 0; count < element_count; count++)
      result += array[count];

    return(result);
  }

float sum(float *array, int element_count)
  {
    float result = 0;
    int count;

    for (count = 0; count < element_count; count++)
      result += array[count];

    return(result);
  }


void main(void)
  {
    int a[5] = { 1, 2, 3, 4, 5 };
    float b[4] = { 1.11, 2.22, 3.33, 4.44 };

    cout << "Sum of int values: " << sum(a, 5) << '\n';
    cout << "Sum of float values: " << sum(b, 4) << '\n';
  }
```

C++ 865 Overloading Functions: A Second Example

As you have learned, C++ lets you overload functions, creating two or more functions in your programs that have the same name. The following program, USEPARAM.CPP, overloads the function *swap*. The first function swaps the two values while the second function swaps four. During compilation, the compiler uses the number of parameters to determine which function to call:

```
#include <iostream.h>

void swap(int *a, int *b)
  {
    int temp = *a;
    *a = *b;
```

```
      *b = temp;
  }

void swap(int *a, int *b, int *c, int *d)
  {
    int temp = *a;
    *a = *b;
    *b = temp;
    temp = *c;
    *c = *d;
    *d = temp;
  }

void main(void)
  {
    int a = 1, b = 2 , c = 3, d = 4;

    swap(&a, &b);

    cout << "Just swapped a and b " << a << b << '\n';
    swap(&a, &b, &c, &d);
    cout << "Just swapped four " << a << b << c << d << '\n';
  }
```

Overloading Operators

C++ 866

As Tip 863 describes, C++ lets you overload operators by assigning different operations to an operator. For example, the plus symbol might add two values, concatenate two strings, or even add days to a date structure. During compilation, the C++ compiler will determine how the operator is being used and will determine the correct operation to apply. Before you can overload an operator, however, you must declare a *class* for which the operator will apply. Several of the tips that appear later in this section discuss C++ classes in detail. At that time, you will use the C++ *operator* keyword to overload an operator. The I/O streams *cout*, *cin*, and *cerr* are actually classes that have overloaded the << and >> operators.

Reading a Line at a Time with *cin*

C++ 867

As you have learned, your programs can read keyboard input using *cin*. When your programs want to read input a character at a time, your programs can use *cin.get*. In some cases, your programs might need to perform input operations a line at a time. For such cases, your program can use *cin.getline*, as shown here:

```
char string[256];

cin.getline(string, sizeof(string), '\n');
```

The *string* parameter is a pointer to the string you want cin.getline to read. The *sizeof* operator specifies the number of bytes the string can hold. Finally, the newline character specifies the character that will terminate the read. The following program, GETLINE.CPP, uses *cin.getline* to read a line of input:

```
#include <iostream.h>

void main(void)
  {
    char string[256];

    cout << "Type in your full name and press Enter\n";
    cin.getline(string, sizeof(string), '\n');
    cout << string;
  }
```

Experiment with *cin.getline*, changing the termination character to possibly a letter of alphabet and then note your program's results.

C++ 868 Using *cin.getline* in a Loop

In Tip 860 your programs used *cin.get* and *cout.put* to display redirected input as uppercase. The following program, ALLUPPER.CPP, uses *cin.getline* and *cout* to perform similar processing:

```
#include <iostream.h>
#include <string.h>

void main(void)
  {
    char string[256];

    while (cin.getline(string, sizeof(string), '\n'))
      cout << strupr(string) << '\n';
  }
```

As you can see, the program loops until *cin.getline* returns 0, which indicates the end of the redirected input. Because the *cin.getline* function does not place the newline character into the string, *cout* must write the newline for each line.

Changing *new*'s Default Handling

As you have learned, when the *new* operator cannot allocate enough memory to satisfy a memory request, it returns NULL. Depending on your program's function, there may be times when you want new to perform other processing when memory can't be allocated. As it turns out, when *new* cannot allocate memory, it calls the function pointed to by a global pointer to a function named *_new_handler*. By assigning the *_new_handler* variable to point to a custom function, you can direct *new* to call your own function when memory cannot be satisfied. The following program, NEW_HAND.CPP, uses the *_new_handler* function pointer to direct *new* to call the function *no_memory* when a memory request cannot be satisfied:

```cpp
#include <iostream.h>
#include <stdlib.h>

extern void (*_new_handler)();

void no_memory(void)
  {
    cerr << "There is no more memory to allocate...\n";
    exit(0);
  }

void main(void)
  {
    _new_handler = no_memory;

    char *ptr;

    do {
      ptr = new char[10000];

      if (ptr)
        cout << "Just allocated 10,000 bytes\n";
    } while (ptr);
  }
```

Note: *If your handler cannot allocate the memory for the program, the handler must end the program, or an infinite loop will occur.*

C++
870

Setting a New Handler with *set_new_handler*

In Tip 869 you learned that C++ lets you define your own handler that gets called when the *new* operator cannot satisfy a memory request. To assign a new handler, your program assigned the address of your handler function to a global variable named *_new_handler*. To simplify this process, many C compilers provide a function named *set_new_handler*:

```
#include <new.h>

void (* set_new_handler(void (* custom_handler)())))();
```

The following program, SET_NEWH.CPP, uses the *set_new_handler* function to install a custom handler:

```
#include <iostream.h>
#include <stdlib.h>
#include <new.h>

void no_memory(void)
  {
    cerr << "There is no more memory to allocate...\n";
    exit(0);
  }

void main(void)
  {
    char *ptr;

    set_new_handler(no_memory);

    do {
      ptr = new char[10000];

      if (ptr)
        cout << "Just allocated 10,000 bytes\n";
    } while (ptr);
  }
```

Determining a C++ Compilation

C++
871

Many C++ let you compile standard C programs. Depending on your program's statements, there may be times when you want to terminate a standard C compilation. When many C++ compilers compile a C++ program, they might define a constant that you can test within your programs. For example, the Borland C++ compiler sets the constant *__cplusplus* when it is compiling a C++ program. The following program, TESTCPP.CPP, uses this constant to determine if the compiler is performing a C or C++ compilation:

```
#ifdef __cplusplus
#include <iostream.h>
#else
#include <stdio.h>
#endif

void main(void)
  {
#ifdef __cplusplus
  cout << "C++ compilation";
#else
  printf("C compilation\n");
#endif
  }
```

Compile this program as a file with the CPP extension. Next, copy the contents to a file with the C extension and compile the file. Note the processing the compiler performs.

Structures and C++

C++
872

As you have learned, a structure lets your programs group related information of different types. When you declare a structure in C, you can specify a *tag* (or name) with which you can later declare variables of the structure type:

```
struct tag {
    int member_a;
    float member_b;
    char member_c[256];
};

struct tag variable_one, variable_two;
```

When you declare a structure in C++, however, the structure tag becomes a type, with which your programs can later declare variables without specifying the *struct* keyword:

```
struct tag {
    int member_a;
    float member_b;
    char member_c[256];
};


tag variable_one, variable_two;
```

As you can see, the C++ structure does not require the keyword *struct* before the tag in variable declaration.

C++ 873 Functions as Structure Members

When you create C programs, the C compilers lets you use pointers to functions as structure members, as shown here:

```
struct tag {
    int member_a;
    int  (*member_b)();  // Pointer to function that returns int
};
```

C++ lets you take this concept one step further, letting you place actual functions within a structure:

```
struct tag {
    int member_a;
    int member_b();
};
```

When you declare the corresponding function, you have two choices: As shown in Tip 874, you can define the function code immediately within the structure, or you can define it outside of the structure, as shown in Tip 875. To invoke the function, your program simply refers to the structure member, as shown here:

```
variable.member_b(parameters);
```

Defining a Member Function Within a Structure

As you have learned, C++ lets you programs place functions as structure members. When your structure contains a member that is a function, you can define the corresponding function code within the structure. The following program, FUNC_MBR.CPP, defines the function that corresponds to the member *show_msg*:

```
#include <iostream.h>

struct Msg {
  char message[256];
  void show_message(void) { cout << message; }
};

void main(void)
  {
    struct Msg book = { "Jamsa's 1001 C/C++ Tips" };

    book.show_message();
  }
```

In this case, the program invokes the member function *show_message*, which in turn displays the *message* member. In this case, the program defined the function within the structure. In Tip 875, you will learn how to define the function outside of the structure.

Declaring a Member Function Outside of a Structure

As you have learned, C++ lets you place functions as members in a structure. In Tip 874 you define the function *show_message* within the structure itself. The following program, FUNC_TWO.CPP, defines the function outside of the structure. To correspond the function with the *Msg* structure, the program precedes the function name with the structure name, followed by two colons:

```
#include <iostream.h>

struct Msg {
  char message[256];
  void show_message(char *message);
```

```
};

void Msg::show_message(char *message)
  {
    cout << message;
  }


void main(void)
  {
    struct Msg book = { "Jamsa's 1001 C/C++ Tips" };

    book.show_message(book.message);
  }
```

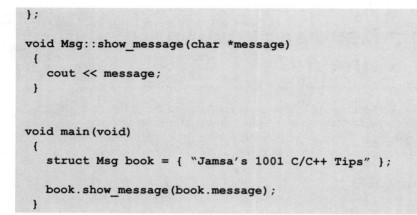

876 Passing Parameters to a Member Function

As you have learned, C++ lets you place functions as a member of a structure. Tips 874 and 875 have used the member function *show_message* within a *Msg* structure. When you place a function as a structure member, you can treat the function just as you would any other C++ function, meaning that you can pass parameters to and declare local variables within the function. The following program, FUNC_THR.CPP, passes the value 1001 to the function *show_title*:

```
#include <iostream.h>

struct Msg {
  char first[256];
  void show_title(int value)
    {
      cout << first << value << " C/C++ Tips";
    }
};

void main(void)
  {
    struct Msg book = { "Jamsa's " };

    book.show_title(1001);
  }
```

Multiple Variables of the Same Structure

In Tip 874 you defined a structure that contains a function as a member. The program then declared a variable of the structure type. The following program, MULTSTRU.CPP, declares several variables of the type *Msg* assigning each a unique character string and then displaying the message using the *show_message* function:

```cpp
#include <iostream.h>

struct Msg {
  char message[256];
  void show_message(void) { cout << message; }
};

void main(void)
  {
    struct Msg book = { "Jamsa's 1001 C/C++ Tips\n" };
    struct Msg section = { "The ABC's of C++" };

    book.show_message();
    section.show_message();
  }
```

Different Structures with Same Function Member Names

As you have learned, C++ lets your programs place functions as members within a structure. When your programs use different structures, there may be times when two structures have the same member names. The following program, SAMENAME.CPP, creates two different structures that both use the member function *show_message*. As is the case with nonfunction members, the C++ compiler differentiates between the function names:

```cpp
#include <iostream.h>
#include <string.h>

struct Msg {
  char message[256];
  void show_message(void) { cout << message; }
```

```
};

struct UpperMsg {
    char message[256];
    void show_message(void) { cout << strupr(message); }
};


void main(void)
 {
    Msg book = { "Jamsa's 1001 C/C++ Tips\n" };
    UpperMsg book_upr = { "1001 C/C++ Tips\n" };

    book.show_message();
    book_upr.show_message();
 }
```

In this case, the structures define the functions within the structure itself. In Tip 879, however, you will see how to differentiate the functions that are defined outside of the structures.

C++ 879 Different Functions with Same Member Names

In Tip 878 you learned that the C++ compiler will distinguish between function members of different structure types. The following program, DIFFNAME.CPP, defines member functions outside of the corresponding structures. To differentiate between the member functions, the program precedes each function definition with the structure named, followed by two colons:

```
#include <iostream.h>
#include <string.h>

struct Msg {
  char message[256];
  void show_message(void);
};


struct UpperMsg {
    char message[256];
    void show_message(void);
};
```

```
void Msg::show_message(void)
  {
    cout << message;
  }

void UpperMsg::show_message(void)
  {
    cout << strupr(message);
  }

void main(void)
  {
    Msg book = { "Jamsa's 1001 C/C++ Tips\n" };
    UpperMsg book_upr = { "1001 C/C++ Tips\n" };

    book.show_message();
    book_upr.show_message();
  }
```

Understanding Objects

In the simplest sense, an *object* is a *thing* or a real-world entity. When programmers create programs, they write instructions that work with different things, such as variables or files. Different *things* have different *operations* that your programs perform on them. For example, given a *file* object, your program might perform such operations as reading, writing, or printing the file. As you will learn, C++ programs define objects in terms of a class. An *object class* defines the data the object will store and the functions that operate on the data. C++ programs often refer to the functions that manipulate the class data as *methods*. Most of your C++ programs have already used the *cin* and *cout* objects. In the case of these objects, the I/O stream was the *thing*, and functions such as *cin.get* and *cout.put* were the *operations* on the object.

Understanding Object-Oriented Programming

To programmers, an *object* is a collection of data and a set of operations, called *methods*, that manipulate the data. *Object-oriented programming* is way of looking at programs in terms of the objects (things) that make up a system. One you have identified the objects, you can determine the operations normally performed on the object. If you have a *document* object, for example, common operations might include printing, spell-checking, faxing, or even discarding. Object-oriented programming does not require a special programming language such as C++. You can write object-oriented programs in such languages as COBOL or FORTRAN. However, as you will learn, languages described as "object-oriented" normally provide class data structures that let your programs group the data and methods into one variable. As you will learn, object-oriented programming has many advantages. The two primary advantages, however, are object reuse and ease of understanding. As it turns out, the objects that you write for one program can often be used in another. Rather than building a collection of function libraries, object-oriented programmers build *class libraries*. Likewise, by grouping an objects data and methods, object-oriented programs are often more readily understood than their nonobject-based counterparts (at least after you learn the syntax of the programming language used). C++ is often called an object-oriented extension to C. Many of the tips that follow examine the C++ object-based capabilities.

882 Understanding C++ Classes

Throughout this book, programs have used structures to group related data. As you have learned, C++ lets your programs use functions as structure members. A C++ *class* is best viewed as a structure extension. A class, like a structure, describes a template for future variable declarations—it does not allocate memory for a variable. A class has a name (tag) and member fields. The following definition, for example, illustrates a simple class named *Book*:

```
class Book {
  public:
    char title[256];
    char author[64];
    float price;
    void show_title(void) { cout << title << '\n'; };
    float get_price(void) { return(price); };
};
```

As you can see, the class definition is very similar to a structure. The only new item is the *public* label. Tip 884 discusses the public label's purpose. The following program, 1STCLASS.CPP, uses the *Book* class to display information about a book:

```
#include <iostream.h>
#include <iomanip.h>
#include <string.h>

class Book {
  public:
    char title[256];
```

```
      char author[64];
      float price;
      void show_title(void) { cout << title << '\n'; };
      float get_price(void) { return(price); };
};

void main(void)
  {
    Book tips;

    strcpy(tips.title, "Jamsa's 1001 C/C++ Tips");
    strcpy(tips.author, "Jamsa");
    tips.price = 39.95;

    tips.show_title();
    cout << "The book's price is " << setprecision(2) <<
      tips.get_price();
  }
```

Using or Omitting the Class Name in Declarations

C++ 883

As you have learned, a class defines a template for future variable declarations. After you define a class, your program can declare a class using the class or simply by specifying the class name (tag), as shown here:

```
class Book {
  public:
    char title[256];
    char author[64];
    float price;
    void show_title(void) { cout << title << '\n'; };
    float get_price(void) { return(price); };
};

// Declare variables of the class type
class Book tips;
Book diary;
```

As you can see, C++ treats class tags in the same manner as structure tags, using them to create a type, with which you can later declare other variables.

Understanding the *public:* Label

In Tip 883 you created a simple class, named *Book*, that contain the *public:* label, as shown here:

```
class Book {
  public:
    char title[256];
    char author[64];
    float price;
    void show_title(void) { cout << title << '\n'; };
    float get_price(void) { return(price); };
};
```

Unlike a structure, whose members are all accessible to a program, a class can have members the program can directly access using the *dot operator*, and other members (called *private members*), that cannot be accessed directly. The *public:* label identifies the class members the program can access using the dot operator. If you want the program to access a member directly, you must declare the member within the class' public members.

Understanding Information Hiding

Information hiding is the process of hiding underlying implementation details of a function, program, or even a class. Information hiding lets programmers treat functions and classes as *black boxes*. In other words, if a programmer passes a value to a function, the programmer knows a specific result will occur. The programmer does not need to know how the result is calculated, but instead, simply that the function works. For example, most programmers don't know the mathematics behind the *tanh* function, which returns an angle's hyperbolic tangent. However, the programmers know that if they pass a specific value to the function, a known result will occur. To use the function, the programmer only needs to know the input parameters and the values returned.

In object-oriented programming, an object may have underlying implementation details. For example, in the case of a document, the data may be stored in Word, Excel, or some other format. To use the document object, however, the program should not need to know the format. Instead, the program should be able to perform read, write, print, and even fax operations without knowing the object details. To help programmers hide an object's underlying details, C++ lets you divide a class definition into private and public parts. The public data and methods can be directly accessed by the program, while the private data methods cannot.

Using the *private:* Label

As you have learned, C++ lets you divide a class definition into public and private parts. The public data and methods can be accessed directly by the program using the *dot operator*. The private data and methods, however, cannot. The following class definition expands the *Book* class to include public and private data and methods:

```
class Book {
  public:
    char title[256];
    char author[64];
    float price;
    void show_title(void) { cout << title << '\n'; };
    float get_price(void) { return(price); };
    void show_book(void) { show_title(); show_publisher(); };
    void assign_publisher(char *name) { strcpy(publisher,name); };
  private:
    char publisher[256];
    void show_publisher(void) { cout << publisher << '\n'; };
};
```

The data and methods that reside in the public section can be directly accessed by the program using the dot operator. The only way to access the private data and methods, however, is through the public methods. Tip 887 presents a program that manipulates both the public and private data.

Using Public and Private Data

887

As you have learned, C++ lets you divide a class definition into public and private data and methods. Programs can access the public data and methods using the dot operator. To access the private data and methods, however, the program must call the public methods. The program cannot directly manipulate or invoke private data and methods. The following program, PUB_PRIV.CPP, illustrates the use of public and private data:

```
#include <iostream.h>
#include <iomanip.h>
#include <string.h>

class Book {
  public:
```

```
      char title[256];
      char author[64];
      float price;
      void show_title(void) { cout << title << '\n'; };
      float get_price(void) { return(price); };
      void show_book(void) { show_title(); show_publisher(); };
      void assign_publisher(char *name) { strcpy(publisher,name); };
   private:
      char publisher[256];
      void show_publisher(void) { cout << publisher << '\n'; };
  };

void main(void)
  {
    Book tips;

    strcpy(tips.title, "Jamsa's 1001 C/C++ Tips");
    strcpy(tips.author, "Jamsa");
    tips.price = 39.95;
    tips.assign_publisher("Jamsa Press");

    tips.show_book();
  }
```

As you can see, the public method *assign_publisher* initializes the private member *publisher*. If the program had tried to directly access the *publisher* member, the compiler would have generated an error. In a similar way, the program uses public method *show_book*, which in turn invokes the private method *show_publisher*. Again, the program cannot directly access the private method.

C++ 888 What to Hide and What to Make Public

As you have learned, C++ lets you divide class definitions into private and public sections. One of the most difficult tasks programmers who are new to object-oriented programming face is trying to determine what should be hidden and what should be public. As a general rule, the less a program knows about a class, the better. Thus, you should try to use private data and methods as often as possible. In this way, programs have to use the object's public methods to access the object data. As you will learn in Tip 889, forcing programs to manipulate object data using only public methods can decrease programming errors. In other words, you don't normally want a program directly manipulating an object's data using only the dot operator. Making use of private data in this way improves information hiding.

Public Methods Are Often Called Interface Functions

As you learned in Tip 888, your programs should try to place most of an object's data in the private section of a class definition. In this way, programs can only access the data by calling the class public methods. In this way, the public methods provide your programs *interface* to the object data. Using such interface functions, your programs can verify that the value the program wants to assign to a member is valid. For example, assume the member *melt_down* in the *NuclearReactor* class should only contain the values 1 through 5. If the member is public, a program can assign an invalid value using the dot operator as shown here:

```
nuke.melt_down = 99;
```

By restricting access to the *melt_down* member to the public method *set_melt_down*, the object can verify the value, as shown here:

```
int set_melt_down(int value)
  {
    if ((value >= 1) && (value <= 5))
        {
          nuke.melt_down = value;
          return(0);
        }
    else
        return(-1);   // Invalid value
  }
```

By restricting access to object data to the public methods, the only operations a program can perform on the data are those defined by the object itself.

Defining Class Functions Outside of the Class

Several of the preceding tips have created simple classes that define function members within the class itself. As the size of the class functions increase, you will eventually define the functions outside of the class. The following program, BOOKFUNC.CPP, defines the functions for the *Book* object outside of the class itself. As you will see, the program identifies the class functions by preceding each function name with the class name and double colons:

```
#include <iostream.h>
#include <iomanip.h>
#include <string.h>

class Book {
  public:
    char title[256];
    char author[64];
    float price;
    void show_title(void);
    float get_price(void);
    void show_book(void);
    void assign_publisher(char *name);
  private:
    char publisher[256];
    void show_publisher(void);
};

void Book::show_title(void)
  { cout << title << '\n'; };

float Book::get_price(void)
  { return(price); };

void Book::show_book(void)
  { show_title(); show_publisher(); };

void Book::assign_publisher(char *name)
  { strcpy(publisher, name); };

void Book::show_publisher(void)
  { cout << publisher << '\n'; };

void main(void)
  {
    Book tips;

    strcpy(tips.title, "Jamsa's 1001 C/C++ Tips");
    strcpy(tips.author, "Jamsa");
    tips.price = 39.95;
    tips.assign_publisher("Jamsa Press");

    tips.show_book();
  }
```

Defining Methods Inside and Outside of Classes

As you have learned, C++ lets you define methods inside and outside of the class declaration. The decision you make on where to define the method function affects the code the compiler creates for the program. When you define a method within the class, the compiler will treat each method reference as an *inline* function call, placing into the object code at each method reference the function's corresponding instructions. As you have learned, using inline code can improve your program's performance, but it also increases your program size. When you define a function outside of the class, on the other hand, the compiler does not use inline code. Instead, the compiler will generate code for a function that is called at each method reference. Thus, if your class has a common operation that is small, you might want the compiler to generate inline code for the method. If the method is larger, do not direct the compiler to generate inline code.

Understanding Object Instances

Many C++ books and articles refer to *object instances*. In short, an object instance is a object variable. As you have learned, a class defines a template for future variable declarations. When you later declare an object, you create an object instance. In other words, when the compiler allocates memory a variable, an object instance has been created. All instances of the same class have the same characteristics. For the purposes of this book, an instance is a variable of a specific class.

Object Instances Should Share Code

As you have learned, C++ lets you define class methods within the class or outside of the class. When you declare class methods outside of the class, instances share the same copy of the methods. If, for example, you have a class with three methods, and you create 100 instances of that class, your program will only contain the three methods. If you include code inline, however, the code is not shared. Inline code should be reserved for small commonly performed operations, where operation performance is more important than program size. For example, the following program, SHRBOOKS.CPP creates two instances of the *Book* class:

```
#include <iostream.h>
#include <iomanip.h>
#include <string.h>

class Book {
  public:
    char title[256];
    char author[64];
    float price;
    void show_title(void) { cout << title << '\n'; };
    float get_price(void) { return(price); };
    void show_book(void);
    void assign_publisher(char *name) { strcpy(publisher,name); };
  private:
    char publisher[256];
    void show_publisher(void) { cout << publisher << '\n'; };
};

void Book::show_book(void)
    { show_title(); show_publisher(); };

void main(void)
  {
    Book tips, diary;

    strcpy(tips.title, "Jamsa's 1001 C/C++ Tips");
    strcpy(tips.author, "Jamsa");
    tips.price = 39.95;
    tips.assign_publisher("Jamsa Press");

    strcpy(diary.title, "All My Secrets...");
    strcpy(diary.author, "Kris Jamsa");
    diary.price = 9.95;
    diary.assign_publisher("None");

    tips.show_book();
    diary.show_book();

  }
```

If you compile this program using Borland's C++ compiler to produce an assembly language listing, you will find that the instances do not share code for inline methods, but do share the code defined outside of the class. To produce the assembly language output of this program, invoke the Borland C++ compiler as follows:

```
C:\> BCC -S  SHRBOOKS.CPP  <ENTER>
```

Understanding Constructor Functions

When your program creates an object instance, the program will then normally assign initial values to the object data members. To simplify the process of initializing a object members, C++ supports a special function, called a *constructor*, that automatically executes when the instance is created. The constructor function is a public method that uses the same name as the class. For example, using the *Book* class, the constructor function would have the name *Book*, as shown here:

```cpp
class Book {
  public:
    char title[256];
    char author[64];
    float price;
    void Date(char *title, char *author, char *publisher,
        float price); // Constructor
    void show_title(void) { cout << title << '\n'; };
    float get_price(void) { return(price); };
    void show_book(void) { show_title(); show_publisher(); };
    void assign_publisher(char *name) { strcpy(publisher,name); };
  private:
    char publisher[256];
    void show_publisher(void) { cout << publisher << '\n'; };
};
```

Your programs can define the constructor function within the class itself or outside of the class. When your program later declares an object, the program can pass parameters to the constructor function, as shown here:

```cpp
Book tips("Jamsa's 1001 C/C++ Tips","Jamsa","Jamsa Press", 39.95);
```

The constructor function will automatically execute. Tip 895 presents a program that uses a constructor function to initialize instances of the *Book* class.

Using a Constructor Function

As you have learned, a constructor function is a special class function that automatically executes when you create an instance of a class. Programs normally use constructor functions to initialize a member values. The following program, CONSTRUC.CPP, uses the constructor function *Book* to initialize members of instances of the *Book* class:

```
#include <iostream.h>
#include <iomanip.h>
#include <string.h>

class Book {
  public:
    char title[256];
    char author[64];
    float price;
    Book(char *btitle, char *bauthor, char *bpublisher,
        float bprice);
    void show_title(void) { cout << title << '\n'; };
    float get_price(void) { return(price); };
    void show_book(void) { show_title(); show_publisher(); };
    void assign_publisher(char *name) { strcpy(publisher,name); };
  private:
    char publisher[256];
    void show_publisher(void) { cout << publisher << '\n'; };
};

Book::Book(char *btitle, char *bauthor, char *bpublisher,
  float bprice)
  {
    strcpy(title, btitle);
    strcpy(author, bauthor);
    strcpy(publisher, bpublisher);
    price = bprice;
  }

void main(void)
  {
    Book tips("Jamsa's 1001 C/C++ Tips", "Jamsa", "Jamsa Press",
      39.95);
    Book diary("All My Secrets...", "Kris Jamsa", "None", 9.95);

    tips.show_book();
    diary.show_book();
  }
```

In this case, the constructor function *Book* precedes each of its parameter names with the letter b to distinguish the names from the class members. As you will learn in Tip 897, however, your programs can precede variable names with the class name to resolve name conflicts.

Constructor Functions Do Not Return a Value

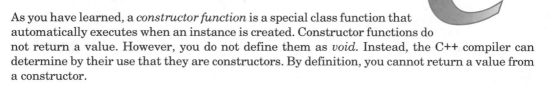

As you have learned, a *constructor function* is a special class function that automatically executes when an instance is created. Constructor functions do not return a value. However, you do not define them as *void*. Instead, the C++ compiler can determine by their use that they are constructors. By definition, you cannot return a value from a constructor.

Resolving Name Conflicts in a Constructor Function

In Tip 895 you created the *Book* constructor function to initialize members for instances of the *Book* class. To differentiate between parameter and class member names, the program preceded each parameter name with the letter b:

```
Book::Book(char *btitle, char *bauthor, char *bpublisher,
  float bprice)
{
  strcpy(title, btitle);
  strcpy(author, bauthor);
  strcpy(publisher, bpublisher);
  price = bprice;
}
```

In this case, the parameter names *title*, *author*, *publisher*, and *price* are more meaningful and preferred. Because the names conflict with member names, the function must resolve them using the class name and double colons, as shown here:

```
Book::Book(char *title,char *author,char *publisher,float price)
{
  strcpy(Book::title, title);
  strcpy(Book::author, author);
  strcpy(Book::publisher, publisher);
  Book::price = price;
}
```

The companion disk to this book contains the program CONSTR2.CPP, which presents the complete program source code used to access objects of the type *Book* using the constructor function *Book* just shown.

C++ 898 Using a Constructor to Allocate Memory

As you have learned, constructor functions let your programs initialize member variables. If the member variable uses arrays, the constructor function can allocate the desired memory amount. For example, the following program, CONS_NEW.CPP, uses the *new* operator within the *Book* constructor function to allocate memory for the character string arrays:

```cpp
#include <iostream.h>
#include <iomanip.h>
#include <string.h>
#include <stdlib.h>

class Book {
  public:
    char *title;
    char *author;
    float price;
    Book(char *title, char *author,char *publisher,float price);
    void show_title(void) { cout << title << '\n'; };
    float get_price(void) { return(price); };
    void show_book(void) { show_title(); show_publisher(); };
    void assign_publisher(char *name) { strcpy(publisher,name); };
  private:
    char *publisher;
    void show_publisher(void) { cout << publisher << '\n'; };
};

Book::Book(char *title,char *author,char *publisher, float price)
  {
    if ((Book::title = new char[256]) == 0)
      {
        cerr << "Error allocating memory\n";
        exit(0);
      }

    if ((Book::author = new char[64]) == 0)
      {
        cerr << "Error allocating memory\n";
        exit(0);
      }

    if ((Book::publisher = new char[128]) == 0)
      {
```

```
        cerr << "Error allocating memory\n";
        exit(0);
      }

   strcpy(Book::title, title);
   strcpy(Book::author, author);
   strcpy(Book::publisher, publisher);
   Book::price = price;
 }

void main(void)
 {
   Book tips("Jamsa's 1001 C/C++ Tips", "Jamsa", "Jamsa Press",
     39.95);
   Book diary("All My Secrets...", "Kris Jamsa", "None", 9.95);

   tips.show_book();
   diary.show_book();
 }
```

Handling Memory Allocation in a Cleaner Way

C++ 899

In Tip 878 the program CONS_NEW.CPP used the *new* operator within a constructor function to allocate memory for character string members. The code for each memory allocation was very similar, as shown here:

```
if ((Book::title = new char[256]) == 0)
  {
    cerr << "Error allocating memory\n";
    exit(0);
  }

if ((Book::author = new char[64]) == 0)
  {
    cerr << "Error allocating memory\n";
    exit(0);
  }

if ((Book::publisher = new char[128]) == 0)
  {
    cerr << "Error allocating memory\n";
    exit(0);
  }
```

On way to reduce the amount of duplicate code is simply to try to allocate memory for each variable and then test to see how you did after the last allocation:

```
Book::title = new char[256];
Book::author = new char[64];
Book::publisher = new char[128];

if ((Book::title && Book::author && Book::publisher) == 0)
  {
      cout << "Error allocating memory\n";
      exit(1);
  }
```

A second way to reduce the code is to assign a custom handler first that displays the error message and exits when the free space can satisfy the request. Tip 870 discusses the *set_new_handler* function.

C++ 900 Default Parameter Values for Constructors

A *constructor function* is a special class method that automatically executes when your program creates an instance of an object. As you have learned, C++ lets your programs provide default values for function parameters. Constructor functions are no exception. The following program, DEF_CONS.CPP, uses the default values 1, 2, 3 for members of the class *MagicNumbers*:

```
#include <iostream.h>
#include <iomanip.h>

class MagicNumbers {
 public:
   MagicNumbers(int a = 1, int b = 2, int c = 3)
     {
         MagicNumbers::a = a;
         MagicNumbers::b = b;
         MagicNumbers::c = c;
     };
   void show_numbers(void)
     {
        cout << a << ' ' << b << ' '<< c << '\n'; };
 private:
   int a, b, c;
};
```

```
void main(void)
  {
    MagicNumbers one(1, 1, 1);
    MagicNumbers defaults;
    MagicNumbers happy(101, 101, 101);

    one.show_numbers();
    defaults.show_numbers();
    happy.show_numbers();
  }
```

As you can see, the instances *one* and *happy* specify their own member values. The instance named *defaults*, however, uses the default values 1, 2, and 3. By providing default values to your constructor function in this way, you can ensure that class members are initialized to meaningful values.

Overloading Constructor Functions

C901

A *constructor function* is a special class method that automatically executes when your program creates an instance of an object. As you have learned, C++ lets your programs overload functions such that the C compiler will decide which function to invoke, depending on the parameters passed. Constructor functions are no exception. The following program, NEEDVALS.CPP, provides two constructor functions for the class *Book*. The first constructor function assigns the values passed as parameters. The second constructor displays a message stating that the program must provide parameters for each parameter and then exits. The second constructor only executes should the program try to execute a function without specifying initial values:

```
#include <iostream.h>
#include <iomanip.h>
#include <string.h>
#include <stdlib.h>

class Book {
  public:
    Book(char *title, char *author,char *publisher,float price);
    Book(void);
    void show_title(void) { cout << title << '\n'; };
    float get_price(void) { return(price); };
    void show_book(void) { show_title(); show_publisher(); };
  private:
    char title[256];
    char author[64];
```

```
    float price;
    char publisher[256];
    void show_publisher(void) { cout << publisher << '\n'; };
};

Book::Book(char *title,char *author,char *publisher,float price)
  {
    strcpy(Book::title, title);
    strcpy(Book::author, author);
    strcpy(Book::publisher, publisher);
    Book::price = price;
  }

Book::Book(void)
  {
    cerr << "You must specify initial values for Book instance\n";
    exit(1);
  }
void main(void)
  {
    Book tips("Jamsa's 1001 C/C++ Tips", "Jamsa", "Jamsa Press",
       39.95);
    Book diary;

    tips.show_book();
    diary.show_book();
  }
```

Understanding Class Scope

902

As you have learned, an identifier's *scope* defines the locations within the program for which the identifier is known. C++ classes, like types and variables have a scope that begins at their definition and exists to the end of the block within which they were defined. To increase the scope of a class, you can define the class outside of all program blocks. In addition, if a class is defined as *extern*, the class is known throughout the entire program. If a class is defined as *static*, the class scope remains the same as if the class were automatic, but the class existence remains for the duration of the program.

Understanding Destructor Functions

As you have learned, each time you create an object instance, your program can automatically execute a constructor function that you can use to initialize the instance members. In a similar way, C++ lets you define a *destructor function* that automatically runs when the instance is destroyed. Destructor functions typically run at one of two times, when your program ends or when you use the *delete* operator to free memory allocated to hold an instance. Destructor functions have the same name as the class. Destructors are differentiated from functions in that their name is preceded with the tilde character (~). The following program, DESTRUCT.CPP, creates a simple destructor function that displays a message stating an instance is being destroyed. The program invokes the destructor function for each instance as it ends:

```cpp
#include <iostream.h>
#include <iomanip.h>
#include <string.h>

class Book {
  public:
    char title[256];
    char author[64];
    float price;
    Book(char *title,char *author, char *publisher, float price);
    ~Book(void);
    void show_title(void) { cout << title << '\n'; };
    float get_price(void) { return(price); };
    void show_book(void) { show_title(); show_publisher(); };
    void assign_publisher(char *name) { strcpy(publisher,name); };
  private:
    char publisher[256];
    void show_publisher(void) { cout << publisher << '\n'; };
};

Book::Book(char *title,char *author, char *publisher, float price)
  {
    strcpy(Book::title, title);
    strcpy(Book::author, author);
    strcpy(Book::publisher, publisher);
    Book::price = price;
  }
```

```
Book::~Book(void)
  {
    cout << "Destructing the instance " << title << '\n';
  }

void main(void)
  {
    Book tips("Jamsa's 1001 C/C++ Tips", "Jamsa", "Jamsa Press",
      39.95);
    Book diary("All My Secrets...", "Kris Jamsa", "None", 9.95);

    tips.show_book();
    diary.show_book();
  }
```

C++ 904 Creating an Array of Class Variables

Several of the tips presented throughout this book created arrays of structures.
In a similar way, your programs can create an array of class instances. The
following program, LIBRARY.CPP, creates an array that contains the specifics
about four books:

```
#include <iostream.h>
#include <iomanip.h>
#include <string.h>

class Book {
  public:
    void show_title(void) { cout << title << '\n'; };
    void show_book(void) { show_title(); show_publisher(); };
    void assign_members(char *, char *, char *, float);
  private:
    char title[256];
    char author[64];
    float price;
    char publisher[256];
    void show_publisher(void) { cout << publisher << '\n'; };
};

void Book::assign_members(char *title, char *author, char
*publisher,
    float price)
  {
```

```
      strcpy(Book::title, title);
      strcpy(Book::author, author);
      strcpy(Book::publisher, publisher);
      Book::price = price;
   }

void main(void)
   {
      Book Library[4];

      Library[0].assign_members("Jamsa's 1001 C/C++ Tips", "Jamsa",
         "Jamsa Press", 39.95);
      Library[1].assign_members("Jamsa's 1001 Windows Tips","Jamsa",
         "Jamsa Press", 39.95);
      Library[2].assign_members("1001 Word for Windows Tips","Wyatt",
         "Jamsa Press", 39.95);
      Library[3].assign_members("Rescued by C++", "Jamsa",
         "Jamsa Press", 19.95);

      for (int i = 0; i < 4; i++)
         Library[i].show_book();
   }
```

Constructors and Class Arrays

As you have learned, C++ lets your programs declare arrays of a specific class type. When you declare an array, C++ automatically invokes the constructor function for each array entry. For example, the following program ARRCLASS.CPP, creates an array of the class type *Employee*:

```
#include <iostream.h>

class Employee {
  public:
    Employee(void) { cout << "Constructing an instance\n"; };
    void show_employee(void) { cout << name; };

  private:
    char name[256];
    long id;
};

  void main(void)
    {
```

```
    Employee workers[5];
    // Other statements here
}
```

When you compile and execute this program, you will see that the program automatically calls the constructor function five times, once for each array element.

Overloading an Operator

906

As you have learned, when you overload a function, the C++ compiler determines which function to invoke, based on the parameter number and types. When you create a class, C++ also lets you overload operators. When you overload an operator, you must continue to use the operator in its standard format. For example, if you overload the plus operator (+), the overload must still use the operator in the form *operand + operand*. In addition, you can only overload existing operators. C++ will not let you define your own operators. The overload you create only applies to instances of the specific class. For example, assume that you create a *String* class and overload the plus operator such that the operator concatenates two strings:

```
new_string = string + target;
```

If you use overloaded plus operator with two integer or floating-point values, the overload will not apply. Finally, C++ will not let you overload the following operators:

Operator	Function
.	Member operator
.*	Pointer-to-member operator
::	Scope-resolution operator
?:	Conditional-expression operator

Overloading the Plus Operator

907

You have learned that, to overload an operator, you must create a class for which you want the overload to apply. Next, within the class public methods, place a line that defines the operator. For example, the following program creates a *String* class and overloads the plus operator so that it concatenates strings:

```
#include <iostream.h>
#include <iomanip.h>
#include <string.h>
```

```
class String {
  public:
    char *operator +(char *append_str)
      { return(strcat(buffer, append_str)); };

    String(char *string)
      { strcpy(buffer, string);
        length = strlen(buffer); }

    void show_string() { cout << buffer; };
  private:
    char buffer[256];
    int length;
};

void main(void)
 {
    String title("Jamsa's 1001 ");

    title + "C/C++ Tips";

    title.show_string();
 }
```

The program begins by assigning the member *buffer* the string "Jamsa's 1001 ". The program then uses the overloaded plus operator (+) to concatenate the characters "C/C++ Tips". Note that the operator overload is a simply a function that receives a parameter. The function receives only one parameter. The parameter is the second operand. The instance operand is implied by the operation.

Overloading the Minus-Sign Operator

C++ 908

In Tip 902 you created a *String* class and overloaded the plus operator. The following program, STRMINUS.CPP, overloads the minus operator (–), using it to remove all occurrences of a specified character from the class *buffer* member:

```
#include <iostream.h>
#include <iomanip.h>
#include <string.h>

class String {
  public:
```

```
      char *operator +(char *append_str)
        { return(strcat(buffer, append_str)); };

      char *operator -(char letter);

      String(char *string)
        { strcpy(buffer, string);
          length = strlen(buffer); }

      void show_string() { cout << buffer; };
    private:
      char buffer[256];
      int length;
};

char *String::operator -(char letter)
  {
    char target[256];
    int i, j;

    for (i = 0, j = 0; buffer[j]; j++)
      if (buffer[j] != letter)
        target[i++] = buffer[j];
    target[i] = NULL;

    for (i = 0, j = 0; (buffer[j] = target[i]); i++, j++)
      ;
    return(buffer);
  }

void main(void)
  {
    String title("Jamsa's 1001 ");

    title + "C/C++ Tips\n";
    title.show_string();

    title - '0';
    title.show_string();
  }
```

C++ 909 Understanding Abstraction

Abstraction is the process of looking at an object in terms of its methods (the operations) while temporarily ignoring the underlying details of the object's implementation. Programmers use abstraction to simplify the design and implementation of complex programs. For example, if you are told to write a word processor, the task might at first seem insurmountable. However, using abstraction you begin to realize that a word processor actually consists of objects, such as a document object that you will create, save, spell-check, and print. By viewing programs in abstract terms, you can better understand the required programming. In C++ the primary tool for supporting abstraction is the class.

Allocating a Pointer to a Class

As you work with class variables, there may be times when you want to allocate dynamic arrays or dynamic lists of the class type. The following program, DYNCLASS.CPP, for example, creates an array of pointers to variables of the class type *Book*:

```cpp
#include <iostream.h>
#include <iomanip.h>
#include <string.h>

class Book {
  public:
    void show_title(void) { cout << title << '\n'; };
    void show_book(void) { show_title(); show_publisher(); };
    Book(char *title,char *author,char *publisher, float price);
  private:
    char title[256];
    char author[64];
    float price;
    char publisher[256];
    void show_publisher(void) { cout << publisher << '\n'; };
};

Book::Book(char *title,char *author,char *publisher, float price)
  {
    strcpy(Book::title, title);
    strcpy(Book::author, author);
    strcpy(Book::publisher, publisher);
    Book::price = price;
  }

void main(void)
  {
    Book *Library[4];

    int i = 0;

    Library[0] = new Book("Jamsa's 1001 C/C++ Tips", "Jamsa",
```

```
                   "Jamsa Press", 39.95);
      Library[1] = new Book("Jamsa's 1001 Windows Tips", "Jamsa",
         "Jamsa Press", 39.95);
      Library[2] = new Book("1001 Word for Windows Tips", "Wyatt",
         "Jamsa Press", 39.95);
      Library[3] = new Book("Rescued by C++", "Jamsa",
         "Jamsa Press", 19.95);

      for (i = 0; i < 4; i++)
        Library[i]->show_book();
   }
```

As you can see, each time you create an instance using *new*, the class constructor function is invoked.

C++ 911 Discarding a Pointer to a Class

In Tip 910 you created an array of pointers to structures of type *Book*. Each time the program created an instance, the *Book* constructor function is automatically invoked. In a similar way, if the class has a destructor, the function will automatically invoked when each instance is destroyed. The following program, DYNDESTR.CPP, adds an destructor function to the *Book* class. The program also uses the *delete* operator to discard each instance:

```
#include <iostream.h>
#include <iomanip.h>
#include <string.h>

class Book {
  public:
    void show_title(void) { cout << title << '\n'; };
    void show_book(void) { show_title(); show_publisher(); };
    Book(char *title,char *author,char *publisher, float price);
    ~Book() { cout<<"Destroying the entry for "<< title <<'\n'; };
  private:
    char title[256];
    char author[64];
    float price;
    char publisher[256];
    void show_publisher(void) { cout << publisher << '\n'; };
};
```

```
Book::Book(char *title,char *author,char *publisher,float price)
  {
    strcpy(Book::title, title);
    strcpy(Book::author, author);
    strcpy(Book::publisher, publisher);
    Book::price = price;
  }

void main(void)
  {
    Book *Library[4];

    int i = 0;

    Library[0] = new Book("Jamsa's 1001 C/C++ Tips", "Jamsa",
      "Jamsa Press", 39.95);
    Library[1] = new Book("Jamsa's 1001 Windows Tips", "Jamsa",
    "Jamsa Press", 39.95);
    Library[2] = new Book("1001 Word for Windows Tips", "Wyatt",
      "Jamsa Press", 39.95);
    Library[3] = new Book("Rescued by C++", "Jamsa",
      "Jamsa Press", 19.95);

    for (i = 0; i < 4; i++)
      Library[i]->show_book();

    for (i = 0; i < 4; i++)
      delete Library[i];
  }
```

Understanding Encapsulation

C++
912

As you read articles and books about object-oriented programming and C++, you might encounter the term *encapsulation*. In the simplest sense, encapsulation is the combination of data and methods into a single data structure. Encapsulation groups together all the components of an object.
In the "object-oriented" sense, encapsulation also defines how an object's data can be referenced. As you have learned, C++ classes let you divide your data into public and private sections. Programs can only access an object's private data using defined public methods. Encapsulating an object's data in this way protects the data from program misuses. In C++, the class is the fundamental tool for encapsulation.

C++ 913 Discarding Leading White Space on Input

As you have learned, the *cin* I/O stream uses white space as delimiter for input data. When you use *cin*, there may be times when you will want *cin* to ignore leading white space. In such cases, your programs can use the *ws* manipulator as shown here:

```
cin >> ws >> buffer;
```

The following program, WS.CPP, uses the *ws* manipulator to eat leading white space:

```cpp
#include <iostream.h>

void main(voi)
  {
    char buffer[256];

    cout << "Enter a word with leading blanks\n";
    cin >> ws >> buffer;
    cout << "==" << buffer << "==";
  }
```

Experiment with this program, removing the *ws* manipulator and changing the leading whitespace input.

C++ 914 Understanding Class Libraries

As you have learned, object libraries make it very easy for your programs to reuse functions. A *class library* is very similar to an object library, in that it contains code to which your programs can link. Unlike an object code library, which contains a collection of callable functions, a class library contains class methods. To use the methods, your programs must use the corresponding class structures. In other words, your programs cannot simply call class library functions without using a class. Throughout this book, your programs have made extensive use of the C++ *iostream* class library to perform I/O operations using *cin* and *cout*. Just as you may eventually create object code libraries that contain the functions that you create, the same is true for class libraries. By creating your own class libraries, you make it easy for future programs to use existing objects.

Place Your Class Definitions in a Header File

When you create a class that might be used by other programs, you should place the class declaration in a header file that is based on the class name. For example, the class declaration for the *iostream* class is contained in the header file iostream.h. Do not place your class methods in the header file. Instead, compile the class methods and place them into a class library, as discussed in Tip 914. By placing the class declaration in a header file in this way, you make it much easier for a program to use a class. Rather than having to know the complete class structure, the program simply needs to include the class header file and can then use only those members it requires.

Using *inline* with Class Member Functions

As you know, the *inline* keyword the compiler to place a function's code inline at each reference. Using the *inline* keyword trades increased program size for improved performance. When you define class member functions, C++ lets you place the functions within the class itself or outside of the class. When you place a function definition inside the class, C++ generates inline code each time it later encounters an invocation of the method. When you define the function outside of the class, however, C++ does not use inline code. If you have a method that you have defined outside of a class for which you want the compiler to generate inline code, simply precede the function name with the *inline* keyword. The following function definition, for example, directs the compiler to generate inline code for each invocation of the method *show_book*:

```
inline void Book::show_book(void)
    { show_title(); show_publisher(); };
```

Initializing a Class Array

As you have learned, C++ lets you declare a class array. When you declare a class array, the program will automatically invoke the constructor function for each element. When you declare an array of structures, C++ lets you initialize the array member, as shown here:

```
struct Employee {
    char name[64];
    long id;
} workers [2] = {{ "Kris", 1} , "Happy", 2}};
```

When you declare a class array, C++ does not let you provide initial values. Thus, assigning the member values can be challenging. The following program, ARRAYASN.CPP, uses the constructor function to assign each array element:

```cpp
#include <iostream.h>
#include <string.h>

class Employee {
  public:
    Employee(void);
    void show_employee(void) { cout << name << endl; };
  private:
    char name[256];
    long id;
};

Employee::Employee(void)
 {
   static int index = 0;

   switch (index++) {
     case 0: strcpy(Employee::name, "Kris");
             Employee::id = 1;
             break;
     case 1: strcpy(Employee::name, "Happy");
             Employee::id = 2;
             break;
    };
 }

void main(void)
 {
   Employee workers[2];

   workers[0].show_employee();
   workers[1].show_employee();
 }
```

The constructor function uses the static variable *index* to determine which element it is initializing. As you can guess, the constructor could become quite messy, depending on the number of elements and class members.

Inline Class Code Allows Changes

918

As you have learned, C++ lets you place method functions inline within the class or outside of the class. When you are determining which functions to place inline or if any functions should be inline, keep in mind that placing method code inline exposes the code to changes. For example, the following class uses several inline functions:

```
class Book {
  public:
    char title[256];
    char author[64];
    float price;
    void show_title(void) { cout << title << '\n'; };
    float get_price(void) { return(price); };
    void show_book(void);
    void assign_publisher(char *name) { strcpy(publisher,name); };
  private:
    char publisher[256];
    void show_publisher(void) { cout << publisher << '\n'; };
};
```

When another programmer uses this class, the programmer can easily change the class methods because the code is contained within the class itself. If you instead place the class methods within a class library, the programmer must have access to the library source code in order to change the class methods. In this way, using the class library insulates the class from spur-of-the-moment changes.

Public, Private, and Protected Section Order Is Unimportant

919

As you have learned, a class can contain public and private (and you will learn about protected) data and methods. When you declare a class, C++ does not care about the order of the sections within your class. In other words, the public members can come first or the private members can come first. The order makes no difference to the compiler. However, you should choose a declaration format that you use within your programs and then stick to the same format throughout your programs. In that way, readers who are familiar with your programs always know that within your class declarations, the public members come first followed by the private members, for example. In the advanced section of this book, you will learn that C++ also supports protected members. I normally use the following template:

```
class Name {
   public:
      // Public members
   protected:
      // Protected members
   private:
      // Private members
};
```

The template shows class methods from most accessible to least accessible.

C++ 920 By Default, Everything Is Private

As you have learned, classes normally contain public and private members. When you declare a class, members, by default, are private. For example, the following class contains three private members and two public members:

```
class Employee {
    char name[256];
    int id;
    float salary;
  public:
     Employee(char *name, int id, float salary);
     void show_employee(void);
};
```

As you can see, the class does not explicitly specify its private area. However, because the class does not state otherwise, the first three members are considered private. Rather than make another programmer guess or have to understand the default, your classes should explicitly label their public and private members.

C++ 921 Understanding the Static Store

As you have learned, C++ documentation refers to the heap space as the *free store*. As you read through articles and books on C++, you might encounter the term *static store*. In the simplest sense, the static store is a global memory region from which data can be allocated by the compiler. When you create global or static variables, the memory for the variables is allocated from the static store. In most cases, the scope of objects allocated from the static store is the entire program. In other words, the objects are global.

Synchronizing iostream Operations with stdio

As you have learned, C++ programs can use the standard output functions, such as *printf* and *scanf*, that are defined *stdio.h*, or they can use the extractor and inclusion operators with the iostreams *cout* and *cin*. To improve your program's readability, you should normally choose one technique or the other. However, there may be times when you just can't get around using both. For such cases, you can synchronize operations between the two I/O techniques using the *sync_with_stdio* function. The function directs the two I/O techniques to use the same input buffer and the same output buffer so that the same data is accessible to both. The following program, SYNCIO.CPP, illustrates the use of the *sync_with_stdio* function:

```cpp
#include <iostream.h>
#include <stdio.h>

void main(void)
  {
    ios::sync_with_stdio();

    printf("This is book is ");
    cout << "Jamsa's 1001 C/C++ Tips\n";
  }
```

Understanding C++ I/O Streams

Almost all of the C++ tips presented throughout this book have made extensive use of the *cin, cout,* and *cerr* I/O streams. In the Advanced C++ section of this book you will learn about *inheritance*, which lets objects of one class inherit the characteristics of another class. As it turns out, C++ provides the base class *ios* (input output stream), which defines the fundamental I/O operations. Using the *ios* stream, C++ derives an output stream class and an input stream class. When you closely examine the header file iostream.h in the Advanced C++ section of this book, you will find a class definition for *ios* and then class definitions for C++ output and input streams discussed next. Note that the streams are defined in the files iostream.h, fstream.h, and strstrea.h.

924 Understanding the C++ Output Streams

Throughout this book, your programs have made extensive use of the *cout* output stream. In the simplest sense, an *output stream* is a destination for bytes. For most of the discussion presented, we have assumed that C++ provides an output stream used by *cout, cerr,* and *clog* and an input stream used by *cin.* As it turns out, the header file iostream.h actually defines three different output streams. Table 924 briefly describes each output stream's use.

Output Stream	Function
ostream	Used for output to cout, cerr, and clog
ofstream	Used for file output to disk
ostrstream	Used to perform buffered output to a string

Table 924 *Output streams defined in iostream.h, fstream.h, and strstream.h.*

Several of the tips presented throughout this section discuss ways your programs can use these streams.

925 Understanding the C++ Input Streams

As you have learned, the header file iostream.h actually defines three different output streams, one for screen output, one for file output, and one for use with strings. As you might guess, iostream.h also defines three input streams. Again, in the simplest sense, an *input stream* is byte source. Table 925 briefly describes the function of each.

Input Stream	Function
istream	Used for input from cin
ifstream	Used for file input from disk
istrstream	Used to read buffered input from a string

Table 925 *Input streams defined in iostream.h, fstream.h and strstream.h.*

Several of the tips that follow discuss ways your programs can use these streams.

Opening a File Stream

C++ 926

As you have learned, C++ provides the *ifstream* and *ofstream* (input and output) file streams. Within your C++ programs, you can perform I/O using these two stream classes, or you can use standard C file I/O operations using *fopen, fgets, fputs,* and so on. To open a file stream, you must declare a variable of the corresponding class (ifstream or ofstream). Assuming you want to perform input and output operations, your declaration might appear as follows:

```
ifstream input;
ofstream output;
```

Next, to open a file stream, you might use the *open* member, as shown here:

```
input.open("FILENAME.EXT", ios::in);
output.open("FILENAME.OUT", ios::out);
```

In addition, to using the *open* member , you can use the constructor function (see the Advanced C++ section for a discussion on constructors) when you declare the stream variable, as shown here:

```
ifstream input("FILENAME.EXT", ios::in);
ofstream output("FILENAME.OUT", ios::out);
```

The *ios::in* or *ios::out* parameters select input or output. In addition to these two values, your programs can use combinations of the values listed in Table 926.

Value	Meaning
ios::app	Opens the stream in append mode
ios::ate	Opens a file for either input or output, moving the file pointer to the end of the file
ios::in	Opens a file for input
ios::out	Opens a file for output
ios::nocreate	Opens a file only if it already exists
ios::noreplace	Opens a file only if it does not already exist
ios::trunc	Truncates an existing file
ios::binary	Opens a file in binary mode

Table 926 *Value open mode values for ifstream and ofstream.*

927 Closing a File Stream

As you learned in Tip 926, your programs can open C++ iostreams using the *open* member or using a constructor function when you declare a stream variable. When you have finished using the file stream, your programs should close the stream using the *close* member:

```
input.close();
output.close();
```

By default, when your program ends or if you destroy the class variable, the file stream is closed. If you want to associate the file stream with a different file, however, you will need to use the *close* member.

928 Reading and Writing File Stream Data

As you have learned, C++ lets your programs open file streams of the class *istream* for input operations. To read data from an input file stream, your programs use the *read* member:

```
input.read(buffer, number_of_bytes);
```

As you can see, the program must provide a buffer into which the data is a read and the number of bytes to read. In a similar way, if you have opened an output stream, your programs can write data to the output stream using the *write* member:

```
output.write(buffer, number_of_bytes);
```

Note that the read and write members *do not* return the number of bytes successfully read or written. Instead, they return references to the stream. To determine the success or failure of an operation, you must check the status members, as discussed in Tip 929.

929 Checking the Status of a File Operation

When you perform file I/O operations using the *ifstream* and *ofstream* class streams, your programs can determine the success of an open, read, or write operation using the members listed in Table 929.

Member	Example	Function
bad	variable.bad()	Returns true if an unrecoverable error was encountered
fail	variable.fail()	Returns true if an unrecoverable or expected error such as a file not found was encountered
good	variable.good()	Returns true if the operation was successful
eof	variable.eof()	Returns true if an end of file was encountered
clear	variable.clear()	Clears the status flags
rdstate	variable.rdstate()	Returns the current error state

Table 929 *Member functions that return I/O success or failure information.*

Putting File Stream Operations Together

930

Several of the preceding tips have discussed C++ file streams and the various member functions your programs can use to perform file I/O. The following program, FILECOPY.CPP, uses several of these member functions to create a simply file copy program that copies text files a character at a time:

```cpp
#include <iostream.h>
#include <stdlib.h>
#include <fstream.h>

void main(int argc, char **argv)
 {
   char buffer[1];

   ifstream input(argv[1], ios::in);

   if (input.fail())
    {
      cout << "Error opening the file " << argv[1];
      exit(1);
    }

   ofstream output(argv[2], ios::out);

   if (output.fail())
    {
      cout << "Error opening the file " << argv[2];
      exit(1);
    }
```

```
  do {
    input.read(buffer, sizeof(buffer));
    if (input.good())
      output.write(buffer, sizeof(buffer));
  } while (! input.eof());

  input.close();
  output.close();
}
```

To copy the file FILECOPY.CPP to FILECOPY.SAV, you would invoke the program as follows:

```
C:\> FILECOPY FILECOPY.CPP FILECOPY.SAV <ENTER>
```

C++ 931 Performing a Binary Copy Operation

In Tip 930 you created the program FILECOPY.CPP, which copies the first text file specified in the command line to a file with the name specified by the second command-line argument. If you want the program to copy binary files, you need to change the open operations to use the *ios::binary* flag, as shown here:

```
ifstream input(argv[1], ios::in | ios:binary);

if (input.fail())
  {
    cout << "Error opening the file " << argv[1];
    exit(1);
  }

ofstream output(argv[2], ios::out | ios::binary);

if (output.fail())
  {
    cout << "Error opening the file " << argv[2];
    exit(1);
  }
```

The companion disk that accompanies this book contains the program BIN_COPY.CPP, which performs a binary file-copy operation.

Controlling the File Stream Pointer

As you have learned, the *ifstream* and *ofstream* file streams provide member functions that your programs can use to perform file I/O. When your program perform file I/O operations, there may be times when the programs need to position or determine the position of the file stream pointer. To position the file pointer, your programs can use the *seekg* (for input) and *seekp* (for output) members:

```
input.seekg(byte_offset);
output.seekp(byte_offset);
```

The byte offset is a *long* offset value, that unless specified otherwise, is applied from the start of the file. To apply the offset from a location other than the start of the file, use one of the following values:

```
enum seek_dir { beg=0, cur=1, end=2 };
```

In a similar way, if your programs need to determine the current file pointer position, your programs can use the *tellg* and *tellp* members, as shown here:

```
offset = output.tellp();
offset = input.tellg();
```

Understanding Character String Streams

In the C section of this book you learned that your programs can use the *sprintf* and *sscanf* functions to output and input data to and from a character string. To help you perform similar operations, the header file istrstream.h defines the *istrstream* class. When your programs create a string output stream, you essentially bind the stream to a specific character string. For example, the following statements create a string output stream named *str* and binds it to the variable *string*. The following program, FILL_STR.CPP, creates a variable of type *istrstream* and fills it with the characters "Jamsa's 1001 C/C++ Tips":

```
#include <iostream.h>
#include <strstrea.h>
```

```
void main(void)
 {
   char string[256];

   ostrstream str(string, 256);     // Bind the string

   str << "Jamsa's 1001 C/C++ Tips" << ends;

   cout << string;
 }
```

C++ 934 Understanding the *ends* Manipulator

In Tip 933 you created a string output stream and used the insertion operator to output the *ends* manipulator to the stream. The manipulator places a NULL character into the stream, much like the *endl* manipulator inserts the newline character. When you use the insertion operator to place text in a string buffer, you will use the *ends* manipulator on a regular basis. The following program, ENDS.CPP, uses the *ends* manipulator with several string output streams:

```
#include <iostream.h>
#include <strstrea.h>

void main(void)
 {
   char title[64], publisher[64], author[64];

   ostrstream title_str(title, sizeof(title));
   ostrstream pub_str(publisher, sizeof(publisher));
   ostrstream author_str(author, sizeof(author));

   title_str << "Jamsa's 1001 C/C++ Tips" << ends;
   pub_str << "Jamsa Press" << ends;
   author_str << "Jamsa" << ends;

   cout << "Book: " << title << " Publisher: " << publisher
     << " Author: " << author << endl;
 }
```

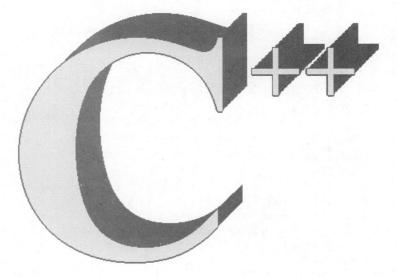

935 Understanding Polymorphism

When you begin reading books and articles on C++, a term you will encounter is *polymorphism*, which lets programs apply the same operation to objects of different types. In this way, polymorphism lets programmers use the same interface to access different objects. In C++, *virtual functions* provide access to polymorphism. In the simplest sense, a virtual function is a pointer to a function that is resolved at run time. Depending on the function pointed to by virtual function, the operation performed will differ. As a result, a single interface (the virtual function) can provide access to different operations. Tip 980 discusses virtual functions in detail.

936 Invoking One Object from Another

As your C++ programs become more complex, they will begin to use more than one type of object, and there will be times when one object will use another. For example, the following program, TWO_OBJS.CPP, creates two different object types: an object that contains information about a reader and an object that contains information about a book. The *Reader* object invokes the *Book* object to display information about a reader's favorite book:

```cpp
#include <iostream.h>
#include <string.h>

class Book {
  public:
    Book(char *title) { strcpy(Book::title, title); } ;
    void show_book(void) { cout << title; };
  private:
    char title[64];
};

class Reader {
  public:
    Reader(char *name) { strcpy(Reader::name, name); };
    void show_reader(class Book book) {
        cout << "Reader: " << name << ' ' << "Book: ";
        book.show_book();
    };
  private:
    char name[64];
};
```

```
void main(void)
  {
    Reader reader("Kris Jamsa");
    Book favorite_book("Compiler Internals");

    reader.show_reader(favorite_book);
  }
```

Understanding Friends

937

As you have learned, a class can contain public and private data and methods. Normally, the only way to access private members is through the public or interface methods. As your programs begin to work with more than one type of object, there may be times when one the object calls another object or uses another object's data members. In Tip 936, for example, the *Reader* object used the *Book* object method *show_book* to display the title of a book. The only way the *Reader* object could access the *Book* object private data was through the *show_book* method. Depending on your program, there may be times when you want one object to have access to another object's public and private data. In such cases, you can specify a *friend object*. Given the previous *Reader* and *Book* program, the *Book* object could declare the *Reader* object as a friend. The *Reader* object could then directly access the *Book* object's private data, displaying the book's title without having to call the *show_title* method. The remainder of the program code could not directly access the *Book* object's private data. The only object that could access the private data would be *Book* object's friend, the *Reader*. Before you can specify a friend, however, you should tell the compiler about the friend's class, as discussed in Tip 938.

Telling the Compiler About a Class

938

When one class references the identifier for a second class that has not yet been declared, you must tell the compiler that the identifier corresponds to a class that will be declared later in the program. To do so, you can simply place a statement in your program that contains the *class* keyword and the class name:

```
class class_name;
```

For example, assume that the *Book* class wants to tell the compiler that the *Reader* class is its friend. If the *Reader* class has not yet been declared, you can place the following statement in your program that tells the compiler that you will define the class later in the source code:

```
class Reader;
```

Tip 939 uses this technique to inform the compiler about the *Reader* class before referencing the *Reader* class within the *Book* class.

C++ 939 Declaring the *Reader* Class as a Friend

As you have learned, C++ lets you specify one class as the friend of another, which provides the friend with access to the classes private data and methods. The following program, READBOOK.CPP, uses the *friend* keyword to specify that the *Reader* class is a friend of the *Book* class. As such, objects of type *Reader* can access the private members of a Book object. In this case, the *Reader* class accesses the *Book* class private data member *title*:

```
#include <iostream.h>
#include <string.h>

class Book {
  public:
    Book(char *title) { strcpy(Book::title, title); } ;
    void show_book(void) { cout << title; };
    friend Reader;
  private:
    char title[64];
};

class Reader {
  public:
    Reader(char *name) { strcpy(Reader::name, name); };
    void show_reader(class Book book) {
          cout << "Reader: " << name << ' ' << "Book: " <<
book.title; };
  private:
    char name[64];
};

void main(void)
  {
    Reader reader("Kris Jamsa");
    Book favorite_book("Compiler Internals");

    reader.show_reader(favorite_book);
  }
```

As you can see, within the *Book* object, the following statement tells the compiler that the *Reader* object is a friend, thus permitting the *Reader* object to access the *Book* object's private members:

```
friend Reader;
```

Eliminating the Need for the *class class_name* Statement

As you have learned, when one class references an identifier for a class that has not yet been declared, you can inform the compiler that the identifier corresponds to a class using a statement similar to the following:

```
class class_name;
```

By including such a statement, the class can refer to second class using only the class identifier, as shown here:

```
friend class_name;
```

If you place *class* between *friend* and *class_name,* you eliminate the need for the "forward" declaration:

```
friend class class_name;
```

The following declaration of the *Book* class uses this technique to inform the compiler that the *Reader* class is a friend:

```
class Book {
  public:
    Book(char *title) { strcpy(Book::title, title); } ;
    void show_book(void) { cout << title; };
    friend Reader;
  private:
    char title[64];
};
```

Restricting a Friend's Access

As you have learned, C++ lets you specify that one object is a *friend* of another, which lets the friend have access to the object's private members.

To control the friend's access to the private members better, C++ lets you specify specific methods within the friend that can access the private members. The friend's other methods have no access to the members. For example, assume that only the *show_book* member of the *Reader* object needs to access the *Book* object's private members. Within the *Book* class, you can place the following statement:

```
friend Reader::show_book(void);
```

The following program, FRIEND2.CPP, uses this format to restrict the *Reader* class access to the *Book* object:

```
#include <iostream.h>
#include <string.h>

class Reader {
  public:
    Reader(char *name) { strcpy(Reader::name, name); };
    void show_reader(class Book book);
  private:
    char name[64];
};

class Book {
  public:
    Book(char *title) { strcpy(Book::title, title); } ;
    void show_book(void) { cout << title; };
    friend Reader::show_reader(Book book);
  private:
    char title[64];
};

void Reader::show_reader(class Book book)
  { cout << "Reader: " << name << ' ' << "Book: " << book.title;};

void main(void)
 {
    Reader reader("Kris Jamsa");
    Book favorite_book("Compiler Internals");
    reader.show_reader(favorite_book);
 }
```

Name Conflicts and Friends

942

When your classes use friends to access the members of another class, there may be times when member names conflict between the two classes.

When such conflicts occur, the member of the current class is used. The following program, MEMCONFL.CPP, illustrates a member name conflict between friends:

```cpp
#include <iostream.h>
#include <string.h>

class Book {
  public:
    Book(char *title) { strcpy(Book::title, title); } ;
    void show_book(void) { cout << title; };
    friend class Reader;
  private:
    char title[64];
};

class Reader {
  public:
    Reader(char *name) { strcpy(Reader::name, name); };
    void show_reader(class Book book) {
        cout << "Reader: " << name << ' ' << "Book: " <<
book.title; };
    void show_book(void)
       { cout << "The book's reader is " << name << endl; } ;
  private:
    char name[64];
};

void main(void)
  {
    Reader reader("Kris Jamsa");
    Book favorite_book("Compiler Internals");
    reader.show_book();
    reader.show_reader(favorite_book);
  }
```

As you can see, both classes use the member name *show_book*. When you compile and execute this program, the *Reader* class member is used, as shown here:

```
C:\> MEMCONFL  <ENTER>
The book's reader is Kris Jamsa
Reader: Kris Jamsa Book: Compiler Internals
```

C++ 943

Understanding Inheritance

As you have learned, C++ lets objects of one type call and access of objects of a different class type. In addition, C++ lets you build one object using another. For example, assume that you have defined a *disk_drive* class, a *keyboard* class, a *screen* class, and a *mouse* class. By combining all four classes, you could create a *computer* class. As the number of classes you create within C++ programs increases, you may find that many of your newer classes are simply extensions of classes you have already created. To help you reuse your existing classes (saving your considerable programming time), C++ lets you combine objects to build a new class. *Inheritance* is the ability of one class to inherit (use) the characteristics of another class. When a class is built from two or more existing classes, the term *multiple inheritance* is used. C++ supports multiple inheritance. Many of the tips that follow discuss inheritance in detail.

C++ 944

Understanding Base and Derived Classes

When you build one class using an existing class, the new class inherits the characteristics of the existing class. The characteristics include the data and methods as well as their access (public and private). As you read through magazines and books on object-oriented programming, you will encounter the terms *base class* and *derived class*. The base class is the original class whose characteristics are being inherited. The derived class is the class being created. A base class can be used by many different classes. A derived class can be built from several different base classes.

C++ 945

Inheritance in C++

C++ supports *inheritance*, which lets you derive a new class from an existing or base. When you derive one class from another in C++, you will use the following format:

```
class derived_class: public base_class {
    public:
        // Derived class public members
    private:
        // Derived class private members
};
```

For example, the following program, BLD_LIB.CPP, creates a base class named *Book* and then derives a class named *LibraryCard* from the base class *Book*:

```cpp
#include <iostream.h>
#include <string.h>

class Book {
  public:
    Book(char *title) { strcpy(Book::title, title); };
    void show_title(void) { cout << title << endl; };
  private:
    char title[64];
};

class LibraryCard : public Book {
  public:
    LibraryCard(char *title, char *author,
      char *publisher) : Book(title)
      {
        strcpy(LibraryCard::author, author);
        strcpy(LibraryCard::publisher, publisher);
      };
    void show_library(void) {
        show_title();
        cout << author << ' ' << publisher; };
  private:
    char author[64];
    char publisher[64];
};

void main(void)
  {
    LibraryCard card("Jamsa's 1001 C/C++ Tips", "Jamsa", "Jamsa
Press");
    card.show_library();
  }
```

Tip 946 discusses this program's processing in detail.

Deriving a Class

In Tip 945, the program derived the class *LibraryCard* using the base class *Book*. The first line of the Library class declaration informs the compiler that *LibraryCard* is a derived class that uses the base class *Book*:

```cpp
class LibraryCard : public Book {
```

The remainder of the class declaration is very similar to those with which you have been working, with the exception of the constructor function. As you can see, immediately following the declaration of the *LibraryCard* constructor is an invocation of the *Book* constructor:

```
LibraryCard(char *title, char *author,
  char *publisher) : Book(title)
  {
    strcpy(LibraryCard::author, author);
    strcpy(LibraryCard::publisher, publisher);
  };
```

When the *LibraryCard* constructor is called, it will first call the constructor for the base class (for *Book*). If you do not specify the base class constructor in this way, the compiler will generate a syntax error.

947 Understanding Base and Derived Constructors

When you derive a class from a base class that has a constructor function, you must invoke the base class constructor from within the constructor of the derived class. The following program, BASEDERI.CPP, illustrates the processing that gets performed during the derived class constructor invocation:

```
#include <iostream.h>

class Base {
 public:
   Base(void) { cout << "Base class constructor\n"; };
};

class Derived:Base {
 public:
   Derived(void) : Base()
     { cout << "Derived class constructor\n"; };
};

void main(void)
  {
    Derived object;
  }
```

When you compile and execute this program, your screen will display the following:

```
C:\> BASEDERI  <ENTER>
Base class constructor
Derived class constructor
```

As you can see, the base class constructor executes before the derived class constructor.

Understanding Protected Members

As you have learned, C++ lets you categorize class members as public or private. A member's private or public categorization controls how your program can access the member. When you use inheritance to derive one class from another, C++ adds a third member category: protected. A *protected member* is essentially in the middle of a private and public member. For a base class, the protected members can be accessed by derived objects just as though the members were public. Outside of the derived objects, however, the protected members can only be accessed through the public interface routines. The following class adds two protected members:

```
class Book {
  public:
    Book(char *title) { strcpy(Book::title, title); };
    void show_title(void) { cout << title << endl; };
  protected:
    float cost;
    void show_cost(void) { cout << cost  << endl};
  private:
    char title[64];
};
```

In this case, objects derived from the *Book* class can access the members *cost* and *show_cost* just as though the members were public. Outside of the derived classes, however, the members are treated as if they were private.

Putting Protected Members to Use

In Tip 948 you learned that C++ lets your programs declare *protected* class members, which are fully accessible to classes derived from the base class. The following program, PROTECT.CPP, illustrates the use of protected members:

```
#include <iostream.h>
#include <string.h>

class Book {
  public:
    Book(char *title) { strcpy(Book::title, title); };
    void show_title(void) { cout << title << endl; };
  protected:
    float cost;
    void show_cost(void) { cout << cost << endl; };
  private:
    char title[64];
};

class LibraryCard : public Book {
  public:
    LibraryCard(char *title, char *author,
      char *publisher) : Book(title)
      {
        strcpy(LibraryCard::author, author);
        strcpy(LibraryCard::publisher, publisher);
        cost = 39.95;
      };
    void show_library(void) {
        show_title();
        show_cost();
        cout << author << ' ' << publisher; };
  private:
    char author[64];
    char publisher[64];
};


void main(void)
 {
   LibraryCard card("Jamsa's 1001 C/C++ Tips", "Jamsa",
     "Jamsa Press");
   card.show_library();
 }
```

As you can see, within the derived class *LibraryCard,* the class statements have full access to the protected members.

When to Use Protected Members

As you have learned, protected class members can be accessed by derived classes. As you create your classes, you need to decide which members to make public, private, or protected. As a rule, you should create each class with the intention that it will later be used by a derived class. As such, decide which members should be public and protected. If the class is never used as a base class, the protected members are essentially private. Should you later use the class a base class, predetermining the protected members will save you programming time.

Understanding Multiple Inheritance

As you have learned, *inheritance* is the ability of one class to inherit the characteristics of another. *Multiple inheritance* is the ability of one class to inherit the characteristics of more than one base class. C++ supports multiple inheritance. When a derived class inherits characteristics from more than one base class, you simply separate the base class names as shown here:

```cpp
class derived_class: public base_class_1, public base_class_2 {
    public:
        // Derived class public members
    private:
        // Derived class private members
};
```

Likewise, when you later declare the constructor function for the derived class, you must call the constructor functions for each base class. Tip 952 illustrates a simple use of multiple inheritance.

A Simple Multiple Inheritance

As you have learned, multiple inheritance is the ability of a derived class to inherit the capabilities of a two or more base classes. The following program, SIMPMULT.CPP, illustrates the use of multiple inheritance to create a class named *Book*, which inherits the base classes *Page* and *Cover*:

```
#include <iostream.h>
#include <string.h>

class Cover {
 public:
   Cover(char *title) { strcpy(Cover::title, title); };
 protected:
   char title[256];
};

class Page {
 public:
   Page(int lines = 55) { Page::lines = lines; };
 protected:
   int lines;
   char *text;
};

class Book: public Cover, public Page {
 public:
   Book(char *author, char *title, float cost):
     Cover(title), Page(60)
   {
    strcpy(Book::author, author);
    strcpy(Book::title, title);
    Book::cost = cost; };
   void show_book(void) { cout << title << endl;
                          cout << author << '\t' << cost; };
 private:
   char author[256];
   float cost;
};

void main(void)
 {
   Book text("Jamsa", "Jamsa's 1001 C/C++", 39.95);

   text.show_book();
 }
```

953 Constructor Order and Base Classes

Multiple inheritance is the ability of a derived class to inherit the characteristics of more than one base class. When you create a derived class using multiple inheritance, the derived class must invoke the constructor functions for each base class. The order of constructor invocation depends on the order in which the derived class specifies the base classes. The following program, MULTINV.CPP, illustrates the order of constructor invocation when three base classes are used:

```
#include <iostream.h>

class One {
 public:
   One(void) { cout << "Constructor for One\n"; };
};

class Two {
 public:
   Two(void) { cout << "Constructor for Two\n"; };
};

class Three {
 public:
   Three(void) { cout << "Constructor for Three\n"; };
};

class Derived: public One, public Three, public Two {
 public:
    Derived(void) : One(), Two(), Three() {
      cout << "Derived constructor called\n"; };
};

void main(void)
 {
    Derived my_class;
 }
```

When you compile and execute this program, your screen will display the following output:

```
C:\> MULTINV  <ENTER>
Constructor for One
Constructor for Three
Constructor for Two
Derived constructor called
```

As you can see, the program invokes the constructor functions in the same order as the base class names appear in the class header:

```
class Derived: public One, public Three, public Two {
```

C++ 954 Declaring a Base Class as Private

Each of the previous programs that have illustrated multiple inheritance have used the keyword *public* in front of the base class names:

```
class Derived: public One, public Three, public Two {
```

When your create a derived class, you can precede the base class name with *private* or *public*. When you use the *public* keyword, public members within the base class can be directly accessed using the derived class. When you use the *private* keyword, however, the base class members can only be accessed through the derived class members. The following program, PRIVMULT.CPP, precedes two base class names with the keyword *private* and one with *public*:

```cpp
#include <iostream.h>

class One {
 public:
   One(void) { cout << "Constructor for One\n";
               one = 1; };
   int one;
};

class Two {
 public:
   Two(void) { cout << "Constructor for Two\n";
               two = 2; };
   int two;
};

class Three {
 public:
   Three(void) { cout << "Constructor for Three\n";
                 three = 3; };
   int three;
};


class Derived: private One, private Three, public Two {
 public:
    Derived(void) : One(), Two(), Three() {
      cout << "Derived constructor called\n"; };

    void show_value(void)
      { cout << one << two << three << endl; };
```

```
};

void main(void)
  {
    Derived my_class;
    my_class.show_value();
    cout << my_class.two;
  }
```

Because the base class *Two* was declared as public, the program can directly access the member *two* without having to use interface functions. The program could not, however, directly access the values *one* or *three*.

Destructor Functions and Multiple Inheritance

955

As you have learned, when you derive a class from a base class, the base class constructor function is called before that of the derived class. In the case of destructor functions, however, the opposite is true: the derived class destructor is called followed by the destructors for each base class. The following program DESTMULT.CPP, illustrates the calling sequence of base and derived class destructor functions:

```
#include <iostream.h>

class One {
 public:
   One(void) { cout << "Constructor for One\n"; };
   ~One(void) { cout << "Destructor for One\n"; };
};

class Two {
 public:
   Two(void) { cout << "Constructor for Two\n"; };
   ~Two(void) { cout << "Destructor for Two\n"; };
};

class Three {
 public:
   Three(void) { cout << "Constructor for Three\n"; };
   ~Three(void) { cout << "Destructor for Three\n"; };
};

class Derived: public One, public Two, public Three {
 public:
```

```
    Derived(void) : One(), Two(), Three() {
      cout << "Derived constructor called\n"; };
    ~Derived(void) {
      cout << "Derived destructor called\n"; };
};


void main(void)
  {
    Derived my_class;
  }
```

When you compile and execute this program, your screen will display the following output:

```
C:\> DESTMULT  <ENTER>
Constructor for One
Constructor for Two
Constructor for Three
Derived constructor called
Derived destructor called
Destructor for Three
Destructor for Two
Destructor for One
```

As you can see, the program invokes the destructor functions in the opposite order of the constructors.

956 Name Conflicts Between Base and Derived Classes

When you derive a new class using one or more base classes, there is a possibility that a member name in the derived class is the same as member name in one or more of the base classes. When such conflicts occur, the derived class member name is used. The following program, CONFLICT.CPP, illustrates a member name conflict between a base and derived class member name:

```
#include <iostream.h>

class Base {
 public:
    void display(void)
      { cout << "This is the base class" << endl; };
};

class Derived: public Base {
```

```
  public:
    void display(void)
       {cout << "This is the derived class" << endl;};
};

void main(void)
  {
    Derived my_class;

    my_class.display();
  }
```

When you compile and execute this program, your screen will display the following output:

```
C:\> CONFLICT  <ENTER>
This is the derived class
```

Resolving Class and Base Name Conflicts

As you learned in Tip 956, when a derived member name conflicts with a base member name, the derived member name is used. There may be times, however, when your program needs to access the base class member. To do so, your program can use the global resolution operator (::). The following program, RESNAME.CPP, uses the global resolution operator to access the base class *display* member:

```
#include <iostream.h>

class Base {
 public:
    void display(void)
       { cout << "This is the base class" << endl; };
};

class Derived: public Base {
 public:
    void display(void)
       { cout << "This is the derived class" << endl; };
};

void main(void)
  {
    Derived my_class;
```

```
    my_class.display();
    my_class.Base::display();
}
```

When you compile and execute this program, your screen will display the following output:

```
C:\> RESNAME  <ENTER>
This is the derived class
This is the base class
```

958 Overloading the << Operator

When your classes contain several members whose value you want to output in a specific way, using *cout* and extraction operator can lead to considerable code. For example, assume you are working with a class whose members include a name, sex (M or F), age, and phone number that you want to output as follows:

```
Name: John Doe          Sex: M  Age: 43     Phone: 555-1212
```

Using *cout*, your programs must include the following statement each time they want to display the output:

```
cout << "Name: " << name <<  "\tSex: " << sex <<  "\tAge: "
  << age << "\tPhone: " << phone << endl;
```

A better alternative would be to overload the extraction operator, as shown in the following program, OUTOVER.CPP:

```
#include <iostream.h>
#include <string.h>

class Employee {
 public:
   Employee(char *name, char sex, int age, char *phone) {
     strcpy(Employee::name, name);
     Employee::sex = sex;
     Employee::age = age;
     strcpy(Employee::phone, phone);  };
     friend ostream& operator<< (ostream& cout, Employee emp);
 private:
   char name[256];
   char phone[64];
   int age;
```

```
       char sex;
};

ostream& operator<< (ostream& cout, Employee emp)
  {
     cout << "Name: " << emp.name << "\tSex: " << emp.sex;
     cout << "\tAge:" << emp.age << "\tPhone: "<< emp.phone << endl;
     return cout;
  }

void main(void)
  {
     Employee worker("John Doe", 'M', 43, "555-1212");

     cout << worker ;
  }
```

The program overloads the extraction operator within the *ostream* class. The operator is only overloaded when it is used with the *Employee* class. As such, the output operations that occur within the overload itself are not overloaded. Because the operator must access the data members of the *Employee* class, the operator is declared as a friend of the class.

Mutual Friends

As you have learned, C++ lets you specify other classes as *friends* of a class, which lets functions in the friend class access a class's private methods. As you examine C++ programs, you might encounter one cases where two classes are *mutual friends*. In other words, the functions in one function can access the private data of another and vice versa. The following program, MUTUAL.CPP, illustrates the two classes that are mutual friends:

```
#include <iostream.h>
#include <string.h>

class Curly {
 public:
    Curly(char *msg) { strcpy(message, msg); };
    void show_message(void) { cout << message << endl; };
    friend class Moe;
    void show_moe(class Moe moe);
 private:
    char message[256];
 };
```

```
class Moe {
 public:
   Moe(char *msg) { strcpy(message, msg); };
   void show_message(void) { cout << message << endl; };
   friend class Curly;
   void show_curly(class Curly curly);
 private:
   char message[256];
 };

void Curly::show_moe(class Moe moe)
  { cout << moe.message << endl; };

void Moe::show_curly(class Curly curly)
  { cout << curly.message << endl; };

void main(void)
 {
   class Moe moe("Nuck, nuck, nuck...");
   class Curly curly("Whoop, whoop, whoop...");

   moe.show_message();
   moe.show_curly(curly);

   curly.show_message();
   curly.show_moe(moe);
 }
```

In this case, because of the use of the *friend* qualifier, the mutual friends Moe and Curly can access each other's private data.

C++ 960 Understanding Inheritance

As you derive classes using C++ inheritance support, it might help you to draw pictures that illustrate the relationships between classes. As you will find, one class that you derive from one or more base classes might very well become the base class for other classes. As you begin to define your classes, start with general characteristics and work toward specifics as you derive new classes. For example, if you are deriving classes for types of dogs, your first base class might simply be *Dogs*, which contains such characteristics as a name, origin, height, weight, and color—in general, all the characteristics common to all breeds of dogs. Your next level might become a little more refined when you create the classes *DogsWithSpots* and *SpotlessDogs*. Both of these class types would inherit the common characteristics that you defined in the *Dogs* base class. As you further refine pedigrees, however, you can use these second level classes as base classes for other class definitions. As such, your levels of base classes might grow, conceptually similar to a family tree. Tip 961 illustrates a C++ program that supports several levels of inheritance.

One Derived Class Can Become Another's Base Class

C++ 961

As you learned in Tip 960, C++ lets you create an inheritance hierarchy, allowing one class to inherit the characteristics of a base class which itself inherited characteristics. The following program, THREELVL.CPP, derives 3 levels of classes. As you will see, each successive class inherits the characteristics of each class that has gone before it:

```cpp
#include <iostream.h>

class Base {
 public:
    void show_base(void) { cout << "Base class message\n"; };
};

class Level1 : public Base {
 public:
    void show_level1(void) {
        show_base();
        cout << "Level 1 message\n"; };
};

class Level2 : public Level1 {
  public:
    void show_level2(void) {
        show_level1();
        cout << "Level 2 message\n"; };
};

class Level3 : public Level2 {
  public:
    void show_level3(void) {
        show_level2();
        cout << "Level 3 message\n"; };
};

void main(void)
  {
```

```
    Level3 my_data;
    my_data.show_level3();
  }
```

When you compile and execute this program, your screen will display the following:

```
C:\> THREELVL  <ENTER>
Base class message
Level 1 message
Level 2 message
Level 3 message
```

962 C++ Using Protected Members in Derived Classes

Each time you create a new class, make that assumption that the class might eventually become the base class for other class derivations. As such, you should take advantage of protected members to limit access to class members to instances of the current class and future derived classes. The following program, PROTDERI.CPP, illustrates the use of protected data in a derived class, which in turn, has become a base class:

```cpp
#include <iostream.h>
#include <string.h>

class Base {
  public:
    Base(char *str) { strcpy(message, str); };
    void show_base(void) { cout << message << endl; };
  protected:
    char message[256];
};


class Level1 : public Base {
  public:
    Level1(char *str, char *base) : Base(base) {
      strcpy(message, str);};
    void show_level1(void) { cout << message << endl; } ;
  protected:
    char message[256];
};

class Lowest : public Level1 {
  public:
```

```
        Lowest(char *str, char *level1, char *base) :
          Level1(level1, base) { strcpy(message, str); };
        void show_lowest(void) {
           show_base();
           show_level1();
           cout << message << endl; };
     protected:
        char message[256];
   };

void main(void)
   {
     Lowest bottom("Lowest message", "Level1 message",
        "Base message");

     bottom.show_lowest();
   }
```

Because each class has defined its data as protected, the derived classes can directly access the data if they so desired. In this case, however, the derived classes still used the interface functions.

Static Class Data

C++963

When you declare class members, C++ lets you precede a definition with the *static* qualifier. For example, the following class definition uses static and nonstatic data members:

```
class SomeClass {
   public:
     static int count;
     SomeClass(int value) { count++; my_data = value; };
     ~SomeClass(void) { count--; };
     int my_data;
};
```

Normally, each object instance receives its own data members. If you precede a member definition with the *static* keyword, the member becomes shared by all object instances. If one instance changes the data, the change is immediately visible to all of the instances. A static member definition does allocate memory for the member. Instead, you must declare the static variable outside of the class, as shown here:

```
int SomeClass::count;
```

The following program, SHARE_IT.CPP, uses the *static* keyword to share the member variable *count* (which tracks the number of object instances):

```cpp
#include <iostream.h>

class SomeClass {
  public:
    static int count;
    SomeClass(int value) { count++; my_data = value; };
    ~SomeClass(void) { count--; };
    int my_data;
};

int SomeClass::count;

void main(void)
  {
    SomeClass One(1);
    cout << "One: " << One.my_data << ' ' << One.count << endl ;

    // Declare another instance
    SomeClass Two(2);
    cout << "Two: " << Two.my_data << ' ' << Two.count << endl ;

    // Declare another instance
    SomeClass Three(3);
    cout << "Three: " << Three.my_data <<' '<< Three.count << endl;
  }
```

Each time the program creates a new object instance, the *static* variable *count* is incremented. After three instances, *count* contains the value 3. As you can see, the *static* member can be shared by all three instances.

C++ 964 Initializing a Static Data Member

In Tip 963 you learned that C++ lets you declare *static* data members that are accessible to all instances of the class. When you use static data members, you need to determine the best way to initialize the member. One way is simply to let the first instance pass the desired value to the constructor function. To do this, you overload the constructor function to support one or two parameters. If two parameters are passed, the second parameter is assigned to the *static* variable. The following program, STAT_INI.CPP, overloads the constructor function in this way to initialize the *static* member to 999:

```
#include <iostream.h>

class SomeClass {
  public:
    static int count;
    SomeClass(int value) { count++; my_data = value; };
    SomeClass(int value, int static_value) {
      count = static_value; my_data = value; };
    ~SomeClass(void) { count--; };
    int my_data;
};

int SomeClass::count;

void main(void)
  {
    SomeClass One(1, 999);
    cout << "One: " << One.my_data << ' ' << One.count << endl ;

    // Declare another instance
    SomeClass Two(2);
    cout << "Two: " << Two.my_data << ' ' << Two.count << endl ;

    // Declare another instance
    SomeClass Three(3);
    cout << "Three: " << Three.my_data <<' '<< Three.count << endl;
  }
```

As you will learn in Tip 965, your programs can also directly access a public static member to assign or reference the member's value.

Direct Access of a Static Data Member

C++965

In Tip 964 you overloaded a constructor function in order to initialize a *static* data member. When a static data member is private, your programs can directly access the member's value. As such, the program could have initialized the member using two different techniques. First, when the member was declared outside of the class, the program could have assigned the value, as shown here:

```
int SomeClass::count = 999;
```

In addition, the within the program itself, the program could have accessed the *static* member directly, as shown here:

```
void main(void)
 {
    SomeClass::count = 999;

    SomeClass One(1);

    // Other statements
 }
```

When you declare a public static member, the program can directly access the member's value *even if* no instances of the class exist. To better protect static members, use static private, as discussed in Tip 966.

C++ 966 Static Private Data Members

As you have learned, C++ lets you declare static class members that are accessible to all instances of a class. If the member is also public, the member can be directly accessed by the program itself, bypassing the class instances. To protect the static member better, you can declare it as *private*. In this way, the member can only be accessed by class member functions. The following program, PRIVSTAT.CPP, illustrates the use of a private static member:

```
#include <iostream.h>

class SomeClass {
  public:
    SomeClass(int value) { count++; my_data = value; };
    SomeClass(int value, int static_value) {
      count = static_value; my_data = value; };
    ~SomeClass(void) { count--; };
    void show_values(void)
      { cout << my_data << ' ' << count << endl; };
  private:
    static int count;
    int my_data;
};

int SomeClass::count;

void main(void)
 {
    SomeClass One(1, 999);
    One.show_values();

    // Declare another instance
```

```
   SomeClass Two(2, 1000);
   Two.show_values();

   // Declare another instance
   SomeClass Three(3);
   Three.show_values();
 }
```

When you declare a private static member in this way, your program can initialize it with a constructor or by assigning a value at the initialization that appears outside of the class definition.

Understanding Static Member Functions

As you have learned, C++ lets you use static class data members, whose values are shared by each instance. In addition to static data members, C++ also supports static function members. However, static function members are not often used. In general, there only use is to manipulate static data members. Unlike other function members, which have access to instance data using the *this* pointer, static function members do not. The only time you will use a static function member is when you have a function that does not manipulate instance data. The following program, STATIC.CPP, illustrates the use of a static function member:

```
#include <iostream.h>

class SomeClass {
  public:
    SomeClass(int value) { some_value = value; };
    void show_data(void)
      { cout << data << ' ' << some_value << endl; };
    static void set_data(int value) { data = value; };
  private:
    static int data;
    int some_value;
};

int SomeClass::data;

void main(void)
 {
   SomeClass my_class(1001);
   my_class.set_data(5005);
   my_class.show_data();
 }
```

C++ 968 Direct Access of a Public Static Function

As you learned in Tip 967, C++ lets you define public static functions within a class. When you declare such functions as public, the functions are fully accessible throughout the program, even if an instance of the class has not been created. To access the public static member function, your program uses the global resolution operator (::), as shown here:

```
class_name::member_name(parameters);
```

The following program, GLOBSTAT.CPP, illustrates the direct access of a public static member function. Note that the program uses the function, even though no instances of the object exist:

```
#include <iostream.h>

class SomeClass {
 public:
    static void message(void) { cout << "Hello, world!\n"; } ;
};

void main(void)
  {
    SomeClass::message();
  }
```

C++ 969 Spicing Up Class Members

For simplicity, most of the examples presented throughout this section have used class members that were *int*, *float*, or *char* values. As your class definitions become more complex, however, your class members might be pointers, references, enumerated types, and even nested classes. The following program, NEAT_MBR.CPP, illustrates the use of more interesting class members:

```
#include <iostream.h>

enum Days { Monday, Tuesday, Wednesday, Thursday, Friday };

class NeatClass {
  public:
    int *lucky_number;
    enum Days lucky_day;
```

```
  };

void main(void)
  {
    NeatClass wow;
    int lucky = 1001;

    wow.lucky_day = Monday;

    wow.lucky_number = &lucky;

    cout << "My lucky number is " << *(wow.lucky_number) << endl;
    switch (wow.lucky_day) {
      case Monday: cout << "My lucky day is Monday\n";
                   break;

      default: cout << "My lucky day ain't any day but Monday\n";
    };
  }
```

Nesting a Class

As you learned in Tip 969, C++ lets your class members be any type, including other classes. The following program, NESTCLAS.CPP, illustrates the use of a *nested* class:

```
#include <iostream.h>

class Outer {
 public:
   Outer(void) { cout << "Just instantiated an outer\n";
                 outer_data = 2002; };
   class Inner {
     public:
       Inner(void) { cout << "Just instantiated an inner\n";
                     inner_data = 1001; };
       void show_data(void)
          { cout << "Inner: " << inner_data << endl; };
     private:
       int inner_data;
   } inside_stuff;
   void show_all_data(void) { inside_stuff.show_data();
    cout << "Outer: " << outer_data << endl; };
 private:
   int outer_data;
```

```
};

void main(void)
  {
    Outer my_data;

    my_data.show_all_data();
  }
```

When you compile and execute this program, your screen will display the following:

```
C:\> NESTCLAS  <ENTER>
Just instantiated an inner
Just instantiated an outer
Inner: 1001
Outer: 2002
```

As a rule, nested classes can become very difficult to understand, and they can decrease your program's reuse. A better solution would be to implement two distinct classes, using the class *Inner* as a base class from which you can derive the *Outer* class.

C++ 971 Understanding Subclasses and Superclasses

As you read other articles and books on C++, you might encounter the terms *subclass* and *superclass*. The terms relate to class inheritance. In general, the term *subclass* can be interchanged with *base class*. Likewise, the term *superclass* can be exchanged with *derived class*. For your discussions on C++, stick with the terms *base* and *derived* class.

C++ 972 Inline Assembler in a Method Function

As you have learned, many C and C++ compilers let your programs place inline assembly language statements within the program code. As you will learn here, class methods are no exception to this rule. The following program, CLASBEEP.CPP, creates two members, *beep* and *beepbeep*, that use inline assembly language statements to sound the computer's built-in speaker:

```
#include <iostream.h>

class Beepers {
 public:
    void beep(void);
    void beepbeep(void);
};

void Beepers::beep(void) {
   asm { mov ah,2;
   mov dl,7;
   int 0x21; }}

void Beepers::beepbeep(void) {
   asm { mov ah,2;
   mov dl,7;
   int 0x21;
   mov ah,2;
   mov dl,7;
   int 0x21; }}

void main(void)
  {
    Beepers noise;

    noise.beep();
    noise.beepbeep();
  }
```

When you use inline assembler, most C++ compilers will require you to declare the corresponding member functions outside of the class.

Class Members Can Be Recursive

C++ 973

As you learned in the Functions section of this book, a recursive function calls itself to perform a task until a specific ending condition is met. When you define class functions, the functions can be recursive. The following program STRCLASS.CPP, creates a string class with two recursive functions, *str_reverse* and *str_length*:

```
#include <iostream.h>
#include <string.h>
```

```
class StringClass {
 public:
   void str_reverse(char *string) {
     if (*string)
        {
          str_reverse(string+1);
          cout.put(*string);
        }};
   int str_length(char *string) {
     {
        if (*string)
          return (1 + str_length(++string));
        else
          return(0);
     }};

   StringClass(char *string)
     { strcpy(StringClass::string, string); };
   char string[256];
};


void main(void)
 {
   StringClass title("Jamsa's 1001 C/C++ Tips");

   title.str_reverse(title.string);

   cout << endl << "The title is " <<
     title.str_length(title.string) << "bytes";
 }
```

C++ 974 Understanding the *this* Pointer

Each time your program creates a class instance, a special pointer called *this*, which contains the address of the instance, is created. Actually, the pointer is only defined when a nonstatic member of the instance is executing. The instances, in turn, use the *this* pointer to access the different methods. Normally, however, the use of *this* is transparent. The compiler assigns *this* and performs the necessary redirections. Your programs normally don't need to use the *this* pointer, but they can. The following program, SHOWTHIS.CPP, uses the *this* pointer to display the values of several instance members. The program also displays the values without using *this* to illustrate that the compiler automatically inserts instructions to perform the correct indirection for you:

```
#include <iostream.h>
#include <string.h>

class SomeClass {
 public:
   void show_with_this(void) {
     cout << "Book: " << this->title << endl;
     cout << "Author: " << this->author << endl; };

   void show_without_this(void) {
     cout << "Book: " << title << endl;
     cout << "Author: " << author << endl; };

   SomeClass(char *title, char *author) {
     strcpy(SomeClass::title, title);
     strcpy(SomeClass::author, author);
   };

 private:
   char title[256];
   char author[256];
};

void main(void)
  {
    SomeClass book("Jamsa's 1001 C/C++ Tips", "Jamsa");

    book.show_with_this();
    book.show_without_this();
  }
```

How *this* Differs from Other Functions

C++ 975

In Tip 974 you learned that each time your program invokes an instance method, the compiler preassigns a special pointer named *this* to point to the object instance. The *this* pointer is unlike other pointers because its value changes with different instance invocations, so your programs need to use *this* with care. As you examine C++ programs, you might encounter statements that return the value to which *this* points:

```
return(*this);
```

In many case, the compiler will convert the pointer to value to a reference, allowing a method to return a reference to an instance. Check the return value of the member closely to determine if a pointer or reference value is being returned.

C++ 976 Understanding Early and Late Binding

When you read articles and books on resolving function calls, you might encounter terms such as *early* (compile time) and *late* (run-time) *binding*. The terms describe when the address for the functions your programs will call are *resolved* (made known to the program). To this point, all of the class member function addresses have been resolved at compile or link time. Address resolution at this time is called early (sometime static) binding. C++ also supports dynamic binding through the use of *virtual* functions. Dynamic binding occurs at run time and gives programs that use multiple inheritance tremendous flexibility. Several of the tips that follow discuss virtual functions in detail. Virtual functions provide C++ with the ability to support polymorphism, which was introduced at the start of this section.

C++ 977 Pointers to Classes

As your programs become more complex, you might eventually work with pointers to objects. For example, the following program, PTR_OBJ.CPP, creates a simple base and derived class. The program uses the *new* operator to allocate dynamically instances of each class type. Using pointer indirection, the program invokes each instance's methods:

```cpp
#include <iostream.h>

class Base {
 public:
   void base_message(void) { cout << "This is the base class\n";};
};

class Derived: public Base {
 public:
   void derived_message(void)
      { cout << "This is the derived class\n" ; };
};

void main(void)
  {
    Base *base_pointer = new Base;
    Derived *derived_pointer = new Derived;

    base_pointer->base_message();
    derived_pointer->derived_message();
  }
```

Using the Same Pointer to Different Classes

In Tip 977 you created dynamically instances of the *Base* and *Derived* classes. To do so, your programs used two different pointer variables—one declared as a pointer to type *Base* and one as a pointer to type *Derived*. As it turns out, when your programs use inheritance, C++ lets you use a pointer to the base class to point to a derived class. Using the pointer, however, you can only access members of the original base class. You can access the derived class members. The following program, BASEPTR.CPP, assigns the base class pointer to point to the derived class. The program then uses the pointer to access the base class member *base_message*:

```cpp
#include <iostream.h>

class Base {
 public:
    void base_message(void)
        { cout << "This is the base class\n"; };
};

class Derived: public Base {
 public:
    void derived_message(void)
        { cout << "This is the derived class\n" ; };
};

void main(void)
  {
    Base *base_pointer = new Base;
    base_pointer->base_message();

    base_pointer = new Derived;
    base_pointer->base_message();
  }
```

As you will learn in Tip 979, when a derived class and base class have the same member names and you use a pointer in this way, you might not get the results you expected.

C++ 979 Base and Derived Name Conflicts with Pointers

As you learned in Tip 977, C++ lets you point to a derived class using a pointer declared as a pointer to the base class. The following program, BASENAME.CPP, uses a base class pointer to point to a derived class. The base and derived class both have the member name *show_message*:

```cpp
#include <iostream.h>

class Base {
 public:
    void show_message(void) { cout << "This is the base class\n";};
};

class Derived: public Base {
 public:
    void show_message(void)
        { cout << "This is the derived class\n" ; };
};

void main(void)
  {
    Base *base_pointer = new Base;
    base_pointer->show_message();

    base_pointer = new Derived;
    base_pointer->show_message();
  }
```

When you compile and execute this program, your screen will display the following output:

```
C:\> BASENAME  <ENTER>
This is the base class
This is the base class
```

By default, when the base and derived class use the same function names and you use a pointer to the base class, the C++ compiler will resolve the pointer to the base class function. As you will learn in Tip 980, however, there may be times when you want the compiler to invoke instead a derived class member. To do so, however, you must use virtual functions.

Understanding Virtual Functions

As you have learned, when one class inherits the methods of another, there may be times when the names conflict. If you are using a base class pointer to access a derived class and you invoke one of the members with the same name as a base class member, the base class member will execute. If you want C++ to instead invoke the derived class member, you need to define *virtual functions*. Using virtual functions is really not that much different than the operations you have been performing. To create a virtual function, you simply precede the function name with the *virtual* keyword. The function return type and parameter list must be identical for each virtual function. The following program, VIRT_ONE.CPP, defines the *show_message* function as a virtual function within the *base* and *derived* class:

```cpp
#include <iostream.h>

class Base {
 public:
   virtual void show_message(void)
      { cout << "This is the base class\n"; };
};

class Derived: public Base {
 public:
   virtual void show_message(void)
      { cout << "This is the derived class\n" ; };
};

void main(void)
  {
   Base *base_pointer = new Base;
   base_pointer->show_message();

   base_pointer = new Derived;
   base_pointer->show_message();
  }
```

When you compile and execute this program, your screen will display the following output:

```
C:\> VIRT_ONE  <ENTER>
This is the base class
This is the derived class
```

As you can see, using virtual functions the pointer correctly invoke the base and derived class methods.

Implementing Polymorphism

As you read at the start of this section, *polymorphism* is the ability of the same object to take on different forms. C++ supports polymorphism using virtual functions. Using virtual functions, the same object (a pointer) can perform different operations. The following program, POLYMORP.CPP, creates a base class and two derived classes. The program then uses the pointer *poly* to invoke different methods:

```cpp
#include <iostream.h>
#include <stdlib.h>

class Base {
 public:
    virtual int add(int a, int b) { return(a + b); };
    virtual int sub(int a, int b) { return(a - b); };
    virtual int mult(int a, int b) { return(a * b); };
};

class ShowMath : public Base {
    virtual int mult(int a, int b)
      {
        cout << a * b << endl;
        return(a * b); };
};

class PositiveSubt : public Base {
    virtual int sub(int a, int b) { return(abs(a - b)); };
};

void main(void)
  {
    Base *poly = new ShowMath;

    cout << poly->add(500, 501) << ' ' <<
      poly->sub(1500, 499) << endl;
    poly->mult(1001, 1);

    poly = new PositiveSubt;
    cout << poly->add(800,201) << ' ' << poly->sub(0,1001) << endl;
    cout << poly->mult(1, 1001);
  }
```

When you compile and execute this program, each function invocation results in the display of the value 1001 on your screen. Note that, depending on the instance pointed to by *poly*, the operation *poly* performed might differ.

Understanding Pure Virtual Functions

You have learned that when you derive one class from another, C++ lets you use virtual functions to control which class's functions are invoked when a base class pointer is used to point to a derived class. When you read more about virtual functions, you might encounter the term *pure virtual function*. A pure virtual function is similar to a prototype that is declared in the base class for which the base class requires the derived class to provide an implementation. Within the base class, a pure virtual function appears as follows:

```
virtual type function_name(parameters) = 0;
```

The symbols = 0 that follow the prototype indicate that the function is pure virtual function for which an implementation must be provided. The following program, PUREVIRT.CPP, illustrates a pure virtual function:

```cpp
#include <iostream.h>
#include <string.h>

class Base {
 public:
   virtual void show_message(void)
      { cout << "Base class message" << endl; };
   virtual void show_reverse(void) = 0;
};

class Derived : public Base {
 public:
   virtual void show_message(void)
      { cout << "Derived class message" << endl; };
   virtual void show_reverse(void)
      { cout << strrev("Derived class message") << endl; };
};

void main(void)
  {
   Base *poly = new Derived;
   poly->show_message();
   poly->show_reverse();
  }
```

Jamsa's 1001 C/C++ Tips

983 Understanding Abstract Classes

In Tip 982 you learned that a pure virtual function is a function prototype for which the base class requires a derived class to provide an implementation. When a class contains a pure virtual function, C++ refers to that class as an *abstract class*. In general, an abstract class provides a template from which your programs can later derive other classes. C++ will not let you create a variable of an abstract class type. If you try to do so, the compiler will generate a syntax error.

984 Overloading *cout*'s Insertion Operator

Most of the programs presented throughout the last two sections of this book have made extensive use of the *cout* iostream to display output to the screen. The following program, COUT_UPR.CPP, overloads the *cout's* insertion operator for character strings, directing *cout* to always display character strings in uppercase:

```cpp
#include <iostream.h>
#include <string.h>

ostream& operator<<(ostream& cout, char *string)
  {
    char *str = strupr(string);

    while (*str)
      cout.put(*str++);

    return(cout);
  }

void main(void)
  {
    cout << "This is a test";
    cout << "\nJamsa's 1001 C/C++ Tips";
  }
```

The insertion operator returns a reference to an I/O stream and hence the function header:

```cpp
ostream& operator<<(ostream& cout, char *string)
```

Within the function itself, the statements use the *strupr* function to convert the string to uppercase and then use *cout.put* to display characters one at a time. The function could not use *cout*'s insertion operator to display the string or an endless series of recursive calls would have resulted.

Defining a Output Stream Manipulator

985

Several of the tips in the Getting Started with C++ section of this book used output stream manipulators such as *hex* and *endl*. The following program, MANIPUL.CPP, creates a new output stream manipulator called *attention*, which sounds the computer's built-in speaker to get the user's attention. Use the *attention* manipulator within the *cout* stream as follows:

```
cout << attention << "I think your disk is bad!";
```

The following code implements MANIPUL.CPP:

```
#include <iostream.h>

ostream& attention(ostream& cout) {
 return(cout << '\a');
};

void main(void)
  {
    cout << attention << "The boss is coming in your office...\n";
  }
```

It's Time to Take a Look at iostream.h

986

In the Getting Started with C++ section of this book, you were warned not to take a look inside the header file iostream.h. Now that you have mastered classes, overloading, virtual functions, and the basics of object-oriented programming, you should not only take a look in the file, you should start analyzing each line. To begin, print a hard copy of the file to which you can later refer as you create your own classes. There are several very interesting programming techniques used by the C++ masters in iostream.h. Second, make a copy of the file, naming it iostream.nts. Next, spend time every day reading the file and adding comments that explain the file's processing. If you cover two pages of the file every day, you will be through it in less than a week. Not only will you be an expert in C++ I/O operations, you will learn a great deal more about the ins and outs of complex class definitions.

C++ 987 Using *sizeof* with a Class

As you know, the *sizeof* operator returns the number of bytes required to store an object. As your programs work with objects, there may be times when you will need to know an object's size. For example, assume that you reading a file of objects. Using the *sizeof* operator you can determine the object's size. The operator returns only the size of the class data members. The following program, SIZEOF.CPP, uses the *sizeof* operator to determine the size of two classes. The first class is a base class and the second class a derived class:

```cpp
#include <iostream.h>
#include <string.h>

class Base {
 public:
   Base(char *message) { strcpy(Base::message, message); };
   void show_base(void) { cout << message << endl; };
 private:
   char message[256];
};

class Derived: public Base {
 public:
   Derived(char *dmsg, char *bmsg) : Base(bmsg) {
     strcpy(message, dmsg); };
   void show_derived(void) { cout << message << endl;
     show_base(); };
 private:
   char message[256];
};

void main(void)
 {
   Base some_base("This is a base");
   Derived some_derived("Derived message", "Base message");

   cout << "The size of the base class is "
     << sizeof(some_base) << " bytes\n";

   cout << "The size of the derived class is " <<
     sizeof(some_derived) << " bytes\n";
 }
```

When you compile and execute this program, your screen will display the following output:

```
C:\> SIZEOF  <ENTER>
The size of the base class is 256 bytes
The size of the derived class is 512 bytes
```

Private, Public, and Protected Can Apply to Structures Too

Several of the tips in this section have used private, public, and protected class members. When your C++ programs use structures, you can also have private, public, and protected members. By default, all structure members are public. However, using the private and protected labels, you can identify members for which you want to control access. The following program, PRIVSTRU.CPP, illustrates the use of private members within a structure. As you will see, most of the capabilities C++ provides for classes also exist for structures:

```cpp
#include <iostream.h>
#include <string.h>

struct MyBook {
  char title[64];  // Public by default
  void show_book(void)
    {
      cout << "Book: " << title << " Price: $" << price ;
    };

  void set_price(float amount) { price = amount; };
  void assign_title(char *name) { strcpy(title, name); };
  private:
    float price;
};

void main(void)
  {
    MyBook book;

    book.assign_title("Jamsa's 1001 C/C++ Tips");
    book.set_price(39.95);
    book.show_book();
  }
```

In this case, the structure specifies the *price* member as private. As such, the only way to access the member is using one of the structure's public methods. If you find that your structures require this type of protection, you should start working with classes instead.

C++ 989 Understanding Class Conversions

As you know, when you pass a value of type *int* to a function that requires a *long* value, C++ promotes the int value to the correct type. Likewise, if you are pass a parameter of type *float* to a function that requires a value of type *double,* a similar conversion is made. When you work with C++ classes, you can also specify the conversions that C++ should perform to convert class values to a standard data type (such as *int* or *long*) or even to a different class. Conversions are very common when a parameter of one type is passed to a constructor function for a class of a different type. For example, assume that the class *BookStuff* normally receives three character strings as functions to its constructor:

```
BookStuff (char *title, char *author, char *publisher)
  {
     // Statements
  }
```

Assume, however that periodically, the program invokes the constructor with a structure of type *BookInfo,* as shown here:

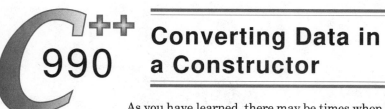

```
struct BookInfo {
    char title[64];
    char author[64];
    char publisher[64];
    float price;
    int pages;
};
```

The class can create a second constructor that converts the data as needed. Tip 990 illustrates a program that does just that.

C++ 990 Converting Data in a Constructor

As you have learned, there may be times when you need to convert data from one format into a format that the class expects. An easy way to perform such a conversion is using different constructor functions. The following program, CONVERT.CPP, uses such a constructor function to convert information contained in a structure of type *BookInfo:*

```
#include <iostream.h>
#include <string.h>

struct BookInfo {
  char title[64];
  char publisher[64];
  char author[64];
  float price;
  int pages;
};

class BookStuff {
  public:
    BookStuff(char *title, char *publisher, char *author);
    BookStuff(struct BookInfo);
    void show_book(void) { cout << "Book: " << title << " by " <<
        author << " Publisher: " << publisher << endl; };
  private:
    char title[64];
    char author[64];
    char publisher[64];
};

BookStuff::BookStuff(char *title, char *publisher, char *author)
 {
   strcpy(BookStuff::title, title);
   strcpy(BookStuff::publisher, publisher);
   strcpy(BookStuff::author, author);
 }

BookStuff::BookStuff(BookInfo book)
 {
   strcpy(BookStuff::title, book.title);
   strcpy(BookStuff::publisher, book.publisher);
   strcpy(BookStuff::author, book.author);
 }

void main(void)
 {
   BookInfo book = {"Rescued by C++", "Jamsa Press", "Jamsa",
     19.95, 256 };

   BookStuff big_book("Jamsa's 1001 C/C++ Tips", "Jamsa Press",
       "Jamsa");
   BookStuff little_book(book);

   big_book.show_book();
   little_book.show_book();
 }
```

Using the constructor function to perform the conversion in this way is really no different than the overload operations you have been performing throughout this section.

C++ 991 Assigning One Class to Another

In Tip 990 you created a constructor function that converted the data contained in a structure of type *BookInfo* into the data fields for an instance of the *BookStuff* class. As you examine C++ programs, you might encounter statements where one class type is assigned to another, as shown here:

```
class BookStuff big_book;
char title[256];

title = big_book;
```

In this case, the class *big_book* is being assigned to a character-string variable. To support such operations, your program must tell the compiler the correct conversion to apply. To do so, you must create a member function within the *BookStuff* class that performs the conversion. In this case, the function will assign the book title to the string. There are some rules that the conversion function must follow. First, within the class, the function must be defined as an operator:

```
operator char *();
```

Second, the corresponding function code must return a value of the converted type, which in this case is a pointer to a character string. The following program, CLASSASN.CPP, uses a member conversion function to assign the class to a character string. In this case, the conversion function assigns the book's title to the string:

```
#include <iostream.h>
#include <string.h>


class BookStuff {
  public:
    BookStuff(char *title, char *publisher, char *author);
    void show_book(void) { cout << "Book: " << title << " by " <<
        author << " Publisher: " << publisher << endl; };
    operator char *();

  private:
    char title[64];
    char author[64];
    char publisher[64];
};
```

```
BookStuff::BookStuff(char *title, char *publisher, char *author)
  {
    strcpy(BookStuff::title, title);
    strcpy(BookStuff::publisher, publisher);
    strcpy(BookStuff::author, author);
  }

BookStuff::operator char *(void)
  {
    char *ptr = new char[256];

    return(strcpy(ptr, title));
  }


void main(void)
  {
    BookStuff big_book("Jamsa's 1001 C/C++ Tips", "Jamsa Press",
      "Jamsa");

    char *title;

    title = big_book;

    cout << "The book's title is " << title << endl;
  }
```

Using conversion functions such as this, your programs can convert from one class to another as needed.

Use Friends for Conversion

When you perform conversions between one class and another, there may be times when you need to access the private members of another class. As you have learned, by specifying a friend class or friend function, you can allow another class to access the private data without making the data visible to other parts of your program. If a class needs to access the private data of another class to perform a conversion, specify the conversion function as a friend of the class.

C++ 993 Determine When Operators Improve or Reduce Readability

As you have learned, when you define a class, C++ lets you overload one or more operators. Before you overload an operator, however, you need to determine if the overload will make the program easier or more difficult to understand. For example, the following program, STR_PLUS.CPP, overloads the plus operator for the *String* class. The program then uses the operator, as well as the function *strapd*, to append one string's contents to another. Examine the program and determine which technique is most understandable:

```cpp
#include <iostream.h>
#include <iomanip.h>
#include <string.h>

class String {
  public:
    char *operator +(char *append_str)
      { return(strcat(buffer, append_str)); };

    String(char *string)
      { strcpy(buffer, string);
        length = strlen(buffer); }

    void show_string() { cout << buffer; };

    void strapd(char *source) {
       strcat(buffer, source); };

  private:
    char buffer[256];
    int length;
};


void main(void)
 {
    String title("Jamsa's 1001 ");
    title + "C/C++ Tips\n";
    title.show_string();


    String book2("Rescued");
    book2.strapd(" by C++");
    book2.show_string();
 }
```

There is a tendency for many new C++ programmers to overload more operators than are *really* necessary. The decision you have to make is whether or not the overload improves your program's readability.

Understanding I/O Streams That Use _*withassign*

994

As you examine the contents of the header file iostream.h, you might find class definitions that include the qualifier _*withassign*, as shown here:

```
extern istream_withassign _Cdecl cin;
extern ostream_withassign _Cdecl cout;
extern ostream_withassign _Cdecl cerr;
extern ostream_withassign _Cdecl clog;
```

In short, _*withassign* tells you that the class variable has been assigned to one of the standard input or output sources, such as stdin, stdout, or stderr.

Understanding Exception Handling

995

As you create class libraries, there will be times when you can anticipate in advance the types of run-time errors a program will encounter while working with the class (such as overwriting array bounds or passing too large a value). Unfortunately, there may be many times when you cannot actually write code to trap such errors when they occur within another program. For such cases, many C++ compilers support *exception handlers*. In general an exception handler is software that executes when such an error occurs. Within the class library code, you would test for the possible error. If the error has occurred, you would raise (C++ calls it *throw*) an exception. The user program that experienced the error is responsible for *catching* and handling the exception—which means the program must provide exception-handling software. Unfortunately, most C++ compilers do not yet support exception handling. The good news, however, is that such support is coming. To support exception handling, the C++ compiler provides the following keywords:

Keyword	Meaning
catch	Catches the thrown exception
throw	Initiates an exception handler
try	Attempts an operation to test for a possible exception

C++ 996 Understanding Templates

As you program, there many times when you must often duplicate a function just so the function supports parameters of a different type. For example, the following function, *compare_values*, compares to values of type *int*, returning the larger value:

```
int compare_values(int a, int b)
  {
    return ((a > b) ? a: b);
  }
```

If your program later needs to compare two floating-point values, you must create a second function, identical in processing, the only difference being the types supported:

```
float compare_values(float a, float b)
  {
    return ((a > b) ? a: b);
  }
```

If the two functions appear in the same program, you must select unique names for each function. To help you reduce such duplicate functions, C++ provides *templates*. In short, a template provides just that—the format of a function and type placeholders. The following is general format of a function template, where *T* is a type that the compiler will later replace:

```
template<class T>  T function_name(T param_a, T param_b)
   {
      // Statements
   }
```

For example, consider the following function template for *compare_values*:

```
template<class T> T compare_values(T a, T b)
  {
    return((a > b) ? a: b);
  }
```

As you can see, the compiler could replace the letter T with the type *float* or *int* to create the functions previously shown. Several of the tips that follow discuss templates in detail.

Putting a Simple Template to Use

As you learned in Tip 996, C++ supports the use of template functions. The following program, COMPARE.CPP, uses the *compare_values* function template to compare values of different types:

```cpp
#include <iostream.h>

template<class T> T compare_values(T a, T b)
  {
    return((a > b) ? a: b);
  }

float compare_values(float a, float b);
int compare_values(int a, int b);
long compare_values(long a, long b);

void main(void)
  {
    float a = 1.2345, b = 2.34567;
    cout << "Comparing " << a << ' ' << b << ' ' <<
      compare_values(a, b) << endl;

     int c = 1, d = 1001;
    cout << "Comparing " << c << ' ' << d << ' ' <<
      compare_values(c, d) << endl;

    long e = 1010101L, f = 2020202L;
    cout << "Comparing " << e << ' ' << f << ' ' <<
      compare_values(e, f) << endl;
  }
```

In this case, the template at the start of the program specifies the function statements and the type placeholders. When C++ encounters the prototypes that appear before *main*, it creates the necessary functions. Later, the compiler determines which function to use, based on the type of the parameters passed (*float*, *int*, or *long*).

C++ 998 Templates That Support Multiple Types

When you work with C++ templates, there may be times when the template requires more than one data type. For example, consider the following function *add_values*, which adds a value of type *long* and *int* and returns a *long* result:

```
long add_values(long a, int b)
  {
    return(a + b);
  }
```

To create a template for this function, you need to specify two types (such as *T* and *T1*), as shown here:

```
template<class T, class T1> T add_values(T a, T1 b)
  {
    return(a + b);
  }
```

In this case, the compiler will substitute each occurrence of class *T* with the type specified and each occurrence of class *T1* with the corresponding class. The following program, TEMPLATE.CPP, uses the *add_values* template:

```
#include <iostream.h>

template<class T, class T1> T add_values(T a, T1 b)
  {
    return(a + b);
  }

long add_values(long a, int b);
double add_values(double a, float b);

void main(void)
  {
    long a = 320000L;
    int b = 31000;

    double c = 22.0 / 7.0;
    float d = 3.145;

    cout << "Adding " << a << ' ' << b << ' ' <<
      add_values(a, b) << endl;
```

```
    cout << "Adding " << c << ' ' << d << ' ' <<
       add_values(c, d) << endl;
}
```

Where to Place Templates

As you have learned, C++ templates let you reduce the duplicate functions that differ only in parameter and return types. When as you create templates, you should place them in meaningfully named header files so you can easily reuse them within other programs. Because the number of templates you will initially create is likely to be quite small, you may want to use the header file template.h. As the number of templates increases, you can assign them to other header files, based on their function.

Templates Also Eliminate Duplicate Classes

As you have learned, C++ templates can reduce duplicate functions that differ only in parameter and return types. In a similar way, your programs can use templates to eliminate similar classes. For example, consider the following classes:

```
class ShortDistance {
   public:
     ShortDistance(int distance)
        { ShortDistance::distance = distance; };
        ShowDistance(void) { cout << "The distance is " << distance
          << " miles" << endl; };
   private:
        int distance;
};

class LongDistance {
   public:
     LongDistance(int distance)
        { ShortDistance::distance = distance; };
        ShowDistance(void) { cout << "The distance is " << distance
          << " miles" << endl; };
   private:
        long distance;
};
```

The following program, CLASSTMP.CPP, combines these two class types into a generic *Distance* class.

```cpp
#include <iostream.h>

template<class T> class Distance {
  public:
    Distance(T distance);
    void show_distance(void) {
       cout << "The distance is " << distance << " miles\n"; };
  private:
    T distance;
};

template<class T>
Distance<T>::Distance(T distance)
  { Distance::distance = distance; };

void main(void)
 {
    Distance<int> short_distance(100);
    Distance<long> long_distance(2000000L);

    short_distance.show_distance();
    long_distance.show_distance();
 }
```

When you compile this program, the C++ compiler will create classes using the correct types. As you will learn in Tip 1001, class templates such as *Distance* are often called a *generic class* or *class generator*.

1001 Understanding Generic Classes

As you learned in Tip 1000, C++ lets you use templates to define generic classes. When you specify a class template, you must always specify the corresponding name followed by angle brackets and a type (either the placeholder type or the actual type), as shown here:

```cpp
Distance<T>
```

or

```cpp
Distance<int>
```

As you examine C++ programs that use class templates, you might find templates defined that use parameters:

```
template<class T, int array_size = 64> class SomeClass {
   // Statements
};
```

n this case, the template not only specifies a type placeholder, it also specifies a parameter that can be used within the template. When the program later uses the template, it can pass a parameter value to template, as shown here:

```
SomeClass<int, 1024>  my_instance;
```

Templates are one of the most powerful features provided by C++. Take time to experiment with their use.

Index

Index

M

Machine code, definition, 1
Macro, invoking and changing, 719
Macros
 creating, 154
 header file, location in, 146
 line wrapping, 153
 MIN and MAX, 156
 naming, 134
 semicolon in, 155
 spaces in, 158
 SQUARE and CUBE, 157
 typeless, as compared to functions, 160
 undefining, 143
main, 274, 276, 676, 678
 declaring as void, 682
MAKE
 command lines and, 706
 creating a simple file, 703
 explicit and implicit rules, 708
 file commenting, 705
 multiple dependency files and, 704, 707
 performing conditional processing with, 711
 simplifying application building with, 702
 using *!error* directive with, 715
 using *!include* with, 713
 using macro modifiers with, 714
MAKE macros
 predefined values for explicit rules (table), 710
 predefined values for implicit rules (table), 710
 predefined, 710
 testing for, 712
 using, 709
_makepath, 385
malloc function, 189
 dynamic memory allocation, 593, 594
 limitations, 597
Math coprocessor
 checking for, 721
 support, 800
Math errors, detecting, 724
Mathematical base system modifiers, 832
Mathematics operators. *See* Arithmetic operators
matherr, 349
max macro, 337
*_memavl_* and *_memmax*, 570
Member. *See* Function; Member function
 private, 884
Member function
 outside of structure, 875
 overloading, 901
 passing parameters to, 876
 within structure, 874
memcmp and *memicmp*, 591
memcopy, 589
_memmax, 570
memmove, 589
Memory
 1Mb barrier, 576
 allocating for *huge* array, 600
 allocating, 596
 allocating, reducing code, 899

 allocating, specific function call, 599
 changing allocated block size of, 601
 conventional, 573
 conventional, accessing, 575
 conventional, mapping of, 574
 determining free core, 570
 different types, 572, 573
 DOS vs. C, 575
 peeking into a specific location of, 608
 poking values into, 609
 releasing, 595
Memory handling. *See new* operator, C++
 set_new_handler, C++, 870
Memory model, 575, 613. *See also* Memory
 compact, 617
 constants table, 620
 determining current, 620
 huge, 619
 large, 618
 medium, 616
 small, 615
 tiny, 614
Memory range
 assigning value to, 588
 copying to another, 589
 copying up to specific byte, 590
Memory-mapped I/O, 610
memset, 588
Methods, 880, 881
Microsoft C++, *extern static* example, 258
Microsoft C, determining stack space, 586
min macro, 337
mkdir, 380
MK_FP macro, 569
mktemp, 404
mktime, 644
Mode. *See* Binary mode; Text mode
modf and *modfl* function, 338
Modulo (remainder) arithmetic, 82
MORE command, writing your own, 659
movetext, 319

N

Name space, 267
Naming conflicts, 252
 global vs. local variables, 224
new operator, C++, 839
 delete, releasing memory with, 845
 far pointers, with 844
 free space, testing for, 842
 memory allocation, with 840
 memory handling, calling, 869
 multiple array allocation, with, 841
Newline character, to display output, 7
 adding with \n or *endl*, 861
no linkage, 792
no_change, 251
node->previous->next, understanding, 750
nonlocal goto, performing, 728
Normalized pointer, 799
Normalized pointers, understanding, 799
Nosound, 558
NULL loop, 119
num_bytes parameter, 588, 589
 comparing ranges, 591
 copying memory range, 590
 swapping bytes, 592